FRAMING OUR PAST

Canadian Women's History in the Twentieth Century

EDITED BY SHARON ANNE COOK, LORNA R. McLEAN, AND KATE O'ROURKE

McGill-Queen's University Press • Montreal & Kingston • London • Ithaca

Legal deposit second quarter 2001
Bibliothèque nationale du Québec

Printed in Canada on acid-free paper

This book has been published with financial help from the Faculties of Education
and Arts, and the Institutes of Canadian Studies and Women's Studies, all at
the University of Ottawa; the Canadian Studies Program of Canadian Heritage;
and the Millennium Fund through a joint project with Making Waves Productions.

McGill-Queen's University Press acknowledges the financial support of the
Government of Canada through the Book Publishing Industry Development
Program (BPIDP) for its activities. It also acknowledges the support of the Canada
Council for the Arts for its publishing program.

Canadian Cataloguing in Publication Data

    Framing our past : Canadian women's history in the twentieth century

Includes bibliographical references.
ISBN 0-7735-2172-0

    1. Women–Canada–History–20th century. I. Cook, Sharon A. (Sharon Anne),
1947- II. McLean, Lorna R. III. O'Rourke, Kate

HQ1453.F72 F2001   305.4'0971'0904   C00-901501-9

This book was designed by David LeBlanc and typeset in 10/12.7 Minion

To Harriet Ethel Killins, a much loved and admired mother, and to Tracey Lynne Cook, teacher extraordinaire and valued friend
– from Sharon

To Hazel Margaret McLean, a courageous and caring mother, and to Heather Lorna and Andrea Ruth Robertson, joyous daughters with inspiring personalities
– from Lorna

To Maureen Patricia O'Rourke, a strong and lively spirit, and to Owen Edward Lee, whom I gaze at with wonder every day of my life
– from Kate

Contents

* Unless otherwise indicated, vignettes are authored by the editors.

The editors gratefully acknowledge the generous contributions to this project from the following academic institutions, federal departments, and companies:

Institute of Canadian Studies
University of Ottawa
Institut d'études canadiennes
Université d'Ottawa

Faculté d'éducation
Université d'Ottawa
Faculty of Education
University of Ottawa

Institute of Women's Studies
University of Ottawa
Institut d'études des femmes
Université d'Ottawa

Faculté des Artes
Université d'Ottawa
Faculty of Arts
University of Ottawa

Institut d'études canadiennes
Institute of Canadian Studies

Faculté d'éducation
Faculty of Education

Faculté des arts
Faculty of Arts

Canadian Studies Program
Canadian Heritage
Program d'études canadiens
Patrimoine canadien

Canadä

Making Waves Productions

Making Waves Productions

L'institut canadien de recherches
sur les femmes
Canadian Research Institute for
the Advancement of Women

Bureau du Canada pour le millénare
Millennium Bureau of Canada

2000
Canadä

Foreword

The writing of women's history during the past three decades has been at the forefront of a fundamental rethinking of the making of contemporary Canada. In the case of the twentieth century, *Framing Our Past* illustrates how this rethinking has revived and greatly expanded our understanding in three key ways that are also central to the work of the Institute of Canadian Studies.

First, the contributions to this volume reflect the value of connecting university campuses to the wider community. Indeed, the writing of women's history has emphasized the inappropriateness of images of "ivory towers" both for the actual discovery of knowledge about the past and for its dissemination within Canadian society. Secondly, *Framing Our Past* demonstrates the key difference between opinions and perspectives supported by archival research, or, in the terms of the institute's mandate, evidence-based interpretations. In rediscovering and analysing a diverse range of historical sources, the authors reject unexamined assumptions in order to offer insights based on the actual traces of thought and behaviour during the past century. Thirdly, this volume emphasizes the extent to which Canadian women's history is not only about Canada but also about the larger international history of the twentieth century. Throughout all the essays and vignettes, on topics ranging from everyday life to education, politics, health, and economics, we can see how women in Canada have both contributed to and been influenced by the transformations of societies around the world.

For these and many other reasons, it has thus been a privilege for the Institute of Canadian Studies to have contributed to the completion of *Framing Our Past*. By connecting the campus to the community, by focusing on evidence, and by situating the Canadian experience in an international context, this volume promises to contribute significantly to the prospects of a healthy and just society as we move forward in the twenty-first century. On behalf of the Executive Committee and the Advisory Board, I extend our heartfelt congratulations to the editors and all the authors for their splendid work.

CHAD GAFFIELD
Professor of History and Director
Institut d'études canadiennes
Université d'Ottawa
Institute of Canadian Studies
University of Ottawa

Preface

There has always been a women's history in Canada. Women's historians, especially, have been recording it both orally and in writing since storytelling began. First Nations women, teaching and nursing sisters in New France, nineteenth-century British imperialists, and early twentieth-century feminists are only some of many who, individually or collectively, have passed down stories or have documented Canadian women's lives. There were accounts of mythic women, like Aataentsic, or of mortal heroines, like Madeleine de Verchères, Laura Secord, and Lady Aberdeen, but there were also social histories of and historical novels about ordinary Canadian women. It is surprising, then, that women's history had to be rediscovered in the last three decades of the twentieth century. For those of us involved in that exciting task, there at first seemed little to go on and only gradually did we become aware of the abundance of fascinating work that had preceded our own women's history movement.

The reasons for the relative inaccessibility of this early women's history are many. Mid-century "professional" historians defined themselves almost exclusively as university-trained and university-employed men; women historians were for a time almost shut out of the business. History, as defined by those boundary-creating professionals, was about political, military, and diplomatic events, with perhaps a little economic history thrown in. Cultural, labour, local, or domestic matters, of interest to many women and to some men, were seen to be of little or no importance. Such prejudices sadly continue, although fortunately they are shared by fewer and fewer historians, both inside and outside of the academy.

A prejudice that academic historians have had a harder time shaking is their bias against writers of popular history. For those who care about women's history, this is a dangerous bias. It was, after all, the problematic line drawn between the professional and the amateur historian that in part accounted for the old sense that women were not really part of the Canadian historical record – or capable of being historians. Popular history (much of which is regional or local history) has never lost its appeal in Canada and women historians never ceased to write, but many academics dismissed both. With that dismissal, it could be argued, also came the dismissal of women's history. This present book demonstrates what a mistake that was.

It is thus with great pleasure that I have followed the work of the editors who created this book. The past quarter-century has seen the development of a vibrant literature dealing with the history of Canadian women; there are now many collections of scholarly essays and we also have both English and French textbooks on the subject. Documentary collections exist as well, although they are not as easy to find, even in the university bookstores where most women's history books are sold. What we need more of, however, are well-researched and well-written works of a more popular nature, intended for the general public. This volume addresses that need.

Historians from all over Canada have contributed to its pages. They bring us their research about individual women, the obscure as well as the better known, and about women's groups and activities across the country. They also introduce us to a kaleidoscope of historical sources and show us the ways in which different kinds of historians approach their female subjects. We learn that although the historian's task is sometimes one of criticism and analysis, it can also be one of celebration and storytelling. The words of these historians – and others – conjure up images of women who were still pioneering well into the twentieth century, in remote parts of Canada or in fields of endeavour new to women, as well as of women who were simply carrying on in territories that were more settled or better known to them. The editors and writers have enriched these mental images with visual ones, reminding us that pictures, too, are part of the historical record and tell their own part of women's stories.

I hope that this book finds the appreciative readership it deserves. I hope, further, that it inspires those of us who love history to work for the preservation of women's records, to tackle new subjects in women's history, to join a local women's history network, or to teach or promote the teaching of more women's history in the schools. Women need to know their history – and men, too, need to know women's history. The essays and vignettes that follow contribute to making the history of Canadian women in the twentieth century more widely available to all of us. Readers will get much pleasure, as well as instruction, from these pages.

ALISON PRENTICE
Professor Emerita
Ontario Institute for Studies in Education
University of Toronto
and
Adjunct Professor
University of Victoria

Acknowledgments

In the course of working on this project we have incurred numerous debts; it gives us great pleasure to acknowledge these supporters and contributors. We sincerely appreciate the generous remuneration and research support provided by Dean Johanne Bourdages, Faculty of Education; Director Chad Gaffield, Institute of Canadian Studies; Director Ruby Heap, Institute of Women's Studies; and Dean David Staines, Faculty of Arts, all of the University of Ottawa. The funding provided by the Millennium Fund through a joint project with Sylvia Spring of Making Waves Productions and the Canadian Studies Program of Canadian Heritage was invaluable to the completion of this volume.

Beyond financial contributions, we benefited from the advice and assistance offered at critical points by Chad Gaffield of the Institute of Canadian Studies; Phillip Cercone of McGill-Queen's University Press; Joy Harrison of Heritage Canada; Sandra Coney, author of *Standing in the Sunshine*, which served as an inspiration for our book; Pam Harris, documentary photographer; Lise Martin and Linda Clippingdale of the Canadian Research Institute for the Advancement of Women; and Lina Beaulieu of Teacher Education, University of Ottawa. Thanks to Melanie Abbott of Artworks Inc., whose creativity and eye for design helped us sell the idea of this book to others, and Robert Crabtree, for his financial-planning and fund-raising advice. As well, Terry Cook, Amber Lloydlangston, Eileen O'Connor, and Heather Robertson completed vital research and editorial tasks.

We are appreciative of the contributors, whose names appear in the table of contents and list of contributors, who sent us images, documents, and essays. In addition, many archivists and gallery and museum curators from across Canada assisted us with our research. Our thanks go to Angela Wheelock and Suzanne den Ouden, Yukon Archives; Pierrette Boily, Musée de Ste Boniface; Judi Schwartz at Hart House Gallery; Jim Burant, Françoise Chartrand, and Monique Benôit, National Archives of Canada; Wendy Thorpe, Nova Scotia Archives and Records Management; Anneke Shea-Harrison, Winnipeg Art Gallery; Marion Byard, Ontario Black History Society; Raven Amiro, National Gallery of Canada; Leslie Boyd, Dorset Fine Art; Christine Braun, Art Gallery of Hamilton; Mario Robert, Ville de Montréal Gestion de documents et archives; Marc Monette, Public Works and Government Services Canada, Parliamentary Precinct Directorate and Digital Simulation Laboratory; Mary Ledwell, Lisa Singer, James Allen, and Raymonde Cadorette, Archives of Ontario; and Frances Wright of the Famous Five Foundation. Finally, the editors wish to thank Judith Turnbull for her meticulous editing and Joan McGilvray for her wise counsel.

Members of the editorial committee generously reviewed submissions and several graciously agreed to write introductory essays. Our thanks are extended to Linda Ambrose (Laurentian University), Katherine Arnup

(Carleton University), Marilyn Barber (Carleton University), Nancy Bouchier (McMaster University), Ruth Compton Brouwer (King's College, University of Western Ontario), Gail Campbell (University of New Brunswick), Joanna Deans (Carleton University), Karen Dubinsky (Queen's University), Deborah Gorham (Carleton University), Viviane Gray (Department of Indian Affairs and Northern Development), Ruby Heap (University of Ottawa), Linda Kealey (Memorial University), Margaret Kechnie (Lakehead University), Ann Leger-Anderson (University of Regina), Eva Major-Marothy (National Archives of Canada), Alan McCullough (Parks Canada), Wendy Mitchinson (University of Waterloo), Gabrielle Nishiguchi (independent researcher), Susan North (Victoria and Albert Museum), Diana Pederson (Concordia University), Geneviève Postolec (National Archives of Canada), Alison Prentice (Ontario Institute for Studies in Education), the late Barbara Roberts (University of Northern British Columbia), Melissa Rombout (independent researcher), and Veronica Strong-Boag (University of British Columbia). In addition, we want to thank the anonymous reviewers of McGill-Queen's University Press for their thoughtful critiques of the manuscript. We are grateful for their having undertaken this sizeable task on our behalf. We also want to express appreciation to Joan Fairweather, who, along with Kate O'Rourke, originally conceived and launched this project.

Each of us has been sustained by a personal network of family and friends, to whom we extend our love and gratitude. Sharon's family has lived with this project longer than they would have wished, with an unplayable pool table, an unusable gazebo, and a dining table burdened with essays and images as the price paid for scholarship. Despite these hardships, sons Timothy and Graham, and partner Terry have mustered unflagging enthusiasm and encouragement during this adventure. Sharon is certain that a special place in heaven awaits Terry for his editorial skills and generosity during the preparation of the manuscript. Lorna's family heard firsthand about many of the essays and photos, and shared her excitement as the project began to take shape. Gord, Heather, and Andrea tolerated her weekend absences during marathon editing meetings, and Heather graciously stepped in and sorted out computer glitches. Lorna wants to thank her family for their unfailing support and good humour throughout the evolution of this book. Kate is indebted to her family and friends; their enduring patience through missed family events and their endless words of encouragement when the project seemed to stall will not be forgotten. Her special thanks go to Sandra and to Chris and Sherry for always being her Ottawa "homes" over the years and for providing food, shelter, and love at the end of long editorial days. Thanks also go to Mary and Lisa, her colleagues and friends, for listening patiently to the challenges faced on what no doubt seemed like a daily basis. Most importantly, Kate would like to express her deepest thanks and love to Lawrence, whose belief in and support of her work on this book sustained her throughout.

We have dedicated this book to women who, in our personal lives, have influenced, nurtured, and cheered us. These include our mothers, the women who have gone before us earlier in this century, who forged new paths while continuing to maintain families and build communities. Like the quilts we pull about us, they have provided us with warmth, beauty, and comfort; in turn, their support has allowed us to experiment in our own lives with new ways of living and learning. We dedicate this book to the next generation of young women and men around us, who will carry us into the twenty-first century with verve and compassion. Together, their lives have inspired this book.

Introduction

Canadian Women in the Twentieth Century

Sharon Anne Cook, Lorna R. McLean, and Kate O'Rourke

> She lives in you and me, and in many other women who
> are not here, for they're washing up the dishes and putting the
> children to bed. But she lives; they are continuing presences.
>> Virginia Woolf, *A Room of One's Own*

This volume analyses Canadian women's experiences during the twentieth century as rooted in the archival record. While stimulated by reflections on women's role during "Canada's century," the book is not intended as another millennial celebration of progress from Victorian constraints to women's liberation. In the following text and images, there is tragedy as well as triumph, frustration as well as joy, shadow as well as light, abuse and discrimination as well as barriers toppled and voices found.[1] We believe that women's stories and women's history, which build on those narratives, are important and should be offered to a wide readership.

In the last three decades, women's history has emerged as part of the larger social history project that seeks to recover the lives of "ordinary" people. Early efforts that had focused on the "woman worthies" later expanded to encompass women's paid and unpaid work, women's social and political organizations and institutions, and, most particularly, women's demand for the vote. Dominant themes included issues of class, ethnicity, immigration, and, to a lesser extent, culture and religion. More recently, women's history has turned its critical eye to probe new areas of specialization, exploring aspects of race and sexuality and the complexity of women's multiple identities.[2] This collection, in part, reflects this evolution and includes many of the themes and interpretive frameworks in the study of women's history.

We do not claim the book to be completely representative of the total experience of twentieth-century Canadian women. The process of soliciting manuscripts has meant that some topics are well represented and others under-represented or omitted altogether. The sample found here is also constrained by the limitations of formal archival collections. Most public archives in Canada, by their nature and mandates, reflect the figures and historical events of the dominant culture. As part of that culture, they have not acquired the same volume of representational material for non-dominant groups. Even where there exist archival records that document women's experiences, accessing them can be difficult.[3] The language used in catalogues, and other finding aids is based on concepts that mask women's particular contributions. Accessibility to these records has improved, however, as archivists have become more aware of inclusive terminology and of the gender implications for archival policies relating to acquisition and description.[4]

Archives have been the lesser-known treasure-trove of consumable information in comparison with either the museum or the gallery. The unique and fragile nature of archival holdings and the sometimes difficult access to them do not readily translate into an easy interaction between the records and the public. In addition, limited public-awareness opportunities, such as exhibitions, the mainstay of museums, have further intimidated the public from actively encountering archives. We hope that this book helps to bridge the gap between the public and archives, allowing those unfamiliar with these repositories a point of departure for their own forays into the records.[5]

GOALS

A book with so many authors and topics requires some introductory comment on our goals, methodology, structure, and organizing themes. First, our prime objective is to give voice to the experiences and accomplishments of Canadian women during the twentieth century as documented in archival records.[6] Some of the resulting essays and vignettes treat famous Canadian women such as Charlotte Whitton, Lotta Hitschmanova, and Pauline Johnson, but far more investigate women unknown beyond their own families or local community. Their history is lodged within the vast network of private archives and public institutions across this country.

Secondly, we hope to find the voice of our foremothers through historical analyses undertaken by writers from a variety of communities. To this end, we actively solicited papers in scholarly and community journals, on Web sites, and at symposia and conferences. We were thrilled to receive, over a five-year period, submissions from independent researchers, archivists, curators, students, and private citizens, as well as from some of Canada's most respected historians. Many contributions were sent to us by first-time authors who felt compelled to write about a woman, event, organization or group that had an impact on a corner of Canadian society. The essays, never published before, record how society has been enriched by so many little-known women, women who often expanded the boundaries of acceptable behaviour or pioneered new activities. Drawn from diverse sources, the papers together culminate in a symphony of women's voices, layered, each different from the other, yet frequently harmonizing across time and space.

Thirdly, this collection aims to engage both academic and public readerships. The diversity of the authors' backgrounds illustrates both the interdisciplinary nature of women's history and the potential for future projects to combine accessible archival records with historical interpretations. We hope that this collection will serve to bring underutilized documents to the fore and to provide archivists as well as private citizens with an opportunity to share what has rarely – indeed in some instances never – been seen publicly before. In so doing, we hope to stimulate further discussion about the preservation and interpretation of historical sources, particularly the vast range found in personal and public archives.[7]

METHODOLOGY

Just as women's varied contributions to Canada's public and private cultures have waited a long time to be recognized, collected, researched, and recorded, this book too has been a number of years in preparation. Initially conceived as a means to tap one major archival collection and to organize the research findings into a popular history focusing on oral testimony and visual documents such as art, photographs, and moving images, the project evolved into more than eighty selected and edited written contributions and more than two hundred images from personal holdings and private and public institutions across Canada. These contributions draw on the gamut of archival sources and testify to the rich heritage available in private and public archives, one from which our history as Canadian women can be crafted. Diary accounts remain an important resource, as is demonstrated by Jo Fraser Jones's analysis of Alice Barrett Parke (#23). Letters, both official and casual, are another prime source of knowledge about women, privileged and not. Katherine Arnup uses these poignant archival records to discuss the women who supplied milk to the Dionne quintuplets (#30). Veronica Strong-Boag's study of Pauline Johnson (#10) and Catherine Vye's of Zoé Laurier (#22) are other examples of letters-based research.

Archives also contain the records of organizations and these too are significant in charting women's lives. Patricia Dirks examines two important organizations for young women in twentieth-century Canada, the CGIT and the Girl Guides, through documents they produced for their members (#33). Paintings and quilts as well as dressmaking patterns and milliners' records not only tell us about the furnishings and fashions of the day, but also reveal the talent and labour of women who created items of beauty and function. Two of many examples are Christina Bates's study of milliners' records and hats (#71) and Anne Newlands's survey of ten artists working in various media(#20). Posters and advertisements, also found in archival collections, provide insights into women's place in society. Dianne Dodd and Ellen Scheinberg (#25 and #68) discuss the use of such promotional tactics with respect to women. Other archival documents are generated by official bodies, including government. These present a window on contested public policies, often representing the strands of public discourse as pressure is applied on one side or the other. Candace Loewen's study of the Voice of Women (#49) provides one such insight through the archival record.

One of the most surprising and rewarding aspects of this wide-ranging project was the contribution made by essays based on oral history and descriptions of oral history projects. Several examples of first-person oral history through reminiscences are presented, as, for example, in the pieces by Marjorie Levan (#8) and Joan Wheeler (#24). We have highlighted one oral history narrative in the essay by Christine Zaporzan (#67) and an oral history project in the essay by Wilma MacDonald (#65). Elizabeth Smyth's discussion of the critical importance of the archival records of women religious, particularly those arising from oral testimony in shrinking communities, stands as a warning to all historical researchers (#7). Without archival records like these, the writing of women's history would be an impossible task.

STRUCTURE

This book can be utilized in a number of ways. First-time readers of women's history are encouraged to consult the introductory essays for each of the book's six parts. These brief introductions establish the context of each theme and offer some preliminary comments on the individual elements that follow. Students of history will also find these introductory essays invaluable, as they serve to contextualize the diverse papers, vignettes, and images, and provide a framework of recent themes, interpretations, and debates in women's history.[8] Notably, each introductory essay is conceived as part of the whole project, but each also reflects the specific subject, section content, and author's interpretation. As such, they are constructed as stand-alone essays framed around selected topics.

While the organizing principle of the book is thematic, the parts are porous and the selections overlap, much like women's lives. Part 1, "Living Women's Lives," points to the lived experience of women during the past century. It includes a selection of the fundamental verities by which many women lived out their lives: social rituals with other women, organized sporting clubs, philanthropic efforts, study and reading groups, spirituality and aesthetics – identified by some historians as women's culture. Part 2 focuses on women's roles as nurturers and keepers of the hearth, with all that that prescribed, including family management, economic contributions, child care and health, and values development. Part 3 considers Canadian women's varied contributions within the formal and informal educational systems. Here, women appear as teachers, as curriculum developers, and as learners. Part 4 surveys some of the forms assumed by women's activism in the modern Canadian nation, but far more than political activism is discussed in this section. Of course, women were instrumental on the political stage, especially after being granted the right to vote in federal elections in 1918 and with their victory in the *Persons* case in 1929, but beyond this they exercised their public voices in social work, consumer activism, peace movements, royal commissions, and cultural expressions. Part 5 examines some of the myriad ways in which Canadian women in the twentieth century shaped health care and scientific investigations. Women's germinal positions as nurses and physiotherapists have been widely acknowledged, but their contributions as researchers in many fields have received less attention. The concluding section, Part 6, on women's work, is as diverse as women's forms of labour have always been in this country. From servants to dressmakers, from broadcasting to banking, women working within and outside the home have consistently shored up and supported family and nation through their labour.

The creation of vignettes around specific topics represents our attempt to introduce images from archival and private collections, thereby to add another dimension to our understanding of selected topics as represented through the written word. Images are too often under-utilized as archival resources, commonly relegated to illustrating a textual point. In contrast, a vignette like "Not Just Rosie ..." (#83) illustrates the typical war work performed by women in munitions factories and shows with minimal textual assistance the many other ways that women contributed to the war effort through their labour. In many cases, the vignettes stand apart from the essays in developing new understandings and in expanding the themes of the parts. In addition, these images bridge the gap between today's visually literate culture, which often relies on the image as a means of information, and the past, which relied far more heavily on the printed word. Who among us does not have a family photograph album documenting our own ancestors, or modern treasured photographs that we send to others or post on the Internet? In this sense, these vignettes document the lives of our foremothers in pictures, creating a kind of composite photograph album or a static Web page for the past.

Many of these essays and vignettes could easily be placed in two or more of the book's parts. While framed by the century, this collection is only broadly chronological within each part, again simulating women's lives with their multiple identities, interests, and responsibilities. Moreover, the book makes no attempt to "cover" each decade or every major historical event on the premise that many women lived their lives within the changing terrain of family, marriage, birthing, work, and care. Rather than being neatly compartmentalized in response to national events, women's lives proceeded according to their own and their families' rhythm, shifting boundaries as the exigencies of the moment demanded.

THEMES

Taken as a whole, the essays in this volume demonstrate a number of themes. In sorting the written selections and images to somehow give "order" to women's experiences and contributions, the editors have been powerfully reminded of the limited value of categories as they apply to women's lives. As members of institutions and groups and as organizers of campaigns on which they left their mark, women were at the same time part of family units, active in the culture of their day, participants and frequently leaders in education, and often politically engaged. And certainly all of them worked, sometimes paid and often not. To which category, then, does each profile belong? These decisions have not been easy and represent for us the blurred lines between the boundaries of women's multiple tasks, activities, and pleasures. Moreover, there is no particular order to the parts or the selections, just as there is no order to most women's lives, other than that of the life course.[9]

The mutability of these categories also serves to underpin a number of subtexts common to the experience of many of the women in this volume. Rarely do the essayists fail to note, for example, that the contributions made by any woman who chose to marry and raise children were carved out of a day largely devoted to the needs of others, even if that woman was privileged with position and money. The women in this book assumed numerous family responsibilities as part of their roles as care givers, claiming an hour here and there for "outside" or public endeavours, but never having sufficient time to approach their life work without a sense of carrying a heavy burden. A second subtext suggested in a large number of contributions is the variety of training provided to many Canadian women through their religious involvement. The influence of spiritual values is clearly demonstrated in many of the essays.

The essays also place before us evidence of the systemic barriers in women's paths. While most of these women were not revolutionaries, they persevered and found ways to achieve their objectives. Many were given encouragement and active mentoring by their mothers and fathers and then by their life partners, teachers, and employers. Where women elected not to marry and raise families, they created communities of understanding that acted as support groups, both privately and publicly. This volume contains many instances of women creating or changing, rather than simply enduring, the conditions of their lives. The solutions they found to their individual and our collective problems validate "women's ways of knowing" that are achieved through cooperation and flexibility, sharing and networking within the parameters of patriarchal culture.

Many aspects of women's lives during this century have not found a place in this book. Issues such as women's sexuality, racism, or violence against women[10] have only recently developed as research fields in Canada. In other instances, silence reflects the very private and personal nature of a specific topic. Certain communities of women will not find themselves represented in this collection despite our efforts at inclusivity. As well, it can be readily seen that the bulk of the articles and images in this book are situated in the first half of the twentieth century. To a degree, this should not be surprising to those engaged in historical analysis or archival work: a certain span of time must elapse before records make their way to archives and measured historical analysis is possible. Moreover, in recent decades the print- and text-based media have expanded their coverage of women and "women's issues" – largely as a result of the feminist movement of the sixties and the subsequent expansion of women's history as a legitimized branch of historical study, in Canada and beyond. Thus, our emphasis on events and women in the first half of the century serves, in part, to reclaim the experience of women from an earlier era for a wider public audience.

Taking these gaps and inclusions into consideration, we offer the following analogy for the collection's organizing concept. In our view, at the very root of women's lived experience – termed by some "women's culture" – is a shared discourse grounded in understandings associated with family, community, work, and spirituality based on nurturing, cooperation, connection, and feeling. We imagine the overarching significance of these lived experiences to be rather like the piece-work quilts on which countless Canadian women have laboured in this century and before, combining their well-honed practicality with their less-recognized artistry within a community of women.[11] The backing, binding, and batting of the metaphoric quilt is the common cultural bearing of many generations of Canadian women. The patterns created by swatches of fabric comprising the quilt top and the styles of stitching that link the quilt top to the backing and batting give each quilt its distinctive, harmonious quality. Some of the patterns give emphasis to individual blocks. Others hold to a single standard design, such as the much-reproduced Log Cabin motif, providing the impression that each quilt is much like the next. While it is true that each quilt also holds to certain common principles in order for it to be called a quilt at all, they are all different in some way, each one a unique blend of fabric, texture, pattern, and skill.

The making of quilts has in the past and continues to this day to be undertaken as a group project where women blend conversation with the passing on and refinement of home-craft knowledge, good works with networking opportunities, social ritual with domestic productivity, spiritual growth with women's mutual supportiveness in times of trial. Many a woman's political or moral campaign has been planned and rehearsed around the quilting frame! And if not the field on which revolution is plotted, the quilting frame has traditionally been a safe place where women have shared their stories of common life passages and uncommon challenges. It has also been the place where younger women have listened and learned. This, then, has been a prime setting where women's history has been passed down through the oral tradition. This book builds on that heritage. The swatches of fabric that comprise the quilt are something akin to archival records; interpretation and skill allow the historian/quilter to fashion a different product while using common materials and techniques as expressions of individuality and choices made. We thus hope that this collection inspires readers to collect, record, and recount their own histories in similar volumes and other forums. Like their real and metaphoric quilts, women's lives are "continuing presences" that, as Virginia Woolf says, "[live] in you and me."

SUGGESTIONS ON HOW TO USE THIS BOOK

Framing Our Past is designed to provide a wide variety of archival sources and interpreted articles to the general reader and the student of history. It does so by drawing on archival material presented as single images, groupings of images in vignettes, and essays based on documentary and oral sources. Other archival resources are identified on the part and essay/vignette charts in Appendix 1. Cross-referencing of essays to companion pieces, vignettes, and introductory essays is provided in a listing in Appendix 2. Sidebars appear throughout the text to amplify particular themes in the articles and to identify topics that have not been included. A list of suggested readings for further exploration of the general themes of this book is provided on pages 485–8. Finally a set of guiding questions, both historical and archival, for the reader's consideration as a further entry point into this book.

• From an archival perspective, what kinds of records are considered to be "archival"? How do these differ from those held in libraries? What kinds of archival records are held by families? Among the archival sources presented in this collection – diaries, manuscripts and correspondence, art, textiles, oral history, organizational records, posters, advertisements, and photographs – what limitations and constraints exist for each? For example, how does one confirm the accuracy of diary accounts or oral histories? Using another case, how do the record-keeping practices of institutions obscure the decisions or choices made by women? In addition to the repositories for archival records presented here, where else can archival records to document women's history be found?
• From an historical perspective, how do the articles in this book utilize archival records while using a variety of methodologies? How do the diversity of resources and methodologies contribute to our understanding of women's history? What conventional notions of women's historical experiences are challenged by the articles and archival resources presented in this volume? What aspects of women's diversity and commonalities are presented through a comparison of time periods, regions, class, ethnicity, religiosity, and patterns of work? What do the themes found in this book explicate or obscure in our understanding of women's experiences during the twentieth century?

PART ONE

Living Women's Lives

1 Introduction

Veronica Strong-Boag

To the extent that women live lives different from men, they create different cultures, different ways of being in the world. To the extent that they differ from each other, women also form non-identical, even discordant, cultures. This tension between similarity and difference has attracted much scholarly attention, both positive and negative, but ordinary people have also been fascinated by and often deeply committed to the belief that women and men, girls and boys, think and behave in ways determined by biology and confirmed by social organization. Twentieth-century writers, such as the socio-biologist Lionel Tiger in his *Men in Groups* (1969), often informed or misinformed by readings of Freudian psychology, took for granted women's rivalry with one another and unfitness for cooperation. Only men, some observers argued, could form natural alliances. In fact, historical research presents quite another story. Historians like Carroll Smith Rosenberg and Janet Guildford and Suzanne Morton point out, for example, that the middle class in nineteenth-century North American societies drew a sharp distinction between female and male worlds and, in the process, created substantial opportunities for female sociability and community.[1] Female culture continued to be expressed in the twentieth century in such varied sites as artists' studios, the stage, the shop, women's clubs, religious communities, and sports venues.

While intensity and form vary, no community has been without some form of female culture. Women often play, work, and politic together, as seen in Illustration 1.1, a photograph of Native women in the Homemakers' Club. Veronica Strong-Boag discovers intense relations among women in English Canada between the world wars,[2] and the Clio Collective recount many stories of vibrant female communities, both religious and secular, in Quebec.[3] Similarly, Varpu Lindstrom-Best celebrates the solidarity of immigrant Finnish domestics,[4] while Dionne Brand turns to the testimonies of Ontario's Black women[5] and Jean Burnet presents a collection that recognizes the experience, often the collaboration, of women of diverse origins.[6] For many Canadian women throughout the century, the small town has been the site for a vibrant women's culture, as is profiled in the vignette for Nelson, British Columbia (#5).

FANNY "BOBBIE" ROSENFELD, 1903–1969

Shortly after Fannie Rosenfeld's birth in Russia, her family emigrated to Canada, settling in Barrie. An all-round athlete, "Bobbie" excelled in hockey, basketball, tennis, and softball. She held several long-standing Canadian track and field records and the world record for the 100 metres. She led the Canadian women's team to victory at the 1928 Amsterdam Olympics with a gold and silver medal. Arthritis ended her athletic career in 1933, after which she became a prominent Toronto sports columnist. In 1949 Bobbie was chosen Canada's outstanding female athlete of the half-century. (Courtesy of Parks Canada)

1.1 Native women at Homemakers' Club, Northern Ontario, 1949 (F884, Archives of Ontario)

Even when men have been especially powerful, perhaps especially then, girls and women have moved from birth on within worlds shaped and informed by those of their own sex. From childhood to old age, women have found rewards in their relations with one another. Kathleen Wilker's description of her grandmother's clothing club in turn-of-the-century Newfoundland captures one such example(#2). Experiences such as these frequently begin within the family. Mothers and daughters, sisters and cousins, and extended kin as well have been accustomed to each other's company. Such bonds often formed the bedrock of women's worlds but intimate relations have also been formed in a diversity of sites, including classrooms and schoolyards, workplaces and churches, and sporting, artistic, and political arenas. The women of the Canadian Negro Women's Association, for example, encouraged young Black women to pursue educational goals. While bitterness and dissatisfaction have existed, so too have affection, admiration, loyalty, and passion. The daily demands of personal education, health, and welfare, not to mention those of earning a livelihood, keeping a house and family, and having a good time, have regularly brought women into close proximity, sometimes to become allies, friends, and lovers. When male worlds, whether of work, religion, politics, or athletics, have been closed, women have all the more readily turned to their own sex for recognition and assistance.

When they have, by choice or necessity, resided alone or only with men, women have frequently observed customs and practices – from meal preparation and personal hygiene to holiday celebrations and diary and letter-writing – that spring from what Carroll Smith Rosenberg termed "the female world of love and ritual." The vignette concerned with tea rituals (#3) illustrates one ceremony that underpins women's distinct cultural experience, and that on "Yukon Women Pioneers" (#15) demonstrates quite another set of practices developed by women in a different time and place. The photograph of the bride in Illustration 1.2, taken at her wedding in an elegantly decorated church, offers yet another instance of a prized ritual to mark a happy occasion. The wearing of a fashionable wedding dress in the remote Yukon further demonstrates the importance of this event in the lives of the participants. Many of these rituals are observed in the presence of men; yet to convey the significance of female company, the Canadian mixed-race writer E. Pauline Johnson (profiled in essay #10 and known in the Mohawk community as Tekahionwake) described the loneliness of her short-story character Mrs Lysle, the wife of a Mountie serving in the North: "There are times even in the life of a wife and mother when her soul rebels at cutting herself off from all womankind, and all that environment of social life among women means, even if the act itself is voluntary on her part." Later on, "during days when the sight of a woman's face would have been a glimpse of paradise to her," she "almost wildly regretted her boy had not been a girl – just a little sweet-voiced girl, a thing of her own sex and kind."[7]

1.2 Rural wedding, Yukon, c. 1900 (National Archives of Canada)

Through shared custom and ritual, women have created distinctive cultural artifacts and historical documents, the basic organizing principle for this collection. Some of these records are textual, as discussed by Elizabeth Smyth in her analysis of documents produced by women religious within an English Canadian cloistered community (#7), and by Marilyn Färdig Whiteley in an examination of minute books kept by Protestant women's Ladies' Aid Societies (#6). These records attest to the fortifying role served by female spiritual culture in Canadian women's lives over the course of this century. Textual records are further represented here by the formal papers written and presented by members of women's study and reading groups in Winnipeg between 1900 and 1940 (#4). Other documents are orally based, attesting to the vibrancy of an oral women's culture. Marjorie Levan's account of her mother's life as a missionary, and of the family culture to which she contributed both in China and Canada, demonstrates the power of this form of historical record (#8). Of her

LUCY MAUD MONTGOMERY, 1874–1942

Internationally renowned author Lucy Maud Montgomery was born in New London, Prince Edward Island. After her mother's death in 1876, she lived with her maternal grandparents until 1911, when she married and moved to Ontario. While residing in Cavendish, P.E.I., she wrote her first novel, *Anne of Green Gables* (1908). A series of popular sequels and other successful novels followed, but the enduring fame of Lucy Maud Montgomery has been firmly established with her creation of Anne, one of the most loveable children in English fiction. Montgomery died in Toronto and is buried in Cavendish, P.E.I. (Courtesy of Parks Canada)

1.3 Canadian Handicrafts Guild exhibit of rug-hooking, c. 1900 (Courtesy of Canadian Guild of Crafts, Quebec)

distinguished themselves as writers, as in the case of Gabrielle Roy and Mairuth Sarsfield (#11), and as performance artists. They have drawn on societal expectations of their civilizing responsibilities to produce a sustained record of artistic expression. Several pieces in this collection focus on these forms, including the contributions by Kirstin Evenden, Sharon Cook, Sonia Halpern, and Helen Diemert. Anne Newlands argues that several key artists articulated twentieth-century society through a female world-view of the visual arts.

Women, both marginalized and mainstream, have found opportunities to develop distinctive cultural artifacts through "handicrafts" that blend artistry and utilitarianism. As shown in Illustration 1.3, a photograph from the Canadian Handicrafts Guild, and supported by Ellen McLeod's biographies of May Phillips and Mary Alice Skelton Peck (#16) and by Jessica Tomic-Bagshaw's study of the development of Inuit print-making as a cottage industry (#18), women have traditionally sought cultural expression through crafts. Here we see attractive and practical blankets, rugs, table-runners, wall hangings, prints, quilts, coverlets, baskets, trays, household containers, dolls, furniture, clothing, draperies, and much more, all confirming women's desire and ability to combine work with leisure and beauty. In this setting as in others, women have expressed difference and solidarity through their construction of a rich tapestry of cultural expressions.

mother, she writes, "Mildred Armstrong's life was unique, but in many ways typical of the women at the turn of the century who were challenging the traditional expectations of womanhood. She was a strong woman with courage, a zest for life and compulsive idealism." Mildred Armstrong's life experiences were much more common in early twentieth-century Canada than is true today, but she remains an important study of the strengths found in our grandmothers.

A good many of the cultural artifacts from our foremothers can be classified as art and, as represented in this volume, especially as visual art. Women have also

A list of readings on this topic is provided on page 485.

2 "Club": Laundering Clothing in Newfoundland

Kathleen Wilker

Grandma has her own distinct history, a history she has been sharing with us for as long as I can remember. I've heard many of her stories many times. But as I get older, she adds details to make the stories relevant to my changing life. So even if I've heard a story more times than I can count, I always listen carefully for surprises. Last Christmas, after I shared some of my feminist ideas with her, Grandma told me a new story. I'll share it as I remember it.

Shortly after she was married in St John's, Newfoundland, Grandma became a founding member of a special club. I've heard her speak of "club" for years, but I always assumed this was a short form for one of her many bridge clubs – the kind of abbreviation that members use with other members. She and Mom laughed when I told them that. Sometimes Mum assumes that I know a lot more about Grandma's life than I do.

Anyway, in those days – the middle of the Second World War – there weren't organizations like the Salvation Army or Goodwill to provide clothing for poorer families. Not in Newfoundland. (Grandma smiled at my patchy jeans, which she knew were a second-hand bargain.) So Grandma and some of her newly married friends decided to pass along their old clothes. Their project required some tact because no one likes accepting charity.

Fortunately, one woman's brother was a priest. It was okay for him to ask families, during his pastoral visits, if they could use some clothes and, if so, in what sizes. He would then discreetly pass along the ages, sizes, and sexes of those needing clothing to the president of Grandma's club. This lady would contact each club member and let her know what garments she should bring to the next meeting. That way the women could pack a box with one outfit for each person. The priest did the deliveries.

I'll pause here to explain a few details. The club women were friends from church who each had other circles of friends. So between them, the club ladies had a large network of women from whom they accepted old clothing for their Tuesday night meetings. Once there, they would sort the clothing and each woman would take home the garments – say men's trousers or girls' dresses – that she was in charge of, to wash and press them.

The women were quite strict about the kind of hospitality that was to be offered when they all met in one another's homes. The hostess was allowed to serve tea, coffee, and one kind of dessert like cookies or one savoury treat like biscuits and cheese. Not both. They were not meeting to out-do each other in a hospitality contest. Grandma made that perfectly clear.

A new president – whose duties included keeping in touch with the priest and letting the other women know what they should bring to each meeting – was nominated every two years. But the other executive position, "Shopper," was a lifelong job. Each week the women would bring twenty-five cents for the underwear kitty and every few months Shopper would take this money and cajole the local shopkeepers into giving her a real bargain.

I asked Grandma what the men did at club. She said, "Oh, the husbands … sometimes they'd stand in the doorway and talk for twenty minutes or so, but we got down to work." I'm not sure what the children were doing while their mothers were busy, out at meetings or hosting club. I didn't ask and she didn't say.

Grandma's club celebrated its fiftieth anniversary last time she was in Newfoundland. It's a lot smaller now. Many of its members, her dearest friends, have died or are dying. But every time she returns, Grandma's remaining club friends have a good visit with her. Sometimes they take her out for a drive. Other times they go for lunch at Signal Hill, where there's usually a nice spread.

Club has always been officially anonymous. They wouldn't have it any other way. But one time in church, the priest said something about a group of ladies who … and Grandma didn't mind being mentioned at all.

Vignette

3 Stirring the Pot

The ritual of the tea service, while an ancient one embedded in social tradition in places such as Japan and China, has come to symbolize in the Western world the gathering place where women talk and connect. In pioneer settlements, women often clung to the civility of serving afternoon tea when all else around them was rough and forbidding (Illustration 3.1). Through much of this century, tea cups were given to brides at all-female wedding showers to better equip their new homes, and in some families, china tea services were passed on from one generation of women to the next as part of a precious family heritage. Organized teas have also served as the site for many social and reform causes. Women's groups such as church auxiliaries, Women's Institutes, and branches of Hadassah have used the "tea" to raise funds for libraries, shelters, schools, war efforts, and, in rural areas, medical services (Illustrations 3.2, 3.3, and 3.4). The photographs reproduced here illustrate the social tea rituals that women have created. Regardless of type, be it black, herbal, Earl Grey, Darjeeling, Oolong, or green, the pot of tea will always symbolize the gathering of women to share their experiences.

3.1 A tea party, 1901 (1996–174, Nova Scotia Archives and Records Management)

3.2 Fund-raising tea in honour of servicemen, Halifax, 1940s (1996–174, Nova Scotia Archives and Records Management)

3.3 Tea time, 1950s (1996–369, 48, Nova Scotia Archives and Records Management)

3.4 Hadassah Wizo tea party, 1960s (C57262, National Archives of Canada)

4 Winnipeg Women Getting Together: Study Groups and Reading Clubs, 1900–1940

Jody Baltessen and Shelagh J. Squire

Thank you for re-electing me as a member of this unique Club. The years I was unable to participate were indeed frustrating, as my spirit was ever with the group every second Friday of the month.[1]

Canada has a rich history of women organizing and forming groups devoted to personal, social, political, and economic improvement. In a 1916 book, *The Woman – Bless Her: Not as Amiable a Book as It Sounds*, Marjory MacMurchy (Lady Willison) estimated that one in eight Canadian women belonged to a national women's organization, such as the Women's Canadian Club.[2]

Despite the far-reaching influence of national organizations, many women chose instead to join local groups dedicated to "improving the quality of community life."[3] These included missionary societies and church groups affiliated with various religious denominations, as well as clubs whose members shared professional interests like nursing or teaching. Women also organized locally to address child welfare, poverty, immigrant settlement, wage reform, political equality, and other social issues. It was, for example, a group of women – members of the Christian Endeavour Movement's Relief Committee – who undertook the first social welfare survey for the city of Winnipeg in 1894. Winnipeg women also campaigned actively for female suffrage, launching the Manitoba Equal Franchise Club and the Winnipeg Political Equality League.[4]

While attention has focused on women who organized around charitable causes or political issues, less study has been devoted to the activities of women who met specifically for intellectual stimulation.[5] Drawing on collections held by the Provincial Archives of Manitoba, this essay highlights the range of study groups formed by women in Winnipeg between 1900 and 1940, with particular emphasis on the Social Science Study Club (sssc), a group that integrated academic improvement with social activism. This chapter's opening quotation, taken from a paper presented to the sssc, suggests the importance of such clubs to their members.

Building on its early history as a fur-trading post at the forks of the Red and Assiniboine Rivers, Winnipeg established itself as the principal city (and capital) of the new province of Manitoba soon after its incorporation in 1873. Through a succession of booms and busts, Winnipeg grew quickly to reach a population of 163,000 by 1916. During these years, the city was both a destination and a transfer point for immigrants and goods moving west, as well as the administrative centre for prairie agriculture. Billed by its promoters as the "Chicago of the North," Winnipeg sustained a vibrant cultural life and was characterized by neighbourhoods with distinctive ethno-cultural identities.[6] To the south, River Heights, Fort Garry, and Fort Rouge were home to the city's large British population, typically well-educated business people and professionals. The North End, centred by Selkirk Avenue, housed a succession of new immigrants, particularly Jews and Eastern Europeans in the early years of this century. And to the northeast was St Boniface, the long-established centre of the French-speaking population. By 1941, the pace of Winnipeg's growth had slowed. The city was then home to 221,960 residents.[7]

Within this context, women gathered together. Why and how Winnipeg women organized themselves was influenced by diverse factors. As in other cities, social class, ethnicity, education, leisure time, and external circumstances influenced their organizing activities.[8] Globally, the period between 1900 and 1940 was punctuated by the First World War and the onset of the Second, as well as by severe economic depression. For Winnipeg, the General Strike of 1919 had particular social and political implications. All of these factors combined to shape the character of Winnipeg's women's groups.

Records attest to the enthusiasm with which Winnipeg women organized and to the range of concerns they addressed. In addition to documenting women's roles in charitable and community work, such sources show that women gathered together to pursue self-education through research, study, and discussion.[9] The Searchlight Book Club (SBC), established in 1910, typifies this kind of group. Its purpose, the mutual aid and improvement of its members, was accomplished through a yearly program of books for study. As one woman reflected on SBC activities for 1923:

To me it has been most interesting, and our Club, consisting mostly of ladies much occupied with home duties, unless we were members of this Club and forced to review and delve into these poems, we would be inclined to relegate the same to some period when we might have greater leisure and consequently the time would probably not ever arrive. But, when we find ourselves with papers to prepare and poems to be read with a purpose, we derive a great benefit therefrom, and for this we must be grateful to our membership and such a Club as ours.[10]

Other clubs operated in a similar fashion. The Twenty Club (TC) – membership was limited to twenty so that meetings could be held in members' homes – set an annual program of papers around a particular theme. Over the years, topics ranged from finance and social welfare to travel, the arts, and history. TC records suggest that members were especially interested in women's accomplishments in artistic and professional fields.[11]

Records also show that clubs were organized in particular neighbourhoods. For example, members of the Fort Garry Reading Club (FGRC), founded in 1932, lived in that area and met regularly to discuss assigned books. And the Hawthorne Women's Club (HWC) was organized in 1923 by women living near Hawthorne Avenue in East Kildonan. The HWC aimed to "promote amongst its members the study of Literature, Art, Music, Education, Current Events, and kindred matters and also to foster a community spirit."[12] HWC members met fortnightly around a program of study set each year by the program committee and the club's executive. Minutes detail presentations by members and invited speakers on topics spanning child psychology, British literature, Japanese poetry, European and Canadian politics, labour, and laws pertaining to women.

Evidence also suggests that clubs interacted with each other and enjoyed a favourable profile in the community at large. In a history of the Fort Garry Reading Club, the writer notes that in 1934 a joint meeting and luncheon for reading clubs was held at the Lower Fort Motor Club, a popular motoring destination of the period.[13] As well, the president of the Women's Canadian Club spoke at a meeting of the Hawthorne Club in 1924, and in 1933 members of the Fort Garry Reading Club reflected on an "entertainment" sponsored by the Twenty Club.[14] In 1919 the T. Eaton Company ordered books for the Searchlight Book Club's program and members were encouraged to buy their books from that store.[15] One year later, the SBC agreed to allow its papers to be read at country club gatherings.

In addition to the social network that emerged and was fostered by the organized nature of women's reading clubs, the public profile of the clubs was further enhanced by their involvement in charitable and social welfare activities. Clubs typically distributed hampers to needy families, contributed to the war effort, and participated in discussions about civic reform. They also responded to other requests for assistance. For example Mrs Curry of the Fort Garry Reading Club received a request for reading material from a "pioneer mother of ten children."[16] The FGRC sent ninety pounds of reading material and several bundles of clothing to Mrs Rudolph of Laurier, a small town northwest of Winnipeg.

In club records at the Provincial Archives of Manitoba, private and public narratives intertwine. Since these groups were formed primarily to meet personal needs, intellectual discussion is reported alongside notes about members' lives and families. Although biased towards the social elite and women who were literate, these records "open a window into the private lives of women and their circles."[17] They also raise questions about intersections between private and public forums. The Social Science Study Club, in particular, illustrates this convergence.

In June of 1912, Georgena Margaret (Mrs H.H.) Smith proposed forming a women's club to study the social sciences. SSSC members later recalled that Mrs Smith was concerned about the number of intelligent women who spent their afternoons playing euchre.[18] At the founding meeting, members agreed that the purpose of their new club would be "the study of social and economic conditions and the means of improving the same."[19] A constitution was drawn up and a slate of officers was elected to develop a program for the club's first year.

Sadly, Mrs Smith died before the SSSC met again in the fall of 1912. However, Vice-President Eva Jones assumed the presidency and led members through the club's first program, a detailed study of education. As principal of Winnipeg's Havergal Ladies College (later Rupert's Land School for Girls) and a past president of the Women's Canadian Club of Winnipeg, Miss Jones was well qualified for the task. Following her successful leadership through the SSSC's first year, she was elected as president for the upcoming season.

Like Miss Jones, many SSSC members were active in other organizations and issues related to social and political reform. For example, as the SSSC worked through its 1913–14 program on the "City and Its Health," Miss Jones, Edna Carley (Mrs Claude) Nash, and Margaret (Mrs R. F.) McWilliams were surveying the working conditions and wages of women factory and shop workers in Winnipeg. Their findings were presented to the SSSC as part of that year's program and were later used to support a brief carried to the Manitoba Legislature by the University Women's Club. Soon thereafter a minimum wage for women became law. After her work on this issue, Mrs Nash was appointed "Lady Member" of the Winnipeg Civic Charities Bureau. The newspaper announcement of her appointment tells of her involvement in a number of other agencies: the Labour Bureau for the Unemployed, the local Council of Women, and the Winnipeg Training School for Household Assistants. Though she was a busy woman, she served as president of the SSSC from 1919 until 1921 and maintained her membership well into the 1940s.

In 1919 the ranks of the unemployed were swollen by soldiers returning from the First World War, and Winnipeg was soon shaken by labour unrest and political turmoil. These events concerned most citizens, and members of the SSSC were no exception. Under Mrs G.D. Lynch's presidency, the 1918–19 program was devoted to the study of "Labour." A surviving paper presented to the sssc in January 1919 addressed the topic of strikes and lockouts, a portent of the General Strike that was to occur that summer. The writer noted:

Clearly, when all their benefits can be obtained in other and better ways, strikes are a social crime and ought to be abolished. If we would do away with strikes, we must find something to take their place. Several methods of preserving industrial peace are now being used. Wealthy corporations have built model villages and libraries, hospitals, amusement halls, and the best working conditions. But this method is not a success. A notable "model village" strike occurred a few years ago at Ludlow near Springfield, Massachusetts, where the men, after receiving the best social conditions, struck for higher wages. The difficulty lies in the law of human nature that men will not let benevolence take the place of justice.[20]

While this paper suggests distaste for civil disobedience, it is tempered by an understanding of human nature and the power differential between employer and employee. What makes this view particularly interesting is that most members of the sssc were married to men prominent in business and the professions, belonging thereby to Winnipeg's social elite. Yet, sssc members did not defend the actions of business towards its workers. Rather, the selection of topics in this and subsequent years reflects an academic distance between the women and the subjects they chose to study.

After 1919 Winnipeg settled somewhat into the routine of a bustling urban centre. As in other cities, growth and development were accompanied by social change and a visible need for welfare work and civic reform. In a 1954 paper on the Social Science Study Club, Mary (Mrs H.M.) Speechly, a long-time member, noted that a major focus in the early 1920s was the reorganization of private charity in Winnipeg. She wrote: "[T]o bring order into the 'welfare field,' to cut out duplication of services and to fill new needs that were emerging, the Central Council of Social Agencies was formed, with our Club one of its first affiliates."[21]

Concern for social reform continued to preoccupy sssc members into the 1930s. Following the club's study of "The Family" in the 1930–31 season, six members became active proponents of the Winnipeg Birth Control Society (later Planned Parenthood Manitoba). sssc members also supported the formation of the Family Bureau, an organization that provided advice and temporary assistance in the home to families "not yet in serious trouble."[22]

As the Depression years of the 1930s drew to a close and war loomed once again, sssc energies were directed to war work and the study of political issues central to the emerging conflict. During these years, the club was involved in the formation of a Central Volunteer Bureau "to bring into a central point the enrollment of volunteers and to place them where they were most needed and could be most useful."[23] As with many other initiatives supported by the sssc, the idea behind this venture continues today as the Volunteer Centre in Winnipeg.

Following the war years, sssc programs detail the members' continued interest in issues related to social and civic reform. For example, the 1949–50 program was devoted to Public Health and Government Responsibility. In other years, members analysed the findings of various government commissions and discussed topics as varied as world population, the United Nations, personal liberty, and extra sensory perception. However, as the sssc entered the 1960s, new recruits became harder to enlist and the program committee began to have difficulty securing papers for the season. The minutes of 17 June 1966 foreshadow the sssc's final meeting: "Miss Dafoe attempted to find out how many would give papers in the coming season, with very little response."[24] Later that year the members considered three options for the future of the sssc: reducing the number of meetings per season, sponsoring discussion groups rather than inviting formal papers, or disbanding the club entirely. After much discussion, a motion to disband the sssc was brought before the meeting: "In view of changed conditions, individual members find themselves unable to prepare papers for the program, therefore, we move, with sincere regret, that the Social Science Study Club be disbanded as of this date, October 14, 1966."[25] The motion carried unanimously.

In retrospect, and as related to the history of Winnipeg women's study groups, the Second World War can be seen as an important social-cultural marker. Most of the clubs discussed here continued to meet throughout the war years, with members engaged in war work. Changes wrought by the war, however, altered fundamentally women's roles and opportunities. While some groups persisted long into the postwar era, their functions shifted. And, like the Social Science Study Club, most eventually disbanded for reasons ranging from the ill health or advancing age of members, to difficulty recruiting new members, to existing members turning to other interests.

What, then, is the legacy of these clubs? As MacMurchy wrote in 1916, "Few things are more unhealthy for a woman whose work is keeping house to remain indoors alone, all day, every day."[26] Until recently, and certainly when these groups flourished, most women were "confined to [that] private sphere."[27] Clubs like those discussed in this paper offered women opportunities for socializing and community activity. In this sense, club records provide insight into how some women in the past used their leisure time to forge important personal, social, and political alliances. Such engagements also stimulate questions about how women used these clubs to gain a "voice" when outlets for their concerns were more limited. As well, these records suggest questions about the women themselves. How did they find time to read and write the papers required of them? What was their source material? Was this kind of study lent an air of legitimacy by the formal structure of the group? Was the group a source of strength and support outside scheduled meeting dates? And were these women's husbands supportive of their wive's club work?

In no small way, this record of Winnipeg women getting together contributes to our understanding of a particular time, place, and world-view. And now the legacy left by these women affords us opportunities to integrate their experiences into the present-day writing of Canadian women's history.

5 Life in the Town of Nelson, British Columbia

Brenda Hornby

5.1 Edith Attree and her family (Nelson Museum, Kootenania Collection, #782)

Life in small-town Canada has been the subject of many works in Canadian literature. Records held in small municipal archives and by local historical societies are a rich source of information on the life experiences of many Canadian women in small towns during the twentieth century. This vignette is a scrapbook that illustrates aspects of life in Nelson, B.C., during the first half of this century. The records of the Nelson Museum's Women's Project show that women worked at a multitude of jobs in addition to raising families, attending school, and socializing with each other at the Women's Institutes, thereby weaving a fabric that sustained not only themselves and their families, but also their community.

Edith Attree emigrated to Canada with her family in 1910 (Illustration 5.1). This excerpt from a letter written home to England explains, without regret, some of the hardships she had endured since her arrival:

We are quite glad we came out, for everything is most promising. The only difficulty, of course, is tiding over the first two years. The settlers, eleven in number, are all very satisfactory people whom we like very much and all seem anxious to work well together. The settlers have formed themselves a Fruit Growers Association, meeting every fortnight to discuss affairs and invite experts to come and give their experiences … There is splendid fishing in the Bay so we hope the men will be able to fill our larder, if we are able to get a boat. But there are so many implements needed I'm afraid that it will come last … We are quite settled in our new home having gone from varied countless hours of comfort and discomfort since leaving old England.

During the First World War, women were hired as waitresses on the Canadian Pacific Railway's Kootenay Lake sternwheelers to replace the men who had previously worked as waiters on the boats (Illustration 5.2). Mrs Lillian Williams worked as a supervisor in the dining room and at the Captain's Table. She was also responsible for taking tickets and for monitoring the gangplank. Lillian received sixty dollars a month plus room and board, which at the time was a reasonable wage, considering that teachers made the same salary. Almost all the women had to leave these jobs when the men returned from the war.

5.2 Staff aboard the *Nasookin* sternwheeler, 1913 (Nelson Museum, Hunt collection, 84.123.9)

The matchblocks produced in the Powell Match Block Factory, as seen in (Illustration 5.3), were shipped to the Eddy Match Company in Hull, Quebec or sent to markets in South Africa, India and the United Kingdom. The factory, which operated for nearly fifty years in Nelson, was one of the two factories in town that employed women early in the century, the other being the MacDonald Jam Factory. Men operated all the machinery, while women, many of whom were unemployed nurses or teachers, worked as choppers and sorters on an assembly line. Using a small hatchet, the women worked in cubicles, cutting out knots and holes in the wood and sending them down the line. In the 1920s and 1930s, women worked without coffee breaks, standing all day long, six days a week for eight hours a day, and were paid twenty-five cents an hour. The old plant burned down in 1945 and was replaced by a modern building. The Powell Match Block factory closed in 1964.[1]

5.3 The Powell Match Block Factory, 1948 (Nelson Museum, *Nelson Daily News* Collection, 92.97.168)

On 10 November 1909, a public meeting was held in the Eagles Hall for the purpose of forming a Nelson branch of the Women's Institute. Adopting the national motto "For Home and Country," Nelson women enthusiastically joined the organization. The main objective of the WI was to improve the living conditions for rural women and their families. Community-minded and determined to bring "civilized" order to a rough mining settlement, Nelson-and-area women financed the maintenance of libraries and parks, sponsored educational lectures, and lobbied for adequate health facilities. The first Nelson community baby and dental clinics were established by the WI in 1921. During both world wars, the Institutes' members knitted and sewed clothing, made bandages, and prepared hundreds of pounds of jam to send to Britain (Illustration 5.4).

5.4 Women's Institute Fortieth Anniversary, 1949 (Nelson Museum, Women of Nelson Collection, #2060)

Born in Regina in 1884, Helen Reynolds moved with her parents to Nelson in 1897, where her father joined the management of the Hall Mines Smelter. Her first published work appeared in the *Nelson Daily News* in a series of articles about pioneer days in Nelson. Later, when she lived in Vancouver, Helen wrote regular articles on art and artists for the *Vancouver Province*, but she would become best known for her novels. The publisher of her first book, Ryerson Press, encouraged Helen to use the masculine name Dickson Reynolds as a *nom de plume*. It wasn't until the 1940s that Helen revealed herself as a woman writer. Her novel *He Will Return* depicts the life of farmers near Nelson during the Depression and draws on her own life as a widow striving to support herself and two small children by keeping chickens and harvesting fruit.

5.5 Helen Reynolds by Kathleen Shackleton, 1939 (Nelson Museum, Women of Nelson Collection, 91.51.1)

5.6 Gwen Scott-Lauder and her family, 1922 (Procter-Hattop Book Committee Collection, #837, Nelson Museum)

Gwen Scott-Lauder was three years old when she and her mother came to Canada from Edinburgh to join her father, a settler on Kootenay Lake (Illustration 5.6). Inexperienced homesteaders, Scott-Lauder and his brother purchased wilderness land and built a home without such comforts as running water. Adopting a similar lifestyle, a total of ten families settled in this area and lasting friendships were made. Gwen recollects one of her mother's undertakings for her new community:

My mother, an avid reader, was in charge of the Government Travelling Library. This important service allowed isolated settlers to keep up with current affairs and literature. She also ran a small grocery store, however, she proved unsuitable to the business of trade – she was too soft in her billing of overdue accounts. It must have been a hard and lonely life. Looking back, I now realize how very homesick she must have been – she was constantly talking about Scotland and the old country.

At age nine Audrey Richardson decided that one day she would become a nurse. At that time her younger brother had contracted double pneumonia and Audrey had watched, transfixed, as a young nurse brought him back to good health. Years later the vigorous three-year nursing program offered in Nelson brought Audrey to the area. She graduated in 1935 (Illustration 5.7). The young women undertook three months of lectures from resident doctors prior to being introduced to practical training. Twelve full months of strenuous training constituted the first year at the school, with the second and third years permitting students a month's summer holiday. The young women received room and board and were paid a meagre salary for their practical efforts. The training nurses worked twelve hours a day, six and a half days a week, and were on call twenty-four hours a day.

5.7 Kootenay Lake Hospital graduates, 1935
(Nelson Museum, Women of Nelson Collection, 92.77.1)

6 "Doing All the Rest": Church Women of the Ladies' Aid Society

Marilyn Färdig Whiteley

We've put a fine addition on the good old church at home,
It's just the latest kilter, with a gallery and dome,
It seats a thousand people – finest church in all the town,
And when 'twas dedicated, why, we planked ten thousand down;
That is, we paid five thousand – every fellow did his best –
And the Ladies' Aid Society, it promised all the rest.

We've got an organ in the church – very finest in the land,
It's got a thousand pipes or more, its melody is grand.
And when we sit on cushioned pews and hear the master play,
It carries us to realms of bliss unnumbered miles away.
It cost a cool three thousand, and it's stood the hardest test;
We'll pay a thousand on it – the Ladies' Aid the rest.

They'll give a hundred sociables, cantatas, too, and teas;
They's bake a thousand angel cakes and tons of cream they'll freeze.
They'll beg and scrape and toil and sweat for seven years or more,
And then they'll start all o'er again, for a carpet on the floor.
No, it isn't just like digging out the money from your vest
When the Ladies' Aid gets busy and says, "We'll pay the rest."

Of course; we're proud of our big church from pulpit up to spire;
It's the darling for our eyes, the crown of our desire,
But when I see the sisters work to raise the cash that lacks,
I somehow feel the church is built on women's tired backs.
And sometimes I can't help thinking when we reach the regions blest,
That men will get the toil and sweat, and the Ladies' Aid the rest.

In Kitchener, Ontario, some member of the Methodist Ladies' Aid pasted a clipping of this poem, "The Ladies' Aid," inside a book containing the society's minutes. This group was typical of hundreds across Canada organized by women in support of their churches. The Kitchener women bought fruit trees for the parsonage garden, paid to have a hardwood floor installed in the church, sewed for those in need, and even, in September of 1919, took over the debt on the parsonage. The woman who placed the poem in the minute book silently testified to the women's pride in their work, but also to their weariness and occasional frustration.[1]

Women of many religious affiliations have joined together to express their faith in practical ways, but the groups that they organize take different forms accounting to the different tradition of their members. Each Ladies' Aid responds to the needs of a particular church at a particular time. Early in the twentieth century, Methodist women most frequently came together to care for parsonages and church buildings, although their activities expanded far beyond what they first saw as their responsibility. After the Methodists became part of the United Church of Canada in 1925, groups of women continued to meet the needs of church and community as these changed throughout the century.

In the Methodist Church, the ministers were itinerants: they were assigned to churches and could stay there for only a limited term. When ministers moved, they and their families took with them only their personal effects; the congregations supplied furnished accommodation. A trustee board (made up of men from the congregation) rented, purchased, or built a parsonage. But who would see that it was appropriately furnished and cared for?

This seemed a natural job for women, who, after all, did just this sort of thing in their own homes. And so in many Methodist churches, the ministers, the men who were the congregation's officers, and the women themselves supported the creation of Ladies' Aids. Women of the Aid frequently took on the challenge of furnishing a new parsonage, as well as the continuing task of keeping it comfortable for the minister and his family. Members cleaned, papered, and painted, or hired others for the tasks, and often initiated such improvements as plumbing, electricity, and telephones. They responded to the request of the minister and his wife, but they also tried to anticipate those requests by inspecting the property themselves.

The church buildings also required care, and often the women carpeted the churches, kept them clean, and furnished them with hymn-books, collection plates, and communion sets. They stocked church basements with dishes and silverware, and carefully locked these away in cupboards; the women who had provided these supplies kept the keys and decided who could borrow or rent them.

The women often showed financial acumen. In August of 1914, the group in Airdrie, Alberta, decided to collect all the money before purchasing an organ, "as it was thought we could get it much cheaper by paying cash." They also had standards. The small group of women in Seldom Come By, Newfoundland, paid only five cents a month in dues, and they set the admission price for their teas at twenty cents. Yet in 1917, when they decided to collect money for an organ, they agreed "[t]hat the organ cost not less than $300."

When trustees wished to improve or replace a church building, frequently one of their first acts was to wait upon the Ladies' Aid, describe their plans, and ask how much the group was willing to pledge. Sometimes, the women did not wait for men to take the initiative. Committees from the Aid called on the men, laid the matter before them, and urged action on an expanded church or a new parsonage. And if the women's influence was not enough and no action was forthcoming, some of the groups devised ways to exercise their power. In 1908 the women of Georgetown attempted to mobilize their congregation when they "decided that the Ladies Aid would paint the outside of the church provided the trustees repaired the windows and roof and the Epworth League [youth group] repainted the schoolroom." When this first strategy was unsuccessful, the women tried again the following year; they voted "that the Amt. on hand and all money raised, be used for that purpose alone until the required sum is attained. The money to be handed to the Trustee Board for that use exclusively." This time the painting got done.[2]

These ventures required money. Yet most of the Ladies' Aid members had little money of their own. Some paid a small annual fee to the Aid, while others, like the women of Seldom Come By, paid monthly, but fees alone would not build a parsonage or purchase an organ for the church. Other methods were required. For decades, church men had been asking women to collect funds for missionary work or for other worthy causes. Now the women of the Ladies' Aids began canvassing their city, town, or countryside for projects of their own.

And the women worked. They did "plain and fancy" sewing and other kinds of needlework, they baked and cooked, and they sold their wares at bazaars. They produced quilts to sell, and for a fee they quilted tops that others had made. They put on teas and socials and dinners and entertainments, they offered meals at fall fairs, and they catered dinners for groups that would hire them. Some people – mainly men – criticized dinners and socials as improper ways to raise money for church purposes. The minute books show that many women's groups would gladly have given them up, and in fact tried to do so, because they required a great deal of work. Yet the simple fact was that women did not have enough cash to support their projects by direct giving, and dinners and bazaars allowed them to earn money by using their skills – skills in organizing as well as in cooking and needlework.

Sometimes the women used individual initiative as well. A member might take from a few cents to a dollar of "talent money" from the group's funds. A few weeks or months later she brought to a Ladies' Aid meeting the proceeds of whatever investment she had made – in fabrics for sewing, in ingredients for baking, and so on. When individual women reported their successes and shared their methods, the group celebrated not only an increase in its treasury, but also the ingenuity and dedication of its indefatigable members.

The women's efforts were not all focused on their own church's needs. In 1905 the newly organized Dawson Ladies' Aid attempted to furnish a women's ward in the hospital. When they were unable to arrange for that, they did the next best thing and furnished a men's ward and sitting room instead. They were also concerned with the poor and the sick in their community, and like women in many groups across the nation, they sewed and cooked and distributed clothing and food to those in need.

The First World War brought new needs, and many Aids mobilized for action. In April of 1917 women in Walkerton, Ontario, organized a shower to which people might bring "candles, money, maple sugar, socks, fruit cake, khaki hdk'fs, gum, short bread" to be sent to the soldiers. Those in Kitchener also sent boxes to the boys overseas; in addition, they raised money for the Red Cross, knitting and sewing needed supplies. Many other groups undertook one or more of these activities. And women in Halifax, Saint John, Toronto, and other places entertained the "khaki boys" who were located temporarily in their communities.[3]

In 1925 the Methodists entered into union with the Congregationalists and a majority of the Presbyterians to form the United Church of Canada, but for Methodist women and for those who had laboured in the parlours and kitchens of the other uniting churches, the work went on as before. Whether the groups called themselves Ladies' Aids or went by the new name,

Women's Associations, they responded to the needs of the times. During the Depression, some groups put on plays or concerts not so much to raise money, for there was little money to be had, as to offer inexpensive entertainment in their communities. Another community service at that time was the distribution of clothing – some new, made in sewing circles, some used, collected and mended. The garments were given away or offered for sale at modest prices. And during the Second World War, the women in local congregations once again responded to new needs, but this time under additional stress, as many of them had entered employment connected with the war effort and little time for meetings and church suppers. In 1962 the Women's Associations joined with the Woman's Missionary Society to become the United Church Women, and the new local groups combined assistance to their congregations with support for missions as well.

Throughout their history, women's groups had often appealed for more workers, but gradually these cries became more urgent. In many congregations, fewer women, and in particular fewer younger women, became members. As more women began working outside the home in the latter part of the twentieth century, many committed church women simply had no time to give to this kind of activity, while others felt more comfortable working outside the churches to express the same concern for others that had motivated their grandmothers. While they might continue to distribute food and clothing to those in need, they would do it now through a neighbourhood food bank or women's shelter unconnected with any church.

Something else changed, too. When the women of Georgetown had wanted their church painted in the earlier part of the century, they had had to work from outside the recognized positions of church power. Women were not trustees who handled the property matters of the congregation, and only rarely did they serve as members of the board that dealt with the church's other business. In the latter part of the twentieth century, women's status within the church altered dramatically as they took their places as members of the boards and committees of their congregations and in regional and national groups, as well as formally behind the pulpit. If a church at the end of the century considered building an addition or buying an organ, it was no longer just men who made the decision and the down payment. Women, too, were involved in deciding and in committing their resources. Consequently, many women no longer felt the need their grandmothers had for an organization of their own to act out their faith and to ensure that their voices were heard.

Yet a significant number of women at the close of the twentieth century still found that a women's group offered them a way to honour their responsibility to God and to humankind. They still chose the toil and sweat, and they still looked forward to the rest.

7 Preserving Habits: Memory within Communities of English Canadian Women Religious

Elizabeth Smyth

7.1 The first Canadian Religious Congress, 1954, Ville St Laurent, Quebec (Archives of the Grey Sisters of the Immaculate Conception, Pembroke, Ontario)

The multiple and varied roles played by communities of women religious comprise one of the great, largely unwritten chapters of English Canadian women's history. Although some of the pre-twentieth-century history of women religious has appeared as a list of female firsts – the first teachers, nurses, hospital administrators, and college presidents – the impact that women religious has had on the development of education, social services, heath care, organized religion, and even government in the course of the twentieth century has yet to be explored. This essay probes some of the reasons for gaps in the historiography of English-Canadian women religious, and outlines the experience of one historian mining the treasure-trove of material – a treasure-trove of people, artifacts, structures, and documents. It gives examples of the sources available to researchers working in this field, some of the sensitivities required, and the potential richness of the results.

It is important to note that the state of this scholarship in English Canada differs significantly from both the international and the French Canadian scene. The international scholarship on the roles played by women religious in social, educational, and intellectual history has grown substantially within the past few years. Natalie Zemon Davis includes the pioneering Ursuline educator of New France, Mother Marie de L'Incarnation, as one of the three subjects of *Women on the Margins: Three Seventeenth Century Lives* (1995). In *The Creation* of *Feminist Consciousness* (1993), Gerda Lerner notes that women religious were self-supporting and economically independent women whose community lifestyle created a context for cultural affirmation, including the celebration of their past.[1] Hunter College's Jo Ann Kay McNamara's *Sisters in Arms: Catholic Nuns Through Two Millennia* (1996) is a monumental work on the significance of women religious across the ages. The array of scholarship on French Canadian women religious includes, but is by no means limited to, such works as Marta Danylewycz, *Taking the Veil* (1987); Micheline Dumont and Nadia Fahmy Eid, *Les Couventines* (1986); Therese Hamel, *Un siècle de formation des maetres au Québec* (1995); Emile Lamirande, *Elisabeth Bruyère* (1993); and Nicole Laurin, Danielle Juteau, and Lorraine Duchesne, *La Recherche d'un monde oublié* (1991). Yet, with a few exceptions, the analysis and assessment of the significance of English Canadian women religious on the larger canvas of the academy have yet to emerge.

Why is this the case? Why is it that the role of English Canadian women religious is either neglected (they are simply ignored) or dismissed (by authors employing infamous lines such as "… and the good sisters taught/nursed/ran orphanages," commentary that frequently followed litanies of every priest, bishop, or layman who took any role in the enterprise)? The answers are complex. Some may be methodological. Historians of French Canada, to craft their studies, have more quickly adapted a variety of sociologically based analytical tools and applied them to sources located in a variety of public and private archival sources. Other reasons may be related more to the nature of the subjects.

For most of their existence, the lived experience of women religious embodied multiple tensions. First, the roles assigned to vowed women were separate from and unequal to that of vowed men. Secondly, women religious saw their role as one of silent serving. Many communities viewed the vow of obedience as embodying humility and thus did not campaign for public recognition of their achievements or for a more active voice in ecclesiastical decision making. Thirdly, as the communities' archives are private, historians seeking to analyse the roles of women religious found that access to them was restricted. It has only been with the renewal of religious life stimulated by the Second Vatican Council that women religious, both on their own and collaboratively with secular historians, have begun to analyse their historic and historical roles. Significantly, this has occurred at a time when History as a field has been changing. Feminist scholarship has provided exciting new frameworks that such communities can use in exploring their past.

J.S. Moir, noted historian of religion in Canada, identifies the collaboration between religious archivists and historians as a necessary step in the growth of scholarship in the field of the history of Canadian Catholicism. He writes: "Without historical records there will be no historical research … The churches [and religious communities] fear that the researcher may be unsympathetic to their particular positions (and in a minority of cases they are probably right) but in fact they are doing no more than denying their own creatureliness. Mistakes will be made by historians, but the road to truth is surely paved with mistakes and with their rectifications."[3]

Moir is right. Without the collaboration and support of the religious communities, the much needed research into the historical experience of women religious cannot be undertaken. Unless religious and lay researchers are allowed access to the relevant materials, what will emerge will be an incomplete picture of the historical record, a picture based on documents drawn from other public and private repositories. It is fortunate that as women religious journey further down the path of the writing and recording of their history, their collaboration with secular scholars is increasingly evident; as each year passes, more scholars are allowed access to community records. At present, religious and secular scholars are collaborating in the preparation of work for both the larger academic community and the public at large.[4]

Researchers wishing to consult archives of religious communities must understand some of the particularities of life in such communities. Within the Roman Catholic and Anglican traditions, "nuns" and "sisters" are women who accept a call (a vocation) to a life of service to God, living in community. Although the terms nuns and sisters are used as synonymous, they represent different types of religious life. While both nuns and sisters take vows of poverty, chastity and obedience, nuns take vows that are deemed, in Canon Law (the body of ecclesiastical jurisprudence), to be solemn and permanent, whereas sisters take vows that are deemed "simple." The orientation of nuns is to a life of prayer in cloister, whereas sisters live in non-cloistered spaces, spending their days in prayer through their work in education, health care, and social service.

Currently there are some 153 Roman Catholic institutes of nuns and sisters in Canada, made up of 24,091 members.[5] Many of these women live in communities that embody institutional memory. There is a continuum of age and experience, from postulants – generally younger women exploring their suitability for religious life – to elderly women who have spent their lives in religion. Many live in motherhouse residences, large buildings that affirm the stability of their communities. While the religious themselves have frequently moved from mission to mission, they come and go from a central home, one that offers them a structure of community stability that supports them and makes it possible for them to preserve their records and stories. In addition, Canon Law instructs that community records be maintained in a "properly equipped and carefully arranged" archive.[6] Among the community records prescribed by Canon Law are the annals.[7]

The annals, also known as chronicles, were (and are) kept by each local house in which the religious lived.

They were the permanent records of community events. The keeping of annals was usually one item in a long list of other duties typically executed by a woman who had no historical training. In the motherhouses, the task fell to the community secretary; in local houses, it was an additional chore assigned to a sister engaged full time in other activities. Annalists were directed to record "any remarkable or edifying occurrence,"[8] and in following this instruction, they often included vivid accounts of community life and its evolution. Annals provided a running commentary on daily life and work and were often complemented by scrapbooks of printed reports from both the religious and secular press documenting community events. Typically, these scrapbooks contained notices of public ceremonies in the life of the community and its enterprises. The notices were often cross-referenced in the annals, which frequently named the community member who wrote the copy or provided the background information. The title "annalist" was commonly used, appearing in community records in reference to the woman who kept records of community events. Yet, in spite of the dictates of Canon Law, there were often gaps, sometimes several years in length, when no one was appointed to keep the annals. Explaining the occasionally sporadic and non-sequitur nature of some of the entries, one annalist noted as a postscript to her work that "in the early days of the Community, no one had the time to keep records."[9]

While the death of a member was listed and briefly commented upon in the annals, a separate volume, a necrology, was also kept by the annalist. Typically, a necrology contained "a short account of each deceased Sister, the year, day, and place of her death and burial, with an abridgement of the principle which characterized her during life and the offices she held in the Community."[10] Since, with a few exceptions, women religious rarely left personal diaries or other pieces of personal writing, necrologies are often the only accounts historians have of individual lives. Necrologies were a temporal and spiritual memorial. They were also a personal history of the community and its evolution.

Necrologies, annals, scrapbooks, community publications such as constitutions and guides to practices, financial records, photographic collections and personnel records are among the many records housed within convent archives. Convent archives are private archives. They are the records of a community which continues to live. The researcher using these resources does so as the guest of the community and must abide by community policies. While the archival collection generally is rich, the holdings are sometimes informally catalogued. The researcher is directly dependant upon the archivist for the identification of and access to the relevant material. Materials are brought to the researcher and browsing through the collection is frequently prohibited. To undertake research on women religious one must accept these challenges and work within the regulations established by the community.

Convent archives occupy a unique place in the world of historical archives. They are administered by an archivist who has three roles: preserver of the corporate memory, guardian of the privacy and dignity of the members, and, where the archivist is a religious, guide to the culture of the community. In many communities, the role of the archivist may be one of many jobs given to a retired religious by her community leadership. Limitations of time and resources may pose challenges to researchers working with these archivists.

A further challenge evolves from the governance structure of many of the religious communities in English Canada. Communities are either pontifical (with centralized administration) or diocesan (originally confined within the boundaries of a diocese). Central administration generally means that sources are housed in one area. One can trace decision making through the relevant channels and gain an overview of how the individual community houses acted within the framework of the larger unit. For diocesan communities, sources become scattered as daughter houses separate and become independent foundations, adding a complexity to the study of the operations of an order. It is important to see these community archives as a part of the complex mosaic of social history. Materials found in one collection can dovetail with another. Thus, a researcher may find that materials not released by one archivist may, in fact, be in the public reading room of another community.

Amid these challenges, convent archives offer rich sources to those studying women's experience in the twentieth century. Take, for example, the study of the life experience of teaching sisters. In addition to gaining new knowledge on such varied topics as administration of schools, curriculum development, and the expansion of school systems, the researcher gains another insight into teachers' lives. Unlike their secular counterparts, teaching sisters dedicated their lives to the service of God and neighbour through lifelong careers in education. Some communities of teaching sisters arrived in Canada as immigrants, with the goal of catering to the educational and spiritual needs of their immigrant communities. Teaching for these women was neither a temporary venture into public employment, a stopgap between their own schooling and their lives as wives and mothers, nor a means to economic independence or social advancement. Teaching was the actualization of their vocation.

For historians interested in oral history, women religious represent a declining resource. In 1993 the Canadian Religious Conference reported that 40 per cent of women religious in Canada are over seventy-five years old. Their numbers are declining, by death, at the rate of some 12 per cent a year. Unless the stories and experience of these women religious are documented now, the details of their lives and work, as told in their own voices, will be lost forever.

This essay offers a glimpse into how convent archives can be used as a rich resource for social and women's history. Mother Marie De L'Incarnation wrote that "writing teaches us our mysteries."[11] Through reading their written records and viewing their visual reources, we can learn a great deal about these communities of women: how in the past they adapted to changing conditions and today are reallocating their resources and actions to address the realities of the new millennium.

8 Mildred Armstrong and Missionary Culture

Marjorie Levan

This is the story of my mother, Mildred Armstrong. I myself am a woman of eighty-three, born in China in 1918, the daughter of two missionaries who met and married there. I bring a particular perspective to this story. Partly it is the perspective of a child – we left China when I was nine – but it is also the perspective of an older woman who has been active in Christian ministries all her life and is the daughter, wife, and mother of ministers. I am not a scholar, but I have many firsthand memories of my mother. Mildred Armstrong's life was unique, but in many ways typical of the women who were challenging the traditional expectations of womanhood at the turn of the century. She was a strong woman with courage, a zest for life, and compulsive idealism.

From the viewpoint of the new millennium, we may question the wisdom of the missionary venture. We are beginning to understand the damage done by colonial powers that divided up countries for their own trade advantages. Britain forced opium on China after a war with a weak empress. Missionaries were encouraged to follow to "save" the Chinese. Young men and women were sent to China without language training or an understanding of Chinese culture. They lived as privileged people, inside walls, seemingly secure in their own superior financial position. We certainly question the sense they had of their own superiority. While today's perspective may be valid when applied collectively, it is less so at the level of personal and conscious motivation. Many individuals embarked on years of selfless endeav-

our and sacrifice, their behaviour motivated by the desire to serve a perceived higher cause, not by a selfish wish for power or domination.

In dealing with the story of an individual woman, my mother, I can affirm that she strongly felt that what she was doing was right and according to the will of God, for His glory and the genuine benefit of the Chinese, and not for herself. My memory of my life in China is very positive and rich in love and appreciation of the Chinese.

Mildred Armstrong came from the Annapolis Valley, near Annapolis Royal in Nova Scotia. She was born on August 1885 to apple farmers of Scottish and United Empire Loyalist stock. When she was sixteen, Mildred taught in a one-room schoolhouse near her home. She went from there to Truro Normal School. After teaching for a time and motivated by a desire for an education and a great curiosity in learning, she enrolled at Mount Alison University (1908–11), very unusual for a woman at that time. She believed she could make a career as an independent woman. Her interest in study was mathematics, but she talked of making fudge in her chemistry class and skating on the marshes around Sackville. At the formal "promenades," couples would walk up and down to music (dancing being considered sinful).

Mildred's family were staunch Methodists. The women of the family had an interest in the *Boston Cook Book* and on rare occasions, travelled to Boston by boat to shop. They were also strongly drawn to the Women's Missionary Society (WMS) of the Methodist Church, and the need to help the "heathen" abroad became the focus of much of their energy. In contrast to the Methodist Church and society at large where men made the decisions, the WMS afforded women the freedom to plan and carry out programs for the betterment of people at home and abroad. In a very real way, the WMS pioneers were "the church's first feminists, struggling not so much for personal rights as 'the right to serve.'"[1] For Mildred Armstrong and young women like her, the summer would include at least one trip to a Burwick Camp meeting, near her home.[2] The camp meeting generated a great deal of evangelical enthusiasm. China was portrayed as a heathen land that needed saving, and volunteers were needed for this task.

Mildred's missionary enthusiasm was further fuelled during her years at Mount Alison, a Methodist university. In 1910 John R. Mott, one of the founders of the Student Volunteer Movement,[3] came to speak, painting a picture of the needs of the world. Mildred was very moved by his call of "the world for Christ in this generation"; she joined study groups in which the need for change was debated and discussed, and applied to the WMS to become a missionary. Besides her desire to save the world and make her life, as a woman, count, she was motivated by a high sense of adventure.

First, she was required to attend the Methodist National Training School in Toronto. After that, she was appointed to Kitamat on the coast of British Columbia to teach in an Indian school. The practical objective of the women of the WMS executive was to test her, to see if she could withstand isolation and family separation. Mildred took the long train ride out to British Columbia and then waited for the monthly supply boat, which took her up the coast to Kitamat, stopping, at every little port along the way. Her students, the boys and girls of the junior school, came each day to the large, two-storey, white-frame building where four other teachers and the (male) principal taught. My mother's stories were of the good

times she had with her students, the concerts and plays and outings. When the monthly supply boat came into harbour, classes were dismissed for the day and everyone would go down to see what had arrived.

Finally, in April of 1912, the executive committee of the WMS approved her appointment to the Methodist Mission in Szechuan Province, West China.[4] Again these astute women selected the work task that would fit the candidate. Mother was to teach. Several conditions were set. She had to stay at her appointed place for seven years. She was not to marry. She was expected to maintain the lifestyle and station of a middle-class lady. In return, she would be paid well and regularly. In order to help her establish herself, she was given two hundred dollars to buy what she would need to put up a household for seven years. This included bedding, silver, linen, clothes, shoes. I still have several pieces of the embroidered linens and monogrammed silver that she took with her. A humorous story of my growing years was that mother expected to live with another missionary whose surname began with "A." Not to confuse their table silver, she had hers engraved with "M" for Mildred. In addition, she took along many drugs, such as quinine, aspirin, cod-liver oil, and drugs for de-worming. These last made them particularly popular as missionaries, because worms were so common in China.[5]

With high expectations, mother embarked for the western part of China near Tibet, the province of Szechuan. This was the area left to the Canadian Methodists after the other Protestant churches of the world had divided up the country. Her six-month trip was the subject of many stories. The vastness of the country overwhelmed her, particularly the beauty and grandeur of the Yangtze River. The trip up the Yangtze alone took two months. Holding as many as a dozen people with their tons of luggage, the Chinese junk was extremely slow. It was sailed, poled, and in the Yangtze gorges pulled by men trackers. They would tie up at night. Mother talked of walking on the river bank on the days that the boat could be pulled only a few feet against the river current.

After she arrived in Kaiting (now Leshan), Szechuan, she had to take language study and learn about the Chinese culture. She lived in a large WMS missionary house, presided over by a wonderful woman, Mrs Lily Hockin, and she began to teach Chinese girls. Until the arrival of the missionaries, Chinese girls were not expected to receive an education. As common to the lives of many women, they had no voice. Their marriages were arranged, and they lived in their husband's home, at the beck and call of their mother-in-law. They lived for the time when they themselves produced sons and became the ruling mother-in-law. Mother enjoyed her pupils and loved the Chinese people. Of course she was lonely, but the missionaries bonded to one another as a family. Her stories included picnics and a trip to Mount Emei in the summer for a month's holiday.

It was in this period of time that my mother met my father, a Scotsman who had responded to the missionary call in Edinburgh and come to China in 1910 under the China Inland Mission, a faith mission that believed "the Lord would provide." He was directed to walk across China from Shanghai to Chengdu, Szechuan Province (in Canadian terms, a distance equivalent to that between Ottawa and Brandon, Manitoba). Without knowledge of the Chinese language and in the mountainous terrain, he must have found it quite a trip. Chengdu today is about a four-hour bus ride from Leshan – in those days, several days' walk. Hearing that a junk with a number of young women missionaries was coming up the Yangtze, father rented a small boat with a Chinese oarsman to meet it. Unfortunately, the boat was caught in the strong river currents, and mother's junk sailed past. This story was a family joke. It was more than a year after this that my parents finally met, at one of the missionary gatherings, and they were married in 1917.

Another favourite story was about ordering a wedding dress from Eaton's in Toronto and having it arrive late!

As a married woman, Mildred was required to resign from the WMS mission, despite her years of training and her knowledge of the language, but her work did not stop – it was simply now unpaid. She continued to teach women and girls in the town of Leshan, and her work in her home increased when I and later my two brothers were born.

After seven years in China, missionaries were required to take a furlough, so my parents spent two years in Canada. My father completed his bachelor of divinity degree at Knox College in Toronto. My mother spent some time in Nova Scotia with her family and gave birth to my eldest brother. She took up painting at this time, and some of her paintings are still hung in my and my brothers' homes. While in Toronto, my father was approached by an evangelical American mission and encouraged to return with his family to China. This time they travelled to Nanjing near the mouth of the Yangtze to train Chinese men and women as preachers and leaders. Mother taught in a training school for church workers. Father worked with a band of Chinese preachers to make converts and preach the need for a better life.

American missions were well established in Nanjing, a big city and a southern capital. There was a large university, training colleges, hospitals, and many schools, as well as large missionary compounds. We were completely dependent upon the Chinese for our well-being. Hot and cold water was carried into the house in buckets by coolies, and all waste was carried out. Our light was provided by a generating plant.

My first memory of my mother is in the dining room of the three-storey brick house in Nanjing. The house was inside a large walled compound that separated the white community from the Chinese, though it is only from the perspective of adulthood that I appreciate the significance of this. My child's memory is one of love and warmth and being held and talked to in Chinese and English by all sorts of people. There was our amah, an indomitable Chinese woman, with her hair in a tight bun, completely committed to caring for all my physical needs and those of my younger brother. She lived on the lower floor of this brick house along with the cook, table boy, and cleaner/laundress. I remember our amah washing our diapers at the edge of the pond in the compound. I used to watch the woman at the gatehouse dress her hair with a silk tie into a smooth, sleek bun, which she preserved by sleeping on a wooden pillow. Once I saw her take the bindings off her wizened feet, which were about six inches long. These servants, and others who came to our house to perform set tasks, formed the rich, loving atmosphere of my early life.

The North Americans lived on the upper floors. At the first level, there was a dining room, kitchen, living room, sun porch, and a large entrance hall. Mother had an office off this hall, where she kept accounts and held interviews. Bedrooms were on third floor and in the attic area. There was a fireplace in the dining room, and in the few cool months we would gather around the fire to hear and absorb the family stories. Mother would talk of her family home because she was lonely and isolated. My mother was the centre, the guiding force, in our home. My father provided the fun and excitement. He acquired a gramophone. I have strong memories of music – records of Harry Lauder singing "Roamin' in the Gloamin'" mixed with evangelical hymns like "All the Way My Saviour Leads Me." I remember evenings when we sang Methodist hymns or played rook. (Rook was a form of bridge without face cards, which were considered evil. I remember my grandmother in Canada once burned my cousin's cards because they had faces on them.)

The church was a beautiful Chinese building, gold with dragons. My Sunday school teacher was Pearl Buck, whose first husband taught at the university. Periodically, the church held rummage sales of unwanted clothes and other goods that had been sent by congregations in North America. I remember one group of Chinese men excitedly trying on used corsets to use as mudguards for their legs when they operated the rickshaws (the knees went in the breast cups).

At five I was taken by rickshaw outside the compound wall to a Chinese school, where our class would repeat Confucius sayings after a teacher. This was so I would have the proper tone when I spoke Chinese. I was fascinated with life outside the compound. Every imaginable thing was carried by humans and offered for sale. Farm carts and rickshaws jostled with people walking and gossiping. Chinese life took place on the street. There were many opium dens where people smoked their lives away. There were also many tearooms where men in particular gathered. Vendors would sell me sweetened rice balls, truly forbidden because of the danger of infections. At six, I walked alone outside and up the hill, around rice paddies and a large cesspool (used for fertilizing the fields), to the American School. Besides the missionary children inside the compound, I had Chinese friends, the children of my father's pastors. I loved visiting their small, one-storey courtyard homes on the street. To eat Chinese food and play on the brick shelf that held a fire by day but a bed at night was a great treat.

In general, we ate a bland North American diet – meat or fish, potatoes, boiled vegetables. Many of these we had to grow ourselves. On the lower floor, the Chinese ate delicious food, such as chicken and noodles, which we were only served upstairs on rare and special occasions. When the cook made noodles, they would be hung from a pole in the kitchen. I remember sneaking downstairs, into the laughing warm atmosphere of the Chinese living quarters, when they were eating. People would pick out choice tidbits with their chopsticks and put them in a bowl for me.

In the hot humid summer, we all packed up and went up the Yangtze to a mountainous but urbanized area called Guilin. Many thousands of missionaries gathered here, which was why it was sometimes called "Methodist alley." The adults and servants walked, but my brother and I were carried in a double-seat sedan chair on the shoulders of "coolies." The mountain trip took a full day. For me, Guilin was paradise. I could roam the hills, play tennis, and go swimming in the pool that had been built in the White Russian community. We drank condensed milk. There was an ice-cream parlour. I saw my first movie, starring Harold Lloyd, who in one scene hung perilously from a clock tower.

Mother gave birth to her third child in the hospital in Guilin. This did not relieve her of her many responsibilities in connection with a large conference centre for training Chinese church leaders. The centre had numerous dormitories, which housed about two-dozen people each, and a large auditorium. Mother was responsible for the accommodation of North Americans who came as speakers. Because there was a lack of suitable hotels, our home in Nanjing was also open to many visiting missionaries travelling up and down the Yangtze. One family stayed for six months because of illness. Visitors filled our big dining-room table most of the time. It took a woman of unusual ability to manage this household. Of course, mother had help from Chinese servants, but a great deal of her skill was required when it came to negotiating between the different cultural norms, particularly the Chinese practice of graft. For example, the cook would routinely go out to buy fruit and vegetables, dicker down the price, and pocket his profit.

Outside the compound was "The Work." It took precedence over everything else in my parents' lives. The prime concern was to "save" the Chinese for eternal life. However, as time passed, raising the social condition of the very many poor people became a great concern. In the 1920s much of China was in turmoil. Warlords controlled fiefdoms, fighting one another and pillaging the countryside. After years of unfair trade advantages being given to foreigners, anti-foreign feeling was high – I remember being called a "foreign devil" as I rode in my rickshaw. Famine was rife and increasingly my parents' work became the care and feeding of the homeless. My father worked full time for the Red Cross, establishing emergency relief. I remember desperate people coming to the compound to dig up various weeds in our lawn that they could cook for vegetables. Tree bark was eaten. Mother and Father became exhausted. Finally, soldiers arrived and in 1927 all missionaries were ordered out.[6]

We arrived back in Canada early in 1928. We had left a life and people we loved for a Canadian city, Vancouver, that was foreign to us. Here I was teased and called "Chink" (though I am not Chinese), and I felt utterly friendless. Although Mother did not complain, the adjustment for her was tremendous. From being the mistress of a large household, she became a poor minister's wife, having to learn to cook and run a limited household during the Depression. She had never had to cook before. I remember in particular a lemon pie that was hard and black and an occasion when my father made fun of her in front of company – I felt almost like crying that time. One by one, carpets, chests, dishes, and other treasures from China were sold, just to eat. My mother died of breast cancer only eleven years after our return from China, when I was just twenty.

Mother and Dad's hearts were in China, but because of their children, they felt they could not return. They would go down to the docks in Vancouver when missionaries were sailing back to China to bid them goodbye. I remember them all singing together "Blest be the tie that binds / Our hearts in Christian love / The fellowship of kindred minds / Is like to that above."

Was my mother's missionary effort misguided? Mission work has changed completely in my lifetime. We still appreciate the need to help a suffering world, but we go now as partners at the invitation of the local people to help them accomplish a task of human betterment. The original goal of mass conversion was an impossible dream: "even thousands more missionaries would have been but a curiosity to the Chinese, so vast and insulated was their country, so proud their culture."[7] Despite this, I profoundly believe that my mother's life was worthwhile. At a time when Chinese women and girls were not encouraged to seek an education, let alone a career, mother's teaching work was of real value. Chinese girls and women were very good students. At the end of my mother's time, they were travelling to the United States for advanced study. By the end of the China missionary period, they were running their own modern schools.[78] They staffed the hospitals and were active in procuring rights for women. Presently, they are a strong voice in the indigenous Chinese Christian Church. As the wonderful principal of a Chinese live-in kindergarten said to me in 1984, when I finally returned to China for a visit, "It is right that women should have careers. After all, they hold up half the sky." And, not to be discounted, the dedication of women like my mother to the care of people, with love, had a profound influence on my own life, and I believe, on the lives of my children.

Vignette
9 Women's Spiritual Lives

Elizabeth Smyth notes in essay #7 that "the multiple and varied roles played by communities of women religious [and, we might add, of religious women of all faiths and languages] comprise one of the great, largely unwritten chapters of … women's history." Although scholarship on French Canadian women religious has received more exposure than has that on the English community, neither French nor English women religious have received adequate scholarly recognition. Given the size and authority of Canadian Protestant women's organizations, particularly the Women's Missionary Societies and Ladies' Aids, this "unacknowledged quarantine" is the more surprising.[1] In essays #6 and #8, Marilyn Färdig Whiteley and Marjorie Levan provide evidence of the impressive range of contributions made by these organizations. Further, this is one of many areas where the photographic record of women's involvement often provides more vivid testimony than does the textual.

In this collage, we are introduced to the Ladies' Aid Society of Metcalfe Methodist Church (Illustration 9.1), near Ottawa. Like the women missionaries of the United Church of Canada (Illustration 9.2), these conventional and disciplined women found their strength in spiritual purpose and communal effort. Among the many tasks of the members of all such organizations was the socialization of young women, helping them assume the duties, learn the skills,

9.1 Ladies' Aid Society, Metcalfe, Ontario, c. 1905 (PA 103926, National Archives of Canada)

9.2 Missionaries, United Church of Canada, 1942 (PA 108350, National Archives of Canada)

9.3 B'nai Brith Junior League Degree Team, 1938 (C 57260, National Archives of Canada)

9.4 Presbyterian Sunday School, Prince Rupert, 1911 (PA 95665, National Archives of Canada)

9.5 St Mary's Convent School, Quebec, 1949 (PA 80937, National Archives of Canada)

and develop the refined comportment of properly reared, spiritually awake women. Four illustrations offer examples of this task in process: the members of the B'Nai Brith Junior League Degree Team in 1938 (Illustration 9.3); the children, along with their young female teacher, of the Presbyterian Sunday School of Prince Rupert in 1911 (Illustration 9.4); the group of girls posed at St Mary's Convent School in Quebec in 1949 (Illustration 9.5); and older and younger women of the Ottawa Muslim Women's Auxiliary selling homemade pickles and crafts (Illustration 9.6).

9.6 Muslim Women's Auxiliary, International Bazaar, 1973 (Photo courtesy of Farook Tareen)

10 E. Pauline Johnson: Mohawk-English Writer and Performer

Veronica Strong-Boag

In the high age of Anglo-Saxon imperialism and patri- archy, E. Pauline Johnson, Mohawk-English performer and author of the best-selling poetry collection *Flint and Feather* (1912) and *Legends of Vancouver* (1911), challenged both the racial divide between Native and European and the conventions that constrained women.[1] Her vision of the First Nations, of women, and of Canada itself was very different than that set forth by the Fathers of Confederation in 1867. From her birth on Six Nations territory in Ontario until her death in Vancouver, Pauline Johnson tested and expanded the meaning of Canada.

Though she was the daughter of an Iroquois chief and an English woman, by Canadian law and by personal sympathy Johnson (or Tekahionwake as she increasing- ly identified herself) was Mohawk. She also found com- mon cause with Euro-Canadian feminists who chal- lenged misogynous conventions, and she joined an English Canadian intellectual elite of her day that endeavoured to shape the imagination of the new dominion. Like the Knights of Labor or the suffragists, who "dreamed of what might be," she chronicled and questioned prejudice and oppression. As post-colonial theorists would now say, she "talked back" to the domi- nant culture, disturbing the conventions that reckoned First Nations peoples and women as properly subject to an imperial and imperious masculinity.[2] Her public championship of a more inclusive and tolerant nation- ality was a fragile, but recurring, accomplishment that

10.1 Pauline Johnson (s 898, Archives of Ontario)

presaged such end-of-the-twentieth-century First Nations writers as Lee Maracle and Jeannette Armstrong.

Pauline Johnson was the product of one country, Canada, which was, for the most part, committed to a politics of white racism; of a nation, the Six Nations Iroquois, which desperately sought accommodation for its own traditions; and of a family that sought to maintain itself as part of a mixed-race elite. The bicultural aspirations of her parents, George Henry Martin Johnson and Emily Susannah Howells, shaped their daughter's imagination and her understanding of the British Empire and Canada itself.[3] Until the end of her life, Pauline Johnson embraced the possibility of a Native-European alliance.

Her 1884 and 1886 memorial odes to the First Nation heroes Red Jacket and Joseph Brant demanded redress and recognition for the Iroquois who had come north as Loyalists after the American Revolution. The protest of the Northwest tribes and Métis in the 1885 Rebellions won her ready sympathy. Rage at imperial Canada's brutal military response inspired her extraordinary poem "A Cry from an Indian Wife" (1885), which shocked and moved white audiences when she featured it at literary evenings. While caught up in making a liv-

ing, Johnson did not forget the desperate situation on the prairies, returning to this subject in her short story "A Red Girl's Reasoning" (1893) and in the poem "The Cattle Thief" (1894). Continuing hope for inclusion and for inter-racial alliances nevertheless spurred her exploration of a brighter future in both verse, as in "The Indian Corn Planter" (1897), and prose, "Among the Blackfoots" (1902). By the end of her life, when Johnson turned to British Columbia tribes for intimacy and inspiration, anger at injustice still echoed through her words, but sadness dominated her narratives. As *Legends of Vancouver* made very clear, First Nations peoples were perishing at the hands of greedy, brutal invaders.

That bleak future haunted Pauline Johnson as she established herself as a career woman who questioned the conventions that hobbled her sex in the middle-class Euro-Canadian world to which she also belonged. While she tended to locate oppression primarily in racism, Johnson articulated a doubled vision: "I am a Redskin, but I am something else too – I am a woman."[4] An amateur performer and enthusiastic writer since her teens, Johnson resisted maternal opposition to a stage career and self-consciously elected to make her way as a new woman in North America and Britain. On stage and in print, she developed close ties to the Anglo-imperial world, including friendships with feminists such as Nellie L. McClung. While remembered best as a poet, Johnson wrote travel accounts, short stories, comic sketches, and literary criticism. Like many woman writers, she made a living by publishing with magazines like *Saturday Night* (Toronto), *Mother's Magazine* (Chicago), and *Boys' World* (Chicago), which increasingly catered to the growing market of female readers and consumers.

Johnson joined the outspoken of her sex in challenging prejudices that subordinated women. Her writing made it very clear that women were neither men's play-

EMMA ALBANI 1847–1930

Albani, one of the great sopranos of her generation, was born Emma Lajeunesse at Chambly, Quebec. After studies at home, in Paris, and in Milan, she was for twenty-four years a principal artist at Covent Garden and a favourite of Queen Victoria. She was mistress of the Italian, French, and German repertoires, and ranged stylistically from oratorio, through bel canto operas, to Wagner. In demand in all the musical capitals of the world and welcomed home enthusiastically during her North American tours, Albani became a Dame Commander of the British Empire in 1925. She died in London, England. (Courtesy of Parks Canada)

things nor mere domestic ornaments. In her mind's eye, the "natural" woman, whether the Iroquois matron or the liberated sportswoman and influential mother, provided the critical moral and productive centre of a superior social order. An avid canoeist, she advocated an outdoor life and comfortable clothing to improve women's health and competence.[5] Her commitment to equality drew on specifically Native traditions. As she explained in the *London Daily Express* in 1906, "I have heard that the daughters of this vast city cry out for a voice in our councils; she [the Iroquois matron] has had it for upwards of four centuries … From her cradle-board she is taught to judge men and their intellectual qualities, their aptness for public life, and their integrity."[6]

Johnson grew up and created an artistic and personal life in a transatlantic community stirred by feminist and Native protest.[7] On stages across North America and Britain, she portrayed active women, the humanity of Native people, and the rapacious self-interest of white settler society. Her poem "The Cattle-Thief" captured these preoccupations in its presentation of a Cree woman defending her father's body against white vigilantes:

You say your cattle are not ours, your meat is
not our meat;
When YOU pay for the land you live in, WE'LL pay
for the meat we eat.
Give back our land and our country, give back our
herds of game;
Give back the furs and the forests that were ours
before you came;
Give back the peace and plenty.

Compiled near the end of a life that was cut short by breast cancer, *Legends of Vancouver* capped Johnson's persistent efforts to present the Canadian imaginative landscape as the rightful inheritance of Natives and women also. One story rejected the idea that the twin mountain peaks that rose to the north of the city were "the lions," as appropriated by some foreign-born settler with a mind for the exotic or the patriotic but "without the love for them that is in the Indian heart."[8] Johnson reminded her readers that the mountains had a far older indigenous history as "the sisters" of Indian mythology. Her retelling of Squamish legends, much like similar efforts by other Native Canadian writers, unnamed the land colonized and dominated by European men and located a powerful earlier inheritance at the centre of human history. This vision, with its inspiration in her commitment to the First Nations and to a fair deal for her sex, made Pauline Johnson one of the most remarkable of her generation of Canada's new women.

In some ways, nevertheless, Pauline Johnson resembles the imperialists considered by Carl Berger in *The Sense of Power* (1907). Her perfected Canada is the heir of British virtues. She was ultimately intensely idealistic, counting on the awakening of friendship and mutual respect and the power and authority of British justice and the North-West Mounted Police. She looked to virtuous elites, notably great men – British aristocrats and others of nature's nobles – and motherly women – both English-speaking and Native – to inspire and lead a young nation confronting the corruption and aggression she condemned in the United States.

For all its limitations, Johnson's legacy was unique among the Confederation generation of literary figures. No one else tried to take Canada and the Empire to task for their treatment of Native peoples or advocated an ongoing role for the original bicultural partnership between Native and European. Few imperialists accepted women's right to independence and authority. More than the vast majority of her leading contemporaries, she envisioned the possibility of fair play and inclusion. Insisting on the humanity of women and Natives and the culpability of European settlers, Pauline Johnson challenged the moral status quo in post-Confederation Canada and won a significant popular audience in her day and later. Her funeral in March 1913, organized by middle-class white feminists and occasioning a civic day of mourning with Indians and whites lining Vancouver streets to take their last farewells, aptly commemorated Johnson's hopes for Canada.

11 Two Perspectives on Urban Living

Mairuth Sarsfield

Mairuth Hodge Sarsfield

Mairuth Hodge Sarsfield was born in Montreal. Her successful novel, *No Crystal Stair*, depicts life in "Little Burgundy," the area of Montreal where she grew up. As she later recounted, "It's the women of colour, mainly Black, who gave the novel its spine. They wouldn't let poverty hamstring them." The book clearly delineates the strength of women oppressed by race, class, and the social perception of others. Published in 1997, the novel sold widely across Canada and appears on many syllabi for women's studies courses.

Early in her career, Mairuth Sarsfield worked as a professional theme coordinator, helping a team of creative young Canadians develop Expo '67 in Montreal and later the award-winning pavilion for Expo'70 in Osaka, Japan. She has travelled extensively, studied in various places, including Columbia University and the University of Ghana, and held a position as a foreign service officer in Washington and Japan. She worked as a housewife while residing in Papua New Guinea and later, in Nairobe, Kenya, as a creative communicator responsible for global information themes for the United Nations Environment Program. In Canada, she served for many years on the Board of Directors of the Canadian Broadcasting Corporation.

Mairuth Sarsfield is the recipient of the Chevalier de l'ordre national du Québec and was honoured in Cleveland, Ohio, with a "Mairuth Sarsfield Day." In recognition of her ongoing endeavours, she received the African Canadian Achievement Award. Retired, but still active as an author and social activist, she lives in Ottawa with her husband, Dominick.

11.1 Mairuth Sarsfield at Canada House, London
(Courtesy of Derek Russell-Stoneham)

MARGARET MARSHALL SAUNDERS, 1861–1947

Born in Milton, Nova Scotia, Margaret Saunders was educated at Edinburgh, at Orleans, and at Dalhousie. A prolific writer, she produced some twenty-five books of which fourteen were animal stories. *Beautiful Joe*, a gentle rather than heroic autobiography of a dog, was her first and by far her most successful work. Published in 1894, it went on to sell approximately one million copies in fourteen languages and many editions. Margaret Saunders displayed her passionate interest in animal welfare, not only in her writing, but by donating most of her royalties to humane societies. She died in Toronto. (Courtesy of Parks Canada)

Gabrielle Roy

Pierrette Boily

Gabrielle Roy was born in St Boniface, Manitoba, the youngest of eleven children. Her parents, Leon Roy and Melina Landry, were originally from Quebec. Roy's mother strongly encouraged her to go into teaching, as academic success came easily to her. After finishing Normal School, Roy taught in small towns in Manitoba before accepting a permanent position at the Provencher Academy. She was active in the theatre community and managed to save up some money in the Depression years so that she could study dramatic arts courses in Paris and London, where she lived from 1937 to 1939. Following a disappointing start in the theatre, she gave it up to pursue writing.

Roy returned to Canada and chose to live in Montreal. She earned her livelihood as a journalist and in 1945 published her first novel, *Bonheur d'occasion*, which was an instant success, earning her France's Prix Fémina and Canada's Governor General's Award. The English version, titled *The Tin Flute*, was selected by the Literary Guild of America and subsequently became a best-seller. Roy was the first woman admitted to the Royal Society of Canada.

In 1947 she married Dr Marcel Carbotte of St Boniface. After spending some time in France, she took up permanent residence in Quebec City. Throughout her lifetime, she often drew on her experiences in Manitoba, describing its landscape and characters in her novels. All her works have been translated into English. She died at age seventy-four in the process of writing her autobiography.

Above:
11.2 Gabrielle Roy (centre, front row) and her class at St Joseph (Société Historique de Saint-Boniface, Le Musée de Saint-Boniface)

11.3 Gabrielle Roy (third from left) with friends (A. Corriveau Collection, Le Musée de Saint-Boniface)

12 Ada Gladys Killins: Sacrificing for Art's Sake

Sharon Anne Cook

Ada Gladys Killins was a Canadian painter of distinction who accepted poverty for the sake of her art. She began her working life as a teacher and, indeed, was descended from a long line of teachers, several of whom had strong artistic leanings.[1] Her great-grandfather had come to Canada from Belfast in the early nineteenth century as a minister of the Church of Ireland. However, he had ended up teaching school at Mono Mills, about sixty kilometres north of Toronto, near Orangeville. Her mother, Rachel (Swick) Killins, and both paternal aunts had also taught at elementary school; they had painted, too, copying the masters as part of their teacher training at Normal School.

Born in Caistor Township, Lincoln County, Ontario, in 1901, Gladys Killins was one of three children and the only daughter born to Robert and Rachel Killins. Killins was a good student in a family that demanded much of its children. During her high school years, she took advantage of the art courses offered, early on showing considerable promise. She also took private lessons from a neighbour and in this way developed her craft further. Killins' family was proud of her artistic talent, and her brother remembers their parents' efforts to provide as much instruction as a limited budget would allow. For years, she took summer courses at the Ontario College of Art in Toronto.

Killins completed her senior matriculation and then Normal School, obtaining her first teaching appointment at the newly opened Memorial School in Niagara Falls, Ontario, in 1924. Here she spent her entire teaching career, until she left the city and teaching in 1947, moving into a rural cabin near Orangeville, not far from her great-grandfather's school. In company with so many Ontario women before her, Gladys Killins early understood the importance of formal education, particularly for women and most particularly for women intent on pursuing artistic careers. Yet despite two decades of urban life and her career in education, she never lost her close identification with rural Ontario, instilled through long family association. Her father and later her brother, Harold, were farmers in the Niagara Peninsula, and it was here that the artist's eye was first caught by the beauty of rural landscapes. The family had briefly homesteaded in Alberta between 1909 and 1912, but it was the Ontario countryside, not the Albertan, that shaped her consciousness and technique.

Throughout her years in teaching, Killins developed her own artistic talent, but she also studyied with Franz Johnston and later, between 1935 and 1938, with Carl Schaefer in his summer classes at Geneva Park, Lake Couchiching. Her early experiments in watercolour were significantly enhanced through her association with these two famed watercolourists. Indeed, the post-impressionist style of the Group of Seven, of which Johnston was a formal member and Schaefer a student and close associate, profoundly influenced Killins throughout her career. Her use of colour, subject, and bold renderings all spoke to the hold that the Group of

12.2 Landscape with house on hill
(Collection of Sharon Cook)

12.1 Landscape with church
(Courtesy of Sharon Cook)

Seven maintained on Canadian art throughout this period.[2] That she chose the rolling hills, wood stands, and farmsteads of central Ontario instead of the more rugged northlands promoted by the Algonquin School,[3] whose artists painted "the mighty forces of Canada in all their primeval power,"[4] meant that she could experiment with the softer hues and gentler shapes of this region, while still reflecting Algonquin techniques. By 1938, as a result of this growing sophistication of style and technique, her work was shown publicly for the first time in the Eleventh Annual Exhibition of the Canadian Society of Painters in Water Colour (CSPWC), which took place at the Art Gallery of Toronto.

The personality requirements, skills, and social demands of teaching are not necessarily easily blended with artistic endeavours. For every Doris McCarthy,[5] who seemed to thrive in both worlds, there are undoubtedly many more who discover that a choice must be made between teaching and painting. Gladys Killins

had impressed her friends and family from the beginning as extroverted, serious-minded, and intelligent. But she was also highly strung and could be sharp-tongued and argumentative. And she became increasingly eccentric, quick with a personal kindness but also given to censorious judgment. She found teaching art to restless elementary schoolchildren increasingly frustrating and stressful. Given this clientele and a temperament that seemed to require that she win every debate, every contest of wills, it seemed that she was better suited to artistic pursuits than educational ones.

But in leaving teaching, this talented single woman also denied herself a steady, if modest, income.[6] Like many other independent women intent on pursuing artistic careers, she took on the additional burden of harsh poverty and deep loneliness, living in an isolated shack without amenities. Above all, her painting was done alone. Unlike the Group of Seven, who enjoyed a close camaraderie, working and camping together when they chose, women like Gladys Killins and Emily Carr engaged in a solitary artistic life. While she was still teaching, Killins needed to remain especially vigilant of the social constraints placed on teachers as moral exemplars in the community; female art teachers could not with impunity embark on mixed-sex painting expeditions!

Despite her financial instability, she held few exhibitions in her later years and never advertised her work or allowed any gallery to promote her. In fact, she had ever more difficulty in parting with her paintings at all,[7] though she did occasionally sell or, more often, give paintings to those she liked. It has been observed that, surrounded as she was by so much poverty, she naturally would have wished to hold on to her beautiful paintings. Such decisions on her part also speak to the insecurity suffered by single women engaged in a difficult craft with neither major financial support nor a sustaining network of other like-minded artists.

Gladys Killins painted buildings, still lifes, and, in particular, rural landscapes, the latter in the Niagara Falls area and, after her move in 1947, in the Orangeville and Hockley Valley regions of Ontario. One of her earlier works, *Town Hall*, hung in the Niagara Falls City Hall, was selected for the Canadian exhibition at the New York World's Fair in 1939. In that same year, her *Factory Closed*, a sombre watercolour with a strong social message, appeared at the Canadian National Exhibition. She was elected a member of the Canadian Society of Painters in Water Colour in 1939, and her paintings were represented in almost every show sponsored by the CSPWC from that date to 1959. Her output steadily increased; in 1942 fifteen of her paintings were included in an exhibition entitled "Four Canadian Painters" at the Art Gallery of Ontario, and in 1954 she mounted a single exhibition of thirty pictures. By this date, her work was exclusively landscape-based; she had become, as one reviewer of the exhibition noted, "strictly an out-of-doors painter and her pictures express a strong love for her environment."[8]

12.3 House in town (Collection of Sharon Cook)

12.4 Landscape in the fall (Collection of Sharon Cook)

That environment was deeply rooted in rural Ontario. The buildings of her earlier pictures of the 1930s and 1940s are often sharply detailed – town halls, churches, factories, houses, yards, and barns. The lines are precise, the details clear, and nature is usually the backdrop, not the focus, even for rural settings. When she did render landscapes during this period, it was with the same precision, with clean cuts. By the 1950s, buildings are almost a blurred oddity in her paintings, small structures perching uneasily in an otherwise majestic scene. Nature now seems to overpower, even mock the human. There is no sign of life, no people, no animals. Some of the buildings are operational, most are abandoned and very often in ruin. For Killins, it was the land that lived, that was alive with colour and movement. That the land was central to her vision, however, does not suggest a harmonious balance between natural features. Her lines, while contoured, are often oddly, even menacingly, juxtaposed. The general sense of threat and of moodiness is always reinforced by an angry, grey sky.

In the later period, the colours change, too, from deeper hues richly applied to muted washes of autumnal greens and yellows, browns and earth tones. And the scenes are almost always set in the fall, with many trees blackened, bare of leaves. It is as if her paintings are themselves returning to the land as she had done. The details of the scenes were less important to her than the mood they evoked. In this period, the scenes are more impressionistic, shapes suggested by washes rather than by precise lines, as if what she felt was more important than what she saw. In these later pictures, Killins found her voice, painting less what was around her and more of what was in her. For women in many fields, finding a voice can come at a significant cost. For Killins, it was a sacrifice she was evidently prepared to make.

Gladys Killins died unexpectedly and tragically in 1963, leaving a small but substantial collection of slightly over one hundred works. While her artistic output must be measured against the economic and social odds ranged against her, these watercolours remain as testament to the evocative power of the Ontario landscape and to her own fierce determination to express herself. Her legacy of Ontario landscapes during the second quarter of the twentieth century offers an example of the work produced by independent women artists during this period, and shows that "invisible" women's voices (and visions) are there to be heard (and seen), if Canadians will but listen (and look).

13 The Road Less Taken – The Single Woman as Artist

What follows are two case studies of women artists who remained single and pursued their artistic ambitions. At times this life choice meant relying on labour other than art to supplement unstable incomes. These women achieved their goal of pursuing artistic careers without the conventional support provided by spouses.

The Unmarried Woman Artist: Emily Carr

Sonia Halpern

Unlike most other women at the turn of the century, Canadian landscape painter Emily Carr (1871–1945) remained unmarried. Born in Victoria, British Columbia, to middle-class, orthodox Christian parents, Emily and her four sisters were expected to marry, rear children, manage a household, and do volunteer good works. Carr wanted to paint professionally, however, and when she was in her twenties and thirties, the age by which most women would have married, she travelled extensively, studying art in San Francisco, London, and Paris. She also made numerous trips alone by canoe to the northwest coast of Canada to paint.

Carr's decision to remain single, despite the inevitable economic hardship, was likely based in part on the presumption that marriage would impede her artistic ambitions.[1] Indeed, an examination of other women artists throughout history indicates that this has usually been the case. More often than not, when professional women artists married, their artistic production dramatically declined or was obliterated altogether.[2] Wives' duties included the care of husbands and children and increased domestic responsibilities, which ultimately deprived them of the privacy and time required for creativity. Domestic duties have clearly had a debilitating effect on the professional artistic pursuits of married women. Artists such as Paraskeva Clark, Peggy Nichol McLeod, Christiane Pflug, and Mary Pratt all struggled with the conflicting needs of career and family life, either addressing the issues directly in their art works or in their correspondence with family, friends, and gallery officials.

Although spinsterhood offered many advantages to aspiring artists, it could also prove detrimental to women artists' freedom. Aging single daughters, for example, unlike their married sisters with families of their own, or their brothers, married or not, were expected to assume the long-term care of elderly and ailing parents and grandparents. These obligations

13.1 Emily Carr as a young woman, 1901 (B-00877, British Columbia Archives)

13.2 *At the Dance*, by Emily Carr (PDP06166, British Columbia Archives)

might have precluded the possibility of other life choices. Spinsterhood could also invite poverty. There were few safeguards to protect single women like Carr (or deserted, divorced, and widowed women) who lived outside the patriarchal family model. Having been orphaned when she was a child and with no male kin to rely on, Carr was forced to supplement her income as an artist by resorting to a host of money-making ventures. She conducted art classes for children, ran her own boarding house, grew and sold fruit, raised hens and rabbits, bred dogs, and sold pottery and rugs that she had made herself.[3] The time and energy that Carr expended on these enterprises and the modest income they garnered compromised the amount of time she could devote to artistic productivity. For a period of about fifteen years she stopped painting altogether. Today her paintings are seen in galleries across the country, but it was not until late in life that Carr generated a substantial income from her paintings.[2]

Isabel and Helen Stadelbauer: Art Teachers in Calgary

Helen Diemert

Isabel and Helen Stadelbauer were born into a family that travelled to the mountains for part of their holidays. There the children enjoyed camping in the natural beauty of the Rockies. Their interest in drawing and painting was fostered during these holidays and remained a strong force throughout their lives.

After high school graduation, Helen and Isabel attended Teachers' College. With her teacher's certificate, Isabel taught art at the high school level. Her instruction provided many students with the opportunity to pursue suc-

cessful careers in art, while she herself undertook higher degrees in education and art. Helen's career took a different turn. After Teachers' College, during the 1930s, she was unable to find a teaching position, so instead she completed the first year of a university degree from the University of Alberta. That was a difficult year at home; their mother became ill and Helen assumed the household duties in addition to her studies. In the next four years, she earned an advanced diploma in fine arts and a certificate from the Royal Drawing Society of London, England. She finally secured teaching positions near and in Calgary, spending her summers painting under the tutelage of outstanding Canadian artists in Banff. Eventually, Helen earned advanced degrees from Columbia University.

13.3 *Approaching Storm over Grotto Mt.*, 1941, by Helen Stadelbauer
(Courtesy of Helen Diemert)

When the University of Calgary was founded in 1966, Helen fought hard for the inclusion of a faculty of fine arts and soon found herself as acting head of that new faculty as well as of the art department itself.

Isabel and Helen spent many summers painting the landscapes around Calgary and Banff (see Illustrations 13.3 and 13.4). They completed hundreds of watercolour paintings that reflect local scenes during the wartime years. They also travelled extensively around the world and documented some of those many trips in artworks in the form of prints as well as sketches, paintings, and photographs. Able and talented single women, Isabel and Helen Stadelbauer supported each other and taught art in order to act on the artistic vision they shared.

13.4 *Corner Banff Avenue*, 1940, by Isabel Stadelbauer (Courtesy of Helen Diemert)

14 A Sense of Place in Alberta: The Art and Life of Annora Brown

Kirstin Evenden

14.1 *Foothills Village* (CN 57.46.1, Glenbow Museum and Archives. Courtesy of the Estate of Annora Brown)

The history of Alberta art is a story of struggle and success that even today remains relatively unknown to Canadians. Itinerant artists who travelled west with survey expeditions, the North-West Mounted Police, or the Canadian Pacific Railway in the latter half of the nineteenth century were just that – itinerant. They depicted certain aspects of Alberta for specific enterprises, per-

haps to document the arrival of settlers in the Canadian West or, in the case of the CPR artists, to serve the economic interests of the company that employed them. Those that depicted Alberta in their works were rarely residents of the province, it was not until the 1930s that there emerged a community of artists with an interest in Alberta, as a distinctive region and as their home.

Even less known is the contribution that women artists made to the development of early art schools and the arts community of southern Alberta. Annora Brown was one such artist. In the words of biographer Helen Collinson,

Annora Brown was one of the first native Albertans to return to the province of her birth to continue her career in relative isolation and often trying circumstances. A full appraisal of her significant contribution to the artistic life of Alberta has not yet been done ... however, there appears to be ample evidence of an active mind which must have affected her students during the 1930's and 1940's when she taught community art classes for the University of Alberta, in such places as Lethbridge, Fort MacLeod and Medicine Hat.[1]

Although Annora Brown was known locally in the communities where she lived, her work has remained relatively obscure in the broader narrative of Canadian art history today. It is the purpose of this article to explore her career in art and its legacy.

Annora Brown was born in 1899 just outside Red Deer, Alberta, and grew up in Fort MacLeod. Her father, originally a member of the North-West Mounted Police, was present at the building of Fort Steele in 1887 and came to Fort MacLeod, via the Crowsnest Pass, with the famous Kootenay Brown as guide. Her mother, Elizabeth Brown, had moved to Fort MacLeod, from Ontario, and became one of the first schoolteachers in the community.

Years before, Elizabeth Brown had taken painting lessons from Florence Carlyle, a Canadian artist of some reputation who was based in Ontario and had herself spent a summer sketching in the Canadian Rockies.[2] Encouraged by her mother to draw and paint, Annora Brown also gained a love for this region that was her home. Along with H.G. Glyde and A.C. Leighton, she was one of several artists in the 1930s and 1940s who made a commitment to developing art schools in Alberta. Not only were these artists actively teaching art, but their work attests to an interest in articulating a sense of place about Alberta itself, thus contributing to the development of a regional identity.

That Annora Brown was interested in representing the world she knew, southern Alberta, was no surprise. She trained at the Ontario College of Art under such well-known Canadian artists as Arthur Lismer, Lawren Harris, and J.E.H. MacDonald, who at the time were advocating a new kind of modernism for Canadian art, one that truly contributed to the development of a Canadian identity for the nation. The schooling that she received advocated that artists should develop their own individual style, and encouraged an interest in the representation of Canada and its distinctive regions. Brown was successful at the college, receiving scholarships during her schooling and graduating with honours. Her interest in depicting the landscape in geometric and abstract forms is indicative of her training under Lawren Harris, while her use of bold colour to create

striking landscapes and moving images of people reflects her commitment to modernism. She met other artists from Alberta at the college, such as Gwen Hutton and Euphemia McNaught (she referred to them as "Westerners"), who gave her friendship and support. Brown would later go on sketching trips with McNaught once back in Alberta.

Upon completion of her diploma, she returned to her home province and in 1929 began teaching at Mount Royal College in Calgary, assuming responsibility for the development of the college's art program. Only four years after starting at Mount Royal College, Brown was obliged to move back to Fort Macleod, where she would stay for several years, caring for her ailing parents. Despite the economic hardship, her nursing responsibilities, and the discouraging advice of friends, she nonetheless maintained a studio and a commitment to her art. While living in Fort Macleod, Brown worked for the extension department of the University of Alberta, travelling to Lethbridge, Medicine Hat, Brooks, High River, and the Crowsnest Pass to teach art and crafts. Brown worked as an illustrator (contributing to six books and numerous magazine articles), designer, and amateur naturalist, there being only a handful of artists during this period who were able to earn a living from their art practice. She was versatile in a number of media, including oil, watercolour, and print-making. The subject matter of her painting was the landscape of southern Alberta, the Native people around Fort Macleod, and botanical images of native Alberta wildflowers. Through these subjects, she articulated her sense of place and her vision of Alberta.

A devoted gardener of wildflowers, Brown reared nearly one hundred specimens of the flora of the prairie and foothills. Accounts document that she knew the name of each plant and bush, how they got their names, and why. Brown's knowledge of native plants and their uses had developed during her childhood for practical

14.2 *Waterton Lake, Alberta* (CN 60.32, Glenbow Museum and Archives. Courtesy of the Estate of Annora Brown)

reasons, as wild plants were useful and crucial, in fact, to settlers dependent on ox-cart deliveries from the East.

I was a small child when the dandelion reached Macleod. Our text-books were those in use in Eastern Canada, with their stories about plants and flowers native to that part of the Dominion. Few even knew their names. The dandelion, you know, came to Canada for "greens." Up at Fort Churchill the gentlemen adventurers watered … their dandelion patch so that they might vary heavy meat meals. Teachers ... had told us of it, and when it was reported out on the prairie, the class rushed off to see the wonder. It was nicer than we had hoped, but now I can't keep them out of my garden.[3]

Brown went on to publish her own book, *Old Man Garden* (1955) on the plants and flowers of southern Alberta. In the 1950s, she was commissioned by the Glenbow Foundation to create two hundred images of Alberta wildflowers, particularly the rarer flowers peculiar to the foothills and mountains. Executed in her preferred medium, watercolour and casein, the project took over two years to complete and required special trips in search of a specimen of each flower at its peak of bloom. Serving as a record of the many wild plants of the region, some of which have become extinct, these works are housed in Glenbow's art collection today.

While living in Fort Macleod, Brown submitted her paintings to exhibitions, and was included in shows at Glenbow and the Coste House (the local Calgary art gallery of the period), as well as in exhibits on the Western Canada Art Circuit. Her work was carried by Canadian Art Galleries, one of the very few commercial galleries in Calgary. In 1951 Brown travelled to England and France, a trip that was an important affirmation for her. Her contact with other artists confirmed her own sense of identity and validated her determination to depict what she knew and identified with best, the

Canadian West. Her isolation as an artist in Fort Macleod – a state she claimed to prefer – was perhaps actually the inevitable consequence of being close to her chosen subject.

Brown also worked as an instructor at the Banff School of Fine Arts, mostly during the summers, from 1945 to 1950. She was a member of the Alberta Society of Artists and an honorary member of the Alberta Handicraft Guild. In 1971 she received an honorary doctorate from the University of Lethbridge.

In her autobiography, *Sketches from Life* (1981), Brown wrote eloquently about her life in Alberta. Her words indicate her strong sense of the importance of local history and her desire to document the region that was her home. She recounted one meeting with a local person in Fort Macleod, early in her career, who came upon her sketching a grain elevator:

"Doing elevators, I see, he said … "Why do you waste your time doing ugly things like that?"

"I don't think they are ugly. They belong to the prairie and they are practically the only vertical lines. They catch lovely lights and shadows, and make interesting silhouettes against the clouds and sunsets."

"But nobody ever paints pictures of elevators," he protested. No. No one ever had. I was breaking trail and finding it hard going. I knew that the townspeople regarded me as an oddity.[4]

Brown then told of how fifty years and two generations later people sought her out to create images of grain elevators:

"Paint me a picture of elevators," they said. "Paint me a picture of wheat fields, mountains, prairie without mountains, cactuses, buffalo beans, meadow larks, gophers."

I painted, painted, painted … "Too bad," they said. "There are so many things to paint."[5]

14.3 *Hoop Dance, Blood Indian Reserve*
(CN 57.46.2, Glenbow Museum and Archives. Courtesy of the Estate of Annora Brown)

This account was presented by Brown with little explanation of its meaning. As a curator who lives in the region of southern Alberta, I was struck at how radical the art of this woman must have appeared in the context of rural Fort Macleod in the 1940s. Brown, an artist who was essentially conservative by nature, nonetheless contributed substantially to an awareness of art in Alberta. Her artistic sensibilities helped form and still reflect Alberta's sense of place and regional identity.

In 1965, leaving her family home behind, Brown moved to British Columbia, where the climate was more temperate and the gardening easier than in Fort Macleod's rocky soil. After living for some time in Sidney, she moved to Deep Cove, where she found friendship within a colony of artists, writers, and musicians. There she lived until the age of eighty-eight.

Vignette

15 Yukon Women Pioneers

Women have played a key role in the development of the
Yukon. The Yukon Archives, along with other archives
and historical societies in rural and remote communities,
have established programs to document the lives of
selected individuals who have contributed to their community. These vignettes are based on archival acquisi-
tions, such as personal papers and photographic collections, that document everyday life.

Edith Josie: "These Are the News"

Charlene Porsild

Edith Josie has contributed to the social fabric of her
community by writing about the daily events in Old
Crow, Yukon, in her newspaper column "These Are the
News." In it, she informs people in surrounding communities of the comings and goings in her town.

15.1 Edith Josie – journalist
(PHO 279 [85/25], Yukon Archives)

Josie was born in 1921 into the Vuntut Gwich'in community in Old Crow. She began her
journalism career in 1962 when *Whitehorse Star* publisher Harry Boyle asked Sarah Simon,
wife of the Anglican minister at Old Crow, to find someone to act as a local correspondent.
Simon chose Edith because she didn't have a "husband to look after her" and thus needed a
job to support herself. Since 1963, Josie has chronicled day-to-day life in her community.
Although a native Gwich'in, she hand-wrote in English, and her column has appeared in
magazines and newspapers around the world. She was
profiled in *Life* magazine in 1965.

In addition to being a journalist, Josie has always been an active member of her
church as a lay reader, and taught classes in the Gwich'in language in her hometown
of Old Crow.

Martha Louise Black (1866–1957)

Martha Louise Black was a young mother living in Chicago in 1898 when Klondike fever struck North America. She started for the Klondike with her first husband, who subsequently abandoned both Martha and the trip. Martha persevered, despite being pregnant, and crossed the Chilkoot Pass with her brother George. She made the Yukon her home and went on to become a successful businesswoman, owning a mining camp and managing a sawmill. Later, she married George Black, who would be appointed commissioner of the Yukon. In 1935 at the age of seventy, she became the second woman to be elected as a member of Parliament in Canada. Awarded the Order of the British Empire for her volunteer work in Britain during the First World War, she was also made a Fellow of the Royal Geographical Society for her research into Yukon flora.

15.2 Martha Black, c. 1900
(87/79, Yukon Archives)

16 Alice Peck, May Phillips, and the Canadian Handicrafts Guild

Ellen Easton McLeod

Exhibition of Arts and Handicrafts

Montreal Branch of the Woman's Art Association of Canada

UNDER THE PATRONAGE OF
HER EXCELLENCY THE COUNTESS OF MINTO

Art Galleries, Colonial House, Phillips Square

From Oct. 22nd to Nov. 3rd, 1900

16.1 Advertisement for Montreal Branch of the Women's Art Association, 1900 (Canadian Handicrafts Guild, Quebec)

Until the Women's Art Association of Canada (WAAC), under the direction of Alice Skeleton Peck and Mary Martha (May) Phillips, began promoting handicrafts as legitimate artistic expressions, these creative products of Canadian women were disparaged and neglected. Peck and Phillips were far ahead of their time in recognizing the artistic and social value inherent in handicrafts that represented women's household tasks, cultural voices, and creative energies. The two women co-founded the Canadian Handicrafts Guild in 1905, remaining its joint source of inspiration for many years.

Alice Skeleton grew up in a family that valued both culture and public service. Following her early education in Montreal, she married Montreal businessman James Henry Peck in 1879. Alice Peck had seven children by 1892; she was widowed in 1903 and left as the head of the family. Nevertheless, her privileged status gave her freedom to participate in the new women's organizations of the 1890s. In 1892 she was a charter member of the Montreal Ladies' Morning Musical Club.

Born in Montreal in 1856 to a notary father and a surgeon's daughter, May Phillips taught art and painted for most of her long life. Phillips never married, living amicably with a younger brother. In 1894 she and Alice Peck began the Montreal branch of the Women's Art Association of Canada, an organization for women interested in the arts founded by Mary Dignam in Toronto. Alice Peck was elected first president of the Montreal WAAC, which operated a studio, held sketching classes, ran a

reading and lecture program, made artist studio visits, and held art exhibitions. Peck and Phillip's most important collaboration was the founding of the Canadian Handicrafts Guild.

Aware that some WAAC activities in the fine arts duplicated classes and exhibitions held at the Art Association of Montreal, they felt their energies might be better spent reviving Canada's neglected arts and crafts. Attracted first by the French Canadian home arts of vegetable dyes, hooked rugs, and weaving, they soon embraced the basketry, bead, and quill-work of Indian women, and the weaving, embroideries, and laces of immigrant women. Alice Peck and May Phillips admired the colours, good design, fine workmanship, and originality of all of these. However, they saw that Indian arts were beginning to decline in quality, and feared that ready-made goods from catalogues would replace local home-arts production and that new settlers would lose their traditional handicrafts as they adjusted to a different country. If they could positively encourage these arts, they would help women who had no other means to earn money and at the same time preserve the country's aesthetic foundation. As early as 1896, Alice Peck and May Phillips together made Indian arts and home handicrafts a priority of the Montreal WAAC. Long before Canadian anthropologists, cultural historians, and art historians were interested in contemporary crafts, Alice Peck and May Phillips understood their artistic and social value.

Their first big initiative was an arts and handicrafts

16.2 Exhibit of textile work, Canadian Handicrafts Guild (Canadian Handicrafts Guild, Quebec)

exhibition held in Morgan's department store in October 1900. Many prominent Montreal citizens loaned their decorative arts, and the WAAC invited women to send in their contemporary handicrafts for exhibition and sale. The exhibition's success sparked further initiatives and a manifesto. In 1890 Alice Peck wrote and hand-printed a tiny pamphlet entitled "Scheme for the Promotion of Home Arts and Handicrafts." It outlined the Montreal WAAC's goals to collect, exhibit, and sell women's hand-made arts and to ensure high standards of workmanship and materials.

An all-Canadian home-arts exhibition followed in March 902, but this time it was held at the Art Association of Montreal gallery (now called the Montreal Museum of Fine Arts). Bringing handicrafts and home-arts into the art gallery confirmed their artistic merit. When in June 1902 the Montreal WAAC opened its own store – Our Handicrafts Shop – the first permanent outlet to sell Canadian handicrafts, another precedent was set. The shop's non-profit mandate assured that the craftspeople earned money from their work. The Montreal WAAC retained a small commission to offset organ-

Right:

16.3 Quill-work box (Canadian Handicrafts Guild, Quebec)

Far right:

16.4 Wood carving example, 1905 (Canadian Handicrafts Guild, Quebec)

ization costs for the many exhibitions of handicrafts it sent out across Canada, the United States, and abroad under the national WAAC banner.

As handicrafts gradually became more important to the Montreal WAAC, issues of jurisdiction, money, and control began to create a rift between the Montrealers and the WAAC head office in Toronto. Alice Peck and May Phillips wanted Montreal to be considered the headquarters of the handicrafts movement. A series of meetings and negotiations within the WAAC failed to reconcile the two sides, and over the objections of WAAC national president Mary Dignam, Peck and Phillips founded the Canadian Handicrafts Guild in 1905 as a separate organization from the WAAC. In 1906, with help from prominent men in law and government, Alice Peck and May Phillips secured a Dominion charter incorporating the Canadian Handicrafts Guild.

Growing out of a women's art organization, the Canadian Handicrafts Guild consisted initially of a group of volunteer women who supported the making, exhibiting, and selling of handicrafts by other women. The guild soon expanded to include men among its officers and exhibitors, although women always did most of the work. From 1905 to 1936, the guild held national exhibitions every year at the art gallery in Montreal. It also sold

Canadian handicrafts at the guild's shop and through agencies in Canada and the United States. The guild held annual prize competitions and ran educational programs such as a lecture series on multicultural crafts, classes for immigrant children, and later a weaving school. In 1909, guild president Alice Peck proposed that the Canadian Handicrafts Guild acquire some of the best handwork for its permanent collection. Today numerous Canadian museums and art galleries – for example, the McCord Museum of Canadian History, the Montreal Museum of Fine Arts, and the Royal Ontario Museum – own early examples of Canadian craftsmanship collected and preserved by the guild. In Montreal the Canadian Guild of Crafts (as the guild was renamed) still retains an impressive permanent collection of Inuit and Indian art.

Alice Peck and her colleague May Phillips founded and gave important early direction to the Canadian Handicrafts Guild, an early and important outlet for women's voices and creative expression. The guild was the first national patron for the handicraft arts of all Canadians, including aboriginal peoples and new immigrants. Today, the guild's legacy includes the continuation of many superb craft skills, but also an increased respect for Canada's multicultural traditions.[2]

Vignette

17 Life in a Native Community

17.1 Girls bringing home the fish (7184, Yukon Archives)

Life for most Canadian women includes domestic chores and the maintenance of the home, as discussed by Cynthia Comacchio in her introduction to Part 2, "Family and the Home"; by Dianne Dodd in essay #25, "Women and Domestic Technology"; and by Allan McCullough in his introduction to Part 6, "Earning Their Bread." In this vignette, Native women are highlighted. Several photographs were taken by John Macfie during his travels as a trapline management officer with the Ontario Department of Lands and Forests. Photographic and written records were often produced by people working in northern Canada for various levels of government, and this material frequently comes to the archives because of the creator's status. Macfie's photographs, like those from the Yukon Archives, capture moments in the lives of Native women in Canada's North as they prepare food (Illustrations 17.1 and 17.2), care for children (Illustrations 17.3 and 17.4), and engage in leisure activities (Illustrations 17.5 and 17.6).

17.2 Woman drying meat, Deer Lake, Ontario, 1956 (C 330-9-0-0-26, Archives of Ontario)

17.3 Woman with children, Port Severn, Ontario, 1955 (C 330-9-0-0-18, Archives of Ontario)

Left:
17.5 Jessie Mann playing the accordian, 1957
(86/61 A1, #145, Archives of Ontario)

Below:
17.6 Woman with pipe, Landsdowne House,
Ontario, 1955
(C 330-9-0-0-7, Archives of Ontario)

Above:
17.4 Woman with baby on back
(C 330-9-0-0-18, Archives of Ontario)

18 Helen Kalvak: Pioneering Inuit Print-maker

Jessica Tomic-Bagshaw

Helen Kalvak (1901–84) lived through a period of fundamental change in the Inuit way of life. Born in a skin tent, she lived the semi-nomadic lifestyle of her Inuit ancestors until she settled in the community of Holman as an adult. She can best be described as a woman who was both traditional in her experiences and exceptional in her ability to survive the upheaval of her culture. The changes in Inuit society occurring around her challenged Kalvak to adapt her knowledge of traditional customs to the new Inuit way of life.

As an artist, seamstress, and storyteller, Kalvak produced numerous imaginative drawings, inspired by the creations of traditional Inuit seamstresses, with their well-honed sense of design and form. The Holman Print Collection and Cooperative made over 150 prints from her drawings. Until her death in 1984, Kalvak's work was the mainstay of the cooperative's print shop, which is still producing highly acclaimed prints by Inuit artists today.

Greatly respected in her own community of Holman and in the Inuit art world beyond, Kalvak was elected a member of the Royal Canadian Academy of Arts in 1975 and was among the first Inuit women to be appointed to the Order of Canada in 1978. A school in Holman was named in her honour. Through her art, she made the experiences shared by many of her generation accessible to future generations of both Inuit and non-Inuit. Her importance as an elder did not go unnoticed, and as one of the few remaining Inuit who grew up on the land, she served as a valuable repository of traditional Inuit knowledge and customs.

Kalvak began life as a member of the semi-nomadic Copper Inuit in the high western Arctic. For Inuit to survive in the harsh arctic environment, rigid customs and duties were assigned according to gender. Men were taught the skill and patience needed to hunt, while the complementary talents and duties of women, especially the sewing of skins for clothing and shelter, were passed down from mother to daughter. Having no son, Kalvak's parents, Aluksit and Ingataomik, also taught her to hunt, an exception to the customary Inuit division of labour. She killed her first caribou at the age of eleven, using her own bow and arrow.[1]

Kalvak was also respected for her strength of spirit. Her parents, who were respected storytellers and *angakoks* (shamans), trained her from a young age as an angakok, teaching her their special language and healing techniques. Tattoo marks on her face and arms, indicating power and beauty, were earned only after difficult accomplishments. Shamans were important spiritual leaders who could summon spirit helpers to aid in a successful hunt, settle disputes between camp leaders, heal the sick, and provide encouragement through stories of the past. Only a few Inuit, and for the most part men, were chosen to learn the intricate knowledge and rituals of the shaman.

In 1921 Kalvak married Manayok, another strong hunter and leader. They raised a family together in the traditional manner, and it was not until after Manayok's death in the early 1960s that Kalvak moved "off the land" to settle permanently in Holman. Here she met Father Henri Tardy, a Roman Catholic missionary. Kalvak's reputed skills as a seamstress resulted in a commission from Tardy for a new parka. She made a preliminary drawing of a shamanic seal for her coat. Impressed with her confident style and unfailing sense of line, Tardy had the idea of using her stories and images to establish a print-making project, similar to the one in Cape Dorset. In this sense, Kalvak was the inspiration for a new art form in Holman. With Tardy's encouragement, Kalvak began to draw. Her rich images, a link between past Inuit life and a new cultural reality, were among the first to be made into prints at the new studio.

Kalvak's sense of design and bold subject matter have made her a favourite with many collectors of Inuit art. She depicted with enthusiasm subjects such as animals, angakoks, and people struggling to survive. She was not afraid to tackle sensitive themes like shamanism or stories of violence and betrayal, as in the 1980 stencil print *Fighting a Sorcerer*. Leo Bushman, in a 1988 interview, described how Kalvak "used her hands for placement of animals and figures in various positions to get a feeling of what the composition could be. All the while she hummed or sang and moved slowly and gently as if she were warming up for a dance instead of a drawing session. No drawing or marks were made on paper before going through these rituals of placing her hands on the paper and humming or singing."[2]

For Inuit at this time, there was no distinction made between art and life. Kalvak found inspiration for her drawings in the numerous local myths, legends, and spiritual events in her life. Part of the appeal and significance in her images is their candid exchange and sharing of personal and cultural content. Inuit art now serves as a vehicle for dialogue and communication between cultures, sharing qualities and values so important to Inuit identity. Future generations of Inuit will be able to understand their traditions and customs through the imagery found in the works of Helen Kalvak.

A remarkable women, she has left a rich legacy of prints and drawings, a legacy that reflects her strong spirit and intimate knowledge of Inuit mythology. Holman print-makers have continued to follow Kalvak's example, producing works that are visual expressions of their oral tradition and cultural heritage.

19 Virginia J. Watt: Champion of Inuit Arts and Crafts

Ellen Easton McLeod

Today she is revered for her enlightened support of Canadian crafts and Inuit art, but Virginia Watt's first job was testing ammunition in Montreal. Born in Winnipeg in 1919, she came to live in Montreal during the Second World War. She was hired almost immediately for a job beginning six weeks later, although she first had to qualify by studying day and night to master the required chemistry and physics. Working for the Inspection Board of the United Kingdom and Canada at a firing range at Ste Thérèse, Quebec, she was in charge of the laboratory and did night fieldwork with Oerlikon and Hispano trace ammunition.

However, it was not long before she found employment more relevant to her education. Virginia Watt had trained in Manhattan at the New York Art Students' League and the Traphagen School of Design, where her interest was theatre and costume design. She took life-drawing classes, studied the Brooklyn Museum's clothing collection, and learned to make quick sketches at fashion shows to explore visual impact. She was also taught how to draft patterns for costume construction. These skills were useful to her as a freelance costume designer, sometimes for Malabar's. In this same period, she joined the Shakespeare Society and the Montreal Repertory Theatre (MRT). She attended the costume rehearsals and was soon recruited to appear on stage as well. Watt went on to act in many MRT productions and in Canadian Broadcasting Corporation (CBC) radio plays sent out on short wave during the war. After years

of performing in rented halls, the MRT acquired its own building, and Watt, along with Hans Berends, worked there as technical director. When the building burned down on 5 March 1952, everything was lost, contents as well as the theatre. All of her sketches, designs, and costumes were gone forever. She had to start again.

After a brief stint at designing contemporary clothes, Virginia Watt moved to Hudson, Quebec, where she decided to take up sculpting and run a gift shop to carry the expenses. Unable to afford marble, she turned to clay, learning "to throw" at Macdonald College and researching the chemistry of glaze technology on her own. She built a large studio and from 1955 to 1967 successfully practised as a ceramist. She is a talented quilter and embroiderer as well.

In 1964 Virginia Watt was appointed to the Board of Directors of the Quebec branch of the Canadian Guild of Crafts. The board asked her to update the interior design of the Montreal shop at 2025 Peel Street and to contribute her ideas on modernizing the guild's organization. She was still a volunteer at this point, but in 1968 the guild hired her to be shop manager. Three years later she was promoted to the position of managing director. She immersed herself in learning about all varieties of creative craftsmanship in Canada and in defining the role she saw for the guild. With her artistic background and enormous respect for the pursuit of excellence, she lent her support to the best Canadian crafts. Not only did the guild benefit from her strong direction and astute eye, but many other organizations asked her to jury art exhibitions and select award winners. She frequently shared her knowledge and experience by giving lectures for the guild, presenting papers at conferences, publishing articles, and writing for exhibition catalogues. In 1979 Virginia Watt was made an honorary life member of the Canadian Crafts Council in recognition of her outstanding service to Canadian crafts.

The Canadian Handicrafts Guild had been the first agency to sell Inuit (formerly called Eskimo) carvings. Its successor, the Canadian Guild of Crafts Quebec, also supported Inuit artists. The guild owned many early pieces of Inuit art, and with Virginia Watt's direction and encouragement, it became a leader in exhibiting and selling Inuit prints as well as sculpture. In the late 1970s, Watt was on the board of Canadian Arctic Producers, the wholesale distributor of Inuit art. She served on the Canadian Eskimo Arts Council from 1969 until 1986 and chaired the council from 1977 to 1983. The Eskimo Arts Council provided technical advice to the Eskimo cooperatives, guaranteed artistic quality by approving which works would be released to the public, and made policy recommendations on Inuit art to the government and the coops. When Virginia Watt first joined, the Eskimo Arts Council had only one Inuit on the board. She was instrumental in encouraging the recruitment and training of many Inuit members for the council.

At the World Crafts Organization Symposium in Toronto in 1974, Virginia Watt chaired the exhibition "Crafts from Arctic Canada." She later organized the permanent exhibit and catalogue of the guild's extraordinary collection of Inuit art, entitled "Permanent Collection of Inuit Art and Crafts, Circa 1900–1980." In 1985 Virginia Watt was awarded the Order of Canada in recognition of her years of service to Inuit art and to the artists and craftspeople of the North. She was appointed President of the Inuit Art Foundation in 1989 and made honorary lifetime director in 1997.

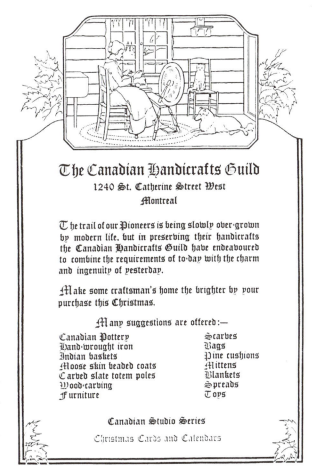

19.1 Canadian Handicrafts Guild Christmas flyer (Canadian Handicrafts Guild, Quebec)

Just before Virginia Watt retired as director of the Canadian Guild of Crafts Quebec in 1986, she unexpectedly discovered a treasure among the decaying cardboard boxes and dusty paper packages in the guild's attic. These unlabelled, forgotten bundles contained a cache of Canadian history dating back to the 1890s: letters, documents, pamphlets, catalogues, and photographs. Until then, the early history of the guild was known primarily through the official minutes. Watt immediately decided to establish a guild archives. As soon as she "retired," she researched the means of setting up a "user-friendly" facility and raised money for acid-free file folders, labels, and sturdy filing cabinets. She recruited Inuit art collector and friend Dr Dorothy Stillwell for assistance. Then, over several years, Virginia Watt meticulously organized the material into an outstanding resource. Besides personally writing numerous articles about the guild's history,[1] especially about its early patronage of Inuit art, Virginia Watt has assisted many scholars in accessing the information she found and organized.[2] She died in March 1999.

18 A Century of Artistic Experience and Innovation

Anne Newlands

Fiction needs its specifics, its anchors. It needs also to pass beyond them … it needs also to fly right through them into the larger universal space.

> Jeanette Winterson, *Oranges Are Not the Only Fruit*

The twentieth century has been a time of war, revolution, social upheaval, technological advancement, and a period that has witnessed unprecedented change. Inevitably this dizzying pace finds itself reflected in art, tendering artistic production that has both mirrored the chaos and provided a refuge. Given this tumultuous context, an introduction to the great accomplishments of Canadian women artists working in a variety of media over the past one hundred years is indeed a daunting task.

This century has seen the growing acceptance and unprecedented recognition of Canadian women artists. Access to art education has been an important factor in these advances, as women were increasingly admitted to art schools and academies where they received an education previously reserved only for men. The expansion in the number of art associations that included women and eventually allowed them to vote in operational decisions, was complemented by new opportunities for exhibitions that made women's work better known and allowed them to establish themselves as professional artists. By the mid-fifties, with the founding of the Canada Council and the achievement of increased equality for women in society, the numbers of Canadian women artists grew by the hundreds. Although the individual economic and social conditions of these artists have varied, each one has made a singular contribution to the history of art in Canada, expanding and enriching its definition and scope.

Not wishing to generalize the considerable accomplishments of Canadian women artists over the century, I propose to anchor our recognition of their contributions in a selection of ten artists from different periods and from different regions. These ten will carve a path of stepping stones from decade to decade throughout the twentieth century. The work of each of these artists embodies a spirit of change and innovation, as well as an exploration of a variety of media. We will examine women's shared attraction to subjects such as the figure, the land, myth, and politics, pondering their transformation though the minds, eyes, and hands of the ever-changing psychological and political realities of artists.

Our first stop brings us to the end of the First World War and a look at the achievements of two important sculptors: Frances Loring and Florence Wyle. These two American-born women trained in leading American art schools before they settled in Toronto in 1913. Within a short time, they had become noticeable on the Toronto sculpture scene, challenging the monopoly of the respected Walter Allward, the sculptor responsible for most of the large public monuments in Toronto at the turn of the century. By 1914 Loring and Wyle were exhibiting with the Ontario Society of Artists, and in

20.1 *Furnace Girl*, by Frances Loring (8502, Canadian War Museum)

1917 Loring became active with the Women's Art Association of Canada.

In 1918 both women were commissioned by the Canadian War Records Office to produce bronze sculptures of various types of factory workers involved in the war industry.[1] In fact, they were the only artists to document in sculpture the contributions of men and women to the war effort on the home front. Their contemporary, Henrietta Mabel May, was commissioned to paint female munition workers by the same office.

Loring's *Furnace Girl* of 1918–19 (Illustration 20.1), depicts a young, lithe woman clothed in the protective garb required by her job, solemnly engaged in the service of industry. Although the dress and action are contemporary, the style employed by Loring is rooted in traditional academic training and its insistence on a faithful and naturalistic rendering of anatomy. While their work was praised in their day for these very qualities, Loring and Wyle would later adopt a more modern, streamlined approach to the figure.

The contribution of Loring and Wyle to the history of sculpture in Canada, both in terms of the art produced and the profile acquired for women sculptors, was enormous. In 1928 they were counted among the founders of the Sculptors Society of Canada, and their studio-home, an old church in Rosedale, became an important gathering place for artists between the wars. Decorated with honorary doctorates in their later years,[2] they blazed the trail for other successful female sculptors of their day, such as Elizabeth Wyn Wood and Jacobine Jones.

Moving along a decade, to the end of the 1920s and the eve of the Great Depression, we encounter Prudence Heward's *Girl on a Hill* of 1929, symbolizing a bold and innovative approach to the representation of the figure at a time when the landscape painting of the Group of Seven dominated the Canadian art scene. As noted in essay #29, Heward studied art in Montreal and Paris, and along with other Montreal artists, such as Lilias Torrance

Newton, Anne Savage, and Edwin Holgate, formed the short-lived (1920–21) Beaver Hall Hill Group. In 1928 she exhibited with the Group of Seven and in 1929 won the Willingdon $200 prize for *Girl on a Hill*. The award boosted her reputation as one of the most celebrated figure painters of the day. In 1933 Heward was a founding member of the Canadian Group of Painters.

Girl on a Hill is typical of Heward's portrayal of women, usually depicted seated or standing at rest. Her subjects gaze at us directly and express an emotional vulnerability that seems at odds with their physical fortitude. Although the model for this painting was in fact the dancer Louise McLea, Heward's depiction transcends the individual and presents a woman of the land, young, solid, and somewhat apprehensive. The subject is seated peacefully under a tree, and her curving forms fill the foreground of the painting and are echoed in the undulations of the land and trees in the background. Painted in 1929 as economic markets began to crash, the work suggests a bleak mood through the dark, sombre colours of the woman's dress and the stark simplicity of the setting, both seeming to foreshadow the hard times of deprivation, poverty, and unemployment to come.

Looking at Emily Carr's *Sunshine and Tumult* of 1938–39 (Illustration 20.2), we move to the beginning of the Second World War, and examine the subject of the land. In her published journals, *Hundreds and Thousands*, Carr protested the hideousness of war – "nations are hating and hissing, striking and wrecking and maiming"[3] – while her paintings of the same time reflect the peace of her immediate surroundings and the inner joy of her soul. In *Sunshine and Tumult*, the rhythmic lines describing the branches of the trees and the patterns of swirling cloud quiver with the excitement of life. Moved by the beauty of the forest, Carr wrote: "When I went into the woods I could rise and skip with the spring and forget my bad heart. Doesn't it show that the good … and inspiring will of nature is stronger than evil and cruelty?"[4] (See the profile of Emily Carr in vignette #13.)

Carr painted this work when she was sixty-eight years old, near the end of her long and arduous journey to find her own artistic voice. From her beginnings in staid nineteenth-century Victoria, she went to extraordinary ends to educate herself as an artist. Following studies in California, England, and France, she returned home and produced colourful depictions of First Nations' villages and totem poles. Her land-ladying years (1914–27) left her little time for art. However, opportunities to exhibit in eastern Canada and to meet the Group of Seven artists fostered a rediscovery of her vision as an artist. Nature, in all of its vast British Columbia glory, became her most powerful subject and her most enduring legacy.

While some artists worked in isolation, as Emily Carr did, independent of group support and affirmation, others chose to form groups based on collective ideals. In Quebec in the 1940s, men and women artists such as Marcelle Ferron, Françoise Sullivan, and Madeleine Arbour banded together under Paul-Émile Borduas to promote a new order for art and society, a plea that culminated in 1948 with the publication of their manifesto, *Refus global*. Signed by artists, writers, and dancers, it called for artistic, social, and political change in the repressive church-dominated society of Quebec during the Duplessis regime.

Artists such as Marcelle Ferron who signed the manifesto were inspired by Surrealist theories of automatism, which advocated working spontaneously from dreams and the subconscious.[5] In *Seafarers' Union* of 1954, Ferron worked abstractly to create a dizzying tapestry of colour. Here, unexpected juxtapositions of deep mauve, brown-red, bright blue, and green weave across the canvas, held in balance by patches of yellow-white. This all-over patterning of colour, where no single element of the composition dominates, may reflect Ferron's belief in social egalitarianism and her interest at that time in Quebec's budding union movement.

20.2 *Sunshine and Tumult*, by Emily Carr (Courtesy of the Hamilton Art Gallery. Bequest of H.S. Southam, 1966)

Taking a northern direction in our journey, we discover that 1948 was an equally auspicious year in the Arctic. That year James Houston, an artist and Canadian government administrator, and his wife Alma were instrumental in encouraging art-making activities among the Inuit as a way for them to supplement their income. The establishment of a printmaking workshop in Cape Dorset followed in 1957, and with it the organization of a printmaking cooperative that facilitated the production and marketing of the artists' prints in the south.

In 1959 Kenojuak Ashevak submitted a drawing to the Cape Dorset Co-operative, the first woman to do so. She later contributed hundreds of images to the annual Cape Dorset print collections and became one of the

20.3 *The Enchanted Owl*, by Kenojuak Ashevak (Winnipeg Art Gallery. Courtesy of West Baffin Eskimo Co-operative Ltd)

most celebrated, widely exhibited Inuit artists. In the mid-fifties, while still living a traditional life on the land, she had begun to make sealskin and beaded objects, as well as a few carvings. By the late fifties, supplied with pencil and paper and encouraged by Houston, she started to draw. Her strong sense of design was rooted in her life on the land, where women were expert in decorating the skin clothing of the Inuit.

The Enchanted Owl of 1960 (Illustration 20.3), with its wide-eyed bird whose head feathers spin out like the rays of the sun and whose tail sweeps up joyously behind it, has become one of the most famous images of Inuit art. Extensively reproduced for its beauty and its striking graphic qualities, it was featured on the six-cent stamp in 1970. Although birds are a dominant subject in Kenojuak's art, she has said that she draws without preconceived ideas and that her goal is to "make something beautiful – that is all." Birds, in their many imaginative permutations, are simply the subject that frequently appears when she begins to draw.

We now return south to Joyce Wieland's *Reason over Passion* of 1968 (Illustration 20.4), and to the feminist revolution of the sixties. Renowned by the mid-1960s as a painter, sculptor, printmaker, and filmmaker, Wieland first turned to quilting while living in New York. There, the effect of being part of the male-dominated New York art world drove her to embrace "the whole feminist thing." At the same time she developed a passionate interest in Canadian history and politics. These pursuits came together in the late sixties in a series of quilts executed in Canada with the help of her sister and other women. They not only celebrated her ardent patriotism, they also addressed feminist issues and the history of the collaborative nature of women's work. She clearly stated her purpose in making quilts: "to elevate and honour craft, to join women together and make them proud of what they had done."[6] In Wieland's eyes, the quilt was more than the traditional form recognized by most people; she hoped that with her contribution it would now be taken in earnest by the art world. Indeed, since the sixties, thousands of artists have embraced the cooperative nature of quilt making as a form of collective artistic expression. This new attitude was most recently illustrated by the quilts created to commemorate the lives of AIDS victims.

The words "Reason over Passion" came from a 1968 statement by the newly elected Pierre Elliott Trudeau, who spoke about the need to place reason over passion in government. Here, Wieland's playful use of bright, colourful letters – hot reds, warm oranges, and soft pinks – seems at odds with the seriousness of the message. The quilt is a study in contrasts: between a political sentiment and an object usually relegated to the privacy of domestic interiors, and between the notions of reason and passion themselves, polarities that permeated Wieland's entire career.

The political activism of the sixties was also reflected in the artistic activities of the First Nations, as Native communities across the country began to assert themselves politically, historically, and culturally. The desire to recover lost languages and identity, compromised by over fifty years of residential schooling, led many artists to give visual form to traditional narratives as well as to the scars of history.

Our next pause is a look at the work of Daphne Odjig, an Ojibway artist born in the village of Wikwemikong on Manitoulin Island. From her earliest childhood, Odjig was interested in art, and her home life on the reserve was happy, until the death of her mother in 1938. The family then moved to Parry Sound, where for the first time Odjig experienced racial prejudice. With the outbreak of Second World War, Odgig moved to Toronto, where job opportunities provided an escape, as well as access to the world of art. For the next twenty years, through marriage and motherhood, Odjig painted both the disintegration of traditional Native life that she had observed on visits to reserves and images based on Indian legends being told again with the resurrection of the

20.4 *Reason over Passion*, by Joyce Wieland (National Gallery of Canada. Courtesy of the Estate of Joyce Wieland)

powwow in certain communities.

Odjig's *Nanabush and the Beavers* of 1969 comes from a series of legends for children about Nanabush, the Algonkian hero. Odjig used her artistic licence to give Nanabush visual form – like a two-headed Janus, the hero looks forward at the sun and back at two mischievous beavers. Although Odjig's bold linear style has been linked to that of the Anishnabe artist Norval Morrisseau, Odjig states that at the time she was not aware of the Morrisseau's work. For all her commitment to Native issues, Odjig's stylistic inspiration comes from elsewhere, "Everyone knows that my favourite is Picasso, I love the way he was able to put down his own feelings … He was never intimidated … I love to distort things … Picasso distorted."[7]

For a short while in the early 1970s, Odjig was a member of a native "Group of Seven" whose affiliation included artists such as Alex Janvier, Norval Morrisseau, and Carl Ray. With these artists she shared the desire to

20.5 *an extended and continuous metaphor – no. 6*, Sorel Cohen, 1983, (Courtesy of the National Gallery of Canada)

employ a modern visual language to explore Native myth and contemporary realities. Recognized for paving the way for a large number of contemporary native women artists, Odjig insisted, "My aspiration is to excel as an artist in my own individual right, rather than to be accepted 'because' I am Indian."[8]

Our next interlude propels us into the 1980s and a stop to look at the work of Montreal artist Sorel Cohen, whose innovative use of photography combines with a feminist aesthetic that contests stereotypical cultural beliefs about women, as well as traditional depictions of their roles. Although women artists have used photography since its invention in 1839, many of those who embraced photography in the 1970s and 1980s were first trained as painters or sculptors; deliberately they chose photography as their medium of expression for the implications inherent in the medium itself.

In *an extended and continuous metaphor – no. 6* (Illustration 20.5) of 1983, we are presented with a large triptych – almost five metres wide and two metres high – in which Cohen critiques the representation of traditional artist-model-viewer relationships and uses herself for all three parties. Borrowing the form of a Flemish altarpiece, Cohen constructs a narrative that begins in the left panel, in which a woman with her back to us holds a red drapery and studies the painting for which she is the subject. In the centre panel, the model watches the artist paint, and in the right, the model examines a blurred reflection of herself as if the painted likeness had stepped out of the canvas. Cohen observed, "I juxtapose the pose of the female model – muse to the male artist … with that of the professional female artist, agent and practitioner of her own work. As I also insert a spectator who is female, a crisis of identity occurs – for they are all clearly the same person."[9]

In exploring and commenting on women's customary domestic responsibilities in the home, such as making a bed or cleaning a window, Cohen exploits the expressive potential of camera art. Her way of composing is striking: large-format colour photography, dramatic lighting, and a slow shutter speed inevitably capture movement as a blur. Because she tends to present her work as a series of images, there is the implication of repetition, suggestive of both ritual and the passing of time. Although her work is rooted in personal experience, the activities represented possess a universal quality that expands their meaning.

Closer to the end of our century, artists and writers increasingly explored questions of personal identity – a topic also surveyed in the work of British Columbia artist Liz Magor. In her *Dorothy – A Resemblance* of 1981 (Illustration 20.6), lead and steel are used innovatively to construct a work of art based on a personal life story. Four steel tables with springs support individual collections of everyday objects cast in lead. One table, for example, features a pile of books, light bulbs, books of matches; another fish and fishing weights; another bread and candles.

One object on each of the tables is stamped with a message that begins, "I have always weighed 98 lbs." The relationship between this assemblage of objects, symbolic of life and survival, and the printed message leaves us puzzled. Returning to the title, we find the answer. Dorothy, a real individual, recounted her life-story to Magor in terms of her weight at particular times. The fluctuations in her weight became landmarks in her life associated with specific occurrences. Her weight was literally the way she measured herself and the passing of time.

The artist has given visual form to this concept, parcelling out Dorothy's sense of herself through a collection of mundane objects cast in lead. While these give us physical equivalents to Dorothy, they tell us nothing of her personality, her hopes, or her dreams. They only hint at a *resemblance* and leave us lost in the gap between outward symbols of identity and internal personal narratives. The work leaves us asking questions: How do we construct identity? How are we known to others and to ourselves? What constitutes a life? It is interesting that

Milan Kundera's novel *The Unbearable Lightness of Being,* published in 1984, explores life's essences in similar terms of lightness and weight.

From the probing of personal identity in Magor's work, we move to the more global questions of one's relationship to society and to a planet threatened by abuse of its resources. The large-scale oil paintings (240 x 320 cm) of Winnipeg artist Eleanor Bond are appro-

20.6 Liz Magor, *Dorothy – A Resemblance,* 1981, (Courtesy of the National Gallery of Canada)

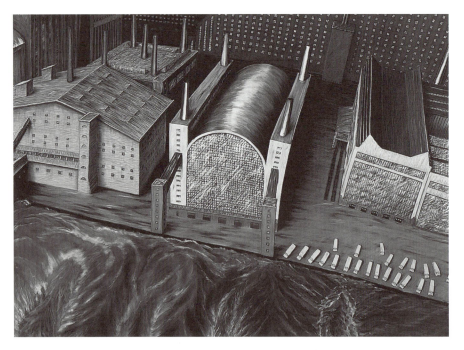

20.7 Eleanor Bond, *Departure of the Industrial Workers*, 1985, oil on canvas 239.5 x 327.5. (Courtesy of The Winnipeg Art Gallery; Acquired with funds from The Winnipeg Foundation (Accession # G-86-140)

feeling of optimism suggested by the bright oranges, reds, yellows, and blues is countered by the ominous monumentality of the factories that cast their sinister shadows on the unpopulated site. Only the rows of yellow school buses on the right and the chevron-shaped wakes left by recently departed boats suggest a human presence. Yet it is a presence that is both regimented and anonymous, suggesting perhaps a loss of individual identity and control in an increasingly technological society.

During our century-long voyage, from Frances Loring's *Furnace Girl* to the fictive landscapes of Eleanor Bond's *Work Station* paintings, we have glimpsed into the minds and hearts of ten very different Canadian women artists. In exploring this highly diverse work, we have been challenged and encouraged to explore different sides of ourselves, questioning our response to nature and the human condition. New forms of visual expression and a variety of media further inspire us to consider new ways of seeing and thinking. More importantly, through artists' creative visions we can travel to worlds that we would othrwise be unable to imagine.

Art like fiction needs its specifics, its anchors, but it needs also to pass beyond the particular into a larger universal space.

priately immense in their interrogation of our place in the world. In 1985 Bond embarked on a series of eight paintings known as *Work Station*; these were inspired by her travels and experiences in cities, towns, and industrial sites, as well as by her interest in the plight of the unemployed and issues of dislocation. The large scale of these colourful canvases fulfils Bond's purpose to engulf the viewer, to overwhelm and create a sense of disorientation. Gigantic buildings loom before us, threatening to tip out of the pictorial space into our own. As Bond has said, "My intention is that the viewer enter this projection, this debate – that these sites function as forums, not as landscapes in the traditional sense."[10]

In *Departure of the Industrial Workers* (Illustration 20.7), 1985, Bond creates bewildering tensions by presenting a fictional urban landscape that seems both familiar and unfamiliar, inviting and frightening. The

PART TWO

Family and the Home

21 Introduction

Cynthia R. Comacchio

"Family," as concept and as relationship, is so closely bound to women's role and status that, until very recently, few dared to question the assumed, exclusive, biological, universal understanding of woman-as-mother. It is, consequently, impossible to think historically about women without giving due consideration to their familial context. The selections in Part 2, both textual and visual, suggest some of the ways in which familial bonds have long defined and limited women. But they also demonstrate how, over a century of whirlwind change, families have also served women as sources of both private and public power. If this power was always confined within the socio-cultural, economic, legal, and political boundaries established by men, women were nonetheless the primary agents of familial adaptation to the forces of change. They were active participants and instigators in the modernizing trends that marked the century's development: industrialization, immigration, western settlement, reform movements, suffrage, and the development of the welfare state.[1]

Despite the force of the male-breadwinner family model, Canadian women of all backgrounds have always contributed significantly to the family economy. As Dianne Dodd indicates in essay #25 and Alan McCullough in the introduction to Part 6, women in colonial, preindustrial Canada were the mainstay of the domestic production that sustained the family economy, at a time when the labour of all family members was crucial to survival and the hope of prosperity. As industrial capitalism advanced in the closing quarter of the nineteenth century, the work of men became increasingly identified with wage labour outside the home, while that of women with the domestic sphere and the unpaid "women's work" within. The home became increasingly a haven and source of nurture rather than of production, at least for those urban middle-class families that could in some measure embrace the Victorian "cult of domesticity" that depicted women as "angels of the hearth."[2]

Achievement of this family model, premised on the male breadwinner and on dependent, stay-at-home wife – emblematic of Victorian middle-class respectability – depended enormously upon the virtue, selfless devotion, and ability of the woman/mother at its centre. Catherine Vye's biographical sketch of Zoé Lafontaine Laurier (#22) shows that this woman's unusual status as "one of the dominant women in Canadian political circles" was due by and large to her skill in meeting the demands of "True Womanhood" through a heavy schedule of domestic management, entertaining, and volunteer activity that would have been familiar, in varying degrees, to many middle- and upper-class women of her time.

Madame Laurier and her fortunate sisters worked hard to meet the standards imposed by a society that measured women's worth in terms of her domestic vocation. But hard, even punishing, labour – and at times deprivation and suffering – was the lot of many other Canadian families that earned their living on

21.1 Mathilde Carrière-Perreault and her family (T. Mymka Collection, Musée de St Boniface)

farms and in factories. We will never know how many women toiled like Alice Barrett Parke (#23), whose story has been reconstructed by Jo Fraser Jones through the diaries that Parke wrote expressly to inform her Ontario family about conditions in frontier British Columbia. These unknown pioneers of dauntless spirit and indomitable will – such as Joan Wheeler, who supported her bank-manager husband in a coal-mining camp (#24) – helped their fathers, brothers, and husbands put down new roots and found new communities. These women were at once obliged to demonstrate "womanly virtues" and to cope with the daily challenges of frontier living. Other women crossed oceans, often following men lured by the promise of free land in the West or, like Marjorie Levan's missionary parents (#8), resuming their Canadian lives in a changed Canada after overseas postings. Some women struggled to maintain their families while living in crowded ghettos of such cities as

Toronto, Montreal, and Winnipeg, frequently remaining there despite their dreams of moving westward. Still others were among the nation's original inhabitants, aboriginal families displaced by racist settlement policies that made white Europeans the choice builders of a modern Canada. The portrait of Mathilde Carrière-Perreault and her family, shown here in Illustration 21.1, illustrates the proud matriarch in 1907, little more than thirty years after the first Riel uprising saw recognition of the rights of Métis families, descendants of French Canadian fur traders and Native women and founders of the province of Manitoba. Yet this promising beginning was betrayed in the completion of various land treaties in the 1870s that resettled aboriginal families on government-regulated "reserves" and placed their children in residential schools that estranged them from their families, communities, and culture.[3] (See the letter reproduced in Illustration 21.2.)

The "new woman" of the early twentieth century, for all her newness, never truly departed from the Victorian ideal of true womanhood. With more schooling than previous generations, the new woman was more likely to work for wages before marriage, often in the mixed-sex environment of the modern office, as shown in image Illustration 21.3. Yet this expansion of women's sphere, including the acquisition of the suffrage in 1918, made the new woman newer in appearance than in the actual, day-to-day experiences of her life. This apparent "new woman" – urban, independent, and forthright – raised fears for the future of the farm family, as Margaret Kechnie describes in essay #26. The Great War intensified the inherent maternalism of prewar social reform movements aimed at "fixing" the worst abuses of industrial capitalism, particularly since it was evident that women and children – judging by such sensitive indices as their illness, mortality, and poverty rates – were the most vulnerable to these. The devastation wrought by war gave women-as-mothers a key role in the hoped-for social reconstruction that would see the dawning of a just and equitable New Jerusalem for all Canadians.

Underlying this sense of rising from the ashes of global war was a profound anxiety about social, often deemed "racial," degeneration. It appeared to many Canadians that the very source of all public good, the family itself, had been greatly undermined by the forces of modernization, now accelerated by war. The solution proposed was not one that aimed to turn back the clock – Canadians were fiercely proud of their modernity – but one that attempted to "modernize" the family by updating its key member: the wife/mother. The "angel of the hearth" would become more "efficient" and "scientific" under the guidance of new family experts emerging from the fields of medicine, psychology, social work, education, and the social sciences generally. The "new day" represented by the war's end saw women firmly reformed in the wife/mother role of tradition, but within an updated, "upgraded" context. These newly professionalized domestic angels were supposed to study instruction manuals, attend domestic science and parenting classes, and heed the advice of doctors and other experts, largely men. Essay #30 presents a dramatic case study of the phenomenon of the male expert in the field of child raising, describing how women from across Ontario were asked to donate their "mother's milk" to meet the needs of the Dionne Quintuplets.

Women were to aspire to manage home and family just as their husbands managed business affairs, and as smoothly and efficiently as any factory where workers clocked in and out. My own contribution to this section, "Saving Mothers and Babies" (#31), shows how worried reformers joined hands with doctors and new state health and welfare agencies in a campaign to address many of the ills of modern Canada through "scientific motherhood." Dianne Dodd's work on domestic technology (#25) also demonstrates the impact on home and family, and therefore on women's work and status, of

Moosehide Y.T.
Aug. 31st, 1919.

Dear Bishop;

I would like my daughter Gladys to come home to me now. I think she has had enough schooling. I want her home to help me; she is 13 years old. I do not want her to stay at school till she is 18; that is too long; when they are too long at school they won't have anything to do with us; they want to be with white people; they grow away from us. We are mothers and we feel it. Please Bishop, I wish you to be kind enough to bring her home to me when you come. I want her while she is young so she will then get used to me. I find it too much to do my house work and help to earn our living. If Gladys comes she will be able to help me; I do not want her to work in town.

My husband is away up the river hunting; he will not be back till the middle of Sept. We are well; we caught a lot of fish this Summer. Jonathan Wood has been ill but he is getting better but is very weak he held a short service for us this morning as Mr Totty is away

I had a letter from Gladys askin

to get her home. I shall look for my daughter to come back with you.

With best wishes I am your friend,

Sarah Jane Esau.

From Mrs Esau.

21.2 A letter from Sarah Jane Esau regarding her daughter, 1919
(COR 257, file 10, Yukon Archives)

this commitment to scientific management to modern household technology. Yet the technology of the early twentieth century was not shared equally between women and men, especially on the family farm. As Monda Halpern reveals in essay #27, farm women protested their unequal status in terms of technology and the lack of recognition of their work and worth on the farm, a lack of recognition deriving from the Victorian ideals of domesticity.

The gender crisis occasioned by the Great Depression actually did little to alter this fundamentally mother-centred domestic model. If the unemployment crisis obliged some mothers to seek work who had never before done so, the male-breadwinner ethos prevailed to the point where state-relief measures were designed above all else to provide for the breadwinner, according to the number of his children, and to discourage women from working in any but the lowliest female categorized jobs, such as domestic labour. As hard times tend to do, the Depression both fostered anxiety about the demise of the family and reinforced public sentiment about "the family" as the only true source of individual and collective nourishment, in its every sense. Many a Depression memoir testifies to the hard labour and sheer force of will that Canadian women brought to bear in keeping their families together, materially and emotionally, through those trying times.[4]

The Second World War saw the unprecedented entry of women into non-traditional wage labour, though ostensibly fuelled by patriotism and only "for the duration." For some women, as Ruth Haywood shows for Newfoundland in essay #28, the war could mean involvement with military personnel and the resulting burden of single motherhood. The state and private charitable organizations combined to "help" such mothers. Yet the war also marked the most notable entry of the state into the "private" sphere of family. Prodded by the experience of the Depression, the federal govern-

21.3 A modern office, 1907
(PA 119420, National Archives of Canada)

ment, in 1940, instituted a nationwide system of insurance against unemployment for certain categories of workers, largely male. Liberal prime minister Mackenzie King's acute political sense told him that the time had come for such a theme. The universal system of family allowances implemented in 1944 was likewise intended to support the male-breadwinner family, allocating public funds to mothers on the basis of number of children in order to maintain the family's buying power in the event of a postwar recession.

Both measures were welcome support for the beleaguered family, even more so as the return to postwar normalcy entailed a renewed cult of domesticity. The angel of the hearth was relocated to a brand-new suburban ranch bungalow, amidst many others equally situated, as the Baby Boom commenced with the close of the 1940s. The 1950s, a period of affluence previously unknown to many Canadian families, was ruled over by the new medium, television, whose favourite icon was the house-wife, ruling queen of the consumer family. Reversing a trend dating back to the mid-nineteenth century, Canadian women married younger and had more children, spaced closer together. Kate Aitken generated a stream of advice literature to Canadian middle-class house-wives in postwar Canada, including "20 Good Luck Lunch Menus," shown in Illustration 21.4.

Where women and family are concerned, we can see clearly how the pace and nature of change have intensified since the Second World War. By the time that the first Boomers, born in 1946, reached adolescence in the early 1960s, a virtual revolution was stirring. With its profoundly aural and visual images emblazoned in collective memory through television and rock music, that decade signified the socio-cultural turmoil associated with youth movements aimed at dislodging inhibitions, personal and societal, and making "freedom" the ultimate catchword. Some of the more lasting effects penetrated the heart of women's historic roles: socio-economic and political equality, sexual liberation, emancipation from the constraints of traditional heterosexual relationships, marriage, and motherhood – much of the latter made possible by the advent of "The Pill."

Quietly discernible even during the home-bound 1950s, the trend that saw married women, often with children, increasingly likely to work for wages also picked up speed. During the 1970s, the "second wave" of feminists in Canada, as in other Western industrial nations, organized to lobby for women's rights to pay equity, abolition of gender discrimination and sexual harassment, maternity benefits that would cease to make pregnancy a penalty, and quality, affordable day care. As illustrated by the example of her art included here in Illustration 21.5, cartoonist Lynn Johnston

chronicles the challenges of contemporary family and gender relations in her syndicated comic strip "For Better or for Worse."

By the 1980s, some 80 per cent of all married women with children under school age were working for wages. The two-income family had become a reality, although women's income still lagged behind men's, and women still found themselves responsible for the larger part of the traditional work entailed in child rearing and house-keeping. Marriage and family obviously remain popular, but women and men are again marrying later, and family size has declined to a new low of approximately 1.7 children per household. The loosening of stringent divorce laws during the 1970s and 1980s is manifested in the demise of one in three first marriages. One in six Canadian children will spend some part of their formative years in a lone-parent household, probably their mother's. Three other important trends have also taken hold since the 1980s: more couples of all classes and ethnic backgrounds are cohabiting before, or in lieu of, marrying more couples are eschewing parenthood altogether; and more mothers are giving birth for the first time after their mid-thirties. In the 1990s, the rights of lesbian and gay couples in regard to legal marriage and parenthood have come to the fore, further expanding our sense of "family," of gender and sexual, as well as, familial relationships.

As we embark upon the new millennium, we are experiencing what some social theorists regard as a "Great Disruption" sparked by the information revolution of the past thirty years.[5] This historic moment has striking parallels in the societal response to the Industrial Revolution of a hundred years ago, especially regarding the subject that concerns us in this section, that of the interrelations of women and family. Previously utilized arguments about the crisis in the family are recovered and updated. This is, as ever, a crisis undermining the very bedrock of society, and one in which, once again, women

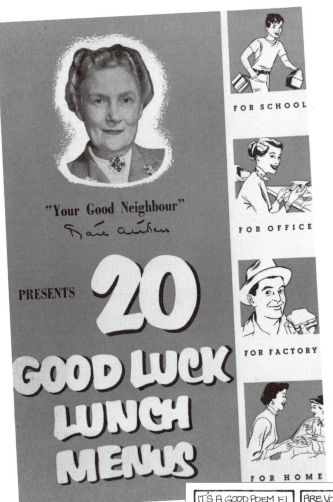

are inescapably implicated. Thus we come full circle. We are without any doubt "a century stronger" as women and as families. Our options are unquestionably more far-reaching than those of our foremothers. Yet we know that in this new century our daughters must face tests both different and achingly familiar to those that twentieth-century women have had to endure and overcome.

A list of further readings in this area is found on page 485.

Left:
21.4 Kate Aitken – "20 Good Luck Lunch Menus" (MG 30, Johnston 206, v. 35 National Archives of Canada)

Below:
21.5 Lynn Johnston cartoon "For Better or for Worse" (C 139135, National Archives of Canada; @ Lynn Johnston Productions, Ltd., United Features Syndicate, Ltd.)

22 Zoé Laurier, Prime Minister's Wife: Family Ideals at the Turn of the Century

Catherine Vye

One of the dominant women in Canadian political circles at the turn of the last century was Zoé Laurier (née Lafontaine), 1841–1921. As is the case today, in the late nineteenth and early twentieth centuries, the activities of prominent people such as prime ministers' spouses were of great interest to a public curious about their politicians. Newspapers of the past recorded details of their conduct, behaviour, and dress to satisfy this curiosity. Unfortunately, relatively little documentation of any other kind related to Zoé Laurier has survived. This is surprising, since she was the wife of Sir Wilfrid Laurier, the prime minister of Canada from 1896 to 1911. Unlike some other prime ministers' wives, Zoé Laurier left no diaries or memoirs and almost no correspondence.[1] As a consequence, it is impossible to know what she thought about her life and times. Historians are left to reconstruct her character and life by gathering information about her from photographs, references to her in the archival collections of other persons such as her husband, obituary columns, anecdotal material published in newspapers, and magazine articles published when she was alive.[2] What textual information we have left to us about Zoé Laurier is coloured by Victorian attitudes about women.

In the nineteenth century, an ideology of domesticity – an idealized vision of home and family – was one of the major tenets of the Victorian world-view.[3] This ideology created a sharp division between the private, or domestic, "sphere" of home and family and the public sphere of commerce and politics outside of the home. It also prescribed a distinct character, behaviour, and set of social roles for each gender. The domestic sphere was assigned to women. The public sphere belonged to men. According to the cult of domesticity, the four main attributes of the ideal woman – of "True Womanhood" – were piety, purity, submissiveness, and domesticity. Woman was considered morally superior to man, but also passive, modest, and pure. It was woman's duty to provide support, cheer, nurturing, and comfort to her husband and children. Woman's role as wife and mother was considered divinely ordained. Her activities focused on the home and the family and included managing the household and the social life of the family, creating a refined and cultured home environment, and ensuring an elevated tone in the family's daily life, and the moral training of children.

Zoé Laurier, as described by her contemporaries, fulfilled all of the criteria of True Womanhood. At her two homes, one in the rural village of Arthabaska, Quebec,[4] and the other in the capital of the nation, Ottawa,[5] she assumed many of the traditional roles of a middle-class woman, keeping close supervision over the activities within the domestic sphere, including the cooking, cleaning, and other work of the servants whom she employed.

Zoé came from a middle-class background of impoverished gentility. The circumstances of her life before her marriage fostered her practical no-nonsense attitude towards life. Her father had abandoned the family when she was a small child, and her mother was forced to work outside of the home teaching piano and music lessons to support the family. Middle-class women in the mid-nineteenth century had extremely limited opportunities for respectable employment; they could work as governesses or as teachers. When Zoé was old enough, she contributed to the family's income with the money she made teaching piano lessons. As the family lacked the support of a male breadwinner, she and her mother probably did most of the domestic labour in their home; hiring even the least expensive of domestic help, the maid-of-all-work, would likely have been beyond their means.[6] Zoé, by necessity, acquired such practical domestic skills as cooking, cleaning, and sewing.

When she married Wilfrid Laurier and became the chatelaine of their household, she was responsible for overseeing all aspects of the domestic sphere. An important part of her role was the keeping of household accounts. Whether pertaining to automobile parts or china dinnerware and fine wines, almost all of the bills and receipts in the Laurier Papers at the National Archives of Canada are made out to Zoé Laurier.

As well as being in charge of domestic affairs, Zoé took special responsibility for her husband's comfort and well-being, and constantly monitored his health and the strain that his activities had upon him. She knew of his semi-invalid condition as a child and youth and that his sister and mother had died of tuberculosis, so she guarded against the chronic bronchitis that afflicted him. When Wilfrid travelled, Zoé insisted that he take his own blankets and bedding so that he wouldn't have to use unclean and potentially "infected" hotel bedding. Zoé's devotion to her husband was matched by his feelings towards her. Whenever he travelled, he often purchased a small gift such as a ring or brooch, because he knew of her fondness for jewellery. Wilfrid and Zoé shared many common interests, and both had a passion for music and a fondness for birds and nature. They

22.1 Zoé Laurier, c. 1905 (C 15561, National Archives of Canada)

were devoted marriage partners. On their golden wedding anniversary, they renewed their marriage vows. During that occasion, Wilfrid referred to Zoé as "a help to me, an inspiration and a comfort, a good soldier alike in prosperity and adversity."[7]

In addition to caring for her husband's physical well-being, Zoé Laurier also acted as a political adviser. She was a fierce supporter of the Liberal party. Like most females who grew up in the middle of the nineteenth century, Zoé did not have any extensive formal education. The purpose of education for girls was to socialize them in correct feminine behaviour and prepare them for their roles as wives and mothers. Despite her lack of formal education, Zoé was a frequent participant in the political conversations that took place in the couple's home. Her warm and friendly personality and political acumen likely played a part in her husband's success. Wilfrid Laurier recognized and appreciated Zoé's wisdom, and liked to tell others that he believed that his political battle was half won when he married his wife.[8]

In the nineteenth century, one of the main responsibilities of middle- and upper-class women was to maintain the social status of the family. This was accomplished by entertaining in the home, where the gentility, wealth, and status of the family could be demonstrated to guests and visitors. At the Lauriers' home, the weekly routine consisted of a heavy schedule of entertaining, which included teas, luncheons, formal and informal dinners, card parties, children's parties, and "at-homes" or arranged times during the day when visiting acquaintances and friends were treated to light refreshments and conversation. Receptions of a formal or political nature were held at commercial establishments such as local clubs or in the elegance of Ottawa's Russell House Hotel.

At the Lauriers' residence in Ottawa, the atmosphere was informal and domestic – that of a family home rather than the formal official residence of the leader of a national political party and the prime minister of Canada. Both Zoé and her husband enjoyed entertaining friends and visitors and their home was filled with the friendly bustle of pets, the chatter of nieces and nephews, special visitors, and friends, and music. Young people were frequent visitors and always a welcome presence. Zoé and Wilfrid were very fond of children, and though they had no children themselves, they had an easy rapport with people younger than themselves and enjoyed their company. Zoé loved music of all types. Every Saturday evening was set aside for semi-formal musical recitals or "musicales." Two of her closest friends were the renowned concert singers Eva Gauthier and Emma Albani. Zoé and her husband were strong supporters of Canadian performing and visual artists. They were the patrons of the painter Marc-Aurèle de Foy Suzor-Coté and the sculptor Louis-Philippe Hebért, and their Ottawa home contained works by both of these artists, as well as by Vigée Le Brun. Turn-of-the-century photographs show that the rooms in their house were decorated with expensive imported furniture and art pieces done in a variety of different media. Artists, politicians, and other famous people of the time, as well as other less prominent visitors, could often be found partaking of the friendly activities at the Lauriers' house. When she was not entertaining friends, Zoé Laurier spent time taking care of her pets. She had a great fondness for animals and kept a small menagerie of birds, cats, and dogs, usually Pomeranians, in her Ottawa home. Apart from caring for her animals, her other favourite pastimes included knitting and playing bridge and poker.

Zoé Laurier, like many other women of her time and class, was involved in philanthropic activities. Canada in the late nineteenth and early twentieth century witnessed a tremendous growth in national women's organizations.[9] Disturbed by the rapid changes in Canadian society and the concomitant social problems created by urbanization, immigration, and a rampant industrial capitalism, many educated, white, upper- and middle-class women established charitable institutions, philanthropic societies, and moral and social reform organizations.[10] Using the ideology of the cult of domesticity as a justification for their activities, they argued that woman's special role as wife and mother, her nurturing qualities, and her elevated moral nature made it natural and right for her to be involved in reform work outside of the home. Many of the voluntary organizations founded by women focused on issues relating especially to, or directly affecting, women and children, such as temperance, public health and sanitation, child labour, poverty, economic and sexual exploitation, and women's suffrage.[11] In the absence of a state-run social welfare system, voluntary and philanthropic organizations provided a range of different types of assistance, including the provision of clothing, food, moral guidance, emergency housing, and charity to the respectable working poor.

Zoé Laurier was an active patron of a number of charities and organizations, including the Sons of Scotland, the Salvation Army Rescue Home, the Saint John's Ambulance Association, and the Canadian Immigration Guild. She was also a member of the Ottawa branch of the National Council of Women of Canada and served a term as its vice-president. Founded in 1893 by Lady Ishbel Aberdeen, the wife of the governor general of Canada, the National Council was a coalition of women's organizations that lobbied the government to pass legislation to improve the lot of women and children. The council was active in campaigns to raise the age of consent, strengthen obscenity and anti-procurement laws, establish of women's and children's courts, and grant women's suffrage.[12] In addition to her formal philanthropic activities, Zoé Laurier seems also to have engaged in more personal forms of charity. In the Laurier Papers, lists of monthly household accounts record the names of groups and needy individuals to whom she regularly gave money.[13] Her generosity and many small kindnesses made her well loved by Canadians from all walks of life. When Zoé Laurier died in 1921, the country felt a deep and genuine sorrow for the loss of its former first lady.

23 "A Hardier Stock of Womankind": Alice Barrett Parke in British Columbia

Jo Fraser Jones

In August 1996 the Vernon Archives received an unexpected donation: a cardboard box filled with old and fragile scribblers, the journals of Alice Barrett Parke. Port Dover, Ontario, resident Harry Bemister Barrett, her great-nephew, delivered them in the hope that they would be a useful addition to the collection of archival materials. Such a rare acquisition delighted archivist Linda Wills. She wanted the preparation of a transcription to begin at once, so I agreed to undertake the assignment. Little did I know that I would be working on the journals for the next fifteen months. Wills told me only that she had learned that they had been kept by "the wife of a former Vernon postmaster" and that the entries recorded the nine years from 1891 to 1900.

I began the project in the expectation that the process would be protracted and monotonous,[1] but the opposite proved to be true. By the end of the second volume I found myself totally involved in this marvellous tale of the life and adventures of an exceptionally dynamic and capable woman. Her words, filling page after faded page, were still so full of vitality. By the time she made her final entry, in May 1900 at the dawn of the new century, Alice Barrett Parke had written nearly half a million words. Convinced that here was a book waiting to be written, I transcribed her text, creating as I went along a database of footnotes on the pioneers, places, and events she recorded; her work has spawned nearly eighteen hundred citations.[2]

Alice Butler Barrett was the descendant of Irish war-

riors and aristocrats who had settled in Ireland as early as 1170.[3] Her father, Theobald (Toby) Butler Barrett, born at Banagher, Ireland, in 1817, was thirteen years old when he and his family set sail for Canada on the *Bolivar*, and eventually making their home in Sorel, Quebec. Toby Barrett had a total of fifteen siblings. In 1850 he married Emily Langs, of Pennsylvania Dutch heritage, and the couple moved to Port Dover, where Toby Barrett obtained a position as an officer in the Department of Customs and Excise. Toby and Emily became the parents of eight children; Alice was the fifth born and youngest daughter. She was born in Port Dover on 5 November 1861 and received an unusually thorough education for a girl at that time, including instruction in Latin and French. Her father wanted his children to expand their knowledge of English literature, so a wide variety of reading material was provided. Since he had helped to build St Paul's Anglican Church and was a lay reader there, all the Barretts accompanied him to church twice every Sunday. Alice was raised in a large, boisterous, and God-fearing family; she was continually challenged intellectually, while being showered with loving support and approbation.

In March 1891 twenty-nine-year-old Alice Barrett had no idea what to expect as she journeyed from her home in the East to the southern interior of British Columbia, but she was prepared for adventure. She was a tall, slim, young woman with penetrating brown eyes and jet-black hair, and she had long regarded herself as a spin-

23.1 Alice Barrett Parke (MS 172, Alice Barrett Parke fonds, Greater Vernon Museum and Archives)

ster without expectation of marriage. She had agreed to travel to the Okanagan Valley at the request of her adored younger brother, Harry, who had moved west many months earlier in order to run their Uncle Henry's 320-acre Mountain Meadow Ranch, situated in the Spallumcheen Valley north of Otter Lake. The two men intended that she should take over domestic operations so that they could devote their own time and energies to ranching and construction activities; she had agreed to try the arrangement for one year. The five-day trans-Canada train ride was crowded and uncomfortable, and she found herself confined with many "very common" people. When she descended from the train at Sicamous, she received a joyful welcome from the brother she had not seen for so long. Although conditions in the Spartan living quarters at the ranch – a three-room cabin – were daunting and utterly new to her, she set about bringing a touch of home to her surroundings, bringing amazing powers of will and resoluteness to the daily round of pioneer life.

Harry Barrett urged his sister to begin a journal because he wanted their "home ones" in Port Dover to learn about their life in the Okanagan. Alice undertook the task reluctantly – it was the first time she had ever kept a journal – but once she had begun, she felt a strong sense of duty both to continue her writings and to engage her audience. Before long, her self-assured and heavily slanted handwriting had filled hundreds of pages. She bought scribblers of varying quality for the task: some entries were written on paper that has withstood well the passage of more than a century; others, on pages whose edges crumble if they are handled with less than a delicate touch. Although her routine of housework and meal preparation was strenuous, she settled down every day to write the entries that would continue for more than nine years. Not long after arriving in the valley, she wrote:

There is no doubt in my mind that woman's sphere is, as a rule, in the house. Of course, genius may force her out of it, or dire necessity drive her forth to soar – or to struggle in higher flights or harder paths, but the quality of a house maker is essentially woman's, and perhaps if she did her work better in this line, men might be stronger and nobler. One can see that, at the very first, her presence is almost an impossibility in a new country. It needs a hardier stock of womankind – both physically and mentally – than is often produced by our eastern civilization to stand the loneliness and hardships of this western life, but oh! how the country needs women strong in character, gentle in words and ways, to soften while they strengthen the rougher manners of the men.[4]

She quickly realized that the "rougher manners" frequently concealed gentlemanly origins: "I have been much struck with the kindliness and real politeness of the men here to a woman. Men who talk atrociously ungrammatically, who have dirty hands, and dirtier clothes, seem to take quite a courtly air, and more real

chivalry of manner than many so-called polished gentlemen, when they address a woman, and there seems to be no limit to their kindness of heart."[5]

Barrett participated enthusiastically in the social life of her Spallumcheen neighbours. Having learned how to ride a horse, she travelled to other valley communities to take part in balls and informal socials; she went canoeing and was the first recorded white woman to ascend the Enderby Cliffs. She found swift acceptance from her neighbours, who soon realized that a teaching resource of the first order had come their way. When she was asked to accept young women like Nonah Pelly[6] and Lucy Crozier as pupils, she offered what she called "readings" of politics, literature and history to enhance their education.

The Okanagan Valley was at the threshold of an important period of expansion. Prospective settlers were arriving daily and the region was undergoing massive change. The area was witnessing the development of numerous cattle ranches, flour mills, sawmills, and brick works. Hotels and homes were being built, government offices and jails constructed, and communities incorporated under new names. Dairy and grain operations dotted the landscape as farmers claimed land and completed the work necessary to acquire deeds to their property.[7] The Shuswap and Okanagan Railway's spur line, under construction between Sicamous and Okanagan Lake,[8] would render obsolete the stagecoach service at the northern end of the valley. Sternwheelers would soon transport passengers and freight from Okanagan Landing west of Vernon to Penticton. There was an air of tumultuous exhilaration and enthusiasm; settlers believed that this was another Eden and that opportunities were limitless.

Within a month of her arrival, Alice Barrett had a suitor, Harold Randolph Parke of Port Colborne, Ontario.[9] In him she met her match intellectually and emotionally, and he proved to be a versatile man of great ability. Parke was born on 25 January 1846 into a well-to-do family, the youngest of four lawyer sons of the Honourable Thomas Parke, a London builder and architect,[10] and Harriet Rose Wilkes. Young Parke was sent to Upper Canada College but ran away to enlist in the Confederate forces during the American Civil War; after being wounded in action, he was eventually rescued by his father's agent. Parke then tried to settle down in a respectable profession and, after completing law studies, worked for a time at his brother Ephraim's law firm in London. He married the twenty-year-old Edith Barrett (no relation to Alice) in Port Colborne in 1868 and was deeply saddened by her death. In time the young widower began to yearn for a more adventurous life and enlisted in the North-West Mounted Police. He served in the force for two years, and while under the command of Major Walsh at Wood Mountain Fort he took part in an extraordinary confrontation with Sitting Bull. After leaving the NWMP, he remained in the West.

Hal Parke first caught sight of Alice Barrett while she was visiting friends in Enderby. By that time he was a forty-five-year-old freighter driving an eight-mule outfit, hauling goods and equipment between Vernon and Enderby. He was also a partner in a sawmill and brick kiln in Vernon. While he said nothing to Alice then, he obviously wanted to know more about her, for he made a private arrangement with her brother to stop over twice a week at Mountain Meadow Ranch with his freighting team. Alice was dismayed by this arrangement, but in May 1891, intrigued by this outwardly unprepossessing man, she wrote: "Mr. Parke got here quite early Monday, & came in before tea to get warm & dry. I did not much care for his appearance – a short, fair man, partly bald & evidently over forty. I was half sorry Harry had let him come, but at tea time I knew he was a gentleman. One can always judge pretty well of a man's place in the social scale by the way he eats, & in the evening I found by his conversation that he was an educated man as well.[11]

Parke soon became devoted to her, and the journals describe his wry and appealing sense of humour and his great thoughtfulness, amiability, and loving disposition. He was enterprising, dependable, and proficient at almost any task (including cooking) and pursued Barrett tenaciously. She found it painful to be asked to choose between allegiance to her family in Ontario and marriage to him.

Mr. Parke asked me quite a long time ago to marry him and I said no – a good many times – because I could not bear the thought of ever coming so far from home. But at last I have written home about it, and this mail brought an answer from Mother and Wese[12] – I am afraid it has made them unhappy, and that grieves me terribly. I don't love him well enough to marry him unless they are perfectly willing at home. I cannot imagine any woman loving one man so well that it dulls her love for those who have been near & dear to her all her life.[13]

The journals offered a delightful overview of the development of their romance, as Parke progressed from being "the freighter," to "Mr. Parke," to "Harold," and finally to "Hal." As planned, Barrett returned to Port Dover at the end of her promised year, but despite her repeated refusals, Parke finally prevailed; their wedding took place in Port Dover on 5 January 1893. She had married into an illustrious and respected family, and her love for her husband would never waver. The couple enjoyed a three-week honeymoon and then boarded a CPR train for the return trip to Vernon. During the journey they endured a severe blizzard and they arrived two days late at Sicamous. Parke returned to a job as assessment officer for the newly incorporated City of Vernon. He later became unofficial deputy to his former partner and now postmaster Robert McDougall, and afterwards he accepted several government positions: provincial constable, superintendent of roads, and finally postmaster in his own right. He also managed the BX Ranch from 1896 to 1898. Parke added entries to the journals when asked to by "The Boss," as he called his wife, whenever she was absent on visits to family and friends. Alice and her husband became devoted, caring, and faithful companions, and she rejoiced in her status as the wife of a government servant and prominent citizen.

From their cottage in the centre of the small town Alice carried out a methodical daily schedule of visits, extending her circle to include the wives of all the other leading citizens in the valley, as well as those who were less fortunate. She did not forget the lessons of her religious upbringing and she demonstrated admirable qualities of sympathy and compassion. She could often be seen by her neighbours, in times of need, delivering a pot of cream here or a jug of beef broth there. She remembered birthdays and anniversaries, prepared a posy of flowers to celebrate a newborn or a marriage, and extended condolences upon a death. She loved to see the gleam of anticipation in the eyes of her little pupils at Sunday school as they awaited the distribution of Christmas gifts from the tall tree standing in the church.

Yet, characteristic of her generation, she was at the same time unabashedly racist; I winced as I read the many references to "Japs," "darkies," "Siwashes" (Indians), and "Chinamen." Soon after she had moved to the BX Ranch (where her husband had just become manager) and had met her Chinese cook, Loo-Yee, she wrote: "I wish I could get over my prejudice against Chinamen. I know it is a prejudice, for any that have worked for me – my different washermen in Vernon and now this man – have been most polite and obliging – still I don't enjoy having them around."[14] Her behaviour towards Loo-Yee, however, soon caused her husband to remark that she had "certainly won Lou-ee's [sic] heart, for he always has some extra little dainty ready for our table, without ever being told to do so."[15] She was willing to learn and adjust,

and through her subsequent close daily dealings with Loo-Yee, Alice gradually changed her attitude:

Tonight Lou-ee [sic] came to me & said he would do my washing tomorrow. He knew I had hurt my hand, & he offered. I think it was so kind of him, because of course he is not supposed to do that kind of work for me, being very busy in his own kitchen. It just shows that Chinamen have the same feelings and natures that other men have. We have always been kind to Lou-ee, & he is willing to go out of his way to return the kindness. So many people advised me when I first came to be very strict & exacting with the Chinaman – they said "You can't give them any privileges, or they will impose on you" – but I think it is a mistake, & I often think where their knowledge of our language is so imperfect we cannot preach or teach Christianity to them except through our actions – & if these have not even a basis of "brotherly kindness" how can we claim so much as toleration for our religion, to say nothing of respect and belief.[16]

Indeed, by the end of the journals, Alice's attitude had mellowed to the point that she paid a formal call on the youthful bride of Kwong Hing Lung, the wealthiest Chinese merchant in town.

Alice's friendships were steadfast and abiding, and she nurtured them with care. She came to cherish and respect pioneers such as Clara Cameron, Addie Cochrane (wife of prominent lawyer Maurice "Pa" Cochrane), Kate Martin (married to hardware store owner William Martin), Sophie Ellison (American-born wife of the wealthy Price Ellison), Gertie Costerton (married to the unreliable Charlie Costerton), and Jessie MacIntyre (Kate Martin's aunt). All these women were active members of organizations that helped others, such as the Ladies' Aid Society, the committee to establish a cottage hospital, the Woman's Christian Temperance Union, and the local branch of the National Council of Women (NCW).[17] Alice herself had a profound aversion to committee work and preferred to carry out individual acts of compassion.

Canada's governor general at the time, the Earl of Aberdeen, owned two large ranches in the Okanagan Valley,[18] which he and his family visited regularly. Alice had never come into contact with anyone like the vigorous and aristocratic early feminist Ishbel Aberdeen. She was impressed by Ishbel's forceful character, while respecting her competence at achieving her goals:

Lady Aberdeen wants to get up some Woman's [sic] Council here ... I don't know, of course, what they want me to do, but I won't take any leading part, for a good many reasons. First, I have sense enough to know that I have no executive ability – I mean for business meetings and organizations, & managing & leading others. Then I really haven't time to give to any public working – I have my house to look after – Harry & Nonah to help sometimes – a frequent neighbourly kindness to do, many little calls on my time which I don't think it would be right to neglect ... I suppose if I were to see Lady Aberdeen I'd listen meekly to all she has to say, & never air one of my old fashioned notions – but I'd "scissors"[19] to myself just the same. I think she is a good woman, with an honest desire to improve & to help those she is among, & I wouldn't want to discourage ever so little (for of course my opinion would be "ever so little") any thing she may attempt. So I was not sorry I had rheumatism in my shoulder, which, for the present, makes a simple & conclusive excuse for taking no active part in her efforts.[20]

Despite her misgivings, Alice became a member of the Aberdeens' circle and reluctantly permitted herself to be persuaded to become the first corresponding secretary of the Vernon branch of the National Council of Women. Emily Langs Barrett was extremely upset that her daughter contemplated such a move, as evidenced by this journal entry from Alice: "I had a letter from Mother today. She is quite distressed that I have anything to do with Lady Aberdeen's Society. I confess I feel a little distressed myself over the thought of having to read a report in public – however perhaps there won't be very many people there and I am not going to usurp any of men's duties & responsibilities I am sure."[21] Mrs Barrett had brought up her daughters to know their place; in her still mid-Victorian world, women and men fulfilled totally separate roles. Ever the dutiful child, Alice hastened to assure her mother that she had not forgotten what she had been taught. Meanwhile, Lady Aberdeen continued to solidify support for her project: "About five I had a visit from Lady Aberdeen. She drove up in great style, with her coachman and footman, and paid me quite a long visit. Of course it was all about the Woman's [sic] Council, but Hal laughs at me & says I'll be very puffed up after 'hob nobbing' with a Countess. It really is a pleasure & a privilege to be associated with a woman like she is – but oh! she is large! I felt quite like a pigmy beside her. She is so tall, & stout as well."[22] And Alice continued to placate and reassure her mother:

After tea we went to Lady Aberdeen's meeting. I won't attempt to report her speech. I was convinced that I had a wrong impression of the aim & objects of the Woman's National Council. It in no way promotes "Woman's rights" in an offensive acceptation of the phrase – nor does it encourage the new woman in the very slightest. It seems to me simply a movement to promote greater unity of feeling between women of all sects and denominations by affording a platform of common interests upon which they may meet and confer together – and to awaken and strengthen patriotism by making women in all parts of the Dominion cognizant of, and interested in, the good works in which the different provinces are concerned. Hal says he thinks it is a splendid scheme. Of course we do not hope very great things from our own little local branch (for one has been established here) but 'many a mickle makes a muckle'[23] and we can but do our best.[24]

But she did not enjoy committee work of any kind, and membership in the Council of Women did not change her views: "My year as Sec will be up in October and I will then resign. I am not fitted for *society* work – I am not tactful or enthusiastic enough to be a leader and not humble enough to follow without arguing, so I'd better give it up."[25]

Alice Barrett Parke produced entertaining word portraits of many of the most respected pioneers of the day. She brought to her entries a sometimes wickedly accurate eye and ear for physical form and foreign accents, and could capture a person's appearance and character in just a few brief phrases. She came to love and admire Vernon's earliest settler, Luc Girouard, "The Old Man" as everyone in town called him: "I was introduced to old Girouard on the way out, a queer old Frenchman, with a beard he braids up and tucks under, a queer, wild-looking old fellow with just one front tooth in his upper jaw, which hangs down so far and makes him look like Red Riding Hood's wolf – but he is very kind, & has a lovely orchard."[26]

The remarkable Catherine Schubert, too, became a firm favourite. Schubert had been the only woman among the group of Overlanders who crossed the country from Winnipeg to British Columbia in 1862, and she told Alice the tale of her feat as the two enjoyed coffee one day.[27] Alice had an amazing affinity with elderly people, and they were always among those she visited most frequently.

Price and Sophie Ellison, Vernon's best-known residents, quickly became close friends.

I think I never saw a more truly generous man than Mr. Ellison, & Mrs. Ellison seems to agree with all he says & does. It does not seem kind to say it even here (though none but the home ones will ever see this) that it is a terribly shiftless household. If they were poor it would be very much on the Micawber plan[28] – as they are rich it is better, but there is no system, or order, or even tidiness. Mrs. Ellison is a tiny sweet-tempered, smiling little body, who thinks that everything which 'Pawpa' does is perfection, & who lets said 'Pawpa' arrange & *do* almost everything, cooking included, now that they have no Chinaman.[29]

The disparity was wide between the disorderly Ellison household and the sedate home of A.L. Fortune.[30] At the latter's Enderby home, propriety was of the utmost importance:

Both are comfortable homes, with evidence of easy circumstances, but theirs [the Ellisons'] is a happy-go-lucky, disorderly place where good temper & extreme generosity reigns – three little children, who do exactly what they please, tear the house upside down – while here there are no children, Mrs. Fortune is exceedingly prim, order reigns supreme, no mat is awry, no speck of dust to be seen. The sudden jump from one to the other almost takes away one's breath. I'm afraid I enjoyed the disorderly establishment most.[31]

Though deeply religious, Alice detested the effete minister at the local Anglican church, Reverend T. Williams Outerbridge, and avoided him whenever possible. She became eclectic in her church-going and frequently attended Methodist or Presbyterian services. She needed to feel inspired by the sermons she heard, but was often disappointed in the intellectual calibre of the local clergy:

I was sorry the sermon was quite lacking in interest. It seems strange to me that with such a subject men can be so dull. It is a pity that men who have not the gift of preaching are sent out as preachers – surely there must be some other work they could do better.[32]

[In Vancouver] we went to a little church nearby yesterday morning, and listened to a smooth-faced little man talk – not preach. Oh! I wish I could hear someone who would stir me up.[33]

However, the young Reverend Wilson was different and certainly more to her liking: "We all went to church in the evening to hear Mr. Wilson. He certainly does not speak with cunning words of men's wisdom, but he is so good & self forgetful that one always feels a desire to do better after hearing him – & I think his humility is a little infectious, though I am conscious that humility is a Christian Grace of which I am sadly lacking."[34]

Throughout their years in Vernon, the Parkes shared a cozy and welcoming home, which was the centre of their lives, though Alice was always happier than her husband to go out calling on friends. She rationalized this need for human interaction when she wrote one day:

I know Hal does not care for going out, & sometimes I feel very selfish in wanting to go – then again I feel that it is really better for both of us to get shaken out of our jog-trot now & then. It is a very happy contented jog-trot I will allow, but the social instinct should be encouraged out here. I am sure we are too apt to look for all our happiness just inside our own home – and it isn't fair to ourselves or our neighbours to narrow joy down to that one spot. No doubt a life cannot be a happy one unless home is the fountain of its peace & refreshment, but we don't want to keep all the waters of a fountain shut up in their source – it would be of little use then, and so I think a happy home ought to strengthen and beautify our character that its influence may be more wide spread.[35]

After 1898 it is apparent from the ever-longer intervals between entries that the journals were becoming more and more an onerous task rather than a pleasure. By May 1899 Alice was a working woman, having taken a job outside the home, albeit an unpaid one. Upon her husband's appointment as postmaster, she worked daily behind the office wicket (and time available for her writing grew ever more scarce). It is quite apparent that her welcoming and efficient manner was appreciated by the post office's customers, though she herself downplayed her role as Hal's deputy postmaster.

I do feel awfully sorry for some of the men who come day after day & get nothing - it reminds me of that mournful song Hubert[36] used to sing about the letter that never came. Hal says he's going to put a stop to all these "wicket flirtations" of mine. He says everyone is far too attentive, & they'll be making me conceited but indeed I think I'm about as conceited now as I'll get, & I'm sure acts of kindness are more apt to make us humble than vain. People seem more grateful for a little kindness than the occasion demands.[37]

Hal says there is one part of the Post Office work I excel him in and that is in remembering the children – such a number of little ones come in, & they must be careful as we never hear any complaints about their losing mail.[38]

The journals ended abruptly – in the middle of a sentence – on 16 May 1900; the end coincided almost exactly with the conception of the Parkes' only child, Emily Louisa. The baby was born on 14 February 1901, but tragically she died nine months later, on 13 November.[39] Little Emily Parke's funeral procession was the longest ever seen for a child in Vernon up to that time. She was interred in the old cemetery near Old Kamloops Road, but the remains were moved to the present location on Pleasant Valley Road when it opened in 1904. Her grave can be seen in the pioneer section of the cemetery, a tiny white marble cross at its head.

Alice did not take up her pen again while she remained in the Okanagan. During their final years in Vernon, the Parkes' influence remained widespread and they were held in the highest esteem. A large crowd was present at the station in the fall of 1905 when the Parkes returned to Port Dover after Hal's retirement from the post office. Jack McKelvie, their friend and editor of the *Vernon News*, wrote:

A pleasant surprise awaited them at the station. Just before the train pulled out, G.A. Henderson, W.R. Megaw, S.C. Smith and other gentlemen called the popular postmaster and his wife apart from the group of friends who had assembled to bid them farewell, and, on behalf of the people of Vernon, presented Mr. Parke with a handsome gold chain and diamond ring, and Mrs. Parke with a gold watch and chain. The accompanying address expressed appreciation of the unfailing courtesy, untiring attention and the manner generally in which Mr. Parke had conducted the business of the Vernon post office during the past six and a half years, and also of the way in which Mrs. Parke had seconded his efforts, and of her kindly manner which always made business with the office a positive pleasure.[40]

The following spring Alice and Hal Parke returned to Vernon to sell their property and settle their affairs; they then left the Okanagan Valley permanently. The couple spent a few years in Ontario, but by 1910 Hal had grown restless, and they moved west again – this time to Fort Saskatchewan, Alberta, where they operated a small market garden. Hal's health began to decline, and by the fall of 1914 his wife was anxious to get him back to Ontario. With Wese's help she was able to do so. The sixty-eight-year-old Hal died a few short weeks after their return to Port Dover, on 30 November 1914, from a combination of thrombosis and myocarditis. His widow returned to Alberta the following spring to sell their house and effects, and then headed back to the old family home in Ontario. She lived there contentedly with Wese and survived Hal by thirty-eight years. She died on 8 December 1952, aged ninety-one, after suffering a massive stroke.

The donor of the journals wrote from Ontario: "I keep wondering what Aunty Alice would think of the stir she has created. I expect she would be amazed and a bit shocked, but secretly pleased."[41] His insightful comment is helpful in understanding this complex woman, who so often found herself in situations where her conservative upbringing was at odds with her innermost feelings. By turns opinionated, outspoken, and independent-minded, she was required by society to be restrained, deferential, and respectful even towards those men whom she recognized as her intellectual inferiors. Throughout the journals, we are witness to the ongoing tension between her perceived need to demonstrate all the traditional "womanly" virtues of the nineteenth century and her more personal need to summon the abundance of her other talents in order to cope with the rawness and crudity of pioneer life in the West.

The women of that time left behind very few documents other than letters, but this woman bequeathed to us a marvellous history documenting her region and period – the southern interior of British Columbia at the end of the nineteenth century. In particular, Alice's work brings into sharp focus the lives and struggles of the women of that era, clarifying for us the ideals of nineteenth-century womanhood that were both reinforced and challenged in the harsh conditions on the frontier. Their pioneer spirit sustained them as they worked long, physically punishing hours to create livable homes, raise families, collaborate with their neighbours, and make a contribution to community affairs. It is the very minutiae of the journals that endow them with such exceptional power. Alice did not shy away from chronicling the social problems and disasters of her time, writing with great feeling about ranching life, birth, marriage, death, alcoholism, domestic violence, disease, political ineptitude, poverty, inequality, floods, droughts, and earthquakes.

In a short piece like this, it is not possible to render a comprehensive portrait of Alice Barrett Parke; her journals are too extensive and wide-ranging. During her life, the scribblers remained tucked away in a small rawhide box in the attic; she herself never made any attempt to publish them – modesty and reticence forbade. It gives me undeniable satisfaction that I have been able to rescue her work from the twilight in which it has lain hidden for more than a hundred years, allowing this exceptional and engaging woman to become known.

24 Life on the Frontier: Remembering the Coal Mining Camp at Cadomin, 1929–1934

Edith Wheeler

In October of 1929, my husband was told to report for duty as manager of the Bank of Nova Scotia branch in a coal mining camp in the Alberta Rockies. It was a new assignment for Ted and one that he found very exciting. Although he had served in several branches, it had always been in a clerical position. One learned by trial and error the job of being manager, since there was no special training in those days. So, it was with great expectation, timidity, and excitement that we set out on our three-day and two-night train journey, feeling very inadequate for what lay ahead. We were newly married and this move was a great challenge, an adventure that was taking me from my sheltered life and my mother in Winnipeg.

The journey was tedious and the last lap of seventy miles into the mountains took a whole day. The countryside was desolate with no sign of human life. At noon, the crew left the train for lunch at a wayside camp. We were the only passengers and all we had to eat was the sandwich we had bought the previous night, which we had been advised to do. Finally, about 5:30 p.m., we reached Cadomin, our destination. Five thousand feet above sea level and situated in a valley with mountains rising all around, the town was quite beautiful – if we kept our eyes above the blackened buildings. Mount Cheviot, always snow covered, rose in the west and was a never-to-be-forgotten sight as the sun sank behind it. Such a contrast with flat Manitoba! Ted and I agreed we would like this place, but at this point we had seen nothing.

Cadomin had no roads and no cars. Access was by train twice a week. We were met at the station by the local delivery man in a horse-drawn democrat which had one seat up front. It was important that Ted sit with him and make conversation, asking about the people, the weather, and so on. Dick, our driver, also asked questions, but he did not wait for the answers! He assured us that he would not want to live anywhere else but in Cadomin and that we should consider ourselves fortunate to have been sent here. I had climbed up onto the floor in the back of the wagon and was properly shaken up (not only physically) as we made our way over ruts and stones to the bank, a distance of about half a mile.

What a let-down that was! The building was a low, square, five-room structure, covered with green shingles, with THE BANK OF NOVA SCOTIA displayed in large letters across one side. The other side comprised the living quarters, consisting of a large kitchen, running across the back of the building, and three small rooms on the other side. We did not see our living accommodations on our first visit.

We were told that the former manager was off in the hills shooting wild deer. His wife and two small children still occupied the rooms that were to be our home, but we did not meet her. We later heard that her husband had been fired for not attending to business. The humiliation must have been too cruel for her. My mind raced forward: "Would we go through the same embarrassment two or three years down the line if things did not work out?" A substitute manager had been sent from Edmonton to hold the fort until Ted arrived. He knew little about Cadomin and was most anxious to get back to his own branch.

For the next week and until our furniture arrived, we had a room at the "Black Beetle." Before seeing the place the name frightened me, but it proved not too bad, being warm and clean. This long, black, tar-papered structure housed the single men and served three meals a day. Two long tables were laid out with huge platters and bowls of food – all one could eat for fifty cents and it was good. I felt that we would put on pounds! The cook was a hard-working woman whose daughter of nineteen helped her in the kitchen.

The hub of activity was the town square with the general store, the bank, the barbershop, and the meeting hall. The post office, the only place that handled pennies (stamps cost three cents), was a short distance from the Black Beetle. The houses were built in rows on the flats to the rear of the square. All were one storey because of the severe winds. Timber logs were used, with mortar between, which gave the place a look of uniformity. Each had its own outhouse and, to my horror, the bank's little "retreat" opened onto the main square. This meant that I could be seen whenever I used the facility … and the Eaton's Catalogue! Hallowe'en came soon after our arrival and the local teenagers overturned the toilets all along the main row. The young fellows returned the next morning and, under instruction, rectified their mischief.

The mine manager, the accountant, and the doctor lived in the staff quarters near the mine entrance, a half mile from the town. Their quarters, which were equipped with inside plumbing, made me green with envy. The six-bed hospital, owned and operated by the mine, was also in this area and had a nurse on duty. It was there primarily in case of a mine accident, even though there were only two such accidents in our four years in Cadomin, and I could not go to the hospital when my first child was

born. There was also a superstition that women should not be allowed to enter the mine, so when Ted was invited I stayed home!

It did not take long to realize that life would not only be a challenge, but also a hardship. After a week's delay, our quarters were vacated, our furniture arrived, and we could move in. The place was a shambles! Talk about roughing it! Ted and I looked at each other and he said, "What did we expect for fifteen dollars per month, plus fuel?" Needless to say, we did not expect what we were seeing. The kitchen was the size of the bank, with congoleum on the floor, but a large piece was torn from its centre. The walls had been painted a very dark green, but the painter had run out of paint on one wall. The trap door in the floor led down to the freezer room, which was just a dirt dugout. One look convinced me I would never use it, for I could see the mice had taken over!

There were no cupboards in the kitchen, just three open shelves with a table below, holding two bins for keeping flour. There was a cookstove with a reservoir on the end to heat water. The oven door was broken and propped open with a piece of wood. Thoughts rushed thoughts my mind: "Was I going to stay here or was it grounds for a marriage break-up?"

But Ted was excited about his new posting. It would lead to better things if he was successful, and so, successful he must be! But now I must support Ted – and we could have the stove repaired and the kitchen painted. Fortunately, I enjoyed cooking and would soon learn how to use wood and coal. Needless to say, the making of meals was done the hard way. There was no place to keep leftovers, so shopping and cooking were daily routines.

One side of the kitchen had a door that led into the bank, right at the teller's cage, an old-fashioned type, caged all around with wire. The only heat, apart from the cookstove, came from two Quebec heaters. One was in the bank office and the other was in our living room and had to heat all three rooms. The winters were long and cold, which meant getting up at least once during the night to stoke both heaters. Many times one or both would be out. Ted and I had to constantly encourage each other. Our duties got us down at times – his was the fire and mine was the cooking.

There was a shed, four by six, just outside the kitchen door, which housed the coal and wood and was the entrance to our home. The bank's entrance was at the front of the building. Wood was delivered in huge blocks from the sawmill, which was about five miles away. Ted had to chop the blocks before we could use them. The coal was also delivered and it was mostly slag, which could not be sold to the railway. There was, however, a wonderful seam of hard coal, which was very much in demand. Water had to be carried in buckets from across the roadway. I quickly learned how to conserve it, since whatever came in had to be carried out.

After unpacking and settling in as best we could, I realized that we did not have even the essentials. We decided that I should take the train to Edmonton to buy the things we needed: a new floor covering, curtains, a wash tub – which would also serve as our bathtub – and numerous other things. The list was long. I shopped quickly and was able to return on the next train, in three days! My purchases, however, did not arrive for another week, at which time there was a terrific wind storm. Cadomin was noted for such storms, and the boxcar carrying our things was blown onto its side off the track. Our floor covering was damaged, but I learned to live with such things. Needless to say, it was an effort for me to make the place liveable and like a home, but I did. I soon learned that a much easier way to shop was via the Eaton's Catalogue.

During the frequent wind storms, we could see our footprints in the resulting coal dust on the floor. My comb on the dresser would leave its teeth marks in the soot. Sealing all the windows did not keep the dust out. Dishes had to be washed before each meal, and when the storm abated, a real house-cleaning had to be done – until the next time. It was a never-ending chore, as the storms were fortnightly. The winds were so strong that men, crossing the little bridge from the mine, had to do so on their hands and knees. During one such storm, a house on our row caught fire, but neighbours quickly recovered the furniture, much of which had blown around the town site. All the men turned out and eventually got the blaze under control.

There were not great privacy standards at first. Our kitchen, for example, was often used as a "waiting room" if the manager was busy with a customer, and I would usually offer tea. It bothered me, however, that folks would walk in without knocking, so we purchased a lock and key, much to the annoyance of one customer, who said, "The kitchen has always been open!" From then on, anyone wishing to wait his or her turn had to knock first!

Electricity was connected for our building, but since we were neither part of the mine nor its employees, we were rationed as to how much we could use. We were not allowed a washing machine, so after months of scrubbing on a washboard we decided to send our heavy wash by train to a laundry in Edmonton. It would be returned in ten days.

Life was not all humdrum. Although we very much missed a tennis court and a skating rink, we soon found ourselves in a community of party people. Something was taking place most evenings in either the homes or the hall. Plays were put on the second and fourth Saturdays of each month, beginning at 11 p.m., to allow the late shift of miners to attend. The mine manager directed a six-piece orchestra and the music was terrific. Most of the camp turned out for the dances and everyone had a wonderful time.

On the Saturdays, which were pay-days, the bank remained open until 6 p.m., something unheard of elsewhere where banking hours were from 10 a.m. to 3 p.m., and closed on Saturday. These hours enabled miners to cash their cheques and send money orders to Edmonton for liquor. This was a disastrous situation for many of the miners, their wives, and their families.

The three churches had been built of rough lumber and had only rough benches to sit on. The United Church was the best attended, chiefly because it had a resident minister. The Anglicans had a struggle with only five families, including us. The Anglican minister, Mr Matthews, a man of seventy, came from Edmonton every six weeks to minister to his congregation. After the Sunday service, he would set out on foot on the railway tracks to Mountain Park, a distance of nine miles west, returning by train on Tuesdays and travelling on to Luscar, which was six miles north. Mr Matthews carried a sack of clothing on his back for the needy. His visits were always a highlight. His Saturday evenings were spent in our home, where we all enjoyed a game of bridge. It was a treat, too, for us to hear news from the outside world, where the Great Depression was in full swing. Living as we were, where there was steady employment with good wages, we had no conception of the struggle that was taking place elsewhere.

On the Sundays when there was no Anglican service, we attended the United Church, where there were two services, morning and evening. After the evening service, a black-and-white silent movie was shown in the dance hall. Ted and I were amused to see the people rush from the church, down the hill and into the hall. The young minister lived in one room attached to the rear of the church. We became good friends with Merrill Ferguson and were pleased to see him at our door. One morning, looking out the window, we saw Merrill crawling down the path that led to the bank. He had a ruptured appendix and had been in severe pain all night, unable to contact anyone because he had no phone. Phones were very rare in Cadomin and no one I knew had one in their home.

The doctor, who had lost a local child to appendicitis two months earlier, now performed the operation single-handedly and brought the patient through beautifully. It was a case of doing the surgery or letting the patient die. With no roads and only two trains a week, he had little choice. The doctor carried a heavy load, with over a thousand people in three camps to care for, and there was always the fear of a mine disaster. He was in his late fifties, made house calls, and had no transportation.

Gifts of wild meat were often left at our door. Mountain sheep was our favourite – the most delicious meat I had ever tasted, although deer steaks were almost as good. Moose, which was more plentiful, was lean and tough and required special cooking. Our diet was restricted because there were no fresh vegetables or fruit, except apples and potatoes in the fall. We never had any lettuce or tomatoes, but we did not go hungry.

Everything came in cans, even the milk! A small dairy herd of eight cows supplied milk to the few families with children. One day government inspectors arrived and condemned the whole herd because of tuberculosis. All the cows had to be destroyed. You can imagine the uproar, but the children were healthy and survived. In our own case, I had boiled the milk for our baby, so had no fears in that regard. Speaking of children, the school was built at Cadomin on the flats and consisted of eleven grades with three teachers. Many of the older students, however, were sent to school in Edmonton.

A new teller, a good-looking fellow of twenty-two, arrived on the Friday train. The community dance, which always took place on Saturday evenings, seemed to be a fitting place for Ted to introduce him to the young schoolteacher, a lovely girl of twenty-one. She was delighted, and we thought it was the beginning of a nice relationship. At the next dance, two weeks later, our teller decided to take another girl. The teacher was so upset that by midnight, when he had not called, she drank Lysol. How much no one knew, but surely she just wanted to frighten him. In spite of all the doctor could do, she died. The whole community was devastated.

Undeserved blame was laid heavily on the teller, and he had to be quickly transferred elsewhere.

During our third year, Ted wrote to the head office asking that some improvements be made in our living conditions. After all, he had brought the branch "out of the red." To our great delight and without delay, head office instructed Ted to have a room added to our quarters, to bring in water (which would mean no more carrying buckets in and out), to put a bathroom with a septic toilet in the corner of the kitchen, to purchase a modern heater for the living room (which would burn for more that eight hours), and to arrange with the mine manager for us to have an electric washing machine. The bathtub was a particular delight, even though the water was cold and had to be heated by kettles of boiling water. Some of our friends also enjoyed an occasional bath!

Our fourth year was our last at Cadomin. Living there had become much easier, but shortly before the Christmas of 1934, Ted received a transfer to manage a branch in Calgary. After four years and three months we could now look forward to city living. Ted would have a larger office, more staff, and, of course, more responsibility, but we were delighted. For me, the thought of having a proper house, a garden and lawn, running hot and cold water, and a flush toilet was overwhelming.

The camp folk said their "goodbyes" in many wonderful ways. We knew we would miss them. Many of them also had the dream of leaving Cadomin one day. That one dream came true when, a few years later, the seam of hard coal ran out and Cadomin became a ghost town. But, as you can see, Cadomin lives on in my memory. Difficult as those years were, I look back on them as a time of challenge and growth from girlhood to womanhood. I realize now that I was given a valuable opportunity to experience a very full range of human life and behaviour.

25 Women and Domestic Technology: Household Drudgery, "Democratized Consumption," and Patriarchy

Dianne Dodd

Commencing in the colonial period and continuing to the present, the complex process of industrialization dramatically transformed domestic technology from simple pots and pans to a myriad of electrical and gas-powered devices designed to cook, clean, sew … everything but raise the children and care for the elderly.[1] Just as the tools of domestic work have been industrialized, so too has the social organization of domestic labour. Centred on the family, the new system dictates who does domestic labour, when, where, and under what conditions.

The everyday sameness of domestic labour, its low status as unpaid "unproductive" labour performed by women in the home, as well as the difficulty in finding sources to document it, have led to a scholarly neglect of this subject. With the emergence in the 1970s of social history and women's history, however, the causes and consequences of changes in domestic technology, together with the related question of the impact of industrialization on the home, are being examined more thoroughly. Has changing domestic technology led to alterations in the social organization of domestic labour and related reproductive work in the home? Or, conversely, did social and economic changes create the need for, and hence the development of, domestic technology? The impact of domestic technology is also unclear. Did it save middle-class housewives' labour as the advertisers claimed, or did it reinforce the sexual division of labour that tied women securely to the domestic role – or perhaps both? What did women expect from domestic technology? And how much input did they have into its development, marketing, and utilization? This essay, which examines domestic technology from the colonial period to the introduction of modern domestic electrical technology in predominantly urban, middle-class homes in Ontario in the 1920s and 1930s, will explore these questions.

The family economy dominated social organization in the earliest homes in Canada and was characterized by a relatively high degree of household autonomy. Here women played an important productive role, making everything for their family's consumption, from clothing to food products to soap and candles. Although family members were mutually dependent, labour was divided along age and gender lines. Women were responsible for housekeeping tasks such as cooking, sewing, infant and child care, and ironing, as well as for care of the sick, candle-making, dairy production, maintenance of the kitchen garden, and the making of preserves. Although the women sometimes helped the men with sowing and reaping crops in busy seasons and in time of exceptional need, men rarely helped women in their domestic sphere of work.

In this preindustrialized family economy, householders used fairly simply domestic tools – axes for chopping wood, pots and kettles for cooking, and looms for weaving. Such tools could be made, used, repaired, and maintained fairly autonomously and were not dependent on networks of energy or transportation sources outside of the control of the average householder.[2] The price of this autonomy, for most, was a low standard of living. With the exception of the very wealthy, who employed numerous servants to maintain a grand lifestyle, standards of cleanliness were low, the only heat available emanated from one central fireplace, and cooking consisted mainly of one-dish meals, supplemented by coarse breads. All of that changed in the mid-nineteenth century when industrialization began to influence the household economy. Yet industrialization had an uneven, if eventually major, impact on Canadian homes, with wealthy urban householders in central Canada and the Maritime provinces the first to take advantage of new products and services, while the poor, rural residents and western and northern settlers followed much later.

Industrialization led to the mechanization of numerous household processes. The production of clothing moved out of the home in stages. By the mid-nineteenth century, most women were freed from the chores of spinning and weaving, and made clothes from manufactured textiles. While ready-made clothing became available in the early nineteenth century, first with men's clothing, then later with women's and children's, it was not until the development of standard sizes following the American Civil War that the textile industry prospered. Gradually the task of sewing the family's clothes was transferred from home to industry, until by the 1920s home sewing had become a hobby.[3]

The production of food underwent a similar transformation. Flour began to be milled outside the home in the earliest colonial towns, and buying bread was common among the industrial working class, although the middle class made their own better-quality breads. The dairy industry emerged in the later nineteenth century, first in central Canada near large urban markets, gradually in less populous areas. As dairying moved from individual farms to factories, women's participation in the production of cheese and butter declined and ready-made dairy products were available for purchase.[4] Finally, home preserving began to decline, first in the cities and only much later on farms. By the turn of the century, food-packaging and -processing industries offered consumers goods of comparable quality and cost under nationally advertised brand names. Although the cost of these goods and services remained prohibitive for many householders throughout much of the nineteenth century, by the early twentieth century advertisers were appealing to lower-income groups. They promised lower prices and greater accessibility to the products of consumer capitalism through the benefits of mass production and mass consumption.

Social services such as health care and education also moved from the domestic to the public sphere. The first nurses' training school was opened in the General and Marine Hospital in St Catharines, Ontario, in 1874. Many more followed in the 1880s and 1890s as hospitals transformed themselves from charitable, custodial institutions to centres of scientific or curative medicine. Thus, the seriously ill were less frequently cared for at home by women. Throughout the late nineteenth century, free schooling and compulsory attendance laws in most Canadian provinces – despite the hardships these imposed on the labouring poor and farmers – confirmed the public school rather than the home as the principal education site.[5]

The introduction of technological systems for water, sewage, gas, and electricity revolutionized mid-nineteenth-century households, although the impact initially favoured wealthy urban residents. Urban middle-class households situated in the earliest-settled regions of Upper Canada, Lower Canada, and the Maritime provinces enjoyed access to these systems as much as a century ahead of the urban working class, who, even then, could only partially take advantage of them owing to the prohibitive cost of both the services and the installation of related appliances and indoor plumbing. Although many of the first tasks to be eliminated, such as carrying water and chopping wood for fuel, were men's and boys' chores, the new technologies did lighten the housewife's work as well. By the end of the century, most urban households had access to a public water system, even if it meant only a tap outside the door. Sewage systems tended to lag behind waterworks by several decades, but by the second decade of the twentieth century, most city dwellers, both rich and poor, had water, sewage, and indoor plumbing, eliminating the need to maintain the private privies that had been prevalent in the slum areas in the early twentieth century and had been a major public health concern. Pioneer settlers in the West and North as well as rural inhabitants across Canada generally had to wait, some of them until after the Second World War, for full access to those technologies.

Innovations in heating and cooking began with the introduction of the wood stove, widely available by the mid-nineteenth century to replace the inefficient open fireplace.[6] Gas was first introduced for commercial and streetlighting purposes as early as the 1830s, and with the introduction of natural gas in the 1890s, domestic uses were possible, initially for lighting but eventually also for cooking and hot water heating. By the late nineteenth and early twentieth centuries, gas stoves had begun to replace the more burdensome and less clean wood or coal stoves, which had been the technological marvel only a few decades earlier.

Although local electric companies preceded it, in 1905 the Hydro Electric Power Commission of Ontario was formed to harness the wonders of Niagara Falls for all Ontarians. Electricity was soon available as an energy source for home appliances. The electric iron had been patented in 1882; electric washing machines were introduced in 1916 to replace hand-operated machines; powered vacuum cleaners, patented in 1907, soon replaced brooms and carpet beaters. By the 1920s, stoves, refrigerators and water heaters in urban home had begun to be powered by electricity.[7]

The introduction of new domestic technologies, as well as of commercially prepared products, steadily reduced the physical workload of many middle-class women managing households from the mid-nineteenth century onward. However, the separation of work from the home also reduced the amount of domestic help these women could draw on in their own family. The expansion of waged labour and the introduction of compulsory school attendance laws took some single relatives and children out of the household. Further, as factories, shops, and offices hired women workers in greater numbers, the availability of domestic servants declined sharply. Many middle-class women were left to search for solutions to the "servant problem," at times using technology as a replacement.

Domestic technology failed to provide increased leisure for women as its advertisers continually promised. This had little to do with the technology itself and much to do with the social organization of domestic work. Throughout the nineteenth century, as the home declined as a productive unit, it took on an increasingly important emotional role. A "cult of domesticity" resulted, whose proponents cajoled nineteenth-century women into a confining domesticity intended to safeguard the health and morality of husband and children then being increasingly exposed to the harsh realities of a competitive market economy.

Organizationally, women responded to all of these changes. Perceiving that the traditional family was threatened by the loss of many of its former productive functions, women hoped to modernize the home and raise the status of domestic work. A new breed of domestic reformers emerged to keep women abreast of the dramatic changes occurring not only in domestic technology, but also in the home. Household or domestic science classes were first directed at housewives and servants through institutions such as the Young Women's Christian Association, the Woman's Christian Temperance Union, and Women's Institutes.[8] Domestic science courses were also introduced into the public school curriculum, and by 1903 institutions to train domestic science teachers had been established, such as the Macdonald Institute in Guelph, Ontario, and Macdonald College in Ste Anne de Bellevue, Quebec.[9]

At the same time as the domestic reform movement began to respond to the effects of industrialization on the home, advertisers, the spokespersons of an evolving consumer capitalism, were promoting "democratized consumption." Beginning as early as the 1890s and gaining considerable momentum by the interwar period, national advertisers promised that mass production would transform luxuries into everyday products. To this end, emotional appeals were directed at women and lower-income groups. Creating Mrs Consumer, advertisers assigned women the task of purchasing all of the new store-bought, manufactured goods and appliances. If mass production was designed to lower prices, promote economic growth, and improve access to consumer products, women must do their part by purchasing nationally advertised goods. This strategy promoted not only economic growth, but social and labour stability as well. It also effectively channelled worker discontent into consumption.[10]

Perhaps it was inevitable that, given the combined forces of capitalism, the state, and patriarchy, domestic reform would merge with the democratization of consumption to produce an essentially conservative "social construction" of domestic technology. Although a few radical schemes were envisioned by domestic reformers to fully socialize housework, these failed.[11] It is ironic that, at a time when most other forms of work were being centralized and rationalized, domestic tasks such as child care, laundry, and cooking became increasingly

privatized and centred on the fully equipped family home as an ideal. The Canadian government's 1930s Home Improvement Plan, for example, was intended to promote economic activity through encouraging home improvement and, with that, of course, increased purchases of domestic technology. The plan used as its model the male-headed household, with a stay-at-home wife and two to three children occupying a single family dwelling.[12] Men benefited not only as workers and consumers in a revitalized economy, but also as individuals, by retaining patriarchal authority in their homes, newly transformed with new comforts. The following examination of the advertising and advice literature pertaining to domestic electrical technology in Canada in the interwar years will focus on middle-class women's participation in the face of these capitalist, state, and patriarchal forces. Did middle-class women acquiesce and adopt a domestic technology that did not serve their needs? Or did women have more input than has formerly been acknowledged?

The introduction of domestic electrical technology to urban Ontario households in the interwar years was guided by the aggressive marketing of some of the municipal electric utilities that constituted part of the Hydro Electric Power Commission (HEPC), later known as Ontario Hydro. The HEPC was one of the first major publicly owned electric utilities in North America and a pioneer in the early twentieth-century consumer capitalist strategy of the democratization of consumption. Like its manufacturing counterparts, which used mass production techniques to create lower-priced consumer goods, the HEPC kept domestic rates low in hopes of encouraging increased electricity consumption. The gamble paid off spectacularly. Throughout the first two decades of the twentieth century, domestic electricity consumption increased and rates fell, justifying the commission's advertising slogan, "The more you use, the cheaper it gets." *The Hydro Lamp*, a promotional flyer, was sent to Ontario householders along with their electricity bill in the early 1920s. Directed at a lower-income group than HEPC's national advertising would have targeted, it was particularly sensitive to women's perspective. *The Hydro Lamp* stressed the practical, labour-saving benefits of domestic technology and did not assume that users employed servants.

Both *The Hydro Lamp* and national advertising stressed domestic technology as a central feature of democratized consumption. Illustration 25.1 shows the advertisers' view of electricity, which purportedly brought comforts "that kings would have envied" into the homes of workers: "All the vaunted luxury of ancient kings fades into insignificance beside the comforts made possible in every modern home by the simple turn of an electric switch." *The Hydro Lamp* associated electricity with modernity. Illustration 25.2 shows the cover of two issues of the flyer. Depicted on the left is the pre-modern coal cookstove. The woman's face has a haggard and prematurely aged expression as she attempts to cook amid oppressive heat. As well, the ever-present child is threatening to track coal dust all over the house, or worse still, may suffer serious burns. All this serves to illustrate the dirt, inconvenience, and danger of the old-fashioned technology. By contrast, on the right we see the modern electric range, presided over by a young, modern housewife who appears relaxed and happy. The child-under-foot is replaced by an appreciative young man awaiting a splendid meal, which the Ontario housewife is able to prepare thanks to the benefits of clean, cool, safe, and convenient electric cooking.

These advertising images were largely male-centred, the home being portrayed as a retreat from the harsh realities of the modern world. Each ideal family was headed by a male worker who owned his own private family dwelling. His wife stayed at home to preside over this realm, raising his children, cooking, shopping, and

25.1 "Comfort that Kings Would Have Envied"
(*Maclean's*, 1 November 1930)

A Hot Day in the Kitchen

He knows a treat's awaiting him
Every single day
For Mother's meals are always good
Cooked the Hydro way.

ELECTRIC COOKING NUMBER

25.2 *The Hydro Lamp* August 1924 and April 1925

generally making his life comfortable. However, women were invited to share in these domestic benefits. In the idealized family shown in Illustration 25.3, the wife has the leisure to go out with her son while the electric range presumably cooks the dinner unattended. She is also shown seated at the breakfast table with husband and child, presiding effortlessly over a meal prepared with the aid of tabletop appliances such as a coffeemaker, toaster, and grill. Tellingly, it is only father who is enjoying symbolic access to the outside world through the medium of electric radio, while mother works alone in attending to the laundry task.

Despite the emphasis on leisure, which gave the false impression that the housewife had little to do, advertisers seemed to ask more and more of her. Bolstered by the proliferation of child-care advice literature in the interwar period, which was legitimized by the new Department of Health's publication of the *Canadian Mothers' Book*,[13] advertisers set increasingly strict standards of cleanliness, diet, and health. Middle-class housewives were urged to vacuum with their new electric vacuum cleaners once a week to prevent the spread of infectious diseases. Exploiting fears surrounding the deadly scourge of "infant diarrhea," often caused by contaminated milk, advertisers advised middle-class housewives to use modern refrigeration techniques. Cleanliness and higher domestic standards were also promoted for their aesthetic appeal. The availability of ready-made clothing increased the items in an individual's wardrobe, and an electric washing machine put pressure on the housewife to do laundry more frequently. The availability of numerous commercial food products and home refrigeration lead to demands by those who could afford it for a more varied diet, which the woman would prepare.

The advertising of domestic electrical appliances reflects the reality that women were clearly not "in control." Institutional advertisements by Canadian General Electric, Northern Electric, and even the HEPC painted

25.3 "Better Living … and Money Ahead" (*Maclean's*, 15 May 1938)

Once--Woman's Work Was Never Done

FORTY years ago the housewife's life was an endless round of drudgeries . . . task heaped on task. But forty years have seen great changes . . . the emancipation of millions of slaves to brush and broom, scrubbing board and scorching cook-stove.

The heavy burdens of household toil have been removed from women's weary backs on to the broad shoulders of electricity.

The wood stove is gone . . . and with it the sad-iron. The wash-tub and scrubbing-board are rarely seen. Brush and broom have been relegated to basement and back-porch. Oil-lamps, with their smoke-soiled chimneys, are now

relics of a dimly remembered past.

Today, electrical servants perform the household tasks. At the cost of a few cents they cook the meals, do the washing and the ironing, clean the rugs and draperies.

The hours that once were spent in menial labor, the woman of today devotes to recreation, to social activity, to culture and to the moulding of her children's character.

Since its inception the Canadian General Electric Company has been constantly devising new methods of lightening household work through the development of electrical apparatus and appliances for the home.

Canadian General Electric Company supplies Canadian homes with Hotpoint Ranges, Water Heaters, Toasters, Irons, Percolators, Heaters, in fact electrical devices of all types to lighten housework and brighten the home.

CANADIAN
GENERAL ELECTRIC Co. Limited
HEAD OFFICE: TORONTO—Sales Offices in all Principal Cities

25.4 "Once – Woman's Work Was Never Done"
(*Maclean's*, 1 May 1928)

technology as a knight in shining armour and women the lucky but largely passive recipients. Advertising copy projected an image of electricity as a powerful, effective and clearly male-engineered technology. Illustration 25.4 shows a Canadian General Electric ad that used gendered language to convey the message that domestic technology had liberated women from work. While once woman's work was never done, now "the heavy burdens of household toil have been removed from women's weary backs on to the broad shoulders of electricity." The advertising message's generalized association of technology with masculinity gave men a vicarious enjoyment of a technology from which women were excluded.

Despite their relative exclusion from engineering and industry, which at this time were almost exclusively male preserves, female domestic science experts had some input, albeit largely unrecognized. Some women played a limited role advising industry as well as women in the home. They found their niche in the advertising and marketing of domestic technology and in advising other women on changes occurring to household work. Women household advisers, many of them graduates of the domestic science courses established a few decades earlier, worked as journalists for women's magazines, junior advertising copy writers, demonstrators and retailers of appliances, and managers of the household departments of large municipal utilities. Household advisers did not question the sexual division of labour, which assigned technological creativity to men and homemaking to women, but they did question the denigration of domestic work and added a gendered perspective to the otherwise masculine advertising message. They believed that women had a right to domestic technology and that they welcomed the improved household standards that meant cleaner homes, healthier children, and more varied diets for everyone. The domestic technology that these advisers enthusiastically promoted in the interwar years benefited many Canadian urban women, particularly significant segments of the working class, and a few rural households. These latter women, who had rarely enjoyed the benefits of domestic servants, experienced a real rise in their standard of living and conditions of domestic work.

Although most rural and many working-class Ontarians had to wait until after the Second World War to enjoy the benefits of this new technology, it was being disseminated to an increasingly broad socio-economic group in the 1920s and 1930s. HEPC statistics on the degree of market saturation of various appliances throughout the interwar period, in both urban and rural markets, were based on appliance ownership in households that were wired for electricity.[14] In 1934, 26.1 per cent of urban customers with electricity had an electric range, 38.9 per cent a clothes washer, 28.6 per cent a vacuum cleaner, 29.9 per cent an air heater, 93.6 per cent an iron, 10.9 per cent an electric refrigerator, 52.2 per cent a toaster, 9.1 per cent a grill, and 60.7 per cent a radio. Among the few wealthy rural householders, electricity was being employed as much for its domestic applications as for its agricultural ones. Not surprisingly, farm use of most appliances lagged behind that of urban dwellers, with the significant exception of the washing machine and radio, which enjoyed greater acceptance in the rural market. Illustration 25.5 indicates the steady increase in appliance usage throughout the 1920s and 1930s.

Although household advisers allied with industry in promoting domestic technology, they also followed a divergent path. Recruited to present the women's perspective, some advertising writers tried, largely unsuccessfully, to gain for housework a measure of recognition as skilled, productive labour comparable to that accorded paid or professional labour. Their voices can be heard in subthemes in the dominant advertising message – particularly in advertisements specifically directed at women, such as those promoting smaller, lower-

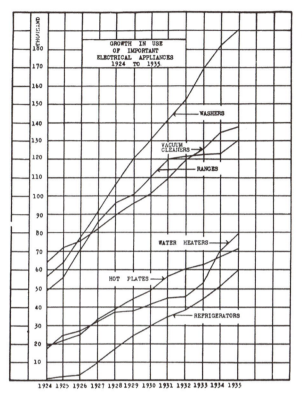

25.5 "Growth in the Use of Important Electrical Appliances 1924–1935" (*The Bulletin*, December 1936)

priced appliances. By contrast, ads selling the ideal of an electric home were more male-directed. Reflecting women's input, the women-directed ads often compared women's work in the home with workforce participation. In one issue of *The Hydro Lamp*, for instance, a young business-girl-turned-housekeeper justified investing in an electric stove by noting that "men in offices and factories, even on farms, provide themselves with every labour-saving device."[15] Household advisers also demanded financial autonomy or a recognized share of the family wage for the modern homemaker, comparing the cost of household conveniences with that of automobile accessories or cigarettes, products primarily identified with men. Advertising women chastised men who failed to provide the latest technology for their wives, and asserted that when the health and happiness of the homemaker were taken into account, appliances were not expensive. Of course, this message reinforced the traditional patriarchal view that the man was responsible for the health and happiness of his home.

Household advisers failed to have domestic labour recognized as skilled or productive labour, not least because of their unequal alliance with consumer capitalists. Still, their rejection to the twentieth-century notion that the housewife's work has no value and requires no skill suggests what they expected of the new domestic technology. They sought to improve working conditions and status for middle-class housewives, but they did not envision women escaping such work. Ironically, by the post–Second World War period, women began, in increasing numbers, to abandon housework as a life-long, fulltime occupation in favour of paid employment outside the home. Today, thanks partly to further technological developments, housework is often done at night or on weekends, in addition to jobs in the labour force. In summary, technology has not improved the status of domestic labour. It remains as unrecognized and undervalued at the dawn of this new century as it was at the beginning of the last.

26 Defining the Lives of Rural Women: Laura Rose on "The Womanly Sphere of Woman"

Margaret Kechnie

During her fifty-year association with Women's Institutes in Ontario, British Columbia, and Quebec, Laura Rose championed life in the countryside and the role that wives and daughters of farmers had to play in strengthening country living. In "The Womanly Sphere of Woman," an address delivered at the annual meeting of the Ontario Women's Institutes held at the Macdonald Institute in Guelph in 1905, Rose expressed concern over the future of rural institutions, particularly the farm home.

The organizations known as the Women's Institutes was founded in 1897, and its purpose was to introduce farm women to the principles inherent in the new discipline of domestic science, much as the Farmer's Institutes taught farmers the latest advances in farm technology. Educated in the domestic arts, the new "ideal" farm woman would be in control of her work, a mother devoted to the maintenance of an up-to-date home, one who used modern methods in the care and feeding of her family. While Adelaide Hoodless has often been identified as the organization's founder, it was Laura Rose with her fifty-year association with the Women's Institutes who was its conscience and ideologue.

Even though the wives and daughters of farmers were often involved in agricultural work that produced income vital to the family, in "The Womanly Sphere of Woman" Laura Rose attempted to apply the notion of separate spheres to the farm family arguing that women's and men's roles should be separate. As Rose

put it, man is "the breadwinner – the producer; woman is "the home-maker – the dispenser."[1] The answers to the questions Rose posed in her address, "The Womanly Sphere of Woman"–"what does woman really want?" and "what is her proper and congenial sphere?" – are a reflection of the conviction of many of her middle-class contemporaries caught up in the turn-of-the-century Country Life Movement. The movement emanated from the United States in the late nineteenth century and grew out of a sense of foreboding on the part of urban-based educators, religious leaders, and other public figures regarding the threat posed to rural institutions by the loss of the farming population to the cities. These agrarian idealists embraced the rural myth. They believed that the countryside would always be the cradle of essential social values and the moulder of national and personal character.[2] For Rose and other reformers like her, the problem was not just that people were leaving the farm. Rev. John MacDougall's book *Rural Life in Canada*, published in 1913, documented that women particularly were turning their backs on the countryside.[3] Holding tenaciously to the belief that farmers are the bulwark of the nation and their sterling character the greatest asset of the state, MacDougall asserted that 85 per cent of those listed in *Who's Who in Canada,* as well as 99 per cent of the ministers of the gospel had been born in rural areas.[5] With so many young women choosing higher education and jobs in Ontario's growing urban centres over life in the coun-

日八月二十年十和昭　念記年三廿　　　　　　　　　　　　　　　會人婦人本日一キロ八

26.1 Haney Women's Institute twenty-fifth anniversary (B-1022, British Columbia Archives)

tryside, Country Life reformers questioned who would mother the nation's leaders in the future.

The daughter of a well-to-do miller, Rose was born in Georgetown, Ontario, in 1866.[5] When still a young woman she moved to her brother's farm in North Dakota. As his housekeeper, she was responsible for all the domestic work, which included caring for the poultry, tending the garden, making butter, and performing the work associated with the hired men. Typical of the times, the domestic work was done without the aid of running water or electricity. Besides her work in the home, Rose taught in a nearby school. Throughout her life she would claim that it was her experiences in North Dakota that allowed her to identify with the problems women faced in farming communities.

When her brother married, Rose returned to Ontario

to attend Alma Ladies' College in St Thomas. Later she enrolled at the Ontario Agricultural College (OAC) in its short program in dairying. After completing her studies with distinction, she was hired by the Ontario Department of Agriculture to work in its travelling dairies project. In 1898 Rose was the first woman appointed as an instructor in dairying at the OAC, and she taught there for thirteen years. Throughout her career Rose was in great demand as a speaker and as a judge at rural fairs. Her articles appeared in numerous farm journals in both Canada and the United States. *Farm Dairying*, written by Rose and published in 1911, was widely used as a text in dairy schools. Like all of her writings, the book consistently reflected her belief that women's place was in the home. Even in terms of dairying, work that was integral to early twentieth-century Ontario farm women, Rose felt women's only role in the dairy was to keep the milking utensils clean and the male milkers' clothing spotless.

To a large extent it was fear of social breakdown that motivated "The Womanly Sphere of Woman." Rose pointed out that the decision of young country women to seek higher education and paid work in the city might aid the campaign to achieve equality with men, but in doing so would create "complicated social problems." Like other urban-based reformers associated with the Country Life Movement, Rose believed rural women would find the satisfaction they were yearning for in country living by becoming ideal mothers and exemplary homemakers, and she promoted the "cult of domesticity" among rural families.

County Life reformers generally believed in a theory of social evolution according to which an increasing division of labour would lead to a better life, if modelled after reformers' own middle-class experience.[6] As contradictory as it may seem, Country Life reformers were convinced that the economic problems of the farm would be solved and rural institutions renewed if the country became more like the city.[7] Ignoring the fact that many married working-class women did a variety of paid work both inside and outside the home to augment the family income, middle-class reformers such as Rose idealized middle-class urban homemakers whose lives were centred primarily on the care of their own families. While she felt that it was important to ask, "What can we do to keep our boys on the farm or turn them again to the land?," for Rose a more important question to national well-being was "What can we do to keep our girls in the *kitchen*?" Ignoring the harsh economic realities of farming in Ontario in the first two decades of the twentieth century, Rose insisted on seeing the problems of the countryside and the reasons for the migration of young people to urban centres in simplistic terms. She was convinced that if country women would accept their proper sphere – their place in a modernized country home – the problem of keeping men on the farm would disappear. In a modern rural environment, country people would want to stay on the farm and a revitalized farm community would start a back-to-the-land movement.

In addressing her audience of mostly rural homemakers at the Women's Institutes' annual meeting, Rose clearly meant to instruct, if not scold, the women sitting before her. She often upbraided farm women for failing to acquire modern equipment for the home.[8] She pointed to the way farmers readily purchased the new reapers and binders to ease farm labour and claimed that farm women were by nature less willing to spend money on equipment that would reduce their work. At the same time, it was typical for her to blame women for farmers' economic woes. This is evident in her "The Womanly Sphere of Woman" address when she said that "many a woman only becomes a millstone around her husband's neck, and by her extravagance drags him to the brink of bankruptcy or suicide." When assigning guilt for young women's attraction to the city, Rose again blamed women. It was the mothers who were at fault when they allowed their daughters to go to secondary school, where education might divert their attention from home and its concerns. Her essential cry was "Let us be womanly." "Real womanhood," for Rose, began and ended with a "proper education," that is, one limited to the elementary level, unless, of course, that education was dedicated to teaching women a love for the home and for homemaking. "My greatest hope in the good work the Macdonald Institute[9] may do is that it may turn the young women back to home life, and that their true pleasure will be found in administering to the comfort of the inmates of their own homes." While her argument does not quite parallel that of Edward Clark, who argued in *Women and Education*[10] that higher education could render women sterile, Rose did see physical consequences for such women: "muscular flabbiness" and "sharp-featured irritability."

While rural mothers disappointed Rose, young women, too, had failed the countryside, in her view. When attending secondary school, they allowed themselves to be caught up in the crushing burden of school work, and school work replaced learning the most important aspect of life for a young woman: a love for home life and the work associated with it. In fact, young women willingly admitted to knowing nothing about housework. Once they began to work outside the home, the problem worsened. Not only did these educated working women "fritter away" their lives "indulging themselves in luxuries," but they began to exhibit a "spirit of independence … which does not tend toward matrimony." Even though Rose was a forty-year-old, single, educated woman who chose life away from the farm, she wondered at the growing number of employed women in America and questioned whether their emancipation had not made them unattractive marriage partners. Women, she argued, who remained at home and assisted their mothers with home work were content;

unlike their working sisters, they had a proper attitude and did not spend money foolishly. In answer to her question "What do women really want?," Rose claimed that regardless of feminist demands for equality in education and paid work, women really wanted the "contentment of their own 'happy, thrifty households.'" "Home girls" would attract the attention of men, and "maids must be wives and mothers to fulfil the entire and holiest end of women's being."

Just as farm women in the United States ignored Country Life reformers, the wives of Ontario farmers paid little heed to directions on how to update their homes.[11] For decades male farmers had argued that farming could not be learned from books, and now their wives both resented and resisted the domestic science instruction offered by the Department of Agriculture through the Women's Institutes. Nor did they encourage their daughters to attend Macdonald Institute for a domestic science education. The Women's Institutes grew in Ontario because they adapted their agendas to meet the interests of middle-class women in hundreds of small towns throughout Ontario and not only because they found a following among some farm women. That is not to say, however, that farm women rejected modernization itself; rather they repudiated the message promoted by leaders of the Women's Institutes such as Laura Rose who wanted women to adopt the homemaker role to the exclusion of income-producing work. For them, it was an issue of practicality, not a conscious challenge to patriarchy or an endorsement of feminist principles. They simply could not afford Rose's philosophy.[12] Besides, while farm women, no doubt, found their work roles difficult without modern equipment, their income-producing work gave them a sense of autonomy that housework alone could not provide.[13]

The class bias in "The Womanly Sphere of Woman" is palpable. The same prejudice permeates most of the addresses to Ontario's rural women by middle-class, urban-based, domestic science experts and by professional women such as Rose, who both accepted the philosophy of the Country Life Movement and dominated the leadership of the Women's Institutes in its early years. The root of farm women's discontent with the countryside, these advocates would argue, could be found in their misguided rejection of the homemaker role and their erroneous attempts to achieve equality with men by seeking higher education and jobs in the city. Rose could answer her question "What is her proper and congenial sphere?" with confidence: it was the home and the work associated with the care of family members. For those who resisted this calling, the warning was clear. Only those women who chose "the womanly sphere" would know that "the eyes of the world and of the God above rest with favour upon her, and her reward in the hereafter is sure." Many Ontario farm women seemed intent on working for a reward here on earth instead.

26.2 Nakusp Women's Institute parade, 1939 (C-04671, British Columbia Archives)

27 "Such Outrageous Discrimination": Farm Women and Their Family Grievances in Early Twentieth-Century Ontario

Monda Halpern

In early twentieth-century Ontario, the survival of the family farm enterprise necessitated interdependence and cooperation between women and men in their differing roles on the farm.[1] The presumption that this mutuality nurtured an egalitarian partnership between wives and husbands, however, not only overstates women's power within the patriarchal farm and family, but implies that little or no conflict existed between women and men within the farm family. The alternative view that women martyred themselves for the sake of the farm, a disempowering conception of women, also suggests the general absence of gender discord. Women were indeed dedicated to the success of the farm, but they themselves recognized their disadvantaged status and discerned that their interests and needs often opposed those of their men. Indeed, farm wives and daughters decried their unmerciful workload and the devaluation of their labour, and in so doing asserted a shared recognition of female oppression for which many of them impugned farm men.

The first decades of the new century in rural Ontario were a time of dramatic change. The increasing availability of hydroelectricity, the tractor, and the automobile was revolutionizing life on the farm, making chores more time- and energy-efficient. As well, mixed-crop farming had emerged as the choice farming strategy for widening urban markets, one that would prevail until the advent of crop specialization after 1945.[2] Significantly, farms steadily declined after 1911, when they numbered just over 200, 000, but their average size steadily increased.[3] In 1911 the typical farm claimed 110 acres; in 1941 it comprised about 20 acres more.[4] The expanded acreage of increasingly fewer farms reflected a shrinking farm population. The 1931 census, which was the first to specify the proportion of rural dwellers who resided on farms, reveals that the farm population for that year consisted of 786,000. By 1941 this number had dropped to 695,000.[5]

The rapid modernization and transformation of rural Ontario, however, did little to change the fundamental nature of farm women's work. Most of the farm wife's time continued to be consumed by arduous household demands. These included domestic, productive, and reproductive work, and the care not only of husband and children, but of infirm relations and farmhands.[6] A 1912 article entitled "Is Marriage a Failure?" chronicled the farm woman's typical day: "Up in the morning early, breakfast over, hurry to milking, separating milk, washing dishes, (minding babies in intervals), tidy house, get dinner [i.e., lunch], wash dishes, do mending, sewing, gardening, berry picking, helping in field if necessary, washing, ironing, baking, with the thousand and one interruptions, which come through the day; get supper, put sleepy babies to bed, milk, wash dishes, sew or mend again till bed-time."[7] Reflecting upon her work, Frontenac County farm woman Helen Campbell declared that "on the farm, I emulated a camel – the original beast of burden."[8]

27.1 Harvesting oats, 1915 (RG 16-274, album 3, p. 59, Archives of Ontario)

It was, in fact, a widely held belief in early twentieth-century Ontario that because of interminable monotony, overwork, and exhaustion (vacations from the farm were rare and brief), countless farm women had gone hopelessly insane and were alarmingly overrepresented in the province's lunatic asylums.[9] This topical issue appeared in farm journals of the day, such as *The O.A.C. Review*, which in 1912 detailed the farm woman's descent into madness:

So during the [childbearing] years when she is entitled to a certain amount of care and rest, the woman on the farm struggles along, bearing burdens which should only be borne by those who are physically strong. She is unable to cope with her work, and she lets some of it go. Then she shrinks within herself, lest some neighbor should drop in and find her unprepared. Her appearance begins to suffer. Her shoulders stoop and her whole figure assumes ... an attitude neither graceful nor proper. Her clothes wear out and she has little time to spend on having them replaced. Her teeth go, and she cannot leave the babies long enough to have them attended to ... And all this comes in the nine or ten years which follow her courtship and marriage. Is it any wonder that many a young woman finds the change from girlhood to such strenuous wifehood too great for her mental or physical strength? She succumbs. She is laid away in the churchyard or she is taken to the asylum for the insane ... If she is dead they lay flowers on her grave. If she is insane, she gets care and rest: She is surrounded by green lawns and flowers ... But it is too late.[10]

In describing the way in which insanity impeded the ability of women in their childbearing years to keep house, maintain their appearance, and repair their clothes, this account ignored the general symptomology of insanity and underscored its gender-specific manifestations as they related to the distinctiveness of women's work.

It is true, however, that the rigours of farm life took an emotional toll on its women and were sometimes too overwhelming to bear. Louisa Good, for example, experienced excessive strain and fatigue in her unsuccessful effort to attack the staggering workload at Myrtleville, her parents' large farm near Brantford. She was acutely aware of her inability to conform to the demanding domestic role expected of her as a woman – especially a farm woman. These feelings no doubt contributed to her stay at a small private hospital in Toronto in 1911 and at the Ontario Hospital in Hamilton in 1912. She suffered from various "nervous" conditions, and endured these ailments for the remainder of her life.[11] Selina Horst of St Jacobs, outside of Kitchener, remembered that after the birth of her youngest sibling, the family's ninth child, her mother "had sort of a breakdown." Horst cited too many people to care for and too little privacy as the reasons for the collapse.[12]

In a 1905 article entitled "Farmers' Wives and Insanity," however, doctors testified to the fact that farm women were no more prone to mental illness than other groups of people, especially given their "idyllic" surroundings. Dr Groff, of the Pennsylvania Board of Health, wrote that "'less farmers' wives become insane than of any other class, owing to the joyous elements of country life.'" Dr C.K. Clark, superintendent of the asylum in Kingston, asserted that he had "'a great deal of faith in the level-headedness of the farmer's wife, and cannot understand why she should develop insanity more readily than the city woman surrounded by more artificial conditions.'" And Dr Daniel Clark, superintendent of the Toronto asylum, declared that "'it is my opinion that farmers' wives, as a rule, are a healthy class with healthy work in the fresh air, and who are, as a whole, contented.'" Farm women were largely represented in insane asylums, these doctors believed, only because they comprised one of the largest occupational groups.[13]

In their effort to dispute the myth about the pervasiveness of insanity among farm women, these doctors might have overstated their case. Many farm women found few "joyous elements of country life" and hardly felt "contented." But most did not go "insane," nor did they stoically suffer in silence. Rather, farm women expressed with much clarity and candour their displeasure with the volume and nature of their work, and in so doing presented a challenge to the gendered family and work relations on which their own survival depended, as indeed did that of the farm.

A forthright Mrs Hopkins of Russel County outlined the most distressing issues for farm wives in her 1912 letter to *Farm and Dairy*, declaring that "in no other occupation are we offered so great a contrast between the superior advantages of the male and the acquiescent humility of the female … so poorly paid, so complacently considered as only a chattel, a mere machine, a possession valuable only according to her work and childbearing capacity."[14] The frustration expressed by Ontario farm women led author John MacDougall to address the topic in 1913, in a book chapter entitled "Social Causes of Unrest," and also prompted a writer in *The Farmer's Advocate* to declare in 1920 that "this 'restlessness' that we are reading and hearing about all the time is not growing any less throughout the country, to put it mildly."[15] Indeed, American farm women were no less agitated, as exemplified in 1913 by a series of six articles in *Harper's Bazaar* entitled "The Revolt of the Farmer's Wife!"[16]

Sympathy for the plight of the overworked farm woman was evident in the women's pages of the agricultural press, where women – farm wives, farm daughters, and journalists – revealed the extent to which farm women's domestic labour went unappreciated on the farm. They put the devaluation of women's work squarely on the shoulders of farm men. One presumably female author in *Farm and Dairy*, frustrated by the farmer's relative privilege and arrogance, summarized the prevailing sentiment: "'I am a self-made man.' How often we hear this assertion now-a-days made with great pride and satisfaction by men who in a comparatively few years and with few opportunities have raised themselves from poverty to affluence … The self-made farmer … owe more to their wives than any other class of self-made men … These self-made men make me tired. Why cannot they tell the whole truth and give to the woman in the case her due credit?"[17]

One article written by a man, and seemingly directed to male readers, warned them of the possible repercussions of their neglect:

Have you ever thought what the result would be if all the farmer's wives and housekeepers in this country were to form a sort of labor-union and then go out on strike, for something under an eighteen hour day and a pay-envelop [*sic*] every night? … the fact that the 'female of the species' has always been more faithful to her home and family in the past than she has been to any 'union' or organization is no argument proving that she will always remain in that attitude, or frame of mind … Surely, we say, let the woman of the farm go out on strike. There are a whole lot of things in this world that are hers by rights, and she hasn't been getting them.[18]

Clearly, farm wives and their supporters knew that the productive work of farm wives, however extensive and however integral to the survival of the farm, did not give them sexual equality within the male-owned enterprise or within the legally sanctioned patriarchal farm family.[19] Indeed, while reciprocity was evident between farm husband and wife, "family relations could stress hierarchy and control as often as mutuality."[20]

The absence of modern labour-saving devices in the home was at the core of the farm woman's frustration with farm life.[21] In particular, many farm women were infuriated by the fact that the barn, viewed by their husbands as the "real soul" of the farm,[22] was better equipped with labour-saving devices than was the kitchen, and that, by extension, men's labour could be done in a more timely and efficient fashion than could theirs. Farm women did not anticipate at this time that domestic "labour-saving" equipment could potentially raise the standards and increase the pace, and thus the time and amount, of their work. Indeed, owing to their awareness that "women were the last to get anything for the household," feminism for farm women, asserted one article in 1921, was defined by their struggle for and acquisition of modern appliances for the home:

Feminism in the city may mean many things. It may mean a combination of short hair and knickerbockers or of babies and jobs. It may mean equal pay for equal work and equal pay for equal misbehaviour. But on the farm and homestead from the east to the west, feminism means something else … it means: A power-machine for the house for every tractor bought for the farm. A bath-tub in the house for every binder on the farm. Running water in the kitchen for every riding-plow for the fields. A kerosene [sic] cookstove for every automobile truck. A fireless cooker for every new mowing-machine.[23]

As this passage indicates, farm women and their supporters consistently drew analogies between the requirements of the barn and those of the home. The warm, well-lit environment that the farmer and modern technology offered the barn prompted many farm women to complain that the animals lived a more comfortable life than did the farmer's own family.[24]

While some argued that the lack of modern conveniences was attributable to the farm woman's fear of machinery and her reluctance to try new ways, many women claimed that it was the fault of the notoriously conservative and frugal farmer, who had the power to sanction the purchase of devices for the home but who underestimated their value in easing his wife's work.[25] His ignorance in this regard was problematic for his wife, who understood that "the installation of machinery in most farm homes will have to come through a man's understanding of its need and in the case of power machinery, his teaching on how to operate it."[26] Women, then, knew that their acquisition of labour-saving devices was dependent upon both the tenuous goodwill and earned capital of men, as well as upon their presumed knowledge of domestic machinery, in truth likely very little. Many women felt cheated by "such outrageous discrimination," and although they intellectually understood the survival strategy of "the Barn First school of farming," they certainly demonstrated some resentment towards this dictum.[27]

The gendered opposition set up between the barn and the farm house at this time masks the fact that, while farm men seldom assumed responsibilities in the home, farm women, although absorbed first by domestic concerns, were very much involved with the workings of the barn.[28] Poultry raising was deemed the most suitable barn work for women. Ontario farm women seemed to have agreed with their American counterparts that poultry raising was "a nice ladylike branch" of agriculture – one in which inherently female attributes proved advantageous over those of men. Women's ability to nurture (especially small creatures) and to keep house (coops had to be cleaned) and their attention to detail and fondness for order also served poultry raising well.[29]

More often than not, however, the farm wife's earnings from the sale of poultry and eggs went immediately to household expenses, which left her little or no personal money by the end of the year.[30] This scenario prompted Mrs Dawson, who had resided on a farm for six years, to assert in 1912 that the husband "claims that he supports her, but he is mistaken. The truth of the matter is that she supports him." In contrast to the farm wife, her husband "comes to the end of the year with a nice bank account to his credit. He has sold his grain, his cattle, his horses, his pigs, and the proceeds are all his. … Then what about the wives and daughters?"[31] Member of Parliament Agnes Macphail, herself of the farm, quipped that "'in farming women break fifty-fifty with the men … fifty dollars to the men and fifty cents to the women, and I doubt if that is overstating the case.'"[32] Mrs Dawson recommended that "[e]ither the farmer should recognize the fact that his wife and daughters have made his large bank account possible and should give them some tangible interest in that bank account, or he should pay his share toward the board and clothing of his family and allow his wife and daughters the privilege of starting a bank account of their own."[33]

Even a male contributor to *Farm and Dairy* stated, in a rare confession, that "we farmers too often share the profits with our partner in a grudging spirit as if we were giving them something that belongs rightfully to us." He called for "more true cooperation. Let us divide the profits of the firm graciously and justly."[34] The significance of this entire issue was not lost on one woman who in 1921 saw feminism to mean "our share of the farm income."[35]

Whether or not farm wives should engage in traditionally male barn work involving large livestock and should labour in the fields alongside men was a contentious matter of gender in rural Ontario.[36] Indeed, a 1914 article, entitled "What Is a Woman's Work on the Farm?," referred to the issue as "this Oft Times Burning Question."[37] There were those few farm men who insisted that their wives perform barn and field work, an assignment that a handful of women welcomed.[38] Some were keenly interested in agricultural issues and wanted to experience all aspects of the farm; others simply welcomed the pleasures of outdoor work and freedom from domestic drudgery.[39] The majority of farm folk, however, opposed women's outside labour. Mrs T.H. Bass

bitingly declared that "real men prefer to do their own work themselves." She added that "it is quite possible to train a man to expect a woman to do the 'chores' outside the house. I have seen this done, but it never struck me that the gratitude of the man was proportionate to the energy expended by his 'other half.'"[40] Mrs Bass would have approved of one agricultural speaker who, when asked at a meeting if his wife milked cows, searingly replied, "My wife, sir, does nothing on the farm that a man can do for her."[41] In fact, many men supported this viewpoint, deriding those members of their own sex who turned their wives into "the pack-horse of the family … a sort of upper servant or slave."[42]

Underlying both male and female arguments against women's barn and field work was the shared belief between the sexes that a wife's rightful place was in the home.[43] But, as many women knew only too well, a role exclusively within the home did not shield them from the kind of heavy labour or emotional strain that they were feared to experience had they worked outdoors. Indeed, despite the proposed correlation between women's overwork in the home and insanity, many farmers failed to realize that women's taxing workload in the house posed as much of a health risk as their "male" outdoor work.[44]

Although women were told that farm men should share in the concerns of homemaking, many wives felt that their husbands did little to lighten their household burdens and rarely acknowledged their labour.[45] One woman wrote in 1914 that, "in speaking of 'Woman's Work on the Farm,' we are dealing with a difficult problem for reasons that are obvious – lack of help, lack of convenience, and lack of consideration of the husband."[46]

In an era that promoted the companionate marriage, farm women also complained that husbands, as a whole, made phlegmatic partners. In March of 1923, Ethel Hillier of Vyner, near Sarnia, attended a "Literary Evening" that entertained the following debate: "Resolved[:] that books are more companionable and of more use to a woman than a husband."[47] Kenneth Cragg remembered his mother's frustration over her husband's excessive time in the barn, away from his family: "The way he would hang around the stable at night was a constant annoyance to mother. 'I've given up trying,' she would tell her relatives in her resigned way. 'If he has no more respect for his wife and family than to spend all his time with his horses …' … Sometimes she tried sarcasm. 'Well have you at last got the horses tucked away for the night?'"[48] Mrs Cragg was not alone in her frustration. David Densmore confirms that "for farmers, a house was a place to rest between workdays, and many a farm wife over the generations has lamented that her man seemed to prefer the company of the barn to that of the house."[49] With all of the liabilities associated with farm life, Ontario farm women, like their Manitoban sisters, were no doubt left musing "Should My Daughter Marry a Farmer?"[50]

It was the adult farm daughter who helped the farm wife with much of the domestic work. For Galt-area daughter Roxie Hostetler and many young women like her, it meant "housework!: raising children; scrubbing floors; milking cows; making butter; baking bread and coffee cakes and pies."[51] As the eldest of four children and the only girl, Ethel Hillier performed countless household chores, and she often remarked in her diaries that she was "very busy," "real busy," and "busy as usual."[52] Ethel was so consumed by domestic work that she was obliged to forgo high school and only left her parents' farm when she married relatively late at age thirty-five.[53] Unlike Ethel, who in fact married a farmer, one group of country girls, repelled by the prospect of continued domestic drudgery on the farm, "declared out and out that no farmer need propose to them."[54]

Most adult daughters provided savings for their fathers by performing unpaid domestic work in place of the "hired girl," and they were cognizant of their eco-nomic function and lack of reward. Alice Ferguson, in "Should Daughters Be Compensated for Their Labor?," observed in 1914 that "money is always forthcoming for the payment of hired help, but apparently little for the daughter who does the same work. The girl feels this is not just to her."[55] Kingston-area farm daughter Jennie A. Pringle, in a letter addressing "What Girls Need Most in a Rural Community," firmly pointed out in 1926 that "the hired girl and man get wages. If she were working in the city, she would be paid. Why not on the farm? … Fathers, why wait to give us our share on our marriage or your death?"[56] The disparity between the treatment of farm daughters and sons intensified the resentment by daughters. It prompted one outspoken woman to proclaim that "the girls who stay at home should be paid for their services. Why not? When the son comes of age, if he stays at home, he enters into a business-like agreement with his father as to the wages he shall receive, and is not regarded as mercenary in the least. Why should the daughter be regarded as a minor child, a ward of her father or of some male relative, till legally delivered over into the care and keeping of her husband?"[57] Farm daughters agreed that the absence of an income "is the bane of the farm girl's life … It hurts her self-respect to ask for spending money continually."[58] Farm daughter Edna I. Brown confirmed in 1926 that "the lack of any such provision in most farm homes is the chief reason why Daughter leaves; almost the only reason why she is discontented if she stays."[59]

For older "spinster" daughters who had long remained on the farm and cared for aging parents, bachelor or widowed brothers, or the children of married siblings, poverty and dependence were a consuming fear.[60] Elizabeth McCutcheon, in her 1911 article "The Single Woman in the Country[:] Can the Spinster Remain on the Farm and Be Independent?," asked "if those who choose this self-sacrificing sphere are not paid for their labor, what have they ahead of them? … When old and helpless, their existence may be a continual misery because of the ingratitude of those whom they have served."[61]

This ingratitude was no more profoundly expressed to the devoted and overworked spinster daughter than in the pages of her father's will, which unjustly and consistently provided far better for the farmer's son (and by extension, his son's wife) than for his daughter.[62] Indeed, "A Farmer's Daughter" wrote in 1908 that she knew of "one case where a daughter came home and tended her father for years, giving him every loving attention, and when he died he left his daughter one hundred dollars, and the son a farm and stock worth thousands."[63] With little or no provisions made for the daughter in her father's will, farm daughters asked, "… and what of the girl? She is left wholly defenceless … She must either marry or go to a factory or domestic service … Think of the shame and disgrace of being forced into a marriage for the sake of a home. Can anyone imagine a worse fate?"[64] They suggested that if fathers "cannot leave their daughters enough to keep them, they should at least take a little and provide them with the means of learning some life-work … the daughter could in time come to be a credit to her parents, instead of, as is often the case, being a stranded wreck on the shores of time."[65]

Plagued by drudgery and the devaluation of their labour, farm women were neither equals, nor martyrs, nor mad. They were dissatisfied workers, who, as the wives and daughters of the male farm owners who undermined them, felt the sting of their oppression all that more keenly. The intimacy that characterized the work arrangement on the family farm meant that farm wives, and the daughters who stayed, were obliged to combat their oppression with much care and finesse and in clever, resourceful ways. In the end, although farm women were duty-bound to the needs of the farm, this obligation did not preclude their demand for dignity, opportunity, and fairness.

28 Between the Rock and a Hard Place: Single Mothers in St John's, Newfoundland, during the Second World War
Ruth Haywood

On the edge of the North Atlantic, Newfoundland was in a strategic position during the Second World War. Both the Canadians and the Americans established army, navy, and air bases in Newfoundland and Labrador. The Americans became the largest contingent with over ten thousand personnel in 1943.[1] The first appearance of the "Yanks'" in 1941 caused great excitement in St John's. Newfoundlanders were looking forward to jobs at American bases at much better pay than they were accustomed to earning, and many women found the idea of working in close proximity to thousands of American servicemen very appealing.

Hundreds of Newfoundland women married American men during and after the war,[2] but many of the women who entered into a relationship with a serviceman were left pregnant and alone. In 1942, the year after the arrival of the Americans, both the number and percentage of illegitimate births in St John's were more than double that of the year before. By 1945 the city had over one thousand infants and small children born to single mothers.[3]

According to Cecelia Benoit, after the war single motherhood "became institutionalized" in Stephenville, a town on the west coast of Newfoundland. In one of Benoit's oral accounts, a former mess hall worker at the Stephenville base described her former colleagues as "so young and still wet behind the ears. They didn't know fellows lied so much, telling them that they was going to marry them and take them back to the States … Being

Catholic, and the priest outrightly refusing to marry you to an American or a Protestant, didn't help much either. How many of them went home to their mothers with a little one on the way!"[4]

Very few women chose to be single mothers; many expected marriage. The majority of single mothers did what they could to support their children, including introducing affiliation cases, as paternity suits were known at this time.[5] A minority of single mothers rejected their children: a small number of women abandoned their babies, several put them up for adoption, and a few were accused of infanticide. Single mothers with little family support often worked full time while contributing a few dollars a week to keep their child in foster care.[6] Children whose parents were unable to care for them were frequently left at one of St John's foster homes or, if possible, at an orphanage. In 1966 the Church of England Orphanage still refused to take an illigitimate child or "a child deprived of support by neglect of duty on the part of a parent."[7]

Young expectant women often spent a short period at the Salvation Army's home for unwed mothers, the Anchorage, and many of them returned to their parents' or a sibling's home with their child. Some women who had worked as live-in domestic servants returned to their employer's home, and a few were allowed to bring their baby with them. Contacted about her "servant" in 1943, Mrs V. replied that she was "taking all responsibility of the girl and her child."[8]

Domestic service represented most of the jobs for Newfoundland women up to and including the 1940s.[9] Of the single mothers who reported their occupation when applying for a warrant, "domestic" was the most frequent response. One former domestic, Irene L., shared other characteristics common to single mothers in St John's in the 1940s: she was young, she had come to the city from an outport, and she had become involved with a serviceman.[10] Seventeen-year old Irene left her home in the autumn of 1944 to work in St John's. Shortly after her arrival she began a sexual relationship with a Canadian sailor, but in April 1945 he shipped out, leaving her pregnant. Irene worked until the last few months of her pregnancy, then returned to her parents' home in Lower Island Cove, where she delivered twins with the assistance of a nurse and an unregistered midwife. One baby was stillborn, the other died within hours, and both were buried in the front yard without a funeral. With no doctor or clergyman to provide a signature, there were no death certificates. This prompted a police investigation.[11] Months later Irene went back to St John's and lived at the Anchorage while bringing a lawsuit against her former lover.[12] The path Irene followed after the discovery of her pregnancy – from charitable agency, to her parents' home, to the home for unwed mothers, to the magistrate's court – was typical of other young single mothers.

The wartime United States consul claimed that Newfoundland women became pregnant "to force the careless soldier" into marriage.[13] While some women might have believed a baby would provoke a proposal, others thought a pre-marital pregnancy or child could be used to circumvent parental objections to a wedding. In Newfoundland until the 1950s a girl under twenty-one needed her parents' permission to marry.[14] This law caused Mildred J. to leave home in 1943. Mildred wanted to get married, but according to the social worker's report, "her mother would not give permissions as she is under

age and her people don't like American soldiers."[15] Unions between Americans and Newfoundlanders were further complicated by the requirement that a serviceman have his commanding officer's permission to marry and by the U.S. military's 1943 ban on marriages to non-Americans.[16] The marriage ban delayed or prevented some weddings and may have contributed to the rise in illegitimate births.

In Newfoundland the rate of illegitimate births was higher than in the rest of North America, almost certainly due to the military presence.[17] As in Canada, which Newfoundland joined in 1949, birth control was illegal until 1969. Despite this, servicemen and civilian workers on military bases were issued condoms to combat the spread of venereal disease. Natural birth control methods may have been used, and before abortions were made available, many women used folk remedies to end a pregnancy or induce a miscarriage.[18]

Birth-control information was also restricted until the 1960s. During the war, Newfoundland censors were told to prohibit, along with pacifist, socialist, and certain religious works, publications such as *Sex, Sexology*, and *Scarlet Confessions*.[19] These restrictions did not stop Newfoundlanders from trying to obtain sexual information. In 1941 the secretary for posts and telegraphs intercepted a package with twenty copies of *Marriage Guide*. "Books … of a treasonable … immoral or indecent character" should be disposed of under the section of the Revenue Act that prohibits their importation, wrote the secretary for justice.[20]

Unwanted pregnancies were certainly related to the lack of birth-control information and devices, but it is possible that many women did not fear becoming pregnant because of the assurances of their lovers. When Olive B. signed a warrant for the appearance of a Canadian soldier in an affiliation case, she said that he had promised marriage "if anything happened." Frequently this was an empty promise. Servicemen were often unwilling or unable to get married; some were already married and some were shipped out before a wedding could take place. There is some evidence that the American military discouraged marriages by tranferring soldiers with pregnant girlfriends out of the area.[21]

A few women suffered an even greater indignity than being left pregnant at the altar. In June 1943 Julia H. signed a warrant for the appearance of the Canadian soldier to whom she was engaged. Julia was pregnant, and a few days before she had expected to be married, the soldier had left the country with eighty dollars he had borrowed from her. Julia had also spent a considerable sum on wedding clothes and a ring. One of Julia's relatives was going to Canada and said he would search for the soldier and try to get Julia's money back. The chaplain of the Lincoln and Welland Regiment informed Julia that the soldier was already married. Very soon after her baby was born, Julia gave it up for adoption.[22]

Most of the single mothers who could not afford to keep their child preferred a foster home or orphanage to adoption. As both wages and the number of employment opportunities for women improved during the war, more women could afford to keep a child in foster care. But women still had the lowest-paying jobs, and the type of day-care facilities that developed during the war in Ontario and in other places where women laboured in defence industries did not exist in Newfoundland.[23] The lack of day care and the high cost of fostering left many single mothers in desperate circumstances, including many of those who obtained some child support.

In 1943 Ethel G. called at the probation office to explain that she had not been paying for her child's foster care because she was out of work, but that she had a new job at the Newfoundland Hotel and would start making payments. Later, a probation officer, as social workers were called, visited the hotel laundry where Ethel worked to ask why she had not yet made the promised payments. Ethel responded that she earned twenty dollars a month and half this amount went to pay her board. Other women were slightly more fortunate. Annie H., a domestic at the "Mental Hospital" (or Hospital for Mental and Nervous Diseases) contributed five dollars towards her child's support and told the social worker that the child's father would also pay five dollars "when working."[24]

One of Newfoundland's first pieces of legislation forced fathers of illegitimate children to make some financial contribution to the maintenance of their offspring.[25] An unmarried pregnant woman could apply to the magistrate to issue a warrant for the arrest of the alledged father of the child. The accused was then obliged to post a bond to ensure his court appearance. If the woman's suit was successful, the father would be required to post another bond. If the defendant was unable or unwilling to "furnish a bond in the amount ordered," he could be jailed for up to twelve months.[26] Some fathers of illegitimate children failed to make payments to the affiliation accounts.[27] As many men left Newfoundland during the war, even a lawsuit could not guarantee the appearance of the defendant in an affiliation case.

The majority of women were successful in their suits against servicemen, and the military put money directly into the affiliation account administered by the Public Health Department. The monthly sums entering the account swelled from $615.53 in 1941 to $2,257.98 in 1953.[28] Both the American and the Canadian military made provisions to have support money deducted from a serviceman's pay.[29] The U.S. government also made welfare payments to single mothers between the end of the war and Newfoundland's union with Canada in 1949.[30]

Under the Canadian Army Act, a soldier could be sued or could enter into a private agreement, but he could not be jailed or otherwise taken out of service unless his debt exceeded thirty pounds "above all costs of suit."[31] In

July 1942 a Canadian private was jailed for twenty days when he could not furnish a bond of $250. The commander of the Canadian troops in Newfoundland complained to the commissioner for justice and defence that, while a soldier should be responsible for the maintenance of "any bastard child," the Army Act stated that no decree in respect of maintenance could be issued "against his person." Further, the commander claimed that no soldier of the Canadian Forces in Newfoundland should be jailed for failing to furnish bonds.[32]

Usually the military tried to help in cases where a serviceman was obviously responsible, but many women lost in court and many who won found the awards pitifully small. Single mothers were rarely awarded more than ten dollars a month. Awards also did not keep pace with the cost of living in Newfoundland, estimated to have risen by 66 per cent between 1938 and 1946.[33] Sometimes compensation for expenses was awarded, but payments were as low as twenty dollars. In one exceptional case a woman was awarded ninety-five dollars to cover the birth and funeral expenses of her baby. A widow was also awarded thirty-five dollars for expenses when her child died at birth. From the amounts of the awards, it appears that young women were treated more sympathetically by the court than were older women, particularly if they were the wives of servicemen separated from their husbands by the war. First-time single mothers were also treated more kindly than women whom the Salvation Army referred to as "repeaters."[34] The Salvation Army's official policy was to refuse single women who had already had a child, but the records show the St John's home making several exceptions.[35]

The Anchorage was the only home for unwed mothers in Newfoundland.[36] While it was a charitable institution, it expected its temporary residents to make a contribution towards the cost of their stay and birth expenses, such as the fee of a midwife.[37] One group of women rebelled against the home's strict discipline and were charged in court with disorderly behaviour.[38] The Anchorage, like many other homes for unwed mothers, offered training in domestic arts and tried to find positions for women leaving the home.[39] A dearth of household help during the war had several prospective employers calling the home asking for a "maid."[40]

St John's social workers also helped to find employment for single mothers and arranged adoptions for women who did not wish to keep their babies. Newfoundland's first Adoption Act was passed in 1940 to address the prior situation when an adoption could be arranged by a magistrate, clergyman, or physician.[41] While adoption records are sealed, the social worker's records reveal members of both the mother's and the father's families adopting illegitimate children. In 1941 Laura B. had a child by William P.; Laura did not bring a lawsuit, and no arrangements were made for support. William and his wife decided to adopt the baby. Laura agreed to this as long as she could see the child occasionally. William agreed to have a lawyer draw up the papers, and two days later the adoption was finalized.[42]

In a later case, an American officer brought the baby he had had with a Newfoundland woman, who had abandoned the child, back to his wife in the United States.[43] Adoptions such as this were often privately arranged. When an approach was made directly to the probation office, older children were sometimes requested. In December 1943 a social worker visited Harbour Grace to see Mrs T., who had requested a little girl of ten or twelve years of age, because she had two sons and no daughter. Provided a social worker found their home suitable, those who desired to adopt a child could get one very quickly. In July 1943 Mrs S., who wanted to adopt an infant, was informed that the home would "have one ready on Monday." Two days later Mrs S. went to the Anchorage to finalize the arrangements.[44]

As the war went into its fifth year, the birth rate and number of illegitimate births continued to be high, and the orphanages and foster homes remained full. In November 1944 Monica R. was informed that "there was no place in town where she could place her child."[45] Some women could not wait for arrangements to be made and abandoned their babies, usually at the Anchorage, which had a small nursery to care for infants.[46] Like other neglected children, these babies became the responsibility of the Public Health Department's Child Welfare Section.[47]

On several occasions the Child Welfare Section gave single mothers funds to return to their outport homes with their children.[48] For many single mothers, the support of family was crucial if they intended to keep their babies. Young mothers often returned to their parents with a baby even when there was very little space. In St John's at the end of the war, Josephine T. lived with her six-month-old baby, her parents, and her seven siblings.

Also in St John's, eighteen-year-old Helen M. and her eighteen-month-old child were living with her mother and five siblings. Across the street from Helen, nineteen-year-old Margaret D., who had had a child around the same time, lived with her baby and her parents. It is like-ly that Helen and Margaret were friends, as they named their daughters after each other.[49] Thus it would appear that some women not only had family for support, but occasionally companions in the same situation.

Single mothers in St. John's struggled to keep their children, and their survival depended on several factors. Those with accepting families, families that not only sheltered the single mother but also folded her child into the family unit and cramped family home, were the most fortunate. Familial supports were critically important in sustaining economically and socially vulnerable women. Those fathers who provided even minimal financial aid or took on the raising of their children alleviated the poverty and anxiety of some mothers – as did the military's financial support. The Salvation Army's Anchorage and the Child Welfare Department tried to provide some emergency care for those children whose needs were greatest, but many single mothers received little or no aid, managing to raise their children under the most difficult of circumstances. These persistent and undoubtedly weary women can also be counted among the survivors of the Second World War.

29 Prudence Heward: Painting at Home

Pepita Ferrari

In the spring of 1994, walking through a remarkable exhibition of art from the 1920s in Montreal's Musée des beaux-arts, I came upon a painting that changed the course of my life. It was a work entitled *Au théâtre* by Prudence Heward. The painting spoke so clearly to me with such exceptional clarity and power of vision that I, who had never done a documentary film, was inspired to research and direct a film, *By Woman's Hand*, on the life and work of this woman and two of her fellow painters, Anne Savage and Sarah Robertson. As I learned through my archival research and many interviews with relatives, surviving contemporaries, and experts in Canadian art, Prudence Heward's work is all the more outstanding when examined within the context of her life.

Efa Prudence Heward was born in Montreal on 2 July 1896 and died in Los Angeles on 19 March 1947. Until recent and long-overdue revisions in Canadian art history books, her name would count as one of the few women mentioned among the litany of male Canadian painters. Lacking both the promotional skills of a personal agent and the "eccentric" nature of an Emily Carr, she remained relatively unacknowledged, but even before her premature death, her works would be hung in Group of Seven[1] and Canadian Group of Painters[2] exhibitions, as well as in widely recognized exhibitions as far away as Paris, London, New York,[3] and Buenos Aires.[4]

From her mother, Sara Efa Jones, who served up four o'clock afternoon teas, to her grandmother, Eliza Maria Hervey, who imported the first Jersey cows to Canada, Prudence Heward was raised and influenced by indomitable women with a strong vision of who they were. When she was as young as twelve, her first sketches of family members clearly showed what Prudence's goal in life would be. These bold, untamed scrawlings, now in the safekeeping of her relatives, have the unmistakable markings of that unlearnable thing – raw, instinctive talent.

Prudence Heward was the sixth of eight children, and family would play an essential part in her life as well as in her art. She was inspired by her elder sister Dorothy, a gifted newspaper illustrator. In her brother Jim, she found a soulmate. With her sister Honor, she shared secrets, laughter, and sorrow. And she would become a caring, involved aunt to her many nieces and nephews. Each in turn would become the subject of a striking portrait.

But family would also prove to be the source of Prudence's greatest sadness. When she reached the age of sixteen, her father, Arthur, died. An amateur musician and theatre buff, he had been a great supporter of her emerging talent. "Where's my Prue?" he would ask upon arriving home[5] from his job in management with the Canadian Pacific Railway. Unthinkably, one week later Prudence lost her adored sister Dorothy, due to complications with a pregnancy. Later that year another sister, Barbara, also died. It was not without good reason that people I interviewed often described Prudence as seeming sad or preoccupied when in public.

Popular art analysis views the works of a strong artist as a reflection of the artist's own life and personality.

Certainly there is an inner pensiveness in any of Prudence Heward's paintings. Landscapes are imbued with a profound solemnity. Even the still-lifes seem rather melancholic – often captured behind windows that look out onto a larger world. There is a tension of great emotion withheld, contained behind the eyes of the sitter in any of her portraits. Young children appear wizened far beyond their years, as in *Rosaire*. Even her portraits of her nieces and nephews, blessed with a less impoverished childhood than Rosaire, display this same inner regard.

Like many women of her generation, Prudence lived on the edge of two colliding worlds – the archetypal Victorian world that her mother inhabited and strictly maintained and the new world ushered in by flapper girls and art deco. It was inevitable that, to satisfy the demands of one and explore the other, she would set herself on a course of continual internal conflict.

Undoubtedly, coming from the middle class allowed Prudence a certain freedom. A widowed mother who needed company and enough family money to support her comfortably provided acceptable reasons for her not to marry. Then there was her private domain – the art deco bedroom and the painting studio on the third floor of the Hewards' Peel Street townhouse in Montreal. Prudence could devote her life to painting. The four o'clock teas and constraints of "appropriate behaviour" might have seemed a small price to pay, but there is evidence to suggest that the price was exacted in the form of ill health. Early in life Prudence displayed a delicate constitution. Then, as the years went by, she was confined to bed for extensive periods with increasingly frequent and persistent heavy colds or asthma attacks. In the end, the price proved too high and led to a premature death.

Life with mother nevertheless had its positive side. Efa Heward ran an orderly household that catered to Prudence's precise scheduling. The day would start with a walk on Mount Royal with one of the several dogs that would become her constant companion. By nine o'clock she would be in her studio ready to paint. As one niece remembered it, "She always sat in a heap. And she always chewed her tongue. And she always wiped her brushes on her shoulder … By December you could hardly lift the old smock because it was so laden with paint."[6] Prudence would work straight through until lunch at one o'clock, except for a short break at eleven. The afternoon would be spent reading, taking another walk, or shopping. Defying the stereotypical notion of an artist, Prudence was a woman who visited the hairdresser twice a week, favoured fine cosmetics, and always wore the latest fashions.

For Prudence, a close-knit support group of fellow women artists would prove critical to her success. While studying at the Art Association of Montreal school as a young woman, she met her painting companion and dearest friend, Sarah Robertson, as well as fellow artists Ethel Seath, Kathleen Morris, and Anne Savage. Then, in 1921, Prudence came into contact with a larger group of Montreal artists calling themselves the Beaver Hall Hill Group of Painters. Through their informal gatherings, she met still other women who, like herself, would defy the expected traditions of marriage and children and devote their lives to their art: Nora Collyer, Emily Coonan, Mabel Lockerby, Mabel May, and Lilias Torrance Newton.

Although the Beaver Hall Group lasted for only a little over a year, its impact was significant. Unlike the Group of Seven, who were out to paint the ultimate Canadian art, the Beaver Hall Group had a much simpler goal, "To thine own self be true."[7] For Prudence and the other women, their involvement in the group marked the beginning of a lifelong support network for one another. It also introduced them to someone who would become an indispensable friend and champion of their work, A.Y. Jackson.

Alec Jackson, as he was called by close friends, was the eternal unsettled bachelor, and he would include a stop at Fernbank, the Hewards' summer home, on his visiting circuit. Each summer Efa Heward would pack up her Montreal household and settle in at the gracious home situated outside Brockville, Ontario, on the banks of the St Lawrence River. This retreat provided both a relaxing lifestyle and endless country vistas to paint. Sarah Robertson and her sisters, Marion and Elizabeth, were often welcome guests, as were Kate Morris and Anne Savage. Fernbank was also a regular summer holiday for Prudence's other close friend, Isabel McLaughlin, who lived in Toronto.

Isabel McLaughlin brought a vitality and excitement to Prudence's otherwise sheltered existence, which centred on life with her mother on Peel Street and at Fernbank. Isabel's easygoing character and her busy social and travel life offered welcome distraction and inspiration to her more serious friend. The unmarried daughter of Samuel McLaughlin, the first president of General Motors, Isabel was herself a dedicated artist. Based in Toronto, she was deeply involved in the social milieu and in exhibitions of the English Canadian art world. It was in 1929, at A.Y. Jackson's suggestion, that Prudence and Isabel met at the Ritz Carlton in Paris for tea one afternoon.

Prudence's first exposure to European culture had come eleven years earlier when her siblings – younger sister Honor and older brothers Jim and Chilion – decided to do their bit for the First World War effort. Ever the true matriarch, Efa had moved house to spend the war years in England nearer the war front and her children. Prudence, eighteen at the time, was ripe for artistic influence – and she found it in the works of the then-popular Bloomsbury Group.

The group's mentor, Roger Fry, maintained that most artists catered to a commonly held notion of any given subject rather than create a true representation of their own subjective interpretation. In Prudence Heward's landscapes such as *Gananoque*, painted many years later,

the influence of the Bloomsbury Group's individualistic style and abstract treatment can still be detected. There is a strong argument to be made that here too, in Bloomsbury, are the origins of the unflinching honesty of her portraiture. This first exposure to the European art world would have reinforced the groundwork established by the two very gifted teachers Prudence had studied with as an adolescent at the Art Association of Montreal, William Brymner and Maurice Cullen. It was Brymner who had already instilled in her the importance of individual style, of leaving her mark.

With her winnings from the Montreal Women's Art Society prize for painting, Prudence headed to Paris in 1925. The objective of this second European trip was to study painting under Charles Guérin at the Académie Colarossi and life-drawing with Bernard Naudin at the École-des-beaux-arts. Perhaps the combined effect in 1925 of having two works accepted at the world-famous Wembley Exhibition and tasting the fruits of the European academic tradition gave Prudence the assurance she needed to begin to assert her artistic vision and establish a name for herself.

Certainly, by the time of her 1929 visit to Paris and her meeting with Isabel McLaughlin, Prudence had achieved recognition on the Canadian art scene. In the previous year, she had received the highest of accolades in the male-dominated art world as an "invited contributor" to the Group of Seven show in Toronto. She was in good company. So contrary to the European tradition of landscape painting were the group's works that their first exhibitions inspired public outrage. She had also won the top prize for Canadian art, the Willingdon Prize, for her work *Girl on a Hill*, which now hangs in the National Gallery of Canada.

In Paris, over long lunches and gallery tours, Prudence and Isabel began a strong and lasting friendship. Together they attended classes at the Scandinavian Academy, one of the smaller art schools in Paris. Prudence had

29.1 *Rollande*, by Prudence Heward (Courtesy of the National Gallery of Canada)

originally planned to attend André L'Hôte's school but decided to join Isabel at the Scandinavian instead. Despite this change in plans, it is interesting that comparisons are frequently made between Prudence's work – in particular, *Rollande* (Illustration 29.1) – and works by the flamboyant Polish painter Tamara de Lempicke, whose works are definitely influenced by her studies with L'Hôte. While Lempicke's portraits and nudes lack the intense pathos of Heward's portrayal of her subjects, there is a remarkable similarity in the arrangement and treatment of the figure and the strong graphic approach.

The early 1930s would bring a series of successes to Prudence both at home and abroad. While *Rollande*, with its bold, confrontational pose and modernistic style established her name in two major American exhibitions, a succession of breakthrough works would create an even greater stir. In 1931, again an invited contributor to the Group of Seven show, Prudence unveiled *Girl under a Tree*. The clash of styles between the more traditionally painted nude in the foreground and the abstracted background was widely criticized. The truth was that the pose was considered too provocative and, worse still, the nude was painted by a woman; female nudes were then considered the exclusive territory of the male artist.

Two years later, in 1933, Prudence launched yet another volley at the art world with her painting *The Bather*. This time she shocked the critics by painting her female sitter in what was considered a most un-ladylike position – bathing-suited, open legged and seated, gazing ahead, somewhat defiantly, at the viewer. The critics – male, of course – responded with biting sarcasm: "Imagine the genius of a painter who could conceive of a woman sitting in a bathing suit, surrounded by nothing and waiting for the salad to grow."[8] The "salad" in question was a spray of water lichen nestled amongst the rocks in the foreground.

The sexual content and defiant nature of Prudence's paintings of women have elicited much debate in recent years regarding her own sexual orientation. That she painted almost exclusively women, whether clothed or naked, and with such candour, has led many to conclude that she must have been a lesbian or at least a closet lesbian. It is important to remember that, by all accounts, Prudence came from a very conservative background and that she continued to live according to those tenets throughout her life. Sexuality had not achieved the political and public profile that it has today, and it would not have been unusual for a woman of her background to live a very asexual existence. My extensive archival research and personal interviews show that, in Prudence's case, an unconsummated love affair with a certain unavailable man is much more likely. Perhaps most importantly, marriage would have meant abandoning her mother and the end of her painting career.

Along with recognition as an artist of stature on the

Canadian scene came the inevitable participation in various art groups. In 1934 a founding member of the Group of Seven, J.E.H. Macdonald, died. By this time there was a growing consensus in the group to sacrifice their exclusive stance for the sake of supporting young, promising Canadian artists. The new and expanded version was known as the Canadian Group of Painters, and Prudence Heward was a founding member. Then, in 1939, she also became a founding member of John Lyman's group, the more *avant garde* Contemporary Arts Society.

Beginning in 1936, Prudence began to accompany Isabel McLaughlin on the occasional holiday to the McLaughlin's family estate in Bermuda. The lush tropical environment and rich colours inspired her to take on a new painting challenge. Prudence's paintings of Black nudes mark the peak of her painting career. While a number of class-related issues could be raised surrounding Prudence's choice of model, it is easy to understand that an impassioned painter like Prudence would have been motivated by the artistic challenge these subjects presented to her. The superb modelling of the body and the incredible subtlety of skin tone make these outstanding works on a technical level, but the paintings are not the typically exotic or academic portraits of Black women being done by other artists at that time. These were profoundly sad, vulnerable women, depicted as being exactly who and what they were – reluctant posers who felt completely out of their element. Gone were the defiant stares and bold posturings of Prudence's earlier portrayals of women. Indeed, failing health and new tragedies in the early 1940s marked a new phase in her own life.

In 1940 Prudence was hospitalized with a serious asthma attack. Shortly afterwards she was in a car accident that left her painting arm affected and damaged her sinuses. It was becoming increasingly difficult, physically, for her to paint. Then, in 1943, a double blow fell. She

discovered that her unfailingly cheerful companion, Sarah, had been diagnosed with bone cancer. And on November 25 her sister Honor, who had been both confidante and staunch advocate of her work, committed suicide. "To me, my personal loss is so great it staggers me. Honor and I have done everything all our lives together," she wrote to her friend Isabel.[9]

Somehow managing to overcome each seemingly insurmountable obstacle, Prudence continued to paint and exhibit over the next few years. But by 1947 more drastic measures were required for her worsening asthmatic condition. She and her mother headed to Arizona, hoping that the dry climate would help. Instead they were forced to proceed directly to the Good Samaritan Hospital in Los Angeles, where Prudence died at the age of fifty-one.

In 1948 the National Gallery of Canada mounted a memorial exhibition of Prudence Heward's work. There were over a hundred sketches and canvases included in the show. A.Y. Jackson, who had once told Prudence, "You take your place amongst the best half-dozen painters in Canada,"[10] wrote the introduction to the accompanying catalogue. Illness and an early death certainly abbreviated Prudence Heward's artistic output and consequently, according to some specialists in the field, her stature as well. She also painted the familiar – those who were close to her, the surrounding countryside – and did not go off on heroic adventures to paint the "uncivilized" north, and she was a women – a distinct disadvantage in a then male-dominated profession. But the continuing retrospectives of Prudence Heward's painting and the frequent inclusion of her work in major exhibitions are testament that her art ranks among the best this country has to offer, by men or women. There is a dignity, a deep pathos, a subtlety and richness of palette in her paintings that leave the viewer profoundly moved in a way that can be achieved only by a great artist.[11]

30 Mothering the Dionne Quintuplets: Women's Stories
Katherine Arnup

The image of the Dionne Quintuplets, five identical, curly haired girls from Northern Ontario, is a familiar one to many Canadians.[1] Born in Corbeil to a poor French-Canadian family on 28 May 1934, in the midst of the worst economic depression in Canadian history, the Dionnes were the first quintuplets to survive more than a few days, and their rags-to-riches story provided hope and inspiration to millions of people across North America and, indeed, around the world.

Removed from their home and placed under the general care of the delivering physician, Dr Allen Roy Dafoe, the "Quints" became a major tourist attraction and cultural phenomenon. By 1943, an estimated three million people had travelled to Callander to view the girls at play. And for those not able to make the trip, there were countless visual images of the girls in magazines and daily newspapers across North America.[2]

So ubiquitous were the images of the quintuplets that people referred to the girls as "our babies." Canadian author Pierre Berton, thirteen at the time of their birth, noted, "I felt that I knew them."[3] Despite this feeling of familiarity, however, most people did not, in fact, know the quintuplets. Rather, they saw and heard about and read stories of the Quints, stories created by journalists, advertisers, and child-care experts. How accurate those depictions were is a subject of considerable dispute. How they affected the lives of ordinary women who identified with them is a question that can be considered by examining the historical record, especially letters from mothers found in the Allan Roy Dafoe Papers.

Capitalizing on the tremendous popularity of the quintuplets, nurses, doctors, psychologists, and midwives who had been associated with the girls all turned their hand to writing about their experiences, using their stories to offer advice to "ordinary" mothers. By far the most prolific among them was Dr Allan Roy Dafoe, the quintuplets' physician from their birth until his resignation in 1942 and, for a time, "the world's best-known doctor."[4] In addition to a 250-page guidebook for mothers and a number of smaller pamphlets on infant care, Dafoe produced some 967 columns for Hearst's King Features Syndicate, which appeared daily in over two hundred newspapers across North America.[5] His radio talks, sponsored by Lysol disinfectant, were broadcast across North America three times a week. As well, his byline appeared on countless feature articles and interviews in popular and medical magazines across the continent, and hundreds of products that carried his endorsement.

Many records reflecting these activities are available on microfilm at the Ontario Archives. Dr Dafoe was a collector, and he appears to have saved virtually every newspaper clipping and magazine article that referred to the Quints and their physician, and had them arranged in carefully prepared scrapbooks. Originally in possession of his family, the Dafoe papers were donated to the Ontario Medical Association (OMA) in 1978; in 1981 the OMA allowed the Province of Ontario Archives to micro-

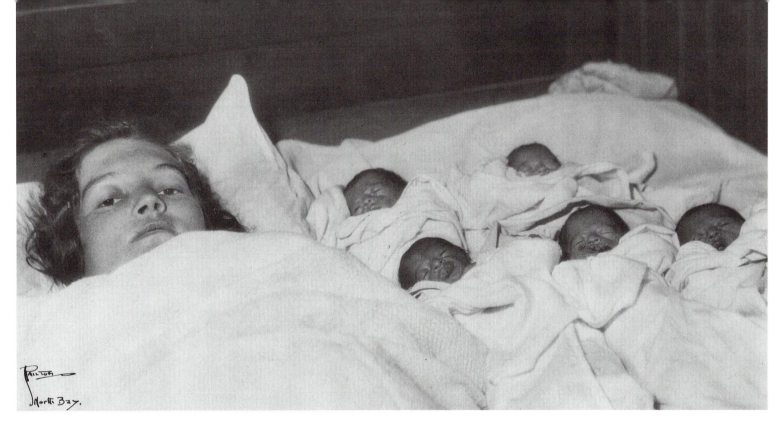

film the collection, thus making it available to a much larger group of researchers. The papers contain extensive medical records, correspondence, photographs, articles, scrapbooks, newspaper columns, and radio scripts, as well as background materials for Dafoe's writing.[6] They provide an amazing record for researchers, not only of the quintuplets, but of Canadian life and politics in the 1930s and 1940s.

For those researching the history of women, the records are particularly noteworthy, for they contain dozens of letters from ordinary mothers trying to raise their children. In this regard, the Dafoe Papers mirror other archival collections. During the interwar years, in a time when mothers found their traditional maternal skills and networks increasingly under attack, women sought the advice of prominent child-care experts. In a phenomenon that seems almost unthinkable today, women wrote tens of thousands of personal letters to public figures like Dr Helen MacMurchy, chief of the

Federal Division of Child Welfare; Charlotte Whitton, director of the Canadian Council on Child and Family Welfare; and Dr Benjamin Spock, author of the best-selling *Baby and Child Care*. And, even more surprisingly perhaps, many of the experts responded, offering personal advice on a vast array of problems. Dr Dafoe, as the personal physician to the world-famous quintuplets, was no exception.

An exploration of the Dafoe correspondence reveals aspects of the preoccupations, concerns, and practices of Canadian mothers during the interwar years. Over the course of the quintuplets' first year, when their health was in jeopardy, many of the letters offered traditional home remedies on infant care; the cure for "summer complaint," for example, ranged from "saffaras [*sic*] tea and catnip tea" to "rye."[7] Once their health was on a more stable footing, however, the majority of writers sought advice in the care and feeding of their own children. Ruby Dunham of Vancouver was typical of those

30.1 Dionne Quints with Elzire Dionne, their mother, shortly after birth, 1934 (C 9-6, Davis-Leroux Collection, box 4, Archives of Ontario)

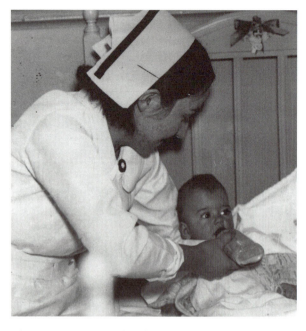

30.2 One of the Dionne Quints being fed, 1934 (C 9-6, Davis-Leroux Collection, box 4, Archives of Ontario)

who wrote to Dr Dafoe: "We have followed with great interest the progress of the Quintuplets … and consider their growth marvellous, so like everybody else we wondered if we could get a little advise [sic] from their doctor."[8] Mrs Lee Wadleigh of Evanston, Illinois, wrote to Dr Dafoe about her son's terrible temper: "I have written before but understand you have so many, many letters that is taking time to read them all, only please try and read this for I feel sure you are the only one who can help me with this problem that is facing me."[9] For many women living in isolated locations, far from friends and family, unable to afford a doctor's visit, this assessment may very well have been accurate. One mother, living in the mountains near Boulder, Colorado, wrote Dafoe a note of thanks for his radio programs: "I have no one to advise me on the care of my three babies, and surely do appreciate your help … Your talks have helped me to care for my ten-month-old baby and also to manage Lunelle and Jimmy who are five and four."[10]

It would appear that these women were not disappointed, for many of the letters to Dafoe expressed gratitude for the help his columns and radio programs brought them. "Words can't express what your messages mean to people in this world if they mean as much to all others as they do to me," wrote another avid radio listener.[11] "I'm sure you don't realize how much we mothers enjoy your kindly radio talks," Mrs Floyd Yates wrote, in a letter asking for help with her daughter's delayed speech.[12] "Just a Granny," a woman from Salem, Massachusetts, with two daughters who were mothers of young children wrote: "Your morning talks seem to be an inspiration and without saying anything [my daughters] begin at once to put your advice into practice."[13]

Despite the help, or perhaps even because of it, mothers frequently expressed shame and guilt about their children's problems, interpreting their own difficulties as an indication of their personal failings as mothers. "An anxious mother" of a three-year-old girl who did not talk "as well as she should" confessed that "I know this is my fault and would like some advice how to overcome this."[14] A Minnesota woman, who was "absolutely ashamed to confess" that she could not get her eighteen-month-old son out of diapers, admitted, "I truthfully believe that it is my fault."[15] "Maybe," she added, "I should have begun earlier – but I didn't have foresight enough for that and let it slide, I'm afraid." Mrs Robert Averbeck, another regular radio listener, wrote: "I try to do everything I think is right for my baby, but since it is my first child I sometimes feel as though I'm doing everything wrong."[16] For these women at least, it appears that the experts' counsel served to increase their feelings of guilt, rather than to provide them with much needed reassurance and help. Already separated from their own mothers by geography and by generation, they may have found that the experts' systematic attacks on "old wives' tales" merely exacerbated their sense of isolation. Perhaps not surprisingly, then, even the mother

30.3 Nurse preparing food for Quints, 1934 (C 9-6, Davis-Leroux Collection, box 4, Archives of Ontario)

who felt she was doing "everything wrong" told Dr Dafoe, "I never miss your broadcasts and believe I've learned more from them than from all the advice given by friends and relatives."[17]

To draw upon the recollections of contemporary women, I sought out another group of mothers: the women who donated breast milk to the babies.[18] From their fourth day of life until they reached the age of five months, the quintuplets were fed breast milk donated by nursing mothers. Initially, the services of a Chicago hospital were used, but soon milk depots at Toronto's Hospital for Sick Children and Montreal's Royal Victoria Hospital were able to supply the necessary milk. The bulk of the milk came from Toronto, where the task of collecting the milk was done by members of the Junior League. "The milk was pooled at the Hospital for Sick Children, boiled, bottled, refrigerated until evening, packed in ice, and shipped by train to Callander."[19] By five months of age, the girls were consuming a gallon of breast milk a day, an amount too large for even the two major Canadian hospitals to supply![20]

I have always been fascinated with the story of the women who decided, shortly after giving birth themselves, to donate their excess breast milk to the Quints. The challenge was to find them. There was no record of their names, and since nearly sixty years had elapsed, they would be at least eighty, if not closer to ninety, years old. To overcome these obstacles, I submitted a query to the "Have Your Say" section of the *Sunday Star* (Toronto), asking for letters from women who had donated breast milk. Within days, I had received more than a dozen responses.

Not surprisingly, given the passage of time, I heard primarily from relatives and children of donors, rather than from the women themselves. One woman, whose mother (now deceased) had donated breast milk, was born two days before the Quints and her mother's doctor and Dr Dafoe's brother (also a doctor) were friends. "I'm afraid I don't know any more about this, except that the money my mother received helped our family, as my father was unemployed at the time."[21] I heard as well from the sister and the widower of donors, as well as from a student nurse who had worked in the nursery and from two women who had donated milk themselves. One of the donors, whose first child was born on 10 June 1934, recalls her involvement with the quintuplets. "The head nurse came to my bedside and asked if I would be interested in feeding the famous quintuplets … I thought it was a wonderful contribution I could make but when I found out I was to be paid, I was really excited." While her husband was fortunate to retain his job during the Depression, the money she received – ten cents an ounce – was a great help to her family.[22] While the women were reimbursed for their efforts, the letters would suggest that the payment was not the women's primary motivation. They were simply pleased to be able to play some role in the miracle of the quintuplets. As one mother recalled, "I suppose my part in the lives of the quints was minimal but it was a small satisfaction for me – and a fun thing for our family."[23]

In addition to these letters, I received an assortment of other responses, including a framed photograph of the Quints that had been hanging in the owner's basement for nearly sixty years and a phone call from the president of the Quintuplets' Fan Club. The strangest of all was an unsigned letter, pencilled all in capital letters:

Where [sic] you there when they were born? My brother, husband and midwife were first to see them. They called the doctor [Dr Dafoe]. He would not come at first because no money, but when he heard there were 3 and more on the way. They were all born before he got their [sic]. I got proof. We pick Mr. Dionne every morning to work on H.Way. The Doc. would not come to my brother's wife, when she was in labour[.] No Money. My family and friends lived all around Corbeil. They will tell you the same. Doc look after Quints because, he knew that there would be money.

Clearly, for this woman at least, her own experiences belied Dr Dafoe's image as the friendly Country Doctor.

As the responses to my query reveal, sixty-five years after their birth the Dionne Quintuplets still hold an enormous popular appeal. For many, they represent the innocence and joy of childhood and the wondrous possibilities of human life; for others, the miracles of science and modern medicine; and for still others, the illusive promise of fame and riches. And now, with their recent successful financial claim against the Ontario government, they also hold out the possibility that the "little guy" can really triumph against the state. Their story, I suspect, is one that will be told time and time again.

31 Saving Mothers and Babies: Motherhood, Medicine, and the Modern State, 1900–1945

Cynthia R. Camacchio

ORGANIZING FOR CHILD WELFARE: THE PROBLEM AND PROPOSED SOLUTIONS

"To glorify, dignify, and purify motherhood, by every means in our power": In the early years of the twentieth century, Dr Helen MacMurchy used these stirring words to rally Canadians behind a crusade to save mothers and infants from preventable illness and death. As a long-time public health activist, the author of the Ontario Board of Health's critical series of infant mortality reports (1910–13), and the first chief of the Child Welfare Division of the federal government's new health department (1919), MacMurchy was ideally positioned to make this call to arms. While contemporary statistics are scarce and unreliable, they indicate that annually one infant in five fell to common respiratory and intestinal ailments in the first twelve months of life. MacMurchy's own *Report on Maternal Mortality* (1928) revealed that approximately fifteen hundred Canadian mothers were lost to complications of childbirth every year. The statistics also confirmed that this was a class mortality, afflicting primarily the ill-fed, ill housed, often recently arrived families of workers.

The joint campaign for child and maternal welfare – the two issues so entwined that they were commonly discussed under the single heading "child welfare" – unfolded within a larger international campaign and was thus closely modelled on earlier initiatives in the United States, Great Britain, and France. As in these nations, the reform-minded volunteers directing Canadian efforts were concerned about deteriorating public health and social conditions in a time of rapid, disruptive socio-economic change.[1] The furious pace of expanding industry, unplanned urbanization, and mass immigration, appeared to be leading the young dominion down a path of social degeneration. Mostly urban, middle class, and Euro-Canadian, whether English or French speaking, Protestant or Catholic, many participants in the Christian activism that fuelled the period's Social Gospel reform campaigns recognized that the scope and nature of the problems they identified were beyond even the most dedicated voluntarist efforts. The "slaughter of the innocents" entailed in the problem of infant mortality could best be approached through a "scientific program" devised jointly by the medical profession and government agencies.

By the early 1900s, international bacteriological research on infant death had pinpointed its three leading causes: prematurity and congenital debility, intestinal disorders, and respiratory diseases.[2] Because medicine remained far more effective in its preventive than its curative aspects, focusing on intestinal disorders seemed the most practical and promising strategy. Doctors maintained that most of these illnesses, often called "summer complaint" because their incidence peaked during that season, were directly attributable to the spreading practice of bottle feeding. More and more women, they charged, were "shirking" their maternal –

31.1 Baby Clinic, 1914 (RG 8-32-334, City of Toronto Archives)

and "patriotic" – breastfeeding duties. The "problem" thus defined could be readily assailed through public education, attempts to regulate the milk supply, and the combined efforts of volunteers and municipal public health departments.[3]

While pasteurization was not effected in most Canadian communities until the 1930s, growing public concern about infant mortality sparked organized attempts to clean up the milk supply, or at least to provide pure milk for the most vulnerable. Babies' dispensaries or milk depots, called "Gouttes de lait" in Quebec, were modelled on their late nineteenth-century counterparts in Britain, France, and the United States. Organized women, including such groups as the National Council of Women, the rural Women's Institutes, the Imperial Order Daughters of the Empire (IODE), the Assistance maternelle, the Fondation nationale de St Jean-Baptiste

(FNSJB), and the Cercles fermières in Quebec, inaugurated related programs involving home visitors (usually municipal nurses, but sometimes volunteers), supervisory baby clinics, public lectures on child care, and "Little Mothers" classes in schools. Some groups arranged medical assistance for poor mothers in childbirth and housekeeping and nursing help during the traditional ten-day "laying-in" period after birth, as well as furnishing layettes for babies. By 1915, in most urban areas the original babies' dispensaries had evolved into general clinics for the supervision and maintenance of the health of infants and preschool children.

What really turned public attention towards infant mortality and intensified calls for state involvement was Dr Helen MacMurchy's series of infant mortality reports, published by the Ontario government between 1910 and 1913. Shocking Canadians across the land, Mac-

Murchy revealed that in 1909 death had claimed 6,932 children under one year of age in the nation's wealthiest province, or more than 10 per cent of the 52,629 children born that year. Toronto alone suffered 230 deaths per 1,000 live births. This mortality may have been associated primarily with intestinal diseases, but as MacMurchy argued, it stemmed from a wide range of societal causes. Ignorance, poverty, and inadequate medical assistance were the most important of these. Her ultimate conclusion was that "[n]ational action, government action, collective action, not individual action, can save the baby."[4] The first systematic, large-scale surveys of the extent and nature of the problem, MacMurchy's reports effectively redirected the campaign.

The second major turning point for organized child welfare was the Great War. The casualties of war, affecting some sixty thousand "young men in their prime" and "future fathers of the race," magnified concerns about "race suicide" and the depletion of "the better stock," as white Anglo-Celtic middle-class Canadians classified themselves according to the racist categories of the day. The voluntarist efforts on the part of women's organizations were helpful but simply insufficient. In the wake of war and the social turmoil that it brought, the "crisis in the family" demanded a state-funded and professionally directed program of regulation to ensure the health of prospective mothers, who would then produce an abundance of healthy infants. This program would also foster the "proper" nurture, maintenance, and socialization of these infants, to assure the future health and well-being of the nation.

Since the problem of child welfare was defined in terms of "health" in its broadest sense – physical, mental, moral, social, economic – then who better to lead these noble efforts than the members of the newly organized, newly scientific (as they proclaimed themselves) medical profession? Doctors played a crucial role in delineating both the period's targets of social and moral reform and the means to approach these.[5] The Great War experience renewed public commitment to "regeneration" through social reform, especially in regard to the health and welfare of families. Canadians, who saw the federal government manage the war economy and extend that management to "philanthropic" concerns such as the maintenance of soldiers' dependants through the Canadian Patriotic Fund, were impressed by the peacetime possibilities of such state intervention.

By the war's end in 1918, child welfare had become a joint enterprise of the medical profession and newly created agencies at the municipal, provincial, and federal levels of government. Women continued to help in their voluntary capacity, largely by supporting and promoting the government campaigns based on a combination of free educational literature, visiting public health nurses, and Well Baby Clinics. The campaign's leadership, however, was firmly in the hands of medical professionals and state agencies. The exception was Quebec, where a historic anti-statism and the traditional social involvement of the Roman Catholic Church permitted a continuing leadership role for women that was not matched anywhere in English Canada.[6]

INFANT HEALTH AND FAMILY POVERTY: THEORIES AND CONCLUSIONS

Many of the early assessments of the Canadian infant mortality problem reflected the social and medical considerations of the British and American studies inspiring them. They repeated a complicated and confused logic that recognized the link between poverty and ill health, yet refused to see poverty itself as the primary cause.[7] Many Canadian families of the time were barely able to get by on the wages of a sole breadwinner. In the Dominion Bureau of Statistics' estimation, a "decent family budget" required about $95 per month for necessary expenses. Approximately 46 per cent of the labour force of seven major industries earned less than $20 per week in 1918. At this time, under the fee-for-service health-care system, a doctor's attention cost at least $5, not including drugs or dental care. Medical attendance at childbirth ranged from $15 to $25, constituting a full week's wages for many male breadwinners.

As the child welfare campaign expanded and flourished across Canada during the interwar decades, doctors persistently discounted environmental factors in high infant and maternal mortality. They were also inclined to downplay, ignore, or dismiss the simple fact that all too many Canadian women either did not have access to or could not afford medical care during pregnancy, childbirth, and the critical first twelve months of the infant's life. Isolated women in northern resource communities, in coastal fishing villages, on the sparsely settled prairies, and on subsistence farms in eastern Ontario and Quebec, aboriginal women on impoverished reserves, African-Canadian women, and many recently arrived eastern and southern European and Asian immigrants struggling in urban ghettos – these mothers were fortunate if they had the assistance of family and friends at delivery, and even more so if they were attended by an experienced midwife.

The economic collapse occasioned by the Great Depression naturally made matters worse for families already living on the margins. Identifying herself as "A Worried Expectant Mother," a woman from Wabewawa [Northern Ontario] wrote a heart-wrenching letter to the federal health department in 1932. She assured officials who were undoubtedly inured to such pleas that she was not writing to beg food or clothing, "though I am in need of both." As she told it, the "thing that worries me the most" was her imminent delivery. By the age of twenty-five, she had borne five children in as many years, all without medical help – at great cost to her health and much risk to the infants. No doctor would

come to her isolated homestead for less than twenty-five dollars, a sum far beyond her family's means. "It is a tragic thing," she concluded, "that the mothers of the land must suffer." Many similarly plaintive personal stories from across the nation provide stark testimony to the very real relationship between material circumstances and individual and familial health.[8]

Successive lobbying attempts by organized women, including farm and labour groups, led to heated debate in medical and state circles respecting the need for trained midwives in isolated areas, state-supported health units in sparsely settled districts, government-salaried physicians and dentists in these areas, maternity benefits so that pregnant and nursing women would not be obliged to work outside the home, and national health insurance to offset the high costs of medical care. Midwifery was a particularly contentious issue, despite the obvious need. The Canadian Medical Association's political influence ensured that midwives remained outlawed, as they had been in most Canadian communities since the late nineteenth century. With the exception of Saskatchewan's experiment with salaried rural physicians and Ontario's medical relief program, both necessitated by the Depression emergency, few public initiatives on behalf of mothers and children materialized before the Second World War. Neither organized women nor farm and labour groups had the political representation and influence necessary to persuade governments to take action that smacked of "state medicine" in a time of ambivalence about state intervention and of adamant opposition by organized medicine to any perceived threat to private practice.

Consequently, the official stand of the medical profession and government health agencies did not waver throughout these years, even in the face of stark evidence. They insisted that the explanation for high infant mortality lay with maternal ignorance. The poor were providing the victim's sanction by refusing to take responsibility for their own health and welfare and that of their children. They had to be made responsible by means of "a better and broader education in all that relates to the child and child life." Paradoxically, while mothers were the source of the problem, they were also its principal solution. What they needed was the guidance and supervision of doctors, foremost among the coterie of new "family experts."[9]

SCIENTIFIC MOTHERHOOD: TRAINING MOTHERS AND INFANTS

The response to the crisis in the family, therefore, was the promotion of a maternalism depicted as regenerative while operating in a fundamentally regulatory manner. Medicine and the state would see that mothers were "educated," that they were, in effect, modernized, upgraded, reformed, so that families could meet the needs of modern industrial society while preserving their traditional form and relationships.[10] If mothers accepted their "national duty," they could minimize "inefficiency and waste" at their source by improving the health of their children through expert-designed scientific child-care methods. Once physical welfare was assured in infancy, mothers could manage and train their children all along the path to healthy, productive, and efficient adulthood.[11] By promoting and facilitating "scientific motherhood," the state could best do its work "to see that the rights of the children are not ignored and that the mothers have the opportunity given them of learning how best to rear their children." The result would be a modern Canada defined by the favourable – rather than the adverse – implications of modernity: progress, efficiency, productivity, and the triumph of reason signified by advances in science and technology. The enthusiastic maternalist platforms of various reform organizations, women's groups, and voluntary agencies, together with the establishment of a federal

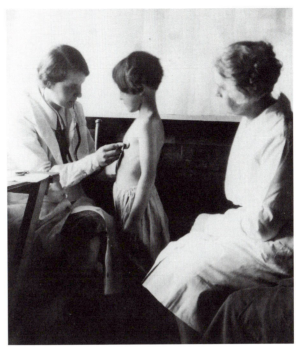

31.2 Health test in rural community (RG 16-274, album 3, p. 11, Archives of Ontario)

health department and various provincial divisions with stated commitments to child welfare by the early 1920s, facilitated popular acceptance of attempts to "modernize" motherhood.

The clinics, home nursing visits, and advice literature that became the campaign's hallmark service, were meant to complement but never to replace regular attendance by the family physician, despite the fact that most of the client families could not avail themselves of such medical care. The campaign's foremost advice to all classes of mothers was that they should see their doctors regularly and take no counsel from non-professional, traditional sources, such as their own network of family, friends, and neighbours. The clinics were purely diagnostic and advisory. No treatment was permitted. Mothers were often required to have the written permission of their regular physician before attending. Nurse visits to homes were also advisory in nature and limited to "demonstration" of child-care techniques in order to impress upon mothers the value of raising children and keeping house in the sanctioned "scientific" way, the only "proper" way. Child welfare nurses were kept under close surveillance by the public health departments for any suspected overstepping of bounds, usually respecting artificial feeding, which was supposed to be by doctor's prescription only. And disclaimers were published on every item in the extensive body of government-produced parenting literature to the effect that, while "expert" in origin, this information was meant to serve as a "guideline" only. Mothers were repeatedly warned that each individual case demanded the personal attention and specific consultation of the physician.

Through the medium of advice literature, predominantly medical in authorship or at least in inspiration, directives for "perfect parenting" were issued. During the interwar years, advice literature was produced apace by medical professionals and by new health and welfare agencies at all levels of government in conjunction with private insurance companies and voluntarist health and social service organizations. It was further popularized in the advice columns and "women's pages" of mass-circulation magazines and newspapers, through government-produced radio shows and short films, and by public health nurses who held "demonstrations" at baby clinics and in homes. The advice strove to establish doctors as maternal mentors, to associate maternalism with national interest, and to reformulate motherhood and consequently childhood.[12] Science and state lent the weight of their combined authority to social constructions depicting the ideal mother, the ideal child, and ideal family relationships.

While disparaging modern women, the advice literature nonetheless called for the creation of a new, improved, scientific mother, a thoroughly modern mother befitting the new industrial order. "Management," an almost uniquely masculine role, was the core concept of the experts' child-rearing program. Just as "efficiency" and "productivity" became keywords of modern industry, scientific management ideas were transferred to the home. Modern motherhood was infused with the spirit of industry, with its unrelenting demands for regularity, repetition, scheduling, systematization, discipline, and productivity. Effective maternal management of children, it was hoped, would quickly transform them into "little machines." The tremendous public admiration for science and technology made this a noble objective: the machine represented the most evolved human type.

The role of the state, meanwhile, was given much rhetorical significance, but in practice, it was always cautiously defined. Governments at all levels, but mainly municipal and provincial, gradually expanded their participation in the child welfare campaign during the interwar years. State involvement, however, was restricted to the administration and direction of educational measures. While child welfare advocates promoted the idea of the child as "national asset," they did not intend this to mean that the state was directly responsible for the health of mothers and children; it meant, instead, a new obligation on the part of mothers regarding their duty to the nation.

Maternal education was not the easy way out so much as it was an approach that fitted the limitations of its proponents' position and outlook. It allowed doctors greater scope for their professional authority. Just as important, it upheld traditional concepts of feminine roles at a time when political enfranchisement and new opportunities in education and employment were challenging those constructs. Motherhood was a science, "a profession of the highest order," not a mere biological or instinctual function. As physicians argued, "Intelligent motherhood alone can give to the infant that which neither wealth nor state nor yet science can offer with equal benefit to mother or child." The goal of scientific motherhood dictated the direction that the campaign would take and the nature of its measures throughout its course. In a wider sense, this goal also shaped new relationships between doctors and mothers, mothers and children, and ultimately, women, the family, and the state.

CONCLUSION: EFFECTS AND PROSPECTS

By the end of the Depression decade, the child welfare campaign was diminishing in intensity. The massive reorganization necessitated by the outbreak of the Second World War meant that governments at every level focused their resources on the war effort. This war, too, would nonetheless prove an important breakthrough. The combination of the Depression experience, full-scale state intervention for the war effort, and public pressure about postwar reconstruction pushed and pulled the nation towards the welfare state. It seemed that Canadians who had suffered through the 1930s with minimal state assistance were not going to sacrifice themselves and their children in another war unless money could also be found to better their lives during peacetime.

Mackenzie King's Liberal government was at last prepared to consider the need for effective, coherent social security legislation. McGill University social scientist Leonard Marsh was asked to prepare a report for the House of Commons Committee on Reconstruction and Rehabilitation. Marsh's *Report on Social Security for Canada*, presented to the committee in 1943, attempted to establish a justifiable social minimum for all Canadians. The report proclaimed that children "should have an unequivocal place in social security policy." After much criticism and consternation, the Family Allowances Act was passed in 1944. Produced the same year as the Marsh Report, Dr J.J. Heagerty's health insurance recommendations for the Committee on Reconstruction, with their comprehensive measures for health insurance and public health grants, were largely jettisoned because of the perpetual inability of the provin-

cial and federal governments to agree on fiscal terms. Moreover, if their own Depression experience encouraged some doctors to look favourably on state medicine, the majority continued to insist that complete state control of health-care services would undermine the quality of medical care and consequently the health status of the people. Further measures would have to await the economic affluence and "baby boom" of the 1950s.

The maternalist ideals at the basis of the child welfare campaign affected the way that Canadians regarded motherhood and the way that governments shaped social policy. But neither these ideals nor government attempts to regulate maternity necessarily made women the passive and submissive "patients" that doctors wanted them to be. Far from simply taking in the entire "modern motherhood package" presented by the new experts, women themselves recognized the limits of these ideas and practices. Ultimately, the way that most women in this period raised their children had more to do with the material circumstances of their lives, and how these constrained their choices, than with any amount of advice or medical supervision provided through baby clinics, nurse visits, and, especially, the heaps of free literature. Most women did not resist their definition as mothers, and many responded gratefully to medical instruction and supervision; but they also wanted tangible help in the form of affordable health care for themselves and their families. They believed that such assistance was owed to them by the state as a right of citizenship.[13] Maternalist politics failed, however, to deliver on promises to have organized medicine and the state serve as joint guardians of the beleaguered modern family.

The improvement in the mortality indices during the interwar years was real, though it masked the extent to which class and regional inequalities persisted. Peaking at 5.8 per 1,000 live births in 1930, maternal mortality was 4 per 1,000 a decade later, at that time the lowest point ever in Canada. Starting in 1926, the infant mortality rate declined even more sharply. By 1940, it had dropped 45.1 per cent, signifying 11,100 lives saved. In Ontario, the rate was 76 per 1,000 in 1920 and 49 per 1,000 in 1940. Even taking into account the multiple contributory factors, including the great strides in medical therapeutics with the introduction of sulphonamides, antibiotics, and incubators by the late 1930s, the return of prosperity probably had the most significant effect on the health of Canadians of all ages. The postwar boom obviously did not eliminate class, gender, and regional disparities, but the improvement in real income was felt by more people than ever before.[14]

The child and maternal welfare campaign of the early twentieth-century contributed significantly to the ongoing trend towards increasing "expert" authority and state intervention. Doctors and nurses acquired new status and influence as government consultants. Moreover, as doctors increasingly persuaded parents to look to them in childrearing matters, their power to influence social customs expanded. By the Second World War, the care of expectant and parturient women and their children was firmly in the hands of the medical profession, a monopoly over health services only challenged within the past few years. Institutionalized childbirth and child-care supervision became the social norm for middle-class women and, increasingly, for their working-class sisters. Hospital births were the experience of the majority of Canadian mothers by the mid-1950s, and remain so.

Saving babies and modernizing mothers required, first, public recognition of the mother-centredness of national welfare; second, maternal education and supervision by an emerging coterie of child-rearing professionals, especially doctors, public health nurses, child psychologists and social workers; and ultimately, in order to sustain and promote the first two requirements, the subtle process of state regulation. Doubtless many women and children gained from services provided under the aegis of state child and maternal welfare divisions, limited as these were. However, in striving towards the twin goals of saving babies and modernizing mothers, doctors gave scientific authorization to traditional gender roles and the traditional family, supported by the power of the state.[15] Despite their evident inadequacies in the face of the socio-cultural changes that have unfolded since Dr Helen MacMurchy first issued her pleas for collective action on behalf of Canadian mothers and children, these understandings of gender, motherhood, family, and the state's role in child welfare have tended to persist.

PART THREE

Teaching and Learning

32 Introduction

Nicole Neatby

As with many fields of history we study today, the history of women's education is a relatively recent one. Publications started emerging at a steady rate in the mid-1970s when converging developments around that time inspired historians in greater numbers to ask questions about women's educational past. At a societal level, the second wave of the women's movement encouraged several historians to turn their study to this neglected field. Their efforts not only fill a void in our understanding of the past, but also explain in part present-day women's status and experiences. In the sub-field of the history of education more generally, many historians began to apply stimulating questions, findings, and approaches of social history. Until the 1970s, historians of education had focused their attention mainly on the history of institutions, laws, and public policy, usually quite divorced from wider social developments. By the late 1960s, an effort was made to draw more explicitly the links between the world of education and society, communities, and families, including women.

The practitioners of this "new education history" or "revisionist" approach rejected a fundamental tenet of traditional education history, which assumed that the evolution of education has consisted of a succession of victories over ignorance, of improvements that have led to remarkable present-day accomplishments that will give way to an even greater future. Revisionist historians of education in the 1970s did not believe that the road of education had necessarily always progressed upwards.

Historians of women's education felt particularly comfortable with this analytical framework. The study of the past made it clear that, as far as women were concerned, progress was either slow in coming or non-existent. Some schools and most universities only reluctantly opened their doors to women as teachers, professors, and students, and when they did, the classroom often continued to perpetuate negative, confining stereotypes about women's abilities and social roles.

One of the first questions that attracted the attention of historians of women's education revolved around the status of women elementary public school teachers. These women were at the centre of a fascinating and puzzling development, and their plight illustrated quite starkly the gender inequalities that characterized the field of education. During the second half of the nineteenth century and in the early decades of the twentieth, women slowly, yet steadily, replaced the majority of male primary public school teachers, earning salaries considerably less than the men's, as they were needed to fill the lower echelons of a rapidly expanding school system. This phenomenon begged for an explanation and raised interesting issues for historians ready to question Whiggish interpretations of the past.

Visual documentation of women public school teachers, particularly those in one-room rural settings, is reasonably common in archival collections. The visual images provide evidence of the centrality of the school and its teacher in the social and cultural fabric of the

32.1 One-room school, Ukrainian settlement, Alberta, 1909 (F 1075-9-0-11, Archives of Ontario)

rural community. The school often doubled as a meeting hall, an exhibition space for school fairs and agricultural exhibits, and a social clubhouse. In Illustration 32.1, a one-room schoolhouse dominated by girls in a Ukrainian settlement of Alberta in 1909 attests to young women's interest in joining the circle of the formally educated. In Illustration 32.2, Native young women receive instruction in spinning as part of a domestic science course. The young female teacher in Illustration 32.3 posed with her prized bicycle and her pupils, some of whom match her in size, if not maturity, in this rural scene from the Gordon Township School on Manitoulin Island, Ontario, *circa* 1900. Further evidence of the importance of the young female teacher in her one-room schoolhouse is provided by Pat Trites in essay #39, a reminiscence of Shamrock School at Fardy's Cross, Newfoundland.

Two of the first historians to study the issue of public schools' feminization were Alison Prentice and Marta Danylewycz, who focused on Ontario and Quebec teachers respectively.[1] They suggested that school boards' desire to save money was a key factor as the staffing requirements of large urban schools increased and school systems became more bureaucratized and hierarchical. Over the years, new findings have led these historians and others to qualify their interpretations and take into account a wider range of factors behind the feminization of elementary teaching. Indeed, Prentice notes that "although gender was clearly a powerful force, other factors were also important as communities made decisions about who should teach in their local schools." Thus, for instance, regional differences emerged in historical analyses. Historians discovered that poor rural areas were quicker to hire women than urban centres and that communities with immigrant men were less likely to take on women teachers.[2]

More recently, scholars such as Susan Gelman have noted a comparable development at the public high school level as of the 1870s in Ontario.[3] In her essay, "Educators Confront the 'Feminization' of the High School" (#36), Gelman confirms that despite a stubborn reluctance to expose young male students to female teachers at the high school level, school boards, heavily burdened with financial difficulties and expanding enrolments, eventually overcame their misgivings. By 1905, 23 per cent of collegiate institute and high school teachers were women.[4] Just as in the case of elementary school teachers, budgetary constraints encouraged officials to revisit earlier assumptions about appropriate gender requirements in the classroom. Women were frequently hired to teach extension courses to adults. Illustration 32.4, for example, shows a female teacher instructing a class of adult learners in Nova Scotia on the intricacies of mathematics. However, as Gelman makes clear, many efforts were made by male educators to reverse the feminizing trend in secondary education. Their lack of success speaks to women's ability to take

Clockwise from top left:
32.2 Women learning to spin, Prince Rupert–Queen Charlotte Islands, c. 1900 (B-03573, British Columbia Archives)

32.3 Gordon Township School, Manitoulin Island, 1900 (C-119-1-0-0-14, Archives of Ontario)

32.4 Adult education class (1966-277, Nova Scotia Archives and Records Management)

advantage of the new opportunities before them, but it also reveals the arduous road faced by women at a time when many men concluded that high school teaching was "no longer considered a respectable occupation."[5] Women did not respond to these attitudes with passivity. Women teachers, in particular, have spoken out against the way they were treated in the profession.[6]

Women's history scholars have also been drawn to tell the story of women who have been excluded from various educational institutions during the nineteenth century and part of the twentieth, specifically institutions of higher learning. These historians, have recounted how pioneer women fought for admission to universities across the country.[7] While women started to attend universities in the 1870s, admittance at the various professional schools, such as medical and law schools, came later. Yet, although university administrators eventually agreed to co-education, they nonetheless maintained a traditional understanding of gender roles. Indeed, many educators argued that university-educated men needed the company of well-educated wives and mothers, and that an undergraduate degree for capable young women who could afford tuition could serve that purpose. Occasionally, these well-educated women carved out a space for themselves in the educational enterprise – such was the achievement of Isabel Murphy Skelton, historian and textbook author. Beyond this, however, the idea of a professional education for women clearly challenged many strongly held assumptions about women's roles as wife and mother, and thus admission to academic professional schools and to disciplines less accommodating to women's demands proved much more difficult to obtain.[8] The Microbiology 11 class shown in Illustration 32.5 at the University of Montreal in 1947 is an example of the fact that even if women were reluctantly admitted to classes, the instructors were male.

The study of women's higher education has opened up many other ancillary avenues of research, that have fur-

32.5 Microbiology lab, 1947
(PA 162818, National Archives of Canada)

ther enriched our understanding of society's attitudes towards women – some changing, others remaining stubbornly resilient. Thus, for instance, in order to make sense of university administrations' long-standing opposition to the admission of female students, women's historians have explored the history of psychology and medicine. Opponents of university co-education from these fields once argued that the rigours of a higher education would put women's health in jeopardy, even threatening their reproductive functions. Furthermore, in asking why women wanted a university education, historians have examined the world of women and work and more specifically women and the professions.[29] Anna Lathrop, for instance, in essay #41, provides telling examples of the pioneering experiences of women entering the male-dominated field of physical education.

Historians have also discovered that even when women were accepted into the male preserves of higher education, their experiences on campus and in the classroom revealed that they were not considered the equals of their male colleagues. Alyson King, in essay #34, doc-

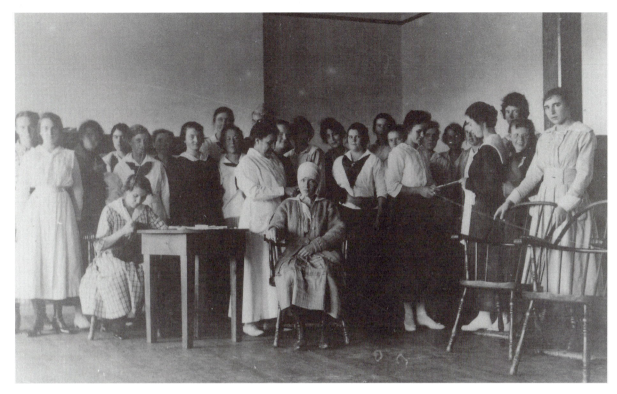

uments the differences in the male and female experiences in a comparative study of several Ontario universities.[10] Also in this volume, Jean O'Grady explores one distinctive element of a university woman's social and academic life, that of the authoritative role model, the dean of women (#35). One of the most memorable, Margaret Addison, stirred the pride and aspirations of young women when she addressed them as "Women of the University."

Very early on, women's history scholars, along with their colleagues in other areas of education, appreciated the extent to which children and adults learn outside the classroom environment. This has proven to be all the more true in the case of young girls and women, since they were excluded for so long from so many settings in which formal education took place. As a result of this exclusion, many young girls and women turned to private and voluntary associations and clubs for instruc-

tion and self-improvement. Thus, women's education historians have had to further extend their net of inquiry to study the initiatives of groups such as the Girl Guides and Canadian Girls in Training, described in essay #33 by Patricia Dirks. The 4-H Clubs, Junior Farmers, and Women's Institutes all provided education in Home Economics, first aid (Illustration 32.6), and financial management for farm women. One self-improving example is the reading room provided by the Imperial Order Daughters of the Empire between 1939 and 1945 in Halifax, Nova Scotia, shown in Illustration 32.7. Both the IODE and its sister organization, the Woman's Christian Temperance Union (WCTU), were founded in the nineteenth century but remained active throughout the twentieth. Both were concerned with self-education, one purpose being to reach others through extracurricular networks. In addition to reading rooms, which were a common initiative of many women's groups, the WCTU

PLEDGE.

I hereby promise, by the help of God, to abstain from the use of all intoxicating liquors, including wine, beer, and cider, as a beverage, and from the use of tobacco in any form, and from all profanity.

Top:

32.7 Volunteers at the IODE library, c. 1939 (PA 135178, National Archives of Canada)

Bottom:

32.8 WCTU pledge card, early twentieth century (MU 8397-3, WCTU fonds, Archives of Ontario)

focused its attention on childhood "purity" education. One instance of the WCTU's educational efforts is shown in Illustration 32.8: a WCTU pledge card through which users of alcohol, tobacco, or foul language forswore such intemperate behaviours.[11]

In addition to women's education historians shedding light on these other centres of learning for women, they have also explored the extent to which women are affected not only by issues of gender in the education world, but also by issues of class and ethnicity. Not all women were excluded from society's educational "services" in the same way or to the same extent. Enriched by the analysis of the various social history approaches and interpretations, historians have explored the impact of poverty and minority status on the individual's educational experience. Thus, for example, several articles have appeared on the experience of aboriginal students within the infamous system of the residential schools.[12] In her study of private education for French Canadian female students at the Rideau Street Convent in Ottawa,

presented in essay #38, Isabelle Bourgeois documents the school's mission to transmit culture as well as the three Rs to young French Canadian women.[13] The available studies point to the particular challenges of linguistic and ethnic minorities and their distinct responses to the dominant culture. They encourage us to be wary of generalizations and certainly confirm the need to analyse each case separately. Researchers in this field would concur with historian Paul Axelrod, who has recently cautioned that one cannot presume that people's responses will be based on their minority status, social origins, or the period under study.[14]

These various lines of inquiry have been accompanied more recently by a growing interest in the experiences of students in the classroom and the role and priorities of parents. A focus on the recipients of education and how they interact with the policy makers and school reformers reveals that the interaction between all these players has yielded a variety of results. In keeping with this desire to capture the life experiences of the participants, whether teachers or students, several historians have turned to biography and used oral history research methods when possible. This approach is particularly appropriate when studying women, since they have generally left fewer written records.[15]

As this brief overview confirms, the field of women's education history is forever casting a wider net in an attempt to catch the full reality of women's educational and learning experiences. At times, women's history scholars have concentrated on certain issues more than others, but looking back, one can see that, by widening their lenses, they progressively reveal in richer focus the multifaceted history of women in education.

A list of further readings in this area is available on page 486.

33 Shaping Canada's Women: Canadian Girls in Training versus Girl Guides

Patricia Dirks

The widespread social change and dislocation generated by the economic boom in early twentieth-century Canada heightened Anglo-Protestant fears of moral and national degeneration. Concern about the potential corruption of teenagers was heightened because of the popularity of G. Stanley Hall's child development theories, which had identified adolescence as the crucial period of moral and religious decision making. Canada's Anglo-Protestant middle-class parents, more and more of whom were urbanized, faced the challenge of ensuring that their teenagers made the "right" choices. Increased secondary school attendence, moreover, meant that many of these teenagers had "time on their hands" in settings where the temptations of demoralizing, commercial entertainments abounded. Initially attention was focused on providing adolescent boys, the cause of greatest concern, with worthwhile leisure activities. The women who ran the Young Women's Christian Association (YWCA) and the new breed of professional Protestant religious educators, however, soon turned their attention to meeting the needs of the nation's adolescent girls.

When Girl Guides came to Canada in 1912, the program for female adolescents modelled on Lord Baden-Powell's Boy Scouts, Anglo-Protestants, including YWCA officials, eagerly embraced the organization. By the First World War, however, Protestant religious educators under YWCA leadership had developed a unique fourfold training program for Canadian girls under a different umbrella, the Canadian Girls in Training (CGIT).

The objectives and operational principles of Girl Guides and the made-in-Canada alternative, Canadian Girls in Training, are set out in the two documents reproduced in Illustrations 33.1 and 33.2. The "Aims and Ideals" of the Girl Guide movement in Canada were drawn up by Lady Pellatt, who was appointed chief commissioner for Canada in 1912, and by the other prominent Toronto women who were named to the first Dominion Girl Guide Council. These women, many of whom held high offices in the country's leading women's organizations or were married to leaders in business, education, and the church, initially considered the YWCA a valuable ally for the Girl Guide movement and looked to Canadian branches to sponsor Guide companies. Many YWCA branches did just that and, indeed, were encouraged to do so by association publications that praised the Girl Guide movement.[1] Problems of a religious and political nature, however, soon troubled the relationship between Girl Guides and the YWCA. Religious, class, and generational factors all contributed to the appearance of the Canadian Girls in Training, so shortly after Girl Guides had been imported from Britain.

As early as December 1913, the YWCA's National Executive was urging the Dominion Girl Guide Council to issue an edition of the *Girl Guide Handbook* more adapted to Canadian conditions and needs.[2] With respect to religion, YWCA officials objected to the fact that Guiding left religious education to a girl's church. In their view,

33.1 Ontario Council Archives, Girl Guides, First Canadian Fashion and Home Exhibition, Arena, Toronto, October 20–25, 1913, Program, Monday, October 20, Evening … Girl Guides Display – Platform, 3–5.

THE GIRL GUIDES*

AIMS AND IDEALS OF THE ORGANIZATION

The Girl Guide Movement was founded by Miss Agnes Baden-Powell, sister of Lieut.-Gen. Sir Robert Baden-Powell, for the purpose of making girls useful and self reliant and of developing those qualities of character which make good women and good citizens …

GIRL GUIDE MOVEMENT IN CANADA

Lady Pellatt, of Toronto, received her warrant as Chief Commissioner of the Dominion of Canada from Miss Agnes Baden-Powell in August, 1912, whereby the head office at 37 Wood St., Toronto, was constituted headquarters for Canada …

A Dominion Council has been formed, the members of which are representatives of Dominion-wide Movements …

WHAT THE GUIDES ARE

Girl Guides promise on their honour:

"To be loyal to God and the King."
"To help others at all times."
"To obey the Guide Law."

Their motto is "Be Prepared," and they are being prepared by their discipline and training to help themselves and other people.

Their training includes: 1. Work for the Home – Cookery, Housekeeping, First Aid, Home Nursing, Making Clothes, Care of Children.

2. Physical Development – Swedish Drill, Laws of Health, Saving Life, Outdoor Games.

3. Woodcraft – Camping, Natural History, Map Reading, Boating, Swimming, Signalling.

4. Discipline – Obedience to those in authority, Self-Sacrifice, Sense of Duty, Self-Reliance, Good Manners.

For most of these subjects Girl Guides can earn Badges.

CANADIAN GIRLS IN TRAINING*

Prepared and Issued by the
CANADIAN NATIONAL ADVISORY COMMITTEE
FOR CO-OPERATION IN GIRLS' WORK

A Standard for Girls
I. – PHYSICAL … II. – INTELLECTUAL … III. – RELIGIOUS … IV. – SERVICE

The Physical Standard

As health is the first essential in a girl's normal development, and as present-day business conditions make it necessary for many girls to spend much of their time in-doors, thus depriving them of regular exercise, the importance of emphasizing the "Physical Standard" is self-evident …

The Intellectual Standard

Every teacher has a great task in showing girls the place of the mind and reason as the controlling force in life. They need to see what a heritage God has given them in the power to enter into intellectual and scientific interests …

This standard aims at creating in every girl a desire to continue her own education, whether at school, or at home, or through trade training …

The Religious Standard

As religion means a girl's relationship to God, this standard touches the very motive power of her life …

… remembering that these adolescent years are by far the most fruitful for life decisions, this standard reminds us of the necessity of a conscious choosing of our Lord Jesus Christ as Master and Saviour …

The Service Standard

Life is … lived in social groups … and the Christian law for these relationships is that of service, actuated by love …

The power to carry out such ideals may often be stimulated through self-governing classes or clubs …

The new opportunities coming to women for sharing in the duties of citizenship make a very real reason for including under this standard some understanding of and sharing in the various civic and community efforts of to-day.

33.2 National Archives of Canada, Canadian Girls in Training Papers (CGIT), MG 28 I 313, vol. 12, file 311, "Canadian Girls in Training: Suggestions for the Mid-Week Meetings of Sunday School Classes, Clubs, etc., For 'Teen-Age Girls,'" Prepared and Issued by the Canadian National Advisory Committee for Operation in Girls' Work. Price 5 cents. (1917 edition.)

fulfilment of a girl's potential included acceptance of Christ. A training program was therefore needed "to help forward girls into the joy and fruitfulness of full Christian womanhood." As the theories of religious education current among early twentieth-century evangelical Protestants asserted that adolescents must be won for Christ by linking their mid-week activities to Sunday school, it was thought to be counterproductive to divorce religion from a girl's leisure activities. These differences, combined with opposition to the Girl Guide program's competitive element and emphasis on unquestioning obedience to authority (see Illustration 33.1), inspired the development of CGIT and its fourfold "Standard for Girls" (Illustration 33.2). While the women behind CGIT also rejected the competitive nature of Canadian Standard Efficiency Tests, an element of the comparable boys' program, they wanted Canadian girls to have equal opportunity to improve in every aspect of life.

CGIT's designers, several of whom were college graduates, applied the teachings of modern psychology and educational theorists in their planning for the all-round improvement of Canada's girls.[3] Although they agreed entirely with the Girl Guide objective of training girls "to be useful and self-reliant and good and loyal citizens," they believed that the rigid organization of the Guiding movement would stand in the way of girls realizing their potential as self-reliant Canadian citizens.

CGIT's designers objected to the prescriptive nature of Guiding. They disliked the fact that the character-building requirements were predetermined and inflexible. The requirement that all girls learn exactly the same things to be officially enrolled and pass the same tests to progress through successive levels was equally objectionable. The badge system also came in for criticism because Guides earned badges for mastering set standards and rather than working to their fullest capacity in an area and because they were tested on material chosen by a Headquarters committee. Moreover, while girls could choose from a wide variety of badges, they had no direct say in determining what areas these were in. Finally, Guiding's competitive element, which pitted girl against girl and patrol against patrol, conflicted with the latest self-expressive and cooperative educational theories espoused by the women involved in girls' work through the YWCA and various Sunday school agencies.

The very format of a Girl Guide company meeting restricted individual initiative, as Guides were expected to do as their captain instructed in a set pattern when certain whistles blew. The young women behind the Canadian alternative to Girl Guides were fundamentally opposed to Guiding's objective of training girls to obey authority and perform assigned duties. They rejected the authoritarian leadership role played by the Guide captain because it went against the progressive educational theories endorsed by Canada's evangelical Protestant religious educators. Girls' work, according to these theories, was best done in self-governed groups under the direction of an adult leader who, acting as a "guide," helped group members to draw up a program tailored to their interests and particular needs.

These concerns, together with worries about the inability of Sunday schools to hold the interest of adolescents, brought CGIT onto the Canadian scene as a "progressive" alternative to Girl Guides at the height of the social dislocation associated with the war effort. The religious, political, and social values of Canada's evangelical Protestant middle class had been incorporated into a training program that promised to shape Canadian girlhood.

The underlying assumption of CGIT was that every girl – and every group of girls – was unique and required the application of different means to achieve the common objective of Christian citizenship training. Adult leaders were therefore to adapt the fourfold program on the basis of consultation with the girls in small, church-controlled groups. CGIT members were to exercise initiative rather than be passive recipients of a prescriptive program package.

Despite this flexibility, the choices offered to the girls were all intended to develop the skills and Christian character that program planners felt would bring about a more fulfilled girlhood and womanhood. CGIT's designers were as concerned to shape the character of Canada's girls as was the Girl Guide movement, but they chose different content and methodology for their training program. They did not think that Guiding would produce adult females with the faith, initiative, and ability to make a meaningful contribution to the realization of Canada's potential.

When CGIT was originally put together in 1915–16, its program reflected the conviction that competition was undesirable because it encouraged girls to try to excel over others rather than to realize their own potential and develop their life interests. Even with the introduction of "A Standard for Girls" in 1917, there was no system of grading.

As Canada emerged onto the world stage following the First World War, the young women responsible for CGIT reiterated the importance of the program's commitment to self-government and group spirit. In 1922 a book for CGIT leaders emphasized the national importance of their work with girls. The fourfold development was seen as vital if the women of Canada were to overcome their inability to fulfil their duties as citizens because of their lack of proper training and "vigour of mind." The nation's girls needed to be helped to value study and education, to see the necessity for definite vocational training, and to be interested in world affairs. Without detracting from her training in homecraft, the CGIT girl's experience must provide her with the skills and the confidence she would need to operate effective-

ly as a fulfilled and fully participating member of society at large.

By the 1920s, the Canadian Girl Guide movement thus faced a formidable, home-grown rival girls' organization that had been endorsed by the country's major Protestant Sunday school agencies. The Guide movement's new and younger leaders' vigorous response to CGIT's challenge ensured Girl Guides an ongoing role in shaping future generations of Canadian women. During the decade in which Canada attained full independence within the British Commonwealth, CGIT and Girl Guide leaders considered the possibility of amalgamation in the interests of reaching a larger proportion of the nation's future female citizens, but the movements' differences prevailed. While both programs changed with the times, CGIT and Girl Guides continued to shape Canada's twentieth-century girls through alternative training schemes.

33.3 Meeting of members of the CGIT, c. 1919 (PA 125872, National Archives of Canada)

34 The Experience of Women Students at Four Universities, 1895–1930

Alyson E. King

Between 1877 and 1895, Ontario universities gradually opened their doors to women students (Table 34.1). These enrolments were accompanied by much dissension and spurred debate regarding the type of higher education women should receive.[1] Research on the early years of women's attendance at universities in Canada, the United States, and Britain has expanded,[2] although there is still little known of the experience of women students from the late 1890s to the end of the 1920s. These years are important because of the steady increase in the number of women attending Ontario's universities and the expanding participation of women students in all aspects of university life. This essay provides an overview of the impact of women students' enrolment between 1895 and 1930 at Queen's and McMaster Universities and the Universities of Toronto and Western Ontario.

During this period, several changes occurred that profoundly affected the character of education and academic life for women students. From the physical setting of new women's buildings to the offering of courses designed for women, the opportunities for women students seemed to increase dramatically. Nevertheless, the vast majority of women students sought out a more traditional arts education. With this increase in female enrolment, some feared that traditional academia was becoming feminized. Overall, reactions to the large number of women in the arts faculties varied, as did the women students' strategies to create a space for themselves within the traditionally male institutions.

The number of women enrolled in the faculties of arts at these four universities rose steadily over the period. By 1900, 250 women were enrolled in the Faculty of Arts and the affiliated colleges of the University of Toronto, 117 at Queen's University, and 17 at McMaster (no accurate statistics are available for Western University, but the numbers were low). By 1929, enrolment at Toronto had reached 1,666; at Queen's 1,117; at McMaster 113; and at Western 416.[3] Nationwide, women were more likely to attend an arts faculty, even after the introduction of courses aimed at women, such as household science and nursing. Between 1901 and 1930, women composed between one-quarter to one-third of the student body in arts and science. The percentage of

---

GRACE ANNIE LOCKHART, 1855–1916

Grace Annie Lockhart was the first woman to earn a university degree in the British Empire. Founded exclusively for the education of men, universities in the nineteenth century gradually began opening their doors to women. Mount Allison College became co-educational in 1872. This change built on the pioneering commitment to female education of the associated Mount Allison Ladies' Academy and of denominational schools in the United States. Lockhart, a student of the Ladies' Academy, took courses at the college, formally enrolled in 1874, and graduated with a degree of Bachelor of Science and English Literature on 25 May 1875. (Courtesy of Parks Canada)

women in courses aimed at them may have been higher, but the actual numbers show that more women chose arts and science.[4]

The number of women in the faculties of arts did rise, but the proportion of women to men increased only slightly, certainly not enough to pose a real threat to the dominance of men at the universities. Why then did commentators and administrators believe so strongly that the university was becoming feminized? A look at the honours-level courses that women students tended to take may shed some light here. Despite the introduction of "women's courses," women students tended to dominate the modern language courses numerically. In this case, it might seem as if women were beginning to outnumber the men. In fact, men continued to dominate all other programs. At University College (part of the University of Toronto), for example, a large number of women took the Honours Moderns Course, second highest after the General Course (Table 34.2). Similarly, at Western few women enrolled in courses outside of the Arts Department. As at University College, women students at Western appeared to select language rather than science courses. For example, in 1929, one-quarter of Western's graduating women students had taken modern languages (Table 34.3)[5] The heavy enrolment of women in a few fields would have lent credence to the perception of an increasingly feminized university. Of course, some women did enrol in such courses as mathematics and economics and in graduate programs. In 1904 Jessie Rowat was described in Western's student newspaper as having enrolled in advanced courses without blinking an eye, and in 1905, as being brilliant at math and prose.[6] In 1916 Lily Bell (BA 1915) wrote an article for the Western University Gazette describing her graduate research work on early Canadian literature undertaken during a summer spent at the National Archives in Ottawa.[7] In the 1924 yearbook, Mary Routledge was described as courageous for "being the only

Table 34.1 Admission of Women to Ontario Universities

University of Toronto's affiliated colleges	
Victoria	1880
University	1884
Trinity (St Hilda's College – 1888)	1886
St Michael's (St Joseph's and Loretto Abbey Colleges)	1911
Queen's University	1880
McMaster University	1890
University of Western Ontario	1895
Brescia College	1919
Ottawa University	1919

Sources: McKillop, *Matters of Mind*, 130, 234; LaPierre, "The First Generation," 60–1; *Baptist Yearbook*, 1889, 79–81; *McMaster University Monthly*, June 1891, 89.

girl in the economics course."[8] The situation at Queen's and McMaster was much the same.

Why then did women choose the courses they did, despite these exceptions? Women were directly and indirectly influenced to take modern languages instead of mathematics and sciences. Bessie Scott, for example, took math in her first year at the University of Toronto in 1889. After only two weeks, for no apparent reason, she records in her diary her decision to switch to Moderns the following year. She did so in spite of being better at math than at languages and of enjoying her "beloved Math."[9] Certainly some women managed to persevere in the sciences despite barriers. Elizabeth Laird, for example, was denied the University of Toronto's 1896 physics scholarship because she was a woman, yet she went on to study physics in the United States and Germany before becoming a professor at Mount Holyoke in the United States.[10]

Academic work was only one aspect of student life. Extracurricular activities also played an important role in women students' experience at university. While some differences are apparent at the four universities, the similarities are stronger. Although groups were formed to

Table 34.2 Registration of Women Students, University College, 1912–1913

	1st Year	2nd Year	3rd Year	4th Year	Total
General Course	35	37	24	28	124
Honours Arts					**146**
Classics	2	2	3	2	9
English & History	1	3	3	1	8
Classics, English, & History	0	1	2	0	3
Moderns	19	12	26	21	78
English & History (Mods.)	18	7	3	9	37
Moderns, English, & History	4	1	1	1	7
Modern History	0	0	0	1	1
Philosophy	0	1	2	0	3
Honours Science					**27**
Mathematics & Physics	7	4	4	5	20
Science	2	0	0	0	2
Physics	0	0	0	1	1
Biological & Physical Sci.	0	0	1	0	1
Physiol. & Biochemical	0	0	1	0	1
Biology	0	0	2	0	2
Household Science					**33**
Household Science	14	4	5	5	28
Physiol. & Household Sci.	0	3	2	0	5
TOTAL	102	75	79	74	330

Sources: University of Toronto, *President's Report*, 1912–13.

promote involvement in missionary work, religion, and athletics, among the most important societies were the Literary Societies, with various names, at each university. The Literary Society was usually the first club established and it often oversaw many of the student activities. At Queen's and Toronto, the Alma Mater Society (Queen's) and the Literary and Athletic Society (University College, Toronto) were already well established when women were admitted. Sara Z. Burke notes that, at the University of Toronto, women students chose to regulate their own behaviour in order to pre-empt the restrictions imposed on them by the president of the university, Daniel Wilson.[11] Women students at Queen's University also appear to have excluded themselves from the main student group, the Alma Mater Society.[12] Whether they were formally or informally excluded, women students were usually not active members of the existing groups at the two larger universities, at least initially. Thus isolated from the main culture of the male-dominated university, they were forced to create their own groups. Yet these separate women's clubs were formed for other than simply reactionary reasons, and they had important implications for women's development and progress within the university and beyond. Women's clubs, both religious and secular, provided women with the opportunity to develop the skills necessary to pursue careers and social activism and to foster alliances and networks that would often last through life. The success of such women's clubs, however, did not mean that women did not eventually participate in the central student groups earlier dominated by men.[13]

At McMaster University, both women and men were members of the Literary and Theological Society, later called the Literary and Scientific Society, from at least 1892.[14] Although women appeared on the program for the open meeting in 1893, it was not until 1895 that they were even nominated to any executive position.[15] The 1896 elections established the tradition of electing a woman as second vice-president and as assistant editor of the *McMaster University Monthly*.[16] The male students controlled the more prestigious positions of president and editor-in-chief, but the women did establish their presence on the executive of the Literary and Scientific Society long before the women students at Queen's and Toronto did. It was not until 1914, however, that McMaster women attempted to gain the presidency of the Literary Society.[17] At Western in 1907, both the vice-president and treasurer of the Literary Society were women.[18] Women at Western were also part of the 1904 founding of the student newspaper, *In Cap and Gown* (later

Table 34.3 Graduates, Bachelor of Arts, May 1929, University of Western Ontario

Course	No. of Women	Total	% of Women	% of Total
General	9	25	36	28.1
Gen. - Secr. Sci.	4	4	100	12.5
Honours Biology	2	3	66.7	6.3
Hon. B. Admin.	0	9	0	0
Hon. Chemistry	0	9	0	0
Hon. Classics	1	2	50	3.1
Hon. Econ. & Pol. Science	0	7	0	0
Hon. English & History	5	6	83.3	15.6
Hon. English & French	3	4	75.0	9.4
Hon. English & German	1	1	100	3.1
Hon. French & German	3	3	100	9.4
Hon. French & Spanish	1	1	100	3.1
[Total in Modern Languages]	[8]	[9]	[88.9]	[25.0]
Hon. Math & Business	0	1	0	0
Hon. Math & Physics	0	5	0	0
Hon. Science	1	6	16.7	3.1
Hon. Romance Languages	2	2	100	6.3
TOTALS	32	88	36.4	

Sources: Derived from the Minutes of the Faculty Meeting, May, 1929, University College of Arts, University of Western Ontario.

renamed *Western University Gazette* and then *Western U Gazette*). Women at Queen's, however, were not elected to the executive of the Alma Mater Society until 1916. At Toronto's University College, the men's Literary and Athletic Society and the Women's Undergraduate Association finally merged in 1949, although they had cooperated prior to this.[19]

At both Western and McMaster, women students were a significant part of university life. They were active in the same clubs and organizations as the men and were among the founding members of the central clubs and organizations. Women students played an important role earlier at Western and McMaster for two reasons. First, women were among the first students enrolled when Western University's art college reopened in 1895 after refinancing was arranged. Secondly, the small student population led to a closeness not felt at larger institutions. In the spring of 1900, three women graduated from Western, making a total of five women graduates since the reopening. Although the number of graduating women students increased each year between 1895 and 1930, only 360 women in total had graduated from Western by 1930.[20] These smaller numbers meant that for the clubs to be successful, all of the students had to be involved. Indeed, the women were able to take on leadership roles in the formation and running of co-educational clubs. Western's Modern Language Club, for example, was formed in 1903 by mostly women students. Only two of the ten founding members were men, one of whom was a professor.[21] Similarly, McMaster had a small number of students, but in addition its Baptist philosophy of education had from the beginning encouraged women to participate fully.[22]

At most universities, the first stage of the development of a separate culture for women students was the designation of a room for their use. All four universities provided at least one room or parlour, of various sizes and quality. At McMaster, the room was explicitly intended "to maintain efficient discipline in the movement and intercourse of students within the building."[23] At Western, the ladies' room was used for formal meetings and as a gathering place between classes where the women ate lunch and prepared hot drinks. Since conversations among students were discouraged in the halls, most socializing had to be done in rooms set aside for that purpose. Having a separate room also promoted a sense of community. The physical separation of the women's room from the men's space quickly encouraged separate student organizations and cultures.

At all four universities, separate societies for women were important. Although as noted above, most McMaster women maintained membership in both co-educational and separate societies, it was the separate groups that provided them with unique opportunities not available in larger, co-educational groups. Estelle Freedman argues that the founding of separate female-oriented clubs was a strategy used by early feminists to develop skills and community among like-minded women.[24] The McMaster Ladies Literary League, originally formed in 1891 as the Modern Language Club, was influenced by the feminism of the women's movement of the period, as seen in its choice of topics for discussion, the seminars on careers for women, and the encouragement of women students in developing skills formerly associated only with men. Indeed, the influence of the women's movement can be seen as early as 1899, when, at the reading of the new constitution, an amendment was moved that the name be changed to the "Women's Literary League."[25] Although the motion was unsuccessful at that time, in 1907 the name of the Ladies Literary League was changed to the Women's Literary Society.[26] Western's women students also created their own unique culture by forming separate societies, despite being involved in the same organizations as men from the beginning.

At the two larger universities, the women's societies were seen as necessary for the development of skills for women's future roles in society. At Victoria College, for example, women students saw membership in the Women's Literary Society as providing many advantages:

Here we learn something of speaking, listening, replying, and the methods of business procedure, which are useful to us every day of our lives. In no other phase of college life do we have this indispensable training. Certainly it is not in any course in the curriculum. The work of any college organization is to promote culture and to fit one to become a useful member of society. We claim that the

Literary Society is a potent factor in the accomplishment of this purpose.[27]

The writer went on to state that this training would allow women to occupy prominent positions after graduation.

Although propriety was carefully observed, it did not limit the development of friendships between the women and the men and the enjoyment of a wide range of co-educational social events. At McMaster's Literary Society meetings, for example, the women arrived in a group, after the men were seated, and sat well apart in the west side of the chapel. Women and men were discouraged from mingling, talking was forbidden in the halls, and the men were reminded not to flirt with women passing in the street.[28] Yet the students shared jokes and pranks, despite such efforts of the administration to keep the men and women apart.

Social activities, in fact, played an important role in university life. The Methodist, Anglican, and Baptist communities all sought to train their children to take an active role in Canadian society.[29] An important aspect of this was developing their social skills and helping them establish contacts with appropriate members of the community. The social life of the students included the receptions, sleigh rides, skating parties, and promenades held as part of the regular round of events each year. At McMaster, for example, Founder's Day was the main public event to which friends of the university were invited. At the 1900 Founder's Day, there were more than six hundred guests in attendance.[30] By 1922, however, such events were in decline. That year both the professor of mathematics and the head girl commented on the Founder's Day activities. Professor William Findlay felt that they should find a more consistent and sustainable way of introducing McMaster students to "the best social life of the Baptists of Toronto."[31] Florence Marlow noted that there was declining enthusiasm for standard social functions such as Founder's Day, one of the main reasons being that dancing was not permitted.[32] Efforts had been made in earlier years to maintain the interest of students in these events – such as the introduction of promenading and the serving of refreshments – but these met with limited success. Students at all the universities held many events, which included more informal class parties as well as formal receptions. The women's groups frequently held a tea and invited women from the community. University administrators recognized the importance of such activities, noting in one case that they helped "to develop McMaster men and women into the fulness of stature."[33]

During the thirty years after the turn of the century, the presence of women at Ontario universities gradually strengthened. Women students took an active role in all aspects of university life, from the classroom to the clubs and social life. The university administrators attempted to control aspects of the student culture by restricting women to one room when not in class and ensuring that all social activities were carefully chaperoned. Students at Western and McMaster, however, aided by their small numbers, subverted attempts at physical separation by maintaining co-educational clubs. At the same time, women appeased the university authorities and parents by creating separate groups for some activities. Certainly the models provided by women's clubs at the University of Toronto and Queen's University, and by those outside the university, played a role. By the time women at McMaster and Western were planning their own organizations, the women at Toronto and Queen's already had well-established separate societies and activities. While many women were active in clubs and activities beyond their own separate societies, their interactions carved out important feminist space and established networks that advanced women's presence at the university and later in Canadian society.

35 Margaret Addison: Dean of Residence and Dean of Women at Victoria University, 1903–1931

Jean O'Grady

When young Esther Trewartha entered Victoria College in 1925, one of the high points of her year was the welcoming talk given by the dean of women, Margaret Addison, who addressed the new students as "Women of the University."[1] Esther felt she was being ushered into a splendid intellectual community with all its challenges and responsibilities, and the moment left its mark on all her subsequent life. Many other women students could report a similar experience. For twenty-nine years, as dean of residence and then dean of women at Victoria College, Addison inspired, guided, and – it must be said – sometimes irritated a whole generation of women at Victoria. She herself belonged to the first wave of Canadian women to attend university, and her work as an administrator helped to define the conditions for the second wave, those attending when higher education for women was no longer a novelty but not yet widespread. By her tactful policies, she eased the transition to a modern era, when the expectations for women's careers were to be transformed.

One of Addison's strengths was her openness to what the future might hold for women. Her evangelical Christian faith left her comparatively free of secular ideology. Neither a fierce "women's righter" nor a proponent of domesticity, she believed that the proper role of women had yet to be defined; thus far they had not made the full contribution to society of which they were capable. She was convinced that intellectually women were the equal of men and deserved the same education. At the same time, their essential femininity predisposed them to nurturing, to fostering harmony, and to appreciating beauty. How best to harness these qualities for the greater good was for her one of the major questions to be worked out in the twentieth century. Meanwhile, her part was to ensure that the young women she supervised had both the moral strength and the intellectual equipment to meet all challenges.

When Addison herself attended Victoria College, then a Methodist institution in Cobourg, there were only a handful of women enrolled; in 1889, graduating with some twenty young men, she was the sixth woman ever to obtain a bachelor of arts from Victoria. She and her fellow female students were janey-come-latelys in an overwhelmingly male environment, where the college newspaper referred to the student body as "the lads" and it was a mark of honour to be "one of the boys." While many of these boys lived on the third floor of the college building in close proximity to their professors, the women were scattered around the town in boarding houses. The Methodist Church was somewhat ambivalent about female college students, supporting their right to knowledge, but uneasy about their participation in a rowdy culture of sports, debates, class meetings, and hijinks.

Addison's experience at Victoria convinced her that winning a BA was only half the battle – that a complete education involved not just attending lectures, but also entering into a community of learning, where all the powers of mind, body, and spirit could be developed. This impression was reinforced by a seven-month trip she took to Europe and Britain in 1900. The six weeks she spent in Oxford and Cambridge, touring the women's colleges, were a revelation to her. At Newnham, Girton, Somerville, and the other residential colleges, she encountered what she considered ideal societies: communities of women, animated by a common vision of scholarship, and led by older women who were role models. Such women's colleges could not be duplicated in co-educational Canada, but they inspired her with the notion of a college education designed to answer the needs of women. Measured against their yardstick, Canadian girls were getting only half an education.

Addison kept in touch with her old college during the thirteen years she worked as a high school teacher of French and German, first at the Ontario Ladies' College and then at Stratford Collegiate Institute (1889–1903). Meanwhile, Victoria College affiliated with the University of Toronto and left Cobourg; it had fourteen women students when it opened its doors in Toronto in 1892. When the idea of building a women's residence was first introduced by Mrs Burwash, the president's wife (who had also visited the English colleges), Addison was an enthusiastic backer of the scheme. She saw it as a way of establishing women's presence in the university, of enriching their education, and at the same time of providing a Christian and homelike environment acceptable to families who might otherwise hesitate to send their daughters away. In the Alumnae Association (which she helped to found in 1898) and in speeches and letters, Addison threw herself into the difficult task of raising funds from a sceptical church membership.

When at last Annesley Hall was erected in 1903, it was no surprise to find that Margaret Addison was asked to be its dean. Suddenly she became one of the most influential women – indeed, one of only four women – in academic office at the University of Toronto[2] and a spokesperson for educated womanhood. Initially, how-

ever, her position was somewhat precarious. The residence was slated to open in the fall of 1903 with fifty-five girls, but by the first of September, only five rooms had been let. Victoria women were appalled at the fees of five dollars a week, and needed to be convinced of the superiority of the residence to the cheaper YWCA or boarding houses. Because of a carpenters' strike, the downstairs rooms were still full of paint-pots and saw-horses on opening day, and the last beds arrived only twenty-four hours before their occupants. But these teething pains passed, residents signed up at the last minute, and in that and subsequent years Addison had a full house to mould into her desired community.

As dean, Addison had two main tasks: to secure acceptance of the venture by a fairly conservative church and to create a form of community life that would further women's development. Many of the rules of conduct she had established to lull the fears of parents and guardians, obviously had the underlying purpose of controlling sexuality. Visitors were generally restricted to young women and family members, though gentlemen might make formal calls in the downstairs area on the second and fourth Fridays of the month between 7 and 10 p.m. and on Sunday evenings. After supper the hall doors were closed, and a young woman could not go out unless she had the dean's permission and indicated her whereabouts in writing. Though late leaves were given to third- and fourth-year students, basically all the girls had to be home and accounted for by 10:30. Annesley women could not attend a dance or public entertainment without a chaperone such as the dean; they could be escorted by a young man if their parents had approved of his name in writing, but on no account were they to go out driving or walking after dinner with young men of any description.

Such rules were necessary in a restrictive era, when young women were generally regarded as innocent goslings needing protection. Addison was responsible to a fairly conservative body of women, the Committee of

Management, who represented the church and the community. In one report to this group, she explained that as women were on suffrance in formerly male institutions, they "could never be in advance of public opinion concerning their freedom. But as public opinion changed, so could their freedom expand."[3] Gradually the rules were relaxed; the students of the 1920s rocked with laughter when the dean read out the rules of 1903.[4]

Other early procedures and practices enhanced the character of Annesley Hall as a gracious home, with the dean as a sort of surrogate mother; it was a place of repose, order, and dignity, where character could mature. The reception rooms were tastefully furnished, thanks to the efforts of the Victoria Women's Association, and included a library and music-room. No clumping shoes were allowed indoors, and no housecoats or nightwear downstairs. Dinners were a communal gathering, very different from the cafeteria-style mayhem of today: the girls changed their clothes for the meal, ate at designated tables served by maids, and waited until everyone had finished before getting up. Each year the dean explained that it was bad form to talk about the food, the servants, or personalities. Her apparent preoccupation with social niceties had the serious purpose of fostering a thoughtfulness and consideration for others that the girls would carry over into their own homes.

Another part of her mission was cultural. To ensure that intellectual development did not take place in a vacuum, she escorted the residents to concerts, plays, and recitals. Annesley Hall had a picture committee which, through the good offices of Professor Currelly of the Royal Ontario Museum, obtained several paintings a year, including an A.Y. Jackson and a Tom Thomson. Addison encouraged awareness of contemporary issues by inviting speakers such as Marie Stopes, a colourful, unconventional figure, though not yet embarked on her advocacy of birth control; Mrs Pankhurst, the British suffragette; and Olive Schreiner, the South African early feminist novelist. In later years there were conferences exploring new careers in education, church and YWCA work, nursing, libraries, writing, and business. The needs of the body were taken care of in a basement gym where all were required to take exercise; those of the soul, by optional Bible classes, Sunday evening talks, and prayers before meals.

Unfortunately, the young women of the time did not always appreciate the in *loco parentis* function of the residence. They would slip out without signing a form, eat in downtown restaurants, and (in later years) visit prohibited dance halls. At times Dean Addison appeared as a Gorgon, stalking the halls to ambush latecomers. Indeed, the first year of the residence was, according to her, a disaster, with disobedience and selfishness rampant. As she wrote in her 1905 report, the patriarchal form of government was evidently not adaptable to large residences, and the analogy with a home could not be pressed too far. The classic solution to the misuse of liberty was the institution of responsible government, and accordingly, in 1906, she introduced a new model, that of the self-governing state. With the formation of the Annesley Student Government Association, or ASGA, students became partially responsible for framing and administering their own rules. Addison liked to compare the adult supervisors to the House of Lords, and the student government to the House of Commons. In truth, the degree of self-government was mild. Nevertheless, it was a bold step for the time, and Addison never ceased to believe in its virtues as training in community living, cooperation, and responsibility. ASGA continues to this day, the oldest residence government in Canada, and with only minor adjustments its constitution became the model for that of many other residences in Canada.[5]

By keeping in creative tension her two models – that of a home and that of a self-governing community – Addison managed to steer a middle course between conflicting demands for freedom and protection. Her success is suggested by the two main crises she weathered, which represent criticism from both extremes. In 1912 Dr Burwash, the president of Victoria College, launched an investigation into the governance of the residence, where freedom seemed to have got out of hand. Rumours had reached his ears that girls were drinking tea in each other's rooms as late as 12.30 a.m. at night, and had been seen at public entertainments unchaperoned. "This is not Methodism," lamented the general superintendent of the church when he heard the allegations; "this is not the pathway of healthful discipline or of sound and safe scholarship!"[6] But Addison was able to show that the rules had generally been honoured and that many of those women given leave to be out in the evening had been attending plays by Shakespeare. The ultimate result was the vindication of student government and the resignation of Dr Burwash.

In 1920 Addison came under fire again, but this time for being too paternalistic and restrictive. Her critics – chiefly Vincent Massey and his wife, Alice – felt that the Annesley women were being treated as dependents rather than as mature adults, and that their intellectual life was being neglected. The Masseys envisaged a merely housekeeping role for the residence, while social and intellectual activities of both men and women would be coordinated by a single body. The Masseys' criticism had some validity and was in tune with "unisex" notions of increased freedom and autonomy for women. But Addison was more realistic about what could be done in 1920. Had the Masseys' views prevailed, there might well have been a backlash against women's higher education. The changes that the Masseys did succeed in introducing, such as moving Addison out of her suite of rooms in the residence, were not appreciated by most of the women students and were gradually rescinded. Eventually, Alice Massey resigned from the Committee of Management.

Addison's difficult position as guardian of the interests of both students and parents took its toll on her health. And so did the minutiae of her job, in which, especially in the early days, she had to chair meetings, make speeches, write all the residence correspondence by hand, collect money and take it to the bank, interview students, assign rooms, buy railroad tickets, make up the piano practice schedule, sign permissions, act as chaperone, direct the household servants, and stay up until midnight every night to answer the door of the residence. During epidemics she was an overworked nurse, and at all times she was on call as an adviser and guide. Small wonder that she was sometimes so exhausted that when she took a few days off to visit old friends in Newcastle, she would crawl into bed as soon as she arrived and not come down till the last day. In 1917–18 she had a year's leave of absence, which she spent at a spa. She called for more help, but the work expanded as the help came; the residence developed satellite houses, and in 1920 she was made dean of women instead of dean of residence, with additional responsibility for the increasing number of city students.

When Addison resigned in 1931, women had been fully integrated into Victoria College – indeed, slightly more than half the students were women. In her final report (4 June 1931), she pointed out that she had lived longer with more university women than had any other woman in Canada; according to her calculations, seventeen hundred women had passed through her hands at Victoria.[7] Her influence was wider even than this, for the example of Annesley Hall provided guidance for many of the women's residences that came later in Canada, on matters ranging from governance to the number of mops and brooms required. After Addison's death, a scholarship was instituted in her name to send a graduate woman student to study abroad. And in 1959 the new women's residence at Victoria was named Margaret Addison Hall. Though she may not have appreciated its popular name, Marg. Add., she would have been gratified at the recognition that her labours on behalf of women were still bearing fruit.

36 The "Feminization" of High Schools: The Problem of Women Secondary School Teachers in Ontario

Susan Gelman

The history of women in public secondary school teaching in Ontario is the history of women entering a new area of public teaching. There is no evidence in the Department of Education records that prior to 1871 women had ever taught in Ontario's grammar or secondary schools, even though, in contrast, by that year women represented a majority of the teachers in the province's common or elementary schools.[1] In the manuscript census for 1861, however, Letitia Youmans is named as an assistant in the Colborne Grammar School.[2] Grammar schools where women were assistants were probably union schools that employed women to teach the common school subjects.[3]

The year 1871 marked the entrance of the first women into public secondary school teaching in Ontario. Despite vocal objections from the province's male educators and efforts to limit the number of women secondary school teachers, their numbers increased steadily during the late nineteenth and early twentieth centuries as they pioneered this new public occupation for women in the province. This is not to suggest that women had never taught at advanced levels, for many had been employed as teachers in the province's denominational private girls' academies since the middle of the nineteenth century. In these schools, indeed, they taught advanced subjects in a formal setting. Thus, the entrance of women into high school and collegiate institute teaching in 1871 must be seen as the entrance of women into public secondary school teaching rather than into

something entirely new to them.[4]

Although the issue of women secondary school teachers did not become contentious until the turn of the century, the problem of gender and secondary teaching first caught the attention of Egerton Ryerson, Ontario's superintendent of education, during the early 1870s. With the passing of the 1871 School Act, high school boards began hiring women teachers to accommodate newly funded female students. In addition, hiring women teachers allowed high school boards to expand their secondary teaching staff while keeping within financial limitations.[5] Although Ryerson approved of employing women secondary school teachers, he stipulated that trustees could only hire "one Female Teacher in every mixed school," increasing their numbers according to the proportion of female pupils.[6] This reflected both the traditional role of the high school as a place to educate boys and the traditional role of women as teachers of girls at the secondary level. Women were seen as a threat to the male culture of the secondary school and the masculinity of adolescent boys. The proper place of women in teaching was considered to be with small children and older girls.

Despite this traditional view of secondary schools and secondary school teaching, the proportion of women teachers increased slowly but steadily during the late nineteenth century. By 1880 women accounted for 9 per cent of the high school and collegiate institute teachers,[7] and by 1890 they reached 13 per cent. After a visit to the eastern United States in 1889, John Seath, the minister of education, speculated that although women teachers were increasing in number, they posed no immediate threat to secondary school education, for "judging from public opinion, it will, I think be long before Ontario's High School staffs [will be] constituted as … those in the United States," where "the large majority of the teachers are women."[8]

By the turn of the century, fewer men were entering and staying in teaching. The consequent growing shortage of teachers in the province, combined with an expanding number of secondary schools, provided increasingly more teaching opportunities for women. By 1900 women represented 17 per cent of the secondary school teachers, a small increase compared to the decade before, but by 1905, they accounted for 23 per cent of all collegiate institute and high school teachers.[9] In reaction, R.A. Pyne, the minister of education, spoke out against this growing trend towards the hiring of women. He warned school boards that they were of "too great a disposition to employ, even for the most advanced pupils, women teachers." Pyne felt that the proportion of women secondary school teachers was not large enough to cause "alarm," but if the present condition was allowed to continue, women teachers would increase in number. Pyne argued that school boards, by hiring women at salaries below that demanded by male teachers, were practising "false views of economy." If the object of education was merely to impart knowledge, then he was willing to agree with the "frequently" heard statement that "the work of the woman [was] as good in the school as that of the man." However, Pyne maintained that since an essential goal of education was character building, women were not suitable teachers of older boys.[10] He therefore recommended that secondary schools not employ more than one woman teacher for every two men on staff.[11]

One way to shift the trend towards women secondary school teachers was to make the profession more attractive to men. A 1904 *Queen's Quarterly* article pointed out that bringing teacher training under the auspices of the university would professionalize teaching and thereby attract more men.[12] It was in this climate that the 1905 Royal Commission on the University of Toronto addressed its report to the province. The commission recommended that the university extend its role into teacher training as a way both to modernize the university in accordance with trends in the United States and England and to raise the professional status of teaching.[13] Just as the university already trained men "for a number of the professions, such as medicine, engineering, mining," it could reasonably be expected to train them to be teachers as well.[14] The following year, the university commissioned its own study on the issue of teacher training. The 1906 report argued that, by transferring the higher levels of teacher training to the university, the expense of a fifth year of study would be decreased. This would attract more university-educated men to teaching and solve the shortage of male high school teachers that the province had been experiencing over the last five or six years.[15]

The Faculty of Education at the University of Toronto opened in October 1907 (renamed the College of Education in 1920),[16] bringing teacher training under the auspices of the university for the first time in Ontario. Provincial male educators hoped, as noted, that the university setting would give teaching the professional status needed to attract more men. The time was thus pivotal for the university to assume its place in teacher training, but would the faculty accomplish what male educators hoped it would?

In a series of articles in the *Queen's Quarterly* in 1909, University of Toronto English professor J.F. Macdonald addressed the problem of women secondary school teachers. He blamed low salaries for the fact that, over the last five years, while the number of secondary school teachers had nearly doubled, the number of men had been declining. Few "college men," he stated, were willing to go on to a fifth year at the Faculty of Education in order to teach when they could earn higher salaries in business and engineering. Macdonald predicted that the tendency towards hiring women secondary school teachers would continue: "Let the experts worry as much as they please over what they call the 'feminization' of the high schools, it is coming in Ontario." However, he hoped that "prejudiced" hiring policies on the part of some school boards – those that were employing women in junior positions and others that were increasing the salaries of male teachers – would arrest what had been an "abnormally rapid increase" in women secondary school teachers.[17]

When Macdonald wrote this article, the faculty had been in operation for three years. During the first two years, women students represented 70 per cent of the total enrolment of the school. By 1909 a small increase in the number of male students had lowered the percentage of women slightly, to 63 per cent. Regardless of a large increase in students during the first two years of the war, the percentage of women students remained relatively constant throughout the decade. A decline in enrolment in 1916 and 1917 brought with it a return in the proportion of women students to 69 per cent, a rate that had not been seen since 1907. This caught the attention of the dean, William Pakenham, who predicted that it was "not likely that the movement of men away from the teaching profession [would] cease after the war."[18] However, Pakenham's predictions were incorrect. In 1918 and 1919, enrolment increased largely because of an increase in the number of male students. By 1919 the faculty saw the largest number of male students, close to double the number just two years before. For the first time, the proportion of male students reached 50 per cent. This increase was the result of special incentives given to male veterans returning from the war. Not only

did the Department of Education pay for tuition and books, but each veteran was given a daily allowance to cover carfare and other expenses, calculated according to marital status and number of children.[19]

The 1920s began auspiciously for the College of Education. As standards were raised, to admit only students with an undergraduate degree, the first two years saw a majority of male students, representing 66 and 60 per cent of the total enrolment. Educators attributed this to a "business depression" during the early 1920s, which made teaching more attractive to men.[20] Moreover, R.H. Grant, the minister of education, maintained that as teachers' salaries had been increasing during the early 1920s, fewer men were entering other occupations. This, he proposed, would "restore the former proportion of men and women teachers."[21] But the increased majority of male students was short-lived. Within one year, their proportion fell to 46 per cent. Although by 1922 women again accounted for a majority of the students at the college, the proportion of women during the middle years of the decade tended to fluctuate between 57 and 44 per cent. Despite the majority of male students during much of the 1920s, most of the men enrolled at the college during these years were already practising teachers seeking further certification. Overall, during the 1920s the number of students increased steadily, bringing an increasing number of women to the profession, and by the end of the decade the percentage of women had increased greatly, reaching 70 per cent in 1928 and 1929. Even the higher admission standards set by the college had not deterred the enrolment of women, as the number of women enrolled in undergraduate university programs in Canada increased during the 1920s.[22]

In 1930 Macdonald again addressed the issue of women teachers. He claimed that poor salaries earned by teachers, compared to those that men could earn in other occupations, could no longer be cited as the major reason why teaching did not hold interest for men. Macdonald quoted one of a number of male university students who had been surveyed on whether or not they would consider high school teaching: "The trouble is that most of the fellows think it is a sissy job." Macdonald concluded that men no longer considered teaching a respectable occupation. The turning point in teaching, he claimed, had occurred over the last twenty-five years: "No one thought it a sissy job twenty-five years ago. The H.S. teacher was then a respected and influential member of the community." In his opinion, the status of the profession had been driven down by the large number of women secondary school teachers.[23]

In 1930, faced with the realization that secondary school teaching had become a woman's occupation, Macdonald changed his tone from that of resignation and concern of 1909 to alarm and disappointment. He was part of a very vocal number of male educators who no doubt realized that the faculty and the college had failed to accomplish what they had thought the school would do, which was to create a core of male secondary school teachers. Instead, it had created an opportunity for women to expand their presence in secondary school teaching. In 1910 the proportion of women secondary school teachers in Ontario increased to 37 per cent, representing a 13 per cent increase from a decade earlier. Ten years later, by 1920, this proportion increased again, to 51 per cent, a percentage that remained stable in 1930. Changing social and economic conditions encouraged women to take advantage of the new opportunity that the faculty and the college had to offer. Despite the disapproval of male educators, women were increasingly making inroads into an occupation that had been seen as the preserve of men.

37 Writing for Whom? Isabel Murphy Skelton and Canadian History in the Early Twentieth Century

Terry Crowley

Although the writing of fiction attracts widespread media attention, much more non-fiction than fiction is published each year. Within non-fiction, history writing has long held an honoured place, but the field until recently has been dominated by men. In the nineteenth century, many women chose to express their interest in history in other ways, such as through active involvement in historical societies. Those who did become authors were most often amateurs who typically pulled at their readers' heartstrings through vivid narratives that made little contribution to historical understanding. Such authors as the Strickland sisters were immensely popular with reading audiences in the United Kingdom, who readily purchased their series on the queens of England. The men who monopolized positions in university history departments seldom allowed women access or paid them any attention. They wrote to influence other male intellectuals. As a result, women tended to be handmaidens who assisted with research and writing, but the results were published under male exclusive authorship. Nevertheless, collaboration between the sexes occasionally marked the efforts of such renowned British and American couples as Barbara and J.L. Hammond, Alice Stopford and J.R. Green, and Mary Ritter and Charles Beard.[1]

Even though she did not fit any of these categories, Isabel Murphy Skelton (1877–1955) became a successful historical author at a time when few Canadian women wrote history. Although she raised three children and had to manage home life for her husband, Skelton produced three books of Canadian history, one edited volume, three short school textbooks, and a number of articles. Her writings showed novelty in selection of topics, in research, and in being composed in graceful prose free of pretense. Publishers were interested in producing her work because Isabel Skelton wrote for an informed audience interested in seeing the past in new ways. She believed that her contemporary male professionals pursued history narrowly by concentrating on politics, diplomacy, and war. She therefore wrote about women, missionaries, literary nationalism, and religion. Combining authorship with roles as wife and mother was often a delicate balancing act for Isabel Skelton, but writing was so important to her that she continued active research until her death at the age of seventy-nine years in 1955.

Isabel Murphy was born in 1877 in Antrim, a hamlet in Carleton County thirty-five kilometres northwest of Ottawa. Her background was ordinary except that she managed to enter Queen's University in 1897 at the age of twenty. Majoring in English and history, she graduated with an MA in 1901. Three years later she married Oscar Douglas Skelton. Marriage framed much of Isabel Skelton's adult life, particularly after the arrival of three children, but the couple was able to afford assistance with housekeeping. Oscar was a political economist with a doctorate from the University of Chicago. A member of Queen's Department of Political Science and Economics, he became a prolific author of books on political economy and Canadian history.

In 1909 Isabel started to publish articles in newspapers and magazines about literary subjects and issues of topical interest such as women's suffrage. As well, she frequently prepared talks for the Women's Canadian Club in Kingston. With Oscar she shared firm commitments to democracy and to liberal nationalism at a time when Canada was still a colony of Britain. She believed that Canadian history could appeal to a broad audience if such writing were based on "careful scientific research," free of prejudice, and written elegantly. This kind of history, she maintained, would "rank as high in the world of cultural interests as the writing of history of an older country would do."[2] Her goal was to secure a wide readership through original research and writing.

Interest in Canada's history exploded early in the twentieth century in response to the Boer War (1899–1902) and the First World War (1914–18). During the latter conflict, Skelton's journalism was noticed by Robert Glasgow, the publisher of the multi-volumed Chronicles of Canada series. He asked Isabel if she would prepare a volume on Canadian heroines for the series, but she considered that subject too hackneyed. Instead, she wrote a book on the history of women in settlements, to which she affixed the inventive title *Backwoodswoman* when it was published by Ryerson Press in 1924. Isabel Skelton's book was the first significant attempt to place Canadian women in history. With a demonstrable thesis that women had played a key role in Canadian settlement, Skelton surveyed the years from the French regime until the middle of the nineteenth century. "Few women are enrolled among the Makers of Canada," she wrote in reference to another series of history

books appearing between 1903 and 1908 under that title. "Yet in all save the earliest years they have formed nearly half the population and have done almost half the work. But historians, absorbed in the annals of war and politics and business, tell us little of the part they played. The woman's stage was not set in the limelight, but in the firelight."[3]

These words were as brave as the approach Isabel Skelton assumed in analysing the lives of ordinary rather than prominent women. Her focus centred on women in their domestic and community settings, but she was also attuned to differences in wealth, culture, and social class. She therefore parted company with such famous nineteenth-century authors as Susanna Moodie and Catharine Parr Traill, whose contemporary accounts had long been accepted as definitive portrayals of early Ontario, despite their British and middle-class biases. "The very artistic refinement and gentle training that made them so appreciative of the distant picture," Skelton wrote of these earlier women writers, "robbed them of all sympathy with and understanding of it [Upper Canada] at closer range, and blinded them to the deep human pathos and tragedy – the toil, the poverty and the sickness that formed its details." Skelton's approach was so new that the reviewer of the volume in the country's foremost historical journal, the *Canadian Historical Review*, attacked her for the book's major strength in recounting the lives of women of no special distinction.

Through her research in archival sources, Isabel Skelton moved successfully beyond depicting women as a general category to portraying them in their cultural settings as part of social and ethnic groups, although aboriginal women figured only cursorily and gender analysis was slight in her book. What was missing in her account was a provocative thesis (most could agree, after all, that women had figured in history) or a consideration of the relationship between women and the larger structures of society. Her history was primarily an affirmation of white women's roles in an effort to make them more visible. She wanted to paint women into the picture rather than adopt a gender analysis that would have questioned the underlying assumptions that governed people's lives. An examination of law or inheritance patterns, as undertaken by her American contemporary Mary Ritter Beard, would certainly have made her account less celebratory. Still, *Backwoodswoman* sold its print run and remained the standard authority on women in New France and Upper Canada for many decades, a shelf life much longer than that enjoyed by most history books. "To attempt to this kind of work," Isabel Skelton wrote, "has made all the difference between a life of satisfaction (comparatively) and one that would have been – and had been – up to that point restless and dissatisfied."[4] Achievement arrived at a cost she would later regret. Writing consumed so much time that the author gave less attention to her first two children than she did to her third. Life entailed choices.

Isabel Skelton wanted to widen history's vistas, but as she was also passionately committed to a country that she hoped would soon be independent of Britain, she chose Thomas D'Arcy McGee as the subject of her second book, which appeared in 1925. Skelton wanted to write a biography of McGee because he had been an Irish immigrant, literary nationalist, journalist, author, poet, and Father of Confederation prior to his assassination in 1868. Research into an entirely different area was required, and it was hard slogging at times. "Work on *Globe*," she noted in 1924 when reading old copies of a Toronto newspaper. "Must push myself more at this kind of work."[5] Her husband assisted by retrieving documents from Ireland's national library on a trip abroad, making con-

tacts for her in Ottawa, and reading her draft for revisions. The resources of Canadian libraries were so weak for the sections of the book that dealt with McGee's life in Ireland and the United States that Skelton had to buy books from a variety of far-flung bookstores. Skelton's *McGee* was a large biography that became the definitive life of its subject and one that all subsequent writers in the twentieth century acknowledged.

After Oscar Skelton accepted appointment as Canada's under-secretary of state for external affairs, Isabel moved with the children to Ottawa in 1925. She was not happy with the social exigencies imposed on the wife of one of the country's top civil servants, but she continued to set aside mornings for reading and writing. She wrote a book of literary criticism that failed to get published, edited a book of McGee's speeches that was published in 1937, and wrote three textbooks for Ryerson Press's Canadian history school series.[6] A scholarly article on prairie novelist Frederick Philip Grove that appeared in 1939 was said by the author himself to be the most insightful criticism of his work that he had ever encountered. When Grove told her that her criticisms cut so close to the quick that they appeared vicious, Isabel Skelton stood her ground in defending what she had done. Those seeking to interpret literary output, she said in defence of her work, needed to digest an author's complete output "objectively and with a free mind," and then "to have the courage of one's convictions and be true to one's standards." She also wrote that unless "a critic is honest according to her lights, her work is of no value whatsoever, whether the comments are favourable or the reverse."[7]

Returning to history writing, Skelton produced a new book-length manuscript in 1939 that was not published until 1947 on account of wartime shortages. Between those dates her husband died, in 1941, and she moved to Montreal to live on her own in an apartment close to one of her children. Her new book was ostensibly a biography of Presbyterian minister William Bell, who had written a fifteen-volume diary in Perth in eastern Ontario after 1818, but the book was really a study of immigration and the processes of colonization. Skelton used Bell's life to weave a rich tapestry of social and cultural history. When Ryerson Press anticipated that the volume would not sell well because William Bell was almost totally unknown, Isabel Skelton subsidized the publication with her own money. "You were fair," University of Western Ontario historian J.J. Talman wrote her after reading the volume, "and yet did not squeeze all the colour out of his life in an effort to be exact. I ... shall count this one of the good books in my library."[8] Skelton then began her last historical project, a study of Tiger Dunlop, the colourful character who served as agent for the Canada Company in southwestern Ontario during the early nineteenth century, but she did not live long enough to complete the manuscript, dying in 1955.

Isabel Skelton wrote not just for herself, but also for a larger audience interested in history and in literary criticism. Because she was supported by her husband financially, her projects were her own in conception and execution. The Skeltons' collaboration with each other's publishing efforts was limited to minor phases in the long process, from gestation to appearance in print, that accompanies the production of books that are truly original. At a time when few women wrote history, Isabel Skelton managed to bridge the divide that separates academic historians from amateurs or popularizers. Through her portrayals of women in their own right and through her interest in a broader cultural approach to history, Skelton served as a foremother for a later generation of women historians in a manner similar to Mary Ritter Beard in the United States.[9] Her books showed originality in thought and research, but they were written in an accessible manner so that they could be enjoyed by the general reader wanting to know about Canada's history. Isabel Skelton extended intellectual Canadian horizons in a manner unacknowledged by university professors concerned with exclusively male conceptions of history.

38 The Rideau Street Convent School: French-Language Private Schooling in Ontario

Isabelle Bourgeois

Franco-Ontarians have a long history of having to struggle to obtain services in French in their home province.[1] One of the longest and perhaps most important battles in this history was the fight for French-language schooling for all French-speaking residents of the province. Since most educational services in French were not granted until the end of the 1960s, Franco-Ontarians have been forced to find ways throughout the years to provide education to their children in French. Many families incurred significant cost to send their children to private schools, established by religious orders, to ensure the preservation of the French language and culture for future generations. Private schools also allowed parents to obtain education of high quality, which in turn provided pupils with the means of upward mobility to escape the poverty of the working class from which most of them originated.

The education of girls was deemed particularly important to the preservation of the French language and culture in Franco-Ontarian homes, since it can be argued that mothers have always been especially charged with the task of language and cultural transmission to their children. Private schools for girls thus played as important a role, one perhaps even more central, in this preservation than was true of those for boys.

Our Lady of the Sacred Heart Convent school is an example of one such private institution. Located on Ottawa's Rideau Street, a few blocks east of Parliament Hill, this private school was open to girls of both lan-

guages, from the elementary course to the bachelor's degree. The Rideau Street Convent School, as it was commonly known, helped to develop a female francophone elite among its pupils. Thus, the goals of the school, its curriculum, and the experiences of the young women who attended the private institution are worthy of study. This essay is based on secondary sources and interviews with two former students of the Rideau Street Convent School, the author's mother and grandmother: Rita Racine-Carrière who attended the school from 1927 to 1942, and Lise Bourgeois (née Carrière) who attended the school roughly from 1955 to 1967.

Before 1841, Upper Canada's (later Ontario's) schools were primarily local, one-room schools started by rural community initiative, where the quality of the instruction was often dependent on the instructor overcoming adverse circumstances. The language of instruction in these schools was based upon the language of the majority of inhabitants in each community. After 1841, however, with the implementation of Canada West's official school system to replace that of Upper Canada, many changes occurred in the way schools were regulated. That same year, the newly established government named a superintendent of education, Egerton Ryerson, who is remembered with respect in francophone communities. Ryerson recognized the legitimacy of French-language schools and facilitated their multiplication and development. Under Ryerson's long influence, Ontario's French-language schools acquired the *de facto* right to exist and

38.1 Grey Nuns class of 1964, junior school, Ottawa (Courtesy of Bourgeois family)

serve the educational needs of Franco-Ontarian students. Unfortunately, few subsequent administrators followed Ryerson's direction, and until 1948 Ontario provided little or no educational services in French to Franco-Ontarian secondary school students.[2] The provincial government also tended to eliminate services offered to French-speaking elementary school students and limited access to French-language books and activities.

In this evolution, the struggle against Regulation XVII, which was passed in 1912, is considered by many to be the most critical battle Franco-Ontarians ever waged for their rights as a minority group. The principal clauses of Regulation XVII stated that English was to become the only language of communication and instruction after the second grade in all public and separate Anglo-French schools. Teaching of the French language was to be reduced to one hour per day per classroom.

Fifteen years of public outcry and political battles followed the passage of Regulation XVII. This ruling was never revoked, but strong pressure from francophone communities and individuals managed to supplant it by Circular 46 in January 1928, which stated that French was equal to English in the instruction of Franco-Ontarian children at the elementary level. However, until 1968 bilingual high schools were the only publicly supported means through which French-speaking students could pursue their studies past the elementary level. In these schools, French was taught as a subject to francophones, but all other subjects were taught in English and school administrators only communicated in English.[3]

In these restricted circumstances, francophones embraced private schooling, especially for their daughters. Private schools received no state funding and were owned and administered by religious orders. In fact, most of Ontario's French-language private schools were established by Quebec's religious orders. This situation prevailed in Ontario until the implementation of Ontario educational standards later in the twentieth century. Private schools usually had boarders as well as day students. The curriculum was infused with religious and culturally based materials. As such, these schools served an instrumental role in the preservation of the French language, culture, and religious identification among Ontario francophones. But in doing so, they paid a price: numerous convents and colleges used significant financial resources to provide access to higher education to all young deserving francophones, who otherwise could not afford to continue their schooling.[4]

In 1967 John Robarts, premier of Ontario, announced his government's formal intention to establish a complete network of services in French to Franco-Ontarian students at the secondary level. Bills 140 and 141, implemented in 1968, ensured the creation of publicly subsidized French-language secondary schools. For the first time in Ontario's history, French would be equal to English in matters of public education.

The Rideau Street Convent School was founded in 1849 by Mother Elisabeth Bruyère, founder of the Ottawa chapter of the Congregation of the Grey Nuns of the Cross, which later became the Sisters of Charity. The school took as its mandate the preparation of an elite among Catholics of both languages by providing superior instruction to that offered in Bytown's smaller parochial school, which had also been founded by the Grey Nuns in 1845.

The main goal of the instruction offered at the Rideau Street Convent School was to produce young women who were conscious of their Christian duties and the importance of their work in the home. Instruction featured moral education and practical skills. The goal of the sisters at the Rideau Street Convent, from the women students' point of view, was to help them become young professionals as well as give them the necessary social and class-based skills required to be the wives of professionals, such as doctors, lawyers, and diplomats. Another objective of the sisters was to invite their young pupils to enter the community life of the order once their studies were completed.

Many factors motivated francophone parents to send their daughters to the Rideau Street Convent School. Most parents recognized its high standards of education and found the means to pay the tuition fees required by the sisters to keep the institution running. The sisters tried to help less fortunate parents by contributing some of the community's funds towards the tuition of worthy students whose parents could not afford to send them to school.

The majority of students attending the Rideau Street Convent School were francophone Catholic girls, but the sisters also accepted girls from other cultures and faiths. While the school offered a full English-language curriculum to those who preferred to study in English, the sisters emphasized francophone culture in their teaching and in the activities organized for students, especially literature and art. But in order to maintain the bilingual character of the institution, pupils of both languages were encouraged to socialize during recess and outings, with French and English alternating every day as the language of communication. Even though all subjects were taught in both languages, thus providing francophones with courses and activities in their first language throughout their studies, bilingualism was an integral part of the school's educational practices.

The Rideau Street Convent School, like all private schools, had a strong code of discipline. The sisters reinforced their teachings with moral, religious, and cultural content to promote the compliance of their pupils. Discipline and religion seemed to be part of the same concept as remembered by school alumna Mrs Racine-Carrière: "It was never an arduous discipline, but we had to follow all of the rules and regulations taught and enforced by the sisters. The sisters also often followed the same groups of pupils from year to year, which made discipline easier to enforce." Mrs Bourgeois provided further details on discipline in the Rideau Street Convent School:

Discipline was very, very strict. We were not allowed to talk to each other in between classes, we had to stand quietly in line. When the Mother Superior or the school's principal came into our classroom, we had to stand up, place our feet a certain way, put our hands one on top of the other, lower our heads, and recite a standard greeting. After lunch, when we came in, the Sisters had an instrument which made a clapping sound, and we would always do the same routine: "clap," stand up, "clap," "clap," turn, "clap," clap, "clap," kneel, and we recited the rosary. That was in high school, every day.

Religion was taught to students as a compulsory subject. It also permeated school activities. Mrs Bourgeois elaborated on the extent of this religious influence: "For instance, in the ninth grade, we studied a specific section of the Old Testament. It was a historical approach which was very interesting, because it was history, not liturgic theories. Of course, we could attend Mass every morning if we wished to do so, and there was a compulsory Mass on the first Friday of every month, with mantillas, hats, and 'Kleenex' on heads … It was just another way of learning religion, that was very cultural."

The range of courses offered at the Rideau Street Convent School changed over the years to accommodate provincial regulations and to meet the changing academic and social needs of the pupils. In the earliest years of the school, all students followed the "Convent Course," a program that had been designed by the convent's teaching sisters and lasted from eight to ten years. This program was offered in both French and English and covered typical elementary-level course content, as well as some secondary course content. Later on, as the requirements of diplomas in teaching, accounting, and health services changed, the sisters reviewed the program offered to students and created the French Classical Course, which included both elementary and secondary course content. This course covered grades one to twelve, and its structure was based on programs offered to students in private schools across Quebec.

Therefore, until 1960, the elementary course, from grades one to six, was based on the Sisters' "Convent Course." After this date, it was based on the provincial elementary schooling guidelines. The most important subject in the elementary course was French, both spoken and written. English was also taught at this level; francophone students had an English lesson every day, and spelling bees every week. Mathematics, history, and geography were part of the elementary curriculum. Religion was taught every day.

Courses offered in the various secondary studies programs consisted of languages and humanities courses such as Latin, French, English, history, and religion. Some science and mathematics courses, such as algebra, geometry, zoology, and botany, were also part of the secondary curriculum. Other courses, such as domestic science, visual arts, and music, were available to students.

From the 1960s, the sisters used manuals produced in Ontario instead of Quebec, in order to follow provincial course requirements. Unfortunately, none of these manuals were written in French. The twelfth grade provincial compulsory examinations also caused problems for the convent's pupils, since these were in English only. Mrs Bourgeois noted: "In order to graduate, we had to pass compulsory examinations provided by the Ministry of Ontario. The subject assessed by these exams changed every year. In 1964, it was Latin, which caused us problems, because we had studied Latin in French, and in the exam, we had to translate from Latin to English. We asked the government of Ontario for a special permission, in order to be able to write the test in French."

Many young girls attending the Rideau Street Convent School considered their postsecondary education as a means of obtaining employment in these professions. Since the University of Ottawa did not accept women in the bachelor's degree program during this period, the sisters decided to extend their educational work to higher education. After negotiating with the administrators of the university, the sisters opened the Collège Bruyère in 1925. Affiliated with the Faculty of Arts of the University of Ottawa, the college prepared its pupils for the university's examinations in a four-year course. Even though the college never received provincial grants, it managed to keep tuition fees low.

The Collège Bruyère emphasized both French and English language skills. All subjects, except for English, were taught in French, and the level of English taught was the same as that taught in English-language institutions. As in the case of the secondary curriculum, the subjects initially included the humanities – philosophy, theology, French, English, Latin, and history – as well as mathematics and biology. This program was later modified and updated to provide more options, including Spanish, Italian, psychology, sociology, and political science. In the 1930s, more courses were added: geology,

geography, physiology, chemistry, social economics, and culinary arts. In keeping with the primary mandate of the Rideau Street Convent School, religion courses were also part of the four-year curriculum. In 1957, the college was granted permission by the Faculty of Pure and Applied Sciences of the University of Ottawa to offer courses at the pre-science level, to prepare the pupils for studies in nursing, medicine, and laboratory technology.

Graduates felt that they had received an education of high quality; Mrs Bourgeois recalls: "People can talk about anything and I can understand what they are saying. In the organizations in which I work, the concepts have remained the same. The ideologies stem from the philosophies that I have studied. For us, there are no mysteries: we know where we come from and where we are going. I really appreciate the knowledge I've acquired: I chose to take even more philosophy courses during my master's degree, because it helped me understand literature and history."

Discipline was enforced at a much more subtle level than during the previous years of schooling. The young women who attended the college wore uniforms as they had done during their elementary and secondary studies, and were expected to act with decorum both inside and outside the college. The pupils were also expected to earn excellent grades in the University of Ottawa's examinations. Mrs Bourgeois explained: "When we finished our degree, we had to take the University of Ottawa's examinations. We always received high grades on these exams, because we worked very hard, we studied every night. The courses were very intensive."

The years spent at the Collège Bruyère were beneficial to the young women who chose to pursue their studies with the Sisters of Charity. Many went on to pursue professional careers, others married and began their work in the home, and still others chose to continue studying in graduate schools across Ontario. Mrs Racine-Carrière noted: "It helped me, especially once I was married, with the children. It enabled me to help them; otherwise I couldn't have. It also helped me understand many other things, through analysis, synthesis, judging situations. It was very beneficial to me." Such a variety of choices would probably not have existed for these women without the opportunity to complete secondary and post-secondary studies in French.

Aside from its more academic training, the Rideau Street Convent School was also well known for its commercial course. This option provided choice to girls who were less academically inclined, giving them employ-ment and career skills.

In summary, the Rideau Street Convent School pro-vided a climate in which French-speaking girls could study in their first language. This emphasis on superior education resulted in an elite group of young women who served a number of important functions in their communities. The graduates became teachers, wives of diplomats, doctors, psychologists, actresses, and nuns. Perhaps the most important role served by these women was that of preservers and promoters of the French lan-guage, its culture, and its values for future generations.[5]

39 "The School on Fardy's Cross": Shamrock School Remembered

Pat Trites

For much of our country's history and well into the twentieth century, many of Canada's children were educated in one-room, multi-grade schools. How did young women teachers in such schools manage to teach so many different grades successfully and address the needs of a variety of students in one room, sometimes with students ranging from grades one to eleven? How did students with special requirements have their educational needs met? Did teachers or students have special attributes that assisted in the operation of these schools? What was the nature of the day-to-day experience for the teacher and the students in a one-room school?

The history of the one-room school has been documented from a variety of perspectives, oral histories being a popular method employed in several studies. The experience of rural female teachers has frequently been presented as a largely unpleasant one, with the teacher often portrayed as a victim.[1] In a study of rural women teachers in British Columbia, J. Donald Wilson states that rural areas were thought to be too "rugged and wild for the delicate sensibilities of the young female."[2]

This essay considers Shamrock School in Lakeview, Newfoundland, examing this small, isolated, rural school from the perspective of sixteen of the students, two teachers who taught there, and two additional teachers from the local high school. The study focuses primarily on Isabelle Woodford, the one teacher whom all the selected students had in common. Information was gathered through personal and telephone interviews and through written responses. Anonymity was assured all participants, a condition that Isabelle Woodford has since waived. By examining one particular school, this essay hopes to contribute to the knowledge of one-room schools in Canada. In particular, it hopes to shed some light on the motivations, challenges, and rewards of one female teacher, Isabelle Woodford, while relating her former students' perceptions of their educational experiences there.

Shamrock School in Lakeview stood at the junction of two roads, a site known locally as Fardy's Cross. Built in 1908, the white clapboard building was forty feet in length, twenty feet wide, with a high peaked roof and ceilings that were at least twelve feet in height. At the back of the school was a large attached porch that served as the school's entrance, with hooks on its walls for the children's outer garments and a large coal bin situated at its rear. Also attached to the back of the school were two outhouses, one for the girls and one for the boys, and these were accessed through a short partitioned hall. During the period of study, the school had electricity but no running water. Thirty-five to forty students seem to have been the average number attending the school at any given time.

Ten tall windows provided plenty of light and sometimes more than adequate ventilation. At the front of the schoolroom were the black boards, while the back contained a few shelves that housed the school's resource materials – a globe, a copy of *The Birds of Newfoundland*,

and a few other books. In the centre of the classroom sat a pot-bellied stove with a sheet of metal beneath to protect the floor boards from sparks. It was here that mittens dried after a winter's recess. On exceptionally cold and windy days, the stove was sometimes taxed beyond its capacity, despite the zealous efforts of the older boys to stoke it until it was red hot. At such times the teacher would dispense with the orderly rows of desks and allow them to be moved around the stove in a roughly circular fashion so that children could better share the limited heat. The lack of a schoolyard did not pose a problem, for the ponds, the woods and Kennedy's Meadow were all easily available, and children organized their own activities during recess.

Isabelle Woodford taught at Shamrock School between 1948 and 1953. Career options for women were fairly restricted at the time, and she recalls that while her mother might initially have preferred that she study to be a nurse, she herself was firmly committed to becoming a teacher. To realize this ambition she completed two years of teacher training in St John's (1946 to 1948) at the prestigious Roman Catholic St Bride's College, or Littledale as it was more commonly known.[3]

Isabelle describes herself as having been very religious and idealistic at the time. She regarded the nuns as exemplary role models who set very high standards: "Littledale and the sisters opened up a different world for me, one that changed forever the way I thought, the things I appreciated. It helped to form not only the teacher but the person I was to become." In the first year of teacher training at Littledale, all courses were taken at the college. The second year involved attending courses at Memorial College, which was not a degree-granting institution at the time, while continuing to board at Littledale. Along with the academic regimen, the sisters at Littledale offered courses that included music, art, elocution, and needlework. (When Memorial College became Memorial University of Newfoundland in 1949, the two years of

teacher training at Littledale were accepted with full credit towards the four-year education degree.) The denominational school system in Newfoundland continued for many years, and each parish priest hired the teachers who taught in his parish. As a Littledale graduate, Isabelle Woodford was a well-qualified eighteen-year-old when she started her career at Shamrock School in 1948, with a monthly salary of forty-eight dollars.

When Isabelle began teaching at Fardy's Cross, the teacher was expected to teach whatever number of students or grades were present. Quite frequently there might only be the elementary and junior grades, since the majority of students did not complete high school. However, when Isabelle began teaching, she discovered among her students a number who she felt would complete their schooling. Because she wanted to see her students through to the Council of Higher Education examinations, which marked the end of high school, Isabelle requested that she be permitted to teach up to grade eleven. The request was granted by the parish priest.

Isabelle remembers her years at Shamrock School vividly and with fondness. She recalls walking more than a mile to work each day, having the younger children vie to hold her hand on their way from school, and being driven by her father by horse and sleigh if the winter weather was particularly bad. She recalls also a pride of ownership in the school, remembering bringing a bucket and washcloths from home so that she could clean the school's windows: "It [the school] was your place and you wanted it to be nice." School days began and ended with prayers; morning prayers were followed by catechism class, and then the days proceeded in a regular pattern. She "heard" the lessons first of the smaller children, assigned work for them, and moved on to work with the higher grades.

Isabelle believed that the first two years of school were critical in instilling a love of education, and she strove to make these years enjoyable for her young charges.

School resources were limited, and with her own money she purchased small teaching aids such as coloured, gummed stars. These stars adorned well-executed work and provided a source of motivation that is remembered by former students more than forty years later. The practice of purchasing their own supplies was continued by subsequent teachers at Shamrock School. Years later, one of the last teachers there recalled purchasing such basic supplies as chalk with her own money, rather than endure a lengthy wait for the necessary funds.

Along with providing academic instruction, Isabelle gave the religious direction necessary to prepare the children for the Catholic sacraments of First Communion, Confession, and Confirmation. She took students occasionally to St John's for events such as the Santa Claus Parade, and she organized Christmas concerts and end-of-year picnics. Perhaps because she was young enough to remember a child's joy in spring and sunshine, when weather permitted she sometimes held classes outdoors in an area known as "The Park." These outdoor classes were extremely popular with students, but it was sometimes difficult for the teacher to maintain strict control in this setting.

Isabelle remembers her years at Shamrock School as being among the happiest in her life and her pupils as "wonderful youngsters, remarkably enthusiastic, and with so much potential." She believes that she worked well with fairly bright students, but still regrets what she believes was an inability to find the hidden talents in some of her charges. Isabelle also regrets her use of the strap, a piece of leather of about sixteen inches in length, supple from many years of use, and notched at one end to better accommodate the teacher's grip. "The Slapper," as it was known by students, was applied for such misdemeanors as not knowing one's Catechism, taking another student's pencil, or causing a disturbance in class. Parents generally accepted its use as legitimate, and one former student stated, "If I got in trouble at school, there

would be punishment waiting at home as well. My parents respected the teacher." The strap notwithstanding, Isabelle is remembered by almost all of her former students as having had a very positive and lasting impact on their lives.

The challenges facing the teacher in a one-room school were enormous and required a variety of coping skills and strategies. Every grade had its prescribed curriculum, and since it was impossible to teach all official lessons to each grade of children on a daily basis, different approaches had to be employed. Periods of time were set aside "to hear" students' lessons, and many students from Shamrock School recall being called up to the teacher's desk as a group for that purpose. Peer assistance was encouraged. Sometimes older students assisted the younger ones when they had finished their own work and the teacher was busy with another class. Bright children assisted slower ones, and students sometimes corrected each other's tests. There was no formal group work, but working in pairs was encouraged as long as it was done in a quiet, studious manner. Overall, despite the mixture of ages and classes in one room, there was a sense of order, not chaos. Isabelle does not recall feeling frustrated by her workload. She believes that the circumstances under which she worked were the norm of the time and as such were taken in stride.

Without the technology that today aids teachers, even the simplest tasks were labour-intensive. There were no photocopiers for example, but copies could be made in a variety of ways. One highly unsatisfactory yet common method involved the use of a hectograph.[4] Papers printed with the hectograph had a purplish colour, and the print was often so faint as to be illegible. Despite its shortcomings, the hectograph seems to have been the method most resorted to in preparing test questions. It saved the teacher considerable time, and she could always dictate the illegible parts to students. When the hectograph was not used, questions might be dictated or written on the chalk board to be copied by older students. Less commonly used was carbon paper, probably because of its cost and limited availability.

There were no regularly scheduled parent-teacher meetings; instead "Education Week" provided an opportunity for parents to come to school and see samples of the students' work posted on the walls. Meetings between parents and teachers seem to have occurred only if something was perceived to be very seriously wrong, such as a major discipline problem. Parental involvement in children's education was of a direct and immediate type. There were no Parent Teacher Associations, no cadre of young mothers who volunteered to come to school and assist with classes. And yet fathers found time from other tasks to construct a stage for the Christmas concert, used their trucks to transport children to the annual school-closing picnics, and cleaned the outhouses. Mothers assisted with costumes and stage props and scrubbed the school's wooden floor once or twice a year. With rare exceptions, parents of both sexes appear to have given the teacher unqualified support. Generally, no criticism of the teacher was countenanced and disciplinary methods were not questioned. As one student stated, "There was no point in complaining to your parents; the teacher was the ultimate law and her discipline was upheld."

Although somewhat intimidating to teacher and students alike, the school inspector is remembered fondly as being well qualified and supportive of teachers. Students looked forward to his visits because he brought with him a film projector and showed films that were often of educational merit. This was a rare treat for children for whom the nearest movie theatre was in St John's, about thirty-five miles away and only visited once or twice a year. The inspector who came to Shamrock School held a master's degree and, despite more lucrative job offers from the mainland and the United States, had returned following his studies to Newfoundland, where he felt he was most needed. A teacher at Shamrock School some

years following Isabelle recalled that the inspector had had a passion for English and would sometimes teach a class when he visited the school. She stated, "We were doing team-teaching before it ever became fashionable."

After five years at Fardy's Cross, Isabelle left teaching and worked with the Children's Aid Society in St John's until 1958. Some former students remembered her tears on the day she announced that she would not be returning to Shamrock School after the summer break. Isabelle recalls that it was a difficult decision, for she loved the children and her work, but she felt that it was time for a new career challenge, as well as time to move away from her home community. She remembers also her pleasant surprise upon learning that the salary for social workers was considerably higher than that for teachers. Isabelle remained with the Children's Aid until she married and started a family. She never resumed working outside the home, a decision not unlike that of many women of her time. It surprises her now that she never considered pursuing additional education. She believes it was part of her generation's approach to the role of women in society and muses that perhaps it was a gender issue. Once a woman embarked on a home-making career, there was little need seen for her to pursue further academic studies.

All of the former students who shared their memories of Shamrock School for this study were taught by Isabelle Woodford for at least one year and most had also had other teachers during their time there. Several themes emerged when former students were asked to comment on the advantages and disadvantages of the one-room schoolhouse. On the positive side, these included independent learning, self-reliance, a ready exchange of ideas, and an ability to learn from other classes being taught. One student recalled being taught according to groups, not grades. Several grades would listen to a language lesson or a poem being discussed and, she reflected, "Really, what difference did it make what grade we were in?"

Students remembered an emphasis on going through the textbooks page by page and completing them rather than following a thematic approach. Students also recalled a sense of community, a sense of safety and comfort at not being separated from siblings or friends, a sense of relaxed mingling that probably assisted socialization, fostered the ability to work with others, and taught tolerance and perhaps some compassion, as there was no segregation of the bright and not-so-bright pupils.

Former students shared their teacher's belief that students in a one-room school had an opportunity to learn from what was being taught to other classes. The setting was also felt to promote a trust between the teacher and pupil. This was evident when the teacher gave students the key to the school and the responsibility of lighting the fire before school started, assigned pupils to help others with their school work, or left students to lock the school after they had finished sweeping it or practising for a school concert.

On a less positive note, several students commented on the fact that there was not much individual attention. One person qualified, saying, "Children in those days did not seem to need as much individual attention as they do today – either at home or in school – so it was not really a problem." Another former student commented that the main objective seemed to be to have at least one student from each grade pass the provincial examinations, with the result that "those of us in the middle often fell through the cracks." The Council of Higher Education in St John's, which initially conducted examinations prepared and corrected in England, was abolished in 1949. However, its function was absorbed by the Department of Education, which continued the system of external examination. The above student's implication that the CHE exam system promoted an emphasis on some students (those preparing to write these examinations) to the detriment of others is echoed elsewhere.[5]

At Shamrock School there was the usual amount of teasing that one encounters in any schoolyard, and most former students either did not comment on it or gave it a very small place in their remembrances of past schooldays. One student, however, remembered being singled out for teasing that reached the point of bullying. She stated, "Shamrock School to me was primarily an experience to be endured, survived, rather than an idyllic pastoral place of learning." This woman described herself as having been "a bookish child," and one wonders if the teasing she endured was the sort of socialization that encouraged children not to outperform their peers. A similar phenomenon was reported as having occurred in a one-room school in coastal British Columbia.[6] Perceptual problems, dyslexia, and other related learning disabilities were not well understood at the time, and no particular accommodations were made for such students.

On the evidence of Isabelle Woodford and her former students who contributed to this study, the experience at Shamrock School would seem to have largely been one of mutual respect between the teacher, students, and parents. Roles were strictly defined within rural communities in Newfoundland at that time, and it was assumed that people, young and old, would live up to what was expected of them. Sanctions against the failure to do so were strict, and in the case of children, these might come in the form of corporal punishment. Perhaps this sense of duty, this conformity to community expectations, was at the heart of the apparent mutual respect between the teacher, students, and parents. It was the teacher's business to teach, the students' to learn, and the parents' to support the teacher's efforts. In serving and being supported by a community, teachers in one-room schools, most of them women, confirmed in turn the community's social, religious, and cultural norms.[7]

40 Women, Team Sport, and Physical Education

Women and Physical Education

Ellen O'Reilly

Part of sport culture is women's physical education. Contemporary Canadian programs of physical education for young women have their roots in nineteenth-century Victorian British notions of health, beauty, and appropriate feminine activity. Although women's sport can be traced to classical times, organized programs of instruction for physical education are a relatively new phenomenon. A combination of science, fashion, and shared cultural beliefs in the propriety of certain physical activities for women culminated in the development of physical education programs for women in the early twentieth century. These programs emphasized femininity, wellness, and attractiveness through moderate physical exercise and games.

40.1 Young women's field hockey team, Alert Bay, 1910 (D-04477, British Columbia Archives)

40.3 Tennis player, c. 1925 (Fader Collection, Nova Scotia Archives and Records Management)

40.2 Basketball team, 1915 (N 9702, Nova Scotia Archives and Records Management)

Left:
40.4 Walking in a road race, c. 1920
(1987-310, #537, Nova Scotia Archives and
Records Management)

Bottom left:
40.5 Female cyclists, c. 1900
(N-8090, Nova Scotia Archives and Records
Management)

Bottom right:
40.6 Fishing, c. 1900
(1992-398, 7, Nova Scotia Archives and
Records Management)

Note in the early photographs the ladylike, genteel poses of the field hockey players (Illustration 40.1) and basketball players (Illustration 40.2). Neither team is pictured on a field or court, but instead appear within the familiar domestic, parlour-like scene. Note also the composed expression of the young tennis player (Illustration 40.3). Sporting costumes, as illustrated by the women who are race walking (Illustration 40.4), preparing for riding a bike (Illustration 40.5), fishing by the lake (Illustration 40.6), or playing on a baseball team (Illustration 40.7), were not very different from everyday apparel. Over time, women's outfits were gradually redesigned to offer more freedom of movement, as seen in the later-day bathing suits (Illustration 40.8) and basketball shorts (Illustration 40.9).

Top right:
40.7 Young women's basketball team, c. 1930
(82/428, #33, Yukon Archives)

Right:
40.8 Girls swimming at Bain Lévesque, Montreal, 1954
(VM105/Z-2102, #3. Ville de Montreal. Gestion des documents et archives)

Below:
40.9 Women's basketball team (1986-516, Nova Scotia Archives and Records Management)

Women and Team Sport

Veronica Strong-Boag

Sports are often taken for granted as part of masculine cultures, but athletic activities have also contributed a good deal to women's sense of personal confidence and camaraderie. During the 1966 Olympics, young women rowers raced proudly for Canada and communicated their enthusiasm for both the sport and their team-mates. Such sentiments are far from new. Just like the figures in Illustrations 40.10 and 40.11, girls and women have sought out a wide range of recreational activities to test their mettle and enjoy themselves. In face of substantial religious disapproval during the French regime, they determined to dance; in the nineteenth century, they dismissed objections to take up the bicycle and hockey stick. Girls still struggled for equality in intramural sports in the last quarter of the twentieth century. Whether in ice hockey, skiing, synchronized swimming, or curling, where Canadian sporting culture has produced champions, women contribute to and benefit from athletic associations and team efforts.

40.10 The Flying Hens soccer team, 1961 (E-07918, British Columbia Archives)

40.11 Curling, 1960s (Harbottle Collection, 6159, Yukon Archives)

Montreal Sportswomen and the Penguin Ski Club

Andrea Winlo

In 1932 during the pioneer days of downhill skiing, a group of eighteen enthusiastic women established the Penguin Ski Club for women. Using the club to initiate ski lessons to improve their basic skill in the sport, they sought out more varied and challenging slopes. They also sought out acceptable lodgings in the Laurentian Mountains for their members at a time when social convention denied females such opportunities. By incorporating themselves into a legal and financial entity in 1938–39, club members circumvented most of the constraints facing women in male-dominated ski clubs; in doing so, they were unique in North America. The Penguin Ski Club owned its own club house at St Sauveur des Monts and all women were invited to join. Most of the members were middle class, both anglophone and francophone. In a forty-year period, the club accepted over three hundred young women into its membership. It conducted ski lessons and races for school-age girls and they managed annual co-educational ski races. In addition, the club was represented on Canadian Amateur Ski Association committees.

40.12 The Penguin Ski Club, Montreal, 1930s (Andrea Wilno)

41 From Elegance and Expression to Sweat and Strength: Physical Education at the Margaret Eaton School

Anna H. Lathrop

In a first-year composition entitled, "Who I Am and Why I Came to College," the young Dora Mavor, nineteen years of age, describes the aspirations that probably typified young privileged women who sought higher education at the turn of the century in Ontario.

I came to college because it was the most convenient way of continuing my education. I want to be able to earn an honest living if I so chance that I may have to. Some people think that it is not necessary for a girl to go to College, but the point that I want to emphasize is that learning to use your brains should not hinder you from being able to do menial work, but rather, lend help. Whatever our vocation in life is, we are all sure one time or another to have some sorrow. How much better will it be to have something to fall back upon; to be able to pick up a book, perhaps of foreign poems, and be able to appreciate it! This is why I came to college.[1]

Dora's hopes reflect a period of transition in higher education for middle- and upper-class women. The advent of university co-educational access had begun to erode the place of nineteenth-century female academies and women were asking for vocational training in addition to courses of study designed to enhance female accomplishment.[2] For the young Dora Mavor, undoubtedly shaped by her father's reformist politics and a home environment enriched by art and theatrical appreciation,[3] the Margaret Eaton School of Literature and Expression was her preferred choice.

The Margaret Eaton School was a private institution of higher learning designed to train young middle- and upper-class women in the fields of literature and dramatic arts and body culture – the first to do so in Canada. The school, originally established as the School of Expression in 1901, was the enterprising work of a young widow from Waterdown, Ontario. Emma Scott Raff opened her studio in a few small rooms at the corner of Bloor and Yonge Streets in Toronto. Here, she offered young women training in "elocution, physical culture, pedagogy and literature."[4] In 1903 Margaret Beattie Eaton attended classes in dramatic expression with Scott Raff. Margaret Eaton's passion for drama and the theatre led her to convince her husband, Timothy Eaton, to provide the funds for a magnificent new facility to be built for the school. In 1907 the building was completed, and Scott Raff's School of Expression became the Margaret Eaton School of Literature and Expression.

From 1907 to 1925, Emma Scott Raff directed this school, offering "[a] professional and practical education for women."[5] Delsartan movement training figured as an important part of this education, and by 1917 there were two distinct streams of study: literature and dramatic art and physical culture. Scott Raff believed that the body should be trained to be a perfect instrument of expression so that literature could be appreciated as a truly "living art." As a widow and single mother who struggled for economic autonomy, she also firmly believed that "[a]ll culture should carry with it a bread-winning power."[6] For the young Dora Mavor – Emma Scott Raff's most famous and beloved student – this ideal was certainly realized. Dora Mavor Moore, a graduate of the school, later became one of Canada's most noted pioneers in the establishment of amateur theatre.[7]

In 1925 the school was substantially reorganized. Although classes in physical culture had been an important part of its early curriculum – echoing nineteenth-century beliefs that light, expressive exercises would prepare women for the rigours of higher education – they became more so as the century progressed. By the first decades of the twentieth century, women's physical education in England and the United States was shifting towards the development of specialist women's physical education colleges and training institutions. The same trend was evident in Canada. As early as 1915 Scott Raff reported that "physical education" was becoming an area of increasing popularity in its own right,[8] and by 1923 students of the school were awarded either a teacher's diploma in literature and dramatic art or a diploma in physical education.[9] In 1925, however, the school building was demolished as a result of the expansion of Bay Street in Toronto, and political events led Emma Scott Raff to resign her position as principal. As a result, the school temporarily closed. Through the efforts of a persistent alumnae association, the school's board was convinced to reopen and relocate the school to the YWCA (Young Women's Christian Association) building on the corner of Yonge and McGill Streets, a property owned by the T. Eaton Company. The curriculum was reorganized into the Department of Literature and Dramatic Art and the Department of Physical Education. Within a year, with falling student registration in the dramatic arts side of the program, the Literature and Dramatic Art Department was discontinued and the school became exclusively devoted to a curriculum of physical education. Despite the fact that Margaret Eaton

wanted nothing to do with physical education, the school continued to honour her in its new shortened name – "The Margaret Eaton School."

In 1926 Mary G. Hamilton, a quiet woman of practical vision from Fergus, Ontario, became the second principal of the school. Hamilton, a graduate of the Sargent School of Physical Training in Boston, was originally hired by Scott Raff in 1911 and had taught classes in games and social dance at the school for a number of years. Like Emma Scott Raff and Dora Mavor, Hamilton relied on a friendship network that was strongly affiliated with the school. These three women remained close friends throughout their lifetimes.

As the new principal, Hamilton hoped to consolidate a course of study that would prepare graduates for the developing field of physical education. Her intent was to ensure that the school's graduates would be "competent to organize and take charge of every branch of physical training for girls."[10] She believed that there was a need for young women to be trained in the field of physical education and that their training must include a rigorous practical and theoretical course of study. Proficiency in games, sports, dance, gymnastics, and wilderness survival were important skills included in the curriculum. In her first year as principal, Hamilton instituted a mandatory month-long camping experience for Margaret Eaton students as part of their training as potential camp counsellors. She took them to Camp Tanamakoon, a girls' camp that Hamilton founded in 1924 in Algonquin Park, Ontario. For the next seventeen years, this camp operated as a girls' camp during the summer months and as a camp counsellor training centre at the beginning of each academic term for the students of the school. Here, as Hamilton asserted, the future graduates of the school were exposed to wilderness experiences that prepared them to be "staunch and rugged and unwilling to acknowledge defeat by weather or circumstance."[11] Student songs about these camp experiences extolled the

41.1 Fundamental gymnastics (*Margaret Eaton School Yearbook*, 1936–1937, Toronto. Courtesy of Anna Lathrop)

joy of swinging an axe, the strain of a challenging portage, and the exhilaration of a successful trek.

Strap a compass and knife and an axe to your belt;
There's a thrill in the woods to be felt
When you chop and you swing, you can hear
   your axe ring!
Oh, the call comes to hearts that are true![12]

Between 1925 and 1941, the Margaret Eaton School prepared over 250 young women to enter the field of physical education. The curriculum included practical training in fundamental gymnastics, remedial gymnastics, aesthetic and folk-dancing, life-saving, and a variety of indoor and outdoor games, which included ice hockey, lacrosse, basketball, and field hockey. Theoretical courses covered anatomy, physiology, hygiene, anthropometry, theory of games and gymnastics, psychology of exercise, methods of teaching, first aid, and home nursing. Hamilton hired full- and part-time faculty from Bedford and Dartford Physical Training Colleges in Britain, as well as from the Boston and Chicago Normal Schools in the United States. Specialists in dance from the Imperial Russian Ballet and the Dalcroze School of Eurhythmics in Geneva were also hired. The school offered the first intensive physical education training centre for women in Canada and was advertised as such across the nation. Hamilton initiated a placement bureau and encouraged directors of private camps and principals of private girls' schools to solicit their graduates directly through her.[13] The academic and activity skills that the school fostered had a clear vocational emphasis. The school calendar published employment statistics that boasted that their graduates found employment in schools, colleges, social centres, settlements, playgrounds, industrial settings, and YWCAS.[14] These graduates entered positions as settlement house workers, YWCA directors, private school teachers, and camp counsellors. Hamilton proudly advertised successful career placements in the school's calendar:

During the last ten years the Margaret Eaton School has granted its diploma in physical education to one hundred and fifty-three young women who have come from Newfoundland, the United States, and every province in Canada. In the fall of 1931 eighty-eight graduates were teaching, six were studying, three were in physiotherapy, three in social service, three in other occupations and fifty in private life. Of those gainfully employed 74 percent were in Canada, 21 percent in the United States, and 5 percent in foreign countries.[15]

Elizabeth Pitt Barron graduated from the Margaret Eaton School in 1925, and her career pattern typified many of the young graduates of this period. A student at the school during the transitional period when dramatic arts was eclipsed by physical education, she recalled both Emma Scott Raff and Mary Hamilton – "Auntie Em and Ham" as their students' nicknamed them – with great fondness. She remembered Scott Raff's exotic handmade European velvet gowns and Hamilton's crisp brown tunic and leotards.[16] As a graduate of the physical education stream, self-described as "one of the physicals" as opposed to "one of the expressions," Pitt Barron had entered a career in physical education that lasted over forty years. Immediately after graduation, she accepted a junior coaching position at Bryn Mawr College in Philadelphia, and later she returned to Toronto to teach at Havergal College. She next accepted a position as the director of the Eaton Girls' Club – a position she ultimately held for twenty-nine years – and served overseas as a member of the Eaton Nursing Division of the St John Ambulance during the Second World War. She served as a director and a counsellor for a number of girls' camps in the province, notably the Eaton girls' camp at Shadow Lake, north of Toronto. In 1951 she became the director of the YWCA in Oshawa, and well into her sixties, she served as the executive director of the YM/YWCA of Welland and the YWCA of Niagara Falls. Later reflecting on her own life history, she commented "I wasn't afraid to be the first at anything. Whenever someone said that I couldn't do something – that made me really determined to do it."[17] When it came to queries of marriage, she explained, "I found I was becoming a career girl, with no time for dates."[18] In fact, after her retirement, at the age of sixty-six, Bess Pitt finally relented to what she described as the "tender trap" of marriage – but only after a long and eventful career. Indeed, Pitt Barron's life echoed the kind of Margaret Eaton pluck that another graduate, Helen Plaunt, wrote about in the 1937–38 student alumnae magazine. In a fictional account entitled "The Awful Truth," Plaunt described a young Margaret Eaton graduate's first job interview with a prospective YWCA employer:

She strode up to me and with a baleful glare, roared – 'We expect you to be able to teach riding, golfing, swimming, diving, tennis, canoeing, hand craft, and nature lore. You must be able to cook and also groom horses and at any time be able to take over the job of director if the present one die or be poisoned – can you do it?'

Bravely I stood up to her and with a sticky accent gave the saccharine reply, 'Margaret Eaton girls can and do everything – they never get their man!'[19]

During the Margaret Eaton School's forty-year history, although the type of education offered to young women shifted from an education in elegance and expression to one of sweat and strength, its young graduates were clearly expected to serve the needs of the nation. Many of them entered the field of physical education at a time when the discourse of social purity focused on body issues such as health and cleanliness. Middle-class women were taught to believe that social "diseases" such as poverty and crime were directly related to personal habits of hygiene and physical training. As Mariana Valverde suggests, they inherited the era of "soap, water and light."[20] This middle-class ideal – to provide service to the nation and "seek the highest good"[21] – was precisely what the young graduates of the Margaret Eaton School heard from Colonel George S. Nasmith, the second husband of Emma Scott Raff Nasmith, on the occasion of the school's commencement exercises in 1918. To the new graduates he proudly proclaimed,

The woman who is receiving her education today is fortunate, for she is living in a period when the old order of things is passing away and a new era is at hand. Today is the day when the idea of public service reigns in the hearts of thinking people, and when men and women will tolerate and follow only those whom they know are true to the best interests and ideals of the nation. There are great opportunities for work in the world today. It is your privilege to serve.[22]

In 1941, despite high enrolments and a successful placement history, the Margaret Eaton School closed. The closure was part of a plan, orchestrated by Stanley Ryerson, assistant dean of the Faculty of Medicine, to begin a new co-educational physical education degree program at the University of Toronto. Florence A. Somers, the last principal of the Margaret Eaton School, had assumed that position in 1935 when Mary Hamilton retired. As an American who came to the school with a distinguished career as an educator in elementary, secondary, and postsecondary institutions, Somers promoted the philosophy of girls' non-competitive physical education and the belief that a co-educational education would enhance the status of women. Formerly the associate director of the Sargent School in Boston, Somers believed that the absorption of the school by the University of Toronto would heighten the profile of the school's graduates and give them the academic legiti-

macy to pursue teaching careers in the public school system. In 1940 Somers submitted a plan for union. Under the terms of the agreement, the school's students, faculty members, and facilities were funnelled into the University of Toronto and a new co-educational bachelor's degree program in physical education was established. Following the merger, the school's curriculum changed. A strongly medical and theoretical configuration of courses took prominence, and courses based on practical experience were reduced in scope and importance. A remarkable chapter in the history of women in higher education in the early part of the twentieth century ended.

The history of the Margaret Eaton School experience has been reclaimed through the personal memoirs of and interviews with graduates. Bess Bitt Barron, who died in May 1998, recalled that it was a period when many young women felt a sense of empowerment and possibility. She remembered that the physical training "made you strong, muscular and fit and able to move into the world with confidence."[23] She also observed, "It's hard to look back on it all and believe that I actually did it; but I did. I felt I was opening up new areas for young girls and women."[24] Indeed, through the efforts of Bess Pitt and other Margaret Eaton graduates like her, many young women entered the professional field of physical education a century stronger.

41.2 Fencing (*Margaret Eaton School Yearbook*, 1938–1939, Toronto. Courtesy of Anna Lathrop)

PART FOUR

Women's Activism and the State

42 Introduction

Joan Sangster

The word "politics" sometimes conjures up images of suffragists in long skirts presenting petitions demanding the franchise for women to disinterested politicians. Indeed, the "Heritage Minute" television vignette depicting Nellie McClung suggests that she was a more witty, astute, and lively politician than her pompous opponents, who were, of course, on the losing end of the suffrage battle.

Politics certainly encompassed the struggle for women's right to vote. The 1916 petition from the Yukon Women's Protective League (Illustration 42.1), politely declares, for example, that its members "do not intend to be the last to place ourselves on record in demanding the rights that have so long been withheld from us." But it also involved much more. If we define politics as all organized initiatives to effect political, social, and economic change, then what historians define as political would include campaigns for access to birth control, policy initiatives to eradicate domestic violence, and attempts to secure women's access to higher education. Illustration 42.2, for example, which shows Ellen Fairclough with representatives of the immigration committees of the National Japanese Canadian Citizenship Association and the Chinese Canadian Association, is evidence of a more broadly defined kind of politics. Even the narrower definition of politics that is applied in this chapter, which focuses on women's public efforts to influence or initiate state policies, involve themselves in political parties and policy making, or influence govern-

ment priorities, suggests how diverse, wide-ranging, and continuous women's political efforts were over the twentieth century.

There is no doubt that the vote was an important emblem of women's initiation into the body politic, symbolizing women's emergence from reliance on a male family member to full rights of citizenship in the public sphere. The struggle for the right to vote was undertaken by different groups of women across Canada, groups that did not always share the same view of women's place in society or even a rationale for why women needed the vote. Some women, largely from middle-class backgrounds and often referred to as social or maternal feminists, argued that women's distinct role as homemakers and mothers and their commitment to family and moral issues – such as temperance – would

---

ADELAIDE HUNTER HOODLESS, 1857–1910

Born in Ontario, Adelaide Hoodless sought to release the full potential of women for social action. An outspoken educator and reformer, she successfully pressed for acceptance of domestic economy as a subject for study in Canadian schools and was largely responsible for founding Institutes of Household Science at Guelph, Ste Anne de Bellevue, Quebec, and Toronto. Active in forming the Young Women's Christian Association, the National Council of Women, and the Federated Women's Institute, she also aided in establishing the Victorian Order of Nurses. She died in Toronto. (Courtesy of Parks Canada)

September 8, 1916.

Commissioner George Black
Dawson, Yukon Territory

Dear Sir:

At the request of our General Assembly, we, the Officers and executive members of the Yukon Women's Protective League and Franchise Movement, have come before you today, actuated by the highest and best of motives – love of home and country – and possessed of a sincere desire to improve the conditions and advance the best interests of the same.

There are some who contend that women's proper place is at home. And we agree with them to this extent, that woman's proper place is at home. But when those critics go farther and insist that woman's interests, energies and activities should be confined within the four walls of her home, and must not extend to the community at large, we wave such assertions aside with all the contempt they deserve.

After all, what is a community but a collection of homes, and what is our country generally speaking, but a vast number of communities, comprising a mighty nation, held together by common interests, regulated by the same laws, inspired by the same ideals.

It is a mighty truism that 'No nation ever rose above the level of its women.' Free men are not born of slaves, and a man in denying his sister woman equal rights, has only strengthened his own fetters.

Looking back through the centuries of time, even to the age of Muscular Force, when man first placed upon woman the bands of conventional restriction, and arrogated to himself the power that was their joint inheritance, we see countless generations of women, patient, sorrowful, but clear eyed and hopeful, working, watching, for the hour when man's eyes will be opened, and he will be able to read the message which God has written upon the heart of every woman.

And we women of the twentieth century count ourselves as 'Blessed indeed, among women' inasmuch as ours is the privilege to hail the dawn of a new existence for us and all the world. For indeed, it is obvious to even the most blind among us, that the day of universal suffrage is at hand, and before many months have passed the women of the English speaking race will be placed on the same political footing as the men.

And we women of the Yukon Territory do not intend to be the last to place ourselves on record in demanding the rights that have so long been withheld from us, and so we have come to you, the head of our local administration, and ask to be instructed as to the best and most speedy method of obtaining the Franchise.

Signed of behalf of the
Yukon Women's Protective League

Lizbeth A. McLean	Dora Dook
Elizabeth K. Murray	Marie Fotheringham
Geraldine E. Sharp	Mrs. Bertha Kunze
Lucile MacMillan	Katherine Rodgers

provide an important antidote to male political perspectives. They eschewed direct political involvement, preferring to devote their reformist efforts to social reconstruction as a precursor to political rejuvenation. Cathy James's article on women in the settlement movement (essay #45) defines this approach. Others argued decisively that women were the intellectual and social equals of men and deserved the same rights. These two arguments were not mutually exclusive, and some women, like Flora MacDonald Denison, a dressmaker, dynamic journalist, and prominent suffragist, combined both strands of thought in her writing.[1] Still other women, generally of the working class and often socialists, supported suffrage and advocated women's "emancipation," but they saw the vote as a means of achieving social equality for working people, not just women. They were sceptical that the vote, without more fundamental economic change,[2] would usher in equality for women.

These very different political views remained a central feature of Canadian women's lives even after the vote was secured. Women had received the federal vote by 1919, but in some provinces the battle for suffrage consumed them into the 1930s and 1940s. Women in Prince Edward Island waited until 1922 for the provincial vote, and in Newfoundland, then a colony of Britain, until 1925 – though in that province they had to be a more "mature" twenty-five to exercise their right, while men could vote at twenty-one![3] Quebec women waited the longest for the provincial franchise, despite the leadership of Idola Saint-Jean (Illustration 42.3), who led the campaign for suffrage through the Provincial Franchise Committee and l'Alliance Canadienne pour le vote des femmes du Québec. Thérèse Casgrain (later a member of the Voice of Women and shown in Illustration 42.4 with Jeanne Sauvé) also championed the campaign throughout the 1930s. Together, they triumphed over the vigorous opposition of the Roman Catholic Church and Union Nationale politicians in 1940.[4]

Top:
42.2 Ellen Fairclough with representatives of Japanese and Chinese immigration committess (PA 117803, National Archives of Canada)

Left:
42.3 Idola Saint-John (C 68508, National Archives of Canada)

42.4 Jeanne Sauvé and Thérèse Casgrain, 1976
(PA 146048, National Archives of Canada)

The existence of two suffrage groups in Quebec again underlines the fact that women never shared one voice or a unitary point of view when it came to politics. Rather, their politics were shaped by class, race, ethnicity, and culture; their political causes varied considerably, crossing a spectrum of political ideologies. The cases of Agnes Macphail and Charlotte Whitton, featured in essays #43 and #47, are a good example. Both women in one sense benefited from their Anglo-Celtic origins and the rural respectability associated with the farming families they came from, both encountered antagonism in their public lives because of their roles as outspoken, intelligent women in a "man's world." Yet their views of Canada were completely different. Whitton, though she was seen as a progressive on the question of the training of social workers, was profoundly conservative at heart.

She embraced the economic and social status quo; during the Depression she had little sympathy for poor and working-class women struggling on relief, supporting policies that could be seen as Victorian in their emphasis on the "undeserving poor." Nor did she sympathize with married women who worked; she believed that they did not belong in the labour force. Macphail, by contrast, embraced unpopular causes involving the dispossessed, like prison reform, promoted concepts like equal pay for women and men, and believed in a welfare state that would provide a social security net for the working classes.

The different political paths of these individual women mirrored larger processes. After the federal vote was won, women did not retreat from politics, as had been feared by some, but directed their political energies to new causes. Five socially and politically prominent western women embarked on a campaign to have women legally declared "persons" so that they could hold Senate seats, and their 1929 victory remains much celebrated in the public memory. It is represented here in a vignette (#44). At the time, their campaign was criticized by communist women who argued that offering a few bourgeois women the perks of political patronage would not ease the drudgery of most women's lives – a view that still might find resonance today.

On the left of the political spectrum in the 1920s, women who embraced, or were sympathetic to, communism joined the Women's Labour Leagues, which in 1926 set up their own paper for women, the *Woman Worker*. Communist women believed in the long-term need for complete social transformation, including the abolition of capitalism; in the short term, they attempted to organize working women into unions, lobbied for birth-control clinics, opposed military education in the schools, and urged housewives to protest rising prices and the social conditions that made the daily work of caring for their families intolerable.[5] As my contribution in this section indicates (essay #48), the organization of house-wives remained an important goal for both communist and social democratic women in the Co-operative Commonwealth Federation (CCF) for decades to come.

Women's participation in the Communist Party persisted and indeed grew in strength in the later 1930s, when the misery of Depression and the threat of European fascism convinced a larger group of women that radical alternatives were necessary. Presented in Illustration 42.5 is Florence Theodore, the first woman to be elected leader of a provincial branch of the Communist Party serving in Saskatchewan from 1942 to 1945. By the 1930s, however, a social democratic option became available for women: the CCF. This forerunner to today's more timid New Democratic Party (NDP) drew on Marxist ideas, Christian socialism (or the social gospel), radical agrarianism, and pro-labour ideas. The socialist alternative thereby created nonetheless focused on parliamentary elections as the means to secure social security and health care, the redistribution of wealth, and international peace. The four women in Illustration 42.6 were members of Ontario's first CCF Women's Committee in 1947. Although women were often found doing essential, but less visible, background organizing for the CCF, a small and vocal minority pursued feminist concerns (though they would not have used that word then), such as equal pay, the increased organization of working women, and even birth control. The latter, for example, was proposed by some of the CCF farm women from Saskatchewan who were involved in the United Farmers of Saskatchewan in the thirties. Though the male leaders of the farm movement buried the women's resolutions, fretting that birth control was too radical for popular consumption, farm women knew that, for them, control over reproduction, was a pressing political issue.[6]

Before the 1960s, socialist women, though perhaps smaller in numbers, were better organized and more vocal than liberal and conservative ones. Indeed, even

42.5 Florence Theodore, Communist Party leader in Saskatchewan, 1942–45 (PA 126370, National Archives of Canada)

42.6 CCF Women's Committee, 1947 (PA 125807, National Archives of Canada)

before the First World War, as Linda Kealey has revealed, women in various socialist parties wrote in socialist papers, worked as travelling organizers and speakers, and debated with fellow socialists the origins of, and cures for, women's oppression.[7] Because the socialist tradition had always claimed women's equality to be part of its mandate, it undoubtedly attracted women who wished to change not only the world, but also their place in it. For some immigrant women from Jewish, Ukrainian, and Finnish backgrounds, communism also provided a comfortable and meaningful political home, as the party addressed both the needs of their struggling families and their concerns relating to racism and ethnocentrism, such as anti-Semitism.[8]

Liberal and Conservative women, however, were not completely invisible. A Women's Liberal Federation was established in 1928, and though largely dormant until 1947 and heavily controlled by the male party's leadership, it provided a small avenue of participation for women, sending some delegates to Liberal conventions and working to mobilize the Liberal vote during elec-

tions (see Illustration 42.7). A very few women also made their way into the ranks of Liberal office holders. Nellie McClung ran successfully on the Liberal ticket in Alberta in the 1920s, and Cairine Wilson, a Quebec philanthropist with impeccable Liberal credentials, was the first woman appointed to the Senate. Wilson, despite her patrician background, made the salvation of European Jews from the Nazis one of her first (though largely unsuccessful) causes in the Senate.[9]

By the 1960s, a few notable women, such as Liberal cabinet minister Judy LaMarsh (Illustration 42.8) and NDP member of Parliament Grace MacInnis, were becoming prominent as federal politicians. At the local and provincial levels, women had always been more politically adventurous; in the 1920s and 1930s, for instance, women associated with labour parties ran for school board positions, advocating equal pay for female teachers and free school textbooks, a crucial issue for working-class families with scarce resources for education. Women's interest in both educational issues and local politics spoke to two recurring themes in their political activism until the 1960s.

First, across many political parties, women expressed a keen interest in issues that spoke to their daily work and worries, including their responsibility for child rearing and management of the household budget. At the same time, women's activism was also circumscribed by the dominant ideology of female domesticity, which saw marriage, motherhood, and the domestic sphere as women's desired, primary, and exclusive role; this made it harder for women to take on political positions and more difficult for them to be accepted in political life. As Gladys Strum, a CCF federal MP from Saskatchewan in the 1940s, once quipped in dismay, "[T]he press wrote about my hats, not my speeches."[10]

Secondly, women's political endeavours actually focused only marginally on federal and provincial electoral politics. In the fifteen federal elections after the

vote was won, women made up only 2.4 per cent of the participating candidates and less than 1 per cent of the elected members of Parliament.[11] Far more evidence of women's activism comes to light when we examine local, community, and non-partisan politics.

For instance, women might react to certain issues as they arose, organizing in an ad hoc manner. During the Depression, when men were preparing the On-to-Ottawa Trek to demand jobs rather than endure the activity at army-run "relief camps," from the ruling Conservatives, women in Vancouver organized a massive demonstration in Vancouver's Stanley Park in their honour, carrying a banner that read "Mothers Abolish the Relief Camps." Or, after the Second World War, when prices were rising after wartime controls were removed, a coalition of left-wing women, with some communist leadership, organized the broadly based Housewives Consumers Association to demand that Ottawa continue to control prices to aid working families.[12]

Even though many women's organizations were non-partisan, they continued to reflect the strong class, ethnic, cultural, and racial divisions in Canada. French Canadian women were often isolated from English-speaking women, and in some organizations, non-white women were discouraged, if not barred, from membership. The National Council of Women, established in the suffrage era, was an umbrella group dedicated to reform, that drew together Local Councils of Women across the country. Its membership was almost entirely Anglo-Celtic and English-speaking, middle and upper class. The council tended to ignore issues such as the need to improve wages and working conditions for working women, and it lobbied against the employment of white girls by Chinese employers. Other women's organizations, like the Imperial Order Daughters of the Empire (IODE), also opposed Asian immigration, thus perpetuating the racist and ethnocentric view that a "white" and "British" Canada was a better Canada.

Top:
42.7 Liberal Women's Club, Saskatoon, 1949
(PA 88646, National Archives of Canada)

Left:
42.8 Judy LaMarsh on the campaign trail, 1960
(PA 126968, National Archives of Canada)

Women thus excluded did not remain unorganized or quiescent. Some used their ethnic or racial identity as a focus for organization. Jewish housewives in Toronto, for example, organized their own housewives league, the "Faryen," to protest rising prices; Ukrainian women organized in ethnic associations to further the interests of compatriots from a common background.[13] Some women also focused specifically on issues of discrimination. As essay #53, on South Asian Women, illustrates, Canada's racist and gender-biased immigration policy, maintained until 1967, was itself the focus of political action by the South Asian community. Women from these communities often drew on the resources of existing organizations representing both men and women to help them fight discrimination and racism. When Viola Desmond was ejected from the "white section" of a segregated theatre in Nova Scotia in 1947, she courageously took her case to court, aided by the Nova Scotia Association for the Advancement of Coloured People.[14]

In Toronto in the interwar period, Afro-Canadian women were important organizers and actors in the Universal Negro Improvement Association, which was based on the ideas of Marcus Garvey, an advocate of self-determination and race pride for Black peoples.[15]

IMPERIAL ORDER DAUGHTERS OF THE EMPIRE

The IODE, a Canadian women's volunteer organization, was founded by Margaret Polson Murray in 1900 during the Boer War, its goal being to encourage service, patriotism, and loyalty to the Crown. Throughout the two world wars, members raised considerable funds for medical and personal supplies for military personnel. Between and after the wars, they directed much of their attention to the care of veterans and their families. Once a symbol of imperial unity, today the IODE is a national service organization that maintains projects in the areas of education, social service, and citizenship. (Courtesy of Parks Canada)

Often, Afro-Canadian and First Nations women joined the men from their communities in tackling pressing political and social issues. Native communities and their leaders, for example, protested to a Senate committee in the 1940s the discriminatory clauses of the Indian Act that removed women's Indian status when they married outside the reserve. Iroquois women supported the claims of their communities, as nations, to self-determination, at the same time laying claim to their own political voice by invoking the matriarchal history and tradition of the Iroquois. By the 1970s, both First Nations and Afro-Canadian women had also established their own women's political groups, such as the Native Women's Association of Canada and the Canadian Negro Women's Association (CANEWA; see Illustration 42.9). CANEWA established student scholarships, led protests against racists policies, lobbied for the teaching of Black history in Ontario schools, and created the original "Caribana" Festival in Toronto.

When we take into account all these activities, the range of women's political organizing is impressive and should lay to rest the idea that there were two waves of feminism (suffrage and the 1960s), with a trough or political wasteland in between. One of the most enduring issues of concern for women from the time of the First World War to the nuclear age was international peace. The Voice of Women (VOW), described in essay #49 by Candace Loewen, had strong antecedents, stretching back to the 1920s and 1930s. In the thirties especially, women were concerned about the rise of fascism in Europe; they were aware of its misogynist tendencies, as well as its threat to world peace. Some women organized into groups supporting Canada's Mackenzie-Papineau Battalion, which fought against Franco's fascists in Spain in 1937–39; others advocated complete non-violence and disarmament in Europe. Many women's peace organizations, such as the Women's League for Peace and Freedom, and individuals

42.9 CANEWA members at Awards Banquet, 1961 (Ontario Black History Society)

like Rosalie Bertell (discussed in #52), who was active in the 1930s, adopted the radical view – for that time – that peace would only be achieved when human rights were recognized worldwide and economic and social equality was made a reality in the world.

Is there no reason, then, to see the 1960s and 1970s as a new era in women's political organizing? It is true that the "second wave" of feminism, beginning in the 1960s, brought new energy, ideas, and organization to women's political activity. A virtual renaissance in feminism occurred, including avowedly feminist forms of cultural expression (see essays #54 and #55). Such international writers as Germaine Greer and Kate Millett provided provocative new feminist treatises, and women in many countries, including Canada, discovered (and celebrated) their own historical roots. A renewed, vital women's movement emerged to be sure, shaped in part by the changing structure of Canadian society. New patterns of women's work outside the home took form, as more and

more married women entered the workforce, while a generation of younger "boomers," with more education and high expectations, began to ask why our so-called society of meritocracy and equality actually reflected persisting inequalities based on gender and race. What followed was a profusion of feminist writing and organizing, from the polite lobbying of governments, to more militant demonstrations and sit-ins, to the establishment of needed services, such as shelters for battered women.[16]

Again, more than one strand of political ideology and organization was visible. On the one hand, a liberal feminist analysis – the kind reflected in the Royal Commission on the Status of Women (see essay #50 by Kimberly Speers) – emerged, shaped in part by its middle-class and professional supporters who desired legal and social reforms to equalize opportunities for women within the present political structures of the state. The culmination of this movement for many was the election of Rosemary Brown to the British Columbia leg-

42.10 Audrey McLaughlin, first woman leader of the New Democratic Party (National Archives of Canada)

set up new organizations to fight for women's right to reproductive control, including abortion, the unionization of women, day-care and social services, and many more issues. As the history of the vow indicates, women might embrace more than one strategy, sometimes moving their organization from "polite" lobbying to militant protest.

Second-wave Canadian feminists were influenced, in part, by the civil rights and women's movement in the United States, but more centrally by Canada's own student and peace movements, anti-Vietnam war efforts, and anti-poverty crusades. Many feminists also became cognizant of their own privilege, in terms of sexual orientation, race, and ethnicity, and the way in which mainstream women's organizations marginalized lesbians and excluded the views and participation of women of colour. As Native Canadians also organized to argue for self-government in the 1970s and women of colour articulated the damaging effects of racism on their lives, the women's movement, including the largest feminist organization, the National Action Committee on the Status of Women (NAC), formed in 1972, readjusted its analysis of inequality to try and take account of racism as well as economic inequality. The Canadian Advisory Council on the Status Women was especially active during the 1980s as an effective pressure group on government. This new attention given to racism and ethnocentrism, as well as to the needs of lesbians – however imperfect and incomplete – especially distinguishes the second wave of feminism from the first.

islative assembly in 1972. Other successes followed: Audrey McLaughlin, as leader of the New Democratic Party, (Illustration 42.10); Kim Campbell, as leader of the Progressive Conservative Party, becoming Canada's first woman prime minister in 1993; and Adrienne Clarkson, named Canada's first non-Caucasian woman governor general, seen in Illustration 42.11 honouring Flora MacDonald, an early contender for the leadership of the Conservative Party. On the other hand, more radical feminists criticized the entirely male-dominated political system, and a socialist feminism emerged, buoyed by a long tradition of socialist and left-wing organizing in the country. Not all socialist feminists embraced party politics as a strategy for change. They

Over this century, Canadian women's political activities have thus crossed a wide spectrum of ideologies, actions, and organizations. They have also changed considerably over time, shaped by the economic and social context, by cultural change, and by women's own ideas and organizing. While this brief overview has tended to stress those politicized women who wished to alter Canadian society by abolishing inequality, discrimination, or oppression, women have also organized for more conservative ends, attempting to secure the status quo from which some women derive considerable privilege. Examples of such women are the reformers described by Tamara Myers in essay #46, who tried to intervene in the lives of young women in east-end Montreal whose sexual and social activities did not conform to middle-class values of respectability.

Nonetheless, since the turn of the century, streams of feminist thought and action – though ebbing and flowing and taking on different ideological forms – have remained a consistent theme in our political history. Despite media questions concerning the "death of feminism" in the 1990s or claims that we have entered a post-feminist era, there is every indication that this feminist interest in social transformation will persist into the next century.

A list of further readings in this area is provided on page 487.

42.11 Flora MacDonald receiving the Order of Canada from Governor General Adrienne Clarkson, Ottawa, 2000 (Courtesy of the *Ottawa Citizen*)

43 History and Human Agency: The Case of Agnes Macphail, Canada's First Woman Member of Parliament

Terry Crowley

This above all: to thine own self be true
And it shall follow as the night the day
That thou canst not then be false to any man.
    William Shakespeare, *Hamlet*

William Shakespeare's lyrical updating of Socrates's injunction to "know thyself" has long stood at the centre of individual consciousness in Western countries. Historians have therefore assessed people in the past according to the principles they espoused and their ability to measure up to those ideals. The recent desire of historians to give expression to a fuller panoply of human experience has tended to detract from the emphasis once placed on human agency in history. Old debates about whether heros/heroines made their times or were thrust into prominence by propitious circumstances have long been abandoned as conundrums as impossible to unravel as whether the chicken or egg came first. Historians now tend to concentrate on discrete groups based on such categories as race, ethnicity, gender, religion, social class, caste, and national origin. In stressing the importance of groups, historians have become increasingly sceptical of the agency enjoyed by prominent individuals.

A strong inclination to enter into the lives of others still remains deeply embedded in the human psyche, however, both fiction and non-fiction afford opportunities for this mental voyage. Fiction allows authors to give full vent to their imaginations, but writers of non-fiction have to respond to their evidence in an attempt to be truthful. For the historian there is the added problem of where to put the emphasis on a particular individual or on the group to which she belonged. Agnes Macphail, Canada's first woman member of Parliament in 1921 and the first woman to be seated in the Ontario legislature in 1943, provides a case in point. Other men and women in farm, labour, and left-of-centre political organizations shared her ideals. Why has she attracted more attention than other women in Canada during the first half of the twentieth century? Were there limits to her human agency?

There was little in the family background or early upbringing of Agnes Macphail to set her apart from many other Canadians. She was born in a log cabin on a farm in southern Ontario in 1891. Her parents decided that she should not go to high school, as it was expensive to board in the county seat where the nearest high school was located. The cost of advanced education for women, it was often argued, would be wasted once they married. Macphail fought her parents' decision and won, finishing high school in two years and going on to Teachers' College in Stratford, where she graduated in 1910. For the next decade she was an innovative schoolteacher in southern Ontario and Alberta, but she was keenly attuned to current events and to discrimination on account of her sex. As organized farmers became increasingly dissatisfied with inequalities in Canadian life, Macphail wrote on the subject to the newspaper of the United Farmers of Ontario (UFO), and its editor invited her to write a column. As her involvement with the United Farmers deepened, Macphail emerged as an organizer for the new agrarian organization. With the 1921 federal election approaching, Macphail took the bold step of abandoning her teaching job in order to secure the UFO nomination in her home constituency of Southeast Grey.

The initiative was bold because she was the sole female contender among the score of those whose names were entered in nomination. With assistance from relatives, Agnes Macphail captured the nomination and became one of only three women in Ontario to stand in the first federal election in which women were able to run. Having honed her speaking skills while organizing UFO branches, Macphail adopted a punchy delivery style that commanded attention through saucy straight talk. She denounced the great discrepancies between enormously rich and abjectly poor, between urban and rural dwellers, and between those who earned their living with their hands and those who shuffled paper. During the campaign she was attacked personally on the basis of her sex and her religion. Her status as an unmarried woman led to insults that she was a threat to wives and the sanctity of marriage. Since she belonged to the Reorganized Church of Jesus Christ of the Latter Day Saints, she also was accused of supporting male polygamy by those who confused her denomination with Mormonism.

In an upset election, Agnes Macphail succeeded in gaining a seat in the House of Commons and remained the only woman there until 1935. As someone prepared to challenge conventional thinking, she emerged as an outspoken advocate of feminism and world peace. From her unique position on the nation's stage, she confronted the shibboleths governing gender relations that had entered government legislation. Immersing herself in English feminism's great classics – Mary Wollstonecraft's *Vindication of the Rights of Woman* and John Stuart Mill's *On the Subjection of Women* – she became an exponent of equity feminism. "I think that what women really want today is perfect equality with men," she said in 1922. "I am a feminist," she declared a few years later, "and I want for women the thing that men are not willing to give them – absolute equality. We will not get it this year, but will get it next."[1] By proposing complete equality between the sexes, Macphail was open to criticism that such views were utopian because women alone bear children. She answered that women could not be happy with all life centred around the maternal role and that men needed to bear greater responsibility in child rearing.

Macphail readily supported efforts during the 1920s to secure gender equity in divorce proceedings in the Prairie provinces and a divorce court for Ontario. She also participated actively in the Women's International League for Peace and Freedom, which wanted an end to war as a means of settling international disputes. She became a speaker on the Canadian Chautauqua circuit, an offshoot of an American enterprise that attempted to enlighten and entertain before radio and cinema displaced such public occasions. Later she addressed audiences in Canada and the United States, securing these bookings through an agent in New York City who also worked for such popular speakers as British politician Winston Churchill, psychologist Alfred Adler, and French writer André Maurois.

Women formed the larger constituency that Macphail addressed, but as her seat in the House of Commons depended on the farmer/labour coalition that helped to get her re-elected in Southeast Grey, she believed that women needed to meet men on their own terrain. The fractiousness of farm and labour organizations posed great difficulties. Members of Parliament representing provincial farm organizations, known as the Progressives, were racked by such internal dissension that by 1930 they were no longer of political consequence. Through her association with Winnipeg labour MP James

Shaver Woodsworth, Macphail acquired a social democratic philosophy that sustained her as farmers ceased being a direct influence in politics. Governments needed to assist the poor, the needy, and those who were simply less fortunate in a capitalist society, she believed. During the early 1930s, Agnes Macphail contributed to the formation of the Co-operative Commonwealth Federation (CCF), which brought farm, labour, and intellectuals into a new movement designed to introduce social democracy into Canadian politics. From 1932 to 1934 she headed the Ontario wing of the movement, but she was unable to arrest its disintegration as a result of internal dissension among warring factions.

Macphail returned to representing the farmer/ labour ticket in her own constituency. She also assumed a personal campaign to reform the country's prisons by drawing media attention to the ways in which the penal system contributed to massive recidivism. Prisoners were still whipped, young male offenders were mixed with hardened criminals, and nothing was done to ensure that prisoners might lead more productive lives upon release. At one point in her campaign during the early 1930s, Macphail had herself locked into a solitary confinement cell at Kingston penitentiary; on another occasion, she pursued a case in court when prison bureaucrats were alleged to have impugned her name. These tactics proved effective. In 1936 a royal commission was appointed to look into prison conditions. The report of that investigation provided the basis for a massive updating of the federal penal system after the Second World War.

Agnes Macphail failed to get re-elected in the 1940 wartime election when she unwisely attacked Prime Minister William Lyon Mackenzie King too vociferously. Taking to journalism to provide an income, she rejoined the CCF and gained a seat in the Ontario legislature for the Toronto riding of East York. She also assumed responsibility for raising a young cousin after the girl was released into her custody following a family tragedy, in which she had shot her abusive father. Macphail lost the election of 1945 but was re-elected in East York in 1948.

At this point in her career Macphail returned to championing gender issues, particularly an end to salary discrimination and to low-paying job ghettos for women. Women had often been paid half or two-thirds what men received for the same work. Men supported a family and women's needs were lesser in the minds of many people, but Macphail and others to the left of centre would have none of this specious supposition, because they knew that it did not correspond to the reality in the lives of working families.

During the Second World War, federal contracts had required employers to provide women equal pay for equal work, but as women seldom did the work of men, few women benefited from such provisions. After investigations by CCF women like Barbara Cass-Biggs, Marjorie Mann, and Edith Fowke, lawyer Andrew Brewin prepared legislation for pay equity that Agnes Macphail seconded when it was introduced into the legislature. Since men's and women's paid employment was rarely comparable, an attempt was made to expand pay equity legislation from equal pay for equal work to equal pay for work of equal value. The Conservative government of Leslie Frost chose instead to legislate the more limited concept of equal pay, but the idea of employment equity resurfaced during the 1980s and entered law in 1994 through legislation aimed at ending discrimination in the workplace against women, aboriginal peoples, people with disabilities, and visible minorities.

Agnes Macphail retired from public life following defeat in the 1951 provincial election. What had she achieved? What were the limits to her human agency? Two perspectives need to be brought to the answers to these questions; one perspective belongs to her own time and the another to ours, the viewpoint of history.

As Agnes Macphail was a member of opposition parties and social movements, her influence on government legislation was naturally slight, much in the same way as was the influence, say, of French Canadian nationalist Henri Bourassa. Opposition is absolutely vital to democratic life in that it prevents abuses of power and the mammoth political swings seen in countries such as China, but opposition most often serves only to moderate and to suggest alternative policies. Governments both create and cancel programs; critics are limited to registering dissent that may or may not be heeded.

Still, Macphail did score a number of significant achievements. She assisted in securing the Old Age Pensions Act of 1927, which was the first significant federal social welfare legislation; in forming the CCF, which later became the New Democratic Party; in securing prison reform; and in prompting the formation of the Elizabeth Fry Society of Toronto, the second such organization in the country to assist women upon release from prison. All these activities were undertaken in concert with other men and women who shared similar ideals.

What is more elusive for the historian is Macphail's larger impact in her own time. Some young women who heard her speak in the first part of the twentieth century attested that she became a role model for what they might become in life. Women's groups and some of her parliamentary colleagues also testified that she was able to communicate with audiences in a manner that few other speakers were able to achieve. As a result, 55 per cent of Canadians asked in a Gallop poll in 1952 said they knew who Macphail was – surely the highest recognition factor obtained by a Canadian woman until that time. Still, history is not a popularity contest; it if were, it would concentrate solely on movie stars.

In the history of democratic societies, individuals rise to prominence through managing to articulate shared aspirations and through working with others to achieve them. Many of the causes Agnes Macphail championed were unpopular in her own day. She did not represent all women, although she frequently spoke on their behalf. Her views appealed only to a minority, but as they gained increasing currency with the passage of time, Macphail became more important from the perspective of history. For this reason Agnes Macphail has been remembered more fully in Canada than Nancy Astor, Britain's first woman member of Parliament, has been recalled in the United Kingdom. Macphail's vision of a more just and equitable society where women would assume positions of importance touched base with the aspirations of later generations. Agnes Macphail was not alone in expressing such ideals, but she achieved a position that allowed her to have a larger impact in her own day and to enter into historical consciousness. Human agency is always limited, but some individuals succeed in leaving their impress on history more fully than others.[2]

44 The *Persons* Case, 1929:
A Legal Definition of Women as Persons
Anne White

On 18 October 1929, five Alberta women were successful in achieving an historic ruling from the highest court in the British Empire regarding the legal status of white women in Canada. The women – Henrietta Muir Edwards, Nellie McClung, Louise McKinney, Emily Murphy, and Irene Parlby – were all prominent social activists. Led by Emily Murphy, these seasoned campaigners united to challenge the existing discriminatory legal definition of "person" within the British North America (BNA) Act, which precluded, among its other implications, any Canadian woman being appointed to the Senate. The case became known as the *Persons* case. This precedent-setting judgment, rendered by the Judicial Committee of the Privy Council in Britain, changed the Canadian constitution so that white women were recognized as full "persons." A photograph of the maquette commemorating the decision (Illustration 44.1) captures the five petitioners celebrating their victory with a cup of tea. The statues were mounted on Parliament Hill in October 2000.

Barriers to women's full citizenship are illustrated in the 1928 cartoon titled "Will She 'Crash the Gate'?" (Illustration 44.2). Prior to the *Persons* case legal challenge, national women's organizations had actively supported the cause. Canadian women's groups, such as the National Council of Women of Canada, with 450,000 members, and the Federated Women's Institutes of Canada, took up the issue and together nominated Emily Murphy as the first female senator in 1921.[1] Several years later, another women's organization, the powerful Dominion Woman's Christian Temperance Union, circulated a national petition signed by both women and men, requesting the appointment of women to the Senate.[2]

Even though the various provincial suffrage acts, dating between 1916 and 1925, and the Dominion Franchise Act of 1918 had acknowledged women as voting citizens, the rights of women and even their identity as persons under the BNA Act remained ambiguous. Within the act, the term "person" used a masculine noun or pronoun, despite the fact that various sections pertaining to "pains and penalties" were interpreted to include the female person. Thus, notwithstanding political gains made by women through voting rights and the privilege to stand for certain offices, their full constitutional identity was still shrouded in this complex legal definition. As we see in the reproduced letter (Illustration 44.3), the five women initially requested clarification on the constitutionality of appointing "a female to the Senate of Canada."

On 24 April 1928, the Supreme Court of Canada ruled unanimously in favour of the Crown, which defended the traditional interpretation of the act (Illustration 44.4). Chief Justice Anglin stated that women, along with children, criminals, and the insane, were not persons under the strict interpretation of the BNA Act and were therefore ineligible to sit in the Canadian Senate.[3] The original application to the Supreme Court states that "the question at issue in this appeal is whether the

44.1 Maquette of the Famous Five sculpture
(Courtesy of the Famous Five Foundation)

words 'qualified persons'… include a woman."

After deliberation and with the support of the attorney general of Alberta and the now-sympathetic government of Canada, the five women decided to appeal the decision. In July 1929 Newton Rowell presented the appeal before the British Judicial Committee of the Privy Council, which then reserved judgment for three months. When the Privy Council reconvened on 18 October 1929, their lordships rendered the historic ruling in favour of the appellants, stating that "the word 'persons' as above mentioned may include members of both sexes."[4] And in conclusion they ruled that "the word 'persons' in Section 24 *does* include women, and that women are eligible to be summoned to and become members of the Senate of Canada" (Illustration 44.5)."[5]

44.2 "Will She 'Crash the Gate'?"
(*Vancouver Sun*, 11 May 1928)

P.C. 1835

IH.

PRIVY COUNCIL
CANADA

Edmonton, August 27th, 1927.

To His Excellency

The Governor-General in Council

Rideau Hall,

Ottawa, Ontario.

Sir:

As persons interested in the admission
of women to the Senate of Canada, we do hereby
request that you may be graciously pleased to
refer to the Supreme Court of Canada for hearing,
consideration and adjudication the following
constitutional questions:-

1.   Is power vested in the Governor-General
in Council of Canada, or the Parliament of Canada,
or either of them, to appoint a female to the
Senate of Canada?

11.   Is it constitutionally possible for
the Parliament of Canada under the provisions of
the British North America Act, or otherwise, to
make provision for the appointment of a female
to the Senate of Canada?

These questions are respectfully referred for your consideration pursuant to Section
60 of the Supreme Court Act, R.S.C. 1906, Cap.139.

We have the honour to be,

Sir,

Your obedient servants,

(Sgd.)   Henrietta Muir Edwards (Macleod)
   "   Nellie L. McClung   (Calgary)
   "   Louise C. McKinney   (Claresholm)
   "   Emily F. Murphy   (Edmonton)
   "   Irene Parlby (Alix)

Kindly address communications to
Mrs. Emily F. Murphy,
11011-88th Avenue,
Edmonton, Alta.

IN THE SUPREME COURT OF CANADA

TUESDAY, THE TWENTY-FOURTH DAY OF APRIL, A.D. 1928.

PRESENT:

    The Right Honourable Francis Alexander Anglin, P.C.,
                                    Chief Justice.
    The Right Honourable Mr. Justice Duff, P.C.
    The Honourable Mr. Justice Mignault
    The Honourable Mr. Justice Lamont
    The Honourable Mr. Justice Smith.

In the matter of a Reference with respect to the meaning to be
    assigned to the word "Persons" in section 24 of the
    British North America Act 1867.

Whereas by Order-in-Council of His Majesty's Privy Council for Canada bearing date the nineteenth day of October in the Year of Our Lord One Thousand Nine Hundred and Twenty-seven "P.C. 2034", the question hereinafter set out was referred to the Supreme Court of Canada for hearing and consideration pursuant to section 60 of the Supreme Court Act, namely, —

Does the word "Persons" in section 24 of the British North America Act 1867 include female persons?

As whereas the said question came before this Court for hearing on the fourteenth day of March in the Year of Our Lord One Thousand Nine Hundred and Twenty-eight, in the presence of Counsel for the Attorney General of Canada, the Attorney General of the Province of Quebec and Henrietta Muir Edwards, and others, petitioners.

Whereupon and upon hearing what was alleged by Counsel aforesaid, this Court was pleased to direct that the said Reference should stand over for consideration and the same having come on this day for determination, the following judgment was pronounced:-

"The question being understood to be "Are women eligible for appointment to the Senate of Canada" the question is answered in the negative."

Ent'd Fol: 133
J. B. n° 9
[signature]

[signature] E. R. Cameron
Registrar

Privy Council Appeal No. 121 *of* 1928.

In the matter of a Reference as to the meaning of the word "persons" in Section 24 of The British North America Act, 1867.

Henrietta Muir Edwards and others   -   -   -   - *Appellants*

v.

The Attorney-General of Canada and others   -   -   - *Respondents*

FROM

THE SUPREME COURT OF CANADA.

———

JUDGMENT OF THE LORDS OF THE JUDICIAL COMMITTEE OF THE PRIVY COUNCIL, DELIVERED THE 18TH OCTOBER, 1929.

———

Present at the Hearing :

THE LORD CHANCELLOR.
LORD DARLING.
LORD MERRIVALE.
LORD TOMLIN.
SIR LANCELOT SANDERSON.

[*Delivered by the* LORD CHANCELLOR.]

———

By section 24 of the British North America Act, 1867, it is provided that "The Governor General shall from time to time, in the Queen's name, by instrument under the Great Seal of Canada, summon qualified persons to the Senate ; and, subject to the provisions of this Act, every person so summoned shall become and be a Member of the Senate and a Senator."

The question at issue in this appeal is whether the words "qualified persons" in that section include a woman, and consequently whether women are eligible to be summoned to and become members of the Senate of Canada.

Of the appellants, Henrietta Muir Edwards is the Vice-President for the Province of Alberta of the National Council of Women for Canada ; Nellie L. McClung and Louise C. McKinney were for several years members of the Legislative Assembly of the said province ; Emily F. Murphy is a police magistrate in and for the said province ; and Irene Parlby is a member of

44.5 Privy Council Appeal, 1928 (National Archives of Canada, Department of Justice fonds, RG 13, vol. 2524, file C 1044)

the Legislative Assembly of the said province and a member of the Executive Council thereof.

On the 29th August, 1927, the appellants petitioned the Governor-General in Council to refer to the Supreme Court certain questions touching the powers of the Governor-General to summon female persons to the Senate, and upon the 19th October, 1927, the Governor-General in Council referred to the Supreme Court the aforesaid question. The case was heard before Chief Justice Anglin, Mr. Justice Duff, Mr. Justice Mignault, Mr. Justice Lamont and Mr. Justice Smith, and upon the 24th April, 1928, the Court answered the question in the negative ; the question being understood to be " Are women eligible for appointment to the Senate of Canada."

The Chief Justice, whose judgment was concurred in by Mr. Justice Lamont and Mr. Justice Smith, and substantially by Mr. Justice Mignault, came to this conclusion upon broad lines mainly because of the Common Law disability of women to hold public office and from a consideration of various cases which had been decided under different statutes as to their right to vote for a member of Parliament.

Mr. Justice Duff, on the other hand, did not agree with this view. He came to the conclusion that women are not eligible for appointment to the Senate upon the narrower ground that upon a close examination of the British North America Act of 1867 the word " persons " in section 24 is restricted to members of the male sex. The result therefore of the decision was that the Supreme Court was unanimously of opinion that the word " persons " did not include female persons, and that women are not eligible to be summoned to the Senate.

Their Lordships are of opinion that the word " persons " in section 24 *does* include women, and that women are eligible to be summoned to and become members of the Senate of Canada.

45 Women, the Settlement Movement, and State Formation in the Early Twentieth Century

Cathy James

Men sometimes talk of 'undesirable immigration,' but there is no denying the fact that the greatness of Canada's future lies in the hands of the people who are coming in shiploads to our shores. These people must be taught our language. They must know our laws and customs, or how else can they live according to them? They and their children must be made cognizant of our ideals in private and public life, or how else can they be expected to support them? They must know the value of sanitation, order and British fair play.

Phamphlet, June 1913[1]

Until recently, most scholars of nineteenth- and early twentieth-century Canada have seen state formation as a male-dominated activity, primarily economic and political in character. Women, when they enter the picture at all, have generally been considered only in light of their efforts to become full members of the state, or as targets or victims of public policies and practices. But an examination of the early history of the Canadian settlement movement can reveal one area in which women were directly involved in state formation, both at the conventional level of institution building and at the level of fostering the development of the state's ideological infrastructure.

It is important to begin by acknowledging that state formation involves much more than the development of government agencies and institutions. Philip Abrams has argued that in order to study properly the nature and role of the state, one must consider the fact that the "state" is not a thing, that it does not exist as a material object of study, whether concrete or abstract. What does exist is the state *system* – the internal and external relations of political and governmental institutions – and the state *idea* – a hegemonic ideal of nationhood, citizenship, and cultural norms and practices.[2] State formation is the process of establishing and maintaining these relations and ideals as normal, inevitable, and just, of striving to assert the cultural hegemony of the dominant group in society. This larger conception of the state provides a compelling framework for exploring the role that some women played, through their participation in the settlement movement, in this developmental process.

Social settlements in Canada were part of a much larger international movement that began with the establishment of Toynbee Hall in the Whitechapel district of London in 1884. The movement was urban in orientation and was based on the Christian socialist vision of a cooperative community in which rich and poor lived in harmony. Fearing the growing geographical and social distance between the classes, settlement advocates proposed that university-educated young people should "settle," or live for a period of months or years as neighbours, in the city's working-class districts in order to come to a better understanding of the causes of and potential cures for poverty. These young people were to serve as models for the poor to emulate, as embodiments of "uplifting" lifestyles, attitudes, values, and behaviours.

Settlement workers believed it was their duty to "reconnect" their peers with those less fortunate than themselves and to provide the relatively wealthy and well-educated with opportunities to use their gifts of cultural refinement and education in meaningful, socially significant ways. They argued that previous approaches to philanthropy only sustained and perhaps even augmented social disharmony. It would be far better, they maintained, for educated men and women to offer leadership, practical services, and inspiring ideals to the poor. Such good examples would eventually teach the poor to help themselves and would ensure that all members of society would adhere to the same values and mores.[3]

The concept of the social settlement rapidly spread throughout Britain, Europe, the United States, and, eventually, Canada. The movement was especially popular in American social reform circles: in 1902, when Canada's first settlement was established, there were approximately 100 American settlements; by 1905 this figure had risen to over 200; and by 1911 there were over 400 settlements in the United States. Britain, for its part, boasted roughly 50 settlement houses in 1911, and Canada, with its proportionally smaller urban population base, claimed 13 settlement houses by the start of the First World War. Canadian settlements, like their American counterparts, were generally located in the most ethnically diverse, working-class city wards.[4]

Most Canadian settlements were independent institutions, drawing much of their support from a variety of sources, including local civic groups, social clubs, entrepreneurs, and philanthropists, but some were linked, loosely, to local universities, and others were directly tied to one of the mainstream Protestant churches. The Presbyterian church was particularly active, opening four settlements in the prewar period. But whether or not they were sponsored by churches, the settlements distinguished themselves, clearly and emphatically, from urban missions. Movement advocates argued that over-

coming the barriers created by religious, ethnic, and racial prejudices would be all but impossible to accomplish if they attempted to evangelize their clientele. Instead, they emphasized a form of "practical Christianity," stressing the need for settlement staff and volunteers to demonstrate acts of service, neighbourliness, and exemplary behaviour in their everyday dealings with district residents.[5]

The vast majority of those in Canada who took up settlement work were young, middle-class Anglo-Canadian women who either had attended or were attending tertiary-level educational institutions – not just universities, but also schools of literature and expression, conservatories of music, and teacher, nurse, or deaconess training programs.[6] Most of these women were nonresident volunteers who donated a few hours of their time weekly during the academic year. Indeed, for a number of students from these institutions, the settlements provided an opportunity to develop professional skills as teachers, nurses, and artists. Prior to 1914, when the University of Toronto created the first department of social work in a Canadian university, the settlements offered a means to enter this emerging profession, and thus they provided middle-class women with a potential career alternative at a time when few options existed. After 1914 the university incorporated the settlements into its formal training program as practicum placements, and the department hired settlement experts to lecture trainees in social-work practice.[7]

But settlement work was not restricted to students or professional social workers. Settlements also offered an opportunity for married professional women, many of whom had been forced to abandon their careers, to continue to utilize their skills and expertise as volunteers. For other married women, the movement offered an innovative, "scientific" approach to the social problems they had long been attempting to ameliorate through traditional forms of charity.

It is not surprising, then, that such women's organizations as local councils of women, church groups, alumnae associations, social clubs, and professional associations were among the strongest supporters of settlement work. A number of prominent figures on the Canadian reform scene championed the movement, including Flora MacDonald Denison, Rosalie Torrington, Alice Chown, and Dr Helen MacMurchy. In the early years, these high-profile leaders were active members of settlement boards of directors, their presence in the boardroom often augmented by a few lesser-known local women's group leaders. It is significant, however, that while women comprised the majority of the settlement movement's workforce, settlement boards were nearly always dominated by men.[8]

Canadian settlements shared many policies: they all had some workers residing in the settlement; they all stressed the importance of accepting every member of the neighbourhood regardless of age, race, class, or religion; they all charged nominal membership dues and small user-fees for classes and services; they all operated under the assumption that settlements should act as laboratories for social research; and they all experimented with and demonstrated a variety of services and activities, with the intention that other public or semi-public agencies would take over the ventures that proved successful. While the urban-based working poor comprised the broad constituency of social settlements, Canadian settlement workers, like their counterparts in the United States, focused most of their efforts on recently arrived, non-English speaking immigrants from eastern and southern Europe; they were particularly interested in serving the needs of the mothers and children of these immigrants.

In fact, the majority of the activities and services offered at Canadian settlements were intended to instruct non-British immigrants in their rights and obligations as citizens in a capitalist democracy, as well as to promote their adoption of values, mores, lifestyles, and aspirations that were distinctly bourgeois and Anglo-Canadian. The whole process, significantly, was termed "Canadianization." The majority of settlement programs were oriented towards children, in part because settlement workers considered school-aged youngsters to be more receptive to the Canadianization process than were adults, but also because the workers found that they could often gain greater access to neighbourhood families through the children. A mutual focus on children's welfare, the workers asserted, promoted goodwill throughout the community and encouraged parental support for settlement endeavours. Community goodwill was central to settlement work, and, settlement staff frequently argued, settlement work was central to the transformation of poor, non-British newcomers into responsible and loyal citizens of the Canadian state.[9]

Settlement members were usually organized into age-specific, sex-segregated clubs, and most were encouraged to participate in settlement programs with their clubs rather than as individuals. Thus, a club for fourteen- to nineteen-year-old working women might have its weekly business meeting on Friday evenings and then take settlement classes on other evenings of the week – say a Monday evening sewing class, a Tuesday evening stenography class, a Wednesday evening gymnastics class, and so on. Clubs and classes tutored settlement members in a highly gendered conception of the state; they encouraged male members to prepare themselves to be educated, law-abiding voters and workers in a capitalist democratic state, while directing female members towards becoming efficient and respectable homemakers and mothers.[10]

Clubs were closely supervised by staff members (workers maintained that even adult club members were too unruly to be left on their own), but these groups were still considered to be self-governing, since they were permitted to vote new members in, to elect new officers at

45.1 Children's sewing class, University Settlement, Toronto (sc 24-68 City of Toronto Archives)

45.2 Central Neighbourhood House English class, Toronto, 1913 (SC 5-58, City of Toronto Archives)

regular intervals, to collect dues and penny-bank contributions, and to plan some of their own activities. Settlers contended that the supervisor's presence, and her insistence that members adhere to parliamentary procedure in club meetings, were essential to fulfilling the underlying purpose of the clubs – to instil democratic principles, tendencies towards self-government, respect for Canadian political institutions, and loyalty to the state. Significantly, settlement workers expected the clubs to regulate the behaviour of their members both in and outside the settlement. Indeed, some observers credited settlement clubs with decreasing the juvenile delinquency rates in their neighbourhoods.[11]

Settlement workers also used other methods beyond clubwork to "Canadianize" their member. For example, they offered sex-segregated sports teams in order to contribute to character development; they organized classes in domestic science as a means to instil Anglo-Canadian approaches to child rearing, family life, and personal and domestic hygiene; they established nursery schools and

kindergartens to acquaint immigrant and working-class children and their mothers to bourgeois Anglo-Canadian cultural norms and approaches to learning and play. Settlers pioneered the creation of childrens' libraries to encourage literacy and to increase their members access to books, especially books written from a middle-class British or American viewpoint. Settlement workers also worked closely with municipal groups in establishing supervised playgrounds, and they encouraged local artists, musicians, and Little Theatre enthusiasts to offer lessons to settlement members and to help them stage exhibitions and performances. These various programs, settlement advocates maintained, provided not only inspiration and enlightenment, but also worthy alternatives to disreputable popular amusements such as vaudeville theatre, dance halls, and motion pictures. They also expected these initiatives to encourage immigrant and Canadian-born alike to see middle-class Anglo-Canadian culture as hegemonic – as "truly Canadian."

Canadian settlements also provided a variety of neighbourhood services, including day-care and employment referrals, medical and dental clinics, English-language instruction, high school upgrading and university preparatory classes, lunch rooms for working women, Well Baby Clinics and pure milk depots, and, prior to the expansion of public health departments in the latter part of the 1910s, district nursing services. Many of those who took advantage of these services were not registered members. Settlement workers and volunteers also provided services to local welfare agencies, sometimes acting as "friendly" visitors, and they helped to foster the development of government welfare services. They conducted or participated in various social surveys of such phenomena as sweated labour, prostitution, public health hazards, and housing conditions in their districts, and their findings were distributed to local civic bodies, to semi-private groups like the local councils of women, and to existing provincial and federal agencies. Settlement workers also worked closely with local schools, offering programs like kindergarten, manual training, and domestic science that the overburdened local boards were unable to mount.[12]

Settlement houses were very popular; indeed, they typically became overcrowded within only months of opening. Not surprisingly, the largest group of settlement members consisted of children between eight and fourteen. A smaller but still considerable proportion of the settlement clientele came from the mothers living in the district. Settlements were less attractive to working teens and to adult men, but even non-members from these groups occasionally attended settlement functions – theatre nights, for example – or utilized settlement medical clinics or English-language classes. By the 1920s, some settlements could claim registered memberships of over two thousand, and active memberships in excess of five or six hundred. It is important to recognize, however, that many who took advantage of settlement serv-ices continued to rely heavily upon their own cultural and religious communities and kinship networks, and usually turned first to the latter for support.[13] Clearly, the settlements did not become the homogenizing force that it was hoped they would be in surrounding neighbourhoods. Nevertheless, the settlements were a significant presence in many members' lives; some participants remained deeply attached to their settlements and continued to attend even after moving away from the neighbourhood. Moreover, even those who did not participate directly in the settlements were indirectly influenced by them through the community services settlement workers pioneered and the social surveys they conducted.

Theorists have argued that the state is "a complex of social forms *organized* so that it inflects all relations of production so that they seem inevitable, natural and just."[14] They maintain that the power of the modern state depends on "including in the governed a sense of permanent visibility, and hence vulnerability, to generalized social forces."[15] Viewed within this framework, settlement workers were clearly involved in the process of state formation. The classes, clubs, and activities they organized helped to determine the tenor of the relationship between immigrants and the Canadian state. The services that the settlements extended, such as the district nursing services and the social surveys, heightened the immigrants' sense of being publicly scrutinized within their working-class neighbourhoods; some agency representative always seemed to be coming around to observe, ask questions, and offer advice. All this provides evidence for the claim that state formation is not a theoretical abstraction but a tangible process, one in which Canadian women were directly involved even before they gained the franchise. Their work in the settlements establishes that fact.[16]

46 The Historical Record and Adolescent Girls in Montreal's Red-Light District

Tamara Myers

Writing women's history is facilitated by the fact that some of the women who pushed the borders of what their society expected of them left good records about their personal lives, work experiences, and volunteer activities. These literate women have thus been written into the historical records in the last twenty-five years, thereby enriching our understanding of the past. Such women include the female reformers who sought to challenge the growth of red-light districts and prostitution during Canada's first major reform period (1880–1920s); Montreal's Committee of Sixteen is one such example. But what of the women and girls who lived, worked, hid, or sought pleasure in these menacing areas? To get at the history of these mostly working-class, impoverished young women and to comprehend their actions, historians have traditionally turned to the largely sensationalist words of the reformers. But other records, such as those produced by policewomen and the juvenile court, can divulge aspects of these young women's lives often not recorded by reformers.

In the last two decades, women's history scholars have created a literature that dispels the assumption that marginalized women – such as prostitutes – were too elusive to be studied in historical perspective. In the 1970s and 1980s a body of historical work emerged on prostitution that relied on largely prescriptive sources complemented by judicial data.[1] This work examined both the social history of prostitution (as part of working-class history) and the antagonism of "respectable"

society to the idea of prostitution as it became ever more visible in red-light districts. The definition of prostitution proved to be a slippery one, as historians who have researched "bad girls" have noted. Some of those young women labelled prostitutes by evangelical reformers were not in fact plying the trade but were creating and exploring new rituals of courting behaviour, albeit in areas thought to be tainted with sin and vice.[2] Building on this work, historians have explored how young women were constructed and policed as sex delinquents.[3] Ideas about the relationship of human behaviour, reputation, and geography also contribute to a deeper understanding about women and red-light districts. According to feminist geographers and scholars influenced by cultural theory, certain urban areas, such as red-light districts, developed reputations for sexual danger, permissiveness, and deviance that contaminated women and adolescent girls who were found there.[4]

In the late nineteenth century, Montreal had one of the most well known and flourishing red-light districts in North America. Occupying a large area to the east of downtown,[5] the district was a preserve of gambling, drug dens, and houses of prostitution, earning the city a reputation as a major port of entry for the white-slave trade[6] and the "Sodom of North America."[7] By the late nineteenth century, this part of Montreal was seen as a shameless challenge to respectable society. In attempting to contain, control, and ultimately eradicate the district and the vice that thrived therein, reformers produced a large body of sensationalist literature on prostitution.

The reformers' pervasive images of fallen women suggested that modern life in industrializing cities such as Montreal was hazardous to female chastity. Social reformers were particularly worried about the danger that the red-light district posed to the innocent, unsuspecting young woman. One social commentator noted that in the red-light district "prowlers and night hawks of every kind and both sexes loiter and lie in waist, like Satan, seeking whom they may devour."[8] Church members and the judiciary in Montreal considered prostitution the modern plague, infecting hundreds of innocents each year.[9] Seduced daughters, outcast unmarried mothers, and diseased and desperate prostitutes made headlines in the period's reform literature and investigative news stories.

Towards the end of the First World War, an organized anti-vice campaign peaked in Montreal with the establishment of the Committee of Sixteen, signalling the end of a period of relative tolerance of prostitution and the red-light district. This committee was largely female, anglophone, and Protestant but did include men, francophones, Catholics, and Jews. Revelations that the police and the courts viewed prostitution with a sense of inevitability spurred the Committee of Sixteen to attempt to abolish the "spectacle of triumphant vice" that Montreal had become and force a reluctant city hall to adopt a more vigilant position. The committee embarked on a study of commercialized vice in the summer of 1918, producing a preliminary report on houses of ill fame and prostitutes working in the red-light district in that year. In this report, however, the Committee of Sixteen focused on a seemingly more manageable problem than commercialized vice: the sexual delinquent.

According to the 1918 report, 124 "delinquent, wayward and immoral" young women, unlike prostitutes, were recoverable.[10] Three-quarters of those studied were under the age of twenty-one and the great majority were not professional prostitutes and were not widely promiscuous. The Committee of Sixteen then turned its attention to young women who arrived alone in the city and were preyed upon by unsavoury characters at train stations who offered them housing or employment. The members of the committee discovered what other contemporaneous organizations already had: that young women needed protection and policing in large urban centres like Montreal. Solutions to the problem of young women alone and unprotected in the city included supervised boarding houses and recreational centres – and an army of older wiser women who would be responsible for keeping good girls good.

Anxiety over good girls going bad led to increased state regulation of their lives. The harshest method of control was the heightened policing of adolescent girls' behaviour. During the First World War, Montrealers, like their counterparts elsewhere in North America and in Britain, appointed women to the urban police force to work as protective officers and used the juvenile court to control girls under sixteen.

In the early decades of the twentieth century, the typical police woman was a social worker armed with the responsibility of policing women and girls in the city. The role of the first policewomen was rooted in female philanthropic rescue work. Policewomen, then, became one of the solutions to controlling the "girl problem" that seemed to grip urban centres in this period. Equipped with experience in new social-work techniques, policewomen sought to clean up an urban landscape that was seen as a threat to proper womanhood.

The push for the hiring of policewomen in the second decade of the twentieth century was a cause that united Montreal's francophone and anglophone women's organizations. Indeed, the impetus behind a female police force was the Montreal Local Council of Women and the Fédération national St-Jean-Baptiste. Information about early policewomen is scanty, but the organizations that promoted women officers kept some records of the city's initial experiments in female policing.

The first appearance of policewomen on the scene in Montreal was short-lived. On 23 April 1915, City Recorder Amédée Geoffrion swore in Lilian Clearihue as the city's sole female officer in the law. Clearihue's background and experience eminently qualified her for the job. A Traveller's Aid worker for the Woman's Christian Temperance Union (WCTU), Clearihue had patrolled the city's railroad stations, meeting women coming to Montreal and directing them to safe lodgings.[11] Clearihue would continue to do her Traveller's Aid work as a policewoman and she was paid by the WCTU.

The nebulous status of Clearihue on the police force discouraged women's organizations in Montreal. They, especially the Montreal Local Council of Women, continued their lobbying efforts and would finally be rewarded when the city established the Committee on Public Safety (Service de la Sécurité publique). The director of public safety was more receptive than the chief of police to the wishes of reform organizations that hoped to eliminate vice, and made way for the first policewomen to work the streets of Montreal. Montreal finally joined a long list of Canadian cities in hiring women officers during the First World War. For a trial period of six months, municipal authorities hired four women (two francophones and two anglophones) to patrol the streets of the city and deal with women criminals and female juvenile delinquents. The woman who led the campaign to install women on the police force had commented: "[M]uch escape[s] the policeman … [and] for a thorough clean-up a finer implement must be shaped."[12] That more delicate instrument would be the woman patrol officer. Women police officers targeted young women on the city's streets, especially those in the red-light district. Because policewomen were hired for the purpose of improving the moral environment of the city, the Montreal Local Council of Women argued for an expansion of the list of kinds of behaviour that could be policed. The Fédération national St-Jean-Baptiste agreed that the goal in hiring policewomen was "l'épuration des moeurs."[13]

Many cases processed by Montreal's policewomen in 1918 concerned women who had disappeared from their jobs or families. The "crime" of disappearing confirmed for some reformers that a white-slave trade existed in the city, or at the very least that those responsible were connected to local rings of prostitution. When the policewomen caught up with the young woman in question, though, the "offender" offered a variety of excuses. If she was not the victim of pimps and procurers, she was labelled a delinquent and often punished.

The disappearance of female adolescents in Montreal in the early twentieth century was widely pursued by policewomen, but also by the city's new Juvenile Delinquents' Court (established in 1912). Called "desertion" by the juvenile court, running away appears to have been a major concern of the court and of Montreal parents in the first half of the twentieth century. The red-light district was a common destination for girls hoping to escape home and work responsibilities. Court documents reveal the variety of reasons why girls ran away and why they chose the red-light district.

Most girls who were tracked down by policewomen or brought to court by parents had deserted their home as an act of resistence to parental authority. Girls confessed in juvenile court that they wanted to hold jobs on their own terms; many had disliked working in the family home and had sought better-paying jobs in factories or in the service sector. For example, Fleurette C., a seventeen-year-old French Canadian, deserted in January 1924 and found herself a job as a domestic servant in the red-light district. In the juvenile court she explained that when her mother had taken ill the previous December, she had been left to look after her eight siblings, ailing mother, and working father. She had kept house for one month, but had found the work arduous; preferring a job that paid, she left home and easily found a domestic service job.[14] In that same year, other adolescent girls had been drawn to the red-light district; it appears to have been seen simultaneously as a danger to them and as an escape.

Girls experienced increasing independence in the early twentieth century, and often their leisure activities put a strain on family life. Many of them ignored the warnings of the social reformers regarding the risks inherent in the red-light district. Most of these girls did not enter prostitution, but instead found the adventure and anonymity that was lacking in residential neighbourhoods. Girls as young as thirteen sought out movies, dance halls, and restaurants, winding up their evenings in the cheap rooms located within the red-light district.[15]

Family tensions leading to a daughter's court appearance often involved a dispute over her choice of boyfriend. Germain C., for example, ran away one night to 188 boulevard St Laurent with her boyfriend.[16] Another defence girls offered to the juvenile court to explain their desertion was that family members had physically and sexually abused them.[17] While the court and its officers often labelled adolescent girls who travelled into the red-light district as sex delinquents, the court records reveal that a range of motivations led girls there.

The extensive availability of cheap rooms rented by the night provided a temporary respite to girls looking to escape a tormented family life. These establishments ranged from the seamy to the respectable. "Chambres à louer" proved to be an effective short-term solution for runaways: inexpensive enough to be attractive, yet too costly to become a permanent home. During the First World War, a room in the district could be had for $2.50 per week, about half what an adolescent girl could earn at that time. Most important, the directors of the establishments in the red-light district did not question their age, their company, or their activities.

Policewomen, reformers, and many parents worried that young women alone in the red-light district risked being led into a life of debauchery. But their separation from family did not necessarily mean that these girls had to negotiate Montreal by night on their own; networks of girlfriends appear to have encouraged and sustained them, frequently accompanying them into the red-light district in search of a place to stay or to have a good time.

Adolescent girls who ventured into Montreal's red-light district were subject to interrogation by reformers, regulation by policewomen, and forced appearances before the juvenile court. The few records of them that remain (in the annals of the Committee of Sixteen, the files of the policewomen, and the proceedings of the juvenile court) allow us to hear their voices and begin to understand why they entered an area of the city where vice reigned. Some girls went to the red-light district to find a good time, others to escape threatening family situations. Their words offer us a different way to interpret the experience of the red-light district in Montreal's past, as well as evidence of the state's growing regulation of women's lives.

47 Charlotte Whitton: Pioneering Social Worker and Public Policy Activist

Judith Roberts-Moore

Will the real Charlotte Whitton please stand up? Is it the aggressive, belligerent, and quarrelsome mayor of Ottawa debating heatedly with City Council and civic leaders? Is it the spunky, quick-witted, intelligent Whitton who mobilized many women's organizations to work for her election and persuaded many Ottawans that she could do the job? Is it the orator capable of searing prose and theatrical antics if the press were nearby? Is it the energetic, insightful, high-minded Whitton who turned a small social agency into a national one respected by governments and public activists as the leading organization in the field of child and family welfare? Charlotte Whitton – "Dr Charlotte Whitton," as she liked to be called – was all of those things. Her dynamic personality, combined with a huge capacity for work and a desire to make a contribution, ensured that she would leave a legacy. But her public image as mayor of Ottawa often emphasized her negative aspects, including a quick temper and a gift for severely "dressing down" anyone who differed with her.

The press played a strong role in perpetuating this view, especially during her second term as mayor, from 1960 to 1964, as it reported on the volatile atmosphere at City Hall. Mayor Whitton's more outrageous escapades, such as almost hitting Controller Paul Tardiff for a sexist remark and pulling out a toy gun during a council meeting, fed the press's appetite for sensation. More recently, the press has sensationalized her possible-but-unlikely lesbian relationship with her long-time part-

ner. Overall, however, the press has ignored the real Charlotte Whitton, the complicated person whose ideas could be visionary or archly conservative and who hated to be labelled or stereotyped. Was she a feminist? Yes. Would she have liked to be called one? No. Yet she would have liked her role in paving the way for women's greater participation in public life to be saluted. But most of all Whitton would have liked to be best remembered for her considerable contribution to the fields of child and family welfare and to the expansion of the social work profession.

Born in 1896 in Renfrew, a small town in the Ottawa Valley, Whitton came from a family with a strong belief in the value of education and the place of religion in life. Charlotte became the first of the four Whitton children to attend a post-secondary institution with the help of several scholarships. By 1918, she had graduated from Queen's University in Kingston with a master's degree and medals in English, French, and pedagogy. Charlotte was also a product of a "mixed" (Roman Catholic and Protestant/Irish and English) marriage; such contrasting circumstances marked Whitton's personal and public life. While her siblings embraced Roman Catholicism, Charlotte remained a staunch Anglican all her life. Instead of making her more tolerant of differences, even within her own family, this situation reinforced her unbending, conservative views on religion and on Canada as a largely Protestant, Anglo-Saxon country.

Upon graduation, Whitton accepted the position of

47.1 Caricature of Charlotte Whitton by Al Beaton for the *Toronto Telegram*, November 1962 (C 146245, National Archives of Canada)

assistant secretary to the Social Service Council of Canada (sssc) in Toronto, a post she held from 1918 to 1922. She learned much about the nature of social work, including its principles and techniques; she developed an understanding of the workings of different charities; and she began to grasp the nuances of legislation governing child protection and welfare. She wrote for and contributed to the editing of *Social Welfare*. The council had its roots in church groups that had long engaged in charitable work, but it also included other reform or community groups, such as the Big Sisters and the Neighbourhood Workers' Association. Whitton persuaded the National Council of Women (NCW) to join the sssc. Her interests in child labour, juvenile immigration, poverty, and housing manifested itself during those years. She also joined the Canadian Council on Child Welfare, formed in 1920, and acted as its unpaid, honorary secretary for several years.

Charlotte Whitton lived in a sorority house at the University of Toronto where she met other women with an interest in social welfare and reform. She cultivated like-minded individuals, largely women, and called on them for aid and support throughout her career. Whitton, along with other Canadian women, believed that the franchise should be extended to include women and that women needed strong political representation. She also believed that women in gainful occupations should receive the same pay as men, a concept that marked her somewhat ahead of her time (at least in the eyes of most male politicians and public figures). She also believed that all employees should be paid a "living wage" by their employers in order to provide adequately for their dependents.[1]

By 1922, Whitton's interests evolved into broader concerns that required liaison and coordination of all the private agencies and lobbying of the federal government

47.2 Charlotte Whitton (right foreground) with friends in Algonquin Park, Ontario (PA 203551, National Archives of Canada)

prepared a number of reports, planned further surveys on relevant topics, held conferences, and published a directory of child-welfare agencies.[2]

After she became the CCCW's executive director in 1926, Whitton's organizational and administrative talents came to the fore as she solidified the reputation of Canada as a leading advocate for child welfare by the end of the decade. Her energy, drive, and commitment knew no bounds. She travelled extensively, spoke to many organizations throughout North America, and maintained her links with the NCW and the Imperial Order Daughters of the Empire (IODE). Under her direction, the CCCW conducted surveys; held conferences; investigated the juvenile justice system; lobbied for improved child-welfare legislation; investigated and reported on the family allowance system, the rights of illegitimate children, and protection of the handicapped child; forged many contacts with federal and provincial officials – not to mention strengthening the membership of private organizations.[3]

The council took up the cause of juvenile immigration, especially the practice of sending British "home children" to work on Canadian farms as "free labour," although nominally the British societies inspected living and working conditions.[4] On the one hand, Whitton fought to end this practice, which she genuinely thought harmful to the children and to the country. Her careful orchestration of the successful campaign to end juvenile immigration displayed her political astuteness and keen organizational skills. On the other hand, troubling undercurrents in her ideas regarding immigrants in Canadian society, especially her tendency to blame them for social problems, offer a darker motive for her pursuing this campaign so vigorously. While opposed to the wretched conditions many children faced, she also believed that the type of immigrant child that entered Canada was mainly undesirable. This "anti-immigrant" attitude (which included certain British groups, as well

to improve legislation and to increase funding. Leaving the SSSC, Whitton moved to Ottawa to become executive secretary to Thomas Low, who represented Renfrew riding in Parliament and became minister of trade and commerce. Her move to Ottawa proved to be shrewd; she knew when to take a calculated risk, a quality that she often displayed throughout her career. Whitton's public and personal life became intertwined as she worked tirelessly after work to build up the Canadian Council on Child Welfare (CCCW) as the national organization that represented children's issues. Whitton and council president Ella Thorburn persuaded organizations at all levels to become affiliated members; a number of individuals also joined on their own. The council

as those with Jewish, central European, and Oriental backgrounds) surfaced a number of times throughout her life. As Professors Rooke and Schnell underline in their study of her career, Whitton believed that Canada should be essentially Anglo-Saxon and English-speaking, and that the ideal immigrant came from the agricultural class in Britain. Ironically, Whitton advanced moderately progressive views on social welfare but clung to racist stereotypes in terms of immigrants and immigration policy. Yet such views reflected the beliefs of a certain segment of the Canadian population at the time.[5] Those who held this conservative outlook looked down on others who did not share the view that a British-influenced society represented the ideal model for Canada. There was no room in such a model for tolerating or appreciating ethnic or cultural differences. Such nineteenth-century biases still permeated large portions of Canadian society during the interwar years and even lingered until well after the Second World War whenever the issue on Canadian immigration policy came under discussion.

Charlotte Whitton adeptly manoeuvred behind the scenes too, utilizing her political contacts and skills to advance her career. She adroitly engineered her appointment as an assessor to the League of Nations' Child Welfare Committee in 1925, serving at the League in various capacities until its demise in 1939.

By 1929, the CCCW was firmly established on the national scene, thanks to Whitton's energetic direction. Adherence to "scientific principles" was a popular contemporary refrain that the council promoted. Whitton applied it to her notions about motherhood as well as social work. Although she never experienced motherhood herself, she subscribed to conventional views on the subject espoused by other professional women, such as Dr Helen MacMurchy of the federal Department of Health's Child Welfare Division. According to the "scientific" approach, women had to be educated for moth-

erhood, since bringing up a baby was women's highest calling. The scientific approach stressed strict timetables and routine along with regular consultations with a doctor both before and after pregnancy. Failure to follow this regimen endangered the well-being of the baby. The council's series of pre- and postnatal publications dispensed advice freely along the scientific line. That some advice was highly impractical for many women did not occur to Whitton.[6]

On the social-work front, she continuously advocated that private and government agencies must adopt modern social-work principles. As part of the scientific approach, the practice of social casework required diagnosing problems and devising treatment that suited the individuals in trouble. Provision of material aid must always be accompanied by personal counselling.[7] Implementing these principles meant hiring professionally trained social workers and placing them in key positions in the organization where they would influence less-qualified workers as well as administer aid effectively. Whitton encouraged municipalities to establish coordinating bodies of all social agencies and recommended the establishment of "community chests" as a form of fund-raising for all members.[8] This became a familiar theme during the Depression of the 1930s. With job loss came destitution, and people resorted to public relief. Private charities' resources strained to care for the unemployed and their families.

Relief, its administration, and its consequences preoccupied much of the council's time during the 1930s as it advised governments and social agencies. The Bennett government hired Whitton to investigate relief for the hardest hit region of the country, Western Canada. Upholding social-work principles, her report advocated national standards for relief administration and the use of trained social workers to coordinate and administer public assistance. It also argued for the separation of relief recipients who were unemployed from those whose need stemmed from other reasons; federally funded relief should be reserved for the victims of the economic crisis. Whitton believed that labour should lobby for better wages and benefits so that people would not have to rely on governments for help. She distinguished between the "deserving poor" and "the poor" (who were authors of their own misfortune); underlying this was a fear that relief was promoting a dependency that in turn would diminish the work ethic and endanger the moral fibre of the country.[9]

Whitton exaggerated relief abuses to emphasize the need for trained professionals who would investigate each case to ensure that only those entitled would receive aid and that all earnings would be reported. Moreover, she believed that relief recipients should not obtain more than the lowest-paid workers. Bennett set aside many recommendations, except for the one dealing with single unemployed men. The idea of relief camps for this group had come from Whitton's report.[10] Probably Bennett feared that further federal involvement in relief would mean greatly increased expenditures. Governments of the 1930s were reluctant to spend great sums of money generally, preferring to maintain balanced budgets and avoid bankruptcy.

Whitton pressed her views at every opportunity. Sometimes her advice was partially heeded. For example, the council recommended to the City of Ottawa that the Ottawa Welfare Bureau be reorganized and that the number of trained social workers be increased to handle the distribution of relief, which was becoming a heavy burden on the agency. Ottawa briefly experimented with hiring professional social workers, but the timing coincided with the worst period of the Depression. The numbers on relief increased and stayed high for several years. The city subsequently disbanded its welfare unit and replaced it with non-professionals who were not interested in social casework.[11] The argument for the engagement of trained social workers to administer and

distribute relief was probably one of the more novel suggestions on how to alleviate the problems posed by the economic crisis. Had it been fully implemented, it is questionable whether it would have made a difference or would have just excluded more people from relief and thrown the burden back on the private charities and church groups.

Whitton strongly believed in this proposal, and her council called for a national relief plan three times during the period 1933–35. Underlying this urgent appeal was the fear that relief would encourage dependency if trained workers were unavailable to reinforce the work ethic.[12] In 1936 the Liberal government hired her to prepare a report on reforming the relief system for the newly established National Employment Commission. The result presented familiar arguments for federal administration of relief directed by professional social workers who would ensure that work was always more attractive than relief. Fearing expensive centralization, Mackenzie King rejected her suggestions.[13]

In the area of relief, Whitton must have felt tremendously frustrated at the rebuffs of her ideas. Perhaps this made her start to question her function and role in the council by the late 1930s. However, on other fronts, Charlotte Whitton achieved recognition of her contribution to child welfare. King George V honoured her as a commander of the British Empire in 1934 in recognition of her work in Canada and at the League of Nations. R.B. Bennett influenced the decision to make Whitton a full delegate and member of the Social Questions Committee of the League. She chaired this committee with her usual verve and succeeded in broadening the definition of child welfare to include more than the guarding of the health of young children. Under her direction, the committee produced a well-received report and film on child placement methods. Whitton persuaded Bennett to transfer the responsibilities of the federal Child Welfare Division to the CWC to broaden the definition of child welfare. This highly unusual move – an early example of "privatization" – was criticized by public health officials.[14] Did Whitton anticipate future trends? More likely she believed this arrangement expanded the council's scope and reflected the conservative notion that only private organizations should be responsible for caring for the poor. Government intervention in administering social programs for the poor was unnecessary in her view. She also believed in strengthening private agencies, since they were usually more community-oriented and understood the needs of the people better. Unfortunately for her, the decision was somewhat reversed in the late thirties when the government created a new unit for maternal and child hygiene.

Her conservative views contrasted with those of a growing number of public figures who questioned an economic system that caused such devastating unemployment and poverty. As the Depression lingered, many Canadian leaders came to believe in the necessity of state intervention to alleviate the grave social consequences of the economic crisis. This approach included concepts of unemployment insurance and expanded family allowances, as well as economic and social planners, largely male academics. Many social workers, still predominantly female, also came to believe that government intervention was necessary. Why did Whitton not also question the prevailing system, since she could see firsthand the terrible results of the Depression and must have known that the poor now included not only the working-class but middle-class Canadians as well? Perhaps because her political views of Canadian society were so strongly entrenched, she could not embrace state intervention.[15] In line with many governments of the day, Whitton believed that further government involvement in the country's economic and social life would dramatically increase expenditures and risk public debt or even bankruptcy. For Whitton, private agencies and individuals rooted in the local community were

still the best means to deliver social services to those who needed them.

Ironically, Whitton found herself under attack from the social-work ranks, especially those who advocated that the administration of all social welfare work had to be handled by university graduates. Whitton had promoted social-work principles and the concept of trained professionals tirelessly since her entry into the field, but she did not believe that everyone involved in the social-work method had to have academic qualifications. Experience and belief in the principles was enough. She found herself isolated by the time the Second World War started. The council executive included more businessmen

47.3 Charlotte Whitton after winning the municipal election, Ottawa, 1954 (Photo by Bill Newton, NFB Collection. Courtesy of the Canadian Museum of Contemporary Photography)

who disliked Whitton's aggressive style. Whitton believed the council lacked clear direction and increasingly argued with council members as well as with former colleagues and friends. Most likely she was exhausted after twenty years of vigorous, hectic activity. Whitton and the cwc parted company at the end of 1941.

For the next nine years, before she turned to politics in 1950, Whitton had no real permanent job. Rooke and Schnell suggest that career aspirations of women in the social service area were thwarted by the many university-educated economists and labour planners who during the late thirties and early forties engaged in social planning and prepared for the coming of the welfare state; they were the policy makers and predominately male. The experienced social workers remained in the child and family welfare areas. They were largely female and saw their power base being eroded and their work unappreciated.[16]

The ambitious Whitton did not "lay low." She embarked on numerous lecture tours and prepared *The Dawn of Ampler Life*, her social strategy for postwar Canada for the Progressive Conservative Party. She gained notoriety again through her work for the IODE in exposing inadequate child adoption standards and methods in Alberta, chronicling these in an article, "Babies for Export," in *New Liberty* magazine. The social-work profession greatly expanded after the war ended; Whitton had helped to lay the groundwork during the two previous decades, but she was ready for a change. In 1950 she accepted the challenge of the Ottawa Local Council of Women and ran for Board of Control in Ottawa, backed by many women's groups. Whitton gained the most votes and became mayor in 1951 upon the death of the incumbent. She held that office until 1956 and again from 1960 to 1964. As a "senior citizen," she sat as a city councillor from 1966 to 1972. Her political years were very public; the media followed her closely to catch her ready quip or pithy comment.

Charlotte Whitton never married or bore children, an ironic circumstance since she was such a strong advocate for the child and the family in her professional life. Her dedication to her post as executive director of the Child Welfare Council and her frequent travels across the country and internationally on behalf of child welfare issues meant long absences from her home in Ottawa. That schedule would have strained any relationship. If her hectic pace did not, then her feisty, no-nonsense personality would have challenged many men of her generation. Whitton, like many other professional women of that time, sacrificed family life in order to have a career.

For Whitton, the choice was clear. Her vocation was to better child and family life through a professional career in social work. Motherhood was the vocation of the majority of Canadian women, who best achieved it by working within the home and devoting themselves to the betterment of their family members. The two choices were, in Whitton's opinion, mutually exclusive. Her staunch views never swayed, even when women, including married women and women with children, entered the workforce in increasing numbers after the Second World War (although this trend was still frowned upon until the "boomers" not only questioned the concept, but proceeded to ignore it during the 1970s). Having a career did not necessarily mean leading a lonely, single life. Whitton's public and personal life was always sustained by a large circle of female friends and colleagues; she also maintained close friendships with a number of women from her Queen's University days. For years she shared a home with another professional social worker, Margaret Grier, until the latter's premature death in 1947. The two women, both members of the first generation of Canadian women to work extensively in the professions, provided mutual support for each other. For these women, a woman's ability to have a career and a "normal" family life would have to wait for a future generation.

Sensitive, personal correspondence between the two women, as well as a series of letters written by Charlotte Whitton after the death of Margaret Grier, recently opened for research at the National Archives of Canada, suggest that the two women were life partners.[17] They found personal fulfilment in their long and loving relationship, but not in a sexual sense, since both held strong religious beliefs that would have discouraged sexual contact. The letters reveal the devastating effect of Grier's death on Whitton, never betrayed in her strong public persona. During the last months of her friend's illness, Whitton spent many weeks away from Ottawa, being closely involved in the "babies for export" investigation and libel suit in Alberta. The fact that she did not make it back to Grier's bedside before her death caused Whitton enormous pain and remorse. For several years after this distressing event, Charlotte Whitton wrote letters to her dead friend that express her struggle to come to terms with her loss. Techniques to cope with grief vary from person to person. Writing was second nature to Whitton; it provided a way to expunge her guilt and express her grief in private. Most likely her move towards public office in late 1949–50 helped to close that sad period and provide a focus for her energies.

The career of Charlotte Whitton is rich material for historians: from her university days, through her building the Canadian Council on Child Welfare into a strong, well-run national organization, her years of public speaking and writing on a wealth of topics, her well-publicized investigation into welfare practices in Alberta, to her exciting, but stormy years in politics, initially as the first female mayor of a Canadian city and later as an "alderman" championing the interests of the elderly. After her death in 1975, her will stipulated that her papers be placed in the National Archives of Canada. The Charlotte Whitton Papers (MG 30 E 256) contain 24.3 metres (79 linear feet) of correspondence, memoranda, reports, minutes, manuscripts, speeches, clippings, and printed material relating to a wide range of subjects: social welfare; her family, friends, and close acquaintances; the Church of England; commissioned studies; and civic politics. The collection affords glimpses into the personal and professional life of a notable public figure. To appreciate her role in the expanding field of social welfare during the 1920s and 1930s, the records of the Canadian Council on Social Development, formerly the Canadian Welfare Council (also in the National Archives of Canada, as MG 28 I 10), must be consulted. These extensive records (over 70 metres or 227 feet for the period 1922–81) are especially useful for documenting the Whitton years, offering many files on the reports, surveys, studies, correspondence, meetings, and conferences undertaken by the council as it examined children's aid, juvenile delinquency, adoption, child care, legislation, mother's allowances, unemployment relief, immigration, the League of Nations, and social-service organizations. It is abundantly evident that Charlotte Whitton demonstrated impressive organizational skills, possessed good political instincts, and worked tremendously hard to foster the social service viewpoint through the works prepared for all levels of government and private agencies across Canada. Her high energy and dedication to her special cause shine through the many letters, reports, and studies she wrote or supervised. The CCSD records are also an important source for research into all aspects of social welfare and will provide insights on the work of other female social workers in Canada at that time.

Although one may disagree with Whitton's political beliefs and regret her prejudices, no one who consults the Whitton Papers and the CCSD records can help but be impressed, if not a little intimidated, by her vigour, forthrightness, and dedication to her job. The real Charlotte Whitton defies labelling. Although she helped pave the way for other women to enter politics, it is as a pioneering social welfare executive and public policy advocate that she made her greatest contribution to Canadian life.

48 Consuming Issues: Women on the Left, Political Protest, and the Organization of Homemakers, 1920–1960

Joan Sangster

When a second wave of renewed feminist activity emerged in the 1960s and 1970s, one of the key issues was housework: why did women always do it; what economic role did it play in reproducing capitalism; how could it be transformed to facilitate women's liberation? A Canadian, Peggy Benston, penned one of the first articles stimulating an international debate concerning housework, using Marxist-feminist theory to decipher its economic role in capitalism and to argue for its transformation in a socialist society.[1]

Ironically, despite considerable ink spilled following Benston's article – later labelled the "domestic labour debates" – by academic feminist writers, this second wave of feminism was also characterized in the media as "anti-housewife." It is true that popular feminists like the American Betty Friedan protested women's involuntary relegation to the role of housewife, arguing that it was more fulfilling to have an education and a career. However, Friedan's middle-class perspective and reflex reaction against the 1950s "cult of domesticity" were challenged by other feminist writers, who were more concerned with how the difficult daily burdens of working-class homemakers could be alleviated, how domestic labour could be shared by men and women, and how housework might be transformed in a socialist economy.[2]

The second irony was that many second-wave feminists did not understand that previous generations of women had also debated the relationship of the homemaker to the capitalist economy and had focused their political energies on alleviating the oppression of the working-class homemaker. These earlier activists were more likely to urge women to organize on the basis of their homemaking duties, not question them altogether. However, they also made trenchant criticisms of the economic and social order, and were acutely aware of the difficulties working-class homemakers faced in their day-to-day work. This article examines left-wing women from the Communist Party and the socialist Co-operative Commonwealth Federation (CCF), from 1920 to 1960, who tried to rouse women into political action around issues pertaining to their role as housewives, particularly those relating to household consumption, such as rising prices. These left-wing women made the compelling argument that consuming issues spoke directly to many married women's daily work lives, especially since most women in this time period hoped to leave the workforce on marriage, rather than combine the two arduous jobs of wage and domestic work. Women's worries about balancing the family budget, stretching the meagre wages of family earners, finding decent housing, and educating their children were thus seen as "women's issues," and communists and socialists hoped that they could both mobilize women to fight for a more secure basis for family life and, at the same time, encourage them to join the communist or socialist movements.

48.1 Housewives Consumers League, Windsor (PA 124366, National Archives of Canada)

COMMUNIST WOMEN ORGANIZE HOUSEWIVES

In one sense, efforts to organize women as mothers and homemakers carried on with the "maternalist" political traditions initiated by the suffragists and even earlier by temperance advocates. Left-wing women who organized after federal women's suffrage was won, however, were far more sceptical of women's ability to create decent homes within a capitalist economy, and they were more militant in their organizing methods and in their opposition to the economic and social order.[3]

In the 1920s, women sympathetic to communism often joined the Women's Labour Leagues, organizations that promoted the unionization of wage-earning women and the mobilization of working-class housewives in support of socialist and union causes. Their newspaper, the *Woman Worker*, criticized the current conditions of homemaking for many women, urged homemakers to set up their own political organizations, and even commented on what might happen to housework in a socialist future.[4]

Some homemakers wrote to the *Woman Worker* offering graphic and detailed descriptions of their homes and daily work. From Cape Breton, Annie Whitfield, a coal miner's wife, described the miners' small "shacks" with their open drains and outdoor toilets. How can the housewife even spring-clean, she asked, when "scrubbing was made impossible due to falling plaster?"[5] The difficulties of feeding a family on a miner's erratic wages and the problems of living on credit in a "company town" were the common complaints of miners' wives from across the country. In another article, a housewife called for a "Minimum Family Budget ... [for] Health and Decency"; she implored women to support the struggle for higher, and especially regular, wages so that families would not have to live "hand to mouth." "If we are to do justice to our homes and families, and have our minds free from the worry of debt ... and to send out children to high school," we must have a more secure family wage, she wrote.[6] Writers for the communist *Worker* also emphasized how "making ends meet" meant that the "housewife's work is never done ... the heavy burdens of feminine life fall hard on women ... it is the financial burdens, the maintenance of home and families that are the nightmares which wear [down] women of the working class."[7]

The *Woman Worker* lauded women's lives in post-revolutionary Russia, not only because women had more economic and legal independence, but because reforms were socializing domestic labour. Communal kitchens, for example, were lightening the load of homemakers and making their work less isolated. This was a distant, somewhat utopian solution; for their own country, the Women's Labour Leagues believed that domestic labour – cooking, cleaning, managing the family finances, caring for children – would remain the responsibility of individual women for some time. As a result, they appealed to women to purchase goods with the union label, to lobby to keep the prices of basic food necessities down, and to press school boards for free schoolbooks and for an end to the militaristic education of children. They also criticized the new system of the Mothers Allowance, initiated by provincial governments in the 1920s for widows supporting minor children, because this program did not provide an income sufficient to properly house and feed a family. The allowance was deliberately kept "below the level of necessity," they

noted sarcastically, to "prevent women's laziness"[8] and to encourage supplementary wage work, a conclusion basically confirmed by recent historical analyses of the Mothers Allowance.[9]

By the mid-1930s, during the Depression, these left-wing women were engaged in communist organizing under the rubric of the "Popular Front," the aim of which was to draw together a wide variety of progressive, socialist, and communist women into broadly based coalitions critical of capitalism and dedicated to socialist reform. Organizing housewives was important to Popular Front politics, for communists now believed that one should organize "where women were at," appealing to them on the basis of their daily concerns, often through local, neighbourhood, or community groups.[10] For example, at the national convention of the Communist Party in 1938, Alice Cooke, who penned a women's column in their paper, the *Daily Clarion*, argued that organizing homemakers in a campaign against rising prices was "the most outstanding opportunity for organizing women," for rising prices "are far reaching [and] bound to be harmful to women. Rent increases mean the food bill will be cut; mothers will deprive themselves of food in order to supply their children's needs; pregnant women are unable to obtain the necessary food to maintain [their] health."[11] Women on relief would be especially concerned, for they were caught in the squeeze between inflation and static welfare rates.

By 1938, these left-wing women had launched, or were supporting, Housewives Consumers Associations (HCAS, or sometimes called Housewives Leagues) in cities like Toronto, Montreal, Vancouver, and Port Arthur.[12] The Toronto HCA, for instance, concentrated its efforts on issues such as children's playgrounds, consumer cooperatives, and especially keeping food prices down. In March of 1938, it devised a plan to reduce milk and butter prices, sending letters to its provincial political representatives asking for changes in the Milk Control Act.[13] "With rising prices," they announced at one meeting, "malnutrition as a problem looms large. Women in [our] associations have deluged MPPS with letters [and] this political activity helped women realize how the corporations are bilking people [and] who the enemy really is."[14] A minor victory was claimed after support from a sympathetic city councillor and their own lobbying brought a half-cent reduction in the price of a quart of milk. Women in other major cities were involved in similar organizations. In Vancouver, the HCA organized a strike against high meat costs, boycotting meat retailers for a week, and in Port Arthur, the association tried to raise relief rates for families.

The HCA's political appeal centred on the need for women to defend the well-being of the working-class family. On the one hand, women's responsibility for domestic labour went unquestioned; the women's column in the communist paper, for instance, included recipes and household hints. However, this column was not supposed to "dull women's class consciousness" and "relegate them to the kitchen" as the mainstream press did, but rather offer advice that would "help women devote more time … to outside [political] activities," such as "fighting for a higher standard of living" for their families.[15] Some writers offered a telling critique of consumerism in monopoly capitalism. Women are encouraged by advertising to want "a whiter than white wash – when most working-class women can not afford the washing machines advertised,"[16] wrote one communist woman in the *Daily Clarion*. Moreover, women's columnists also argued that corporate profits and low wages to workers were the reason why housewives could not make ends meet, not women's inadequate budgeting skills, a charge often levied at families on relief by governments and the more affluent.

During the Second World War, some left-wing women shifted their focus temporarily to wage-earning women; as more women went to work outside the home, issues such as decent wages, equal pay, and unionization naturally came to the fore. By 1942, communist women supported the war effort and, like women in the CCF, thought it important to encourage women's participation in war production. However, homemakers' important contribution to the war, in overseeing price-control efforts, running recycling campaigns, and participating in volunteer work, also kept their daily work in the public eye, and communists remained concerned that they be politicized in the "proper" fashion, for the "hand that rocks the cradle," they commented in a rather paternalistic tone, "must not misrule the world."[17]

During the war, some HCAs lobbied for more housing for working-class families (increasingly a crisis near the end of the war) and child-care centres for working mothers. They also tried to monitor prices, supposedly controlled under the government's price and rationing policies. The HCAs, still drawing on a membership of many left-leaning women, including some communists, urged the government to investigate its own Wartime Prices and Trade Board, which was claiming that prices were rising despite its regulations to the contrary.[18] They, too, were concerned that wages were falling behind prices, and wanted a cost-of-living bonus issued for soldiers' dependents[19] and for workers.[20] By 1943, the Toronto HCA had been in existence for five years, and it began to think of setting up a national association with like-minded groups in Vancouver and Montreal.[21] At least for the time being, however, its strength lay in its local and neighbourhood organizations; these groups could monitor the prices of food in their own area and mobilize women at the local level quite quickly to protest severe price increases.

After the war, when many women, even those in the workforce, were encouraged to return to homemaking, the issue of rising prices again became a crucial rallying point for left-wing women. As wartime price controls

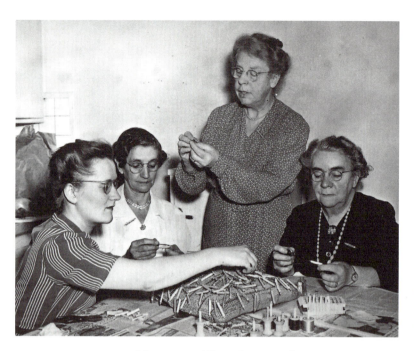

48.2 Women assembling miniature rolling pins
(PA 93677, National Archives of Canada)

were lifted by the government, working-class families were caught in the crunch of inflation; the escalating cost of food created very real stresses on low- and middle-income families. Homemakers were again seen as the key to political protest against the "profiteering" of business and in defence of the working-class family.[22] Leading communist Becky Buhay believed that the majority of women, as homemakers, held tremendous political power: "The majority of Canadian women still fall under the category of housewives and the part of the housewife against monopoly cannot be minimalized … at least one quarter of a million voters in 1945 were housewives … and never have [they] been so articulate over rising prices."[23]

Much of the HCAS' efforts were now directed at federal lobbying. In March of 1947, a Winnipeg delegation presented a brief to the minister of finance asking the government to reimpose price controls, and a few months later, women from eastern cities also sent large delegations to the federal government, the Port Arthur one calling itself "a bread and butter cavalcade" to Ottawa.[24] The issue of price controls was pressing and popular, and the HCAS drew in many women who devised ingenious methods of publicizing their concerns. When the Toronto HCA sent a massive group of protesters to Ottawa, women advertised their efforts by making small emblems, miniature rolling pins, which they wore as badges of political protest. HCAS' also organized smaller consumers' strikes over very specific issues; in Vancouver, escalating bacon prices were protested with a strike against pork in the stores, and in one of the more popular and inventive strikes, children in a number of cities were recruited to picket with signs declaring, "Bring back the 5¢ chocolate bar."

The issue of prices was "ready-made" for protest in the postwar years, remembered Mona Morgan, the leader of the women's auxiliary for the International Woodworkers Union in British Columbia. Along with union issues such as safety in the woods, she made rising prices a theme in her radio broadcasts to loggers' wives, and she found them very receptive to her message.[25] Homemakers, it was recognized, were still in charge of budgeting for family essentials, and escalating prices created considerable strain in their daily work – even in this more affluent era. Moreover, it was not simply the individual family's "self-interest" that encouraged women's protests; the HCAS' critique of monopoly capitalism and of the unrestrained power of business to pursue profit clearly appealed to many working people.

But the HCA campaign, however popular to begin with, was ultimately thwarted by the efforts of two political opponents. The HCAS were caught in the grip of the increasingly vicious Cold War; when labelled a "communist" organization, first by the Royal Canadian Mounted Police (RCMP), then by the press, they were seriously undermined publicly. As Julie Guard has documented using RCMP surveillance files, the HCA women were indeed intensely watched and purposely discredited by the RCMP and government because some (certainly not all) of the leaders were communists.[26] The HCAS had another group of political opponents: CCF women. The CCF, a social-democratic party intent on a milder, evolutionary, and parliamentary brand of socialism, also believed in organizing homemakers – but on their own terms.

THE CCF MOBILIZES HOMEMAKERS

After it was founded in 1933, the Co-operative Commonwealth Federation remained a somewhat decentralized party, with strong local and provincial federations as well as a nascent national structure. In many of these localities, women set themselves the task of drawing more women into the CCF movement, convincing them of the benefits of democratic socialism. The women's columnist of the Saskatchewan CCF paper, for instance, compared the difficulties of women's household labour to the challenges of political activism, and she noted that consumer issues could awaken women's critique of capitalism. Women, she wrote, should turn their thoughts from household tasks, "more patching, scrimping, planning," to tidying up the messy outside world. "So who is in a better position to understand the economic system than the person who is the consumer for the family?" she asked rhetorically.[27]

Because the CCF began with a strong base in the prairies, urging women to organize as homemakers also meant organizing farm wives. During the 1930s, controlling consumer prices on basic foodstuffs was not necessarily the primary concern of farm women, as many farmers did not have, or could not sell, their own produce. However, farm wives could be convinced that a competitive, capitalist economic system contributed to the difficulties of their household labour. Ensnared in debt to the banks, unable to purchase household aids or help, they found that their work day was often endless.

They bore the responsibility of making ends meet, sometimes providing the family's only means of subsistence through poultry or garden produce.

CCF women in other provinces also believed that women were more likely to respond politically to family and homemaking issues. In 1936 Toronto CCF women formed a short-lived but radical women's organization, the Women's Joint Committee (WJC), to raise women's issues, draw women into socialist causes, and train women for leadership in the CCF. Though the WJC did not focus exclusively on consumer issues, as it had a long list of concerns ranging from international peace to the unemployed single woman in Canada, it did see the household economy as key to reaching married women. Since many women were in families in which earners were unemployed and women therefore had to budget on the basis of paltry relief payments, the WJC organized a conference "on relief as it related to the home and children in the home."[28] A homemaker from the nearby suburb of Lakeview attended and asked for support in her fight against cuts to welfare; the WJC responded by writing letters to the Lakeview relief officer, as well as the provincial minister of welfare. One of the WJC's leaders, Jean Laing, undertook an investigation of local dairies, bakeries, and movie theatres, drawing up a list of union and non-union businesses that was widely distributed so that women would know which businesses to support. A boycott of non-union dairies was planned by the women. This classic consumer protest allowed homemakers to flex their shopping muscles by supporting union businesses or forcing others to change their labour practices or lower their prices.[29]

Like communist women, CCF members also saw consumer protest as one of the most effective ways to mobilize women in the postwar period. Although issues relating to women's wage work – such as equal pay and unionization – were promoted by a small number of women in the party, it was felt that the majority of

WOMEN

In Peace As In War

PROTECT YOUR HOME

48.3 "Protect Your Home" (National Archives of Canada)

female voters were in the "occupational group, home-makers" and were thus likely to respond to that which directly touched their role as care-giver in the family.[30] Indeed, CCF election pamphlets directed at women electors just after the war still employed a representational figure used in the suffrage era: the homemaker, with apron and broom, ready to "tidy up" political life and anxious to have her home-centred concerns heard.

In 1947 a Provincial Women's Committee (PWC) was established in Ontario, with the purpose of offering political education, of encouraging and training women to participate in the party, and of drawing more women, especially homemakers, into the CCF. Some feared that homemakers were more isolated and conservative in their approach to politics, but they reasoned that their daily work – homemaking – could be used to raise their socialist consciousness. Not surprisingly, two important resolutions initially passed by the PWC at its formation involved the right to health care for the family, and the issue of rising prices.[31]

CCF women across the country also made rising prices their concern. At first, some joined the HCAs, but soon CCF leaders, hostile to the idea of sharing any organization with communist members, insisted that the HCAs be abandoned and that women instead join the newly established Consumers Association of Canada (CAC). Considerable debate ensued, since the CAC was hardly socialist in its views; as one CCF woman wrote in the Ontario CCF paper, the CAC wanted women to "live with austerity" rather than protest it.[32] CCF women eventually embraced a number of strategies. Despite the "liberal" outlook of the CAC, some CCF women joined, involving themselves in its work by monitoring prices and lobbying for the standardization of consumer products. Other CCF women continued to build their own campaign against rising prices, conducting price surveys and raising the issue within their own party and CCF women's organizations.

By the later 1950s, the urgency of the rising prices issue had abated somewhat, though consumption remained on the party agenda as a key political concern for women. CCF women continued to address women as a distinct political constituency, often assuming their interest, as homemakers, in problems of the home and family, or as one CCF activist put it, using the same political language as the communists, referring to "bread and butter" issues.[33] These were not limited to prices; like communists, CCF women also concentrated on social policy issues such as child welfare, education, Mothers

Allowances, and health care. As one historian has noted, these appeals to women as homemakers were "both a hook and a trap."[34] On the one hand, they recognized the work and worries of women in the home and spoke directly to matters considered key to the well-being of the family. On the other hand, they tended to reproduce an image of women that was linked solely to domesticity, which contributed to the marginalization of women in political life.

Despite this limitation, it is important to recognize the radical critique inherent in these protests concerning consumption, as well as the way they were different from both earlier and later feminist concerns with domestic labour. Communist and socialist women were distinct from the vast majority of earlier, middle-class suffragists, not only in their more militant methods – boycotts, strikes, demonstrations – but also in their socialist critique of consumerism and monopoly capitalism. Both communist and socialist parties saw consumption and the family in general as "women's issues," but these were also understood to be crucial economic issues, related to the rights of poor and working-class families to health, dignity, and material well-being. Fighting rising prices would make women aware of the basic inequalities of capitalism and encourage them to fight for a fairer distribution of wealth, temporarily articulated through women's purchasing power. Though many of these left-wing women would not at that time have used the word "feminist" to describe their protests, they saw women's self-organization and militancy, their defence of women's domestic needs, their putting a value on their labour, and their radical critique of society as a direct challenge to the status quo.

Second-wave feminists, unlike earlier activists, were more concerned with directly questioning women's responsibility for domestic labour. Early on, some liberal feminists assumed that housework could be reduced and that some women would be paid to look after domestic tasks while the more educated women worked outside the home. However, even liberal feminists soon offered a more enlightened view, suggesting better legal protection and wages for household workers and, in particular, urging women and men to share domestic labour. Socialist feminists were also deeply concerned with developing a theoretical understanding of how domestic labour sustained, indeed aided, the growth of capitalism as an economic and social system. With a few exceptions, earlier socialists had been more concerned with organizing women on the basis of their daily housework; they did not challenge it altogether.[35] It was partly for this reason that second-wave feminists appeared to be disinterested in the problems of homemakers, despite the strong support of the women's movement for some policies, such as homemakers' pensions, that would aid women working in the home.[36]

What can we conclude from these very different political responses to women's domestic labour and "consuming issues" by successive generations of women activists? Certainly, political ideology played an important role in shaping the way in which socialist and communist women analysed women's role as household worker and the political actions they took. However, the changing political analyses of women's domestic work over time also indicates how the very definition of what is termed a "women's issue" alters historically, moulded by the changing economic, social, and cultural context. In the 1930s and 1940s, when the married woman's primary work was still perceived to be domestic – shopping, feeding, and caring for her family – rising prices were central to her political world. By the 1970s, when far more married women were doing two jobs, inside and outside the home, her political concerns would encompass new issues, including wage work, and rising prices would more likely be a "social" issue, not simply one for the homemaker to tackle.

49 Making Ourselves Heard: "Voice of Women" and the Peace Movement in the Early Sixties

Candace Loewen

With the world facing an intensified nuclear threat after the failure of the Paris Summit in 1960, the Voice of Women (vow), a Canadian women's peace organization, was born of a sense of urgency.[1] Seeking to channel feelings of anxiety about the future of the human race into action, early vow organizers tried to combine women's traditional supportive role in the family with a public voice in world affairs. As the young organization welcomed women from all walks of life, it sought to bring together two different traditions of women's organizations – support groups and political action groups – in order to advocate peace. vow members, similar in some ways to members of women's associations at the turn of the century, and reflecting the peace concerns of earlier figures, such as Agnes Macphail, believed they had a maternal responsibility as protectors of the world's children to protect the earth from nuclear obliteration. This responsibility involved informing policy makers about their concerns as mothers and encouraging women to unite together for action. The organization used a variety of means to jostle those in power, some more vociferous than others. Although the vow made great strides in many ways, it lost some of its initial respectability and developed internal divisions when it attempted to politicize issues surrounding the traditionally domestic, supportive role of women. Such divisions, combined with external forces confronting the vow in the early 1960s – the press, government representatives, family and friends, and the general public –

created enough pressure to cause a decline in membership and a re-evaluation of the organization's purpose and methods.

The story of the early years of the vow could not be told without sensitivity to the marginalized and obscure voices of stay-at-home, suburban housewives, as expressed in their candid letters to one another. The record shows that women's discourse was different from the mainstream debate. Moreover, the archival records of the vow demonstrate how the private sphere was jolted when confronted with the official record of the public sphere. The very personal and domestic-centred records of concerned women, unlike the press's traditional interpretations of women's concerns in the early 1960s, show that vow members struggled for recognition of a different discourse. These observations are consonant with the findings of noteworthy scholars of women's history. The record women have left throughout the centuries conflicts with traditional accounts; it is rooted in a different experience and different knowledge, and must be lifted out of its isolation so as to add to a growing collective consciousness. Otherwise, as eminent historian Gerda Lerner has written, women of each successive generation will have to prove anew that they have a right to their own thought and discourse.[2]

Underlying all vow actions was the principle that it was women's responsibility to work for peace around the world. The main premise of the vow's "Brief Concerning Motivation, Purpose, Methods of Implement and Organization" stated this clearly: "By working through women's common interests and their instinctive concern for the human family we seek to help create a world climate of understanding favourable to mutual disarmament without fear."[3] The vow welcomed all women interested in world peace, whatever their ideas or background. From the beginning, the organization attempted to be "nonpartisan … just a group of women interested in acquiring as many members as possible."[4]

The first letters from women interested in joining the vow echoed this central premise. One woman wrote: "You are right I'm sure that its [sic] up to the women now to put a stop to all this fighting and atomic fear. We bring life into the world and thus fully appreciate it."[5] Many letters highlighted women's responsibility for the preservation of life: "Security is Womens [sic] business and has been since the beginning of time,"[6] one wrote. As mothers concerned for the world's children, most of these women held strong convictions and did not want others belittling their intelligence just because they stayed at home with their children. One woman expressed it this way: "[L]et the men of our nation realize that we women are not completely helpless … After all, surely a women [sic] has a little added intelligence other than changing diapers, cooking, and mending!"[7] Prospective members were relieved that this proposed organization did not "underestimate the intelligence of the average housewife and her interest in the world of today and tomorrow." These letters made it clear that "a female's main ambition is [not] to gossip over the card table, or sip tea at a bazaar."[8]

Although these "average housewives" were united in their feelings of responsibility and helplessness, the very first letters also revealed different opinions about the definition of, and the means to achieve, world peace and nuclear disarmament. How should the vow make its voice heard? Many letters sent in May, June, and July of 1960, just as the organization was getting under way,

opposed "halfway" measures such as policies of deterrence. Many women wanted heads of state to commit themselves to total disarmament; for them, any nuclear weapon was harmful to their children's future and they were prepared to use action to inform politicians of their feelings. One woman summed it up by writing, "To talk of defence, preparedness, and fall-out shelters is ridiculous. There is no defence against a nuclear bomb and people who talk otherwise are only fooling themselves."[9] Many average housewives favoured an "all or nothing" approach to world affairs, but others were interested in the vow as an organization that emphasized such global peace efforts as goodwill projects and policies of deterrence. These women were concerned that the vow remain a respectable women's organization, influencing the "great women … behind all heads of countries or towns or village[s]."[10] One woman bluntly stated, "I don't want to march on Ottawa!"[11]

The question of how to make the vow's voice heard was wrapped up in the question of image, which in turn was intensified by lack of agreement over the nature of the "voice" itself. If the vow were to draw attention to its cause through demonstrations, it might develop a negative public image. Many women whose lives revolved around the respectability of their homes and families had difficulty envisioning public action that might not be quite proper. Others simply wanted the organization to remain small in number and cohesive in methodology – "a small dynamic band" that "must take a stand."[12] One woman proposed that the new organization use "drastic action" even though she herself realized "that you don't want to be labelled 'militant.'"[13] One local vow group prepared a statement encouraging "women … to enter political life" even if this meant "participation in … demonstrations … of civil disobedience."[14]

In the early 1960s, these differences of opinion became more pronounced as tensions about nuclear weapons increased. In addition to universal fear about the future of the world, various others circumstances exacerbated the dissension that had existed within the vow from the beginning. Some members became impatient when results from related research endeavours were slow in coming and then disappointing. For example, the vow supported a study conducted by Dr Ursula Franklin on the radioactive contamination of milk, and planned to use the results in a brief it would present to the federal government. That work continued well into 1963 and ended unhappily for the vow when it received no encouragement or support from the new health minister, Judy LaMarsh.[15] The organization also supported Dr Murray Hunt of the University of Toronto's Faculty of Dentistry: with vow's cooperation Dr Hunt was supplied with twenty thousand baby teeth.[16] He pulverized these teeth to check how much strontium-90 was being trapped in Canadian children's teeth and bones. His study was conducted to see if the "hysteria" over the residue fallout of the nuclear open-air test explosions "were justified" (this was before a test ban treaty was signed in the summer of 1963). According to one reporter, after the study was completed, Dr Hunt himself said, "We'll kill ourselves a lot faster with air pollutants."[17]

Another example was the vow's financial aid to a peace research organization. Largely as a result of a quarter of a million dollars that the vow raised, the Canadian Peace Research Institute (CPRI) was established.[18] At first the vow enthusiastically supported CPRI, but although it was healthy and active for more than a year, the vow-CPRI union did not last. In the fall and winter of 1962, "C.P.R.I. began to dissociate itself from the whole of the Canadian Peace Movement." According to Ursula Franklin, CPRI wanted "massive support" and, in order to achieve this, needed government acceptance rather than endorsement "by the wrong type (like ban-the-bomb group[s])."[19] In 1962 the press made vow out to be "'soft on socialism' or 'pinko' or just plain Communist,"[20] and so CPRI "turned down [vow's offer of

continued support] because it would look 'partisan.'"[21]

The vow's persistent internal problems were magnified by one precipitous event in late 1962. Frustrated by the organization's failure in lobbying the government, whether through other organizations or its own channels, some members thought that public demonstrations (then uncommon in North America) would be more effective.[22] On 1 November 1962, just after the volatile Cuban missile affair,[23] a vow "peace train," organized by the Quebec branch, left Montreal's Windsor Station, picking up passengers en route to Ottawa. Newspaper editors were encouraged by the vow's national publicity chairperson to "send someone down to cover this story."[24] Once they arrived in Ottawa, three hundred women delegates from different parts of Canada, but mainly Quebec, marched to the Parliament Buildings, tying up noon-hour traffic. Here they pressed Conservative minister of external affairs Howard Green for a straight answer to the question "Are we going to accept nuclear arms or stay away from them?"[25] These women became quite upset when Green did not give a definite answer to their question.

The press eagerly captured the occasion, but some vow members were not at all pleased with the reports. Headlines like "La Voix des femmes revient a 'l'attaque' pour la paix" and "300 Irate vow Delegates Demand Canada Voice Stand on Arms" worried many good souls in the vow.[26] *Le Devoir* described the group as "157 femmes, 12 enfants et 22 bebes" whose questions "pleuvaient drues et aggressives."[27] The *Globe and Mail* drew attention to the vow's "block-long procession [of women with toddlers and babies in arms] tying up noon traffic."[28] Some members were not only upset with the press reports, but also with what they perceived as the "mawkish" and "militant" method of demonstrating. One woman summed it up for many when she wrote as follows: "As far as I can see, if the meeting had been an absolute model of decorum it would have been ignored.

The emphasis was on excited little women and crying babies … Equal emphasis should be placed on the opportunity for women as women … to make their voices heard in a plea for the renunciation of war which from time immemorial seems to have been the prerogative of men."[29]

The peace train episode revealed the vow's awareness of the shift in the methods used by lobby groups in the 1960s, from direct contact with policy makers to the staging of "media events" designed to influence public opinion. But it also revealed differences of opinion within the organization. Could "activists" be harboured within a group many of whose members cherished traditional notions of feminine respectability? For many vow members, demonstrations tarnished the "image of Peace" that the movement wished to portray. Aggressive behaviour seemed unbecoming in a group of mothers for peace; "excited little women and crying babies" painted the vow as "inexpressibly urgent" and probably "irrational."[30] Many members believed that there was a strong connection between motherhood and respectability. One woman wrote that she was "not a feminist or (heaven forbid!) a Communist" but "a married woman with two small daughters" who was content to do what she could from her "ranch-style house in the suburbs."[31]

The "controversy" over the vow "in the National Press,"[32] as one member saw it, reflected a deeper controversy within the vow. Could the organization carry out its mandate while encompassing a broad spectrum of strategies and ideas? Essentially, could the vow maintain peace within its own organization, let alone promote it for the world? Furthermore, the group's attempts to unite traditional maternal concerns with political action failed when the vow confronted external pressures. As an early letter writer implied, being militant for peace seemed a contradiction in terms, as did being a militant woman.[33] By the close of 1962, it was clear that, when stepping outside of their traditional domestic domain, women in the cause of peace encountered problems of image. The ideals of motherhood and the practice of politics appeared contradictory. Certainly the combination was neither acceptable nor respected in Canada in the early 1960s.[34]

50 The Royal Commission on the Status of Women in Canada, 1967–1970: Liberal Feminism and Its Radical Implications

Kimberly Speers

The legal and social status of most women in the twentieth century in Canada has generally benefited from liberal-progressive state initiatives. Yet the experience has not been the same for all women. Other defining characteristics, such as race and ethnicity, sexual preference, age, geographic region, class, or physical and mental ability, have prevented women as a whole from receiving equitable treatment from the Canadian state.[1] Nevertheless, it is important that the state be understood in a gender-conscious way, as many state actions have had a different impact on women than on men.

Much of the literature on the history of Canadian women has been categorized by reference to what is called the first and second waves of feminism. The first wave of feminism generally signifies the end of the nineteenth century and the early twentieth century, when a "vigorous reform movement emerged in which thousands of Canadian women were active."[2] The focus of the first women's movement was on temperance, child welfare, urban reform, public health, child and female labour conditions, and, of course, the attainment of the vote.

By the early 1960s, many people began to challenge traditional ideas on war and peace, civil rights, Quebec nationalism, and women's rights. Many Canadian women became involved in movements that evolved from this political discontent and, in the process, became aware of the patriarchal hierarchy within these protest organizations as well as in society at large. Not surprisingly, these "second wave" feminists began to pressure the Canadian government to address the inequities between men and women.

The Government of Canada responded to the changing nature of the state and the transforming relationship between men and women, and women and the state, by establishing the Royal Commission on the Status of Women (RCSW) in 1967. Although the women's organizations that lobbied for such a commission hoped that it would make recommendations that would generate equality between men and women, the country's traditional liberal political roots, the nature of its women's movement, and the policy process itself hindered any chance for fundamental improvement in the power imbalances in society and thus limited any radical reso-

LADY ISHBEL ABERDEEN, 1857–1939

Raised in Scotland, in 1877 Ishbel Maria Marjoribanks married Lord Aberdeen, who was governor general of Canada from 1893 to 1898. A formidably energetic person, she devoted her life to promoting social causes and served for years as president of the International Council of Women. In Canada, she founded the National Council of Women, helped establish the Victorian Order of Nurses, and headed the Aberdeen Association, which distributed literature to settlers. Lady Aberdeen later organized the Red Cross Society of Scotland and the Women's National Association of Ireland. She died in Aberdeen, Scotland. (Courtesy of Parks Canada)

lution of institutional sexism. As will be seen, the RCSW supported a liberal-feminist or piecemeal approach to equality, not a structural change to all institutions in society, as the means to generate substantive equality between men and women.

Although other strands of feminism had an impact on the political process in the late 1960s, the values and beliefs of liberal feminism prevailed in the Canadian feminist movement at that time. At a broad level, liberal feminism argues that substantial and meaningful change can occur within the existing political, economic, and social systems. There is no need for revolutionary change; indeed, as liberal feminists, they must hold true to the belief that existing democratic structures constitute the essential condition for successful reform. Nancy Adamson further notes that "liberal feminists do not argue against the existence of inequalities of wealth, position and power once the barriers to equality are removed."[3] As such, liberal feminists tend to view the state as a neutral structure – a place to go for protection, services, regulations, and redress.[4]

There has been much criticism of the principles of liberal feminism. One critique argues that incremental changes in legislation and public policy "are incapable of realizing women's equality unless they are accompanied by a fundamental reorganization of society, including the public and private spheres and gender roles [within the two spheres]."[5] Another widespread criticism is that liberal feminism's support of the universal individual does not adequately address the collective discrimination certain groups of people may experience. While the image of the individual appears genderless in liberal rhetoric, its formulation includes fundamental assumptions about the roles of men and women in society.[6] Nevertheless, it is these liberal feminist ideals that influenced the process and the recommendations of the RCSW.

Although numerous women recognized the state to be an institution upholding the status quo, most women still believed that the problems they experienced both in the private and public spheres could be solved by public or state regulation. The decision by women's groups to take their demands to the federal government "set a process in motion that was to fundamentally shape the Canadian women's movement as it emerged in the 1970s and the 1980s."[7] Indeed, the establishment of the RCSW set the stage for a close but unstable relationship between the women's movement and the federal government for years to come.

This changing relationship with the state was met with scepticism by many women during the late 1960s. Even Florence Bird, chair of the Commission, was initially dubious of the government's announcement to establish a royal commission, as she felt it "was a political gimmick to allow women to let off steam and that the final report would be pigeon-holed and forgotten."[8] Nevertheless, after 1966 the state focused largely on integrating the representation of women's interests into the policy-making process and many women came to believe that a state-established body would be the most effective means of bringing forth change.

Established in 1967, the Royal Commission on the Status of Women collected 468 briefs, received over two thousand letters, and conducted over forty independent research studies; approximately 890 people appeared before the commission at its hearings. The issues to be dealt with, as directed by the government, were the political rights of women, married women in the workplace, training programs and education, federal labour laws and regulations, women's employment in federal agencies, federal taxation, marriage and divorce, the position of women under the criminal law, immigration and citizenship laws, and other matters in relation to the status of women in Canada.

In 1970 the commissioners presented their findings and recommendations to the government. The criteria and principles of the report were developed by the commission for the purpose of making recommendations to the federal, provincial, and municipal governments as well as to the private sector. The beginning and underlying message of the report affirmed that "Canada is ... therefore committed to a principle that permits no distinction in rights and freedoms between men and women" and "that equality of opportunity for everyone should be the goal of Canadian society."[9] The overarching argument for "equality of opportunity"[10] made by the commissioners was seen as a matter of simple justice and in line with the priniciples held by the Canadian state.[11] The commission adopted several principles that guided them in developing the recommendations: that everyone is entitled to the rights and freedoms proclaimed in the Universal Declaration of Human Rights; that the full use of the country's human resources is in the national interest; that there should be equality of opportunity to share responsibilities in society as well as privileges and prerogatives; that women should be free to choose whether or not to take employment outside their homes; and that the care of children is a responsibility to be shared by women because of pregnancy and childbirth and that special treatment related to maternity will always be necessary.[12]

The contradiction within these principles shows the inherent limitations, or perhaps the "growing pains," of liberal feminism. At first, the overarching principle declares that no distinction shall be made between men and women in developing rights and freedoms, but further on the report states that special treatment has to be given to women because of their child-bearing capacity. The principles, furthermore, established the limited framework in which the commissioners developed their recommendations. They did not challenge the traditional institutions and structures in society, but instead supported the state mechanisms and social structures already in place. Finally, the principles failed to recognize that other forms of discrimination would often present women with "double" or "triple" types of oppression to overcome.

With these principles in mind, the commission put forward recommendations on the position of women in the economy, the education they receive, their place in the family, and their participation in public life. As well, the commission developed recommendations on the implications of poverty among women, conditions of citizenship, aspects of taxation, and the criminal code as it affects female offenders.[13]

The recommendations were both lengthy and powerful. While some recommendations were enveloped by liberal ideals, such as demanding "equal opportunity for education,"[14] other directives were more radical in substance. For example, the commission recommended "to the provinces and territories that household workers be covered by minimum wage laws, workers' compensation and other labour legislation applicable to other paid workers."[15] In dealing with the family, the commissioners stated that "none of our recommendations are intended to change the role of women who are satisfied to remain in the home. Our aim is to remove as far as possible barriers to real equality of opportunity."[16] In general, the report still supported the traditional nuclear family, but cited flexibility as the key component for the family of the future.[17]

For the most part, the underlying principles of the recommendations did not challenge the traditional structures in society; however, should each recommendation have been implemented, there would have been a significant collective impact on society. While the liberal overtones of the report diminished the potential for substantive change, the policy process itself posed other barriers. The members of the RCSW wanted to advance the changes needed to improve women's status in society, and felt that the most effective way to propose change was to adopt a liberal-incrementalist approach. Given the public's minimal level of understanding, awareness, and tolerance of the women's liberation movement, the report would not have been taken seriously by the public, media, or, most importantly, the government had a more radical stance been taken. The commission therefore managed to encompass in its recommendations the main issues of concern to Canadian women, as determined from the letters, submissions, and town hall forums, in a manner that was familiar and acceptable to the federal government.

The government sent the report to an interdepartmental committee of representatives from all agencies affected by the recommendations for consideration, which turned out to be a lengthy and cumbersome process.[18] Further delays occurred because of the lack of expertise on women's issues within the bureaucracy and the subsequent need to educate many participating officials.

With few exceptions, the process of developing and implementing bureaucratic policy generally involves a patchwork of individual ideas, group preferences, and chance events. This type of incremental policy making inhibits rapid change. Realistically, however, new policy directions are more readily accepted when they take the form of amendments to existing programs than when they entail highly visible, large-scale new programs moving in directions different from existing policy. Given that many of the recommendations, if implemented, would have had dramatic consequences for the social, economic, and political relationship between men and women, the politically safe way for the Liberal government to respond to the recommendations was through a liberal-incrementalist approach.

Given the pluralistic identities and politics of women, the Royal Commission on the Status of Women was a success on many levels. As a forum for providing information and raising consciousness, the report of the commission scored a real triumph. Although statistical and other information on women was available before, never had it been documented in one report in such depth and detail. The report also focused significant public attention on some of the political questions involved in trying to achieve equality between men and women in a liberal state. Finally, the report gave impetus to many women to organize formally and lobby the state more professionally.

While the report successfully brought widespread exposure to the status of Canadian women in society, it did not confront the broader ideas about the political and economic systems that intrinsically oppress women. Although the recommendations made by the RCSW were a positive endorsement of equality for all women, the report failed to realize that not all individuals compete, or can compete, on a playing field that is not yet level. Consequently, the RCSW established a piecemeal type of equality for women – one that is further dependent on class, race, sexual orientation, geography, and ability.

At a theoretical level, what has not been well documented is the fact that, while the report was built on the principles of liberalism, in the end it self-consciously moved away from its liberal roots. Zillah Eisenstein describes this transformation as the radical implications of liberal feminism. Liberal feminism, with its attempt to universalize liberal principles, in fact challenges the individualism of liberalism itself. Carole Pateman argues that "liberal feminism challenges the separation and opposition between the public and private spheres that is fundamental to liberal theory and practice."[19]

Explicit calls for radical change occur throughout the report. The closing chapter, "Plan for Action" offers one such example: "But the Commissioners are aware that true equality of opportunity for women and men can only result from radical changes in our way of life and in our social organizations and probably must go as far as equal sharing by parents in the care of their children and a complete reorganization of the working world."[20] The RCSW had figured out how to use the liberal-feminist position of the state as progressively as possible for women without being circumvented by it. While many of the RCSW recommendations have since been implemented, it is important to note that if all the recommendations had been fully implemented, society's values and structures would have been much more radically altered.

Unlike many other royal commissions, the Royal Commission on the Status of Women is one of the few that has had lasting impact in the policy environment. And beyond its influence of policy making, it has also provided the foundation of the modern women's movement in Canada.[21] Indeed, the report still provides feminists today with a yardstick against which to measure women's achievements over the past thirty years. In an article celebrating the twentieth anniversary of the commission's findings, Florence Bird states:

The Report remains a basic document that can still be used as the foundation on which to build new attitudes, and to draft new laws designed for the advancement of women in the future. Its social philosophy and the principles on which it based its recommendations should act as guides and inspirations for lawyers and politicians when they draft legislation designed to ensure justice for men as well as women in Canada, and for sociologists when they consider the sort of society they want for our country during the decade and century that lie ahead.[22]

51 Florence Bird

Judi Cumming

Florence Bird was born in Philadelphia, Pennsylvania, into a wealthy family. She was well educated and encouraged to travel. She and her husband, John Bird, came to Canada in 1930 and settled in Montreal, where Florence joined a peace study-group and lectured on current events to women's groups. In 1937 the Birds moved to Winnipeg; John Bird became editor-in-chief of the *Tribune* and Florence wrote articles for the paper, using her maternal great-grandmother's name, Anne Francis. In addition to writing for the Winnipeg newspaper, for many years she worked with volunteer organizations. During the Second World War, she was the head of press relations for the Central Volunteer Bureau of Winnipeg, writing a weekly column about women's war work for many years. For two years, she also wrote a weekly column for the *Ottawa Journal*, covering the debates in Parliament that concerned the rights of women. Until the time of her appointment as chair of the Royal Commission on the Status of Women, she wrote a weekly newsletter on Canadian women for the International Service of the Canadian Broadcasting Corporation (CBC).[1]

Starting in the 1930s, she prepared an extensive series of radio broadcasts for the CBC on *Trans-Canada Matinée* entitled "Women at Work," which examined the problem of women as a source of cheap labour. Between 1948 and 1951, her broadcasts emphasized women's need to earn an income, not only to provide for their families, but also to contribute to the national economy. Moreover, she frequently noted that it was unfair that women received less pay for doing the same job as men.[2] Her radio broadcasts also examined women's historical workforce activities, particularly those of domestic factory workers, and suggested ways that would allow women to combine marriage and career.

Bird not only championed women's financial equity, she was also concerned with the needs of women in prison. In 1957 she undertook research that she later used in a series of four ten-minute broadcasts on *Trans-Canada Matinée*. With the aid of the Elizabeth Fry Society, she visited the Prison for Women in Kingston, and discovered that most women had committed crimes against themselves, crimes frequently involving alcoholism, drug addiction, suicide, and prostitution. Many prisoners had been removed from their own communities in other parts of Canada to Kingston, making it difficult for relatives to visit them. She deplored antiquated attitudes towards penal reform as exemplified by the construction of a maximum security prison for women at Galt, Ontario, whose features included steel doors, small prison cells, open toilets, and no windows. Later, the *Report of the Royal Commission on the Status of Women* would recommend that the Prison for Women in Kingston be closed and that changes occur elsewhere to facilitate the rehabilitation of women prisoners.

As the chair of the royal commission, Bird saw her role as ensuring a harmonious working relationship among commissioners of different backgrounds, religions, intellectual capabilities, and levels of education. Believing that the wording of the final report should be written in language that could be read by every woman, she refused to permit the use of technical language. She wrote some of the chapters herself to ensure that the language was clear and simple.[3] Her work on the report reflected her concerns both about women and about the women's movement in the 1960s.

52 Women, Peace Activism, and the Environment: Rosalie Bertell and the Development of a Feminist Agenda, 1970s–1990s

Judi Cumming

Throughout the twentieth century, many women have sought to voice their concerns about peace issues and the military. As the twentieth century drew to a close, these concerns became intertwined with issues related to the environment. Dr Rosalie Bertell, a scientist and a nun, has based her views on nuclear technology and the creation of nuclear weapons on a study of epidemiology, the branch of medical science that relates to the study of the incidence and spread of disease in large populations. Her scientific research has resulted in a call for a moratorium on the use of nuclear technology and an end to the production of nuclear weapons, which she connects to a variety of illnesses in human populations. Her involvement in these issues also reflected a growing feminist consciousness.

Bertell was born in Buffalo, New York, in 1929, to a closely knit family with deeply religious beliefs. Moreover, her mother had a social conscious that she acted upon. For instance, at a time when busdrivers only stopped their buses if white passengers wished to board, she would resolutely stand at bus-stops in black neighbourhoods rather than in her own neighbourhood. Rosalie was something of a mathematical prodigy as well as a deeply spiritual person. At age twenty-one, she took the momentous step of entering the Carmelite order of nuns, where she learned many skills – all in an environment of prayer and hard physical work. Unable to endure such a rigorous life, she suffered a heart attack at the young age of twenty-six and had to leave the reli-

gious life temporarily. Continuing her education, she received a master of arts in mathematics in 1959, after which she once again entered a religious order, this time the Grey Nuns of the Sacred Heart, a teaching order. The Grey Nuns were more compatible with her needs and talents, encouraging her to continue with her education, particularly her doctorate. This she received in 1966 under a fellowship that linked mathematics with biometrics (biometrics is the science of mathematical predictions of medical phenomenon).

Although Bertell has also been a teacher, it was as a cancer researcher in the area of biometrics that she began a lifetime of work studying the effects of various environmental hazards on the human condition. With a post-doctoral grant, she worked as the senior cancer research scientist on the analysis of the Tri-State Leukemia Survey at Roswell Park Memorial Institute in Buffalo, New York. This survey examined the incidence of leukemia in the populations of three American states, Maryland, New York, and Minnesota. The results of the survey indicated to Bertell that the single and most serious variable affecting the rate of leukemia was the diagnostic x-ray. Thus began Bertell's concern with radiation and its effects on the human body. Her research on behalf of persons and groups victimized by ionizing radiation and her work as an expert witness with regard to environmental disasters in various parts of the world have brought her into conflict with proponents of the nuclear industry and the military establishment.

It was while she was working at Roswell that Bertell first became aware of the tensions between the needs of the general public and the interests of the nuclear industry. In connection with the possible establishment of a nuclear power plant at Barker, New York, in 1976. she was asked by a citizens' group to answer questions about low-level radiation. The plant was to be built next to Cornucopia Farms, which produces baby foods. The promoters of the nuclear power plant, all men, tried to assure people that there was no danger from radiation at all. Bertell and the citizens' group, composed entirely of women, presented evidence to the contrary, with the result that the Niagara County legislature voted for a moratorium on nuclear power. In December 1978 she appeared on a public television channel to discuss the Ginna nuclear power plant, angering plant officials. In subsequent speeches and talks, Bertell spoke about the dangers to human health of low levels of radiation.

In October 1979 an attempt was made on Bertell's life while she was driving home to Buffalo from Rochester, New York. Bertell's unimpeachable testimony against the hazards of the nuclear industry not only placed her personally at risk, but made Roswell Park itself vulnerable to reprisals as a research institution. Bertell was accordingly asked not to speak out against nuclear-related issues. Unable to accept such a demand, she went on to help found the Ministry of Concern for Public Health at Buffalo, which allowed her to voice her criticisms against what she considered lax standards for radiation exposure in the nuclear industry.

In 1980 she came to Canada at the invitation of the Jesuit Centre in Toronto and stayed. Canadians seemed to be more open than Amereicans to alternatives to nuclear energy and more interested in "peaceful resolution strategies."[1] She became an energy and public-health specialist and in 1984 founded the non-profit International Institute of Concern for Public Health in Toronto. Its goal was to provide scientific and technical assistance relating to environmental hazards to government agencies, citizens' groups, and labour unions. Through the institute, Bertell has been engaged by many groups throughout the world to offer expert testimony relating to environmental hazards. Concurrent with her warnings about the dangers inherent in nuclear technology and radiation, she also speaks out against the use of chemical and biological weapons against civilian populations.

Her work has not been confined to any one country. A series of case files in the accumulated archival records of Dr Bertell attests to her global work: Bhopal, India; Chernobyl; Ireland; Canada; the United States; Malaysia; the Marshall Islands; Scotland; and beyond. Among the projects in Canada are environmental disasters in Scarborough, Ontario; pollution and the Mississauga First Nations; and the Kiggavik Uranium Mine at Baker Lake. In the United States she has offered expert testimony in connection with nuclear facilities in Oklahoma, Nevada, Colorado, Oregon, and Pennsylvania.

In addition to her research-based work, Dr Bertell serves on boards, commissions and agencies for purposes relating to the environment and health. She has also published extensively, her writings including poetry, religious writings, and scientific research. Her book, *No Immediate Danger: Prognosis for a Radioactive Earth* documents her concerns regarding the possibility of a global dependence on nuclear energy and the military use of nuclear weapons. In connecting the two areas, she writes: "In 1952, the u.s. exploded hydrogen bombs, and when that was successful from a military point of view, the u.s. made a decision to base national security on nuclear weapons."[2] In her writings, she has linked these concerns with human rights and freedoms, and she has participated in women's conferences on the environment and peace.

Bertell clearly sees the development of nuclear weapons as a threat to peace and security around the world.

Moreover, she has identified this threat as being associated with patriarchal ideology and the lack of women's participation and influence in the development of military policy. Throughout the 1970s and the 1980s, her criticisms on this point grew stronger. In this respect, the Women's International Peace Conference chose women's alternatives for negotiating peace as its theme in 1985. The conference statement rejected "domination, exploitation, patriarchy, racism and sexism [... and demanded] equitable distribution of the world's resources."[3] Dr Bertell's presentation made reference to victims of militarism and oppression: she criticized the United Nations Security Council as the "bully system where five nations are given veto power over other nations."[4] She condemned peace negotiations conducted in such a manner that the only winners were military leaders and arms manufacturers, and she called for negotiating teams composed of men and women who would seek an equitable distribution of global resources.[5] Furthermore, she denounced the three nuclear nations who were party to the nuclear non-proliferation treaty for failing to prevent the proliferation of nuclear weapons; she criticized not only Third World countries for testing nuclear bombs, but also the United States, whose six hundred nuclear tests in Nevada have caused fallout across North America, without major complaint from either Canadians or Americans.

Pursuing this theme at the Women and the Environment Conference of 1990, Bertell was more explicitly feminist in her evaluation of women's roles and more aggressively critical of military establishments throughout the world. She stated categorically that women do not have power because decision making and power relate to "basic patriarchal society."[6] She contended that those who do have power are "government, industry, business and resource managers,"[7] but that women, as a group, and as 52 per cent of the world's population, do not have a base of power from which to make impor-

tant decisions regarding nations, the environment, and the quality of life on the planet. Further, women as a group will not, in her opinion, be admitted to the structures of power because power and decision making are grounded in patriarchal values. This patriarchal or masculine approach to power is, she believes, based on the use of force, whether in relation to women, children, the family, or war.[8] Patriarchal norms specifically exclude those feminist norms that are based on cooperation and non-violence.

Over the last decade, Dr Bertell has increasingly linked the environmental crises that have occured around the world to unchecked and covert military activities and to a masculine approach to power and decision making. At the conference, she stated that "most of our environmental crises come from military excess."[9] She reminded her listeners that 2,000 nuclear bombs had been detonated on the planet during this century and that 430 operating nuclear power plants "routinely releas[ed] radioactive material in the air, the water and the land, producing waste that we do not know how to get rid of."[10] All this was accompanied by the development of defoliants and pesticides for the destruction of the jungles of Vietnam and by an expensive military space program that had a deleterious effect on the environment.

By contrast, Bertell envisions a new military establishment where "every military program [would] be submitted to an environmental assessment review" and the military would be used to help people during natural disasters and in peacekeeping operations. Women should have a major voice in all decision making because they are "the nurturers of the world ... the ones primarily responsible for food, ... for the nurturing of children, [and] for the care of the elderly and the sick."[11] That being the case, "every degradation of the life support system affects births and most deeply women and children."[12]

On the issue of women as nurturers, Bertell believes that women's nurturing roles are crucial to sustaining life on the planet, but are dependent on peaceful exis-tence. At the beginning of the twentieth century, femi-nist analysis was frequently grounded in maternal feminism, "the ideology of nurturing motherhood [in combination] with the conviction that women should have equal political, legal, educational, and economic rights with men."[13] Bertell extends this concept by seek-ing women's full participation in major decision and policy making. Her convictions are not dissimilar to the maternal feminists: the nurturing role to which she refers is tantamount to the role of motherhood dis-cussed early in the twentieth century. What is different is that Bertell embraces feminist theory, developed throughout the century, about the roles of men and women and the concepts of patriarchy and power. She may, however, fall short in drawing too strong a connec-tion between the need for women to participate in deci-sion making and the nurturing role and the concepts of cooperation and non-violence. While laudable, these may equally apply to men and women: women are not alone in caring for children and in providing a nurtur-ing environment for healthy growth. Moreover, women in positions of power and decision making are not pre-determined to operate in a cooperative, non-violent manner, and some may launch wars as readily as their male counterparts.

Bertell has placed her accumulated, multi-media archive in the National Archives of Canada, and most of it is readily accessible for research purposes. Spanning a fifty-year period, her records consist of textual and elec-tronic documents, printed matter, audio and video recordings, photographs, slides, posters, and maps. An extensive library was placed with the University of Guelph. The textual and electronic documents consist of her original writings, case files, research files, records of the International Institute of Concern for Public Health, records of the International Commission of Health Pro-fessionals for Health and Human Rights (including an extensive series of printed matter on human rights), records relating to her speaking engagements and awards, and a bibliographic database of the institute that identifies the books, periodicals, reports, and other print-ed matter that formed the institute's library. The photo-graphs, for the most part captioned, depict radiation-related matters such as uranium tailings and nuclear power plants, nuclear test sites and nuclear protests. A series of vibrant posters, bumper stickers, decals, and postcards from Canada, Germany, Australia, the United States, and elsewhere depicts a variety of issues related to her work: nuclear disarmament, nuclear reactors, nuclear weapons, Chernobyl, environmental pollution, and radi-ation. Perhaps the most chilling part of the archive is found in the audio and video recordings, which consist of interviews, lectures, press conferences, and speeches on environmental issues.

With the earth experiencing environmental damage and facing potential disaster, Bertell has now turned to the study of the long-range effects of environmental pollution, be it nuclear or non-nuclear, on the human condition. Her research focuses particularly on the pos-sibility of genetic damage and the consequent weaken-ing of human beings. She brings to this work her great lifelong strengths: feminism, spirituality, and the mind of the educated scientist and mathematician.

53 State Control of Women's Immigration: The Passage to Canada of South Asian Women

Helen Ralston

This paper explores the political and social circumstances that shaped the immigration policies, programs, and actions that determined the admission of South Asian women to Canada during the twentieth century. There seems to have been little recognition by policy makers or by researchers that immigration policies, regulations, and practices have been consistently *gender* discriminatory, even when other discriminatory criteria, such as race, ethnicity, and national origin, have been removed. The paper examines the interconnectedness of gender, race and class in the decision of just who would populate Canada at a particular time.

British pomp and pageantry in celebration of the empire's might and global expansion probably initiated the massive flow of South Asian immigrants to Canada.[1] Punjabi Indian troops who were based in the British Crown colony of Hong Kong and other East Asian colonial outposts twice travelled across Canada on their way to join colonial troops assembled in London, first for Queen Victoria's Diamond Jubilee in 1897, and then for the coronation of Edward VII in 1902.[2] These visits prompted the later migration of Indians from Britain's colonies in the "Far East" across the Pacific to British North America. From 1903 to 1904, about forty Indian men and four Indian women migrated to Victoria and Vancouver. In the following years, this immigration increased rapidly, so that by the end of the 1907 fiscal year there were 5,179 settlers from the Indian subcontinent in Canada – virtually all

of them in British Columbia. All but 15 of the immigrants were men, and they were almost exclusively Punjabi Sikhs.[3]

The perceived racial threat of massive Asian immigration provoked a riot in Vancouver in 1907 and prompted a series of legislative measures to restrict Asians' entry to Canada. In 1908 the federal government approved an order-in-council[4] that required an immigrant to come to Canada by "continuous passage" from the country of national origin or citizenship and with a through ticket purchased in that country. There was a further stipulation that Asian immigrants from countries without "special arrangements" possess at least $25 on arrival in Canada, with the understanding that this amount would be increased should it prove inadequate to deter such immigrants.

Canada negotiated with the British government to restrict South Asian immigration. William Lyon Mackenzie King, as deputy minister of labour, was sent on a mission to England "to confer with the British authorities on the subject of immigration from the Orient, and immigration from India in particular." King reported that "[the British authorities expressed] a ready appreciation of Canada's position … That Canada should desire to restrict immigration from the Orient is regarded as natural, that Canada should remain a white man's country is believed to be not only desirable for social and economic reasons, but highly necessary on political and national grounds."[5]

The rhetoric of racist, sexist and nationalist ideology combined to justify discriminatory policies in the interests of an imperial capitalist economy. The continuous-passage stipulation was aimed specifically at Indians. It remained in effect until 1951 and effectively halted further South Asian immigration. In particular, it banned the migration of wives of South Asian men already settled in Canada. Between 1908 and 1912, only twenty men and six women from South Asia entered Canada.

The Immigration Act of 1910 reaffirmed the continuous-journey stipulation; it overtly used racial terminology for the first time and explicitly restricted Indian immigration.[6] White settlers of British Columbia vehemently opposed any suggestion that South Asian men should be allowed to bring in their wives, for this would mean the establishment of a permanent community.[7] In 1912 the editor of the *Daily Province* reflected public opinion when he wrote that British Columbians did not desire South Asians to "fuse with the white population … We do not want a mixed breed, half Oriental, half Occidental, in this country."[8] In the context of this social and political stance, the editor of the *Vancouver Sun* offered this opinion one year later:

The point of view of the Hindu [in wanting Canada to admit wives and families] is readily understood and appreciated. But there is the point of view of the white settler in this country who wants to keep the country a white country with white standards of living and morality … They are not a desirable people from any standpoint for the Dominion to have … The white population will never be able to absorb them. They are not an assimilable people … We must not permit the men of that race to come in large numbers, *and we must not permit their women to come in at all* [emphasis added]. Such a policy of exclusion is simply a measure of self-defence … We have no right to imperil the comfort and happiness of the generations that are to succeed us.[9]

The remarks of these editors highlight the interconnectedness of gender, race, and class ideologies among ruling – and voting – male white settlers of Canada at that time.

Nevertheless, there was ongoing political action to counter the gender discriminatory nature of the immigration regulations. Isolated exceptional admissions of wives and children were for the most part *class* discriminatory, favouring business and professional men who posed no threat to white working-class men.[10]

After Britain's victory in the First World War, accomplished with the aid of its dominions and colonies, the British Imperial Conferences of 1917 and 1918 affirmed that South Asians already domiciled in other countries of the British Empire should be allowed to bring in wives and children. The Canadian government grudgingly approved this recommendation, and a law was passed in 1920 that allowed a man to bring in his wife and minor children.[11] However, the Canadian government initially failed to set up a process in India for bringing wives and children into Canada. Only in mid-1924 was a practical procedure put into place for the registration of wives in India.

The continuous-passage restriction, together with gender discrimination, led to the very unbalanced age-sex composition of the Indian population in Canada. In the 1951 Census, only 2,148 South Asians resided in Canada, 90 per cent of them in British Columbia. Men outnumbered women in a ratio of two to one.

The pressure for relaxation of Canadian immigration policies became even greater after India achieved independence from Britain in 1947.[12] In 1951, a special quota agreement was passed between the Canadian government and Asiatic members of the British Commonwealth.[13] As a result, the total South Asian population in Canada rose. The majority of immigrants, both adults and children, were male. Of the total number of 3,425 South Asian immigrants for 1951 to 1961, inclusive, only one-third were female. The quota agreement remained in effect until new immigration regulations were introduced in 1962.

The most important provision of the 1962 regulations was the redefinition of categories of persons admissible to Canada as immigrants.[14] The new regulations stressed education, training, and skills as the main qualities for admission, regardless of race, colour, national origin, or country of residence. As economic necessity overruled racist ideology, an immigration policy based on national origins was replaced by a policy that would be universally applied to meet Canada's need for particular skills. In other words, *class*, not race, was the key criterion for selection. However, the occupational characteristics underpinning these notions of skill were *gender* discriminatory in that they more readily applied to men than to women.

The 1967 immigration regulations confirmed a universal, racially non-discriminatory immigration policy.[15] Despite their apparent non-discriminatory character, the 1967 regulations were still *gender-biased* in their implicit assumption that immigrants were, for the most part, male workers who entered the country with or without family.[16] The characteristics of the male adult, who was designated as head of the household, were used to determine eligibility of a married couple for entrance to Canada.[17] Gender bias was compounded by *marital status bias*. While a single woman could apply to enter Canada as an independent immigrant, it was only in 1974 that a woman was allowed to be the principal applicant of a married couple.[18]

Gender discrimination has persisted since 1974 in that most South Asian married women with the educational and skills qualifications to be considered as independent immigrants nevertheless entered Canada in the dependent-wife or family-reunification category. The terms "head of family," "independent applicant," and "principal applicant" were replaced by "labour-destined" member of the family. In the majority of cases, however, the

man in the household is identified as labour-destined, not only by the state but also by the immigrant family itself.[19] Family gender relations and patriarchal definitions of family headship in the source country have socially constructed this cultural definition of gender roles and thus determined the legal status of immigrant wives when they enter Canada.

The Immigration Act of 1976 was the first major revision since 1952. The 1978 immigration regulations revised the point system to place more emphasis on practical training and experience than on formal education. They also introduced the elements "designated occupation" and "designated area" to meet specific skill shortages and to provide a means of steering immigrants away from the major metropolitan areas, respectively.[20] These provisions had a direct impact on the lives of contemporary immigrant South Asian women.[21]

Historical analysis and contemporary research demonstrate the interconnectedness of gender, race, and class in state policies and practices regarding the immigration of South Asian women to Canada. From early post-Confederation years up until the 1960s, racially exclusionary and discriminatory immigration policies were based on principles that were ideological distortions of rational arguments.[22] Racist ideology and classist ideology combined to exclude and discriminate against Indian male labour, which was perceived as a threat to the white, male, working-class labourers in British Columbia. Family and sexist ideologies interacted with racist ideology to preclude South Asian women from accompanying or joining their immigrant husbands and thereby fulfilling their ideologically constructed role of social reproduction. The intersections of sexist and racist ideologies were particularly evident in the special case of Anglo-Indians (the descendants of one Indian parent and one British parent). State policies decreed in 1924 that an Anglo-Indian with a British father and an Indian mother could migrate; however, an Anglo-Indian with a British mother and an Indian father could not. The same patriarchal discriminatory policy was applied to British immigrants with South Asian spouses.[23]

With the explicit elimination of overt racist and ethnic discrimination in 1967, gender discrimination persisted. Sexist and family ideological rhetoric continued to justify Canada's implementation of the "family class" aspect of the 1992 Immigration Plan, which ignored Indian family patterns by limiting a family application to the presumed ideal Canadian nuclear family of husband, wife, and dependent unmarried children of nineteen years or less – despite the empirical reality of various other types of Canadian family.

Moreover, patriarchal ideology in Canadian immigration policy and in South Asian familial relations has continuously constructed married immigrant women as wives of immigrant men. The womanhood and productive role of immigrant wives have been absent from rhetoric and reality. Sexist ideology has deemed all women by implication, and South Asian immigrant women in particular, as breeders of the next generation. Their gender role is defined as social reproduction, not economic production. In point of fact, few married South Asian women with high qualifications enter as principal applicant, even though Canadian immigration law, regulations, and practice now permit them to be the principal applicant of a family.

On 6 January 1999, Lucienne Robillard, minister of citizenship and immigration, announced new directions for Canadian immigration and refugee protection legislation and policy.[24] The new policy aims, among other priorities, to strengthen and support family reunification. In particular, it proposes "to broaden the dependent child to better reflect contemporary social realities of longer child dependency … [by] increasing the current age limit for a dependent child from less than 19 years to under age 22, and [by] maintaining a provision to include older children still in full-time studies and financially dependent on their parents."[25] The extension of the age of dependent children is especially important for South Asian families with daughters, since they, unlike the daughters of English or French Canadian parents, more commonly remain in the parents' household until marriage.

The proposed new act would "shift away from the current occupation-based model; it would seek to choose skilled workers with sound and transferable skill sets; it would emphasize education and experience, while retaining language, age, a job offer and personal suitability as selection criteria; [it would] emphasize flexibility, adaptability, motivation and knowledge of Canada, under 'personal suitability'… In addition, further research would be undertaken to determine how a new selection system might take into account the potential for the social economic contribution of spouses [emphasis added]."[26] This last clause is of particular significance for married South Asian women, who, as already noted, almost invariably enter Canada as the dependent spouse. Such a provision, by "counting" and valuing women's educational, occupational, and English- or French-language skills, as well as their personal flexibility and adaptability, might promote greater gender equality within the family and within Canadian society upon settlement.

As the twenty-first century unfolds, Canadian women of South Asian origin, together with researchers, nongovernment agency workers, and government officials, will undoubtedly monitor the impact that revised Canadian immigration policy will have on all immigrant women and on South Asian women in particular.

54 Making Space: Women Building Culture

Janice Hladki and Ann Holmes

The Toronto Women's Cultural Building Collective (WCB) emerged in 1981. It arose from the need for space – physical, conceptual, and political – in which women could gather to talk about and create culture, and to question and theorize about women's cultural work.[1]

The WCB Collective began with informal discussions between and among women who were engaged in a range of cultural and art activities. By the autumn of 1982, a public statement was prepared and circulated to various women's groups, cultural organizations, and the press. This statement described the WCB activities as those "which address feminist, community and aesthetic issues" through "sponsoring or collaborating on projects brought from the community to the collective; and by projects or activities initiated by the collective itself."[2] Consensual decision making, community-based initiatives, and programming that encouraged "the interaction between artists/cultural producers and community"[3] were outlined in this policy statement.

At subsequent meetings, members expressed their interest in a range of possibilities: producing cultural work in conjunction with other women's groups, organizations, and collectives; proposing a feminist art education program; organizing and producing a series of events as a "festival"; promoting public discussions on mass media in relation to feminist theories; networking with other women's groups; and creating a billboard campaign, a newsletter, exhibitions, panels, and a subway "anti-ad" action. Eventually, many of these general ideas developed more specific frameworks and structures. By December 1982, members were meeting in committees to work on the details of particular events and actions.

The policies and activities of the collective were shaped by factors related to political activity, cultural practice, and community access. Members participated in a range of feminist political organizations, addressing such women's issues as birth control and health, housing, shelters, racism, violence, and leadership of artist-run centres. Collective members were producing feminist work in photography, painting, sculpture, performance art, theatre, dance, music, and writing, and were seeking to create new venues that could underline their feminist perspectives.

By November 1982, the collective had decided to forego the idea of an actual building, choosing instead to emphasize the word "building" as a verb.[4] In order to reflect the ongoing construction of women's art work, the collective often used the slogan "Women's Cultural Building – Building Women's Culture." With this different emphasis, members decided to turn their attention away from concrete locations and towards "alternative" spaces. As one journalist observed, "While a geographic area defines the group's terrain, the space they really want to occupy is in the hearts and minds of women throughout the city."[5]

The WCB undertook several projects in 1982 in order to initiate new arts initiatives, achieve public recognition,

54.1 Postcard for Women's Cultural Building Collective (Courtesy of Janice Hladki)

within feminist concerns about the inclusion and exclusion of women's art in institutional contexts, the marketing of art "stars," and the "invisibility" of women's art.

By 1983, membership in the collective had expanded and a wide range of programming expertise had been developed. For example, as part of A Space Gallery's "Talking: A Habit," nine members of the collective presented an evening of short addresses about issues surrounding feminism, language, and authority, entitled "Documents and Conversations."[8] Other activities included "The Great Store Window Takeover or Women in Windows," "Community in Outreach," and "Women Write."[9] The "Window Takeover" idea was transformed into "Storefronting" and included "installations, displays and wall pieces located along Queen Street West in a pastry shop, a second-hand clothing store, a retail store, a book store, several restaurants and two cultural centres."[10] "Women Write" staged a month-long Women's Reading Series.

Although the WCB had set aside the goal of a permanent space, in late 1982 the collective decided to acquire a temporary public location in downtown Toronto to be used as a base for the feminist cultural activities of the two-month festival of women's art, "Women Building Culture."[11] A storefront at 563 Queen Street West was rented for the festival, with funding obtained from the Canada Council, the Ontario Arts Council, and the Canadian Images Film Festival. Organizing the space coalesced a sense of purpose and community among the members, who came from a range of art disciplines, practices, and experiences. The festival events took place in venues along Queen Street West and East, a busy downtown street that was often a hub for cultural activities in Toronto. Creating several exhibition sites outside of mainstream institutions provided an "alternative exhibition and gallery strategy."[12] This could include, as it did for the WCB, opportunities to decide on spaces for women's artworks, traditionally given little attention,

and engage feminist issues in cultural contexts. Public meetings and marches were held, and buttons, T-shirts, and kits were sold to publicize the WCB and raise initial funding. Members operated a "Feminist Hot Line" and designed banners and a flyer to publicize events: "[A]s women, we know that we have more to say to one another, and to society in general, than the present labels of 'artist,' 'performer,' or 'community worker' allow. Art, culture and social concerns need no longer be seen as separate issues."[6]

An event attended by 150 people, "After the Dinner Party Is Over," was organized to address "some of the aesthetic, political, and economic issues" regarding the exhibition of Judy Chicago's artwork, "The Dinner Party," at Toronto's Art Gallery of Ontario. This collaborative installation was intended to illuminate women's history.[7] WCB members situated the Chicago exhibition

54.2 Group protest (Courtesy of Janice Hladki)

and to bring women together for support, discussion, and networking.

The festival featured a range of cultural events, from performance to film, from visual art to discussions, and encouraged participation across disciplinary lines. The events included the now famous "Five Minute Feminist Cabaret"; a storefront/headquarters launch; a reading series; a slide show, "Finding Lesbian History"; a "Dance-works" performance; and the "Edible Art Show."[13] In addition to screenings of documentaries, animations, and experimental shorts, the "Womanfilm" section of the festival included panels and filmmaker presentations.

The first "Five Minute Feminist Cabaret" launched the "Women Building Culture" festival. The original notion was to provide visibility for those not well known or just emerging in musical, theatre, or performance-based cultural work. The collective's activities in what became an annual event included producing, offering technical expertise, performing, selling tickets, and publicizing the event. In 1989 the cabaret, which had become known as "Fem Cab," was presented by the Nightwood Theatre Company, a feminist theatre group, with the support of the Women's Cultural Building.

Most members of the collective defined themselves as "cultural workers" and "feminist"; some women named themselves "artists." However, understandings of art, politics, culture, and feminism varied within the WCB. A diversity of understanding evolved over the years, necessitating an ongoing process of introspection, including a reclarification, redefinition, and reinvention of the term "collective." WCB members were predominantly white and Western. This determined who participated, who was represented, how decisions were made, and whose

issues were raised. Furthermore, the collective tended to focus on gender difference, while the interconnections of gender with class, race, sexual orientation, ethnicity, and ability were not addressed. Nevertheless, throughout the collective's history, members discussed the politics of their own class and sexual, ethnic, and racialized identities. Moreover, members were concerned with the politics of exclusion and inclusion, that is, with how well *different* women were represented in art work and activities. These issues shaped the collective's curatorial and programming decisions.

Many factors contributed to the WCB "hibernation" after 1984. Some of the women who defined themselves as artists changed their focus from artwork and activism to careers in academia or cultural institutions. The economy no longer allowed them to earn enough money in marginal jobs to afford both time for art work and activism and a living space within the downtown artistic community.

While the WCB no longer exists in its original form, its impact on women and the arts in Canada is lasting. First, WCB leaves a legacy: the possibility of creating spaces and environments in which women can imagine, create, and sustain connection, collectivity, and women's artistic practices. Secondly, many of the collective members have continued to be active in Toronto and other locales, and they offer ongoing contributions to women's cultural activities in Canada and in international contexts. And finally, they remain active in feminist collectives, in feminist art criticism and curating, and in art productions in visual arts, theatre, performance, film, video, dance, and music.

55 Feminist Theatre in Toronto:
A Look at the Nightwood Theatre

Corinne Rusch-Drutz

The study of women's experiences throughout history has been a major focus within the feminist movement. If "history is a form of memory,"[1] then the memories of all its participants are essential for thorough analysis. Yet it is only recently that women's experiences as writers, directors, performers, and technicians in theatre have been given any serious critical or historical attention. Part of the reason is that relatively few plays by women have entered the theatrical canon. Consequently, women are not published, produced, anthologized, and taught as often as their male counterparts, and we are therefore not used to associating women with professional theatre.[2]

The purpose of this essay is to chronicle briefly feminist theatre in Toronto[3] by looking at the work of one of its most influential theatre companies, Nightwood Theatre. It will place the work of this company within the context of mainstream theatre in Toronto by highlighting the importance of feminist theatre and recognizing its contribution to Canadian arts culture.

The rise of the alternative theatre movement dates from 1968.[4] The emergence in that year of Theatre Passe Muraille, soon followed by the Factory Theatre Lab, the Tarragon Theatre, and Toronto Free Theatre, signalled the start of something new.[5] With their collective focus on experimental works, these companies became an alternative to existing forms of professional Canadian theatre like the Stratford and Shaw Festivals or established regional theatres, which were run exclusively by men. "These alternative theatres brought a renewed excitement to theatre in Toronto and, through a series of influential productions and publications, helped to create new patterns for theatre production in Canada."[6]

In addition to these new patterns, alternative theatre became a major innovator in terms of style, thus setting the ground work for feminist theatre. As Amanda Hale notes,

Many of the values promoted by alternate theatre are shared by feminist theatre. Theatre Passe Muraille's artistic director, Paul Thompson, was one of the pioneers of the Canadian collective creation. Collective creation was to become a popular format for both feminist and alternate theatre. A further link between alternate and feminist theatre is the attempt to demystify and popularize what has traditionally been seen as an elitist art form.[7]

In a collective creation, a group of actors work together as researchers on a project of mutual interest, with the intent of forming a theatrical presentation. Using improvisation as the backbone of creation, the group begins to form scenes and vignettes based on the research they have gathered. The semi-scripted material is then discussed and reworked until a complete play is created by all the group members. Often one member will be responsible for writing the actual script, based on notes and materials she or he has gathered during rehearsals. What makes collective creation, or "collaborative creation," as it is sometimes termed, different is its dismantling of the traditional structure within theatre, in which the director maintains authority over the actors by imposing his or her vision of a playtext onto the performance. Hale writes: "In traditional theatre, the director controls and manipulates his actors and the writer puts words in their mouths. In collective creation the power of decision-making is balanced out as far as possible among the group to allow fuller participation. It is a difficult but rewarding process."[8]

Despite early alternative theatre's emphasis on the need for experimental works and popularizing collectivity, it still left women on the sidelines. In *The Status of Women in the Canadian Theatre*, a report compiled for Status of Women Canada, Rina Fraticelli found that of 1,156 productions staged at 104 Canadian theatres between 1978 and 1981, women represented only 10 per cent of playwrights, 13 per cent of directors, and 11 per cent of artistic directors. The report also exposed the average annual income of full-time women artists to be only 39 per cent of that of full-time male artists, and revealed that the percentage of Canada Council individual-grants money going to women artists in the category of theatre was only 28 per cent.[9]

The findings do not overlook the success and achievement of playwrights such as Sharon Pollock, Judith Thompson, Carol Bolt, and Margaret Hollingsworth, who were gaining respect among their male colleagues during the alternative theatre renaissance of the late seventies and early eighties. It should also be noted that many works by contemporary women playwrights were considered feminist merely because their characters and the author were female, while alternatively, many women playwrights refused to label their works "feminist" for fear of "pigeonholing" themselves by mixing their writing with their political beliefs.

Toronto's first response to the exclusion of women in the alternative theatre community was the Red Light Theatre, established in 1974.[10] It survived for three seasons on a federally funded Local Initiatives Program grant, with an average of $10,000 per year to fund three or four productions. This was significantly less than the amount that the "male dominated Toronto alternate theatres such as Factory Theatre Lab, Tarragon, Passe Muraille, Toronto Free and Toronto Workshop Productions received."[11]

Red Light is best remembered for its production of *What Glorious Times They Had*, about the life of Canadian suffragist Nellie McClung. Its repertoire included new works and previously produced plays, but its mandate was to produce works by feminist artists in a collaborative manner while providing women with experience in the technical field of theatre and arts management. Only three years after its opening, the company folded as a result of financial difficulties, lack of community support, and general exhaustion among its members. Though short-lived, the Red Light Theatre lay the groundwork for other companies and pioneered the women's theatre movement in Toronto. By establishing itself as the first feminist theatre company, it expanded the realm of women's artistic freedom within the alternative theatre scene, giving voice to pertinent feminist issues and cultural inequalities, such as sexism in the workforce.

Towards the end of the seventies and the beginning of the eighties, the national theatre community suffered huge setbacks when the federal government began to cut back on arts funding generally. To combat this loss of financial aid, the B.A.A.N.N. Theatre Centre, Toronto's only artist-run theatre facility, opened in 1979. As part of the Theatre Centre, Toronto's only feminist theatre at that time, Nightwood Theatre, emerged as a strong, experimental member of the alternative theatre community.

Nightwood developed a form of theatre that was essentially a collage of visual and poetic dramatic work, punctuated with documentary techniques and based on improvisation. It was a style heavily based on the avant-garde New York theatre techniques developed by Cynthia Grant, Nightwood Theatre's founding artistic director. Through a collaborative process, the Nightwood collective and Grant, in her role as both artistic director and director of many of the company's earlier productions, attempted to bring non-theatrical mediums to the stage by incorporating dance, mime, mask, music, and visual imagery with traditional "spoken word" text.

Nightwood's early plays fell into three categories: adaptations from media other than theatre, works written directly for the stage, and scripted materials. In those early years, Nightwood was a theatrical collective dedicated to developing new work for Canadian theatre, often through adaptation of other art forms such as music, painting, and the short story. Works produced in those early years include *Glazed Tempra*, based on the paintings of Canadian artist Alix Colville; *Mass/Age*, a multimedia piece on human survival in a technological age; *Flashbacks of Tomorrow; Hooligans; The Yellow Wallpaper*, an adaptation of Charlotte Perkin Gillman's novel "Smoke Damage;" and "Pope Joan." With these last three scripted productions, Nightwood began to venture into more feminist subject matter. Grant has responded to some of the concerns of producing overtly "feminist work" at that time: "From the beginning it didn't seem to matter what we were doing, because we were women, we were seen as feminists. The work was looked at in that light and sometimes with the male critics that became a problem … We had concern at one point that maybe by having an audience that might be 60–70% female that we were restricting our audience base, by only appealing to women."[12]

Following collaborative adaptations that were decidedly feminist in content, such as "Penelope," based on Margaret Atwood's *Circe Mud Poems*, and *This Is for You, Anna*, a piece on revenge inspired by the trial of Marie Anne Buchmier, a woman who shot her child's murderer, Nightwood began to move towards more formally scripted material. In the spring of 1986, Nightwood took a definitive step in this direction when it premiered Jovette Marchessault's *The Edge of the Earth Is Too Near, Violette Leduc*, a scripted play that deals with the tormented life of the reclusive French novelist, her battle with clinical paranoia, and society's views of lesbianism. The results of this shift can be seen today, as the company has continued to evolve by profiling playwrights such as Ann-Marie MacDonald, Susan G. Cole, Judith Thompson, Sandra Shamas, and Margaret Hollingsworth.

In 1985 Nightwood underwent a structural transformation when Cynthia Grant and other founding members left the company. Grant continued her work in Toronto and soon after formed the Company of Sirens, where she remains artistic director. Nightwood had been associated with Buddies in Bad Times' Rhubarb! Festival, an annual event focusing on new works. In 1986 it initiated its Groundswell festival. Originally produced in conjunction with International Women's Day, Groundswell runs for eight days and celebrates new work in development by women writers, directors, and performers.

In 1995 Groundswell turned ten years old, marking a decade of influential works-in-progress that continue to advance women's theatre. Throughout its history, Groundswell has highlighted the works of important Canadian women playwrights, including Sandra Shamas, Audrey Butler, and Kelly Jo Burk. Each year the line-up consists of an impressive roster of talent from across Canada, and the performances deal with a breadth of issues, from the plight of immigrant women in public housing to a celebration of women in the sex trade.

By the late 1980s, the company began to turn away from its trademark collaborative style towards the promotion of women's solo works. During this period Nightwood cultivated its most successful play to date, Ann-Marie MacDonald's *Goodnight Desdemona, Good Morning Juliet*, about a Queen's University lecturer who discovers her own strengths while trying to alter the fate of two of

Shakespeare's best-known tragic heroines.The play won MacDonald the Governor General's Award for Drama (1990), and it was an important production for Nightwood, bridging the gap between commercial success and feminist theatre. As one reviewer noted: "This play is one of the wildest and woolliest feminist reappraisals that the theatre has recently seen, and one of the most intellectually ambitious. It confronts, in a creative and witty fashion, the dilemma of women in theatre who find that the greatest writer for the theatre was still limited by the patriarchal and half-civilized culture in which he lived. Shakespeare – love him or leave him. Or rewrite him."[13]

By the late eighties and early nineties, Nightwood was looking at issues of race and identity in its productions and how to interact with the predominantly white, middle-class feminist community. Plays like Monique Mojica's *Princess Pocahontas and the Blue Spots* and Diana Braithwaite's *The Wonder Quartet* marked a distinct change in Nightwood's political and conceptual agenda, as it now focused dramatically on those groups of women whose voices had historically been absent or marginalized from the company's productions. Nightwood also produces the *Five Minute Feminist Cabaret*, known as *Fem Cab*, a ten-year-old celebratory fund raiser that is considered one of the major events of International Women's Week. Originally associated with the Women's Cultural Centre, *Fem Cab* is an evening of feminist fun where local musicians, actors and comics gather to perform their five minutes of material. The five-minute time limit was initially imposed to ensure that even the worst act would be over quickly. But more often than not these days, the audience begs for more.

Today Nightwood has the highest-profile feminist troupe in Canada and it continues to create opportunities for women theatre artists with a decidedly feminist point of view. As its mandate affirms,

Nightwood Theatre has provided a forum for women to explore the complexity of our relationships to each other, to society and consequently, to history. Its identity today is a culmination of accident, serendipity and wilful efforts to have a say in the development of women's culture. We are intrigued by the challenge of seeing the whole pattern, Nightwood's past, present and future, in order to support the contribution that each individual constituent, each artist or script or decision, can make to the whole.[14]

With the strong presence of Toronto's Company of Sirens, and with work being produced by many small theatre groups with a feminist focus, Nightwood is no longer Toronto's only feminist theatre. However, it continues to work with women on a feminist, political, and multicultural level, exploring issues that are both pertinent and entertaining for all theatregoers. In its nearly two decades of existence, "Nightwood has provided opportunities for many women in all areas of theatre. In welcoming novices, it has acted as a training ground as well as a production ground for the more experienced." Its commitment to working with women whose individual vision has challenged the way we see society through their politics and their dramaturgy has remained intact and has helped foster not only the development of new Canadian theatrical work but, through its audiences, tolerance among Canadians generally.

PART FIVE

Health Care and Science

56 Introduction

Wendy Mitchinson

By the beginning of the twentieth century, science had become a major arbiter of truth in Canada. This had not always been the case. For much of the previous century, the various churches had assumed that role. However, the challenges mounted by the Darwinian revolution, geological investigations, and biblical criticism undermined confidence in the religious verities, at least as they applied to the physical world. Science offered Canadians rational objectivity in place of religious "superstition," or so they thought; at the same time, they were encouraged to see in scientific "truths" the patterns of evidence of God's creation. Thus Canadians could have the best of both worlds, belief in a supreme being and belief in the laws of science. Over the ensuing century, the prestige of science increased as Canadians and others looked to it as the foundation of modern prosperity through applied science and multiple inventions, and as the technological fix to a vast array of problems: disease, environmental degradation, limits to resources, and so on. Only in recent decades has this new faith come under scrutiny, with critics arguing that our dependency on science and technology has weakened our sense of responsibility as caretakers of the earth we inhabit. The declining fish stocks, the pollution of our lakes and air, and global warming are testimony to the limited success science and technology have had in protecting us.

Medicine shared in the growing prestige of science. The mid-nineteenth-century introduction of anaesthesia and the later recognition of the role of germs and the

56.1 Marine biology lab, 1947 (1975-305, 472-3, Nova Scotia Archives and Records Management)

need for aseptic surroundings gave physicians the confidence to intervene in the body more than they previously had. This intervention has increased greatly over the last one hundred years. But how much have we benefited from it? Some have suggested that the real success story in health has been improved nutrition and sanitation, not medical therapy.[1] One example of early long-term convalescent care that also featured some medical intervention with improved life conditions is the Toronto-based Home for Incurable Children, described in Magda Zakanyi's essay (#57).

In the twentieth century, we have come to believe in medical experts and depend on them. We look to them

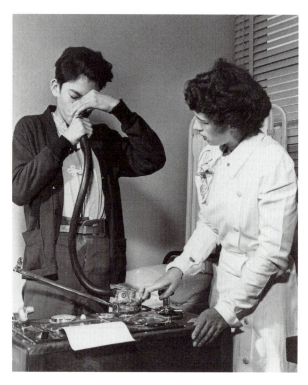

56.2 Testing lung capacity at Camsell Indian Hospital, c. 1950
(PA 138918, National Archives of Canada)

for answers to a myriad of problems we face from the cradle to the grave.

Obstacles to women's involvement in science, medicine, and technology have been many. Science was deemed a rational endeavour, and for centuries Western society viewed women as emotional (assuming this to be antithetical to rationality). For most of the twentieth century, Canadians saw women and men as complements of one another; they were equal but different. Indeed, science provided support for this view. At best, women's role was to help men in their endeavours; they could be the workers of science and technology, not its leaders and thinkers.[2] The young women in Illustration 56.1, for example, worked as technicians in the Halifax Experimental Station in 1947; also reflecting this supportive role, the laboratory technician in Illustration 56.2 tests "patient Archie Half's vital lung capacity with a metabulator" in the 1950s.

Women's perceived social role also limited them. The potential of women to conceive and give birth shaped attitudes towards women.[3] Not only *could* women have children, but most Canadians felt they *should* have children. Canada had long been pronatalist in orientation. The high infant mortality rates early in the century, the loss of life as a result of the First World War, and the influenza epidemic that immediately followed encouraged Canadians to focus on the need to replace those they had lost. The Second World War did the same, with the resulting "baby boom." As the new century begins, concern about the declining birth rate and the unwillingness of Canadians to reproduce themselves has created a crisis in some minds, which many blame on women's entry into the labour force.

Women give birth and many in society have assumed that it was "natural" for them to raise the children as well. Men were to be the family providers. As a result, women's involvement in professional endeavours such as science or medicine was considered inappropriate or even impossible. Universities and professional schools often did not accept women as students. When they did, they limited their numbers and made them feel like intruders. Women entering medicine, for example, were accused of impropriety in studying the male body; few questioned the propriety of men studying the female. Only in the last few decades have training institutions (under pressure) opened their doors equally to women. In medicine, more than 50 per cent of students are now women. However, the percentages are still much less in the pure and applied sciences.

When women persevered and obtained the training necessary, they still had to face the discrimination of

56.3 Researcher in the lab, Halifax, 1946
(N 472-2, Public Archives of Nova Scotia)

56.4 Taste-tasting egg rolls
(PA 148758, National Archives of Canada)

56.5 Nurse reading to children, Royal Victoria Hospital, Montreal, 1953 (PA 133209, National Archives of Canada)

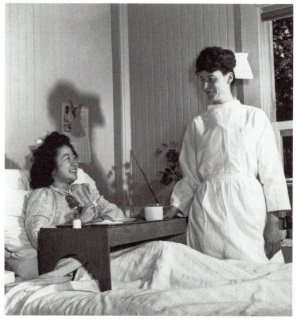

56.6 Nurse with patient, New Denver, B.C., 1945 (PA 132575, National Archives of Canada)

those who held traditional notions of women's capabilities. Was a woman geologist, like Alice Payne in essay #64, as good as a man? Was a medical researcher, such as the woman in Illustration 56.3 or Vera Peters, who developed new techniques to detect breast cancer, considered as skilled as her male peers? Women tended to be ghettoized within fields. In medicine, women gravitated to the care of women and children. They dominated in the dietary sciences, as seen in the image of women taste-testing egg rolls in Illustration 56.4. If a woman wanted to marry and have a family, a career path became even more constrained. Some institutions had formal policies against hiring married women, and even when they did not, they often had informal ones. Even today, many believe that a married woman with a family is unable to give the same devotion to her job as a man with a family. If a woman married a man who was in the same field, which was often the case, then the likelihood of both getting jobs at the same institution was next to impossible because of anti-nepotism regulations. Universities, the major employers of research scientists and medical specialists, were loath to hire married women. They were not, however, unwilling to take advantage of their unpaid labour as adjuncts to their husbands. Many academic wives, well educated in their own right, helped in their husband's laboratories, marked students' papers, filled in when their husband was away, all with little recognition or even pay. They remained on the periphery of their fields.

Women have been central in the health field as nurses. Nursing did not represent a drastic shift from woman's traditional role. After all, most Canadians, including women, assumed that all women were natural nurses. Nursing was an extension of the domestic role; caring for the family was extended to caring for others.[4] (See illustration 56.5) The training and employment of nurses underscored this. Until the 1940s, hospitals used nursing students as free labour, which relieved them from hiring

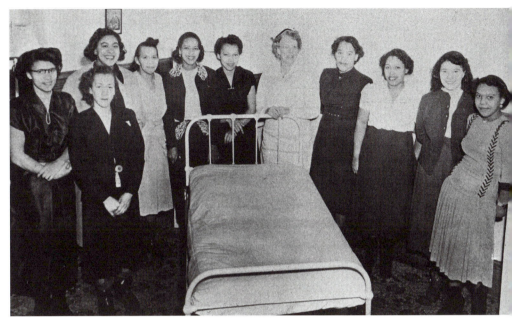

trained personnel to staff their institutions. Trained nurses were free agents, having to find private-duty jobs that provided no job security. Not until the expansion of hospitals and the increasing complexity of medical care were skilled staff in hospitals a necessity.[5] (See Illustration 56.6) But whether hospital or private-duty nurses, such women remained the handmaidens of physicians. Jill Perry's profile of Nurse Ethel Currant demonstrates this principle (#61). Only public and district health nurses or, like Margaret Scott (#58), those who worked in nursing missions, were able to gain a modicum of independence: they were employed on a regular basis by various levels of government, were the first line of medical defence, and at times stepped in and performed the duties traditionally done by physicians. The women in Illustration 56.7 were proudly photographed on graduation from a home nursing course in 1949.

Not all was discouraging for women interested in medicine or science. Many of the women who succeeded

56.7 Home nursing course, 1949 (Courtesy of Mildred Byard, Nova Scotia Archives and Records Management)

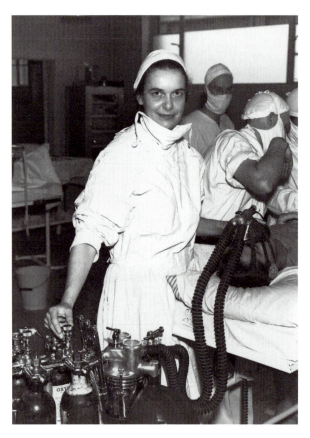

56.8 Anaesthetist Captain Shirley Fleming, Second World War (PA 128186, National Archives of Canada)

Sometimes, the circumstances of society favoured women. The two world wars, for example, drew men out of the labour force into the armed services, leaving hospitals deficient in medical personnel and universities and research laboratories scrambling to find trained replacements to allow them to carry on. Anaesthetist Captain Shirley Fleming (Illustration 56.8) found work at No. 20 Canadian General Hospital in Leavesden, England, during the Second World War. Wars also expanded the traditional roles of nurses, giving them more scope in which to practice their profession. This is described by Linda Quiney in her essay (#59) on the Canadian Voluntary Aid Detachment Nurses; in her contribution (#60), Ruby Heap traces the challenges faced by those who have researched the history of physiotherapy, one of the new professions taken up by nurses in the same period.

Despite the problems faced by women, they carved out areas for themselves. Nurses, who did not share the prestige and status enjoyed by physicians, could comfort themselves that without them hospitals would not run. Married women took any job that would keep them close to their profession even if the job did not utilize the full expertise they had. As noted above, many, like Norah Toole profiled in essay #63, acted as their husband's unpaid assistants. Staying on the periphery was better than being excluded altogether. They were not often able to become the "big" names in their fields, but they did enable others to become so. Many became involved in volunteer work and used the skills they had honed for the betterment of society. They were attracted to areas overlooked by others, responding to needs as they became aware of them. But we should not overlook that these women were products of their society and shared with it the class and racial biases of that society. Most of the women who "succeeded" did not come from working-class or minority ethnic backgrounds. They came from the middle class of mainstream Anglo-Celtic

were fortunate in having the support of their families, especially their belief in the importance of education for both sexes. Some parents who did not give their daughters positive encouragement at least did not place obstacles in their way. They provided them with confidence in their own abilities, even if that confidence took them in directions their families could not have foreseen. Women whose parents directly opposed their goals had to seek support and encouragement elsewhere, and often it was found in wider networks of women.

society. Science necessitated education and higher education necessitated money.

Energy characterized many of the women described in the essays in Part 5. They could not keep still. They pushed themselves to be trained and once trained used their training as best they could. If they could not apply it directly, they rechannelled into other areas the energy and determination that had characterized their push to excellence. Above all, they had a sense of responsibility, a belief in the need to give back to their society what they had received and more. They made themselves and Canada stronger.

A list of further readings in this area is provided on page 487.

57 The Ladies Committee of the Home for Incurable Children

Magda Zakanyi

57.1 First building used for the Bloorview MacMillan Centre, 138 Avenue Road, Toronto, 1900 (Bloorview MacMillan Centre)

In 1899 a group of socially conscious women in Toronto came together to found the Home for Incurable Children. They called themselves "The Ladies Committee." Unlike the members of a modern hospice board, these women did not represent the community at large. Rather, they came from privileged backgrounds, with husbands who were a veritable Who's Who of the time: Osler, Merritt, Gzowski, Harcourt, Gooderham, Cassels, Cox, Dundas, Ryerson, Boyd, Massey. As stay-at-home wives and daughters educated primarily to run large households and entertain, they reflected their upper-middle-class values and attitudes. Aware of the needs of the wider community – in particular, the need to care for chronically ill and physically disabled children – they decided to establish the Home for Incurable Children, to be part hospital and part "nursing home."

The women first met on 15 May 1899. Their priorities were to obtain a building, from which to start their operation, recruit staff, and notify the press of their endeavour. On 2 June 1899 the *Globe and Empire* announced that the committee would have to "appeal to the generosity of the public ... Those who feel liberally disposed will please forward any donations." Then the Ladies Committee began to network; once the word was out among friends and acquaintances, the response was swift and generous. Mr and Mrs George Archibald Cox donated a three-storey house at 138 Avenue Road. (Illustration 57.1).[1] The gracefully proportioned house with its wide porches on two levels allowed the children to enjoy fresh air under the watchful gaze of their nurses.

Donations to furnish the house were also forthcoming: carpets, a gas stove, a dining-room set, iron beds and mattresses. The Avenue Road house required several alterations to make it suitable as a children's hospital. The stovepipe had to be redirected, cupboards installed for the dispensary, and partitions built for the nurses' quarters. Calling on local tradespeople, the members of the Ladies Committee bargained for the best prices, always emphasizing the charitable nature of the enterprise. They were also alert to possible cooperative ventures. A tradesperson wanted to graze his horse on the property and the women agreed, but in return he was paid less cash for his work. After the home was in full operation, regular donations continued to arrive, both in cash and kind. The Gooderham family sent ice-cream every Saturday for many years, and the Massey family sent milk. Typical donations, as recorded in the annual report, included cut flowers, twelve glasses of jelly, a bag of potatoes, eight towels, a cup and saucer, two silk handkerchiefs, candy, and dolls.[2]

Individual women from the committee, some of whom are shown in Illustration 57.2, were assigned to recruit doctors, hire a "Lady Superintendent," and oversee the approval of a Declaration of Incorporation. Note the common appearance of the committee members, who had adopted their own form of "uniform." By mid-October of their first year of operation, the committee had secured five staff physicians, all of whom deferred payment for their work, a nurse, a maid, and a superintendent. The latter, it was decided, would wear a "neat black uniform with white bib and cuffs" while the nurses were to have lilac-coloured calico with white stripes, as shown in Illustration 57.3.

Most of the nursing staff were young, single women, the majority coming from the British Isles. For wages of twelve and fifteen dollars per month, they were obliged to reside in the home, and work from 7 a.m. to 7 p.m., with one hour off to refresh themselves or change their uniforms. In addition to nursing duties, they did some cleaning, sewing, and teaching. On Saturdays they were allowed to go out in the afternoon. Together with the Ladies Committee members, nursing staff also looked after the children's recreation. Labatt's Brewery often provided trucks to transport the children to the Toronto Islands, the Exhibition, and similar places. Long-serving nurses and other staff had their hospitalization expenses paid by the committee as well as salaried holiday time. Miss Underhill, the first lady superintendent, served

more than ten years; her successor, Miss Fleming, stayed for eighteen years.

Applications for admission arrived from parents, doctors and children's homes. The screening process involved a visit by a committee member to each child's home and the evaluation of each child's needs. The two children in Illustration 57.4 are representative of those who were served by the home. Though we know little more about the individual children, the ornate wheelchair, healthy appearance of the younger child, and spacious grounds shown in the photograph all suggest that quality of care was important to the committee. This is confirmed by the assessment of the Ladies Visiting Sub-Committee, which noted disapprovingly in its minute

57.2 Mrs Gooderham laying a time capsule in the foundation of the new centre, 1931 (Bloorview MacMillan Centre)

book that "[t]he visiting committee members were not pleased. The children were not as tidy as they should be, especially Nellie and Basil."[3] On another occasion, "Mrs Ryerson last week found everything in good order, except the unpleasant odour."[4]

Members of the Ladies Committee served long terms. Maria Buchan, secretary/treasurer, served for nineteen years. Miss Freeman, Miss Buchan's niece, who succeeded her in that post, remained for twenty years. Mrs R.A. Donald served for more than thirty years in various capacities on the committee. The most outstanding service record can be attributed to the Gooderham women, both by birth and marriage. For example, Maude Gooderham served for forty-two years, while her daughters, Mary Hogarth and Jesse MacLachlan, were both presidents at various times.

In 1964 the Home for Incurable Children changed its name to Bloorview Children's Hospital. In January 1996 it merged with the Hugh MacMillan Rehabilitation Centre to become the Bloorview MacMillan Centre. Times have changed, and the hospital, which is now referred to as a children's rehabilitation facility, has grown. The 1996 merger was five years in the making and the organization is planning to move to a new single site within a few years. One likes to imagine that the Ladies, who did not have to consult with layers of government, might have accomplished this task in seven months as well! Even so, the goals of the Bloorview MacMillan Centre remain the same: to provide care and support to children and youth with disabilities and special needs.

57.3 Nurses (Bloorview MacMillan Centre)

57.4 Children patients, Bloorview MacMillan Centre (Bloorview MacMillan Centre)

58 Margaret Scott: "The Angel of Poverty Row"

Tamara Miller

On 28 July 1856, Margaret Ruttan Boucher (1856–1931) was born into a wealthy family in the town of Colbourne, Ontario. At the age of twenty-two, she met and married William Hepburn Scott, a lawyer and member of the Ontario Legislature, and settled into a predictable and respectable life as a middle-class wife. However, after the untimely death of her husband in 1881, Margaret Scott's life would adopt a radically different course, earning her the moniker "the angel of poverty row."

Widowed and in need of employment to support herself, Scott obtained a clerical position with Midland Railways in Peterborough, Ontario. Five years later, in 1886, she took up employment with the Dominion Land Office in Winnipeg, Manitoba, where she met the Reverend C.C. Owen of Holy Trinity Anglican Church. Arriving only six years after the incorporation of Manitoba as a province, Scott was struck by the plight of the immigrant poor in Winnipeg's North End and volunteered her services for Reverend Owen's relief work. By 1898, she had given up her position in the Land Commissioner's Office to devote all her time to the work of the Winnipeg Lodging and Coffee House, a hostel for the destitute and transient.

While district nursing had been undertaken in the city of Winnipeg by the Winnipeg General Hospital in 1895, the hospital was unable to incur the continued expense of such a far-reaching program, and by 1901 it had ceased sponsoring district nursing. Through her missionary work with women prisoners, Scott became aware of the plight of sick women who could not afford medical attendance. Without any nursing training and in response to the closure of the Winnipeg General nursing program, she began to care for bedridden women in their homes. Hearing of her endeavours, Ernest Taylor, a local businessman and close associate of Owen's, agreed to pay the salary of a trained nurse for three months. Upon Taylor's death in 1903, the city assumed the full cost of Scott's trained assistant.

In 1904 a group of middle-class reformers, spurred by Scott's charity work, met to organize the Margaret Scott Nursing Mission. After hiring a full-time nurse and securing quarters in the city's immigrant district, Scott moved into the mission house where she would begin her life's work managing one of the most comprehensive home-nursing programs in western Canada. The mission became such an established part of the health-care community that, by 1912, its regular staff had increased to eight trained nurses and it was providing training to both nurses and physicians from the Winnipeg General Hospital.

In addition to nursing attendance, Margaret Scott nurses provided relief supplies, hygiene instruction, and whatever assistance was needed in the homes of their patients, including child care and cooking. Under Scott's direction, the programs initiated by the mission closely paralleled those of well-known social work organizations such as Hull House. Many of the mission's initiatives, such as the child hygiene department and the Little Nurses' League, were adopted and, ultimately, taken over by civic departments. By the time of its incorporation into the Victorian Order of Nurses in 1942, the Margaret Scott Nursing Mission had operated for thirty-seven years, establishing some of the most valuable social welfare programs in the community and contributing to the development of health-care delivery in one of Canada's largest cities.

59 "Hardly Feminine Work!" Violet Wilson and the Canadian Voluntary Aid Detachment Nurses of the First World War

Linda J. Quiney

When Violet Wilson of Edmonton became a Voluntary Aid Detachment (VAD) nurse in the First World War, she joined a special community of more than fifteen hundred Canadian women whose work and experience were quickly lost to Canadian history when the war ended.[1] As Canada entered the war on 4 August 1914, Canadians were eager to "do their bit" for the war effort. Men, like Violet Wilson's brother Charlie, had the choice of enlisting to fight for their country; while women could not take up arms, they could, as trained nurses, enlist with the Canadian Army Medical Corps (CAMC) and serve their country in hospitals overseas.[2] It is likely that Violet's sister, Marjorie, decided to begin nurses' training with the hope of eventually serving abroad, but it was the death of their brother and the loss of three cousins during "that awful summer of 1916" that motivated Violet Wilson to become directly involved with the war effort overseas.[3]

Middle- and upper-class women like Violet had inherited a tradition of voluntarism from their mothers and grandmothers. Thousands of these women chose to give their time and energy to a multitude of war-relief projects at home, but most of these offered little chance of real contact with the war.[4] The only recourse for an untrained woman aspiring to overseas service was to train as a Voluntary Aid Detachment nurse. While there was no guarantee that Violet would be accepted or even posted to an overseas hospital, she abandoned her singing lessons in Edmonton and moved to Toronto, where she took the first steps of enrolling in the required St John Ambulance courses in first aid and home nursing.

The women who became VAD nurses in the Great War were primarily young, single, middle or upper class, of Anglo-Protestant heritage, well educated, and financially secure, the latter characteristic enabling them to volunteer their services without the promise of remuneration.[5] Frequently, their decision to become a VAD nurse had been inspired by the loss of a brother, fiancé, or friend in the fighting. Yet most of these young women had scant knowledge or experience of either hospital or nursing work, and had been little prepared in their early lives for the demands and discomforts of wartime hospital work overseas.

Violet Wilson's own life had been no less sheltered and comfortable. Her father was Edmonton's first family physician, and her mother had once been courted by Sir Henry Pellatt of Toronto's Casa Loma. To ensure her proper education, Violet was sent east to Toronto in 1905 to become a reluctant border at the Bishop Strachan School for Girls. She saw these five years as a hardship, considering herself to be one of "the poor ones" among the daughters of central Canada's elite, with less spending money and fewer party dresses than most of the other girls. She also chaffed under the strict regimen of a Protestant church school and the rigid Victorian attitudes of the teachers. Her spirited nature led her to challenge the rules, sneaking forbidden cigarettes up on the roof, smuggling in contraband food in her bloomers,

VOLUNTARY AID DETACHMENT ST.JOHN AMBULANCE ASSOCIATION OTTAWA.

59.1 Voluntary Aid Detachment, St John Ambulance, Ottawa, 1917 (CA 20071, St John Ambulance fonds, City of Ottawa Archives)

and winking at the choir boys on Sundays.[6]

After graduation, she travelled through Japan and China with her father, the result, she believed, of her lively interest in an unsuitable male admirer back in Edmonton, a journey that kindled a lifelong passion for travel and new experiences. Following the unexpected death of her father in 1909, Violet went east to finish her formal education at the Margaret Eaton School of Literature, and the same year was presented to the governor general at Rideau Hall. The following spring, she and a friend embarked on a year-long journey through Europe, where they attended the Paris Opera, were presented to the pope, and sailed down the Rhine, always managing to have several male admirers in tow. At the end of that year, Violet returned to Edmonton to begin

singing lessons in earnest, unaware of the distant rumblings of the coming conflict.

While Canada had initiated a plan to create Voluntary Aid Detachments in 1914, prior to the summer of 1916 Canadian VAD nurses were not requested for service in overseas military hospitals.[7] Impatient with the long delays, many of these Canadian women financed their own passage to England and applied directly at the London headquarters of the British VAD program to be taken on as nurses in British military hospitals.[8] By the time Violet began her training in 1917, Canadian VADS were being summoned for overseas service at regular intervals. Confident of her success, Violet trained and qualified with the St John Ambulance in Toronto, then worked in a military convalescent hospital as she waited for her overseas posting. Possibly hoping to qualify as a VAD ambulance driver, Violet also took a motor mechanics course and then gained practical experience by working for six weeks in a garage doing repairs. This, she stated, "was considered quite something," since few women drove at that time. An elderly aunt was heard to complain that it was "hardly feminine work!," but Violet thoroughly enjoyed it.

Violet was much less pleased with the "unbelievably ugly uniform" provided for St John Ambulance VADS. The grey cotton workdress was topped by a high, stiff white collar, white cuffs, and long white apron. Her stockings were black cotton, not silk, and the dress uniform comprised a grey woollen dress and a heavy, grey double-breasted great coat. Only the triangular, white nurses' veil was attractive to her, the rest being of "the most frightful cut." The worst item was the dress felt hat with its wide, low crown that had a distinctly "depressing effect." Against regulations, Violet had her hat altered by a milliner, but she was discovered and ordered to replace the hat at her own expense. She complied with the order but kept the altered hat, and once out at sea, "lost" the regulation hat overboard.

Following her selection for an overseas post, Violet became frustrated by the continual delays in her transport and used her family connection to Sir Henry Pellatt, then head of the St John Ambulance in Canada, to secure a promise of quick passage. The interview had been quite terrifying; she described how "this great fat man who seemed as old as the hills to me, pulled me down on his knee and began kissing me!" Yet despite her first experience with a "licentious old man," Violet soon sailed from Montreal as promised, in June 1918, along with a contingent of approximately forty VADS from across western Canada. The sea voyage was long and uncomfortable, three weeks of sleeping six in a cabin designed for two, as they zigzagged across the ocean "to avoid submarines." The food was bad, the weather was

awful, and the women were required to wear lifebelts all day long. The trip was otherwise uneventful, except for a submarine attack on a convoy ship, but Violet managed to defy the rules at least once, accepting a forbidden drink with an old friend she met on board, George Bennett, the brother of the future prime minister, R.B. Bennett.

Once in England, Violet again challenged the regulations and had her uniform altered to look more "presentable." This was hardly necessary, since her first VAD assignment was at Devonshire House, headquarters of the British VAD program, where she was detailed to cleaning up the military cars returned from France. Scraping mud and dirt off vehicles was depressing work – a "waste of trained personnel" according to Violet – but she was soon transferred to the desired nursing post, although again she found her expectations to have been unrealistic. Most Canadian VADS had initially hoped to assist in the care of wounded Canadian soldiers in the Canadian military hospitals abroad. However, the Canadian Army Medical Corps had successfully resisted the employment of volunteers in its hospitals overseas, especially women volunteers. The military medical administration, both nurses and physicians, feared that

MAJOR MARGARET C. MACDONALD, 1873–1948

Born in Bailey's Brook, Nova Scotia, Margaret Macdonald chose nursing as a career. She cared for the wounded of the Spanish American War and then worked with Canadian troops in South Africa between 1900 and 1902. Appointed to the permanent Canadian Army Nursing Corps in 1906, she was made matron-in-chief of the Canadian Nursing Service in 1914. With headquarters in London, England, she was in charge of all Canadian military nurses overseas during the First World War. She retired in 1923 but maintained her professional contacts until her death in 1948. (Courtesy of Parks Canada)

casually trained female volunteers would undermine their professional standards and the military discipline of the hospitals. Only a few Canadian VADs were able to serve in the CAMC hospitals of the First World War, and then only in a non-nursing capacity, at clerical or recreational tasks.[9] The majority of the approximately five hundred Canadian VADs posted overseas served instead in the British military hospitals, alongside British VADs, under the direction of trained British nurses.[10]

Violet was assigned to Gifford House, a British military hospital for amputees in London. The English nursing sisters, according to Violet, did not welcome her as a valued assistant; they were "very antagonistic to all VADs, and seemed to go out of their way to be unpleasant." In particular, in Violet's estimation, the nurses resented "the colonials." Not easily intimidated and lacking the sense of deference that was part of nurses' training, Violet was particularly outraged when the VADs were ordered to rise a half-hour earlier in the morning in order to bring hot water to the nurses' quarters.[11] Violet "rebelled," defiantly announcing that she had come "to help wait on the men, not the nurses," and she emphasized, "I said it very loudly!" In addition to punishment with night duty, Violet was rebuked by the matron, who declared that "[C]olonials, amongst our other awful characteristics, had no sense of discipline!"[12]

Violet's experience was similar to that of Canadian VADs in other British hospitals and Canadian women ambulance drivers with the British Red Cross in France. One driver was reprimanded for being too friendly with the "stretcher-bearers" and warned that this was "a Canadian failing."[13] Most VADs had little concept of the hospital culture, which demanded deference and absolute obedience from junior nurses.[14] Yet the constant influx to already overburdened hospitals of gravely wounded men demanded the assistance of extra hands, no matter how inexperienced. The combination of class differences, culture shock, and inadequate training put a strain on the nurses and VADs alike, allowing little room for patience and understanding.[15]

It was the courage and suffering of the soldier-patients that made VAD service bearable for Violet and others like her. As she described it, "The cheery courage of those men, with no arms or legs, sometimes with neither, was unbelievable!" Violet marvelled at the men's fun in wheelchair races down Putney Hill, oblivious to the consequences of an accident. It was instead the noise of the Zeppelin raids that most upset the men, returning them to the horrors of the battlefield. VADs had to comfort screaming men, desperate to be taken outside rather than be trapped in a bombed building.

Yet VAD life was not all hard work and unreasonable demands, and Violet took full advantage of days off to tour around London with various escorts. On one memorable visit to Kew Gardens, she and her companion forgot the time and missed the last bus. Forced to walk the twelve miles back to Putney, in wartime conditions with no cabs or lights, and having missed the 10 p.m. curfew, they found the gates locked. Gifford Hospital, which had been converted from a large, private house, was surrounded by a high stone fence topped by broken glass. Always ready for a challenge, Violet had her friend boost her onto his shoulders to the top of the wall, where she agonizingly balanced in equal part on her purse and the "pointed glass." With no other recourse she leapt to the ground, "clothes catching and tearing," and "bleeding freely," she eluded the guard. Nevertheless, "the next few days, walking and bending were difficult." She moved painfully around the wards, her "behind plastered with band-aids."

Violet had earlier requested a transfer to a privately funded convalescent home for Canadian officers in France where VADs were accepted, since it was not a military institution. When the request was granted, Violet found herself in a converted Rothschild mansion on a hill overlooking the racecourse at Deauville. The shock of the change was overwhelming, and she admitted to an acute sense of shame while enjoying the luxuries provided by contributions from wealthy Torontonians. The stark surroundings, lack of supplies, and poor food in Gifford House Hospital in London hardly compared with the over-abundant luxury provided for the Canadian officers in France. True VAD work gave way to glorified housemaids' duties, tidying bedrooms, and preparing copious afternoon teas for the Canadians and visitors from local British hospitals. The men here required only rest and good food to recuperate from minor wounds and illness; yet it was too late to transfer back to real VAD duties, as rumours of an armistice proved correct, and within weeks the hospital was dismantled.

Having been granted three weeks leave before taking up duties at VAD headquarters in Boulogne, Violet and two friends set off to tour the empty trenches and the desolate French countryside in December 1918. During this interlude, they spent a night at a former prisoner-of-war camp, two more with a general at a château commandeered as British headquarters, and another cold night in a village, under a partly bombed-out roof. Travelling in various vehicles, with a variety of drivers, they left the countryside for a few days in Paris, finally arriving in Boulogne to an unexpectedly enthusiastic welcome. Help was sorely needed, for as the men returned from the various fronts, the influenza epidemic raged through the camps and hospitals. Violet estimated that one-half of the men invalided to the Boulogne hospital died of influenza, as well as a great many nurses and VADs. Next, Violet volunteered to help at a British Women's Army Auxiliary Corps hospital outside Boulogne, in the process developing a deep appreciation for these "intelligent, cheery, capable women." When this hospital closed, she moved on to a camp at Wimereux, a holding station for men waiting for demobilization papers, where her task was to find some occupation for these "2,000 tired, disillusioned and restless men." Here she made a friend of a British general, once again defying regulations that forbad a British officer accompanying a woman in public. Whenever they met for dinner in Boulogne, they were forced to hide in the darkest recesses of the restaurant. At Boulogne, Violet's final VAD post, she took over the housekeeping of the British Red Cross headquarters in the Hôtel Cristal. This posting greatly enhanced Violet's French vocabulary, as she shopped for the daily provisions in the market and acquired "four-letter words that absolutely horrified my family when I inadvertently used them later in Paris."

After a few months, Violet was called home to Canada when her mother was taken ill. Like many VADs, she described her return to the real world as "too quiet and too sudden a change from all the wartime hustle and bustle," and like the returned soldiers she felt "restless and dissatisfied." Having become accustomed to responsible work and living abroad, Violet applied and qualified for a post as a "woman emigration officer in a Canadian department in Europe." Although veteran soldiers were being given preference for government work, a debate arose over whether a woman's unpaid volunteer work under military supervision qualified her as a veteran. Three months later, her claim was declared valid, and Violet Wilson began a postwar position as a Canadian emigration officer in Glasgow, Scotland.

Like the majority of VADs whose postwar careers can be traced, Violet did not consider nursing as a career. Instead, she worked in turn as a CBC broadcaster in Vancouver, a tourist officer at Lake Louise, matron and hostess at an Imperial Oil camp at Norman Wells in the Arctic, and a tour guide in Europe for fifteen years. After retirement, as long as she was able, Violet continued to travel across Canada and around the world, living in turn in Quebec, Russia, Vienna, and Hungary before finally settling in Victoria, British Columbia. While some VADs entered new careers like physiotherapy, dietetics, or social work, others returned to accustomed roles as teachers or clerical workers and a few used their VAD experience to obtain positions with the Red Cross or St John Ambulance. Many others opted to marry and retired permanently from waged work.[16]

Although her postwar career certainly qualifies as out of the ordinary, it is her work as a First World War VAD, a unique group of Canadian women, that gives Violet Wilson her special place in Canadian history. Though little prepared for the hard work, horrors, and demands that this special service involved, Canadian VADs rose to the challenge, receiving no remuneration and little acknowledgment for their efforts.[17] Violet Wilson's story helps to illuminate the remarkable service given country and empire by the more than fifteen hundred Canadian VADs of the Great War.[18]

60 The Emergence of Physiotherapy as a New Profession for Canadian Women, 1914–1918

Ruby Heap

Books written about the First World War, that "great event" in our history, have traditionally dealt with geo-politics, diplomacy, military strategy, and battles. The main actors are those patriots who governed the country at home or led the armies on the battlefield. But the Great War also evokes images of violence, slaughter, and casualties on a massive scale. Historians have started to pay closer attention to this human cost of war. They have examined the experiences and perceptions of the main victims, the soldiers. These include not only those who were killed in the line of duty, but also the extremely high numbers who became sick, or were wounded, maimed, or permanently disabled. In addition to exploring their lives, historians have studied the way these surviving soldiers were cared for by the military, by the state, and by their family and community when they returned home. Medical historians have thus explored the impact of the Great War on medical techniques and practices. Others have studied the development of social policy aimed at veterans and their families, and the importance attached to the crucial issue of pensions.

If soldiers are now considered valid subjects for study, what about women in wartime? Women, of course, were the mothers, sisters, wives, and daughters of the men who fought, died, or returned home wounded or disabled. Large numbers of women were employed at home in the munitions factories, while middle- and upper-class women got actively involved in volunteer

work. Hundreds responded to the call to service by going to the front to care for wounded soldiers, as professional nurses or as members of Voluntary Aid Detachments (VADS). These "angels of mercy" were direct witnesses to the horrors of war, some of them falling in the line of duty.

One can easily conclude, then, that the study of the Great War, like that of all wars, must consider the lives and experiences of women as well as those of men. However, the inclusion of women in the historical scholarship devoted to the Great War is a recent phenomenon. That male historians have dominated – and still dominate – the field of military history largely accounts for women's invisibility or marginalization. Fortunately, women's historians internationally have started to rectify this situation over the past two decades.[1] They have raised several key questions concerning the experiences of women during the Great War and the impact of this international conflict on women's lives. One question that has led to a new area of historical debate is the role of the war in women's long road toward emancipation. Another concerns the evolution of gender relations during the war, more specifically, how the war disrupted expectations and expressions of femininity and masculinity and shifted the balance of power between the sexes to a degree that is still open to debate.[2]

Canadian women's historians have been involved in this process of rediscovering the Great War from the perspectives of women. They have examined themes such as women's involvement in the war effort on the home front, the feminist struggle for the vote and social reform during the Great War, women and pacifism, and the impact of the war on women's education and paid and unpaid work.[3] Surprisingly, wartime nursing has so far attracted very little attention, despite the fact that the Great War created an unprecedented demand for nurses. That medical historians have, until recently, considered the history of female health-care professions as a minor subset of the history of medicine and that nursing history itself is a relatively young field in Canada largely account for this neglect.[4]

It is not surprising, then, that even less is known about the other female health-care professions, such as physiotherapists and occupational therapists.[5] In Canada, both can be directly linked to the human cost entailed by the war and the policies adopted by the Canadian government to deal with the plight of wounded and disabled soldiers. This essay will chart the different stages of the journey which led to the "discovery" of Canada's first physiotherapists in the archival record, as well as the main themes and conclusions drawn so far from an ongoing study of the emergence of physiotherapy as a new "women's profession."[6]

Interestingly, but perhaps not surprisingly considering the absence of any published scholarly work on the origins of Canadian physiotherapy,[7] our journey of discovery began with an examination of the visual record. Indeed, photographs serve to reveal the nature and significance of the work performed in military hospitals by Canada's first trained "masseuses" in response to the urgent need for rehabilitation services brought on by the ravages of war. For example, Desmond Morton and Glenn Wright's *Winning the Second Battle*, a study devoted to returning Canadian veterans, includes some photographs that speak with eloquence to women's vital role in the physical "reconstruction" of those soldiers wounded or maimed on the battlefield.[8] At the Archives

of the Canadian Physiotherapy Association (CPA), which was established in 1920 by those pioneering physiotherapists who had contributed to the war effort, there are photographs that show young masseuses dressed in white uniform performing the main categories of treatment that constituted physiotherapy at the time: massage, passive exercises, as well as light, heat, hydrotherapy, and electrical treatments. Other pioneer physiotherapists were trained as "muscle function trainers"; they performed muscle tests and also engaged soldiers in a series of exercises involving several types of apparatus. The visual record also provides precious clues regarding the organization of rehabilitation services along military lines, the division of labour in this nascent field, and the short-term emergency training programs dispensed at the University of Toronto's Hart House.

The process of identifying physiotherapists who had participated during the Great War and of reconstructing their lives and experiences at that time involved a major search in three main categories of written historical records: women's archives, which consist mainly in the records of women's organizations and the papers of individual women; university and hospital archives; and the military and political records located at the National Archives of Canada. The first category included, of course, the Archives of the Canadian Physiotherapy Association, originally called the Canadian Association of Massage and Remedial Gymnastics (CAMRG). This collection held biographical information on the founders of the CAMRG, a small group that included mostly women (unlike nursing, "massage" attracted some men, albeit in very low numbers), who had received their training in Europe or in the United States. While these celebrated female pioneers played a prominent role in the organization of wartime physiotherapy services on the home front, including the training of practitioners, some had already been performing massage and other kinds of physical treatment work before the war broke out, either in hospitals or in private practice. This information proved essential in two ways: first, it established a direct link between the Great War and the early stages in the professionalization of a new women's occupation in the Canadian health sector, as demonstrated by the establishment of the CAMRG in 1920; and second, it revealed that some of the approaches that constituted physiotherapy at the time had been introduced in Canada before the war. From this perspective, then, one could not argue that physiotherapy was entirely "born" during the Great War.

To verify this hypothesis, a search was conducted in hospital archives in Toronto and Montreal, where the handful of masseuses working in Canada before the war were concentrated. Indeed, we found that some of them were employed in anglophone hospitals for sick children in both cities. These same archives also helped to establish that, as in Great Britain and the United States, there existed in Canada before the war a close relationship between the development of orthopaedics as a medical speciality and the emergence of physiotherapy. Documentation gathered in other archival sources later demonstrated the significance of this relationship both during and after the Great War, when orthopaedic surgeons were among the main promoters of physiotherapy.

While the material collected at the Archives of the CPA contained vital material on the pioneers who set physiotherapy on the road to professionalization immediately after the war, it was not sufficient to allow us to reconstruct the background of wartime physiotherapy services. Since nurses had played a leading role in the organization of the profession in late nineteenth-century Britain, including the establishment of the Society of Trained Masseuses in 1894, the next step was an exploration of Canadian nursing archives.

A successful search was conducted in the Macdonald Papers, a rich collection of material gathered during and after the war by Matron-in-Chief Margaret Macdonald, in the course of her research for an official history of nursing sisters during the First World War. Indeed, this collection documents key themes in the emergence of Canadian physiotherapy during the war; these include the involvement of nursing sisters and British physiotherapists in the teaching and practice of massage in overseas military hospitals; the conflicting views espoused by nurses, physicians, the military, and federal civil servants concerning the creation of a new group of trained female health workers to whom would be conferred a specific scope of practice; and the granting of non-military status to wartime physiotherapists, a decision that would cause much grief to the leadership in years to come. Unlike nurses, physiotherapists were not integrated into the Canadian Army Medical Corps; although they were paid and had received formal training, they were attached, rather, to the Voluntary Aid Section of the St John Ambulance Brigade, which organized volunteer nursing services during the war. A search in the Archives of the Canadian Nurses Association revealed that the CNA was displeased with the presence of volunteer nurses in military hospitals, as they were considered a menace to the advancement of nursing as a profession. This conflict between volunteer work and professionalism during the war was not lost to the early physiotherapy leaders, which explains their resolve to elevate their occupation to professional status immediately after the end of the conflict.

The issue of professional training was particularly pressing for these pioneers. Material gathered at the McGill University Archives and at the Archives of the University of Toronto provided a clear understanding of this issue. During the war, the McGill School of Physical Education organized a one-year course in massage and medical gymnastics. However, the largest contingent of wartime physiotherapists received short emergency training at the Military School of Orthopaedic Surgery and Physiotherapy, located at the University of Toronto's

Hart House. After the war, the newly established CAMRG was eager to upgrade the formal education required of physiotherapists. It thus started to press for the creation of a university-based course, which was eventually established in 1929 at the University of Toronto. The collected material also shed light on several other important themes related to the beginnings of physiotherapy education in Canada, such as its links with the physical education movement and the gendering of massage and of other kinds of therapies. The records also depict the involvement of professors from the University of Toronto's Faculty of Medicine and emerging Department of Psychology in the development and teaching of new treatments and techniques, as well as the contribution of their colleagues from the Faculty of Applied Science and Engineering, who designed various kinds of mechanical and electrical apparatus utilized by physiotherapists and other staff to treat wounded or permanently injured bodies. Fortunately, visual material has also survived that illustrates these devices and machines and demonstrates the importance of technology in the development of various physical therapies.

The journey we had conducted deep into the archival record had revealed the existence of a large civil, military, and medical administrative infrastructure established during the war, both at home and at the front, with the primary aim of "reconstructing" wounded soldiers as rapidly and as efficiently as possible, so that they could either return to the front or be mobilized into industry if they were sent home. This complex framework was supported by the Canadian government, which for the first time in Canadian history recognized disability and rehabilitation as issues of national importance. It became evident that the beginnings of physiotherapy as a new profession for women had to be situated in this specific context, one that required closer scrutiny.

The last major stage in our journey of archival discovery took us to those very sources that had been used by political and military (male) historians and accordingly did not seem at first to have much to contribute to our project. Located at the National Archives of Canada, these included the records of the Department of Militia and Defence, an agency that oversaw the administration and supervision of all military affairs and expenditures, and the personal papers of Sir Albert Edward Kemp, minister of the department in 1916 and 1917 and minister of the overseas military forces of Canada between 1917 and 1920. Contrary to our initial expectations, both sets of records contained a wealth of information on wartime physiotherapy services and the rationale behind their organization. The department's records, which run to hundreds of volumes, contain pertinent data on the situation across the Atlantic, in overseas medical units, hospitals, curative institutions, and convalescent camps, as well as the records of the (overseas) director of medical services and those of the Canadian Army Medical Corps. The papers of Sir Albert Edward Kemp, for their part, contain a considerable amount of material on the treatment and care of undischarged wounded and invalid soldiers returning from the front. In sum, both sets of records proved to be among the richest we discovered in our attempt to contextualize the origins of physiotherapy, both as a specific form of therapeutic treatment and as a new occupation opened to women in the Canadian health sector.

This journey of discovery in the archival sources demonstrates, once again, that historians of women must resort to a wide array of diverse primary sources to discover women's presence and to reconstruct their experiences. We are all eager, of course, to find those sources where women's voices can be directly heard, such as the Archives of the CPA. Our journey also confirmed the importance of paying close attention to less conventional sources, such as illustrations and photographs, which in this case played the role of launching pads into the discovery of Canada's first masseuses. But our itinerary established at the same time the necessity to go back to, and critically reread, those traditional sources that historians have used intensively to examine "male activities" in war. As Veronica Strong-Boag and Anita Clair Fellman have ably put it, "When fresh questions are asked of familiar data, they will sometimes elicit new answers."[9] In the case of our research project, this approach allowed us to establish a clear link between the Great War and the beginnings of physiotherapy as a new profession for women in Canada. At the same time, a parallel observation was that in Canada, as elsewhere, gender was without doubt an organizing principle of wartime health policy. That only reinforces the necessity to rewrite the history of war in gendered terms by moving women from the edge toward the centre.[10]

61 Ethel Currant: Portrait of a Grenfell Nurse

Jill Perry

In 1918 Ethel Currant graduated from the nurses' training program at Britain's Royal Waterloo Hospital. She was only twenty-five, and just beginning a long and adventurous career. Over the next seventeen years, Ethel worked as a staff nurse in India, a missionary nurse in South Africa, and an outport nurse in Atlantic Canada. She also nursed at government hospitals in Belize, Honduras, and Guatemala. Taking some time off from travel in 1935, she worked as a lecturer at Madonna College in Letchworth, England. It was here that Nurse Currant heard an inspiring speech by Sir Wilfred Grenfell, a British medical missionary who worked in northern Newfoundland and Labrador. Intrigued by Sir Wilfred's description of the medical and social work carried out by the Grenfell Mission, she applied to nurse there. The Staff Selection Committee was impressed with her extensive experience, and she was approved for service.

Although Currant's lengthy résumé may have been atypical, her objective was not. In the first four decades of the twentieth century, more that 350 foreign-born nurses worked as both volunteers and as salaried staff members for the Grenfell Mission. In fact, by the time Nurse Currant arrived, the mission had been posting nurses to northern Newfoundland and Labrador for over forty years. As a doctor representing Britain's Royal National Mission to Deep Sea Fishermen, Grenfell first voyaged to Newfoundland in 1892 to see if this corner of the empire was in need of medical and spiritual salvation. Travelling along the Labrador coast, he encoun-

tered a population composed of the native Innu, the permanent settlers, or "livyers" (descendants of British, Irish, Scottish, and Newfoundland traders and sailors, many of whom had intermarried with the Native peoples), and lastly the migratory fishing people who came north from Newfoundland every spring and summer for the annual fishing season. For all of these groups, survival was a full-time task. For the resident Innu and livyers, "living off the land" in the severe Labrador climate by way of hunting, trapping, and fishing was a constant challenge. And the migratory fishing people fared little better. Though Newfoundland was well known in Britain for its rich cod stocks, there was little "trickle down" economic benefit to those who actually caught the fish. In fact, the economic relationships of the "truck system" – where settlers received food and supplies on credit from local merchants – pinned fishing families in a vicious circle of inescapable debt.[1]

Apart from some Moravian missionaries in the Far North, the people living in these harsh conditions received little outside attention. The colonial government in St John's was preoccupied with the vested interests of an elite merchant class; thus, any initiatives in public health, education, or general welfare were embryonic at best until well into the twentieth century. It was this void that beckoned to the ambitious Grenfell. In 1894 he returned with two doctors and two nurses, and established two rudimentary medical stations on the Labrador coast – the modest beginning of what was to become a large institution. In addition to medical work, Grenfell and his entourage were initially preoccupied with "saving souls," but by the turn of the century, this gave way to a broad agenda of social reform in which a vast army of international workers focused on reforming everything from public health and literacy to leisure activities and general morality. To facilitate these objectives, the mission built up a network of hospitals, nursing stations, schools, orphanages, and cooperatives and, in the process, became a powerful outside influence on the region's people and their way of life.

To date, historians have been concerned primarily with the adventurous exploits and philanthropic initiatives of the mission's founder, Wilfred Grenfell,[2] but the Grenfell Mission was not a one-man show. In fact, 53 per cent of the staff between 1914 and 1938 were women, and it was these women, not the doctors or Grenfell himself, who did most of the day-to-day work. Nurses accounted for 54 per cent of the female workers,[3] the others being employed as teachers and community workers. Though hired as "nurses," women like Ethel Currant actually performed a wide variety of medical and non-medical duties. Such diverse capabilities were essential for nurses who single-handedly staffed remote mission stations, hundreds of miles from other assistance. In this unusual work environment, Grenfell nurses experienced high degrees of independent work and outdoor adventure, often with relative autonomy from male authority figures. Certainly, these experiences were not the norm for nurses, nor for early twentieth-century Western women in general. This portrait of Ethel Currant, a dedicated Grenfell nurse, reflects the exceptional female work experience shared by more that 350 other women between 1894 and 1938. But applause should not be carried too far. An examination of Currant's tenure with the Grenfell Mission also points to some less admirable aspects of the experience. Indeed, an exceptional work opportunity for women "from away" was often inseparable from problematic assumptions about the local people they were there to help.

Nurse Currant joined the Grenfell Mission in 1935. At that time, the mission operated five hospitals and five nursing stations (smaller medical centres with no resident doctor) in northern Newfoundland and Labrador. Currant, however, was not posted to any of these existing hospitals or stations, but was instead assigned to head up a new nursing station at Englee, on the eastern side of the Northern Peninsula. Because the mission had as yet established no facilities in this area, Nurse Currant was to live in, and practice from, one of the local homes.[4] Though the unheated, cramped bedroom was a great inconvenience, Currant spent little time, as it turned out, at her ad hoc station. Assessing the local situation, she quickly realized that the high levels of whooping cough and typhoid in the area required her, as the only medical help for hundreds of miles, to make extensive house calls and inoculation rounds. Between January and May of 1936, Nurse Currant travelled more than nine hundred miles. Reflecting back on her first winter with the Grenfell Mission, she wrote "Englee is one of the most difficult tasks I have ever undertaken."[5]

Nurse Currant's extensive travelling was a large component of this "difficult task." By June of 1936, she had logged twelve hundred miles – an impressive total given the region's arduous travel conditions. An absence of roads and an abundance of snowy, rough terrain punctuated by numerous bays and inlets meant that Ethel Currant relied on a combination of snowshoes, dogsled, motor and row boat, as well as the unpredictable coastal steamers. Each of these modes of travel had its own set of dangers. For winter house calls in her district, Nurse Currant often used a box-like sled, called a *komatic*, that was pulled by a dog-team and driven by a local man whom the mission had hired as her assistant. One winter evening in 1939, Ethel gripped the edge of her komatic seat as they careened crazily around the gaping holes in the ice at breakneck speed. The driver seemed possessed and would not acknowledge her anxious pleas. "The more I tried to caution the driver, the more desperate he became and the quicker the flight," she remembered in a letter.[6] Hopping off when they paused at a village, Nurse Currant did not return to her chauffeur, but ran overland through the dark woods until she arrived at her station and, fearing for her life, barricaded herself inside. When the repentant driver arrived at her door, he confessed that a deep depression made him want to end his life; the hurtling *komatic* ride had actually been an attempted suicide-run. Nurse Currant forgave him and chalked it up to a day's work. Clearly then, a "day's work" for Grenfell nurses could be complicated by hazardous travel in a severe climate.

But when Ethel Currant described her new job as "the most difficult task I've ever undertaken," she was referring to a lot more than dangerous journeys by dogsled. As the sole staff member at an isolated station, Currant was required to fill a number of medical roles. Whether it was pulling teeth, administering anaesthetics, treating devastating epidemics, or performing emergency operations, Ethel Currant routinely overstepped the usual boundaries of the nursing profession. This was not, in most cases, a matter of choice. Although mission doctors were supposed to make routine visits to the isolated nursing station, in reality these visits were erratic and, more often than not, very brief. In 1940, for example, Currant was disappointed that a long-awaited visit from the mission's medical superintendent had lasted only a weekend. "Dr. Curtis was busy most of the time and we naturally felt after he was gone that we had not had time to ask him half the things that we wanted to ask about," she explained in a letter to the London office.[7]

Considering nurses' broad range of duties, it is easy to appreciate the variety of dilemmas that might have arisen. In addition to the intense medical workload, nurses like Ethel Currant were also responsible for looking after the finances, resources, and facilities at their particular station. One of Ethel Currant's main priorities was balancing her station's budget. To this end, much of her time was occupied by various fund-raising efforts. While stationed at Englee in 1937, she organized a district "Jumble Sale." Tickets to the sale included as well a special luncheon, a flea market, and an evening's entertainment by the local children. The event brought in fifty-one dollars – a total that gave Nurse Currant much satisfaction.[8] But the Jumble Sale was about more than fund-raising. On another level, encouraging locals' participation in such events was meant to stimulate a community's sense of responsibility for its own welfare. In keeping with the mission's guiding philosophy, nurses like Ethel Currant were expected not only to treat the ailments of individual people, but also to reform the social conditions in which those ailments arose.

In fact, social work that was aimed at improving the quality of life in northern Newfoundland and Labrador consumed much of nurses' time. Often this work consisted of preventive health measures in the effort to control the region's high levels of disease and malnutrition. At Flowers Cove, for example, Currant organized the regular provision of "milk and cocoa for children all along the bay," and she initiated "Agricultural Shows" to stimulate interest in gardening.[9] Certainly, such endeavours held clear benefits for the local people. But not all of nurses' reform endeavours were as neutral as free milk and improved vegetable growing. Indeed, nurses' social work often reflected their own cultural backgrounds. It should be remembered that most of the Grenfell nurses were a foreign presence in northern Newfoundland and Labrador. And although the local people they sought to help were, for the most part, of the same race as the nurses themselves, they were clearly different.[10] Confronting this difference, nurses, like other foreign Mission workers, often saw themselves as a culturally superior, "civilizing" force in a remote and "backwards" corner of the British Empire. Hence, the social work that kept Grenfell nurses so busy was often influenced by a distinct lack of respect for the region's people and way of life.

A prominent strain of this theme was nurses' tendency to blame local people for their poverty or illness. Upon her arrival in Englee in 1936, one of the first things Ethel Currant noted was "the awful poverty and the utter helplessness of many of the people."[11] Over the course of her stay, Currant often reiterated the idea that a lack of local effort was partly to blame for desperate living conditions. In fact, when it came to making the best of available resources, Nurse Currant ranked the local people abysmally. As she concluded, "sadly, one must acknowledge they are thriftless," since "many a farmer in other parts of the British Empire makes good on less than these people have."[12] And her criticism was not limited to inferior farming. Ethel Currant reserved special blame for the local women, citing substandard domestic management and child rearing as chief causes of the region's woes. In doing so, she was in accord with contemporary reform movements in western Europe and North America that placed great emphasis on women's traditional roles as mothers and housekeepers. As one writer put it, by the turn of the century "women did not merely have babies … through their child rearing they helped or hindered the forward march of [Anglo-Saxon] civilization."[13] Ensuring that mothers aided the development of a "grander, nobler, race" was the objective of reformers who attempted to impose a cultural and class-specific vision of ideal womanhood upon groups – like the working class and immigrant communities – that did not measure up to middle-class standards.[14]

Ethel Currant, like many other Grenfell nurses, was well-steeped in these reform currents. In 1939 she wrote, "I am more and more convinced that the women in the north make or mar the home." And according to Nurse Currant, there were more local women "marring" than "making" the region's homes. "In all my home visiting the thing that impresses me most is the complete lack of ordinary house cleanliness," she declared.[15] Currant did not see domestic filth as an unavoidable consequence of poverty, but rather as the unnecessary result of local women's pathetic efforts. As proof, she offered the example of one home where, despite the presence of six female family members, the extreme squalor was an affront to British, middle-class standards. As she wrote, "I spent two nights there and had several meals … it was almost too much for me. Poverty can inspire one but when accompanied with such an abundance of dirt one becomes somewhat paralysed."[16] On another occasion, Currant was appalled to discover that the local girls hired as domestic servants at the Flowers Cove station were "running amuck with free access to the stores." The result – "two months of butter used up in 5 weeks!" – was, for Currant, a shocking violation of middle-class domestic management. In this case, Currant advocated "a change of maid to begin with," and in the long term, the establishment of domestic science classes to train local girls from an early age. Currant was hopeful that these classes might "make the foundation for … good homes."[17]

The lack of respect for local people in general, and for local women in particular, recurs throughout letters from Ethel Currant's tenure with the Grenfell Mission. At times, she mocked their style of furniture, deemed them intellectually incapable of sarcasm, and, on a bad day, referred to them as "abominable creatures."[18] While the latter may be an extreme example, denigration of the local people and their way of life was certainly not the prerogative of Ethel Currant. Indeed, it was a prominent theme among the foreign nurses at the Grenfell Mission between 1894 and 1938. Gendered and class-bound assumptions of superiority stemmed both from the nurses' own cultural backgrounds and from the mission's "civilizing" agenda. Pointing out these problematic aspects of Grenfell nursing is not meant to deny that

Ethel Currant's service with the Grenfell Mission was admirable in many ways. Taken together, the wide range of duties, high degree of isolated independence, and unusual level of outdoor adventure suggest an exceptional female work experience worthy of applause.

Certainly, it was a work experience that Ethel Currant cherished for the rest of her life. Leaving the mission in 1946, she worked at the Central Sanatorium in Calgary, Alberta, and after marrying in Battleford, Saskatchewan, she moved to Victoria, British Columbia. Wherever she was, Ethel Currant maintained active connections with the Grenfell Mission, corresponding and visiting with former co-workers and giving lectures on her experiences to local church and community groups. Several years before her death in 1974, Ethel Currant received a special award from the St John Ambulance Society, and she was the subject of a feature interview in a Victoria newspaper.[19]

In sum, Ethel Currant, like so many other Grenfell nurses, was a remarkable women. At a time when options for female employment were relatively limited, Grenfell nursing was, undeniably, an exceptional work opportunity for adventurous women. But it is important to balance our admiration against a critical view of nurses' social work. As this portrait of Ethel Currant suggests, the exceptional female work experience was founded on some problematic assumptions about the local people the nurses were there to help.

62 Vera Peters: Medical Innovator

J. Catton and P. Catton

Mildred Vera Peters revolutionized the treatment of breast cancer and Hodgkin's disease, and left behind a legacy in the study of cancer that few others have equalled. Her accomplishments seem even more impressive when one considers that her landmark studies were conducted in the 1940s and 1950s. During this period, the medical community had strict ideas about the "correct" treatment of cancer, and these long-established practices were at odds with her new ideas. Furthermore, as one of the few women oncologists of her time, Dr Peters had to work particularly hard in order for her discoveries to win widespread acceptance in a profession dominated by men. Although the road to success had many barriers, her relentless pursuit of truth, innovative work, and compassion for others laid the foundations for newer and better treatments in the fight against breast cancer and Hodgkin's disease, and established a more humane approach to patient care in the management of these diseases.

Born on 28 April 1911, Vera Peters was one of seven children raised in a little farmhouse in what is now the Toronto suburb of Rexdale. Her early education was in a one-room schoolhouse in Thistletown, a location that is currently the site of the Woodbine race track. An excellent student, she completed all the grades in as little time as possible.[1] At the age of sixteen she had finished high school, but she was too young to be accepted into the Faculty of Medicine, so she enrolled at the University of Toronto to study mathematics and physics. The follow-ing year she transferred to the Faculty of Medicine, hoping the admissions board would not check her age. Fortunately for her, no one did. Between studying for school and playing inter-faculty women's hockey, she worked to earn her tuition money by waiting tables on the ss *Kingston* in the summer, a tourist ship that conducted two-day cruises on Lake Ontario. There she met her future husband, Ken Lobb (whom she married in 1937).[2] She graduated from medical school in 1934.

For two years after her graduation, she trained as a surgical resident at St John's Hospital, where she studied surgical anatomy and newly diagnosed cancers. In 1936 she met Dr Gordon Richards, a pioneer radiation oncologist (radiation oncology is a specialty that involves the use of radiation to treat cancer) and director of the Department of Radiation Oncology at the Toronto General Hospital. At the time, he was the physician who was treating her mother for breast cancer. This chance encounter with Dr Richards would prove to be one of the most important influences in her life, one that encouraged her to study Hodgkin's disease and breast cancer more intensively.[3] Dr Richards was impressed with her determination to learn all she could about the science of radiology. He soon noted not only that she was an excellent clinician, but that she also had the analytical mind and intellectual tenacity of a true researcher. As there was no formal certification in radiation oncology in the 1930s, Dr Peters underwent a kind of personal apprenticeship in radiation oncology under the tutelage of Dr Richards.

At this time, Hodgkin's disease was not considered curable. Until the discovery of X-rays in 1895, little could be done for Hodgkin's patients other than the surgical removal of the affected region in the hope that it would stop the cancer from spreading. Dr Richards had been following the work of Dr René Gilbert of Switzerland, a physician who was experimenting with new treatments for Hodgkin's disease, using stronger and better-directed doses of X-rays. Dr Richards felt that positive results were attainable with this method. Therefore, in 1947 he asked Dr Peters to check all his records of patients treated for Hodgkin's disease and to note things such as the number of treatments each patient had received, the X-ray dosage, survival time, side-effects resulting from radiation, and any other pertinent details. This enormous task took her two years to complete and covered the results of 247 patients treated over a period of twenty years.[4] When Dr Peters presented her study in a staff meeting in 1949, the results were unmistakable: aggressive radiotherapy increased the survival rate of patients with Hodgkin's disease.

In 1950 (the year after Dr Richards died, most probably from radiation-induced leukemia), Dr Peters published her study of Dr Richards's work on Hodgkin's disease. The paper, which became a medical classic, described the effects of aggressive radiotherapy on Hodgkin's patients in Toronto since 1935, showing for the first time that some cases of the disease could be cured. This first publication was greeted initially with a lukewarm response, but a second paper in 1956 aroused great interest. Cancer centres had begun to review their Hodgkin's cases and discovered that they were not treating the disease aggressively enough.[5] By the early 1960s, Dr Peters's conclusions were vindicated as doctors and specialists in all disciplines undertook many more studies based on her observations. As the number of cases increased, Dr Peters was able to define representative patterns of the disease within each stage. This allowed

therapy to be individualized more effectively, and thus a higher cure rate was achieved. Today, thanks in large part to Dr Peters's ground-breaking work, the cure rate for Hodgkin's disease has reached over 90 per cent.

Even before her involvement with Hodgkin's disease, Dr Peters had an avid interest in breast cancer, an interest that was no doubt prompted by her mother's death from the disease. In 1935 the prevailing wisdom was to treat most breast cancers with radical mastectomies (that is, the removal of the cancerous breast) and post-operative radiation. Dr Peters believed that radical surgery in the treatment of breast cancer was excessive in most cases and that a moderate approach was a more effective way to manage the disease. In 1953 she collaborated with a group of radiation oncologists and surgeons at the Toronto General Hospital, and together they assembled sufficient evidence to seriously question radical mastectomy as the only treatment option for breast cancer. Soon she acquired a reputation as a specialist in breast cancer who favoured minimally invasive treatments. As a result, other physicians referred patients to her, especially those women who refused to consent to a mastectomy. After a period of treating these women with radiotherapy following a lumpectomy (that is, the removal of the cancerous lump), Dr Peters sensed that these patients were doing quite well. Based on this observation, she studied all eight thousand of her breast cancer patients from 1935 to 1960 who had had lumpectomies followed by post-operative radiation. She meticulously matched the results of her patients to those of women who had radical surgery, and she discovered that the lumpectomy and radiation group achieved a similar success rate.[6] While the paper she wrote on the subject caused quite a sensation, her findings were again met with scepticism. However, her conclusions ultimately prevailed, and today her insights into disease control and quality-of-life issues are incorporated into the study of breast cancer.

Dr Peters's patient care philosophy was as unique as her innovative studies on cancer. In an age when surgery ruled as the only option in most cancer cases, she discouraged the use of invasive treatments in favour of those that established a greater physical and emotional harmony in the patient. She always believed that the patient played an important role in controlling the progress of the disease, and the stress from chronic emotional tension and traumatic surgery could seriously weaken the body's natural ability to combat cancer. For this reason, Dr Peters advocated a calm, deliberate approach, one that reduced stress by involving as little intervention as possible while still providing effective treatment. She asserted that hasty treatment decisions did not alter prognosis and that a delay of a few weeks after diagnosis gave patients time to deal with their anxiety more constructively. Breast cancer patients, for example, have been shown to fear the loss of pride and self-respect, a diminished personal appearance, and the possible segregation from family and friends. Accordingly, time should be allotted for them to voice their fears and to receive kindly communication from the physician.[7] Above all, Dr Peters recognized that patients had a right to honest information about their situation: the right to seek consultation, to fully understand treatment, to know treatment alternatives, to know treatment ramifications, and to help with treatment decisions.

Vera Peters's unwavering commitment to find a cure for cancer has earned her world-wide acclaim throughout the oncology community. In recognition of her achievements, many honours and awards were conferred upon her. In 1978 she was made an officer of the Order of Canada. In 1979 she was awarded the highest honour offered by her specialty in the United States: the gold medal of the American Society for Therapeutic Radiology and Oncology. She also received the Medaille Antoinne Beclere (1979), the Canadian Breast Cancer Foundation's Profes-

sional Woman of Distinction Award (1988), the R.M Taylor Medal of the National Cancer Institute of Canada and the Canadian Cancer Society, and honorary doctorates from York and Queen's Universities.[8]

In 1976 Vera Peters retired as a senior radiation oncologist at Toronto's Princess Margaret Hospital, where she had been a founding member of the medical staff when the hospital first opened in 1958. After retirement until 1988 she practised as a consultant oncologist at the Oakville Trafalgar Memorial Hospital, responding to consultations from around the world. She died (of breast cancer) on 1 October 1993 at the age of eighty-two.

Dr Peters's legacy of personal and professional excellence has deeply touched those with whom she was associated. Her patients will never forget her sympathetic concern, friendship, and the confidence she imparted while sharing the burden of cancer and its therapy. Her colleagues will always regard her as a consummate clinician and scientist: an insightful listener and observer with an intuitive understanding of cancer and its appropriate treatment. The scientific community around the world will always consider her a pioneer in the study of breast cancer and Hodgkin's disease, one who expanded the frontiers of science, whose dedication and resolve were an inspiration to a generation of women oncologists who followed in her footsteps. Above all, she will be remembered by her family as a devoted wife and mother, someone who seamlessly integrated the often incompatible roles of a full-time professional, wife, and mother at a time when it was not fashionable for women to do so. Despite her many career demands, she always found time for those closest to her: making jam and mending clothes for her children and grandchildren, driving her daughters to music lessons, attending football games with her husband, playing bridge with her friends, and travelling with her family to their cottage at Sunridge.

63 Norah Toole: Scientist and Social Activist

Marianne Gosztonyi Ainley

Norah Vernon Barry, second daughter of Elma Jarvis and Vernon Barry, was born on 29 April 1906, at Smith Falls, Ontario.[1] Her father was a bank manager and the family moved around. Norah attended various schools in Quebec and graduated from the Montreal High School for Girls in 1925. She was interested in sports in addition to a variety of subjects, and decided to study science because she was a poor speller and her parents never told her that science was not a field for a girl. Living in Montreal, it was natural that she enter McGill University, where women had obtained higher education for more than forty years. It is not known why she chose chemistry rather than physics or biology, but she entered the program in 1925 and graduated with a BSc four years later. While at McGill, she met and fell in love with Frank (Francis) Toole (1894–1975), a chemical engineer who returned to university after the First World War to obtain a doctorate in chemistry. After graduation Norah worked as a laboratory technician at the Royal Victoria Hospital for a year, then taught chemistry at the Montreal High School for Girls. In 1934 she married Frank Toole and moved to Fredericton, where her husband taught chemistry at the University of New Brunswick (UNB).

In the mid-1930s, during the height of the Depression, few married women had paid positions. As there were no professional opportunities available for a young faculty wife in Fredericton, Norah took an active part in a collegial circle of UNB professors and their families.

Frank Toole was gregarious and musical and the Tooles did a lot of entertaining. But Norah was unwilling to give up her scientific training, and like many other women married to scientists, she helped her husband with his work. As his unpaid assistant, she helped him mark student exams and clean up the chemistry laboratory. She also acted as an unpaid instructor in chemistry during the summers of 1934 and 1935. It was only during the Second World War, when there was a shortage of (male) scientific personnel, that she obtained her first paid position since her marriage. In 1942 she was hired as a "regular" laboratory instructor in chemistry.

When Norah Toole took up paid employment, she was already the mother of two children (Barry, 1936, and Brigid, 1938) and, like many other women, was fully engaged in contributing to the war effort. She was a member of the newly formed Women's Study Club, which discussed current international affairs, and she helped run a canteen on the UNB campus for army personnel. During this busy period, she also gave talks on being a working woman that were broadcast on CBC Radio's *Trans Canada Matinée*.

With the return of veterans, Norah's workload increased and for a while she taught classes three days and three nights per week. She also continued her involvement with the Women's Study Club and campaigned for women's right to vote in municipal elections, even if they did not own property. She became the first chairperson of the Citizenship Committee of the newly established Fredericton Council of Women. In order to help new Canadians from war-torn Europe, she surveyed existing services and in the process found that the "oldest Canadians" – that is, Canada's First Nations – had little access to social services. This discovery prompted her to organize the Indian/non-Indian Goodwill Association. With other women, she visited various reserves, including the local Malecite one. There, she encouraged the formation of a home and school association and was instrumental in establishing a kindergarten and summer arts program for the children. In later years she actively supported non-status women in their fight to regain their Indian status.

Norah's awareness of racism in Canadian society, combined with her concern and compassion for people, particularly for marginalized ones, led to her increased involvement on the local and provincial levels. In 1946 she was elected to the Board of Directors of the local Young Men's/Young Women's Christian Association (YM/YWCA). In the late 1940s she became the chair of the United Nations Committee of the New Brunswick Home and School Association. She carried on all these activities in addition to being a full time, underpaid, laboratory instructor at UNB.

In 1960 Norah Toole joined a new Canadian peace organization, the Voice of Women. She served as its national vice-president and provincial representative and, in 1966, formed the Fredericton branch of this national organization. The woman who had worked so hard for the war effort twenty years earlier had become a peace activist and feminist. She now campaigned against Canadian policies in support of the war in Vietnam, such as supplying weapons to the United States. Her dislike of public demonstrations never stopped her from taking part in them. She attended countless protests for peace and human justice, believing that demonstrations raise the public's awareness of a cause.

Norah Toole did not publish scientific papers, made

63.1 Norah Toole (Provincial Archives of New Brunswick)

no scientific discoveries, and won no prizes for her scientific work. Nevertheless, as a well-known figure on the University of New Brunswick campus, in the city of Fredericton, and in the surrounding district, she had a major impact on countless numbers of science students. In spite of this, when she retired from UNB in 1971, after nearly thirty years of paid work there, it was without a personal pension. She did not, however, retire from public life. She continued her activism for peace, women's rights, human rights, and the environment until her sudden death on 27 May 1990. Although she never sought honours, Norah Toole's work was recognized by many people and organizations. In 1984 she received the Persons Award from Governor General Jeanne Sauvé. Five years later, the University of New Brunswick conferred on her an honorary doctor of laws degree.

During her long and active life, Norah Toole touched the lives of her students, original and new Canadians, and women and men of all ages. She had friends among the disenfranchised and poor, as well as among the famous and wealthy. As a science instructor she supported all her students, but she took it as her personal mandate to mentor female science students. As a concerned citizen she fought tirelessly for equality, peace, and justice. "She made things happen," her daughter Brigid recalled. "She was a catalyst."

64 Alice V. Payne, Mining Geologist:
A Lifetime of "Small and Difficult Things"

E. Tina Crossfield

Alice Payne's enthusiasm for geology is contagious. Her solid handshake and tall stature speak volumes about a lifetime of doing what she describes as "small and difficult things that add up to quite a lot."[1] She attributes her early success to her father, Thomas Payne, prospector and part owner of Ryan Gold Mines in Yellowknife, Northwest Territories, and a pioneer in northern exploration. He encouraged his brilliant young daughter to join him on field trips, listen in on his business deals, and, later, embark on a university program that attracted very few women. Lacking female mentors and colleagues, she was the only female in her graduating class of 1962 at the University of Alberta. Like most women scientists of her era, she would face rigid barriers in university and industry throughout her career.[2]

The eldest of three children, Alice was born in Edmonton, Alberta, in 1940. She spent much of her youth in Yellowknife, a thriving resource-based town heavily dependent on the mining and outfitting businesses. The Paynes owned a rustic cottage on the outskirts of town, and every summer Alice and her father would prospect for minerals and supervise the work at their gold mine. During this time, her mother, Olga, who worked as a nurse, remained in Edmonton with the rest of the family. Although she supported her daughter's unconventional interests, she would have preferred if Alice had chosen a less rugged occupation. When it came to finishing high school, her parents sent her to a female boarding school in Toronto to learn the art of

becoming "a proper lady." Alice recalled that the experience "teaches you to conform to the rules, but it is hard and unloving."

After graduation, Alice was free to return to Edmonton and enrol in university, where she found the curriculum somewhat disappointing: "I wanted to do geology, but I couldn't believe they weren't talking about mining. I thought lesson one would be how to find a mine or how to drill an oil well." The second problem involved university policy towards women and field trips, which did not change until the 1970s. Alice recalls that at the University of Alberta in the mid-1960s her request to participate on an important outing was flatly denied. When she persisted and found her own means for travel and accommodation, she was told to drop the subject if she ever expected to graduate.

This was particularly exasperating because fieldwork gave geologists the credibility they needed to find gainful employment. Although some science disciplines, like biology, were starting to place more emphasis on laboratory work in the 1950s, in geology, fieldwork was the foundation of the profession. In other words, even sophisticated analyses were considered secondary activities. Most women geologists were confined to the lab as "glorified technicians and assistants" while their more experienced male colleagues did the higher-level interpretative work for better wages.[3]

Underground experience for women geologists was even more difficult to obtain. Because mining was regarded as too dangerous an environment for women, protective legislation barring them from working underground was first introduced in the 1930s and remained in effect until the mid-1970s.[4] Historically, women were thought to bring bad luck underground, and men have refused to work their shifts if women were present. Although there was no real basis to the centuries-old myth, there was a correlation between mine accidents and arguments over female co-workers, and some miners' wives objected because they feared for the physical safety of their husbands. Companies that wished to hire women faced additional obstacles, such as the lack of proper clothing or clean-up facilities. As in government institutions, most women employed in the mining industry were technicians, office assistants, librarians, data collectors, core sample analysts, or vehicle operators.[5]

Yet some women were able to circumvent the rules and go underground despite the legalities of the times. When Alice asked her father if she could see the Cominco mines in 1958, he badgered the company until they relented. "When the bosses saw that the mine didn't collapse after they let a woman in, then I could go down anytime I liked." She still recalls her first time underground with passion and excitement: "I couldn't wait! I was amazed. I couldn't tell how these guys could figure their way around. They ran me up and down two hundred–foot ladders and I didn't fade out. I put on the miner's outfit, the hat and boots, and I never had any problem after that. So now I know what vein gold looks like underground. It looks quite different than what people may think."[6]

For the budding geologist, the importance of going underground was akin to doing fieldwork. After securing her BSC in 1962, Alice joined the Geological Survey of Canada with the intention of going into the field. When they refused, she resigned. "As soon as I found out my job was in the lab, I didn't last very long. I really enjoyed

chemistry and I was good at it, but it was a means to an end, not *the end*!" This experience convinced her to obtain a master's degree, certain that policies would soon change. However, despite graduating in 1965 with an MSC, she never was able to obtain the desired experience. Alice recalls: "You would have a very hard time being a mine geologist if you couldn't go underground. You make the call whether or not to keep drilling, and the mine will go broke if you choose the wrong place." After her father died in 1966, Alice helped to maintain the productivity of Ryan Gold Mines for more than fifteen years by following her instincts and using her knowledge.

By the late 1960s, the restrictions on female students had eased somewhat with changing social norms. Throughout the decade, second-wave feminists had struggled for gender equality, and more and more married women with and without children were participating in the labour force. Geological field trips gradually became available to women, and graduates found limited success in securing jobs outside the laboratory or library. However, the competition for jobs was steep, and many employers sought geologists with ten years of experience. It took another decade before women could acquire the "right credentials" and the government would amend the working rules. Well into the 1970s, the Geological Survey of Canada prohibited women from doing fieldwork, even though petroleum geology and the oil industry were rapidly expanding with the "energy crisis" and there was a shortage of male scientists.[7] Private companies, like Shell, were no exception.

As a practising geologist, Alice found life a constant challenge. Married with two small children by 1969, she planned to stay home as much as possible, but to work during the day when her children entered public school. Realizing that she needed to stay connected to her profession, she found piecemeal projects lasting three or four months each. She often worked for the university, bringing her babies to the lab with her in the evenings or on weekends. "I'd be slicing up rocks and doing thin sections – doing all the little jobs I could hire. My former professor was very kind. He let me write research papers and obtain some scientific credit … but it was tough – it's very hard to concentrate with a howling child in the background." Her strategy paid off because after five years, and relocation to Ottawa, she was still in contention.

Alice returned to Edmonton in 1975, and two years later became a single mother with few personal resources when her marriage ended in divorce. After working with a geological consulting firm, she was hired in 1979 by Gulf Canada in Calgary as an exploration geologist. The transition from hardrock mining to petroleum was demanding: "I didn't know how they did things in the oil business so I kept on doing things the mining way. But I had to learn how to look at soft rock and I spent many nights and evenings studying old textbooks. I was already thirty-nine, and I thought, here are all these people with thirty years of experience and I've only got two years to catch up." Her geology training, however, would not be neglected.

Alice brought a fresh approach to the search for oil and gas by using less traditional exploration methods. She found new wells that had been dismissed by colleagues who had specialized solely in petroleum geology and had interpreted them differently. These successes placed her career back on a solid footing, and Gulf Canada eventually promoted her to first-line supervisor, a rare position for a woman. Finally earning a decent salary, she continued to expand on her knowledge, travelling to Colorado to study ancient sandstones, to the Washington coast for modern sand deposits, and to Florida and the Bahamas for lessons on carbonate reefs. In the interim, a new and happier marriage enhanced her family life.

Cultivating a new circle of friends and associates, she joined the Canadian Institute of Mining, Metallurgy, and Petroleum (CIM), the Geological Association of Canada, and the Canadian Society of Petroleum Geologists (CSPG), becoming the first female president of the latter in 1992. She was director of the Calgary Science Centre from 1995 to 1997 and is currently a member of council of the Association of Professional Engineers, Geologists, and Geophysicists of Alberta (APEGGA). A regular at meetings of the Association of Women in Engineering and Science, she continues to address elementary and junior high school students, where she promotes the study of earth sciences. "My aim in life is to set a good example for people. When I was young, I just wanted to go out and find a mine and carry the canoe through the bushes. Now I want all the young women in the world to consider geology as a career – to go after non-traditional things and not be scared off."

Alice Payne retired from Gulf Canada in 1995 but remains active in both her career and the community. Although the tributes for her accomplishments are numerous, she retains a modest, no-nonsense approach to life. Among her honours are the CSPG President's Award in 1996, a member of the Order of Canada in 1997, and the YWCA of Calgary's Women of Distinction for Science, Technology and the Environment in 1998. In addition, Alberta Venture has named her one of Alberta's "50 Most Influential People."[8] Recently, she has authored a biography of her father, Tom Payne, to whom she attributes much of her vitality and spunk: "I never seriously thought I would starve to death doing geology. I could always take my can of beans and go prospecting."[9] Little did she know then that she would be helping to clear the path for the next generation of women.

65 A Case Study of an Oral History Project

As noted in the general introduction, a number of contributions to this volume present oral histories or descriptions of oral history projects. Here we draw attention to a case study by Wilma MacDonald based on an oral history project organized by Shirley Peruniak. Several of the themes in this study echo those outlined in the introduction to Part 5 by Wendy Mitchinson (#56). This vignette briefly outlines how Peruniak created an extensive public resource based on her personal collection of oral histories. In particular, her recordings have preserved the experiences of people whose life stories rarely appear in written documents – women and aboriginal peoples. Moreover, this oral history project demonstrates the role that photographic images can play in assisting interviewees to recall details and circumstances that they otherwise might not have remembered. As well, this study serves as an example of what Mitchinson describes as "the belief in the need to give back to society." This project undertaken by Peruniak exemplifies that sense of responsibility.

Shirley Peruniak: Naturalist, Historian, Quetico Provincial Park Interpreter

Wilma MacDonald

Shirley Peruniak has made an important contribution to the history and understanding of the northwestern area of Ontario known as Quetico Provincial Park. Since 1973, she has been working with the interpretive program of the Ministry of Natural Resources at Quetico interviewing park wardens and rangers, lands and forest management employees, conservation officers, Ojibwa elders and young people, canoeists and campers. Peruniak's collection of interviews and photographs form part of Quetico's Oral History Project, which is stored in the John B. Ridley Research Library at Quetico's Interpretive Centre.[1]

Established as a forest and game reserve in 1909 and as a provincial park in 1913, Quetico has a history reaching back nine thousand years to the time of the earliest aboriginal peoples. Its land area lies along a major early trading route, northwest of Lake Superior, which was historically used by Native peoples and later by the fur traders. The melting glaciers left a maze of lakes and rivers, best known to the Ojibwa people native to the area and in more recent history to canoeists who come to Quetico to enjoy the wilderness experience while

65.1 Tempest Powell Benson, with a lynx, c. 1930 (Courtesy of Wilma MacDonald)

learning more about the original inhabitants of the land in the centre of the North American continent. The Interpretive Centre is located fifty kilometres east of Atikokan, Ontario.

In 1973, when Peruniak began working in the interpretive program, she set out with conservation officers, park rangers, and friends by truck and canoe to interview anyone who had known the park in its earlier days. The resultant recorded interviews, transcripts, and historical photographs and slides have all been deposited in the John B. Ridley Research Library at Quetico, which also houses the Quetico Archives. The library has three large catalogue databases: one for books and reports, containing 2,100 items on various topics, including specific and general reference materials; a second database for the library's periodicals; and a third, visual, database containing a total of more than 12,500 photographs and slides, all scanned, catalogued, and indexed. Peruniak's method of using old photographs to elicit memories about people and events in and around Quetico Park aided her information gathering. In turn, her oral history interviewing has led to the acquisition of additional archival records, such as family and historical photographs, for long-term preservation. The unpublished documentation collected by Quetico Park's naturalists and interpreters over the years, and especially by Shirley Peruniak, has been used to compile a series of historical albums to document the history of the park area from the 1880s to the 1980s. Arranged chronologically, these albums include excerpts from transcribed interviews, newspaper clippings, and photographs.

In the early days of Quetico Park, women were not employed directly as members of the park staff (this did not occur until the 1970s); nevertheless, a record of generations of aboriginal women and of the wives, daughters, and sisters of rangers and superintendents may be found among the stories, photographs, and biographical material collected by Peruniak. In some cases, the interviews are in Ojibwa, the result of grandchildren interviewing their grandparents; the work of translating these recordings remains to be carried out.

Much of the material in the John B. Ridley Research Library is in an unpublished form. The following extract, for example, is from Peruniak's interview with Dinnah Madsen of Saganaga Lake.[2] Her husband, Art Madsen, was a park ranger at Quetico during the 1920s and 1930s. The oral testimony provides a rare glimpse into the life of a ranger's wife. Dinnah Madsen tells of an experience she had at Ottertrack looking after a friend's daughter one winter. They lived in a tent made of logs and canvas and and had to constantly replenish the wood supply to feed the continually burning "air tight" stove. Madsen's stamina and sense of survival and good humour come across in the following transcription:

I didn't wait until the woodpile was gone … we'd tramp this trail for the toboggan – go down the lake about a mile, mile and a half, and we had to go up this big hill and there was a cliff on the other side of the hill. So after doing this for about a week, I figured, well you know, I've got to save my energy because I didn't have that much energy to be cutting wood every single day and … so this one day, I said: "Okay Bonnie, I'm going to throw the logs over the end of the cliff down to the lake so we don't have to haul them way down this trail." So, I just left the toboggan down there and … I threw all the logs down and I thought "I'm not going to walk way around that trail – I'm going to slide right down." There's all this nice snow you know – it was a beautiful chute down there so I just slid down this cliff and I kept right on going, under the ice. So I just threw myself forward when I got to my waist – man was I scared and it was plenty cold then. So I got out of there and Bonnie was just screaming … we put the logs on the toboggan as cold as I was and tied them on there and took them back to camp there and I changed right away. I never even got a cold out of it.

Tempest Powell Benson (Illustration 65.1) raised three daughters while trapping and living in the bush (Illustraion 65.2).[3] Benson snowshoed long distances during winter in the 1930s to haul out furs from the traplines. Art Madsen admired the fact that, in a vast area with some twenty-five-mile hauls, "the rest of us were dragging and [Tempest] she'd still be going … She would take a steady pace and never let up." Tempest, along with her daughter Janette, also delivered mail with a dog-team.

In her interviews, Tempest talked to Peruniak of her youth and of a succession of pet animals, including moose, deer, fox, beaver, and wolf pups. In one instance, Tempest recounted her unsuccessful attempt to have her pet moose assist along the trapline. She made a pack harness out of canvas and put it on the moose. "Well, she [the

moose] was going along real nice with all this beaver and stuff she had in her pack when something scared her and she took off. (Laughter) We lost all of the beaver skins. Took us five days to find the beaver skins … what we could find and he [her father] was so upset. They wouldn't even let me have the moose inside after that."

In addition to helping to preserve Quetico Park history, Peruniak has been working since the late 1970s with Lac LaCroix First Nations' students, under a Lac LaCroix band council resolution, assembling documentation to preserve some of the Ojibwa history, beginning with Treaty No. 3 in 1873 to more recent times. A thirteen-volume set of these materials, including the recorded interviews of many Ojibwa elders by their grandchildren and translations of Ojibwa by LaCroix students, has been placed in the Lac LaCroix School Library adjacent to the park for use by aboriginal students learning more about their Ojibwa roots. Peruniak is a natural teacher and a nuturing naturalist, attracting a wide range of friends and fellow enthusiasts. Her work has fostered better understanding among cultures that share a common land. In 1998, in recognition of her accomplishments, Peruniak was awarded the third annual Shan Walshe Award for Excellence in Interpretation in Ontario's Provincial Parks.

65.2 Tempest Powell Benson's daughters with beaver pelts
(Courtesy of Wilma MacDonald)

PART SIX

Earning Their Bread

66 Introduction

A.B. McCullough

Work – what it is, who did it, what it meant, and how it was done – has intrigued women's historians. In fact, the study of women and work constitutes the largest sub-field within Canadian women's history. In the 1970s scholars focused on occupational gender segregation and wage disparities. They began with the decades of urbanization and industrialization from 1880 to 1920 and then expanded their studies to include earlier and later periods. They also looked at the feminization of certain industries (teaching and clerical work) and the masculinization of others (dairying). Women's history has had close links with labour history for some time but the history of female entrepreneurs is only beginning to emerge and that of rural women, initially neglected is now recognized as an important field. There is also a substantial body of research on women in some of the resource industries, notably the fur trade and fishing. Housework, the largest field of women's work, remains relatively ignored.

Within the recent past, work was commonly taken to mean "employment, especially as a means of earning money."[1] With a few exceptions, only those who received a wage or who produced goods and services for sale were described as having an occupation.[2] Housekeepers and servants, people who did family and household work for pay, were identified as having an occupation.[3] The unpaid work that women did was made invisible by being categorized as unproductive. Elizabeth Fox-Genovese observed that under the capitalist system the labour expended in producing a loaf of Wonder Bread was productive labour while the labour of producing a home-made loaf was unproductive.[5]

Feminists and women's historians reject this economic definition of work primarily because it ignored the areas – the home and voluntary organizations – where historically women have been most active. The feminist analysis argues that housework, home maintenance, the bearing and care of children, and the care of the aged, the ill, and the employed within the home, as well as the voluntary labour that goes into building and maintaining a community, are essential tasks and as important as those for which people are paid, and should be included within the definition of work. The decision by Statistics Canada to include a survey of unpaid work in the 1996 census is an indication that this point of view is winning wider acceptance.

In considering the working experience of Canadian women, one must keep three sets of statistics in mind. First, until the last third of the twentieth century, most adult women were not part of the paid labour force. In 1901, 86 per cent of adult women were not in the labour force; in 1998, 42 per cent of adult women remained outside of the labour force; the comparable figure for men in 1998 was 28 per cent.[5] Secondly, throughout the century, about 60 per cent of women were married.[6] The first and second points are linked because, especially in the first half of the century, women who were officially in the paid labour force usually left it when they married.

66.1 Mrs Moorhouse doing laundry, 1920 (C 231-1-0-1-139, Archives of Ontario)

It was not until 1980–81 that a majority of married women were in the labour force.[7] Thirdly, until 1921 Canada was primarily a rural country; urban women first outnumbered rural women in 1921.[8] At the beginning of the century, most adult Canadian women lived and worked in the context of a rural, married life, and most did not work for pay during a large part of their lives. By the end of the century, most women lived in urban areas and worked for pay during much of their married lives.

Traditionally, women have done work that was compatible with, or that involved, the care of children. This was work that did not place children in danger, could be easily interrupted, and did not require women to go far from home. It involved a wide range of activities, including housework (cleaning, cooking, sewing, managing subordinate labour, and managing a family budget), the reproduction and care of dependent children (pregnancy and the upbringing of children), the care of working adults (ensuring that they remained "productive" members of society), and the care of dependent adults.[9] Most women worked alone or with the help of immediate family; a minority employed servants. Visual documentation of women's domestic labour is difficult to find for two reasons: first, the subject matter has not been considered worthy for photographers, to capture since photography, an expensive hobby, was typically used to document wealthier people. In domestic scenes with such clients, families appear with no domestic help in evidence. Secondly, archives have not generally chosen to acquire collections with such images in them. Photographs such as Illustration 66.1, which shows Mrs Moorhouse putting out the laundry, are thus rare.

For rural women, work inside the home was usually supplemented by outdoor yard work and some field work. Typically, women had primary responsibility for gardens and smaller animals, notably poultry, and often dairy cattle. Illustration 66.2 shows a farmer feeding her chickens near Edmonton in 1920. In fishing communities, women were often responsible for processing the fish that men caught. The Japanese women in Illustration 66.3 were employed by a canning factory in British Columbia and stood through entire shifts with their babies on their backs. In Illustration 66.4, Haida women also stand stationery while performing the arduous work of shelling and peeling crab. Marion Wright's essay (#69) discusses the many contributions made by women in the Newfoundland fishery. Men as a rule were responsible for much of the heavier outdoor work, but women often served as an auxiliary labour force during harvest or periods when the men were away working in the fur trade, in the forests, fishing, on railway construction, or in the army. Women also often endured hard physical labour as housebuilders (Illustration 66.5), packers, and carriers (note the fatigue on the women's faces in Illustration 66.6).

66.2 Woman feeding chickens, 1920 (C 64815, National Archives of Canada)

Top:

66.3 Women and babies in cannery,
Richmond, B.C., 1913
(E-05041, British Columbia Archives)

Right:

66.4 Haida women in cannery
(F 884, Archives of Ontario)

Although women might assist in field work or, much more rarely, men might assist with housework, most people accepted a division of work along gender lines. The separation between men and women's work became more defined in the nineteenth and early twentieth centuries as men turned more and more to wage labour, which took them away from the home during the working day.

Unpaid tasks within the home occupied most women, most of the time, but many women worked in the waged economy for at least a part of their lives. Most commonly, young women worked for a few years between childhood and marriage. Widowhood, desertion, or the incapacity of a husband sometimes forced women to find paid work. At the beginning of the twentieth century, domestic service, sewing, and teaching were the most common paid occupations for women. All three allowed women to earn an income from services that wives and mothers provided for free in the home.

Domestic service was by far the most important source of paid employment for women well into the twentieth century. It was not always a popular job choice: the hours were long, pay was low, and for live-in servants, privacy was non-existent. Many women were driven to service by poverty and escaped it if they could. Numerically, service was dominated by young women and girls (some not yet in their teens) who went into service for a time prior to marriage and, to a lesser extent, by older women, often widows. The study of a domestic servant presented in vignette #67 makes it clear that some women sought this type of work during both periods of their lives when they were single. Further, the woman in this profile professes to having enjoyed the work, finding acceptance in the host family or among her domestic peers that was otherwise denied her. In the twentieth century, from a third to a fifth of female domestic servants were immigrants, encouraged in this decision to emigrate through a vigorous government recruitment program, as Ellen Schein-

66.5 Doukhobor women and children building a house, Petrovaka, Saskatchewan, 1905 (E-09610, British Columbia Archives)

berg points out in her essay (#68). This was also the result of immigration regulations that favoured the entry of domestic servants.[10]

Sewing was a task that most women did as a part of their unpaid labour in the home; a significant number were able to turn the skill into an occupation. In the first half of the nineteenth century, most seamstresses and milliners were self-employed or were employees of small shops, but by the beginning of the twentieth century, it was increasingly likely that, even if they worked in their homes, they were employed by large firms producing for a mass market. In the 1880s, the garment manufacturer Stanford & Company of Hamilton employed 120 to 160 people to work in its factories and 2,000 to work outside the factories. The inside workers prepared material for the outside workers. The outside workers, mostly women, were organized by subcontractors and worked in their homes or in small shops. Working at home allowed women to take care of young children while they worked, but it left them open to financial exploitation.[12] Some women remained independent, however, and in control of their entreprise. Christina Bates, in

66.6 Women packers, Moricetown, B.C., 1910 (G-04121, British Columbia Archives)

essay #71, observes how "dressmaking and millinery allowed women to transform domestic female skills into lucrative occupations." In the two of the three case studies offered in Part 6 about dressmaking, small businesses were managed by the women who owned them. The essays by Susan Sirovyak, Alexandra Palmer, and Kathryn Church (#72, #73, and #74) all feature women who focused their markets very tightly and who engaged in their craft as workers and as artists. Part 6 also features two vignettes about women who established family businesses (#70 and #80).

In the century between 1850 and 1950, Canada became an urban industrial nation. Industrialization is commonly associated with factory production, but its effects extended beyond the factory. Industrialization accentuated the split between the home and the workplace and reinforced the division of labour by gender. Men became increasingly responsible for providing a family income through paid labour outside of the home. They also became less involved with family affairs, and women became correspondingly more responsible for the family and less responsible for family monetary income. Value was increasingly determined by the market, and women's unpaid work was devalued.[12] These tendencies contributed to the development of the idea of "separate spheres": women were responsible for the private realm of the home, while men went out to work in the public sphere.

Although industrialization encouraged the separation of home and work and the ideology of separate spheres clearly assigned women to the former category and men to the latter, the theory only worked for the relatively affluent. Middle- and upper-class women could sometimes afford to withdraw from market-oriented work. Those who took paying work, usually prior to marriage and raising a family, were encouraged to take respectable jobs – teaching, nursing, clerking, or journalism – which fit in with their traditional roles. Three essays in Part 6

DEPRESSION YEARS
Lara Campbell

Although options for unemployed men were scarce during the Depression, unemployed women had even fewer choices, since relief camps and make-work projects were not open to them. By 1937, only eight thousand women throughout Canada were registered on the relief rolls.[1] Desperation, well illustrated by a letter written to R.B. Bennett in 1934 by a Hamilton woman, was the result for many: "I am faced with starvation and I see no possible means of counteracting or even averting it temporarily! ... First I ate three very light meals a day; then two and then one. During the past two weeks I have eaten only toast and drunk a cup of tea every other day ... Yet before I will stoop to dishonour my family, my character or my God I will drown myself in the Lake."[2]

The only government initiative specifically designed to reduce female unemployment was the development of domestic training programs. To support this program, middle- and upper-class Canadians, experiencing increased spending power because of massive deflation, were encouraged to hire maids. Women who did not were chastised for not doing their part in helping to end the crisis: "It is up to these thousands of women to keep on spending; to spend more than they have in the past ... what could be a stranger anomaly than the sight of women who ... cling tenaciously to their dollars because they are afraid, or selfish – or both?"[3] Domestic service encompassed one-fifth of all women workers, and it was the only profession for women that increased during the Depression.[4] Although it was a job of last resort for women because of its long hours, low wages, and lack of freedom, domestic service did offer a measure of independence for some women.

1 *Canadian Forum* 16 (March 1937): 5.
2 Michael Bliss and L.M. Grayson, eds., *The Wretched of Canada* (University of Toronto Press, 1971), 83–4.
3 See Byrne Hope Sanders, "The Editor's Own Page," *Chatelaine*, February 1932.
4 Leonard Marsh, *Canadians In and Out of Work* (Oxford University Press, 1940), 97. From 1921 to 1931 there was a 7 per cent increase in the number of women in domestic service but a 6 per cent decrease in manufacturing jobs. Alison Prentice et al., *Canadian Women: A History* (Toronto: Harcourt Brace Jovanovich, 1988), 235.

While employers could legally pay women less than men for the same work, a series of minimum-wage laws were passed by the provinces beginning in 1918. However, two royal commissions, established in the 1930s to examine working conditions in the textile and garment industries, found that minimum-wage laws were regularly violated throughout the Depression. Employers knew that the law was unlikely to be enforced, since there were only seventy minimum-wage and factory inspectors for all of Canada.[1] Conversely, the minimum-wage law could place women's jobs in jeopardy. Because it was a form of protective legislation applying only to women, employers found they could fire women and hire men at lower wages. In response, female employees at a Valleyfield, Quebec, textile mill drew up a petition asking the provincial government to spare their jobs by allowing the company not to apply the minimum wage.[2]

1 Census, 1931, *Unemployment Monograph*, vol. 13, 129.
2 Alison Prentice et al., *Canadian Women: A History* (Toronto: Harcourt Brace Jovanovich, 1988), 234–5.

feature journalists in print and radio (#76, #77, and #78), while broadcast leaders such as Florence Bird and Kate Aitken appear in other sections of the book (#51 and #21). Clearly, journalism has operated as a career that is compatible with many women's gender expectations and personal aspirations, providing as well opportunities for community activism.

Working-class men and women were less able than members of the middle class to achieve the separation of work and home. The family wage was seldom adequate to support a family, and many women took work in factories. As well, by displacing home production of many items such as cloth and clothing, industrialization increased the family's need for wages. To pay the bills, older children and youths, both male and female, in working-class families went to work to help support the family. By 1931, 65 per cent of employees in the clothing sector and 50 per cent in the textile sector were women. They were almost always in subordinate positions, at the lower-salary level ranges, where they were supervised by men. On average they were younger than the men

employed in the industry. In the Quebec cotton industry between 1911 and 1931, 74 per cent of female workers but only 42 per cent of male workers were between the ages of fifteen and twenty-four. Most women workers were single, lived at home, and turned their wages over to their family. When they married, they left home and in most cases also left their role as wage earners.[13]

In the late nineteenth and early twentieth century, much office work became "industrialized" in the sense that it was organized into narrowly defined tasks performed on a number of new office machines, such as typewriters, adding machines, and key-punch machines. Traditionally, clerical work had been a male job, and while poorly paid, it provided a range of experience and served as an apprenticeship for higher positions. Similarly, the revolution in communications opened up such areas as telephone operating, discussed in vignette #75. The expansion of a number of industries, notably insurance and banking, with a high demand for routine statistical and correspondence work, enlarged the demand for clerical workers at the same time as the work itself became less attractive as a career starting point. It remained a clean, respectable, white-collar occupation, though now considered suitable for women. Although poorly paid, clerical work may have been attractive to women who, having fewer options than men, may have regarded paid employment as only a short stage in their lives. Women came to dominate clerical work, and some occupations, such as stenographer and typist, were identified as female vocations.[14]

In banking, labour shortages during the First World War led to the recruitment of female clerks. At the Bank of Nova Scotia the proportion of female clerks rose from 8.5 per cent to 40.7 per cent between 1911 and 1916. During the Second World War 60 per cent of Bank of Nova Scotia staff were women and women were accepted as tellers.[15] Still, according to Jane Nokes and Lisa Singer (#79) they remained in a minority in these positions until well into the 1950s. In the federal civil service the employment of female clerks was accepted in the 1890s, and by 1908 seven hundred out of three thousand inside workers were women. The Civil Service Commission was concerned that the domination of lower-level jobs by women would affect training and recruitment into managerial positions and in 1921 moved to exclude married women from the civil service.[16] Ironically, these were the same years in which women were given the vote federally. With the exception of the war years, married women remained barred from the federal civil service until 1955.[17]

In the century 1850–1950, volunteer work emerged as an unpaid occupation for women. Volunteer women in the settlement movement and in groups such as the Unitarian Service Committee, as described in the essay by Grace Hyam (#85), worked to integrate immigrants into Canadian society. During the First and Second World Wars, women who entered the paid labour force in non-traditional jobs attracted public recognition, but "by far the largest contribution made by Canadian women to the war effort was through their unpaid labour in the home and their volunteer work."[18] Volunteer work paved the way for many social services that would be state supported and whose work force would be largely constituted by trained professionals.

Housework, unpaid work in the home, continued to be most women's primary occupation. Technological changes helped to alleviate the heavy work involved in housework, but they did not always lighten the housewife's load. Some of the work that was eliminated, cutting wood for fuel and hauling water, for example, had been the primary responsibility of men and children, not women.[19] Technological changes were also linked, both as cause and effect, to the decline of domestic service as a category of employment. Industrialization also made many non-durable goods available as commodities that had formerly been produced in the home; this substitution created financial stresses that sometimes forced women to take up paid work. Technological changes may have made housework less physically demanding, but they do not seem to have made it less time-consuming. American studies have found that the time devoted to household work by women who had no employment outside the home increased from about fifty-one hours per week in 1926–27 to about fifty-five hours in 1965–66. The time spent in shopping and managing the household and in child care increased, while the time spent in food preparation decreased.[20] In Canada in 1996, 48.5 per cent of women spent over fifteen hours per week doing housework compared to 21.6 per cent of men. Twenty-four percent of women also spent over fifteen hours each week providing child care compared to 12.6 per cent of men.[21] (See Table 66.1.) New technologies also carried hidden costs, such as higher expectations of cleanliness and more elaborate meal requirements. They also contributed to the devaluation of the skills involved in many household tasks.

Both the First and Second World War influenced the nature and extent of women's involvement in paid work. In response to labour shortages as industry expanded and men were drawn into the armed forces, women were hired for non-traditional jobs. In the First World War the thirty-five thousand women who worked in the munitions industry attracted the greatest public scrutiny or admiration. Women also replaced men as farm labourers, streetcar conductors (Illustration 66.7), bank clerks, and telegraph messengers. Most of these occupations reverted to being male jobs after the war, but some, such as bank clerks, did not.[22] In the Second World War women returned to non-traditional jobs, most visibly in the aircraft plants (see essay #85 by Pamela Wakewich, Helen Smith, and Jeanette Lynes) and in shipbuilding. They also embarked on new careers. Illustration 66.8 shows Jewel Butler O'Hanlon, one of the first air stewardesses working on flights between Alberta and the Yukon. Several thousand women had served as nurses in

Table 66.1 Hours of Work Performed in the Canadian Home by Men and Women, 15 Years and Over, 1996 (in percentages)

Number of Hours	Housework	Care of Seniors	Child Care
		Men	
No hours	15.55	86.40	65.69
Less than 5 hours	30.11	9.57	10.89
5 to 14 hours	32.70		10.86
15 to 29 hours	14.26		6.33
30 to 59 hours	5.60	4.03	3.50
60 or more hours	1.77		2.73
		Women	
No hours	7.73	80.83	57.70
Less than 5 hours	15.68	11.97	8.66
5 to 14 hours	28.11		9.60
15 to 29 hours	23.92		7.20
30 to 59 hours	16.93	7.20	6.80
60 or more hours	7.62		10.05

Source: Statistics Canada, 1996 Census *Nation* tables (website).

the first war, and in the second, fifty thousand women were recruited into women only, non-combatant corps of the regular forces. In the later stages of the Second World War, government and industry also began to recruit married women, including those with children, and to provide limited, subsidized, daycare facilities for working women. Women commanded each of the three women's corps in the armed forces, and a few women directed programs that were considered to fall within women's concerns; for example Byrne Hope Sanders, editor of Chatelaine, was director of the Consumer Branch, Wartime Prices and Trade Board.[23] Nevertheless, the war did offer opportunities often not available to women during peacetime. Donna Porter reports in her essay (#82) that servicewomen valued the camara-

derie and authority they were ascribed during their time in the armed forces. Elsie Gregory MacGill was an exception to most rules; an aeronautical engineer before the war, she headed the production and design of a winterized version of the Hawker Hurricane in Fort William, as documented in the essay by Pamela Wakewich (#81).

While the Second World War altered attitudes towards women and paid labour, those changes had no lasting effect. At the end of the war, daycare facilities were closed, women's corps in the armed services disbanded, and women in war industries laid off. Women were expected to resume work within the home. In 1946 women's participation in the labour force fell to 25 per cent (from a peak of 33 per cent during the war) and continued to decline until the mid-1950s. One statistic that did not revert to prewar standards was the employment of married women. In 1931 only 10 per cent of women in paid work were married; during the war the proportion rose to 35 per cent and never returned to its prewar level. In 1951, 30 per cent of women in the labour force were married.[24]

Women's patterns and conditions of paid work have also been influenced by government legislation and regulation. Between 1917 and 1930 most provinces adopted minimum wage laws for women. The laws did not cover the important occupational areas of agriculture, domestic service, banking, teaching, and nursing. Moreover, the pay levels were calculated on the assumption that women working outside the home did not have dependents; as a result, they could be set below the family wage that was set as the ideal for men.[25] Sometimes legislation designed to protect women could work against them. In Quebec, for example, women were not permitted to work night shifts, and after 1925 they were covered by minimum wage legislation; men were not covered by either law, and when wages fell, men replaced female textile workers in some textile mills.[26]

66.7 Maud Foley, during
the First World War
(MG 9, vol. 226, pp. 27–8, Nova
Scotia Archives and Records
Management)

Table 66.2 Adult Labour Force Participation, 1891–1991

	Men in Labour Force (%)	Women in Labour Force (%)	Women as a Percentage of Labour Force
1891	76.6	11.1	12.1
1901	78.3	14.4	13.3
1911	82	16.6	13.4
1921	80.3	17.7	15.4
1931	78.4	19.4	17
1941	85.6	22.9	19.9
1951	84.4	24.4	22
1961	81.1	29.3	27.3
1971	79.9	43.7	34.3
1981	78.7	52.3	40.6
1991	75.1	58.5	44.7

Sources: *Fifth Census of Canada, 1911*, vol 6, xix, Table 10; Leacy, Urquhart, and Buckley, eds., *Historical Statistics of Canada*, series D8–D5. D107–D122; *1971 Census*, Cat #94–701, Table 1; *Canada Yearbook, 1997*, Table 7.2.

66.8 Jewel Butler O'Hanlon, air stewardess
(81–77, Yukon Archives)

Table 66.3 Women as a Percentage of the Work Force in Various Sectors, 1911–1971

Sector	1911	1921	1931	1941	1951	1961	1971	Average
Education	74	74	70	68	63	62	55	61
Personal and recreational services	72	70	70	77	63	64	59	68
Textiles and clothing	67	59	51	52	51	54	58	55
Health and welfare	62	68	67	70	69	73	75	72
Food and lodging	39	40	46	52	49	56	57	52
Retail and wholesale trade	19	19	20	23	28	30	37	28
Other and unspecified mfg.	17	18	19	26	34	32	35	27
Leather and rubber	16	23	26	30	31	35	36	30
Food, beverage, and tobacco	15	18	17	19	22	24	27	22
Finance, insurance, and real estate	11	25	27	31	44	46	51	42
Other services	11	11	26	32	32	35	36	31
Other transport	7	14	13	12	17	18	21	16
Wood products, paper, and publishing	7	8	10	10	12	14	17	13
Chemical, petroleum, and non-metallic products	5	11	9	15	17	17	18	16
Government	5	13	14	20	17	18	25	20
Agriculture	2	2	2	2	4	12	23	5
Metal products, machinery, and transport machinery	2	4	6	9	11	12	15	11
Railway transport	1	4	4	3	5	5	7	4
Coal mining	0	0	0	0	0	0	0	0
Construction	0	0	1	0	2	3	5	2
Electricity and gas	0	0	9	9	10	13	14	11
Fishing and trapping	0	0	0	0	0	0	0	0
Forestry	0	0	0	0	2	2	4	1
Industry unspecified	0	15	2	11	19	27	44	29
Other mining	0	0	0	0	3	5	7	3

Sources: Leacy, Urquhart, and Buckley, eds., *Historical Statistics of Canada*, 2nd ed., series D8–D85.

During the first half of the twentieth century, women's rate of participation in the paid labour force increased gradually from 14.4 per cent in 1901 to 24.4 per cent in 1951. The trend of gradual increases in women's labour force participation was broken in the postwar decades, 1951 to 1971, when participation increased from 24.4 to 29.3 to 43.7 per cent (see Table 66.2). Participation passed 50 per cent in the 1970s and reached 57.4 per cent in 1995 compared with a rate of 72.5 for men.[27] In the 1960s through the 1980s, women were more likely to have a three-stage life work cycle: paid employment until marriage, a period of unpaid child rearing, and then a partial return to the paid work force.[28] The move into the paid labour force seldom relieved women of responsibilities in the home, and many women were burdened with a double work day of a paid job combined with the responsibilities of the home and family.

Through most of Canadian history, the greater part of women's work has been unpaid and most of it has been done in the home. In the twentieth century an increasing number of women entered the paid work force, and many began to work outside of the home for at least part of their lives; most of them retained substantial responsibilities for a wide range of unpaid domestic work. Much of their work, particularly that which was unpaid, was accorded little value by Canadian society. Women's historians and activists in other disciplines have helped to expand our understanding of work and to bring an understanding to the wide range of work that women have done.

A list of further readings in this area is provided on page 487.

Vignette

67 An Oral History Case Study

In Part 5, "Health Care and Science," we highlighted the oral history project organized by Shirley Peruniak (#65). Here we draw attention to an oral history case study. Several of the themes of this study echo those outlined in this section's introduction by Allan McCullough (#66). In the first instance, Zaporzan introduces the history of an immigrant child, Eleanor May Bowden. Bowden's entry into service was influenced by her immigration experience, her health, and family responsibilities. Moreover, Zaporzan's research details the role that charity organizations – in this case, the Barnardo Homes – played in Bowden's migration and employment.

A Barnardo Girl Becomes a Servant at Glanmore
Christine Zaporzan

Glanmore was built for a moderately wealthy banker, John P.C. Phillips, in 1883 at Belleville, Ontario. The house remained in the family until 1971, when it became the Hastings County Museum, and it still retains its original character as a Glanmore National Historic Site. For nearly thirty years, the site's interpretive tours could say little to visitors about the servants who worked in the house. Then, in 1997, a fortunate visit by the granddaughter of one of the domestics shed new light and gave a face and voice to those who had worked "behind the scenes" at the turn of the century.

The Phillips' family correspondence held by the museum contained no mention of the domestic help. Yet, early investigation in the 1891 and 1901 census records turned up the only reference to servants. In 1891 Sarah Colley was living at Glanmore as a domestic servant. She was thirty-four years old, single, born in England, and could read and write. In 1901 Edith Dame was the live-in servant. Edith is registered as married, twenty-four years of age, born in Ontario, and able to read and write. Now there were names for the servants, but little else was known about them.

In 1997 we finally met Eleanor May Bowden through her granddaughter, Patricia.[1] Eleanor had worked for Mr and Mrs Phillips at Glanmore from August 1901 to

67.1 A servant at Glanmore (Courtesy of Christine Zaporzan)

September 1905. She returned to Glanmore in 1945 and had her picture taken in front of the house. On the back of the photograph, Eleanor wrote the following: "This is where I used to live year 1901. These were my happy days." At first this comment seems puzzling given the working conditions of servants at the time. Eleanor would have cleaned a nine-thousand-square-foot home and cooked for John and Harriett and their adopted daughter, Jesse – all on her own to the best of our knowledge. Work days would have been long, and she must have spent her nights "downstairs" in her small room in the basement. To understand how these could be the "happy days" requires more information about Eleanor's life.

Eleanor May Bowden was born on 13 January 1886 in Bath, England, as the fourth of the five children of Ellen and Stephen Bowden. Young Eleanor soon became one of the thousands of young people transported to Canada from England by the Barnardo organization. Between 1872 and 1939, a system of homes for poor children, established by Dr Thomas John Barnardo, was responsible for moving an estimated twenty thousand children to Canada in order to "improve their opportunities."[2] English philanthropists and policy makers were concerned both for public safety and for the religious upbringing of orphaned or deserted working-class children in the late nineteenth and early twentieth centuries, and found a solution by placing children with families in Canada and Australia, a solution that also served to populate the empire.[3]

Eleanor became a Barnardo child after the death of her father. Stephen Bowden was a stone mason who died at age twenty-nine of consumption (tuberculosis) in 1889. Eleanor's mother, Ellen Bowden, worked for the next two years as a charwoman and, during that time, came to live with Mr Davis, by whom she later had a child. In 1898 Davis was removed to the workhouse infirmary, where he was deemed to be a "hopeless cripple," and shortly afterwards, Ellen and her children were evicted from their accommodations. Ellen put her three youngest children in the care of various friends. Eleanor was turned out of her new accommodations during the very first night and found crying in the churchyard by a passing gentleman. This matter came to the attention of the police, and shortly after this incident Eleanor and her two youngest siblings were admitted to Barnardo's Receiving House in London, on 25 April 1898.

Eleanor and her stepsister, Mabel, were soon placed at the Girls Village Home in Barkingside, Essex, where they remained for two years and were presumably taught various domestic skills. Her younger brother remained in London until March 1899, when he set sail for Canada; after his arrival, he was sent on to the Barnardo's Boys Home in Toronto. Eleanor sailed among a party of girls who left England on 7 June 1900, and was sent on to the Barnardo's Girls Home in Peterborough. Mabel arrived in Quebec in July of the same year. Almost a week after Eleanor sailed from England, Barnardo's wrote to Ellen Bowden advising her that "in accordance with the agreement she signed when Eleanor came to Barnardo's she had gone to Canada." Ellen was not given advance notice that Eleanor was being sent thousands of miles away, likely never to return.

On 28 June 1900, at age fourteen, Eleanor was placed in Belleville as a servant for a clergyman's wife, Mrs Gilliard. In June of the following year, she went to work for Mrs G.F. Thompson of Belleville, and two months later she began working for Mrs Phillips at Glanmore. Eleanor stayed at Glanmore until September 1905, when she left for another Belleville employer. By 1910, Eleanor had moved to Hamilton, where she married Daniel Shea in 1912. She had four children and died at the age of eighty in 1966. After marrying Shea, it seems that Eleanor continued to work as a cook for a wealthy family.

In many ways Eleanor appears to have been a typical servant of the time: she was young, literate, single, and an immigrant and she was the only servant at Glanmore. Claudette Lacelle's analysis of the 1871 census for Toronto states that among all servants, 90 per cent were female, almost all were single, 98 per cent were literate, 67 per cent were under twenty-five, most worked in one-servant households, and many of them were immigrants.[4] What is not typical about Eleanor's work for the Phillips family is that it lasted five years. Many different sources suggest that servants frequently changed employers as the result of unpleasant servant-master relationships.[5] The length of Eleanor's stay (which was eighteen months past her eighteenth birthday, when her formal apprenticeship obligations to the Barnardo organization were complete) and her comment on the back of the photograph suggest a positive relationship with the Phillips family, and thus a reason for not switching employers as soon as she was allowed.

A positive relationship would have also been notable in light of the duties for which Eleanor would have been responsible. Glanmore has two floors, plus the basement and the attic. At times she would have been expected to carry heavy objects up and down the stairs. She would have been on call at all times of the night and day. Her work day would have been fifteen to eighteen hours long. She could expect an evening or half-day off once per week, but only after her work was done for the day. If she had become sick for a long period of time, she would have expected to be dismissed.[6] Mrs Beeton's *Housekeeping Book* suggests the following cleaning schedule for nineteenth-century homes, in addition to the daily cooking, lighting of fires, and other duties:

Monday – One bedroom; washing.
Tuesday – Spare room and library.
Wednesday – Dining room; ironing.
Thursday – Mistress's bed and dressing rooms.
Friday – Drawing room and one bedroom.
Saturday – Plate, stairs, and sundries.[7]

Add to this workload the weight of the attitude portrayed in etiquette books, servant handbooks, and household management treatises that asserted that servants were "inferior beings who needed to be supervised and controlled,"[8] and Eleanor's positive impression of her years at Glanmore is even more significant.

Unfortunately, we are unlikely to know the details of Eleanor's relationship with the Phillips family. We can only guess at the advantages for a Barnardo child of working in what appears to have been a good home. Glanmore would have provided Eleanor with a stable home in comparison to her troubled childhood and two years of institutional living at the Girls Village Home in England. She may also have looked back on her years at Glanmore during that visit in 1945 as her "happy days" for their relative simplicity when she compared them to raising four children, living through the Depression and Second World War, and being the only breadwinner for her family at times. Those middle years at Glanmore may have seemed, as her granddaughter Patricia put it, "like being at a tea party!"

68 Bringing "Domestics" to Canada: A Study of Immigration Propaganda

Ellen Scheinberg

During the twentieth century, women interacted with the state in many ways. Some essays in this volume focus on public policy advocates and women activists who attempted to influence state programs that affected the lives of women and their families. Others explore how women's lives were regulated by the state or how women protested over state and economic policies. Yet the state affected Canadian women on a more fundamental way. Its immigration programs actually determined which groups of women were allowed to become Canadians. This essay investigates one such group of women and how the state used varied means to encourage their immigration to Canada.

During the early twentieth century, domestics were a necessary part of the household for many middle-class Canadians. Accordingly, the government of Canada attempted to attract women servants to Canada to satisfy this need. In order to draw the "right" type of immigrant, those who would possess good characters as well as suitable domestic skills, the government focused its recruiting efforts on young women from the British Isles. Between the years 1900 and 1930, approximately 170,000 women from the British Isles came to Canada to work as domestics.[1] The government's success in attracting so many immigrants to Canada can be attributed in large part to the ambitious recruitment campaign it waged through posters, pamphlets, and newspaper advertisements.

Throughout the early twentieth century, the Canadian government spent a great deal of time and money in its effort to recruit three classes of immigrants: farmers, agricultural workers, and domestics.[2] The first two groups were needed to take up land and settle the West. Domestic workers were sought by middle-class Canadian women to assist them with the burdens of housework. Owing to a shortage of servants in Canada, women were recruited from abroad. Few Canadian women were interested in this line of work because of its arduous nature, the isolation, and the low social status associated with this profession.[3] For immigrant women, however, domestic work offered a paying job and free accommodation, as well as an opportunity to start a new life. Domestic service in Canada became, in Marilyn Barber's view, "the main bridge to Canada for women with limited funds."[4]

In addition to attempting to solve the servant crisis, the government used immigration to help redress the gender balance within Canada and to fulfil the nation-building task of populating the country. Rather than encouraging all single women of child-bearing age to enter Canada as domestics, the government pursued a restrictive policy that focused on the admission of only women from the British Isles. It was felt that they would produce children of good Anglo-Saxon stock who would possess the "right" moral and racial characteristics required for a stronger Canada.[5] Although farmers and agricultural workers from the United States, Europe, and the British Isles were targeted during this period, the Department of the Interior focused only on

68.1 Domestic servants arriving in Canada (c 09652, National Archives of Canada)

the British Isles when searching for domestics. Between the years 1904 and 1914, approximately 76 per cent of domestics entering Canada came from the British Isles. From 1919 to 1930, however, this figure decreased slightly, to 60 per cent, owing to a slight increase in domestics from central and eastern Europe.[6]

In order to recruit the "proper" types of domestics to Canada, the Department of the Interior pursued an aggressive advertising drive. A speech given by Minister of the Interior Frank Oliver indicated the centrality of advertising vis-à-vis government immigration policy, stating that "our immigration policy is in the first instance simply an advertising policy – a means of placing the advantages of Canada before such people in other countries as we desire to induce to come to Canada."[7] Harold Troper, in his work *Only Farmers Need Apply*, notes how the government wedded its immigration policy "to contemporary techniques of business promotion, management and advertising know-how – each tempered by a keen awareness of political reality."[8]

In addition to opening offices in major cities in Europe, the department relied on a small but dedicated band of agents who travelled across the British countryside answering questions, displaying posters, delivering lectures, and distributing leaflets, brochures, and pamphlets to the public. Through the use of this strategy, the department assailed both Europeans and Americans with images and information about Canada. Although the message was delivered to a broad audience, the advertisements were very specific as to what type of immigrants would be welcomed to Canada.

Pamphlets, posters, and newspapers were the most popular forms of advertisements used to attract domestics. In addition to carrying out its own mandate, the department cooperated with the private shipping companies, which had their own agents overseas working to recruit suitable immigrants. The government provided the companies with copies of advertisements and also offered bonuses for each immigrant sent to Canada. At the turn of the century, agents were

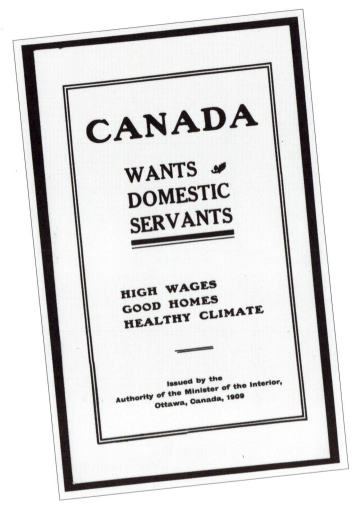

68.2 "Canada Wants Domestic Servants" – pamphlet, 1908
(c 80109, National Archives of Canada)

offered bonuses of five dollars per head for farmers, farm labourers, and domestic servants, and two dollars per head for child dependents.[9]

The immigration pamphlet was one of the most popular of the advertising methods used to attract domestic servants during this period. Although the department produced a large number of general pamphlets, a handful of booklets were created specifically to attract female domestic servants. These pamphlets, in the form of twelve- to thirty-page booklets that contained information on Canada, were circulated by immigration agents in the British Isles. They bore titles such as "Canada Wants Domestic Servants: High Wages, Good Homes, Healthy Climate" (1908), "Canada: The Opportunities Offered in the Dominion for Domestic Servants" (1910), and "Housework in Canada: Duties, Wages, Conditions and Opportunities for Household Workers in the Dominion" (1926). Before the First World War, the government circulated thousands of these pamphlets. In 1910, 100,000 copies of "Canada Wants Domestic Servants" were distributed within the British Isles alone (Illustration 68.2).[10] While production of pamphlets declined during the war years, after the enactment of the Empire Settlement Scheme in 1922 (which sought to attract British settlers to Canada by providing free passenger loans to certain classes of immigrants, such as domestic servants), the production of pamphlets relating to domestics and other desirable classes soared. For example, in 1915 the Department of the Interior issued 51,700 copies of its new pamphlet "Women's Work in Canada," but by 1925, 201,900 copies of this same pamphlet were being distributed in Britain.[11]

Most pamphlets shared a common theme. They stressed the need in Canada for houseworkers or domestics, and clearly indicated that there was little need for other classes of women – governesses, stenographers, typists – occupations typically filled by local women.[12] The pamphlets also offered travelling tips for prospective immigrants; information about Canada, such as the climate, geography, and the political system; and contact points through associations and agents for advice. The pamphlets typically concluded with samples of letters received by the department that year from domestics who had already settled in Canada, as well as letters from satisfied employers.

While a fairly earnest tone was evident within the pamphlets, they often presented an overly optimistic picture of life and work in Canada, downplaying the obviously difficult nature of domestic work as well as the harsh Canadian climate that immigrants from Britain would confront. The department, in fact, played up the benefits of Canada's weather, indicating that "the Canadian climate year round is one which produces hardy, healthy and happy men and women."[13] While the work was faithfully described as representing a full day of responsibilities, prospective domestics were informed that Canadian homes had more modern conveniences than homes in Europe, which made the work easier. Moreover, they were notified that mistresses in Canada generally assisted with the household work, particularly in rural areas. In addition to being informed that the wages and standard of living were better in Canada than in Britain, the women who read these pamphlets were also assured that they would not have to confront the rigid class system that existed in Europe and that they would be treated like "family" within the household. One letter published in a pamphlet was from Minnie F. Duffy, who wrote:

I have been very well treated in every possible way since I came to Canada. In my present situation I am used very much as one of the family. In Ireland I worked for family of six as general servant. I did the work of the whole house including washing and ironing and I just got 14 pounds per year and had one evening out every week from 7 and 10 and every other Sunday. In my present situation I get 43 pounds per year and have easier work. I can also go out every other evening, every Sunday afternoon and one afternoon each week.[14]

Rather than focusing on the isolation of Canadian living, the department emphasized the social opportunities that awaited immigrant women through their participation in churches and women's clubs.

Although the pamphlets were typically sedate in tone, they clearly employed a degree of literary and artistic licence in order to play up the positive aspects of life and work opportunities in the Dominion. Patrick Dunae emphasizes this point, stating that "official publications were rarely guilty of wilful misrepresentation, gross exaggeration, and outright lies, for the government recognized the damage that could result from misleading advertisements."[15] Consequently, in constructing the texts, the department tried to remain as truthful as possible while painting a rosy picture of life in Canada as a domestic. As a result, many domestic workers' experiences did not measure up to their expectations, and subsequently, a significant number of immigrant women attempted to escape domestic work by either marrying or finding other types of employment soon after they arrived in Canada.

The posters that were used by the department were generally one-sided sheets intended to display a slogan alongside very specialized statements. Unlike other types of advertising vehicles, posters were the most effective way to convey a message to a maximum number of people in a minimum amount of time. For instance, rather than distributing hundreds of thousands of posters, the government could simply display one poster in the window of Canada's immigration office in London. Due to the heavy foot traffic near the office, thousands of "respectable" pedestrians would see the poster on a daily basis. The department also produced dozens of posters advertising free land in the West, along

68.3 "Canada Wants Women" – immigration poster
(C 56944, National Archives of Canada)

68.4 "Canada's Call to Women" – immigration poster
(C 137978, National Archives of Canada)

with the accompanying demand for farmers and agricultural workers, and displayed these at exhibition and fairs across the British Isles. Only one poster was created, during the early 1920s, that dealt specifically with domestics. This black-and-white broadside presented the message "Canada Wants Women" for household work (Illustration 68.3). While limited to the space of a single page, the department was able to convey that Canada offered assisted passages for approved applicants who could expect guaranteed employment. The poster also indicated that some domestic experience would be required, and it provided a list of government agents whom women could contact if they were interested in securing a position in Canada.

While the federal government often relied on simple black-and-white posters, private shipping companies often used large-format colour posters that relied on images, sometimes by well-known artists, rather than on text alone, to capture their message. One example of this type of poster was produced by the White Star Line during the 1920s. It bore the simple slogan "Canada's Call to Women," but accompanied it with an image of a fair-skinned young woman standing in a kitchen baking a pie or tarts (Illustration 68.4). The window is open, exposing the beautiful western landscape with sheaves of wheat and the outline of a pleasant town in the distance. In addition to being clad in fashionable clothing and having a modern bobbed hairstyle, the woman in the poster seems to be enjoying a full and healthy life, no doubt thanks to the abundant crops in the West and the fine climate. While the government of Canada was seeking only domestics, this poster developed by the White Star Line held out the promise to immigrant women of future matrimony to a successful farmer. In addition to illustrating plainly the type of woman viewed as desirable by federal and company agents, the image presented the type of life that would entice British women to emigrate to Canada.

Newspapers were the final and most popular method used to promote the immigration of domestics. In addition to being far less expensive than pamphlets and posters, they disseminated a message to a larger audience. Director of Advertising Robert J.C. Stead stated that, in 1921, the department placed advertisements in approximately five thousand papers in the United Kingdom and the United States.[16] While many of these ads were general advertisements about Canada or copies of lectures delivered by immigration officers, a number focused on attracting domestics. Two of the provinces, Ontario and Saskatchewan, joined the campaign to recruit British immigrants to their provinces. One ad submitted by the Ontario government in 1923 read as follows:

Fine opportunity for girls – The British and Ontario governments offer advanced passages by way of loan to Ontario, Canada for capable household workers: good wages and situations guaranteed to approved applicants; girls travel on steamers having a conductress on board, are met on arrival, and stay at the Government Women's Hostel in Toronto until placed in situations – Particulars and application forms free from Miss Duff, Ontario Government Office, 163 Strand, London, w.c.2.[17]

The content of the ad was intended to help allay the prospective domestics' fears about the journey to Canada by emphasizing the type of protection and support that they could expect to receive. This level of support was offered not only to protect these respectable women from harassment, but perhaps more importantly to ensure that they reached their intended destination.

Private companies also relied on newspaper advertisements to entice women to emigrate to Canada. In 1910 the Canadian Pacific Railway published a large advertisement with an image of a woman in a wheat field, which read "Canada for Women" (Illustration 68.5). The text below contained this alarming statement: "Ten

68.5 "Canada for Women" – immigration poster
(C 106840, National Archives of Canada)

thousand Englishwomen could be ranged in a line and shot. No one would be sorry. Everyone would be glad. There isn't any place for them."[18] As part of a quotation from an article written by a Canadian writer, Agnes Laut, it suggested that there were far too many women in Britain to be employed or married off to suitable men (especially after the recent slaughter in the First World War), and that because of its shortage of women and abundance of suitable jobs, Canada was a place where British women could live useful and productive lives. The advertisement effectively blended text and image to illustrate the benefits to British women of leaving the home country for a better life in Canada.

Although the advertisements dedicated to attracting domestic workers were far less numerous than those that targeted male agricultural workers and farmers, they did play a pivotal role in drawing Anglo-Celtic European women's attention to the opportunities that awaited them in Canada. Even though the advertising methods differed, each type of propaganda served the purpose of drawing as much attention as possible to the positive prospects of domestic employment in Canada. While some of the advertisements, particularly the pamphlets, tended to embellish the realities of domestic life in Canada, there was an earnest attempt by the government as well as the private shipping companies to ensure that prospective female immigrants were as informed as possible before they made the decision to venture to the Dominion. Because British women constituted the majority of female domestics who came to Canada during the first thirty years of the twentieth century, it is clear that the potent messages in the advertising proved effective in supporting the Canadian government's initiative to solve the servant shortage in Canada.

69 Women in the Newfoundland Fishery

Miriam Wright

In popular culture, the fishery is usually portrayed as a man's occupation. Images of strong men with rugged features, wearing oilskin coats, hauling their daily catch, come readily to mind. In Newfoundland, however, the fishery has depended heavily on the labour of women. In the nineteenth and early twentieth centuries, women played a central role in preparing the dried saltfish that the families produced for market. In the mid-twentieth century, a new, industrialized fishery based on frozen fish arose and women became fish-plant workers. Although women's contribution to the fishing economy has been significant, an historic gendered division of labour has been a characteristic of the work of the fisheries. The origin of this division is not entirely clear, but it appears to be connected to social perceptions of the proper roles for men and women. Over the years, these practices have been reinforced by the policies of government and business institutions.

From the early nineteenth century to the 1940s, the majority of the population of Newfoundland was involved in the inshore fishery (carried out close to shore, using small boats less than thirty-five feet in length) and the production of dried and salted codfish. The inshore fishery featured a "household economy," meaning that a product for market was made by the family members. Male family members – fathers, husbands, sons, and brothers – caught the fish using small boats and gear such as handlines and cod traps, while the "shore crew" – mothers, wives, daughters, sisters, and younger sons – would split and salt the fish. The women would then take the salted fish and spread it out on wooden fish flakes, or racks, to dry in the sun for a week or so until cured. The women tended the drying fish, taking it in each night or during rainy weather. Besides curing the fish, women also provided the basic needs of the family by gardening, preserving food, and making clothing. This household economy of the inshore fishery had a gendered division of labour, with men doing most of the harvesting and women doing much of the shore work, but there was some flexibility in the roles.

One way of getting a glimpse of women's contribution to the inshore fishery through historic documents is by examining the Newfoundland Censuses of 1891, 1901, 1911, and 1921. Although the censuses taken in Western nations have failed, for the most part, to take into account women's involvement in some areas of the economy, particularly in rural economies where farming and fishing are the main activities, the Newfoundland Census for those years is an exception. From 1891 to 1921, the numbers of both men and women active in the inshore fishery, either as harvesters or curers of fish, were recorded, offering a unique opportunity to see how extensive women's involvement in the Newfoundland fishery of the past actually was.

The figures in Table 69.1 indicate that, in the census years, women made up between 33 and 38 per cent of all people directly involved in the fishery. In some communities, the percentage of females working in the fishery

Table 69.1 Persons Engaged in Catching and Curing of Fish

Year	Males	Females	% Female
1891	36,694	18,081	33
1901	41,231	21,443	34
1911	43,231	23,245	35
1921	40,511	24,937	38

Sources: Newfoundland Census, 1921.

was even higher. For example, in 1921 in Port de Grave, a small inshore fishing community on the Avalon Peninsula with a population of 243, 69 men and 46 women were prosecuting the fishery (that is, women comprised 40 per cent of the total fishery workforce). In Bonavista, a much larger fishing community with a population of 4,050 in 1921, 736 men and 682 women worked in the fishery (women comprised 48 per cent of the fishery workers). In LaScie, a community of 424 people on the northeast coast of the island, 128 men and 67 women worked in the fishery (34 per cent of the total were women).

Other historical accounts of life in the Newfoundland outports confirm the centrality of women's work in the fishery. Women were often acknowledged as shouldering half the load of work in rural households. Indeed, the title of a book by Hilda Murray, *More Than Fifty Percent*, is a reference to the contribution women made to the work of Newfoundland outport families. Apart from the many tasks that women did to feed and clothe the family, the labour of the female shore crews enabled the fishing households to produce a much greater volume of dried saltfish. As inshore fishing families were often never far from poverty, women's toil made the difference between survival and starvation.

Beginning with the Second World War, the Newfoundland fishery, and women's roles within it, changed dramatically. New technology developed in the United States led to the production of packaged frozen fish for home consumption. Newfoundland, with its rich supply of cod, soon became a major supplier of frozen fish, first to Great Britain during the war and later to the United States. Large fishing companies that owned offshore fishing trawlers and frozen-fish processing plants arose in Newfoundland. These firms began hiring men and women – most of whom had been involved in the inshore fishery – as workers at the plants and on the trawlers.

Fish-plant work differed in many ways from fish-curing work on shore. In the fish plants, labour was divided into a number of tasks. After the fish was loaded onto the production floor, the larger cod were put through machines that split, skinned, and de-boned them. Smaller cod, and other species such as redfish, were usually cut by hand. The fish was then sent to trimmers and graders, where it was sorted by size and defects were removed. It was then weighed and packed into boxes or freezing trays and sent to the freezers. After it was frozen, the fish was moved into the cold-storage area where it awaited shipment.

Fish-plant labour, besides being differentiated by task, was also differentiated by gender. Although women regularly performed all of the processing tasks in the shore fishery, from splitting and cleaning, to salting and drying, to loading and stacking the finished product, the range of tasks they tended to perform in the frozen-fish production process was more limited. Since the introduction of the frozen-fish plants in the 1940s and continuing to the present, men have made up the majority of workers involved in the use of machinery, while women have been found in jobs that are defined as less skilled. Men predominate as filleting-, skinning-, and boning-machine operators, hand cutters, freezer operators, and cold-storage operators. Women tend to occupy packing and weighing jobs. Both men and women occupy trimming and grading positions. These divisions are not uniform in all plants. In some plants, women work as hand cutters and skinners, but in others, the gendered division of labour is much more strict. In fact, women who have tried to move into positions considered to be "male" jobs have met with considerable resistance, from both management and male workers.

The reasons for the gendered division of labour within the plants are not entirely clear, particularly when "male" and "female" jobs are not uniform from plant to plant. Common perceptions within our society of appropriate roles for men and women, and notions of what constitutes skilled and unskilled labour, are clearly a part of these designations. The preponderance of men in jobs involving machinery, for example, may be related to the belief that women are not adept at technical work. For the women themselves, one consequence of the division of labour is that they receive less pay on average than the men. The jobs where females predominate – packing and weighing – are among the lowest-paid occupations in the plants. And jobs where males predominate – operating filleting machines and freezing equipment – are the highest-paid jobs. Supervisory and plant manager positions are held overwhelmingly by males. Women have also been underrepresented in leadership roles in the unions of fishers and fish-plant workers.

The census is also a useful tool for looking at women's involvement in the industrialized frozen-fish industry. Table 69.2 shows the presence of women in fish-plant work.[1] The dramatic increase in fish-plant workers in 1981, and of female workers in particular, is related to the expansion in the processing sector after Canada declared a 200-mile fishing limit. Many of the new and expanded plants experienced a shortage in labour and began hiring more female workers to fill the gap. Although useful, these census figures may actually under-represent the involvement of women in the processing sector. Women's work in fish plants is usually seasonal, and women not employed during the week the census was taken may not be included in the totals. Statistics Canada data, which is taken from income tax

Table 69.2 Labour Force – 15 Years of Age and Over – Processors – Fish Canning, Curing, and Packing

Year	Males	% Male	Female	% Female
1961	1,382	79.79	350	20.20
1971	2,925	70.74	1,210	29.26
1981	5,530	42.70	7,420	57.30
1991	4,525	39.23	7,010	60.77

Sources: Canada Census, 1961, 1971, 1981, and 1991.

forms, suggests that the number of women who earned wages from fish-plant work was 10,800 in 1981 and 12,850 in 1990.

Another change in women's involvement in the Newfoundland fishery in the 1980s was the increasing number of women who began fishing. In the years before the 1970s, women were only rarely involved in catching fish. Although much of this was due to social pressures that discouraged women from adopting male roles, government regulations also prevented women from taking to the boats. Since 1957, self-employed fishers have been eligible to collect unemployment insurance during the winter when most cannot fish because of the weather. Those same regulations, however, stipulated that women married to fishers could not collect benefits, even if they fished every day during the fishing season. The assumption was that women who fished with their husbands were only "helping," and their work was therefore not considered valid.

Two major factors lay behind women's growing role as fish harvesters. The first was economic, as years of declining inshore landings had increased the costs of operating a small-boat fishery. More and more women, usually wives of inshore vessel owners, began fishing with their husbands to keep a greater share of the fishing income in the family. The second can be traced to changes in the Unemployment Insurance Act. The discriminatory regulations preventing women married to fishers from col-

Table 69.3 Labour Force – 15 Years of Age and Over – Fishers – Net, Trap, and Line

Year	Males	Male %	Female	Female %
1961	8,166	99.80	16	0.02
1971	6,855	99.28	50	0.07
1981	10,965	97.25	310	2.75
1991	9,575	88.95	1,190	11.05

Sources: Canada Census, 1961, 1971, 1981, and 1991.

lecting benefits were struck down when a woman fisher, Rosanne Doyle of Witless Bay, Newfoundland, successfully challenged them in the Supreme Court of Canada. Suddenly, wives joining their husbands in the boats made economic sense, and the old barriers to women fishers began to come down. By 1991, women made up 11 per cent of the total number of fishers.

In the early 1990s, the cod that have been the mainstay of the Newfoundland fishery for centuries virtually disappeared, as years of over-fishing finally took their toll. In 1992 the Canadian government declared a moratorium on cod fishing on the northeast coast of Newfoundland and Labrador, and it remained closed for seven years. Although the cod fishery has since re-opened, the catch is a small fraction of what it was earlier. Rural fishing communities have been devastated. Although much of the attention has been paid to the plight of the male fishers, women too have been hard hit by this social and economic crisis. Before the moratorium, an estimated fifteen thousand women were directly employed in the fishery as fishers and plant workers. Many others lost jobs in businesses that were connected to the fishery. Nearly ten thousand women were eligible for compensation packages from the federal government, but those programs ended in 1998. As the resource is not yet fully "recovered," the future for women may be difficult. Indeed, competition for licences and fish-plant jobs in the limited fishery that has remained since the moratorium (for example, the shrimp fishery) is intense – and promises to become more so in the future. Despite making up such a large percentage of the fishery workforce, women have had little say in government policy, in union activities, or in plant management.

Women have had a long and varied history in the Newfoundland fishery. Their specific roles have changed over the years, as the household fishery gave way to the industrial fishery, as saltfish gave way to frozen fish, and as the work of the shore crew was replaced by the production line at the processing plant. Women's centrality in the fishery of the future, however, is uncertain. In the long years of the moratorium, women across the fishery have begun to come together to address the specific problems of female workers and to discuss strategies for change. Whether or not women will have fair access to the wealth generated by the marine resources of the future remains to be seen.

70 Madeleine Constant, Leader in the Pasta Industry

Lise Brémault

Madeleine Constant was born in Marseilles, France, to a family that had been in the pasta business for over three hundred years. Henri Constant, her father, came to St Boniface, Manitoba, in 1912, where he began the Excelsior Macaroni Company. Madeleine was raised on the site where her father built both his home and the factory.

With her brothers, Madeleine attended a boys' school, a rare occurrence for the period, and it was here that her teachers tried to steer her towards a career in teaching. She chose instead to join her father, having been involved in various aspects of the business since childhood. In addition to her work in the factory, Madeleine was also responsible for the care of her ailing mother.

In 1928 her father sold the factory, and in 1936 Madeleine and her brother Lucien opened up their own pasta factory, Constant Macaroni Products, in Winnipeg. The factory employed local women (see Illustrations #70.1 and #70.2). Lucien and Madeleine were equal partners in the business, with Madeleine in charge of packaging and distribution. They ran the factory until their retirement in 1972. Madeleine died in 1996.

Top and bottom:
70.1 and 70.2 Interior views of Excelsior Pasta factory, 1930s
(Constant Collection, Le Musée de Saint-Boniface)

71 Creative Ability and Business Sense: The Millinery Trade in Ontario

Christina Bates

Until the 1950s, everyone wore a hat and milliners played an important role in supplying this most essential and often predominant part of women's attire. The millinery trade was important both to female consumers who bought new or remodelled hats at least twice a year and to aspiring young women who hoped to open their own hat shops.

Millinery and its sister occupation, dressmaking, were very different from factory work in the garment industries. Needleworkers and machine operators in clothing factories produced complete, but more often only parts of, garments for wholesale distributors. By contrast, milliners and dressmakers worked independently and often ran their own, though usually modest, businesses and shops. They had control over their products from beginning to end and had direct relationships with their customers.

There is a sizable body of research on the history of women working in clothing factories in Canada, but there is very little information on the history of dressmaking and millinery.[1] Yet these were the two principal skilled trades available to women in the early part of the twentieth century; they were also among the few occupations in the commercial sphere that were considered acceptable for women. Dressmaking and millinery allowed women to transform domestic female skills into lucrative occupations. This is a story of one example of female entrepreneurship that has not yet become part of our understanding of the capitalist market system, usually dominated by male enterprise.

These trades have left behind few traces. Women working with men in factories under organized labour were the subject of many newspaper articles, royal commissions, and government surveys. Unlike male entrepreneurs, businesswomen who ran small custom shops, usually without employees and often in the privacy of their own homes, were seldom mentioned in biographies, city histories, and government and legal records. Millinery and dressmaking, however, form part of an important female economy. This paper will trace the millinery trade in Ontario from 1890 to 1930.

Two main sources yield basic information on the trade. Canadian census data, recorded every decade, contain statistics on the numbers of milliners, and occasionally their gender, age, and ethnicity, in Canada, the provinces, and principal cities. The commercial sections of county and city directories list the names and addresses of milliners in each town or municipality. Although these two major sources present broad outlines of the trade, they do not capture the whole of millinery work. Enumerators and directory compilers did not always consider millinery a viable occupation, nor did all milliners volunteer information about their business, especially those who made hats only on a part-time basis, when domestic duties allowed.

Another source is the millinery and dry-goods trade journals – the *Dry Goods Review* (Toronto, 1891–1980) and the *Canadian Milliner* (Toronto, 1929 only) – which provide insightful but problematic evidence (Illustration

71.1). They were dominated by male contributors writing for manufacturers and large retailers of hats, clothing, and textiles, not for small millinery shopkeepers. Despite this bias, these journals document the encroachment of men in the millinery business and the paternalistic attitudes of men with capital and connections towards female milliners engaged in modest enterprises.

Women did write about millinery in the form of instruction manuals. These guides, such as Isabella Innes's *Scientific Dressmaking and Millinery*, published in Toronto in 1913, proliferated in the early twentieth century and provided a wealth of advice on the techniques, materials, and fashions in women's hat making.[2] Another avenue of research is the study of twentieth-century hats in museum collections. Visual and tactile examination of the actual products of millinery art can offer additional information as to their design and artistry.[3]

A familiar story emerged from these sources about the demise of the hand-made for the assembly line and the usurping of a traditionally female trade by male owners and workers. This trend influenced not only millinery, but all the custom-clothing trades. As industrial activity and mechanization of production increased in Ontario in the early twentieth century, made-to-order dressmaking and millinery workshops gave way to mechanized factory production. In 1901 small but numerous custom workshops employed about two-thirds of all workers (mostly women) in the garment trades, but by 1911, the numbers had dropped to about one-fourth. This trend was especially true of Toronto, which had become a leading industrial centre for clothing manufacture by the end of the nineteenth century. Factories were producing a widening range of ready-made, or off-the-rack clothing, starting with men's garments, including hats, to women's underclothing, shoes, and sports clothes, and by the early twentieth century, coats, tailored blouses, suits, and house dresses.[4]

But women's hats were actually one of the last articles

71.1 Cover of the *Dry Goods Review*, Toronto, February 1897

of clothing to succumb to the ready-made market. At the turn of the twentieth century, when women would buy their underclothing and casual clothes off the rack in department stores, they reserved considerable funds for that important finishing touch, the custom-made hat. So another story emerges from the evidence about the heyday of the hand-made hat, from the 1890s to 1920, and about the skilled milliner and the role she played in virtually every town and community in Ontario (Illustration 71.2).

Throughout most of the nineteenth century, women wore close-fitting bonnets, cradling the back of the head and tied under the chin, often made from draped or shirred fabric.[5] Until the end of the nineteenth century, dressmakers produced these bonnets for their customers to match their outfits. There was no separate column for

71.2 Miss Newton's hat shop, Sarnia, c. 1919 (Lambton County Archives and Library)

milliners in the Toronto city directories until the 1890s, when millinery became a specialized trade. Not incidentally, this occurred at the same time as women were giving up their bonnets for perky hats that perched on the top of the head, surmounted by vertical ribbon bows and feather ornaments. These creations matched the new strong image of feminine beauty; an emphasis on the torso was achieved by clothing with hugely wide sleeves and an s-shaped corset. Early in the twentieth century, hats grew to enormous proportions, covered in velvet or silk cloth, topped with magnificent feathers, flowers, and ornaments. The "girl of the new day," as she was called, was bravely entering careers formerly denied to women, such as medicine and the law, professionalizing the feminine vocations of teaching and nursing, and taking over clerical and sales fields.[6]

Ambitious women who did not have the opportunity to receive formal professional training were attracted to millinery because it was perceived to be a respectable and skilled trade. A few wanted to make millinery a career and hoped one day to own a shop and support themselves on its income. But many more entered the trade in order to supplement their own, or their family's income. They often used their own homes for their business, their clientele restricted to friends and family and their work advertised by word-of-mouth. These small, domestic businesses, with no overhead and only a small outlay of stock, allowed women with little or no capital to earn an income. Another avenue of employment for milliners was in the multitude of dry-goods stores that sold millinery among other clothing and home furnishings. After the turn of the century, a growing number of millinery workshops or factories run by male wholesalers also employed women to make hats to be sold to retail outlets.[7]

In Canada's cities milliners also worked for large department stores, such as Eaton's and Simpson's. A photograph of the Eaton's millinery workroom in 1904 shows the handcraft nature of millinery work at this time (Illustration 71.3). Some women are manipulating loose coils of wire into hat frames (front right). The intersecting wire frames would then be covered with buckram and velvet or other cloth. Other workers are cutting, sewing, and draping pieced foundations or finishing materials.

By 1911, there were 5,567 milliners listed in the census for Ontario, and that figure did not include all the "parlour" milliners who had valid, if hidden, businesses. Toronto claimed the highest number of milliners at 1,215, but other towns had substantial numbers. For example, Hamilton had 175 milliners; London, 200; Kingston, 65; and Guelph, 40. The 1911 census provided figures for only the major towns, but a survey of Ontario county directories indicates one or more milliners for almost every small town, village, and municipality.[8]

One successful millinery business in a moderate-sized town was a store in Galt run by Miss Mantell and Miss Schooley. Like many in the trade, these two women joined forces to fund and manage a millinery store. In an article written in 1914 for the *Dry Goods Review* (one of

71.3 Millinery workroom, T. Eaton Co., Toronto, 1904 (F 229-308-0-1819-3, Archives of Ontario)

the few about small-town milliners), Miss Mantell relates how they have "secured custom" through "attractive parlors and bright windows." These ambitious milliners knew well the importance of being current in millinery fashions, even in a small Ontario town: "We recognized from the start that we had strong competition in Toronto, London, Hamilton and other cities … Our stock had to be right up-to-date; our ideas in trimming had to follow in lines with the fashions."[9]

Millinery was a challenging occupation. Not only did it require considerable skill in drafting, fine needlework, and delicate handling of materials, it also demanded an artistic sense coupled with an aptitude for business. This combination of qualities was discussed in *The Canadian Girl at Work: A Book of Vocational Guidance*, which was published in 1919 for use in Ontario school libraries: "[A] first-class milliner is really an artist. Her hands must be skilful and quick, her touch light and sure. And she must have a sense of colour and form, and originality and creative ability. A girl who combines these gifts with business ability is likely to make a success of an establishment of her own."[10]

A young woman who wished to try her hand at millinery had a choice of training, both formal and informal. By the turn of the century, industrial, technical, and art schools offered both day-time and evening classes in millinery, along with other branches of "Household Science," such as sewing and cookery.[11] But many families could not afford to allow their daughters to stay in school past the elementary level. Girls were expected to work for a wage when they reached the age of fourteen or fifteen. Many entered the garment industry, but a few aspired to millinery and apprenticed in millinery shops, dry-goods shops, or department stores. Millinery was one of the few skilled trades with the possibility of advancement. Indeed, the potential advantages of the trade were lauded in a 1920 vocational survey by the Ontario Department of Labour: "Strong points in favour of the choice of millinery as an occupation are: the possibility of using the knowledge until well on in life, and the opportunity for developing an independent business ... Many women with skill and business ability, but with little capital have succeeded in working up a successful business for themselves in millinery."[12]

Apprenticeship in the millinery trade was informal and not bound by written or legal agreements. If a milliner decided that an applicant had potential, the girl would be hired for six months without pay, in return for training. *The Canadian Girl at Work* cautioned, however, that some employers exploited their apprentices and continued to work them without teaching the whole trade. There were several levels to training. An apprentice began by learning how to make bands for hats and sew in the linings; she would then learn to make wire frames and straw and buckram shapes, after which she would be instructed in covering the frames with silk, velvet, lace, and chiffon. Once she learned to "know intimately and to handle skilfully delicate and costly fabrics," she could become first an assistant milliner and then a first-class maker of hats. If she was artistically gifted, she could be promoted to the work of the trimmer or designer, "one of the most difficult stages in the creation of a hat." The designer was at the pinnacle of the millinery hierarchy, commanding the highest salary.

In small establishments, many of these levels were performed by the same person.[13]

Millinery was a seasonal trade, and this posed the main difficulty for a young woman wanting to make a living. Most of a milliner's stock was made and sold for the spring/summer season and the fall/winter season Women would buy one or more hats that would last the entire season. Prior to each season, an employer would engage apprentices and trained milliners to work very long hours for about three or four months. Once the season commenced, the staff would be laid off for a couple of months, to be rehired for the next season. Therefore, unless milliners ran their own business, or worked full time as heads of millinery departments in large stores, they would receive wages for only six to eight months in the year. Even shop owners had to augment their business during the slack seasons. The *Dry Goods Review* reported that Mrs A. Sorenson, of Mitchell, Ontario, "has found a splendid field in needle-work, paper flower making and reed work. All three lines are sufficient to keep her and many of her staff occupied during the quiet times of the entire year."[14]

Wages for milliners were fairly high compared with factory work or domestic service, but their yearly salary was reduced by the number of weeks of unemployment. The milliner's wage varied greatly depending on the size and status of the millinery shop or department, the level of work, and her personal skills. An assistant milliner could make from $6 to $15 per week. The majority of trained milliners made between $10 and $20. This compares favourably with garment-factory workers, who also often had times of unemployment and made from $8 to $12. Managers of departments, designers, and trimmers could make very high wages, over $25 per week, with employment the year round. A women who owned and operated her own millinery shop could expect an income of $1,000 to $1,500 per year – comparable to the salary of a trained nurse.[15]

The Canadian Girl at Work estimated that a young woman could support herself on a wage of $9–$12 per week. Milliners' salaries certainly fell within this range, except that they only worked from thirty to thirty-five weeks in the year. An assistant, whose earnings were at the lower end of the wage scale could thus barely, if at all, support herself. Milliners were encouraged to seek other employment during the slack seasons – waitressing, working as a saleswoman, caring for children, picking fruit. The difficulty of achieving a living wage for performing women's work was endemic in the early twentieth century, and recognizing this problem is critical to an understanding of occupational gender bias of the period, and indeed of most of the twentieth century. A survey of occupations by the Ontario Department of Labour found that the average weekly wage for the majority of women in 1918 was $10 to $12 per week, whereas the majority of men received $20 to $25. Men working in trades with commensurate training and skill as millinery made over twice the wage of a trained milliner.[16]

We do not know how many young women who trained or apprenticed in millinery actually continued their careers to become head milliners or shop owners. It was accepted at the time that many young women left their jobs to marry. The census of 1921 provides some idea of the relationship between marital status and paid work in general. Of the total female labour force, 50 per cent of all single women were employed, and 20 per cent of widows, but only 2 per cent of married women in Ontario were engaged in paid work.[17] We do not have statistics on marital status for the millinery trade, but age was probably an indicator. Although the vast majority of female workers in Ontario were young, only half of the women working in millinery were between the ages of fifteen and twenty-four. When the alternatives were dead-end jobs in unskilled factory work or domestic service, young women who invested the time and money to learn millinery did not always give it up for marriage and family responsibilities. Compared with the transiency of unskilled labour, women who had trained for millinery tended to stay with the occupation. Writing of the highly skilled millinery trimmer, the Department of Labour stated that "[t]he life of a trimmer is exceptionally full of variety, and the work affords scope for the exercise of artistic ability. A good trimmer has learned an occupation for life."[18]

The vast majority of milliners were Canadian born. In the 1911 Census, only 5 per cent of milliners were immigrants, and of these most lived in Toronto, which had a growing immigrant population employed in the garment trades. The 1921 Census gives more details: almost 80 per cent were Canadian born; 15 per cent had a British birthplace, 3 per cent were from Europe; and 2 per cent were from the United States.[19] The Department of Labour survey remarked on this aspect: "Millinery is an occupation which contains an unusually large proportion of Canadian girls. No doubt this is partly due to the natural aptitude of Canadian girls for the work, and partly to the fact that many of them are not completely dependent on their own resources while learning." The dual message in this statement was that immigrant girls did not have equal access to millinery because their families did not have the financial stability to support their young daughters during their training or apprenticeship, and that Canadian-born girls of British ancestry were nevertheless preferred for millinery, as they were for other prestigious skilled occupations such as nursing and teaching.[20]

In 1920 the picture was rosy for the milliner. The trade was flourishing, and the milliner held a special place in the custom-clothing trade, supplying the most artistic, individual, and conspicuous part of a woman's wardrobe. The milliner had been elevated from craftswoman to artist, on whose unfailing taste her devoted customers depended. Even more than dresses, coats, and other garments, hats had to be up-to-date. The fashion centres of

71.4 Advertisement for the Toronto Hat Co., *Dry Goods Review*, October 1923

Paris, London, and New York established the newest styles, and even the small-town Ontario milliner kept current through trade journals and fashion magazines. Head milliners, like Miss Bernadine, manager of the millinery department in the Right House ladies clothing store in Hamilton, made trips to New York every four weeks and to Toronto every two weeks, to check the very latest styles and make purchases.

Miss Bernadine was an example of the new trend in millinery retailing. She admitted that she did not hire trained milliners to produce hats from scratch, nor did she keep a millinery workroom, because "[t]oday is the day of the ready-to-wear hat." On buying trips to Toronto and New York, it was not unusual for Miss Bernadine to buy three to five hundred hats for her department. Miss Bernadine did, however, employ a trimmer "who is ready at all times to make changes in the ready-to-wear models to suit the tastes of the customers."[21]

The millinery wholesale industry that supplied Miss Bernadine was steadily growing. Wholesalers imported or manufactured hats to sell to millinery, dry-goods, and department stores (Illustration 71.4). In 1900 the *Toronto City Directory* listed nine wholesalers; in 1910 there were thirteen; and in 1920 the number had jumped to twenty-two. Female dominance of the millinery trade was taken for granted except in the case of wholesalers. Out of the over 5,000 milliners in the 1911 Census, 213 were men, mostly wholesalers situated in the industrial centre of Toronto.[22] A wholesale business required a large amount of capital for overhead and stock, for the machinery run on steam or electricity, and for wages for a large workforce. Instead of hats being made from scratch in the workrooms, all or parts of the process were now being performed by machine. Wholesalers both sold hats in their showrooms attached to their factories, but also sent "travellers" on the road to bring the goods to communities across the province. Manufacturers of millinery carried an exclusive line of hand-made hats and employed trained milliners for monotonous work, copying hats from a few models at much reduced wages, sometimes as low as a dollar a day.[23]

The ready-made hat was accepted first in the larger dry-goods and department stores (Illustration 71.5). One by one, these stores eliminated their millinery workroom and staff, as epitomized by an article written by one of the first merchants to embrace the factory hat: "I did away with all the expensive help, which included a milliner, $15 a week; trimmer, $10 a week; three paid hands, average $3 a week … In place of these I engaged a saleslady at $5 a week, thereby saving $29 a week in salaries. I received wholesale, ready-to-wear catalogues and made a selection from these … In all I had about seventy-five ready-trimmed hats … After the first three days' selling I had hardly any hats left."[24]

A further impetus to the industrialization of the making of women's hats was the new vogue for cloche, or bell-shaped hats, beginning in 1918 (Illustration 71.6). The characteristic close-fitting hat of the 1920s was simple in form and decoration, making it ideal for factory production. Often made of straw or felt, these hats were

71.5 Millinery department of the T. Eaton Co., Toronto, 1904 (F 229-308-0-2092-2, Archives of Ontario)

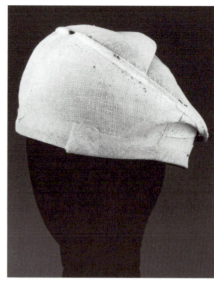

Right:

71.6 Hat from Newton Collection
(Hat D-6558, Canadian Museum of Civilization, s98-77)

Far right:

71.7 Hat foundation from Newton Collection
(Hat D-6752, Canadian Museum of Civilization, s98-05692)

easily blocked by machine. Women embraced the new style, especially young women, and encouraged by the cheaper prices, they bought them in greater quantities.[25]

The acceptance of the ready-made hat by milliners even in smaller towns is evidenced by a collection of five hundred hats, most dating to the 1920s, from Miss Newton's Hat Shop in Sarnia, Ontario. Katherine Newton entered the millinery trade at the age of thirty-five, perhaps by necessity: she was responsible for her older brother, sister, and mother. She opened shop in her hometown of Petrolia in 1918, and the next year opened another shop in Sarnia (Illustration 71.2). She prospered in the 1910s and early 1920s, with two milliners and one apprentice on her payroll. But by 1930, she was "seriously embarrassed financially" and had to close the Petrolia store. It is likely she overstocked during the previous few years and could not sell the hats, which eventually found their way to the Canadian Museum of Civilization. No doubt the Great Depression exacerbated her situation, but her business did not improve afterwards. In 1946 she closed down the Sarnia store. Like the rest of her sister

milliners, Miss Newton followed the general pattern: she opened shop in the optimistic 1910s to find herself foundering by the late 1920s.[26]

Most of the hats in her collection were purchased ready-made. Several have makers' or distributors' labels and handwritten price tags, making it possible to establish the origin of these hats and their price ranges. Miss Newton ordered from a total of forty establishments, most of them in Toronto, but also in Vancouver, Montreal, and New York (Illustration 71.4). Many of the Canadian companies manufactured their own hats, but they also imported hats from the United States, Great Britain, and Europe. Miss Newton's hat shop was far from parochial. She ordered a wide variety of hats from across the country and beyond. The ready-made hats Miss Newton had hoped to sell to the ladies of Sarnia and Petrolia attest to the inroads that the factory hat had made in the millinery business, even outside the large urban centres.

Illustration 71.6 shows a typical example of the ready-made hat. The basic form was easily produced by felting, blocking, and finishing machines. The appliqué decoration was skilfully applied by machine. The manufacturer was the John D. Ivey Company of Toronto, and the hat was priced in the medium range of $8.

Custom millinery did not, however, disappear altogether with the factory cloche. Gertrude Mantell, mentioned earlier, was still in business in 1933, when she wrote an impassioned article in the *Dry Goods Review* entitled "Increase Business by Being a Milliner and Not Just a Seller of Hats." She continued, "Has the Art of Millinery Been lost? Has the ready-to-wear hat submerged and outrun the hand-made hat? We say emphatically No! Never!" Miss Mantell acknowledged that milliners could not go back to "the old days when every hat was made by hand any more than we want to go back to candle-light." She accepted that especially sports and tailored hats (to go with the increasingly popular tailored suits) were suitable as factory made. The important role the milliner should play was in her discriminating selection of ready-made hats, in her ability to alter those hats and to make individual hats for customers who "never were, nor never will be satisfied with the finished article on the stand, and many of whom can be caught at a good profit by the clever milliner who knows how to make or alter a hat to suit the individual."[27]

Katherine Newton was a maker of hats, as well as a seller of hats. Probably most of her commissioned hats left the store with the customer, but one hat in the collection bears the label "Miss Newton's Hat Shop." This wide-brimmed hat was constructed in the traditional manner of wire frame, covered in buckram, and finished with black velvet cloth. The most revealing items in the collection are hat forms in various stages of production. Illustration 71.7 is an example of a buckram foundation for a beret, ready to be covered with finishing material. It is clearly hand-made, probably by Miss Newton. The piecing is complex and indicates a professional hand. The use of both wire frame and flat patterning in buckram shows that Miss Newton made hats

by traditional millinery techniques, in addition to buying hats ready-made.

By the 1920s and '30s, trained milliners offered what large department stores could not: custom work for discriminating customers. But they were at a crossroads, one that Miss Mantell sensed in 1933: "A new day is undoubted approaching , and if we are not too positive what its nature may be, certainly the milliner best equipped for the fray is bound to go over the top. It is a battle, isn't it?"[28]

The custom milliner won the battle, but not the war. Many discovered that the custom trade was disappearing and that they could no longer compete with the larger stores, especially in urban centres where department stores flourished. In 1911 there were 5,567 milliners in Ontario. Despite tremendous growth in population, the number of milliners had dropped to 1,067 by 1931. As millinery workrooms began to disappear, so did young apprentices. The shop owners of the 1920s and '30s were milliners who had excelled in training in the heyday of 1900 to 1920. This created a trend towards milliners who were mature in age. The 1921 census report remarked that for all custom-clothing trades, including dressmaking, "[t]his heavy concentration in the later age groups, while intensified by the exclusion of apprentices, must be mainly attributed to a declining occupation." Nor did wages improve. The 1931 Census reported that in Canada the average salary for a full-time milliner was $760; for a shop proprietor, $1,130. These figures are slightly lower than those in *The Canadian Girl at Work* of 1919.[29]

A series of factors led to the demise of the custom-millinery trade in Ontario. The prominence of the hat in a woman's wardrobe in the first two decades of this century led to an increase in consumer demand, and men with the capital to establish mechanized factories began to enter the millinery marketplace, manufacturing and importing sport and tailored hats initially and later hats for all occasions. Concurrently, the rise of the department store overshadowed the small millinery shops, and department stores were the first to retail the new factory-made hats. New fashions in hat styles were also easily adapted to factory production. These circumstances affected both apprentices and trained milliners who were employed by stores and small workshops, and the businesswoman-milliner who ran her own shop. The millinery workroom virtually disappeared, and shops grew scarce. Hats continued to be a mandatory part of the wardrobe through the 1930s and '40s, but began to fade in the 1950s, and virtually disappeared during the 1960s.

Today most people wear hats only for practical purposes, and department stores sell a limited variety of manufactured straw-brimmed hats and winter toques. But a small number of creative and dedicated milliners are now reviving traditional millinery techniques. The hand-made hat will never again be an obligatory part of our apparel, but the art of millinery may survive.

72 Our Mothers' Patterns: Sewing and Dressmaking in the Japanese-Canadian Community

Susan Michi Sirovyak

Like women from all immigrant communities, pioneer Japanese-Canadian women who came to Canada faced many challenges in the struggle to make new lives for themselves and their families. Most of the Issei (first-generation Japanese-Canadian) women immigrated to Canada in the 1910s and 1920s, joining husbands who had been labouring in British Columbia's primary industries. From the time of their arrival, the women worked outside of the home, on farms, in canneries, or as domestics, to supplement their household income. A significant number of first- and second-generation Japanese-Canadian women also worked as dressmakers or owned dressmaking businesses. The contributions made by these women in the early years, during the period of upheaval in the Second World War, and in the later re-establishment years were considerable. This article examines the experiences of these dressmakers, shedding light on a little-known and previously undocumented area of Japanese-Canadian history and heritage.

In the summer of 1996, with other staff and volunteers of the Japanese-Canadian National Museum and Archives in Vancouver, I had the opportunity to prepare a small exhibition on the role of dressmaking in the history of the Nikkei[1] community. Created through a series of interviews, discussions, and correspondence with Japanese-Canadian women who shared their memories and knowledge, the exhibition was entitled "Our Mothers' Patterns: Sewing and Dressmaking in the Japanese-Canadian Community." From stories of long days over a sewing machine, photographs of sewing classes, and tiny mock-up patterns assembled from brown kraft paper, we began to piece together a picture of dressmaking in the Japanese-Canadian community. We also began to realize the vital role that sewing and dressmaking has played in the lives of Japanese-Canadian women and in the social fabric of the wider community. Almost everyone we spoke with had a mother, grandmother, sister, aunt, or friend who had learned to sew and acquire dressmaker's skills in the decades preceding the Second World War. As one woman, Kay Tatebe, said of that era, "There was a dressmaker on every corner and most of them were Japanese."[2]

Why was sewing and dressmaking so popular in the Japanese-Canadian community? Part of the reason, explains historian Dr Michiko (Midge) Ayukawa, may be traced to Japan, where sewing was considered to be part of the basic preparation for marriage for all young women: "For centuries, in Japan, one of the basic skills that a young woman had to have before marriage, no matter how humble the home, was the ability to sew a kimono. In the rural areas, many started with the raw silk or cotton, made the thread, and dyed and wove the cloth. With the Meiji Restoration and the introduction of western style clothes, Yōsai [or western sewing] often also became a necessary preparation for marriage. In Canada, too, this tradition has continued.[3]

The tradition not only continued, it flourished. From

72.1 Academy of Domestic Arts, Greenwood, 1945 (Japanese Canadian National Museum and Archives Society. Courtesy of Ruth Hamaguchi)

The Academy of Domestic Arts
Greenwood, B.C. April 25, 1945.

the 1910s to the 1930s, dressmaking in Canada was much more than a basic skill for prospective brides; it was one of the primary means by which Nikkei women earned their living. To understand the impact of dressmaking in the community, it is important to realize that there were few employment opportunities for young Japanese-Canadian women entering the work force at that time. Regardless of whether they had completed high school or university, Japanese-Canadians were prevented from entering many occupations, because of racial social discrimination and lack of the franchise. Young Nikkei woman were rarely hired as teachers, nurses, or office workers. While it was possible to find employ-

ment at a Japanese-Canadian business or shop, there were few such openings.

Thus, sewing and dressmaking was an attractive option that offered a reliable way for Nikkei women to make a living. This was especially so for the Nisei, the second generation of Japanese-Canadian women, who began entering the job market in the 1920s and 1930s. According to a 1935 survey of second generation Japanese-Canadians in British Columbia, 85 of 261 female respondents living in urban areas listed dressmaking as their occupation.[4] And although most Japanese-Canadian women in rural areas worked on farms or in fruit canneries, there were also dressmakers among them. Of a total of 254 rural-area respondents, there were 150 farm hands, 69 fruit cannery workers, and 13 dressmakers, leaving only 22 respondents who listed some other occupation.

Since dressmaking was their only option for employment outside of cannery work, housekeeping, or farm work, many young Nisei women chose to attend dressmaking school rather than high school. Throughout Vancouver and its outlying areas, dressmaking classes flourished as early as the 1910s. In people's homes and church basements, informal sewing classes provided young girls and housewives with the skills to sew clothes inexpensively for themselves or their children. Tokuko Inouye recalls attending a sewing class in her Powell Street neighbourhood, dropping in after her housework was finished and as her time allowed.[5]

For students looking to establish a career in dressmaking, a number of formal dressmaking schools taught one- to four-year programs in everything from needlework to pattern layout to dress construction. To name a few, there was the Women's Sewing School, the Marietta School of Costume Design, the Academy of Domestic Arts, and the Girls College of Practical Arts (Illustration 72.1). A healthy competition between the schools for the recruitment of new students is evident from articles and advertisements that ran in the *New Canadian*, the local Japanese-Canadian newspaper. For example, a 1941 article for the Marietta School of Costume Design states: "Miss Haruko Morishita is the Nisei principal of the Marietta School of Costume Design, whose courses in dress designing, drafting and useful arts, are setting a new standard among Niseis in the city. So popular is the Marietta School that prospective students are urged to register immediately to be sure of a place in the classes."[6]

The schools provided comprehensive and individual instruction and awarded the students a diploma upon graduation. Mary Otto (née Ikeda) described her own training in a dressmaking school:

Before the war I studied dressmaking and tailoring at the Matsuzaki School. Craftwork with wool, embroidery, and cutwork were all part of the course for a diploma. My main interest was of course dressmaking and as my aspiration grew my dream and goal headed towards becoming a dress designer. I studied the proportions of sketching a figure and drew my ideas on paper to design and produce a garment … And so during the summer months when many of my friends went to the farms to pick strawberries and tomatoes, I walked Monday to Friday to the Matsuzaki School of Dressmaking and Tailoring [Illustration 72.2].[7]

Drafting the dressmaking patterns, using curved and right-angled rulers, was a highly technical skill. The closely fitted and bias-cut fashions that were popular during the era demanded skill and precision in drafting the patterns. First designed on a small scale, the patterns were then transferred to full scale from which the fabric was cut. Students kept their pattern drafting books for ready reference; many of the women who assisted us with the display still have their pattern books today.

72.2 Women in sewing class, Matsuzaki School of Dressmaking and Tailoring, Vancouver, 1938 (Japanese Canadian National Museum and Archives Society. Courtesy of Mary O'Hara)

Top:
72.3 Sayoko Hattori at her sewing machine, 1953
(Japanese Canadian National Museum and Archives
Society. Courtesy of Sayoko Hattori)

Right:
72.4 Ayako Kohara in front of Sisters Cleaners and
Dressmakers, 1935 (Japanese Canadian National Museum
and Archives Society. Courtesy of Ayako Kohara)

Chie Oya, who studied dressmaking at the Slocan City internment camp, requested that we return her pattern book to her as soon as we could as she still occasionally uses it – over fifty years after she first created it!

Throughout the 1920s and 1930s, Japanese-Canadian women established dressmaking shops and businesses in British Columbia. Sayoko Hattori (nee Tanaka) purchased Bonnie Lass Dressmakers on Dunbar Street in Vancouver in 1936 when she was just twenty-three years old (Illustration 72.3).[8] She had learned her dressmaking skills working for Yayoi Negishi in her corner shop at Broadway Street and Commercial Drive. Sayoko's business thrived, and after she married, she and her husband expanded the shop to include dry cleaning. Another shop-owner was Ayako Kohara (née Yasui), who, together with her sister, Shizue, established Sisters Cleaners and Dressmakers on Alma Street (Illustration 72.4).[9] The two sisters worked side by side designing and sewing dresses for women in the neighbourhood, while their father operated the cleaners. According to Charles H. Young and Helen R. Reid, in 1931 there were eighty-one Japanese-Canadian cleaning and pressing businesses in Vancouver alone.[11] Invariably, these also offered to do alterations and dressmaking, for which the women were responsible.

For these and many other entrepreneurial Nikkei women, however, success was short-lived. In 1941 the Pacific theatre of the Second World War erupted, dramatically changing the lives of all Japanese Canadians who lived along the West Coast. Discrimination and racial tensions that had been brewing for many years culminated in the forced evacuation from the coast of all persons of Japanese origin. By October of 1942 the entire community had been uprooted and sent to internment camps, ghost towns, road camps, or other isolated locations "east of the Rockies." All of the dressmaking businesses owned by Japanese-Canadians in Vancouver closed. Although a few managed to sell their businesses before they were evacuated, most were forced simply to close their shops and leave.

In the internment camps and other isolated locations, the need for sewing and dressmaking became paramount as families scrambled with few resources for adequate clothing. Many families were fortunate to have their treadle sewing machines with them – necessary equipment, as the often crude conditions meant having to live without electric power. There is evidence of the resourcefulness of everyone at that time. In the face of a severe shortage of materials, everything that could be recycled, was: men's dress shirts became small shirts for boys or dresses for young girls; an adult overcoat became the material for children's parkas; rice and flour sacks became sheets, towels, and cushion covers. Tokuko Inouye recalls sewing outfits for her son from the "blackout fabric" her family had used earlier in the war to block the light from the windows.

In many of the internment camps, dressmaking classes and academies that had been forced to close in the Vancouver area were once again established, some by former teachers and directors. There are many photographs of sewing classes from camps and ghost towns such as Tashme, Lemon Creek, Greenwood, Slocan City and East Lillooet (Illustration 72.5). Mary Otto described her attempts at establishing a makeshift dressmaking class in the Tashme internment camp:

Evacuation started and after a year of incarceration in Tashme I decided to share my knowledge in dressmaking with anyone interested. There were many as there was not a clothing store and the girls and young ladies and women were desiring to add new dresses to their wardrobe. I had a Singer sewing machine (treadle) which we were able to have shipped from Vancouver. We started our class on the kitchen table. … Class time was very limited because at mealtime the table was needed.

As I received more requests from would be students we

72.5 Sewing class at Lemon Creek Internment Camp, c. 1945 (Japanese Canadian National Museum and Archives Society. Courtesy of Mary O'Hara)

decided to convert the two bedrooms into sewing rooms by bringing down a flat board over the bed, converting it into a table. When not in use the board was hooked back against the wall and ready as a bed. One of the student's mother loaned out her machine in exchange for her daughter's lessons so with two machines we did all right with four or five students at a time in three shifts: morning, afternoon and evening.

How did we manage without electricity? Coal oil lamps were limited to two per family so we purchased extra lamps by mail order. Our house was well lighted up thanks to my father who had a job as the "Oil Man." I followed the same format of the Marietta School of Dressmaking and those who stayed long enough with my class were able to earn a diploma. After the war we went on our own way but I heard from time to time that the girls and some of the married women were able to find jobs or even supervisory positions in the clothing field.[11]

All the women we spoke with said they felt extremely fortunate that they acquired sewing and dressmaking skills as a means of clothing their families or establishing a career. Marie Saito explained to us the importance of dressmaking in her life and its significance for her and her family after the death of her husband: "My youngest was only four years old so I could not go to work. I was fortunate that I took up dressmaking and I could earn a living at home. It was good to earn extra money but to raise your family on dressmaking was hard work. I had to sew from early in the morning to late at night to make ends meet … When I think back I wonder how I did it with no education, but it was fortunate that I took up dressmaking – I was able to make a living on it."[12]

After the war, some Japanese-Canadian dressmakers established themselves as designers and pattern makers in the clothing industry in eastern Canada. In general, however, there was a decline in the need for dressmaking skills and for the schools to provide such skills. Retail clothing increased in popularity, the job market slowly began to accept Japanese-Canadians into it, and young Nikkei women who were learning to sew discovered commercially made patterns (many received help from their elders to achieve a properly fitted garment). For many years, however, dressmaking had played a vital role in both the Nikkei and the larger community. The dressmakers of that earlier period exemplify a quiet but resolute tenacity to persevere and prevail.

73 Federica and Angelina: Postwar Italian-Canadian Couturiers in Toronto

Alexandra Palmer

The roots of the Italian ready-to-wear fashion industry date back to the post-Second World War period. At that time Italy was struggling to establish itself as an important international cultural and economic force in the areas of industrial design and fashion. Its production process was based upon a craft system of small workshops with limited runs of goods. This general approach was particularly suited to the labour intensity of haute couture, whose many small houses relied on the technical skills of numerous tailors, seamstresses, and embroiderers.

The so-called birth of postwar Italian fashion took place on 12 February 1951 and can be credited to the deliberate and tactical work of an individual, Giovani Battista Giorgini. Following the seasonal buying trip to Paris, he invited a select group of important American and Canadian buyers to his palazzo in Florence to see a fashion show featuring unknown Italian designers. The success of this venture prompted the beginning of more formal presentations. The following July, over three hundred buyers and journalists requested to attend and, from that time onwards, the shows were held in the Pitti Palace.[1] The eager response from the press and fashion world was captured by Bettina Ballard, American *Vogue* reporter then based in Paris. She explained the appeal and sudden success of the Italian fashion scene as follows:

I very soon found out, along with the postwar travel-starved buyers and the fashion press, how pleasant it is to travel on an expense account with the legitimate excuse of looking over new fashion markets. We all flocked, like a migration of well-dressed birds, to Florence [to see] Italian fashions in the Pitti Palace ... it was so manifestly attractive to discover fashion in a country so full of treasures to see, *proscuitto con figi* to eat, and people who were so polite and open-armed and who understood every halting word of Italian we uttered.[2]

The success of the new Italian fashions was indeed partly due to this sense of discovery. However, interest was also heightened by the sense of history and the "Italianness" of the fashions, promoted through touristic fashion shoots in palazzos and typical Florentine settings. Additionally, the presence of aristocrats – Giorgini himself; Emilio Pucci, a marquis; Irene Galitzine, a princess of Russian descent, or Simonetta, the daughter of a duke and wife of a count and couturier, Fabiani – served to strengthen and personify Italy's links to a rich cultural past.[3] Ornella Morelli has suggested that the Italian fashion designers were in fact "compensating for their lack of experience and technical knowledge with their noble heritage of ideas and taste."[4] However, Giorgini had worked as a buying agent for several American department stores and was keenly aware of the North American market in terms of taste and pricing. He tactically advised the designers on issues of wearability, practicality, simplicity of cut, and prices (Italian prices were less than half those of French couture garments).[5] The Italian designs were promoted as feminine and flattering, and not as faddish as French fashion. All of these factors ensured that the fashion appealed to Italian foreign buyers and manufacturers.

Yet Italians working in Italy were not the only ones to profit from this new excitement for things Italian. Italian-Canadians also traded on Italy's new national design identity. At this time, two Italian couturiers, Federica and Angelina, achieved a *caché* that was partially based on this interest in Italian design. In Toronto, Italians had traditionally found employment as tailors and seamstresses working in small ateliers and department stores. The latter had offered custom designing since their inception in the late nineteenth century, although as Susan Porter Benson points out, "shopping changed [in the 1890s] from a straightforward matter of supplying the family's needs into a complex activity involving amusement, diversion, a widening sphere of choice, and class-based standards of taste."[6] In the postwar period, custom-order facilities were still considered part of the traditional service of large retail stores, even though it was an archaic and unprofitable practice.

Immediately after the war, Simpson's and Eaton's in Toronto had fashion designers attached to their couture salons; an in-store designer was perceived as providing a necessary service for a small but important clientele, the same clientele that could afford to purchase imported couture and top-price fashions. A fashion designer's name enabled the store to promote itself during fashion shows, as the in-store creations were always shown with the European couture. Thus, the fashions created by the department store's own designer shared the stage with those of world-famous couturiers, reinforcing the glamour and status of the department store as a source of expertise for taste and design.

In 1951 Simpson's decided to expand its custom salon. Simpson's designer, Vassallo, who was trained as a tailor, went to Italy to hire a dress designer to assist in the salon. He invited a young Italian woman called Federica

to come and work with him and, at the same time, hired a fashion sketch artist.[7] Federica was working in the couture department of a Milanese department store, A La Tessile, as a saleswoman and buyer. She visited the couture collections in Paris twice a year and would buy original models, *toiles* (designs made in muslin), or patterns that were copied or adapted in the store for her local clientele. She was familiar with all the Paris houses, as well as with their suppliers, where she also purchased the textiles and trims. Once back in Milan, she designed a collection for the salon that comprised fifty to sixty original pieces. To price a garment, she calculated the price of the fabric in Italy, the time it took to sew, the price of trims and findings, added 10 per cent, and then doubled the price. The resulting garment would still be cheaper than the same dress made in France. The store then held fashion shows to promote the new designs and took custom orders.[8]

However, once in Toronto, Federica's situation at Simpson's was not what she envisioned. Vassallo had a saleswoman, Mrs Clare, who assisted customers and showed them fabrics, and this was the role that Federica had envisioned for herself, rather than that of designer.[9] Additionally, she felt that the quality of fabric available to her and the scale of the operation were not at all what she had wanted. She soon resigned and opened up her own couture salon.[10]

That same year another new Italian immigrant applied for a job at Simpson's. Angelina Fabbro had learned to sew and cut in a traditional manner. She was born in a small town near Bari, Italy, and began her apprenticeship at a cousin's atelier when she was thirteen years old. She attended a design school for one year, and then began to work professionally as a seamstress when she was eighteen, operating a custom business from her parents' home.[11] Angelina immigrated to Toronto in 1950 and first found employment as a pattern maker at an Italian-owned clothing factory on King

73.1 La Boutique Federica, Toronto, 1950s (Federica scrapbook, Royal Ontario Museum)

Street, in Toronto's garment district. Shortly after, she worked at Simpson's St Regis Room, making custom orders and doing alterations, under Vassallo. Because of her technical expertise she ended up supervising the forty-five tailors, until she again moved on. By the late 1950s, Simpson's had ceased to retain an in-store designer, as the custom salon barely supported itself.[12]

Custom-fashion design was not limited to department stores in Toronto. The 1950s saw a concentrated effort by a small number of individuals to establish a Canadian couture industry.[13] The impetus for this initiative lay in the general economic and cultural growth of the country and was made possible with postwar European immigrant labour. Many new Canadians had not only a strong cultural background in design and textiles, but also the technical skills that allowed them to realize complex design concepts. The new couturiers, primarily postwar immigrants trained in Europe, modelled their salons on the traditional Paris couture house, with showrooms, fitters, tailors, and seamstresses, the employees also being primarily of European extraction. These couturiers produced high-quality original designs

and workmanship that were in step with international design trends.

The location and look of the couture establishment were important. After her brief sojourn with Simpson's, Federica set up her own boutique on Petticoat Lane, off Avenue Road, selling one-of-a-kind couture.[14] She took Angelina with her from Simpsons to help her realize her design concepts, as Federica was not trained as a seamstress or couturier. Her salon was described by a client as "a huge room in front of this big old house. A lot of workrooms were behind … The salon … was big … Gorgeous furniture, Baroque, European … I do remember a big armoire that when closed looked tidy and when open had materials and gorgeous things."[15] A client walking into Federica's salon "would see nothing."[16] She and her customer would talk, Federica would sketch, and they would look at magazines and swatches and the yardage she had in stock (Illustration 73.1).

Angelina set up her own salon in 1953 after working for Toronto couturiers Federica, Olive Smart, and Cornelia. Angelina was the primary breadwinner for her family, and when her youngest son was ill, she needed to be home. So, encouraged by Cornelia, she started working from her home at 1154 Gerrard Street East. This was not a chic area, and one of her clients helped her find a house in a more appropriate location, a house at 303 Avenue Road, where she opened a salon.[17] Angelina's understanding of design, and her four years of apprenticeship in Italy gave her "hands of gold." All the couturiers interviewed unanimously praised her technical skills.[18]

Each Toronto couture establishment had its own system for production, based upon the capability and numbers of the staff employed, as well as on the requirements of the individual orders. However, as all salons emulated the Paris couture system, the couturiers shared many commonalities. As one journalist wrote, "The problems of running a salon in Toronto boil down to one big one, which bedevils all couturiers here: That of finding properly skilled workers."[19] The usual way to obtain help was through word of mouth or advertising. Angelina advertised in the local Italian newspaper and considered herself lucky to have found women who stayed with her. "I had about seven, and I even had a tailor twice. The first was one who was working in Simpson's, he was Italian, he worked for me, Giovanni La Rosa." He came to her when Simpson's closed down the custom department. The other tailor was called Giuseppe, originally a Roman who had worked for an established house called Tritico.[20] During her most intense business period, Federica employed eight to nine women. She trained her own première, who ran the workroom, as it was difficult for her to find someone with the required experience, though other couturiers were reluctant to invest in training staff.[21] Typically workers moved around and knew fellow tailors and seamstresses.[22] Shifting and working within a small circle was typical of the couture system, and couturiers competed for good workroom staff. Toronto couturiers relied upon European-trained immigrants, as noted, and were an especially significant employer for women.

Given the amount of time the couturiers spent with clients as well as designing, getting supplies, overseeing fittings, and running workrooms, it was not surprising that the business of running a couture salon demanded close attention. There was never a large profit margin. Most Canadian clients believed that the couture clothes they were purchasing were expensive, even though they were always below that of an imported couture equivalent. Somehow the status couture imported from Europe and sold locally, even though it was not custom designed or fitted, always outweighed a similar or superior product that was locally produced.

Some couturiers started up with their own funds, while others borrowed, often from clients.[23] Pricing was commonly worked out as follows: the cost of fabric, trims, and thread would be tracked, and the time for cutting, fitting, and sewing would be added. Policies regarding billing differed. Federica, who admitted to being a poor manager, never asked the customers for a deposit, as she felt they should be able to see their purchase because "they didn't know what they were getting."[24] Contrary to her, John Artibello, a second-generation Italian-Canadian couturier trained in Toronto, asked for 25 per cent down on an order and full payment before it left the house.[25]

Each couturier had a core group of repeat clients who were the mainstay of their businesses. This core group tended to be well-off, mature women with an established social position. Angelina had a steady group of about fifty.[26] Some clients had "problem" figures that made buying already made up imported couture impractical, owing to the number of alterations that would be necessitated. By patronizing a local couturier, women not only could be certain of an excellent fit, but could have any design they chose, instead of being limited to a selection of imported couture. A young clientele was more difficult to attract, primarily because of the prices, though it was not unusual for a daughter to became a regular client. Of great importance, too, were clients who ordered special-occasion clothes, such as a daughter's debutante gown, a mother-of-the-bride dress, a bridal gown, or a trousseau.

Designing for Toronto socialites required an understanding of etiquette and appropriate dress for the season and its upcoming events. One instance of this was discussed by reporter and historian Olive Dickason, who wrote, "Toronto's couturiers have never had it so good. They are busy these days … more Canadian women will be meeting Queen Elizabeth in clothes especially created for them than at any comparable occasion in the past."[27] In this instance, Mrs George Wilson, the wife of the head of the Harbour Commission, was meeting the queen as she came ashore from the voyage that inaugurated the opening of the Seaway: "[F]or this Angelina has made an oyster white silk suit, the scissor pleat skirt making it easy to curtsey with grace … For the Royal dinner Angelina has made a beautiful gown of sunlight satin with long chiffon drapery. For Plate Day at the races she will wear a French taffeta in blue and white."[28]

One of Federica's favoured clients had come to her when she had just opened her business on Petticoat Lane. A chauffeur (in uniform) came into the salon and invited Federica to visit and design for a woman living in Grafton, Ontario. She went the following week with her assistant and was warmly met by her client. The next morning Federica was called to her hostess's bedroom and commissioned to make her five dresses, all the same design. The client was a large woman who knew what she wanted: a hostess dress in which to greet her house guests and whose design should suggest a monastic look. This wealthy client never came to Federica's salon, but chauffeured Federica and her fitter to her house for meetings and fittings. Her daughter also patronized Federica. They never asked the price in advance and were the type of client for whom couturiers most enjoyed working.[29]

Torontonians, such as Mrs Jeanie Hersenhoren, were very eager to have high-style couture clothing made locally. As soon as Mrs Hersenhoren heard about Federica through word of mouth, she went to see her. Federica made her "a violet ombre, mid-calf length dress with the top like a tulip and with a black bow, strapless." Later, Mrs Hersenhoren attended a fashion show that featured Federica's designs, and was particularly attracted by a pink satin, crystal-trimmed evening gown.[30]

However, most Toronto couturiers, in addition to a small regular clientele, also had individual champions – socialites or celebrities – who helped to attract the attention of the press. Federica achieved notoriety when Princess Gourielli, better known as Helena Rubenstein, purchased a coat. She later remade this design for a fashion show. Federica's quick success was also reflected by patronage for the socially important occasion of the 1953 Coronation Ball fund-raiser for the Art Gallery of Toronto.[31] Angelina also had her important patrons, including Mrs C. Rudolph Moor, wife of the Swiss consul, who was singled out because of her costume for the opening of the symphony season and "was the centre of envy in a vivid turquoise and gold Indian silk sheath created by the new young Canadian-Italian designer, Angelina."[32]

Toronto's couturiers added to the cultural life of the city through their Paris-inspired salons, which for elite women fulfilled a role similar to that of a private gentlemen's club, and through the production of custom couture that was worn to local and international events. They also created social events focused around fashion shows. Local couturiers were regularly solicited to support charity organizations through fashion shows, and often the charity was one supported by their clients' volunteer work. Federica commented that she never refused to do one. The organizations she supported were varied and included a B'nai B'rith show to raise funds for research scholarships, held at the inaugural luncheon of the Women's Division of the United Jewish Appeal. She also made a conscious effort to use the newly created branch of the Society for Crippled Civilians to embroider and make trims for her, calling the results "Marina Creations."[33] Both her and Angelina's designs were modelled in shows in support of the Association of Volunteers, Ontario Hospital.[34] Fashion shows provided mutual benefits for couturiers and their clients: the show promoted the couturier to a social group that could afford to buy couture, while the couturier supported their clients' professional commitments.[35] But they were costly to produce. Toronto couturiers were constantly having to choose between providing, at their own expense, garments for fashion shows, that would promote their name and business, or not spending the time and money on shows, thereby not reaping the potential, but unpredictable, profit.

Clearly, running a profitable couture salon in Toronto during the 1950s was not easy. Therefore, it is no surprise that Italian-Canadian couturiers, like other European couturiers, were eager to find more profitable outlets for their designs. They did this though the establishment of boutique collections and licensing agreements that presaged *prêt à porter*. Federica and Angelina did too. Federica diversified in the late 1950s and 1960s and rode on the crest of the international success of Italian sport and knitwear. Having established her name through the salon, she expanded her business to include designs for manufacturers. Between 1956 and 1964, she partly designed, and partly copied from Paris, a collection that was made in Milan and flown to Canada. The designs were "one-of-a-kind, and so styled as to fit a variety of sizes with minimum alterations." This collection was shown at the Lord Simcoe Hotel and ranged in price from $150 to $3,000.[36] In 1956 Federica designed rainwear, followed by her first sportswear collection for Daymac, under her own label, "A Federica Original." These were made in cotton prints, called the American Artists series, and French provincial prints, and were exclusive in Canada to Daymac.[37] In 1960 she began to make custom-ordered knitwear on machines she imported from Switzerland, run by operators she brought over from Italy. The garments were all knitted to shape and could easily be adjusted for individual figures by adding or decreasing stitches. This was such an immediate success that the demand could not be met, particularly because of the lack of local skilled operators, all of whom had to be specially trained on her advanced machines.[38] Similarly, Angelina branched out and was commissioned to design an exclusive collection of preteens clothes for Holt Renfrew, called Alina. This was the first such couture collection that was made to order, and the designs were primarily party dresses for special occasions such as graduation.[39] Angelina even designed a new uniform for Girl Guide leaders.[40] Both women undertook these initiatives to augment the couture businesses and

73.2 A suit designed by Federica, 1950s (Federica scrapbook, Royal Ontario Museum)

take advantage of their status as well-known Italian-Canadian couturiers and the contemporary popularity of Italian fashion.

Thus, Toronto's two renowned Italian couturiers in the 1950s followed strategies similar to those of internationally recognized European-based couturiers. While their business practices differed in details, they both struggled to cover their costs and make a profit by drawing from and competing for Toronto's small elite clientele, and they both contributed to the social and community life of the city through their European-style salons and fashion shows. These two Italian emigré couturiers added to the city's cultural capital and attracted clients who believed that a locally designed product, with a bona fide European heritage, could compete with imported international couture and create for them *la bella figura*.

74 Fabrications: Clothing, Generations, and Stitching Together the History We Live

Kathryn Church

How can we learn from history? Not from the formal chronicle of events, but from the subjective feelings and thoughts with which we experience the events of our everyday lives. How do we learn from the history that we live?

Peter Lyman, 1988

MAPPING THE JOURNEY

A Toronto-based sociologist in her early forties returns to her hometown in central Alberta to retrieve pieces of her life. In an unorthodox act of feminist research, she designs a museum exhibit that features the work of a local seamstress. I am the sociologist; my mother is the seamstress; the exhibit is "Fabrications: Stitching Ourselves Together." This is not just a "nice" story about a dutiful daughter "honouring" her mother. It is also a painful story about an ambivalent daughter who, while growing up, was so distressed by her mother's servitude in domestic roles that she dedicated herself to living something different. In mid-life, still struggling to free herself from the grip of the past, she finally turns towards rather than away from the life of her aging mother. Using the exhibit, and in particular the wedding dress form, she revisits the traditional gender relations of her childhood and attempts to come to terms with them.

MY LIFE IN CLOTH: SCRAPS OF AUTOBIOGRAPHY

My mother, Lorraine, sewed for me from the first days of my life to the early years of my marriage. As I was growing up, one of the primary ways that we related to each other was through clothing. We shared in the creation of self through the construction of clothing: looking at patterns, selecting fabric, fitting, wearing, and caring for garments. For most of the special events of my life, I have been dressed in outfits of my mother's making. School pictures and family photo albums document our successes and our mistakes. "Fabrications" begins to work with this deeply contradictory experience: my pleasure in being Mom's chief "model," developing deep attachments to the distinctly feminine outfits that she sewed, while simultaneously feeling at odds with the girl, the young woman, who was produced in this way.

Growing up out west in a family of boys, my preference was for the rough-and-tumble freedom of jeans and T-shirts. I was a tomboy, an aspiring cowgirl, an athlete. It was difficult to own these identities while sustaining a communication with my mother through her sewing. Indeed, as I moved further away from home, deeper into urban life, academic work, and feminist sensibilities, we reached a point where she could no longer sew for me. There was a break in our textural communication, including a post-prairie phase in which I discarded all of my brown clothing, and another during a

74.1 Kathryn and Lorraine Church (Courtesy of Kathryn Church, Red Deer Museum)

protracted illness in which I would wear nothing but black. After many years of separation along this dimension, our dialogue began again through the museum exhibit. I used the project as a way to explore how women use clothing to construct a gendered self.

ACROSS THE GENERATIONS: INTO THE MOTHER-DAUGHTER DIVIDE

My mother and I began to collaborate on what came to be called "Fabrications" in 1997. It has become a journey into knowing and better understanding each other's lives, a door into a different kind of communication. I spent a month living next door to my parents while I interviewed my mother and her former "clients" about their wedding dresses. I kept a journal and a record of my e-mail correspondence during this formative time. These writings mark where I was in relation to the Alberta landscape (familial, social/political, and geo-

graphic) when the project began. What emerged then that has since become very clear and public, was a particular narrative tension: between a woman who exemplifies loving service to home, family, and community, and her daughter who rejects those virtues as traditionally expressed in favour of travel, schooling, and career.

It is a tension familiar to many mothers and daughters whose relationships were formed during the fifties and sixties. This was confirmed for me by women, often academics, who wrote to me in response to the CBC *This Morning*'s broadcast of "Behind the Scenes at the Red Deer Museum." This was a radio documentary (June 1998) in which my mother and I talked openly about our relationship in the context of building the exhibit. Until that time, although I was conscious of working with a volatile emotional thread of my own history, I had little idea how resonant it was with my contemporaries. Through urbanization, greater access to formal education, feminism, and the sexual revolution, we (and here

74.2 Wedding dresses designed by Lorraine Church
(Courtesy of Kathryn Church, Red Deer Museum)

I suppose that I mean women in our forties and fifties) have been enabled to live markedly different lives from those of our mothers. This transformation, including a breach in the nature and transmission of women's knowledge, emerged as a key theme of the museum project. What are the losses and gains that result? What are the challenges for the future?

THE LITTLE EXHIBIT THAT COULD: REDEFINING THE PUBLIC SPACE OF THE MUSEUM

In May 1996 I sat with my mother in the Co-op Cafeteria of the North Hill Mall in Red Deer, Alberta. There, I talked to her for the first time about my desire to create a "one-woman show" of her work. Chasing her salad around her plate, she eyed me with profound disbelief. I felt more optimistic, but much of that was based on ignorance. Because of our class and geographic background, neither of us knew much about museums or galleries. We had no real way of gauging the possibility of implementing my idea. Two years later, along with 160 invited guests, my mother and I participated in the gala opening of "Fabrications" at the Red Deer and District Museum. In March 1999 we were both in Ottawa for the exhibit's official rebirth at the Canadian Museum of Civilization. That is an extraordinary leap along any number of dimensions. How is it that an admittedly homespun, low-budget production was able to make the improbable journey from a local to a national venue?

Part of the answer is that museums are going through a time of tremendous redefinition. Influenced both by economic restructuring and debates over what constitutes knowledge, they are slowly opening to new forms and publics. Thus, there was conceptual space for an outsider such as myself to bring in the biography of an ordinary woman. There was receptivity to a text written from a place of great feeling with the intent of evoking emotions in others. Ironically, such violations of the rules made the exhibit highly accessible. Eight thousand people visited "Fabrications" in Red Deer during the summer of 1998. Most were women. They came from western Canada and beyond; many were not typical museum patrons. In their wake they left a trail of emotional vignettes about themselves, their mothers and grandmothers, and the place that sewing occupies in their lives. It is as if a whole community of women stepped out of hiding. These women and their stories brought the project to life, but none of it would have been possible without women in significant public roles who contributed an impressive array of "non-domestic" skills. Women in their diversity are a huge part of why my mother's story has successfully crossed the private/public divide. The success of "Fabrications'" signifies an important opportunity for other marginalized groups to infiltrate and influence museums in this period, reshaping them as public institutions.

WOMEN'S WORK: THE MORE IT CHANGES

"Fabrications" was billed by the Red Deer and District Museum as "an intimate autobiography of work, women and wedding dresses." While the public responded primarily to the dresses, I have been preoccupied from several directions with questions of work. I have never been comfortable with the private, unpaid, and domestic nature of my mother's work. One of the driving forces of my life has been to establish for myself a different relationship with the labour market. Ironically, in aspiring to this, I inadvertently devalued my mother even further. Over the past few years I have grappled with this dilemma personally and professionally. The museum exhibit is part of this struggle, a way of celebrating my mother's skill in the "domestic arts" while raising questions about its social and economic invisibility.

75 The Telephone Operator: From "Information Central" to Endangered Species

Caroline Martel (translated by Rosemary Covert)

In the middle of the 1870s, an adventure in communications began when the telephone was invented by Alexander Graham Bell. Since that time, the telephone operator has acted as an intermediary between customers and the developing telephone technology. The transition to telephone communication was a difficult one, and telephone companies considered that a "feminine nature" was suited to the work of liaison, as the operator had to be patient and kind with frustrated users. Women were also considered to be physically suited for the job: the fingers of the switchboard operator had to be nimble with the wires. By the end of the 1880s, the job of telephone operator was seen solely as a woman's occupation.[1]

Many considered the job of an operator prestigious because of the key role the operator played in connecting people through communication technology. As well, the operator was seen as a source of general information. People often called her to ask for the time and the weather forecast. This was the golden age of the operator (Illustration 75.1). The introduction of new technologies, however, gradually reduced the dependency of subscribers on operators for this or other information. Full expansion of "self-service" systems in the mid-1920s introduced the rotary dial telephone and enabled subscribers to do their own dialling. Further technological changes in the 1930s paved the way for growth in telephone traffic during the Second World War. By war's end, the number of operators had doubled; in 1946 alone, Bell trained more than five thousand women (Illustration 75.2).

The golden age of the operator began to wane in 1967 with the arrival of electronic exchanges. The first electronic system was installed for EXPO '67 in Montreal, and soon all subscribers gained even more independence from the switchboard operator. Inevitably, with computerization, the operator's position has drastically declined in the telecommunications world. For example, in the late 1990s, about fifteen hundred operators were employed in ten locations in Quebec. Implementation of speech-recognition will further limit human contact with subscribers – including the simple pleasure of hearing a "Thank You."

75.1 Telephone operators,
Toronto, 1911 (SC 244-138, City
of Toronto Archives)

75.2 Marie-Paule Groslouis
operating switchboard
(F 884, Archives of Ontario)

76 Ann Meekitjuk Hanson:
Inuit Broadcaster, Interpreter, and Community Worker

Christine Lalonde

76.1 Ann Meekitjuk Hanson
(Courtesy of Dorothy
Harley Eber)

The second half of the twentieth century marks a time of both cultural upheaval and renewal for Inuit society. The Canadian government's intervention beginning in the 1950s, and particularly the establishment of a cash economy and settlement living, irreversibly altered the tradition semi-nomadic lifestyle of Inuit. For the generation born during this period, this has meant learning to walk the fine line between their own culture and the more pervasive and dominant Canadian society. Ann Meekitjuk Hanson is an Inuk who has adapted to, and even embraced, such changer within her lifetime with grace and optimism. Well known and respected by her fellow northerners, she has acted in various roles to create a bridge of understanding between Inuit and non-Inuit. Although unassuming, Hanson has touched the lives of many through her work as interpreter, radio broadcaster, and free-lance writer. In addition to this, she is a dedicated community worker and has served on numerous boards and committees, including the Science Institute of the Northwest Territories, Northern Sciences Award Committee, Baffin Regional Educational Board, Baffin Regional Health and Social Services, Canada Council, Aboriginal Healing Board, Northwestel, Canadian Geographical Society, and the Judicial Council for Territorial Judges. She was appointed deputy commissioner for the Northwest Territories from 1987 to 1992, during which time she initiated the northern version of the Duke of Edinburgh Awards to encourage young people to become involved in community work.

She was born with the Inuktitut name of Lutaaq in May of 1946, at her family's traditional spring camp, Qakuqtute, near Kimmirut on Baffin Island. Her father, Meekitjuk, was a respected and generous camp leader, while her mother, Uqsiut (her Christian name was Josie), is remembered as a wonderful and talented musician. After the death of her father, when she was just four years old, and the hospitalization of her mother for tuberculosis shortly after, she was cared for by close family and relatives as was, and still is, Inuit custom. As was too often the case for Inuit evacuated for treatment at that time, her mother never returned from the sanatorium in Hamilton, dying there after several years in 1958. Ann sought out her grave thirty-two years later and, in 1995, helped organize a memorial stone recording the names of those who had passed away there and were often buried in unmarked graves. Many people attended the service to mourn family and friends and to attain a sense of closure.

After her mother's death, she returned to Iqaluit to attend school. In 1961 she moved to Baker Lake to live with her maternal aunt and uncle. The unfortunate death of her aunt changed the course of Hanson's life. Fate found her moving to Toronto to live with the family of her non-Inuit uncle. Adapting to culture shock and life in a southern city, she finished grade eight, perfected her English, and attended business school, attaining skills that would serve her well in her developing career.

After three years in Toronto, she returned to Iqaluit and found work with the federal government as secretary and translator. By the 1960s, Hanson was well known as an interpreter and was working for the Canadian Broadcasting Corporation (CBC). She recalls her beginnings as a broadcaster: "My first story was dogs! I was alone in the office when an RCMP member came and said, 'This urgent message must be aired as soon as possible!'... The manager, Ted Morris, noticed that there were no announcers around. He told me to go on the air and announce the message. I did! The announcement said there were too many dangerous dogs around the village and they must be tied up or they would be shot."[1] Although recounted with humour, Ann's story underscores the day-to-day culture clash as Inuit adjusted to settlement life. Sled dogs, previously so important for survival in Inuit culture, were now at loose ends and considered a serious policing problem.

Initially hired to translate the English CBC programs into Inuktitut, Hanson, along with the other interpreters, began incorporating Inuit content and, by 1965, Inuktitut broadcasting was firmly established. The introduction of Inuit-produced programming was a major, and timely, achievement for Hanson and her colleagues, who recognized that language was an essential key to maintaining Inuit culture and identity in the face of outside influences. By listening to broadcasters and journalists such as Helen Hutchinson, Peter Gzowski, and Barbara Frum, Hanson taught herself interview techniques and turned her talents to recording the oral histories of elders and reporting on current lifestyles and events. In the 1970s she travelled to communities across the Arctic to meet with people and collect their stories for the Inuktitut program Tausunni. Her open and empathetic nature encouraged people to speak candidly about their often traumatic experiences, as well as about sensitive areas of traditional knowledge such as shamanism. Recently, the CBC announced a comprehensive project to digitally archive its Inuktitut recordings as a means to preserve them as an invaluable resource.

Having gained a reputation for her language skills, Hanson acted as interpreter for the royal family during their visit to Iqaluit in 1970 and worked with authors such as Dorothy Harley Eber on the published oral histories of Cape Dorset leader Peter Pitseolak and the renowned graphic artist Pitseolak Ashoona.[2] She was the first editor of *Inukshuk*, a community paper that would later become the *Nunatsiaq News* (today the northern equivalent to the *Globe and Mail*). She is also a freelance writer and has contributed to the magazines *Above and Beyond* and *Up Here*. Thousands of tourists and travellers to the Canadian Arctic have benefited from her sensitive essays on Inuit culture and language in the *Baffin Handbook* and the newer *Nunavut Handbook*. She has contributed essays to *Inuit Women Artists: Voices from Cape Dorset* and the commemorative edition of *Nunavut '99*. In addition to this, Ann has published two children's books, *Show Me* and *Tumiit*. She returned to school in 1987 to study journalism at Nunavut Arctic College, graduating in 1989.

Ann Meekitjuk Hanson – and other Inuit women authors, artists, and politicians like her – is an important role model for the younger Inuit who will follow in shaping the future of Nunavut. More than this, her many achievements on both the personal and public level are an inspiration for present and future generations of Canadian women.[3]

77 Cultural Nationalism and Maternal Feminism: Madge Macbeth as Writer, Broadcaster, and Literary Figure

Peggy Kelly

Madge Macbeth (1878–1965),[1] a prolific Canadian writer, cultural nationalist, and maternal feminist, was a young adult at the dawn of the twentieth century and witnessed such tremendous technological innovations as the automobile, the airplane, the telephone, the typewriter, the radio, and electricity. She also lived through periods of immense social upheaval – the Great Depression, the suffrage movement, and two world wars. Macbeth was born to Elizabeth Maffit and H.H. Lyons of Philadelphia, Pennsylvania, and she followed in the footsteps of her maternal grandmother, Adelaide Clayland Maffit, who was a writer, a feminist, and a friend of the famous American feminist and abolitionist Susan B. Anthony. In 1901 Macbeth married a Canadian engineer, Charles William Macbeth; the couple moved to Ottawa in 1903. After Charles's death by tuberculosis, Macbeth remained in Ottawa, where, with the help of both her mother and a housekeeper, she raised their two sons, Charles and Douglas.

In the third decade of her life, the first decade of the twentieth century, Macbeth turned to free-lance writing to support her family; writing was one of the few professions open to middle-class women who wished to remain at home with their children and earn an income at the same time. Macbeth's first short story was accepted by the *Canadian Magazine* in November 1907. Throughout her long career, Macbeth wrote articles, travel literature, short stories, novels, drama, poetry, memoirs, and speeches. In addition, she was active in

77.1 Madge Macbeth (CA 19253, City of Ottawa Archives)

the Ottawa theatre scene as early as 1909, and she acted in, wrote, and directed plays for many years. In 1915 Macbeth was president of the Ottawa Drama League, which is now the Ottawa Little Theatre. She also wrote radio drama during the 1920s, 1930s, and 1940s. For instance, she wrote and produced *Superwoman*, a humorous parody of the New Woman,[2] for one of the first Canadian radio stations, CNRO in Ottawa. Macbeth's mystery series for radio, *Off the Highway*, was produced by the Vancouver branch of the Canadian Broadcasting Corporation (CBC) in 1943.

The CBC, which replaced the Canadian Radio Broadcasting Commission in 1936, was instituted as a means of unifying Canada, and Macbeth agreed with its cultural nationalist goal. In her speeches and interviews, Macbeth urged Canadian writers to write about Canada's land, cultures, peoples, and values; these representations, she believed, were vital to the development of a national literature in Canada. Like many English Canadians of the 1920s and 1930s, she believed in the importance of a national literature to the formation of an autonomous nation-state, a nation-state which, it was generally hoped at the time, would remain predominantly white and Anglo-Saxon. Macbeth was as good as her word; many of her own novels were set in Canada and addressed Canadian issues. *Kleath* (1917) and *Wings in the West* (1935) are adventure romances that take place in the Yukon and British Columbia. *The Patterson Limit* (1923) and *The Great Fright: Onesiphore, Our Neighbour* (1929), the latter co-written with E.L.M. Burns (pseudonym A.B. Conway), are both set in rural Quebec. Moreover, in 1924 Macbeth clashed with expatriate Canadian writer Constance Lindsay Skinner (1879–1939) over the quality of Canadian literature. In a review of contemporary publications by the Canadian writers D.C. Scott, Merrill Denison, and Ralph Connor (Rev. Charles Gordon), Skinner implied that Canada was not producing high-quality literature. Macbeth, supported by her colleagues William Arthur Deacon, Arthur Heming, and Merrill Denison, replied in a series of letters and public speeches in which she defended the existence and quality of Canadian literature.[3]

In 1921 Macbeth joined the Canadian Authors Association (CCA), one of many cultural nationalist organizations founded during the 1920s. A natural leader, Macbeth held the position of national president for three years (1939–41); she also served as secretary of the Ottawa branch of the CCA in 1921 and as its president in 1937. Macbeth was not only the first female national president of the CCA (and the only one until 1962), but also the only national president to be elected three times in fifty-one years (1921–1972). Macbeth supported the CCA's institution of the Canadian Book Week in 1921, a book festival that was reviled by many as merely a vehicle for the sale of mediocre books by commercially oriented Canadian publishing companies. But for Macbeth and other cultural nationalists in Canada, the Book Week was a means towards an end. Macbeth wanted Canadians to read Canadian literature for many reasons: as an expression of their attachment to Canada, as a means of learning about their nation, as a contribution to the development of a national literature, and as a means of supporting those writers who remained in Canada to pursue professional writing careers. In the early part of the twentieth century, many Canadian writers lived in England, Europe, or the United States. The expatriation of Canadian literary talent took place for two main reasons: the Canadian market was too small to support the work of all Canadian writers, and Canadian copyright law favoured publishers and printers over writers who lived in Canada.[4] The CCA lobbied the federal government for copyright reform, and Macbeth was closely involved in these efforts.[5]

Besides influencing her leadership activities in the CCA and her decision to draw on Canadian locales for many of her novels, Macbeth's nationalism was clearly also an important part of her journalism. In 1942 the federal government passed the Civil Employment Reinstatement Act, which forced employed Canadian women to relinquish their wartime occupations upon the return of war veterans. As a widow and a professional writer, Macbeth had a personal interest in these developments, and in 1944 she wrote two articles, "A New Psychological Approach to Home-Keeping Is Needed," and "Raise Her Status and the Worker May Return to the House," for a *Saturday Night* column titled "The Feminine Outlook." In these articles, Macbeth suggested ways to encourage Canadian working-class women to enter domestic service after the war. She claimed that Canadian working-class women avoided domestic service because they accurately recognized its devalued position in relation to other occupations, and she argued that a systemic "prejudice against housekeeping" has a negative impact on the nation-state. "[H]appy, well-ordered homes are a beneficial and cultural influence in a community," she wrote. "[T]hey are an asset to the nation and ... creating and maintaining them is an act of patriotism"(38). Although patriotism was naturally highly valued during the wars, since the nineteenth century, nationalists had been using the metaphor of the nation as a family in order to naturalize women's place in the private sphere. As a means of attracting women to the traditional occupation of housekeeping, Macbeth also called for "a more even distribution of work" among family members, for regular discussions of working conditions, for respectful treatment of domestic workers, and for fair wages and hours of work in the domestic workplace. Macbeth's suggestions were progressive, but her class position as an employer of domestic help was evident in her word choice: she referred to working-class household employees as "girls" and "twirps," and to their middle- and upper-class employers as "women" and "employers."[6]

During her childhood and early adulthood, Macbeth belonged to the American aristocracy. Her mother's family were large landowners in Maryland, and her grandfather was state comptroller. A debutante, Macbeth was educated initially at home by a governess and later in "exclusive private school[s]," including a finishing school in London, Ontario. In her second memoir, *Boulevard Career* (1957), Macbeth described her relatives as "Southern gentlefolk" and "aristocrats," and she explained that, after her father's death, her mother moved to a "modern house" in an "exclusive district." After her mother's losses through poor investments, Macbeth's lifestyle conformed more closely to that of the Canadian upper-middle class; however, she maintained social relations with her Canadian, American, and British upper-class friends and relatives, and she used these connections for writing ideas. For example, between 1943 and 1945 Macbeth published several articles on diplomats' wives in the glossy, upscale Canadian magazine *Mayfair*, including a profile of Princess Juliana of the Netherlands, who spent the war years in Ottawa with her daughters. Under the pseudonym of Gilbert Knox, Macbeth wrote two satirical novels, *The Land of Afternoon* (1924) and *The Kinder Bees* (1935), both based on her personal knowledge of elite political and social circles in the nation's capital. *The Land of Afternoon* created a sensation in Ottawa because it was evident to many readers that the story was based upon Arthur and Jessie Meighen's family life. Meighen was prime minister of Canada from 1920 to 1921 and briefly in 1926. Macbeth knew Jessie Meighen through their mutual involvement in the Ottawa Drama League. In addition, Macbeth was a close friend to Lady Tweedsmuir and Lady Aberdeen, both wives of governors general, and attended state dinners hosted by Prime Minister Mackenzie King.[7]

Macbeth's life and writing combine the values of the New Woman and the maternal feminist. Feminist theorists and historians have distinguished among maternal, radical, socialist, Black, and liberal feminisms, among others.[8] Maternal feminists see motherhood as central to the lives of all women. In the first two decades of the twentieth century, Canadian maternal-feminist suffragists, among them Nellie McClung and Emily Murphy, hoped that women's votes would sanitize politics of corruption and hasten social reform. Their hopes were based on the assumption that women were the moral guardians of society, an assumption also encountered in the values underlying the Victorian figure of the "angel in the house." Macbeth's attempt to reverse the widespread social denigration of housework is an example of maternal feminism. However, Macbeth's interest in the place of housework in society appeared much earlier in her writing. In a 1928 article titled "'Until Love Dies' or the Courts Us Do Part," Macbeth cited crowded apartments and "the tendency to use prepared foods" as causes of the rise in separations among married Canadians; there is no question that, in 1928, Macbeth considered food preparation to be a woman's role.[9] Even earlier, in *The Patterson Limit* (1923), Macbeth introduced a housekeeping metaphor for the heroine's work in a Quebec forest: Ray Lane is not only a New Woman who enters the non-traditional occupation of forest ranger, but also a steward of nature who sees her work as a vocation.

Lane nurtures and protects the forest as a traditional mother does her home and children, and Macbeth's development of Lane's character reflects the values of maternal feminism. However, as a teenager, Macbeth wanted to be a New Woman, and as an adult, she wrote a feminist novel, *Shackles* (1926), the sexual frankness of which shocked Canadian reviewers. Moreover, in the 1930s Macbeth sold to the *Canadian Geographical Journal* several feature articles on her travels to Europe, Mexico, and South America. Like the New Woman, Macbeth made many of these journeys alone.

Macbeth was a highly productive writer and an important figure in the Canadian literary field of the first half of the twentieth century; indeed, in 1963, at age eighty-four, she published *Volcano*, which contains elements of both feminist writing and the gothic novel.[10] However, Macbeth's work is no longer available on the shelves of Canadian bookstores. Students of Canadian literature can access the first editions of Macbeth's writing in their libraries, but her important contributions to Canadian literary politics and to Canadian popular literature have become as undervalued as the occupation of housework.

78 "The Day of the Strong-Minded Frump Has Passed": Women Journalists and News of Feminism

Barbara M. Freeman

In any women's rights struggle, the biggest obstacle feminists have had to overcome has been conservative attitudes about appropriate behaviour for women; such attitudes have often resulted in very mixed messages in the news media about the economic, political, and social concerns of feminists. Over the course of the twentieth century, women have fought for the right to vote, to run for public office, to earn equal pay and promotions, to claim a fair share of their marital property, and, very importantly, to choose if and when to bear children. According to the public record, and their own accounts, women journalists covered these issues extensively, but not always supportively.

This article explores the attitudes and work of several journalists of varying ideologies who wrote for conservative newspapers in Toronto during different feminist eras. Two of them were journalists at the turn of the twentieth century during the fight for women's suffrage. The other two were writing during the onset of what is popularly referred to as the "second wave" of the women's movement, the 1960s and early 1970s, and are representative of the twenty-four journalists I interviewed for this study. For these two generations of journalists, professional expectations placed limits on their political loyalties and their individual commitments to feminist ideals. While they eagerly recorded changes in cultural attitudes towards women, they were reluctant to endorse any perceived "militancy" among women's groups, using this term, or similar ones, at one time or another to describe any feminist who appeared to be transgressing feminine norms.

Kathleen Blake Coleman ("Kit") of the Toronto *Mail* and Alice Fenton Freeman ("Faith Fenton") of the Toronto *Empire* were among the women pioneers of their profession who began writing for the newspapers in the late 1880s. Their editors expected them to adopt suitable pen names and to confine themselves to editing their own "women's page," writing articles about fashions, recipes, and household concerns. Nevertheless, they and several of their female colleagues on other newspapers used the limited space they had to write about broader issues, such as suffrage, which women activists considered a necessary tool to bring about social change. The journalists were not consistent in their support, however. In an era of blatant political partisanship among newspapers, women's page editors

---

JEAN McKISHNIE BLEWETT, 1862–1934

Born at Scotia, Upper Canada, and educated at St Thomas Collegiate Institute, Jean McKishnie was for many years a member of the staff of the Toronto *Globe*, continuing as an active journalist until 1925. Between 1897 and 1922 she published several volumes of poetry. Her poems were admired by her contemporaries "for the directness and simplicity of themes and form and for the occasional whimsical note." She died in Chatham, Ontario. (Courtesy of Parks Canada)

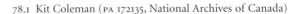
78.1 Kit Coleman (PA 172135, National Archives of Canada)

were expected to adhere to certain positions, regardless of how they felt about the issues. Only the bravest stood up for women's rights in the face of a conservative publisher's anti-suffrage stance.

The later generation, including Yvonne Crittenden and Maggie Siggins of the Toronto *Telegram*, wrote about the liberal and left-wing feminists who pressed the federal government to change many laws that were unfair to women, and for other reforms as well. The liberal or "equality" feminists were interested in making sure that women were treated equally with men in the workplace and at home, and were instrumental in pressuring the government to establish the Royal Commission on the Status of Women (1967–70). After the commission heard briefs from women across the country, these feminists demanded that the government follow through on its recommendations for changes in the country's laws. The women's liberation movement, which took root at the same time and continued for several years, consisted of various groups of New Left and campus activists. Not satisfied with liberal ideals of sexual equality, they went further in challenging the fundamental class and gender structures of Canadian society, which they viewed as capitalist and patriarchal.[1] While both *Telegram* journalists wrote about the demands of the liberal and New Left groups, Crittenden concentrated on the equality feminists and on issues close to the hearts of women working at home, and Siggins covered the women's liberation movement and similar left-wing groups.

Professional limits on all four journalists discussed here dictated what they could write about feminists. "Kit" and "Faith," who both worked for newspapers that were then strongly aligned with the Conservative Party, had to walk a fine line when it came to reporting on the more controversial women's issues. As a single mother

MAJ. GARDINER. FAITH FENTON (COR.) CAPT BILL ROBINSON
STIKINE RIVER CANYON, KLONDIKERS GOING TO GLENORA MAY 1898
B.C. CANADA

HJW 731

78.2 Faith Fenton, 1898
(PA 16892, National Archives
of Canada)

with two children, Kit readily espoused the principle of equal pay, but she did not publicly support suffrage until the cause gained respectability. Her editors opposed it, and she felt too economically vulnerable to endorse it herself "unless so ordered by the powers that be." Further, she was frankly uncomfortable with the more outspoken advocates of the movement; considering them unladylike, she did not want to be associated with them.[2]

In contrast to Kit Coleman, the more daring Faith Fenton took an active role in the National Council of Women, greatly admired its liberal-leaning founder, Lady Aberdeen, and wrote glowingly about her in the *Empire*, also a Conservative paper. In May 1893 Faith attended the International Conference of Representative Women in the Women's Building at the Chicago World Fair, as both a Canadian delegate and a journalist. She defended her decision to write about the generally pro-suffrage conference by declaring that her homebound women readers needed the inspiration her coverage would no doubt provide them – "The time for ridiculing these gatherings is long gone by." Aware that their opponents and many members of the public considered suffragists to be overly intellectual, badly dressed, and shrill, she described the Canadian women attending these meetings as intelligent, well-dressed, and womanly, adding, "the day of the strong-minded frump has passed, and the day of the clever, deep, broad-thinking, daintily-gowned woman has arrived."

A few months later, Kit also visited Chicago and the Women's Building, where debates on women's issues had become a daily occurrence. Unlike Faith, she did ridicule the participants, dismissing the more outspoken ones as "crowing hens," which was another way of saying that these women were behaving in too masculine a fashion for her tastes. Two years later, when the *Mail* took over the *Empire*, it was Kit who remained as the women's page editor and "Faith" who was fired, along with the rest of the *Empire*'s staff. The proprietors of the new *Mail and Empire* were staunch Conservative Party supporters and anti-suffrage in their editorial policies.[3]

From the 1890's Canada's daily newspaper publishers gradually detached themselves from direct political party involvement and grew into major business enterprises which, editorially, still tended to support either conservatism or liberalism. In daily reporting, however, a new convention was taking hold, one that encouraged "objectivity" for journalists covering stories. This meant that their editors expected them to act as outsiders, writing stories in a detached, non-partisan way after interviewing and quoting experts and others with different perspectives.

Journalists and their critics continually debated the true meaning and usefulness of "objectivity" over the years, but by the 1960s it was understood to mean "fairness and balance," if not complete emotional detachment, in one's news coverage. Even so, the 1960s generation of journalists, including the women, were expected to be less politically involved and much more objective than their predecessors. Daily news reporters, as opposed to opinion columnists, could not join any political party, social movement, or interest group and write news articles about it at the same time. To do so was considered a conflict of interest and a transgression of ethical standards.[4]

Some theorists have argued that an undue emphasis on objectivity in any field is an essentially rationalist approach that has no real bearing on reality. For one thing, it does not acknowledge the fact that journalists are products of their own culture, including the gender divisions between the sexes, and are thus influenced by the society around them. Reporters' loyalty to other evolving rules of journalistic writing, such as emphasizing conflict between opposing sides, an unusual angle, or deviancy from accepted social norms, could distort the meaning behind an event as easily as outright bias. So could the pressure of deadlines and competition from other journalists, which demanded brevity and speed in writing stories rather than thoughtful and careful analysis.[5] As a result, even the most careful and committed reporter sometimes produced conflicting messages about the meaning and value of the women's movement, especially its more "radical" aspects.

The truth was that for a purportedly democratic institution, the newspaper industry was itself beset by inequality and unfairness, especially where gender relations were concerned. The men regarded news of concern to women as "soft" news rather than "hard" news, and even barred their female colleagues, whom they did not consider "real" journalists, from membership in most press organizations. By the late 1960s, women journalists, inspired by the women's movement, were pressuring their publishers and editors to allow them more scope in their work. Several journalists even presented briefs on their grievances to the Royal Commission on the Status of Women. A few of the reporters did make it out of the women's department and into gener-

78.3 Women's Press Corps
(National Archives of Canada)

al news, but much of their daily work still involved covering social issues in which many women readers took an avid interest.[6]

Yvonne Crittenden and Maggie Siggins have very different perceptions of how women journalists were treated during the late 1960s and early 1970s at the Toronto *Telegram*, which had always been editorially sympathetic to the Conservative Party. Crittenden, who regarded herself as an "equality" feminist, did not feel discriminated against at the newspaper, partly because all the reporters were unionized under the Newspaper Guild. She recalls that most men, including male reporters, were chauvinists at the time, but she had a supportive husband, who was an editor at the *Telegram*, and she got along with most of them.

Crittenden learned to be a reporter in her native Australia in the 1950s. "I was, you know, trained very strictly … You had to give both sides of the question, you never inserted your own personal views into the story … so I was a very fair-minded, objective reporter." She wrote about many women's concerns for the *Telegram* but became pro-choice in her private convictions after covering several gatherings of vitriolic anti-choice advocates. But to actually join any woman's group would have been out of the question for her as a professional.[7]

Crittenden's younger colleague, Maggie Siggins, worked in general news and specialized in interpretative feature articles on subjects such as poverty, birth control, abortion, and, later, the women's liberation movement, whose ideas attracted her. She became impatient with the snide, sexist remarks and behaviour of some of her male colleagues and, unlike Crittenden, recalls "terrible, fearful screaming matches" in the newsroom about female journalists' capabilities and other issues to do with women's rights.

As the left-wing women's liberation movement gathered strength, Siggins covered their protests and consciousness-raising groups. She was fascinated by their ideals but admits that the term "women's libber" carried "a lot of baggage" and that, as a single woman, she did not want to alienate men she found attractive. At the time, when some women were rejecting men altogether as "the enemy," she wrote the following in a rare opinion article: "Although I agree with much of feminist philosophy, I wonder if I would be brave enough (or is it foolhearty [sic] enough) to be branded as a feminist, to be in a state of constant conflict." As a reporter, however, she could not become actively involved in the movement. Today, she recalls that her professional position as a journalist "was kind of a shield for me" in that she did not have to take a stand. "I was not supposed to march up and down Yonge Street ... I was not supposed to go and sit in at an office, but ... in another way, I was totally committed."[8]

Although both Crittenden and Siggins worked for the same newspaper and had to follow the same professional rules, their personal brands of feminism were very different. Both had their limits, however, and relayed mixed messages to their audiences about the militancy of the women's movements they covered. In one article, Crittenden noted that the issues women brought before the royal commission, such as the need for day care, equal pay, and better job opportunities, "have been in the news for years and are favourite targets of militant women's groups." By "militant," she meant the liberal feminists, whom, she noted, men often denigrated as the "flowered hat brigade" with "whines and gripes." Using quotes from the commissioners, she reported that most

women who appeared at the hearings were not resentful or bitter, that there was no "battle of the sexes," and that the women simply talked about their day-to-day problems. In other words, she was reassuring her readers, many of whom were housewives, that ordinary Canadian women had legitimate complaints, even while she seemed to buy into the "militant" stereotype of the equality feminist then popular among male columnists.[9]

Similarly, Siggins conveyed her ambivalence about the left-wing women's groups. Writing in 1970, she assured her readers that "the girls wearing radical feminist buttons" did not fit the popular image of "a middle-aged, sexually frustrated, bitchy-looking militant," but were "young, attractive and obviously sexually attracted to and by men." When some WLM members left their husbands to live as lesbians in co-op housing with other women, she went through a period of "profound shock" before she came to accept their choices. "I covered a lot of stuff about lesbianism, and I think maybe now, quite unfairly, because I think the *Telegram* was using it as a real kind of freak story ... and I often think that I wasn't careful enough."[10] Clearly, lesbianism as the litmus test of radical feminism initially resounded as loudly for Siggins as the "crowing hens" had for Kit decades earlier, demarking, as they did, the limits of acceptable female behaviour in both eras.

From these brief examples of the working lives of media women, it is evident that their history cannot be separated from the history of Canadian women as a whole. During both the suffrage and women's liberation eras, newspaper editors confined most news of women to the women's pages in the newspapers or, at best, to feature articles on social issues on the general news pages. While this division limited the journalists, it also allowed them to acquaint their wide female audiences with the concerns of the women's movement during times when most male editors were either dismissive or antagonistic towards it. At the same time, the evolving professional standards of "objectivity" in reporting dictated that the women reporters keep their distance from direct involvement in women's groups and issues, especially if they wanted to be taken seriously as journalists.

But, because they as women were themselves harmed by systemic discrimination in law, public policy, and employment, they could not keep an emotional distance, no matter how carefully they covered "both" sides of the story. Generally, they either disassociated themselves from these "militant" feminists by presenting them in headline-grabbing accounts as somehow outside the norm of true womanhood, or defensively encouraged the view that many feminists were really ordinary, non-threatening women with something of value to say. Given the necessity of defending their own professional reputations as journalists, they had little choice, even though neither of these stances was truly objective. Their example helps to explain why the cultural meaning of the term "militant feminist" has constantly shifted, and why the news media have always produced such mixed messages about women's equality.

79 Women in Banking: A Case Study of Scotiabank

Jane Nokes and Lisa Singer

The financial sector since its inception has been dominated by men. Reflecting the social and economic realities of the time, Scotiabank was founded in the nineteenth century by men of vision who held to a strict hierarchical order, starting with juniors (boys of fifteen and a half years old) and progressing through teller and accountant to manager.[1] Executive positions were not attainable to the rank and file, as the president and directors were usually wealthy, well-connected businessmen. Women did not figure into the equation at all until banks and other financial institutions started to expand, necessitating more support staff at Head Office. "Typewriters" were added as a function and were almost always women. By virtue of women's initial minuscule numbers and very specialized skills, and in accordance with the social mores of the late nineteenth and early twentieth century, the advancement of women was not considered a factor by the Staff Department of the Bank of Nova Scotia. The bank's "Manual of Rules and Procedure" focused on character, basic decorum, penmanship, and behaviour deemed appropriate to one's station and to the bank's position in the community.[2] These are all issues that the social historian would expect to find at the core of a large and far-flung operation with a relatively small staff, which included a preponderance of young trainees often living far from their homes. As with church, army, and government postings, young bankers were moved to suit the needs of Head Office.

Contrary to popular twentieth-century opinion, per-haps, women did not dominate the ranks of tellers even after the influx of women to the financial sector (and to all white-collar occupations) during the First World War. Indeed, they continued to dominate only in the growing secretarial, stenographic, and administrative jobs in the Head Office in Halifax and the General Office in Toronto. Typical staff photographs from branches at the time continued to show a lone woman, the manager's secretary.

The Second World War saw a tremendous increase in the number of women staff members in the branch system. By 1944, fully 60 per cent of Scotiabank staff were women.[3] The role of women in the war effort has been well documented elsewhere, but it should be noted that women bank staff sold Victory Bonds and War Savings Certificates. Following the war, women stayed on in their new jobs in far greater numbers than after the First World War. Specifically, at Scotiabank, while fewer than one hundred women were employed as tellers in the bank's Canadian branches prior to the war, in 1953 there were over five hundred women tellers across Canada.[4]

Scotiabank was the first Canadian bank to appoint women branch managers. In 1961 Gladys Marcellus of Ottawa and Shirley Giles of Toronto were appointed, setting an important precedent for women. Both were acutely aware of their roles as pioneers; as Shirley Giles commented, "I really feel that I have to make good. I have to work at it because it seems like all eyes are on me."[5] By 1961, as well, 56 per cent of Scotiabank staff

were women.[6] Women's advancement in the company soon became a public issue for the bank. *The Report of the Royal Commission on the Status of Women* (1970) highlighted that Canadian banks, because of their hierarchical and ultra-conservative structure, were ill-equipped to deal quickly and effectively with the inequity of women remaining in junior positions and being under-represented in the different sectors of banking. Scotiabank inaugurated its Women's Pension Fund in 1967 (and would in 1973 amalgamate it into the Officers' Pension Fund, one of the first pension funds in North America), but this was only a small first step.

Of more significance, perhaps, were the appointments from the early 1940s of women economists. At a time when few bankers had more than a high school education, the bank's need for statistical research led to the hiring of university-educated staff to positions of influence. In Scotiabank's case, Dr Lucy Ingram Morgan joined the bank's Statistics Department in 1942, rising to head the highly respected and renowned Economics Department in 1958. Morgan was the first woman supervisor in Scotiabank. She was eventually joined by Betty Ratz King Hearn, a brilliant protégé of Harold Innis's at the University of Toronto, whose lucidly written "Monthly Reports" were distributed to staff and customers across the country and are still standard references. Betty Hearn's range of interests and abilities led to her running the bank's library, well known as an excel-

79.1 Staff at Edmonton, March 1941 (Scotiabank Group Archives)

significant number of women in increasingly complex specialist positions. One of these, Helen Sinclair, went on to be executive director of the Canadian Bankers Association. The stage was thus set for the bank to examine the hindrances barring women's advancement and to explore ways to help promote a greater number of women to higher positions.

In July of 1993, Scotiabank president Peter Godsoe appointed a special independent task force to find out why so few women held upper management positions (77 per cent of bank staff were women, but only 6.97 per cent had reached positions of upper management) and to determine how to improve this situation.[7] Barbara Mason, head of the task force, stated: "The advancement of women is really about equality of opportunity. The task force is aiming to remove the barriers that have made it difficult for women to even be considered for advancement – historical attitudes, entrenched personal values and beliefs, and structural processes."[8] Nearly ten thousand Scotiabank employees received a confidential survey asking for their perceptions, attitudes, and suggestions on the issue of women in banking. Based on the findings, the task force advanced and implemented a number of recommendations, including an increased focus on ensuring that advancement was based on merit and on finding better ways of communicating job opportunities and measuring skills.

Significant strides have been made by women pioneers in Scotiabank's history. We are confident that Scotiabank's future will see women in even more senior positions.

79.2 Lucy Ingram Morgan (Scotiabank Group Archives)

lent business library. From that base, she launched the Scotiabank Archives, the first bank archives in Canada. The 1950s also saw the hiring of Jocelyn Classy as founding editor of *Scotiabanker*, the bank's staff magazine.

By the early 1970s, Scotiabank was hiring a small but

Vignette

80 The Keroacks, a Family of Business Women

Lise Brémault

Top:
80.2 The Keroack family
(Société Historique de
Saint-Boniface, Le Musée
de Saint-Boniface)

80.1 The Keroack Bookstore
(Public Archives of
Manitoba)

At a time when the range of socially acceptable work outside the
home was limited, Malvina Keroack and her daughters became
professional businesswomen and storeowners. Malvina, the
Keroack matriarch, was married to Maximilien Aimé Keroack,
who in 1882 opened the first French-language bookstore in western Canada, in St Boniface, Manitoba. In 1891 he opened a second store, in Winnipeg. The Keroack family lived above the St
Boniface store on DuMoulin Street.

In addition to serving the thriving readership in their community, the Keroacks supplied books to the French Catholic school
board and made a handsome profit from the arrangement. However, in 1890, with the Manitoba Schools Act and the successful abolition of French-language education, the bookstore fal-
tered. In 1893 Aimé decided to put the store up for sale, and
four years later his two eldest daughters, Eugenie and Blanche,
bought both the Winnipeg and the St Boniface stores from
him and expanded the business. Aimé died in 1899, leaving
Malvina with nine other children to raise. Both Eugenie and
Blanche helped their mother at home. Malvina regained ownership of the stores when her two daughters left to pursue other
interests or get married, and she continued to run the stores
until her own death in 1921.

Faites application à présent
Tous nos arbres sont garantis ou l'argent
est remis.   BLACKFORD & CO.
                   TORONTO, CANADA.

Grande Vente
A Sacrifice !

Ayant acheté un fonds de librairie à
très bas prix, je suis en mesure de
vendre à grande réduction.   Mon
assortiment consiste en

LIVRES, PAPETERIE,
    ARTICLES RELIGIEUX,
        TAPISSERIES, IMAGES,
CADRES de toutes grandeurs et
    OBJETS DE FANTAISIE POUR CADEAUX.
Les ordres reçus par la malle sont promp-
tement exécutés.

B. KEROACK.

29-12 97

Avez-vous besoin d'une Montre ?

6.59   Nous les vendons à si bas
            prix que vous ne pourrez
            pas vous passer d'une mon-
            tre. Nous en avons de tous

Left:
80.3 Advertisement
"Grande Vente à Sacrifice!"

80.4 Malvina Keroack at the counter
(Société Historique de Saint-Boniface,
Le Musée de Saint-Boniface)

81 "The Queen of the Hurricanes": Elsie Gregory MacGill, Aeronautical Engineer and Women's Advocate

Pamela Wakewich

81.1 Elsie Gregory MacGill
(PA 139429, National Archives of Canada)

Elsie Gregory MacGill (Illustration 81.1) is an important figure in twentieth-century Canadian women's history both for her individual career accomplishments in aeronautical engineering and for her contributions to Canadian women's equality rights.

MacGill was born 27 March 1905 in Vancouver to Helen Gregory MacGill, the first woman judge in British Columbia and a prominent advocate of suffrage and the early women's movement.[1] In 1927, after studying at the University of Toronto, Elsie MacGill became the first woman in Canada to obtain a bachelor of applied science degree in electrical engineering. Two years later she became the first woman in North America to graduate with a master's degree in Aeronautical Engineering, which she obtained from the University of Michigan. She accomplished this in spite of the onset of acute myelitis (polio) in her last year of study. MacGill's illness prevented her from taking a full-time post in her field for several years after graduation, although she did commence doctoral studies at the Massachusetts Institute of Technology. In 1934 MacGill was employed as an aeronautical engineer for Fairchild Aircraft Limited in Longueuil, Quebec, where she worked on aerodynamics and stress testing of aircraft.[2]

In July of 1938, at thirty-three years of age, MacGill accepted the position of chief engineer in the aircraft division of the Canadian Car and Foundry Company in Fort William, Ontario. Letters from MacGill to her family at this time convey her excitement at being appointed to such an important post so early in her career and her intense commitment to making a long-term contribution to applied research in aeronautical engineering.[3]

It was at Canadian Car that MacGill designed and oversaw the testing and certification of the Maple Leaf Trainer II.[4] Registered in January of 1940, this was the first aircraft to be designed by a woman. However, an even bigger challenge would be undertaken when Canadian Car began large-scale manufacturing of aircraft for the war effort. When the company won the contract to produce Hawker Hurricane fighter planes for the British government, MacGill, as chief engineer, was put in charge of the operation.[5] This project required a complete revamping of the plant (which had previously been tooled for building boxcars) and the hiring, training, and supervision of a labour force of approximately forty-five hundred men and women, most of whom had no prior experience in aircraft production and few of whom had even worked in an industrial setting.[6] As well, MacGill had to oversee the design and manufacture of the tools and equipment needed to produce the more than sixty thousand parts that made up the aircraft, and ensure that they met with the stringent specifications of the British government.

Despite the difficulties of obtaining a steady supply of suitable materials during wartime, in less than a year the first aircraft was successfully completed, and by war's end approximately two thousand Hurricanes had been produced.[7] MacGill was also credited with developing a winterized version of the Hurricane. The plane was equipped with skis and de-icers to make it safer and more suitable for use in northern climates.[8]

MacGill's expertise and accomplishments were praised in the local, national, and international press during the war.[9] However, as was done with respect to other women working in war industries, articles about her made a great deal of effort to reinforce prescribed notions of femininity – which emphasized women's dec-orativeness and maternal proclivity – and assure readers that despite her work in a "man's field" she was "very much a woman."[10] An article in the *Star* from early 1940, tellingly entitled "She Debates Plane Design Just Like Recipe for Pie,"[11] devotes significantly more space to describing MacGill's feminine appearance and hobbies than to her engineering accomplishments, which are ostensibly the focus of the article. According to the unnamed author, "Reporters wouldn't have been surprised to meet someone with a deep voice and a boyish haircut. Instead they met a pint-size girl, in a modish suit, with a mop of curls and a piquant face that sparkled with friendship and that indefinable thing called personality."[12] Similarly, an article in the *New York Times* from October 1940, reporting on MacGill's successful design of the Maple Leaf Trainer II, assures its readers that "Miss MacGill is all feminine. In a man's engineering world she does not attempt to act like a man. She likes clothes and, though she wears tailored suits at work, they are not severely mannish in style, but have pockets which can hold papers and things. She likes to cook, plays bridge, knits, likes afternoon teas."[13]

A vignette on MacGill entitled "Queen of the Hurricanes,"[14] featured in a contemporary war heroes' comic book, notes the challenges of illness and sexual discrimination from classmates that MacGill had to overcome to make her valiant contribution to the war effort (Illustration 81.2). Yet, it too stresses that "despite her he-man job Elsie is all kindness,"[15] and concludes with scenes of MacGill ordering a stop to production to rescue a lost kitten from an aircraft, as well as overseeing the running of her own home.[16]

In 1943 MacGill married E.J. Soulsby, the former works manager of Canadian Car, and left the plant to open her own office as an aeronautical engineering consultant in Toronto. Over the next several decades she worked for both government and private industry and became recognized as a leading figure in the aeronautics industry.

81.2 "Queen of the Hurricanes" (MG 31 K 7, vol. 16, file 7, National Archives of Canada, C 146539 and C 146540)

ELSIE DEVELOPED A DE-ICER FOR THE HURRICANE, WHICH SAVED MANY BRAVE R.A.F. PILOTS' LIVES.

MISS MacGILL'S NEW DE-ICER SURE KEEPS THE WINGS CLEAR OF ICE!

GOSH, ELSIE MacGILL DRIVES LIKE A WHIRLWIND.

SHE WANTS TO BECOME A PILOT, TOO.

ELSIE RUNS HER OWN HOME...

MUM, THE NEW COOK CAN SPEAK ONLY RUMANIAN. BUT SHE'S VERY GOOD.

GOOD COOKS ARE RARE, AND SHE WON'T HAVE TIME TO LEARN ENGLISH. I'D BETTER GET TO SPEAK RUMANIAN!

DESPITE HER HE-MAN JOB ELSIE IS ALL KINDNESS...

MEW! MEW!

STOP PRODUCTION UNTIL YOU FIND THAT KITTEN. THE POOR LITTLE THING!

THIS, THEN, IS THE AMAZING WOMAN WHO PLAYS SUCH AN IMPORTANT PART IN CANADA'S VALIANT WAR EFFORT. ALL HONOR TO ELSIE MacGILL!

Her technical expertise and research on air-frame design, stress analysis, and certification of aircraft garnered her many honours in the engineering field: the Gzowski Medal of the Engineering Institute of Canada (1940); recognition in the Gevaert Gallery of leading contributors to Canadian business; and the Annual Medal and Citation from the American Society of Women Engineers (1953).[17] During her professional career, MacGill published many technical papers in leading engineering journals and received commendation from her peers for her contributions to applied research.

In addition to her many personal career accomplishments, MacGill was very active in local and national women's business and professional organizations, and was keen to promote opportunities for women in the workplace. Her own chilly reception as a woman pursuing a "man's profession" during her studies and when she first attempted to join peer associations made her aware of the challenges faced by women working in nontraditional areas. Correspondence between MacGill and the director of the Institute of Aeronautical Sciences in New York, in her effort to become a member of that organization in 1936, indicates that MacGill responded to such barriers by firmly and persistently challenging them until she achieved her desired goals.[18] MacGill also challenged barriers on behalf of other women, advocating in both speeches and articles in newspaper and professional publications, the advancement of women in professions such as her own.[19]

For example, in an address to the 14th Biennial Convention of the Federation of Business and Professional Women's Clubs in Toronto in 1954, MacGill humorously, and yet very pointedly, drew links between Canadian women's limited representation in the political arena and the direction of Canadian social and foreign policy. Her speech, entitled "A Blueprint for Madame Prime Minister," details the history of women's enfranchisement and the way in which women have used their voices and votes to shift the political agenda from traditional concerns with finance, trade, and development to social justice issues.[20] MacGill argues for the increased representation of women at all political levels and suggests that the ideal Madame Prime Minister would have three characteristics that sum up women's life experience – "humaneness, cooperation and determination."[21]

MacGill is perhaps best known in Canadian women's history as one of the commissioners on the Royal Commission on the Status of Women, from 1967 to 1970, through which she played, as outlined in earlier essays in this volume, an important role as an advocate for women's equality rights.[22] In her summary reports, MacGill argued for equality in the workplace, access to birth control, the decriminalization of abortion, and amendments to the Federal Income Tax Act and childcare allowances to increase women's financial independence.[23] MacGill showed an astute awareness of the structural barriers to women's equality and their impact on the educational and familial "choices" made by girls and women. As noted in a separate statement filed with the commission report,

Income Tax legislation can encourage or discourage the financial dependency of one group of individuals on another, for example, the child on the father, the wife on the husband. In Canada a great many wives are financially dependent on their husbands and this appears to be a factor in the lower wage rates paid to women as compared with those paid to men. Our findings indicate that anticipation of this dependency often saps the initiative of young girls to take advantage of educational opportunities, and focuses their attention on acquiring a husband-provider.[24]

In the years following the royal commission, MacGill was a member of the Ontario Status of Women Committee (an affiliate of the National Action Committee on the Status of Women); remained active in national women's and business and professional organizations; and continued to lobby for the adoption of the recommendations of the Royal Commission on the Status of Women. In recognition of her efforts, MacGill was named to the Order of Canada in 1971 and conferred honorary doctorates by the Universities of Toronto (1973), Windsor (1976), and Queen's and York (1978).[25]

On 4 November 1980, after a brief illness, MacGill died in Cambridge, Massachusetts, at the age of seventy-five.[26] As aptly noted in the program for her memorial service held at Knox Chapel, University of Toronto, the following passage from MacGill's biography of her own mother, *My Mother the Judge*,[27] "serves as [an] eloquent epitaph for the daughter herself: 'Thus she did what few do – influenced her times for good and left a lasting mark behind her.'"[28]

82 The Women's Royal Canadian Naval Service during the Second World War: An Exploration of Their Archival Legacy

Donna Porter

Many stories have been told about the heroism, courage, and duty of the men in arms during the Second World War. What remains to be examined in much more detail is the work of the women members of our forces during the war and the role they played in making our war effort successful. What follows is a description of some archival sources and collections available to those who may have an interest in pursuing an unfortunately neglected area of our history – the efforts made by members of the Women's Royal Canadian Naval Service (WRCNS).

On 7 May 1942 the Honourable Angus L. Macdonald, minister of national defence for naval service, stood in the House of Commons to announce the formation of the Women's Royal Canadian Naval Service, the third branch of the armed forces to accept women. In July 1941 the air force had formed the Canadian Women's Auxiliary Air Force (CWAAF), which in February 1942 was re-designated as the Royal Canadian Air Force (Women's Division), and in August 1941 the army had formed the Canadian Women's Army Corps (CWAC).

By the end of the war, 6,783 women had served in the WRCNS, freeing men for active sea duty. These women served in naval shore establishments all across Canada and hundreds were posted outside Canada to places such as Washington, Newfoundland, London, Londonderry, Greenock, and Glasgow. Eleven women are known to have died during the war while on active service.

Much of what is known about the history of the WRCNS has been stored in the Directorate of History and Heritage, the Department of National Defence, in the National Archives of Canada, and in the hearts, minds, and memories of the women who served. In September 1998 former members of the WRCNS gathered in Toronto to hold a reunion. Fifty-six years after the founding of the service, many women attending the reunion felt that their time with the WRCNS was the most fulfilling period of their lives, other than their child-bearing years. Women such as Dorothy Robertson felt that the navy had helped make them stronger and better able to deal with the changes and challenges that occurred during the war and throughout their lives.[1]

For the most part, the contribution these women made to the war effort has been overlooked by historians. In 1986 Ruth Roach Pierson published what is considered the first major work on women in the war, *"They're still women after all": The Second World War and Canadian Womanhood*. This work, however, while mentioning the WRCNS, focuses mainly on the activities of the CWAC. The annotated bibliography and footnotes offer the researcher a useful starting point but only touch on the significance of the role played by the WRCNS.

Another interesting book is Jean Bruce's *Back the Attack! Canadian Women during the Second World War – at Home and Abroad* (1985). Bruce uses personal reminiscences, diaries, letters, magazine articles, newspaper clippings, and more than two hundred photographs from both civilian and military women who served in the three services to bring their contribution to life.

Bruce explains in the introduction the reluctance of some women to have their names associated with the stories they told, all of which are rich and colourful.

For anyone attempting to write of the Women's Royal Canadian Naval Service during the Second World War, the Directorate of History and Heritage, the Department of National Defence, and the National Archives of Canada hold a number of key collections that shed light on the activities of this group.

During the 1980s the late Hal Lawrence, while under contract to the Directorate of History and Heritage, undertook the task of conducting interviews with a number of men and women who had served in the Canadian naval service during the Second World War. While copies of the transcripts are available at the Directorate of History and Heritage, the actual taped interviews are available to researchers at the National Archives of Canada. Seventeen former members of the Wrens were interviewed about the work they did during the war. Most of the women interviewed were residents of western Canada and the work done by them varied greatly.

Jenny Pike (née Whitehead) served as a photographer and was sent off to London to help develop the photographs for the D-DAY landing. Jean Hinton (née Davidson) was selected to serve overseas as a pay writer in London between 1943 and 1946. The trade category of cook was one of the hardest to fill. Not many experienced cooks wanted to join the service. Winnifred Mary York joined the WRCNS to serve first as a cook and then as a cooking instructor at the trades school at HMCS. Cornwallis. Her contribution and those of other cooks who provided wholesome and nutritious meals went a long way in keeping up the morale of the service personnel. Alice Adams became a wireless operator. She, along with Lavina Crane, Freda Dougherty, and Eileen Dingwall, intercepted German U-boat signals, passing this information on to Ottawa and London.

The Directorate of History and Heritage also holds a collection of material donated by the Wren's Association of Toronto. The collection is comprised of twenty-two folders of material ranging from pamphlets, handbooks, newspaper clippings, to copies of the *Tiddley Times* (the WRCNS's magazine), reunion programs, and photographs. The *Tiddley Times* magazine was a compilation of news from the various locations inside and outside Canada where Wrens were posted (Illustration 82.1). This magazine was extremely popular among the women, as it afforded them a way of keeping up with events and friends scattered across Canada and abroad. Most interesting are the course notes taken by Wren Helen M. Parsons during her basic training. This beautifully hand-written journal covers the lectures received by the recruits during basic training.

One of the more interesting collections at the National Archives is that of Katherine A. Peacock (née Wayling). Katherine Wayling was a member of the first class of Wrens. It is from this pioneering group that so many of the prominent officers in the organization were to emerge. Her papers are comprised of hand-written course notes taken during her basic training and from later in her career when she attended the officer's training course. Her notes offer insight into the type of instruction that this group received. Many of the classes were instructed by Captain Eustace Brock, Superintendent Joan Carpenter, and Chief Officer Dorothy Isherwood. The women were lectured on topics ranging from "What we are fighting against," delivered by Commander E.H. Bonnycastle of Naval Headquarters, to naval customs and traditions, by Captain Eustace Brock. Other lecture topics included saluting, phraseology and abbreviations, administrative procedures, flags and badges, trade categories and recruiting, as well as hygiene and how not to lose one's feminine side.

The National Archives of Canada holds the papers of the Vancouver Wrens Association. This material came to the archives after the Vancouver Wrens hosted a reunion

82.1 *The Tiddley Times*
(DHH 92/74, Wren Association
of Toronto, file 17, December 1945,
Directorate of History, DND)

82.2 Isabel Macneill, WRCNS (1997-176, #85, Nova Scotia Archives and Records Management)

in the 1980s. This collection includes copies of the *Tiddley Times*, newspaper clippings, photo albums, and membership lists.

The papers of Isabel Janet Macneill are also held at the National Archives. Macneill was a member of the first class of Wrens selected for training in September 1942. She went on to become the first woman in the Commonwealth to command a ship when the women's training centre at Galt was named HMCS *Conestoga*. She was granted an Order of the British Empire in June 1944 for her work with the WRCNS. The citation stated that "Macneill had been responsible for the basic training of almost every member of the Service. Her wide knowledge, her profound sympathy and her unfailing and inspiring devotion to duty have made her contribution one without parallel in the Service"(Illustration 82.2).[2]

The papers of Adelaide Sinclair are also held at the National Archives of Canada. Sinclair had been recruited from outside of the service and sent to England for three months to train with the British Wrens in 1943. With the return to England of Commander Dorothy Isherwood, Adelaide Sinclair became the first Canadian woman to serve as director of the Women's Royal Canadian Naval Service, a position she held from 1943 until the end of the war. Like Macneill, Sinclair was awarded an OBE, receiving this honour in 1945 for her "untiring zeal" and "outstanding ability, tact and judgement," resulting in the WRCNS's becoming a "most efficient and well-disciplined unit."[3] Sinclair's papers hold a number of naval press releases along with many news clippings. One of the more interesting items is a recruiting brochure. The undated brochure spells out the qualifications required of hopeful recruits both to join the service and to work in the various trade categories. Because of the large numbers of women interested in joining the service, very few recruiting brochures were ever produced.

The collection also contains a copy of the report on the Women's Royal Canadian Naval Service. For anyone conducting research on the WRCNS, this document is one of the most useful available. Although undated, it would appear to have been prepared near the end of the war or shortly afterwards, in the hope that it might be useful in the event of another war.[4] The report discusses subjects such as recruiting, basic training, pay and allowance, uniforms, discipline, drafting, advancement, welfare, and rehabilitation. For each topic, the document offers a summary of what actions were taken during the war, what problems occurred, and what could have been done differently. Sinclair's many recommendations demonstrated her commitment to the welfare of the women serving under her. In putting forward the notion that pay and allowances should be the same for men and women, she was well ahead of her time.

Vignette

83 "Not Just 'Rosie the Riveter...'"

Popular mythology surrounding women's work during the Second World War has highlighted their employment in munitions and aircraft factories (see essay #84 by Pam Wakewich, Helen Smith, and Jeanette Lynes). Other archival images, however, identify further aspects of women's paid and non-paid wartime contributions.

In addition to filling the factory jobs vacated by men when they joined the armed forces (Illustration 83.1), women also maintained public transportation by driving trolleys, buses, and trams (Illustration 83.2), farmed (Illustration 83.3) and joined the military as radio and signal operators, nurses, and ambulance drivers (Illustrations 83.5 and 83.6). Women artists also took up the war cause and documented the military and home fronts, their work now stored in the National Gallery and Canadian War Museum. Paraskeva Clark and

Clockwise from top:

83.1 Workers at the Marelco Factory
(C 5-1-0-129-1, Archives of Ontario)

83.2 TTC (Toronto Transportation Commission) drivers
(C 5-1-0-135-3, Archives of Ontario)

83.3 Agricultural workers
(PA 112712, National Archives of Canada)

Pegi Nicol MacLeod both painted women doing war work at home and in the military; Molly Lamb Bobak, a member of the Canadian Women's Army Corps, was hired by the Canadian forces to document military life overseas.[1] The home itself became a site of war work: women were encouraged to participate in the war effort by saving every penny and scrap of cloth or metal (Illustration 83.4). Collectively, women's groups such as the Women's Institutes and the Imperial Order Daughters of the Empire prepared care packages for the men overseas. These included treats such as jam and knitted socks and scarves (Illustration 83.7). All of these contributions, while not as sexy or well known as Rosie the Riveter, were important in Canada's war effort.

83.6 Women of the WRNCS leaving Halifax Harbour
(1995-176, #47, Nova Scotia Archives and Records Management)

Top:
83.4 "Pass the amumunition!"
(C 142649, National Archives of Canada)

83.5 Two members of WRCNS signalling
(1995-176, #21, Nova Scotia Archives and Records Management)

83.7 Nakusp women's jam shipment to troops overseas
(C-04658, British Columbia Archives)

84 Women's Wartime Work and Identities: Women Workers at Canadian Car and Foundry Co. Limited, Fort William, Ontario, 1938–1945

Pamela Wakewich, Helen Smith, and Jeanette Lynes

This interdisciplinary research project examines women's wartime work and identities in a regional Canadian community, and its subsequent impact on their experiences of work and family during the postwar era. The intention is to use this in-depth regional case study to explore the broader theoretical questions concerning women, work, and social change that are currently being debated in women's history and feminist historiography. A central component of this research is the collection of original oral histories of women who worked at Canadian Car and Foundry Co. Limited (CanCar), Fort William, Ontario – an important site of aircraft manufacture during the Second World War. At the height of production in 1944, women made up about 40 per cent of the company's labour force and were employed in all areas of aircraft production.[1] The women's recollections of their wartime work and lives are considered within the broader context of their "full life stories"[2] in order to examine the significance and meanings their wartime experiences hold for them. As Anderson and Jack have pointed out, oral history interviews are "an invaluable means of generating new insights about women's experiences of themselves in their worlds."[3] The interactive nature of this research technique allows the researcher to explore contrasts between dominant representations of women's interests and experiences, and women's own representations framed in their own words and in a less culturally edited form.[4]

A second key component of this research project is its analysis of various local, national, and international textual forms of propaganda whereby women were encouraged both to enter the paid workforce and to maintain socially prescribed forms of "femininity" while they were temporarily occupying traditional "male" roles. Representations of women and women's war work in various forms of media and popular culture are examined, as well as the weekly company newspaper the *Aircrafter* and the Montreal-based *Canadian Car Journal*.

Additional archival data is being collected to help situate the local case study within a larger national and international context. This includes material on women's wartime work and postwar adjustments, the Winston Hall's staff housing for women war workers, and information about Elsie MacGill, North America's first woman aeronautical engineer, who was employed at Canadian Car and Foundry during the early part of the war. Recently rediscovered CanCar personnel records from the war era, provides contextual information on the demographic makeup of the CanCar workforce as well as details on both male and female workers' wages and work histories at the plant.

The twin cities of Fort William and Port Arthur (amalgamated in 1970 to become the city of Thunder Bay) were commonly known as "The Lakehead," being located at the head of Lake Superior. At the end of the nineteenth century, the region ended its primary economic function as a fur trading post and Fort William and Port Arthur came into existence as railway, shipping, lumber, pulp and paper, and mining towns. The population was comprised of a diverse mix of ethnic and immigrant communities, as well as a small but significant number of First Nations' peoples.[5]

The Lakehead was hit particularly hard by the Depression, and war-related manufacturing was a major factor in the region's economic recovery, especially the reopening of the Canadian Car and Foundry plant in 1937.[6] Established in 1912, the Lakehead plant had thrived during the First World War, but a lack of postwar business led the company's Montreal head office to close the local plant from 1921 to 1937.[7] In 1937 the intention was for CanCar to start up again modestly by building small aircraft and hiring approximately "100 people a year from 1939 to 1946."[8]

A key player in helping CanCar become an important war industry was C.D. Howe, Port Arthur's federal member of Parliament, who also happened to be Canada's minister of munitions and supply. Howe, along with the CanCar president, managed to convince the British government that Fort William, being neither too remote nor lacking in skilled labour, could produce top-quality military aircraft for the Royal Air Force. From 1939 to 1943, CanCar built 1,451 Hawker Hurricanes, thirty of which fought in the Battle of Britain. In May 1942, about five months after Pearl Harbor, CanCar obtained the contract to build 1,000 Curtiss Helldivers for the American navy. To fill such orders, obviously the original modest hiring proposal of 1937 would not be sufficient, and with Lakehead men increasingly enlisting in the Canadian armed forces, it was understood that women would have to be hired for jobs other than the clerical ones they had previously held.[9]

The opening up of war-industries employment to female workers at CanCar paralleled the national trend.[10] Initially, single women were selected, but when labour shortages continued, married women without children were hired. According to Burkowski, a concern that the hiring of women with children might destabilize families meant that few married women with children, other than those who were widowed or single parents, found employment at CanCar.[11] Working women who became pregnant were likely to be laid off.[12] Recruitment efforts for the Fort William plant expanded beyond the local area to the prairie region, resulting in an influx of several hundred women from the West to fill vacant jobs.[13]

Women's participation in aircraft production at CanCar began in January 1938 with the hiring of a small group of women to sew fabric wings and tails for aircraft (Illustration 84.1).[14] Over the next five years, women moved into almost all stages of plant production. Women's employment reached its height in 1944, at which time 2,707 of the total 6,760 employees were women and they held more than one-third of the production-line jobs.[15] On the shop floor, women were concentrated in "lighter work" areas such as sub-assembly (see Illustration 84.2 and 84.3). However, some women also found work in more typically male-dominated areas, such as final assembly, and as highly skilled machinists and welders. A small group of women welders took on a legendary status within the plant and the local community for the skill and precision of their work, "in spite of" being women.[16] On 17 August 1945, at the war's end, more than 3,000 CanCar employees were dismissed without notice. Of the 1,200 women employed at the plant in early August, only three were kept on.[17]

A notable exception to the general pattern of women's employment at CanCar was the hiring of Elsie Gregory MacGill as the plant's chief engineer in July of 1938. During her employment at CanCar, MacGill was in charge of production of the Hawker Hurricane fighter plane and oversaw a staff of approximately 4,500 women and men, many of whom came to the plant with little or no skilled work experience.[18] In 1943 MacGill left CanCar to

84.1 First women hired for aircraft production, CanCar plant, 1938 (Courtesy of Pam Wakewich et al.)

open her own office as an aeronautical engineering consultant in Toronto; her career is outlined in essay #81 of this volume.

In the fall of 1996, a brief article about our oral history project in a local newspaper column[19] generated an overwhelming response from local residents who themselves had been employed, or who knew of women who had been employed, at CanCar during the war. Copies of the column sent by local residents to friends and family living outside Thunder Bay generated a number of letters from women across the country who had worked at the local plant, as well as donations of photographs and wartime memorabilia for the project. After compiling a list of names of women war workers at CanCar, we began our oral history interviews with women still residing in Thunder Bay. To date, twenty interviews have been conducted, ranging from two to four hours in length. It is anticipated that interviewing will continue through to the fall of 2002, at which time we expect to have collected fifty to sixty interviews. The interviews are audio-taped and transcribed for analysis.

The oral histories are of particular historical value because of the timeliness of the research and the large number of respondents willing to participate. Potentially the largest case study of women war workers from one local setting, the project will include accounts from women employed in more "traditional" women's jobs, as well as those involved in production-line and skilled trades work at the plant. These women are currently in their seventies and eighties, many have recently become widowed, and some are in the process of moving from family homes to seniors' housing. Because of these sig-

Right:

84.2 Making parts for wings, 1941 (C 190-3-0-0-36, Archives of Ontario)

Below:

84.3 Riveters in sub-plant, 1941 (C 190-3-0-0-47, Archives of Ontario)

nificant life changes, the women are eager to reflect on their own pasts.[20]

Themes explored in the oral history interviews include family history; early work experience; how and why the women came to work at CanCar during the war; job training and the range and experience of women's employment at the plant; male-female and female-female work and social relations during the war era; relations between women working in "traditional" and "non-traditional" jobs at the plant; relations between local residents/workers and women workers who migrated from the West; company-employee relations and the regulation of "femininity" in the work site; postwar work and family experiences; and women's perceptions of, and responses to, wartime representations of their work in media and popular culture.

A number of the women contacted have donated copies of personal photographs that document various aspects of the labour process, the range of women's roles in the plant, the leisure activities of employees (Illustration 84.4), and the layout and organization of the staff residence, Winston Hall, which accommodated 420 female employees.[21] Winston Hall was an important social hub for non-local women workers. They could entertain guests in its enormous lounge, six-lane bowling alley, and cafeteria (where many dances were held), under the strict supervision of residence matrons whose presence reassured anxious parents that their daughter's respectability would be well guarded so far away from home.[22]

Additional memorabilia, kept by the women, and made available to the project, are programs from company social gatherings, dance cards from local social events, newspaper clippings about company employees, copies of pay stubs,[23] certificates and letters of employee achievement recognition, and ration books. These items are important not only as documentary evidence of the women's various interests and activities during the war years, but also as an important statement, in their col-lectivity, about the wartime "memories" that the women have chosen to keep alive.

Of particular interest in our analysis of the interviews completed to date are the early work histories of many of the CanCar women. These challenge the popular perception that women who worked in war production were primarily housewives prior to the war and that war-industry work itself was experienced as non-traditional, or distinctly different from their prewar work. For the many women who migrated from prairie farms to the Fort William plant, as well as local rural women, work with machinery in the plant was not dissimilar in terms of physical demand and skill to the farm work with which they had grown up. For women employed as domestic workers prior to the war, the work at CanCar was described as preferable because of its higher pay, more clearly defined job expectations, more employee autonomy, and workplace camaraderie. While a few of the women spoke of their relief at returning to a more domestic role after the plant's closure, many others indicated that they would have preferred to remain in a similar type of employment at the plant if the opportunity had been available to them.

The *Aircrafter* was the Fort William Canadian Car and Foundry's official plant newspaper. Though its masthead logo – "PUBLISHED FOR AND BY EMPLOYEES" (Illustration 84.5) – implies a type of grass-roots labour publication, much of the paper's content suggests that it was tightly regulated by a management-based editorial cohort. Each eight-page issue typically consisted of the following sections: front-page text and pictorial coverage of war news and news from both the local Fort William plant and the Montreal head office; editorial material on the second page and occasionally a section entitled "Foreman's Forum," which outlined ideal management/employee relations; department news on page three describing the working and social lives of employees (such as engagements, weddings, deaths, ill-

84.4 Women from the Stores Department on top of Mount McKay, 1942 (Courtesy of Pam Wakewich et al.)

ness, and holiday activities) as documented by the employees themselves; a women's page entitled "The Feminine Touch" on page four containing such items as articles on fashion and wartime household tips and recipes; reports of plant sport teams and activities on page five; and additional departmental news and war news in the remaining sections. Scattered throughout each issue were poems written by employees, advertising (especially for War Bond drives), and cartoons created by employees and others supplied by the National Safety Council.

The *Aircrafter* functioned primarily as a didactic vehicle to promote support for both the Allied war effort and the return to a traditionally structured society at war's end.[24] Beginning 7 May 1944 and ending 11 August 1945, the paper reflects the final fifteen months of Can-Car's war production. Sixty-five weekly issues of *Aircrafter* were produced in total; the project archives has now obtained copies of fifty of the issues. To ensure that all employees remained working at full capacity, the paper emphasized themes in line with government propaganda – while differences exist among people based on region, sex, class, and race, those differences must be put aside not only for the greater good of the local community, but for Canada, the Allies, and the World.[25] A key rhetorical device to keep workers united was the constant repetition of the words "teamwork" and "family."

There is a consistent mixed message in the paper's representations of women's war work, regardless of the seeming diversity of textual, discursive, and visual styles and content – whether front-page news, fashions on the women's page, or cartoons. On the one hand, women's work is highly praised and presented as essential to the war's effort; on the other hand, women are depicted and actually referred to as "pin-ups," which emphasizes their decorative, and at the same time incongruous, role in a conventionally male workplace (Illustration 84.5).

Embedded within these depictions is the expectation that, after the war, women will leave the public sphere and return to their proper unpaid role within the supposed privacy of the home.[26]

A central issue in researching women's history continues to be the need to understand the differences and connections between two levels of history: those sources revealing women's prescribed domestic and maternal roles and those more elusive sources revealing women's diverse lived experiences. Times of social upheaval – whether internal revolutions or world wars – provide a key opportunity to investigate the complex relationship between social expectation and personal experience. Ironically, times of social upheaval have tended to destabilize idealized constructions of gender, allowing women to be socially recognized as, and even praised for, functioning in roles conventionally reserved for men. These periods allow historical analysts the opportunity to study the multifaceted complexities of gender construction by analysing the interplay among prewar, war, and postwar ideals and representations, and the various ways in which women actually functioned in relation to these ideals. The era of the Second World War provides a unique opportunity for such studies because of the availability of different and highly sophisticated forms of propaganda directed specifically at women. It is also close enough in time to permit the interviewing of women who were living and working during the war years. However, given the advanced age of most of these women, it is of particular importance that this research be conducted in the near future to ensure that the women's voices and recollections will be heard and preserved.

Much of feminist scholarship concerning women's roles during the Second World War – and their depiction in wartime propaganda – has focused on the question: how was the prewar ideology of women's "natural place" in the private sphere able to remain in place throughout the war, despite women's valued work in the

84.5 *Aircrafter*, 30 September 1944 (Courtesy of Pam Wakewich et al.)

public spheres of home front and battle front, and to resurface with even greater intensity in the postwar era?[27] Deborah Montgomerie, in her 1996 article on representations of New Zealand women's war work, points out that "despite the strengths of this scholarship, we are still struggling to understand the mechanisms by which [this] ideological continuity was maintained."[28] Understanding why the 1950s housewife ideal still holds such influence today in Western society, despite the diversity of women's roles and lived experiences over the past half-century, necessitates understanding why the Second World War did not succeed in shattering the prewar ideals of womanhood.

To grasp the complexities of this continuity demands the analysis of women's work identities and representations of their work in both national and regional contexts, with attention to diverse class and cultural experiences. Canadian women have their own unique stories to tell of what life was like during a time when women were mobilized for war in the military, factories, and agricultural and government sectors, as both paid employees and volunteers. Each story helps us understand the interplay between idealized gender and national identities and women's own constructions and understandings of identity based on region, culture, class, and work experiences. Canada's national war identity was based on a curious mix of the "mother country" Britain and her empire, the American "cousins," and Canada's independent identity within the Allied war effort. Thus, the identities of women at CanCar in Fort William must be studied within this multi-dimensional framework of local, national and international contexts.[29]

85 Foreign-Aid Worker and Humanitarian Lotta Hitschmanova and the Unitarian Service Committee of Canada

Grace Hyam

A small woman who characteristically appeared in an olive-green uniform with "Canada" on the lapel, Lotta Hitschmanova, executive director of the Unitarian Service Committee (USC) of Canada, for many years personified Canadian aid to less fortunate lands. Although other agencies and church groups have also provided aid to people overseas, USC Canada has been particularly active and effective; it has also been noteworthy because of the dominant personal role of "Dr Lotta."

She was born Lotte Hitschmann on 28 November 1909 in Prague, in what is now the Czech Republic. (In the early days of World War II, to distance herself from the Nazis, she adopted the Slavic form of her name, and became Lotta Hitschmanova.) Her family was reasonably prosperous and secure, and her early life was comfortable. Lotta had one sibling, her younger sister Lilly, to whom she was very close. Their parents were Max Hitschmann, a malt producer, and his wife, Else (Theiner), who took an active interest in her daughters' education.

Lotta studied languages and philosophy at the University of Prague and also at the Sorbonne in Paris. She eventually earned her PhD at the University of Prague. She also attained diplomas in five languages – Czech, French, German, English and Spanish – and a postgraduate diploma in journalism. She began work as a journalist, hoping eventually for a diplomatic career. She wrote for several newspapers in Prague, and also served as Prague correspondent for other European newspa-

pers. The 1930s were a very troubled time in Europe and although Lotta did not belong to any political party, her writings clearly indicated her opposition to Nazism.

In 1938, by the Munich Agreement, a large portion of Czechoslovakia was handed over to Hitler. Because of her known anti-Nazi sentiments, Lotta was advised to leave Czechoslovakia before the Germans moved in. She fled to Paris and then to Brussels, where she had friends. In Brussels Lotta resumed her work as a journalist. When the Germans began their advance in the spring of 1940, she joined the flood of refugees and eventually found herself in Vichy France. Conditions were very difficult for all the refugees and there was never enough food. One day, in Marseille, Lotta fainted in the street from hunger and was helped by the Unitarian Service Committee, a Boston-based organization that had been established after the Munich Agreement to assist European refugees. This was her first contact with the USC.

In Marseille Lotta worked with several refugee agencies. She found her work rewarding, but life in Vichy France was unrelentingly tense. Eventually, through the efforts of the Czech government-in-exile, she was granted a visa to Canada for the duration of the war. After a difficult journey, she reached Montreal on 22 July 1942. Although she knew no one in Canada and was not really confident speaking English, she soon found work and began to make friends. In October 1942, she accepted a job as a postal censor and moved to Ottawa, which was to become her home.

As well as working in Ottawa, Lotta joined the Czechoslovakian National Alliance and helped raise money for the Czecholovakian War Services in London; she was also active in the local United Nations group. She worked briefly for the United Nations Relief and Rehabilitation Administration (UNRRA), and maintained her contacts with groups such as the USC that were striving to assist refugees.

When the war in Europe ended, Lotta decided that the best way to make a contribution in the areas of most concern to her would be to set up a Canadian section of the Unitarian Service Committee. In the summer of 1945, with a few associates, Lotta established this new organization, which was to be affiliated with the Unitarian Church in Canada and with the American Unitarian Association headquartered in Boston. The first objective was the relief of distressed people, especially children, in France and Czechoslovakia, and to help in their rehabilitation. Senator Cairine Wilson, well known for her work in assisting refugees, agreed to serve as honorary chairman. The organization of USC Canada included an executive director, a board of directors, and several other officers, but Lotta, who became the executive director, was clearly the dominant personality. On 29 August 1945, the Unitarian Service Committee of Canada was registered under the War Charities Act and authorized to send relief to France and Czechoslovakia. In subsequent years, 29 August was celebrated as the "birthday" of USC Canada.

Meanwhile, Lotta had been trying to get news of her family, having lost touch with them during the war. Happily she reestablished contact with her sister, who, though qualified as an architect, was working as a dressmaker in Hafia, Palestine. (Lilly and her husband later returned to Czechoslovakia, and after the Communist takeover of that country in 1948, they emigrated to Canada.) The outcome of her search for her parents was a sad one. Her parents had stayed in Czechoslovakia when she left, and now she learned that they had been taken from their home and had both died in a holding camp from which they would have been sent to Auschwitz. Lotta was devastated. However, after a period of mourning, her reaction to this personal tragedy was to throw herself even more earnestly into her work of helping others.

The newly created, USC Canada was flourishing. In addition to the head office in Ottawa, branches were formed in Toronto, Hamilton, Montreal, Winnipeg, and Vancouver. Enthusiastic members began to organize the collection of clothing, medical supplies, and personal-care items such as soap and toothbrushes, to be shipped to Europe. At first, USC Canada had been permitted to appeal for funds only to Unitarians and their friends, but in February 1946 the organization received permission to appeal to the general public for money. Lotta set out on her first fund-raising trip to western Canada. Lotta addressed fifty-three open meetings and spoke eleven times on the radio. An expert communicator, she vividly described the conditions in Europe, where millions were homeless and hundreds of thousands were suffering from deficiency diseases because of the shortage of food. She emphasized that even a small contribution could make a big difference, and Canadians responded warmly to this message. Young children donated their allowances. Women's groups undertook to knit clothing, such as sweaters and shawls, and held bake sales to raise money. Men volunteered their time to pack up the donated food, clothing, and supplies. Within a few months, the USC had collected forty thousand dollars in cash, as well as thirty thousand kilograms of clothing.

To a certain extent, USC Canada drew on the spirit of humanitarain concern and volunteerism that was prevalent in Canada during and after World War II. Lotta herself was a professional woman who received a salary (though a modest one) from the USC, but she voluntarily devoted a large amount of her personal time to the organization. And she motivated literally hundreds of volunteers, both men and women, to contribute their time and energy to the cause. Many voluntary organizations, including churches of almost all denominations, as well as the Women's Canadian Club, Business and Professinoal Women, Women's Institutes, the Rotary Club, Kiwanis, and the YMCA and YWCA, assisted and cooperated with the USC. Drawing on the goodwill of others and coordinating USC efforts with theirs was one of Lotta's talents.

In the summer of 1946, Lotta travelled to Europe to assess the conditions firsthand. On the basis of her observations, she made recommendations to the USC Board of Directors on areas of greatest need. In Czechoslovakia alone, some 800,000 children were suffering from serios deficiency diseases and many had no shoes or winter underwear. As a result, USC Canada decided to focus on helping physically disabled children and providing a scholarship program of technical training for young people who had been orphaned or whose parents were ill or destitute, directing its aid to Czechoslovakia and France. Canadians sent foods such as condensed milk, soup, sardines, sugar, and dried fruit, as well as warm clothing, for the disabled children, and money to buy artificial limbs for children who were amputees. Money was also raised for the scholarship program. USC also initiated a foster-parent program. Sponsors were asked for a small monthly contribution that would enable a child to be placed in a Unitarian convalescent home where he or she would receive good food, medical care, and personal attention. To the sponsor in Canada, the USC sent a photo and case history of the little ward, and contact continued through letters. This became a very popular project.

Soon USC Canada expanded its areas of assistance beyond France and Czechoslovakia, sending aid to other European countries, especially Italy and Greece. Lotta had originally intended that the agency would last only a few years, until Europe had recovered from the devastation of the war. But as European countries were recovering, other parts of the world began to request help. USC attention moved to Asia, then to the Middle East and Africa. From the early 1950s to 1978, Korea was a major recipient. Several projects were organized in India. Help went to Arab refugees, especially in the Gaza Strip, and to Vietnam, Lesotho, Swaziland, Mali, Bangladesh, Nepal, and Indonesia. During Lotta's tenure as executive director, USC Canada gave aid to more than twenty countries. Depending on local needs, aid might be food, clothing, or medical care, or it might relate to education or vocational training or other social concerns, such as family planning. As well, the foster-parent plan was extended to many countries.

Lotta developed a routine of spending three months a year fund-raising in Canada and four months visiting USC projects overseas. At these projects she established personal contact with the people and reviewed the administrative and financial arrangements to be sure that the projects were achieving their objectives and that the money was being used responsibly.

Almost always she wore her personal uniform. This idea began with a United Nations requirement in the late 1940s that volunteers of any voluntary agency should wear a distinctive uniform while in the field, so that they could be recognized easily. Lotta modelled hers on the uniform of the American army nurse. She had two versions, an olive-green one for winter and a lighter khaki-coloured one for summer. On each lapel was the word "Canada," reflecting her pride in her adopted country, and a pin bearing the USC insignia, a torch representing hope and freedom. Lotta had never served in any armed forces, and some people questioned her adoption of a uniform that looked military and might seem inconsistent with the peaceful message of the USC. But Lotta found the unifrom convenient for travelling, and it allowed her to avoid the complications of carry-

85.1 Lotta Hitschmanova
(PA 165329, National Archives
of Canada)

ing a variety of outfits and accessories. Perhaps most importantly, it made Lotta readily recognizable.

The Unitarian Service Committee of Canada developed into a large organization, with branches in many other Canadian cities. But even as more people became involved, Lotta's personal role remained paramount. Her dedication and her communication skills were major elements in the success of the organization. She used every available channel to get her message to the public. Through the USC broadcast messages, first on radio and then on television, Canadians became very familiar with Dr Lotta's precise, slightly accented voice. She also made effective use of film. From 1948 to 1972, the USC produced an annual film based on her overseas tour, narrated by Lotta herself. This proved to be very helpful in fund-raising. A composite film, *The USC Story*, provided an overview of twenty-five years of USC work.

After several years of experience, Dr Lotta articulated her basic principles for giving aid: "to come as an open-minded friend and good listener, when offering help; to say goodbye to a project when it can continue on its own; [and] to serve with a personal touch, because a relationship must lift your aid beyond the realm of a simple business proposition and prove that you really care."[2] These principles meant a great deal to Lotta. She stressed the importance of responding to needs felt by the recipients, rather than telling them what they needed. When a project reached the point where the local people could maintain it on their own, the USC would withdraw. And Lotta's personal touch was legendary. In addition to her demanding schedule of travelling to visit overseas projects and to raise funds in Canada, she would hand-sign the letters used for fund-raising and send personal letters of thanks to workers and donors, even for very small services or donations.

Because most people shy away from accepting aid unless they can offer something in return, Lotta always insisted on creating a partnership that placed responsibilities on both donor and recipient, and she insisted that USC should help to develop local leadership. She probably never thought of herself as a feminist, but many USC projects had the effect of encouraging women to take more control over their lives and to develop their leadership skills. It was also important to her that the USC should strive to make a real impact in a few well-chosen areas, rather than spreading itself too thinly, and that it should practise the strictest economy in spending donated money. On the last point, Lotta was extremely scrupulous, and USC concern for keeping costs down was well known. The office was run as economically as possible. Much of the routine work, including the packing of parcels, was done by volunteers. Lotta persuaded newspapers, magazines, and radio and television stations to provide USC publicity free of charge. When USC staff travelled on their fund-raising tours, many hotels would offer rooms at reduced rates as their contribution to the campaign. When Lotta was travelling overseas on USC business, she would not take time out to visit tourist spots, even when her hosts were proud of these and wanted to show them to her. Not all of her associates agreed with such a strict interpretation of responsible financial management, but Lotta felt that she could not use USC funds for touring.

Although the USC was originally affiliated with the Unitarian Church, in 1948 its formal links with this church were dissolved. The organization became, and wished to be recognized as being, non-denominational. To emphasize this point, it had its alternate name, USC Canada, officially registered in 1979. Nevertheless, the USC had, and still has, strong though informal links with Unitarians and with other churches and religious groups in Canada.

Lotta received honours from Canada, France, Greece, Lesotho, and other countries. She was named a Companion of the Order of Canada. In 1982 failing health forced Lotta to retire from the position of executive director of USC Canada. Under new leadership, the organization became a more collaborative agency, less influenced by one person, but it has still carried on the important work of earlier years and has always tried to adhere to its original principles, emphasizing the personal touch, strict economy, and freedom from political influence. Lotta died in Ottawa on 1 August 1990, deeply mourned by many friends and associates in Canada and around the world.

The achievements of USC Canada have depended on a very large number of people, and Lotta always gave great credit to her numerous associates and volunteers. But an enormous amount of the credit must be given to Lotta herself. The agency would never have attained its magnificent level of success without her strong personality, her intelligence and organizational ability, her determination and dedication, and her genuine humanitarian spirit. The fact that USC Canada is still active today, and that it still follows many of the methods and principles that she laid out, is a wonderful tribute to Dr Lotta Hitschmanova.

Appendix One

Archival Sources Identified by Essay/Vignette

Essay/Vignette	Diaries	Manuscripts & Corresp.	Art	Oral History	Textiles	Organizational Records	Posters & Ads	Photos
PART ONE								
1								X
2				X				
3								X
4						X		
5		X						X
6						X		
7				X		X		
8				X				
9								X
10								X
11								X
12			X					
13			X					
14			X					
15								X
16			X		X			
17								X
18			X					
19			X					
20			X		X			
PART TWO								
21			X					X
22		X						X
23	X							X
24				X				
25							X	

Essay/Vignette	Diaries	Manuscripts & Corresp.	Art	Oral History	Textiles	Organizational Records	Posters & Ads	Photos
26						X		X
27				X				
28		X						
29		X	X	X				
30		X						X
31								X
PART THREE								
32								X
33						X		X
34		X						
35		X						
36		X						
37		X						
38				X				X
39				X				
40								X
41		X						X
PART FOUR								
42								X
43		X						
44		X	X					X
45		X						X
46		X				X		
47		X						X
48		X						X
49		X						
50		X						
51		X						X
52		X						
53		X						
54				X		X	X	X
55						X		
PART FIVE								
56								X
57								X
58		X						X

Essay/Vignette	Diaries	Manuscripts & Corresp.	Art	Oral History	Textiles	Organizational Records	Posters & Ads	Photos
59		X		X				X
60						X		
61		X						
62		X						
63		X						
64				X				X
65				X				X
PART SIX								
66								X
67				X				X
68		X					X	X
69		X					X	X
70								X
71		X			X			X
72				X	X			X
73				X	X			X
74				X	X			X
75		X						X
76				X				X
77		X						X
78		X						X
79				X				X
80								X
81		X						X
82		X		X				X
83								X
84				X				X
85		X						X

Appendix Two
Cross-Referenced Essay Index

Essay	Title	Related Essays
27	"Such Outrageous Discrimination": Farm Women and Their Family Grievances in Early Twentieth-Century Ontario	26, 42, 48
28	Between the Rock and a Hard Place: Single Mothers in St John's, Newfoundland, during the Second World War	83, 84, 31
29	Prudence Heward: Painting at Home	12, 13, 20
30	Mothering the Dionne Quintuplets: Women's Stories	31, 56, 67
31	Saving Mothers and Babies: Motherhood, Medicine, and the Modern State, 1900–1945	45, 47, 67
33	Shaping Canada's Women: Canadian Girls in Training versus Girl Guides	40, 41, 46
34	The Experience of Women Students at Four Universities, 1895–1930	35, 36, 40
35	Margaret Addison: Dean of Residence and Dean of Women at Victoria University, 1903–1931	32, 37, 60
36	The "Feminization" of High Schools: The Problem of Women Secondary School Teachers in Ontario	34, 41, 54
37	Writing for Whom? Isabel Murphy Skelton and Canadian History in the Early Twentieth Century	10, 43, 77
38	The Rideau Street Convent School: French-Language Private Schooling in Ontario	32, 34, 39
39	"The School on Fardy's Cross": Shamrock School Remembered	28, 65, 67
41	From Elegance and Expression to Sweat and Strength: Physical Education at the Margaret Eaton School	35, 38, 40
43	History and Human Agency: The Case of Agnes Macphail, Canada's First Woman Member of Parliament	44, 50, 51
45	Women, the Settlement Movement, and State Formation in the Early Twentieth Century	2, 42, 47
46	The Historical Record and Adolescent Girls in Montreal's Red-Light District	33, 45, 47
47	Charlotte Whitton: Pioneering Social Worker and Public Policy Activist	42, 49, 52
48	Consuming Issues: Women on the Left, Political Protest, and the Organization of Homemakers, 1920–1960	25, 52, 54
49	Making Ourselves Heard: "Voice of Women" and the Peace Movement in the Early Sixties	30, 42, 52

Essay	Title	Related Essays
50	The Royal Commission on the Status of Women in Canada, 1967–1970: Liberal Feminism and Its Radical Implications	43, 51, 66
52	Women, Peace Activism, and the Environment: Rosalie Bertell and the Development of a Feminist Agenda, 1970s–1990s	56, 63, 85
53	State Control of Women's Immigration: The Passage to Canada of South Asian Women	67, 68, 72
54	Making Space: Women Building Culture	1, 16, 55
55	Feminist Theatre in Toronto: A Look at the Nightwood Theatre	10, 42, 54
57	The Ladies Committee of the Home for Incurable Children	59, 61, 62
58	Margaret Scott: "The Angel of Poverty Row"	45, 46, 61
59	"Hardly Feminine Work!" Violet Wilson and the Canadian Voluntary Aid Detachment Nurses of the First World War	81, 82, 84
60	The Emergence of Physiotherapy as a New Profession for Canadian Women, 1914–1918	59, 61, 62
61	Ethel Currant: Portrait of a Grenfell Nurse	8, 28, 69
62	Vera Peters: Medical Innovator	63, 64, 81
63	Norah Toole: Scientist and Social Activist	49, 52, 62
64	Alice V. Payne, Mining Geologist: A Lifetime of "Small and Difficult Things"	24, 32, 34
68	Bringing "Domestics" to Canada: A Study of Immigration Propoganda	53, 67, 77
69	Women in the Newfoundland Fishery	28, 61, 66
71	Creative Ability and Business Sense: The Millinery Trade in Ontario	72, 80, 74
72	Our Mothers' Patterns: Sewing and Dressmaking in the Japanese-Canadian Community	66, 73, 74
73	Federica and Angelina: Postwar Italian-Canadian Couturiers in Toronto	70, 71, 79
74	Fabrications: Clothing, Generations, and Stitching Together the History We Live	66, 71, 72
76	Ann Meekitjuk Hanson: Inuit Broadcaster, Interpreter, and Community Worker	15, 18, 78
77	Cultural Nationalism and Maternal Feminism: Madge Macbeth as Writer, Broadcaster, and Literary Figure	15, 37, 51
78	"The Day of the Strong-Minded Frump Has Passed": Women Journalists and News of Feminism	50, 51, 77
79	Women in Banking: A Case Study of Scotiabank	66, 75, 82

Essay	Title	Related Essays
81	"The Queen of the Hurricanes": Elsie Gregory MacGill as Aeronautical Engineer and Women's Advocate	35, 64, 82
82	The Women's Royal Canadian Naval Service during the Second World War: An Exploration of Their Archival Legacy	66, 83, 84
84	Women's Wartime Work and Identities: Women Workers at Canadian Car and Foundry Co. Limited, Fort William, Ontario, 1938–1945	65, 81, 83
85	Foreign-Aid Worker and Humanitarian Lotta Hitschmanova and the Unitarian Service Committee of Canada	6, 45, 49

Notes

INTRODUCTION

1 See Freeman Patterson, *A Photographer's LIfe: ShadowLight* (Toronto: HarperCollins, 1996). Patterson's photographic representations profiling "false starts and periods of regression, as well as sudden leaps forward and periods of sustained development," (p. 7) in his own development were compelling to us as we surveyed and assessed the many articles and images sent to us by contributors.

2 See, for example, Janet Silman (as told to), *Enough Is Enough: Aboriginal Women Speak Out* (Toronto: Umbrella Press, 1994); Peggy Bristow, co-ordinator, et al., *"We're Rooted Here and They Can't Pull Us Up": Essays in African Canadian Women's History* (Toronto: University of Toronto Press, 1994); Andrée Lévesque, *La Norme et les deviantes: Des femmes au Quebec pendant l'entre deux guerres* (Montreal: Les Éditions du remue-ménage, 1989), translated by Yvonne M. Klein as *Making and Breaking the Rules: Women in Quebec, 1919–1939* (Toronto: McClelland and Stewart, 1994); Karen Dubinsky, *Improper Advances: Rape and Heterosexual Conflict in Ontario, 1880–1929* (Chicago: University of Chicago Press, 1993); Sedef Arat-Koc, "Immigration Policies, Migrant Domestic Workers, and the Definition of Citizenship in Canada," in Veronica Strong-Boag and Anita Clair Fellman, *Rethinking Canada: The Promise of Women's* History 3rd edition (Toronto: Oxford University Press, 1997).

3 Joanna Dean and David Fraser, *Women's Archives Guide: Manuscript Sources for the History of Women* (Ottawa: National Archives of Canada, 1991). See also Shirley Spragge, Archival *Source Material Relating to Women's Studies in the Queen's University Archives* (Kingston: Queen's University Archives, 1993).

4 See Helen M. Buss and Marlene Kadar, eds., *Working in Women's Archives: Researching Women's Private Literature and Archival Documents* (Waterloo: Wilfrid Laurier University Press, 2000); and Sharon Larade and Johanne Pelletier, "Mediating in a Neutral Environment: Gender-Inclusive or Neutral Language in Archival Description," in *Archivaria* 35 (Spring 1993): 99–109.

5 For an overview of archival theory, an analysis of how archival concepts and practice have changed significantly across time and space, and an entrée into a large literature on how archivists construct the past, see Terry Cook, "What Is Past Is Prologue: A History of Archival Ideas Since 1898, and the Future Paradigm Shift," *Archivaria* 43 (Spring 1997): 17–63. Additional works that look at the archivist's own historicity include Bernadine Dodge, "Places Apart: Archives in Dissolving Space and Time," *Archivaria* 44 (Fall 1997): 118–31. See also A. Pam Harris, *Faces of Feminsm: Portraits of Women Across Canada* (Toronto: Second Story Press, 1992); and *Documents That Move and Speak: Proceedings from a Symposium Organized for the International Council of Archives by the National Archives of Canada, Ottawa, April 30, 1990–May 30, 1990* (Munich, London, New York, Paris: K.G. Saur, 1992).

6 For other collections of archival documents related to women's history, see Ramsay Cook and Wendy Mitchinson, eds., *The Proper Sphere: Women's Place in Canadian*

Society (Toronto: Oxford University Press, 1976); Beth Light and Joy Parr, eds., *Canadian Women on the Move, 1867–1920* (Toronto: New Hogtown Press and OISE Press, 1983); Beth Light and Ruth Roach Pierson, eds., *No Easy Road: Women in Canada, 1920s–1960s* (Toronto: New Hogtown Press, 1980); and Kathryn Carter, *Voix Feministes/Feminist Voices: Diaries in English by Women in Canada, 1783–1995: An Annotated Bibliography* (Ottawa: Canadian Research Institute for the Advancement of Women/Institute canadien recherches sur les femmes, 1997). On visual history in Canada, see Ken Cruikshank and Nancy B. Bouchier, "Women's History on Film: Requiem for Studio D," *Canadian Historical Review* 80 (1999): 93–113. See also Julie Cruikshank, *Life Lived Like a Story* (Lincoln and London: University of Nebraska Press, 1990); and idem, *Reading Voices: Oral and Written Interpretations of the Yukon's Past* (Toronto, Vancouver: Douglas and McIntyre, 1991).

7 Sadly, despite our goal to demonstrate the diversity of the undiscovered archival resources on women available to historians, we were unable to accept all of the papers and images offered for inclusion in this book. Space limitations played a part in this, but in addition and perhaps more importantly, articles that were not based on the archival record were not included. We regret this, but our commitment to publishing archival materials was paramount.

8 For additional articles and monographs on women's history in Canada see Strong-Boag and Fellman, eds., *Rethinking Canada*, 1st (1986), 2nd (1991), and 3rd (1991) editions. Alison Prentice and Susan Mann Trofimenkoff, eds., *The Neglected Majority: Essays in Canadian Women's History*, 2 vol. (Toronto: McClelland and Stewart, 1977 and 1985); Marie Lavigne and Yolande Pinard, eds., *Travailleuses et féministes: Les femmes dans la société québécoise* (Montreal: Boreal Express, 1983); Le Collective Clio, *L'Histoire des femmes au Québec depuis quatre siècles* (Montreal: Les Quinze, 1982). Translated by Roger Gagnon and Rosalind Gill as *Quebec Women: A*

History (Toronto: Women's Press, 1987); Jean Burnet, ed., *Looking into My Sister's Eyes: An Exploration in Women's History* (Toronto: Multicultural History Society of Ontario, 1986); Linda Kealey and Joan Sangster, eds., *Beyond the Vote: Canadian Women and Politics* (Toronto: University of Toronto Press, 1989); and Franca Iacovetta and Mariana Valverde, eds., *Gender Conflicts: New Essays in Women's History* (Toronto: University of Toronto Press, 1992). For an overall synthesis of women's history, see Alison Prentice et al., *Canadian Women: A History*, (1988; Toronto: Harcourt Brace Jovanovich, 1996); and Wendy Michison, *Canadian Women (A Reader)* (Toronto: Harcourt Brace and Co. Canada, 1996). For additional bibliographic references, see Diana Pedersen, ed., *Changing Women, Changing History: A Bibliography of the History of Women in Canada* (Toronto: Green Dragon Press, 1992). On the teaching of women's history, see Bettina Bradbury et al., eds., *Teaching Women's History: Challenges and Solutions* (Athabasca, Alta: Athabaska University Educational Enterprises, 1995).

9 For one discussion of this term, see Light and Pierson, eds., *No Easy Road.*

10 James Snell, "Marital Cruelty: Women and the Nova Scotia Divorce Court, 1900–1939," *Acadiensis* 18 (1988); idem, "'Till Death Do Us Part': Wife-Beating and the Criminal Justice System in Alberta, 1905–1920," *Alberta History* 36 (1988); Karen Dubinsky and Franca Iacovetta, "Murder, Womanly Virtue and Motherhood: The Case of Angelina Napolitano, 1911–1922," *Canadian Historical Review* 72 (1991); and Annalee Golz, "'If a Man's Wife Does Not Obey Him, What Can He Do?'" "Marital Breakdown and Wife Abuse in Late Nineteenth- and Early Twentieth-Century Ontario," in Susan Binnie and Louis Knafla eds., *Law, State and Society: Essays in Modern Legal History* (Toronto: University of Toronto Press 1995).

11 See Gail Cuthbert Brandt, "Postmodern Patchwork: Some Recent Trends in the Writing of Women's History in Canada," *Canadian Historical Review* 72, no 4 (December 1991): 441–70.

NUMBER 1

1 Carroll Smith Rosenberg, "The Female World of Love and Ritual: Relations between Women in Nineteenth-Century America," *Signs* 1 (1975): 1–29; Janet Guildford and Suzanne Morton, eds., *Separate Spheres: Women's Worlds in the Nineteenth-Century Maritimes* Fredericton: Acadiensis Press, 1994).

2 Veronica Strong-Boag, *"The New Day Recalled": Lives of Girls and Women in English Canada, 1919–1939* (Toronto: Copp Clark Pitman, 1988).

3 The Clio Collective, *Quebec Women: A History* (Toronto: Women's Press, 1987).

4 Varpu Lindstrom-Best, *Defiant Sisters: A Social History of Finnish Immigrant Women in Canada* (Toronto: Multicultural History Society of Ontario, 1988).

5 Dionne Brand, *No Burden to Carry: Narratives of Black Working Women in Ontario 1920s to 1950* (Toronto: Women's Press, 1991).

6 Jean Burnet, *Looking Into My Sister's Eyes: An Exploration in Women's History* (Toronto: Multicultural History Society of Ontario, 1986).

7 E. Pauline Johnson, "Mother O' the Men," in E. Pauline Johnson, *The Moccasin Maker*, with an introduction, annotation and bibliography by A. LaVonne Brown Ruoff (1913; Tuscon, 1987), 182, 187.

NUMBER 4

1 Provincial Archives of Manitoba (PAM), MG 10 C 50, Social Science Study Club (SSSC), Papers Presented, 1954

2 M. MacMurchy (Lady Willison), *The Woman – Bless Her: Not as Amiable a Book as It Sounds* (Toronto: S.B. Gundy, 1916), 10.

3 A. Prentice, P. Bourne, G.C. Brandt, W. Mitchinson, and N. Black, *Canadian Women: A History*, 2nd ed. (Toronto: Harcourt Brace, 1996), 215.

4 Prentice et al., *Canadian Women*, 220.

5 On women's organizing, see ibid. and G.C. Brandt, "Organizations in Canada: The English Protestant Tradition," in P. Bourne, ed., *Women's Paid and Unpaid Work: Historical and Contemporary Perspectives* (Toronto: New Hogtown Press, 1985): 79–96.

6 See J.H. Gray, *The Boy from Winnipeg* (Toronto: Macmillan, 1970); B. Kaplan, *Corner Store* (Winnipeg: Queenston House, 1975); and J. Marlyn, Under the Ribs of Death (Toronto: McClelland and Stewart, 1957).

7 A. Artibise, *Winnipeg: An Illustrated History* (Toronto: James Lorimer and Co. and National Museum of Man, 1977); 202.

8 On women's efforts to build community and women's groups and neighbourhoods, see Veronica Strong-Boag, *The New Day Recalled: Lives of Girls and Women in English Canada, 1919–1939* (Toronto: Copp Clark Pitman, 1988); and Jean Burnett, ed., *Looking Into My Sister's Eyes: An Exploration in Women's History* (Toronto: Multicultural History Society of Ontario, 1986).

9 J. Baltessen, "Getting Together: Women's Study Groups, Collections at the Provincial Archives of Manitoba" (unpublished manuscript, 1994).

10 PAM, MG 10 C51, Searchlight Book Club (SBC), box 1, Annual Reports, 1923.

11 PAM, P5085, The Twenty Club (TC), file 6, Papers.

12 PAM, P882, Hawthorne Women's Club (HWC), Minutes of 9 January 1924.

13 PAM, 5P5389-5P5390, Fort Garry Reading Club (FGRC), 5P5390, file 6, History, n.d., 6.

14 FGRC, P5389, Minutes of 1 November 1933.

15 SBC, Box 1, Minute Book, 1917–1923, Minutes of 13 December 1919.

16 FGRC, P5390, file 6, History, n.d., 4.

17 Baltessen, "Getting Together," 6.

18 SSSC, Historical Sketch, "Changes Sparked by Jubilee-Year Club," by Mary Bletcher, *Winnipeg Free Press*, 10 March 1962, 15.

19 SSSC, Historical Sketch, 10 March 1962.

20 SSSC, Papers Presented, January 1919.

21 SSSC, Papers Presented, 1954.

22 Ibid.

23 Ibid.

24 sssc, Minutes of 17 June 1966.

25 sssc, Minutes of 14 October 1966.

26 MacMurchy, *The Woman*, 17.

27 M. Kinnear and V. Fast, *Planting the Garden: An Annotated Archival Bibliography of the History of Women in Manitoba* (Winnipeg: University of Manitoba Press, 1987), xv.

NUMBER 5

1 Text from Esther Smith, Georgina Judin, and Margaret Valentine, former employees of the factory.

NUMBER 6

1 This poem has been printed in the denomination's newspaper, the *Christian Guardian*, 13 June 1906, and reprinted 28 February 1917. This research is based on Methodist Ladies' Aid minutes found in the archival collections of the United Church of Canada. Those cited are located as follows: the United Church/Victoria University Archives in Toronto holds records of Trinity Church, Kitchener (Berlin), Ont.; St John's Church, Georgetown, Ont.; Walkerton Methodist Church, Walkerton, Ont.; Walkerton Methodist Church, and Parkdale Church, Toronto. Records of Airdie, Alta.; and Dawson, Y.T., are in the Alberta and Northwest Conference Archives, Edmonton; Seldom Come By, Nfld, in the Newfoundland Conference Archives, St John's; and John Wesley Smith Memorial Church, Halifax, and Centenary Church, Saint John, in the Maritime Conference Archives, Halifax.

2 For more on this and other aspects of Ladies' Aid work, see Marilyn Färdig Whiteley, "'Doing Just About What They Please': Ladies' Aids in Ontario Methodism," *Ontario History* 82 (December 1990): 289–304.

3 For a discussion of the activities of groups in some parts of Ontario, see Penny Bedal and Ross Bartlett, "The Women Do Not Speak: The Methodist Ladies' Aid Societies and World War I," *Papers of the Canadian Methodist Historical Society*, (1993–94): 63–86.

NUMBER 7

1 G. Lerner, The Creation of Feminist Consciousness (New York: Oxford University Press, 1993), 249.

2 Communities of religious, such as the Sisters Servants of the Immaculate Heart of Mary of Monroe Michigan (IHM), have labelled their historical project as "Claiming Our Roots: IHM Interdisciplinary Feminist History Project." Their seventeen working Assumptions include the following: "in practice, a range of feminist ideologies exist, but feminist approaches to history accept as a starting point that patriarchy exists in society and in its institutions, including churches." The influence that this project will have, especially through international organizations such as the History of Women Religious Conference (HWR) and its Internet discussion group Sister-L, remains to be seen.

3 J.S. Moir, "Coming of Age, but Slowly: Aspects of Canadian Religious Historiography Since Confederation," CCHA *Study Sessions*, 50 (1983): 97.

4 In the aftermath of Vatican II, many communities of religious adapted a "comic book" format of their history. V. O'Reilly's *Frontier Women: Sisters of St Joseph of Canada – The Canadian Adventure* (Turin: Sadifa Media, 1986), which appeared in the Great Moments in Canadian Church series is one such example. The Sisters of St Joseph of Hamilton commissioned Peggy Savage to prepare a centenary history of health care in Hamilton (P. Savage, *To Serve with Honour* [Hamilton: Dundurn Press, 1990]).

5 Canadian Religious Conference, *Statistics of the Insitutes of Consecrated Life and of the Societies of Apostolic Life, 1 January 1998* (Ottawa: Canadian Religious Conference, 1998).

6 J. Creusen, *Religious Men and Women in the Code*, 5th ed. (1931: Milwaukee: Bruce, 1951, 286.

7 Before the 1917 codification of the Code of Canon Law, the requirements were somewhat more flexible than they became subsequently. Canon 282 of the 1917 Codification required bishops to ensure that "two copies of documents" related to diocesan enterprises and residing "con-

fraternities" be made and that "one copy shall be kept in the respective archives and the other in the episcopal archives." (S. Woywood, *A Practical Commentary on the Code of the Canon Law, 2* vols. [New York: J.F. Wagner, 1926], 1:138) Canon 88 requires Pontifical Institutes to generate quinquennial reports and submit them to Rome. Among the questions that institutes are required to answer is the following: "Are the Archives of the Institute and of the individual houses properly equipped and carefully arranged?" (J. Creusen, *Religious Men and Women in the Code,* 286.)

8 Sisters of St Joseph of Hamilton, *Usual Customs and Observances* (Hamilton: Park Street, 1885), 41 (hereafter *Usual Customs*). The constitutions of religious communities were often accompanied by a companion volume entitle *Customs and Observances*, which contained commentary and elaboration of clauses in the constitutions. Frequently, detailed role descriptions were included. Having such details in a separate volume facilitated revision as amendment of customs and practices did not require the same complex and canonically bound protocols as amendment of the constitutions would have required. (hereafter *Usual Customs*).

9 Postscript, Congregation of the Sisters of St Joseph of Toronto, Annals vol. 1 (1851–1914), 486.

10 *Usual Customs,* 41.

11 Marie de L'Incarnation to Claude Martin, Quebec, 1670, in J. Marshall, ed. and trans., *Word from New France* (Toronto: Oxford University Press, 1967), 371.

NUMBER 8

1 Mary Rose Donnelly and Heather Dow, *Katherine: A Biography* (Winfield, B.C., 1992), 35.

2 These camp meetings still continue today.

3 The Student Volunteer Movement was the forerunner of the Student Christian Movement, which came into being in 1921.

4 Minutes of the Women's Missionary Society, 27 September 1910–3 September 1913, University of Toronto, United Church Archives, Finding Aid 19 C2, file box 003, 136.

5 Donnelly and Dow, in *Katherine*, describe the goods carried by some of the missionaries, who hoped to make this a life-time career (18). These included tuxedos, long gowns for the marriages of yet unborn children, pianos, organs, brass bed-frames, sewing machines, rifles, gramophones, bicycles, and much else. A family might transport several tons of luggage.

6 The young Republic of China was disintegrating into warring factions when the missionaries were ordered out. This dangerous situation was particularly true in the central coastal region.

7 Donnelly and Dow, *Katherine,* 15

8 The China missionary period was at tis heioght between the year 1890 and 1935. By the 1930s, war with Japan and China's inflated economy made missionary work very difficult. War between Chiang Kai-shek's ruling Kuomintang Nationalists and Mao Zedong-led Communists added further problems. When the Communists took over in 1949, the missionaries mostly left. The hospitals, schools, and churches that were left behind were taken over by the Chinese themselves.

NUMBER 9

1 See Ruth Compton Brouwer, "'Transcending the 'Unacknowledged Quarantine': Putting Religion into English-Canadian Women's History," Journal of Canadian Stuides/Revue d'etudes canadiennes 27 (Fall 1992): 47–61. See also her *New Women of God: Canadian Presbyterian Women and India Missions, 1876–1914* (Toronto: University of Toronto Press, 1989).

NUMBER 10

1 See also Veronica Strong-Boag and Carole Gerson, *Paddling Her Own Canoe: E. Pauline Johnson (Tekahionwake) and Her Times* (Toronto: University of Toronto Press, 2000).

2 The essays in Bill Ashcroft, Gareth Griffiths, and Helen Tiffin, eds., *The Empire Writes Back: Theory and Practice in Post-Colonial Literature* (London and New York: Routledge, 1993), provide an excellent introduction to post-colonial writers.

3 For a discussion of the influence of Johnson's parents and family, see Strong-Boag and Gerson, *Paddling Her Own Canoe*, chap. 1.

4 E. Pauline Johnson, *The Moccasin Maker*, with an introduction, annotation and bibliography by A. LaVonne Brown Ruoff (1913; Tucson 1987), 13.

5 In her advocacy of sports and outdoor activities for women, Johnson joined a host of feminists who championed physical activity as a source of empowerment. See Helen Lenskyj, *Women, Sport and Physical Activity* (Ottawa: Fitness and Amateur Sport Canada, 1991).

6 Johnson, *Moccasin Maker*, 232.

7 See Veronica Strong-Boag, "Claiming a Place in the Nation: Citizenship Education and the Challenge of Feminists, Natives and Workers in Post-Confederation Canada," *Canadian and International Education*, Special Issues, 1997.

8 E. Pauline Johnson, *Legends of Vancouver* (Toronto: McClelland and Stewart, 1926), 3. The legend is "The Two Sisters."

NUMBER 12

1 I wish to thank Peggy Carson, Terry Cook, Harold Killins, Brian Killins, and Kate O'Rourke for their help and observations on earlier versions of this article.

2 J. Russell Harper, "Painting, 1840 to 1940," *The Canadian Encyclopedia*, 2nd ed. (Edmonton: Hurtig Publishers, 1988).

3 Dennis Reid, *A Concise History of Canadian Painting* (Toronto: Oxford University Press, 1973), 142.

4 J. Russell Harper, *Painting in Canada: A History*, 2nd ed. (Toronto: University of Toronto Press, 1977), 289.

5 Doris McCarthy, *A Fool in Paradise: An Artist's Early Life* (Toronto: Macfarlane Walter and Ross, 1990).

6 Just how modest may be judged by her surviving paintings, some of which were done on the reverse side of classroom wall charts that she had hand-lettered for her students. In cases where she could afford proper water-colour mats, she painted on both faces of the paper.

7 In this trait, Killins was not unique. It has been observed that other artists – for example, David Milne – reacted similarly.

8 Edward Phelps, "A Brief Sketch of the Life and Work of the Late Ada Gladys Killins, Member of the Canadian Society of Painters in Water Colour" (typescript catalogue prepared for the Gladys Killins Memorial Show held at Oak Hall, Niagara Falls, Ontario, Canada, and sponsored by the Niagara District Art Association, 1967), 4.

NUMBER 13

1 Maria Tippett, *Emily Carr: A Biography* (Markham, Ont.: Penguin Books, 1979).

2 Doris Shadbolt, "Emily Carr: Legend and Reality," in *Artscanada*, June/July 1971: 18.

NUMBER 14

1 Helen Collinson, *Sketches from Life* (Edmonton: Ring House Gallery; and University of Alberta, 1981), 3.

2 Annora Brown, *Sketches from Life*, with a foreword by Frank Lynch-Staunton (Edmonton: Hurtig Publishers, 1981), 84.

3 Freda Smith Mudiman, "Interpreter of the Foothills," *Calgary Herald*, 17 October 1942.

4 Brown, *Sketches from Life*, 8.

5 Ibid., 9.

NUMBER 16

1 May Phillips died in 1937 and Mary Peck in 1943.

2 For further reading, see Ellen Easton McLeod, *In Good Hands: The Women of the Canadian Handicrafts Guild* (Montreal & Kingston: McGill-Queen's University Press for Carleton University, 1999).

NUMBER 18

1 Holman Gallery, Annual Print Collection catalogue, 1972.

2 Leo Bushman, cited in Janet.C. Berlo, "Drawing and Print-making at Holman," *Inuit Art Quarterly* 10 (Fall 1995): 25.

NUMBER 19

1 For further history of the guild, see essay #16.

2 Ellen Easton McLeod, *In Good Hands: The Women of the Canadian Handicrafts Guild* (Montreal & Kingston: McGill-Queen's University Press for Carleton University, 1999).

NUMBER 20

1 Christine Boyanoski, *Loring and Wyle: Sculptors' Legacy* (Toronto: Art Gallery of Ontario, 1987), 21–25.

2 Ibid., 59.

3 Emily Carr, *Hundreds and Thousands: The Journals of an Artist* (Toronto: Irwin Publishing, 1966), 305.

4 Ibid., 325.

5 Ann Davis, *Frontiers of Our Dreams: Quebec Painting in the 1940s and 1950s* (Winnipeg: Winnipeg Art Gallery, 1979), 15–24.

6 Cited in Marie Fleming, *Joyce Wieland* (Toronto: Art Gallery of Ontario, 1987), 81.

7 Cited in Elizabeth McLuhan and R.M. Vanderburgh, *Daphne Odjig – A Retrospective* (Thunder Bay: National Exhibition Centre and Centre for Indian Arts, 1985), #15.

8 Ibid., 20.

9 Cited in Jessica Bradley and Diana Meniroff, *Songs of Experience* (Ottawa: National Gallery of Canada, 1985), 82.

10 Cited in Judith Mastai, *Women and Paint* (Saskatoon: Mendel art Gallery, 1995), 29.

NUMBER 21

1 P. Bourne, A Prentice, W. Mitchinson et al., *Canadian Women: A History*, 2nd ed. (Toronto: Harcourt Brace Jovanovich, 1995).

2 C.R. Comacchio, *The Infinite Bonds of Family: Domesticity in Canada, 1850 to 1940* (Toronto: University of Toronto Press, 1999).

3 J.R. Miller, *Skyscrapers Hide the Heavens: A History of Indian-White Relations in Canada* (Toronto: University of Toronto Press, 1989); and E. Brian Titley, "Indian Industrial Schools in Western Canada," in Nancy Sheehan, J. Donald Wilson, and David C. Jones, eds., *Schools in the West: Essays in Canadian Educational History* (Calgary: Detselig Press, 1986).

4 Barry Broadfoot, *Ten Lost Years 1929–39: Memories of Canadians Who Survived the Depression* (Toronto: Doubleday, 1973.)

5 F. Fukuyama, *The Great Disruption: Human Nature and the Reconstitution of Social Order* (Boston: Harvard University Press, 1999).

NUMBER 22

1 The National Archives of Canada has in its holdings the papers of several prime ministers' wives, including the correspondence of Mila Mulroney, Maureen McTeer, Lady Thompson, Lady Borden, Edna Diefenbaker, Olive Diefenbaker, and the diary of Lady Agnes Macdonald.

2 Christian Rioux, "Sir Wilfrid Laurier's Letters to Zoé Lafontaine," *The Archivist* 19 (1993): 6–9.

3 Barbara Welter, "The Cult of True Womanhood, 1820–1860," *American Quarterly* 18 (1966): 151–74.

4 Her home in Arthabaska is now both a regional art gallery and a historic house and museum, with late nineteenth-century furnishings similar to those the Lauriers might have had.

5 When Zoé Laurier died in 1921, she bequeathed her house to William Lyon Mackenzie King, her husband's successor as leader of the Liberal party and later to be one of Canada's longest-serving prime ministers. Laurier House, today a designated National Historic Site, interprets the lives of three of Canada's prime ministers, Sir Wilfrid Laurier, William Lyon Mackenzie King, and Lester B. Pearson, all of whom spent some of their terms in office there.

6 For a discussion of the amount of manual labour done by middle class women in the home, see, Deborah Gorham, *The Victorian Girl and the Feminine Ideal* (Bloomington: Indiana University Press, 1982), 9–11.

7 *Montreal Herald and Daily Telegraph*, 17 February 1919.

8 *Ottawa Evening Journal*, 1 November 1921.

9 For a discussion of the evolution of national women's organizations, see Veronica Strong-Boag, "Setting the Stage: National Organization and the Women's Movement in the Late 19th Century," in Susan Mann Trofimenkoff and Alison Prentice, eds., *The Neglected Majority: Essays in Canadian Women's History* (Toronto: McClelland and Stewart, 1978), 87–103.

10 For essays on the history of maternal feminism, see Linda Kealey, ed., *A Not Unreasonable Claim: Women and Reform in Canada, 1880s–1920s* (Toronto: Canadian Women's Educational Press, 1979). For an examination of the work and ideas of Protestant moral and social reformers in Canada, see Mariana Valverde, *The Age of Light, Soap, and Water: Moral Reform in English Canada, 1885–1925* (Toronto: McClelland and Stewart, 1991).

11 Organizations that concentrated on gender-related issues included the Woman's Christian Temperance Union, the Young Women's Christian Association, the Girls' Friendly Society, the Dominion Order of King's Daughters, women's missionary societies of a variety of denominations, and the National Council of Women of Canada.

12 Using the ideology of domesticity and contemporary ideas about gender, some women argued that only suffrage and the acquisition of political power would give women the capacity to utilize their special female attributes and domestic skills to effect social reform. This ideology has come to be called maternal feminism. See Carol Lee Bacchi, *Liberation Deferred? The Ideas of the English Canadian Suffragists, 1877–1918* (Toronto: University of Toronto Press, 1983).

13 National Archives of Canada, Sir Wilfrid Laurier fonds, MG 26 G.

1 The transcription process involved a careful reading of each scribbler followed by the keying of its contents into a computer. I took particular pains to maintain the original spelling, punctuation, and paragraph construction. I did not, however, include the scratchings-out that appear occasionally, since these added nothing to the text.

2 Jo Fraser Jones is a former teacher-librarian with degrees in Modern Languages and Education. The working title for her book is *The Land Was Then New*, a phrase found in volume 21 of the journals.

3 Her branch of the Barrett family had its own motto *Omnia virtute non vi* (All by virtue, not by force) and was Norman in origin. It produced warriors who accompanied Richard the Lionheart on his crusades. (A variant on the family ancestry suggested a Mediterranean/Italian heritage, under the name "Barretti"; certainly all of the surviving Barrett children had dark hair, brown eyes, and swarthy features.)

4 Journals of Alice Barrett Parke, 22 March 1891.

5 Ibid. (Hereafter, the journals will be identified by date only.)

6 "Nonah" was the Chinook nickname of Rebecca Julia Pelly, a close neighbour, who quickly became Barrett's friend and, in 1894, when Pelly married Harry Barrett, her sister-in-law. Sadly, Nonah died in 1898 at the age of twenty-two, six days after the birth of her third child.

7 "[U]nder the provisions of the Land Ordinance of 1860, 160 acres of unsurveyed land could be obtained by complying with residence and improvements requirements. The sum of five shillings ($1.25) an acre had to be paid at the time of application, and a further five shillings an acre when the survey was completed and title granted." Margaret A. Ormsby, *Coldstream Nulli Secundus: A History of the Corporation of the District of Coldstream* (Alton, Man.: Friesen, 1990), 3–4.

8 Before the railway spur's completion, Alice made several trips in the six-passenger steam car.

9 Information on the life of Harold Randolph Parke and his family has been culled from several sources. The journals themselves detail his early life, his mother, and family. Other information derives from City of Vernon council records, police records, the "Barrett Family Archives" (unpublished) written by Harry Bemister Barrett, North-West Mounted Police records in the National Archives of Canada, and the records of Lorna G. Kaiser (Parke family historian in Fort Collins, Colorado).

10 The firm of Ewart and Parke had designed and constructed the old Ontario parliament buildings in Toronto and the Gothic-style courthouse in London, and Thomas Parke later held the post of surveyor general in the Baldwin-LaFontaine administration. (See Nancy Z. Tausky and Lynne D. DiStefano, *Victorian Architecture in London and Southwestern Ontario: Symbols of Aspiration* (Toronto: University of Toronto Press, 1986); and the *Dictionary of Canadian Biography*, 8: 281 and 9:618).

11 24 May 1891.

12 Emily Louisa "Wese" Barrett was Alice's devoted elder sister. Born in Port Dover in 1857 she never married, instead remaining in Port Dover to look after her aging parents and orphaned family members. A self-taught artist, she created beautiful paintings and collages for the members of her family and her friends. She wrote voluminous letters and cards, and taught Sunday school regularly. She died in 1938.

13 21 October 1891.

14 27 October 1896.

15 31 October 1896.

16 19 January 1897.

17 The International Council of Women, headed by Elizabeth Cady Stanton and Susan B. Anthony, had held its organizational meeting in Washington, D.C., in 1888. After the Congress of Women at the Chicago World's Fair in 1893, the council was hoping to find a new president in Great Britain and the Countess of Aberdeen was appointed to the position. She became a tireless organizer of local chapters of the NCW in Canada during her husband's tenure as governor general.

18 The ranches were the Coldstream in Vernon and Guisichan in Kelowna.

19 By "scissors," Alice meant that she would cross her fingers behind her back and agree with Lady Aberdeen, but maintain her own ideas all the same.

20 19 September 1895.

21 28 October 1895.

22 25 October 1895.

23 This old Scottish proverb stated that "many a pickle (or little) makes a mickle (a lot)." "Mickle" means the same as "Muckle" and the form Alice used was the corrupted version of the proverb. Her meaning was that every little bit helps.

24 6 October 1895.

25 8 September 1896.

26 Alice Barrett to Wese Barrett, 29 April 1892.

27 The Schubert story covers six pages in volume 4 of the journals (5 March 1892).

28 Wilkins Micawber was a character in Charles Dickens's *David Copperfield* (published 1849–1850). He was an idle optimist who had faith that the future would cater sufficiently to his needs. The author based Micawber on his own unreliable and wastrel father.

29 23 February 1892.

30 Alexander Leslie Fortune had been a leader of the Acton group of men who had become members of the Overlanders' expedition thirty years earlier. A pious man, he had conducted daily prayer services during the journey. See "Records of pioneer A.L. Fortune – History," an unpublished document, and the annual reports of the Okanagan Historical Society, 1925 onwards.

31 25 February 1892.

32 26 June 1894.

33 24 August 1891.

34 24 June 1895.

35 26 November 1894.

36 Hubert Baldwin Barrett (1867–1953), Alice's younger brother, was born in Port Dover. He enjoyed fishing and hunting, and with his younger brother, Clarence, played many tricks on members of the family and friends, according to the journals and family reminiscences.

37 20 December 1899.

38 15 July 1899.

39 No death certificate exists showing a cause of death, but it is probable that Emily Parke died from either typhoid of cholera infantum. (I base this assumption on the fact that outbreaks of typhoid and cholera were frequent at the time, and Emily's illness was of several weeks' duration. Vernon's water supply was still primitive, a heavily polluted open ditch running through the centre of the town.)

40 *Vernon News*, 9 November 1905.

41 Harry Bemister Barrett to Jo Fraser Jones, 25 February 1997.

NUMBER 25

1 Ruth Schwartz Cowan, *More Work for Mother: The Ironies of Household Technology from the Open Hearth to the Microwave* (New York: Basic Books, 1983).

2 Ibid.

3 Susan Strasser, *Never Done: A History of American Housework* (New York: Lantheon, 1982), 125–44.

4 Marjorie Griffin Cohen, "The Decline of Women in Canadian Dairying," in Alison Prentice and Susan Mann Trofimenkoff, eds., *The Neglected Majority* (Toronto: McClelland and Stewart, 1985): 61–83.

5 Alison Prentice et al., *Canadian Women: A History* (Toronto: Harcourt Brace Jovanovich, 1988), 155.

6 Strasser, *Never Done,* 32–49.

7 Ibid., 67–84; 104–24.

8 Diana Pedersen, "'The Scientific Training of Mothers': The Campaign for Domestic Science in Ontario Schools, 1890–1913," in Richard A. Jarrell and Arnold E. Roos, eds., *Critical Issues in the History of Canadian Science, Technology and Medicine* (Ottawa and Thornhill, 1983): 178–94.

9 Prentice et al., *Canadian Women*, 157.

10 Stuart Ewen, *Captains of Consciousness: Advertising and the Social Roots of Consumer Culture* (New York: McGraw-Hill, 1976).

11 Dolores Hayden, *The Grand Domestic Revolution* (Cambridge: MIT Press, 1983).

12 Margaret Hobbs and Ruth Roach Pierson, "'A kitchen that wastes no steps …'": Gender, Class and Home Improvement Plan, 1936–40," *Histoire Sociale/Social History* 21 (May 1988): 9–37.

13 Dianne Dodd, "Advice to Parents: The Blue Books, Helen MacMurchy, M.D., and The Federal Department of Health, 1920–1934," *Canadian Bulletin of Medical History* 8 (1991): 203–30.

14 By the late 1930s, approximately 1.5 million homes, or about 62 per cent overall, enjoyed the benefit of electrical power. These were primarily urban and small-town customers.

15 *The Hydro Lamp*, June 1925.

NUMBER 26

1 Laura Rose, "The Womanly Sphere of Woman," *Annual Report of the Women's Institutes* (1906), 30–4. All quotations are from this document.

2 David C. Jones, "'There is Some Power about the Land': the Western Agrarian Press and Country Life Ideology," *Journal of Canadian Studies* 17 (Fall 1982): 102.

3 John MacDougall, *Rural Life in Canada* (Toronto: University of Toronto Press, 1973; reprint of 1913 edition), 39.

4 Ibid., 211.

5 Ontario Department of Agricultural Archives, Milton, "Induction Profile, Laura Rose Stephen 1866–1963," 12 June 1983. At the age of forty-five Rose married and thereafter used both her own family name and that of her husband.

6 Jane Adams, *The Transformation of Rural Life: Southern Illinois, 1890–1990* (Chapel Hill: University of North Carolina Press, 1994), 186.

7 William L. Bowers, "County-Life Reform, 1900–1920: A

Neglected Aspect of Progressive Era History," *Agricultural History* 45 (1971): 211–21.

8 Laura Rose, "A Plea for Better Dairy Equipment," *F. I. Report* (1900), 146.

9 Macdonald Institute was the school of domestic science that opened at the Ontario Agricultural College in Guelph in 1903.

10 Edward H. Clark, *Sex in Education: or, A Fair Chance For Girls* (Boston: J. B. Osgood, 1873).

11 Katherine Jellison, *Entitled to Power: Farm Women and Technology, 1913–1963* (Chapel Hill: University of North Carolina Press, 1993), 23.

12 Ibid., 182.

13 David B. Dandom, *Born in the Country: A History of Rural America* (Baltimore: Johns Hopkins University Press, 1995), 89.

NUMBER 27

1 This article is a slightly modified excerpt of my forthcoming book *And on That Farm He Had a Wife: Ontario Farm Women And Feminism, 1900–1970* (Montreal & Kingston: McGill-Queen's University Press).

2 David Densmore, *Seasons of Change: Sketches of Life on the Farm* (Toronto: Summerhill Press/Etue and Company, 1987), 9, 81. In mixed-crop farming, wheat, the staple crop of nineteenth-century farms, might have been only one of several grain, vegetable, fruit, and/or livestock cash crops tended on farms now increasingly engaged in dairying. See Tony Fuller, "The Development of Farm Life and Farming in Ontario," in Anthony M. Fuller, ed., *Farming and the Rural Community in Ontario: An Introduction* (Toronto: Foundation for Rural Living, 1985), 6, and Densmore, *Seasons of Change*, 81.

3 Fuller, "The Development of Farm Life," 17, Figure 1.3.

4 Ibid.

5 Ibid., 14–15, Table 1.1.

6 Veronica Strong-Boag, "Discovering the Home: The Last 150 Years of Domestic Work in Canada," in Paula Bourne,

ed., *Women's Paid and Unpaid Work: Historical and Contemporary Perspectives* (Toronto: New Hogtown Press, 1985), 40. Tension often characterized the relationship between farm wife and farmhand. She resented the extra household work that he generated, and he disliked (and often spurned) taking orders from a woman. Farmhands were not unknown to sexually assault farm wives and daughters, particularly when farm owners were away in town. See Karen Dubinsky, *Improper Advances: Rape and Heterosexual Conflict in Ontario, 1880–1929* (Chicago: University of Chicago Press, 1993), 58.

7 "Is Marriage a Failure?" *Farmer's Advocate*, 14 November 1912; 1983.

8 Helen Richards Campbell, *From Chalk Dust to Hayseed* (Belleville, Ont.: Mika Publishers, 1975), 113.

9 Mrs. W. Buchanan, "The Woman on the Farm," *O.A.C. Review* 24 (May 1912): 448; Mrs M.C. Dawson, "The Woman on the Farm," *O.A.C. Review* 24 (May 1912): 406, 407; and Adelaide Hoodless, "The Relation of Domestic Science to the Agricultural Population," December 1896, Hoodless Family Papers, Archival Collections, University of Guelph Library (hereafter UGL), box 1, file – Addresses and Reports, 5.

10 Dawson, "The Woman on the Farm," 406–7.

11 Beth Good Latzer, *Myrtleville: A Canadian Farm and Family, 1837–1967* (Carbondale and Edwardsville, Ill.: Southern Illinois University Press, 1976), 253, 268. These ideas are expressed in much the same way in Monda Halpern, "Beyond the Dell: Farm Women and Feminism in Early Twentieth-Century Ontario," *(SA)FIRE WORKS: More Works in Progress by Students of Feminism(s)*, published by Centre for Women's Studies and Feminist Research, Working Paper no. 10, vol. 2, March 1994, proceedings of "(SA)FIRE WORKS" conference, University of Western Ontario, April/May 1992, 38.

12 Selina Horst (b. 1921), interviewed by Frances Hoffman, 28 March 1990, tape 1, side 2, Oral History Tapes, Rural Women, Grace Schmidt Room of Local History, Kitchener

Public Library (hereafter OHT), OHT 658.

13 "Farmers' Wives and Insanity," *Farmer's Advocate* 40 (4 May 1905): 656. The United States Department of Agriculture circulated a bulletin in 1912 whose object was to counter the notion that farm women were prone to insanity.

14 Mrs W.E. Hopkins, *Farm and Dairy* 14 November 1912, 18, in W.R. Young, "The Countryside on the Defensive: Agricultural Ontario's View of Rural Depopulation, 1900–1914," (M.A. thesis, University of British Columbia, 1971), 40.

15 John MacDougall, *Rural Life in Canada: Its Trends and Tasks* (Toronto: Westminster Company, 1913), 128; and Allan McDiarmid, "Should Farm Women Go on Strike," *Farmer's Advocate* 55 (17 June 1920): 1136.

16 Martha and Robert Bruere, "The Revolt of the Farmer's Wife!" *Harper's Bazaar* (November-April 1912–13). The six articles include "War on Drudgery," "Waylaying Education," "The Social Significance of the Bumper Crop," "The Campaign against Sickness," "The Waste of Old Women" and "After the Revolt."

17 "A Sidelight on a Self-made Man," *Farm and Dairy*, Third Annual Special Magazine Household Number, 5 October 1911, 8.

18 McDiarmid, "Should Farm Women Go on Strike," 1136.

19 See Deborah Fink, *Agrarian Women: Wives and Mothers in Rural Nebraska, 1880–1940* (Chapel Hill: University of North Carolina Press, 1992), 62–3. As Carolyn Sachs points out, "interdependence does not necessarily equal equity." See Sarah Elbert, "The Farmer Takes a Wife: Women in America's Farming Families," in Lourdes Beneria and Catharine R. Stimpson, eds., *Women, Households, and the Economy* (New Brunswick, N.J.: Rutgers University Press, 1987), 174. Under The Married Women's Property Act, a farm wife (like all wives) who made no direct monetary contribution to the purchase or maintenance of marital property, regardless of her indispensable work contributions, was not legally entitled to a share of that property in the event of divorce. In the case of the husband's death, a wife could legally claim only one-third of the estate if her husband did not sufficiently provide for her in his will (that is, if he left her less than one-third). See Suzanne Zwarun, "Farm Wives 10 Years after Irene Murdoch," *Chatelaine*, March 1983: 178; and Allan M. Dymond, *The Laws of Ontario Relating to Women and Children* (Toronto: Clarkson W. James, 1923), 32. As Lori Chambers notes, although The Married Women's Property Act conferred property rights to those wives who held claim to separate assets, "it had done nothing to address the fundamental imbalance of economic power within most marriages or to deconstruct the social belief in marital unity, male authority, and wifely obedience." See Lori Chambers, *Married Women and Property Law in Victorian Ontario* (Toronto: Osgoode Society for Canadian Legal History, 1997), 179.

20 Mary Neth, *Preserving the Family Farm: Women, Community, and the Foundations of Agribusiness in the Midwest, 1900–1940* (Baltimore: Johns Hopkins University Press, 1995), 26. Neth notes that as women had almost no financial or legal protection within the patriarchal farm family, it was in their best interest to promote the mutuality of work and family relations. Mutuality, affirms Nancy Osterud, was "an empowerment strategy" and "a collective response to gender inequality." See Neth, *Preserving the Family Farm*, 18; and Nancy G. Osterud, *Bonds of Community: The Lives of Farm Women in Nineteenth-Century New York* (New York: Cornell University Press, 1991), 275, 276.

21 Young, "The Countryside on the Defensive," 74–75.

22 Densmore, *Seasons of Change*, 123.

23 Elaine Bitz (b. 1928), interviewed by author, 15 April 1993, London, Ontario hereafter Bitz interview; and "Feminism on the Farm," *Farmer's Magazine*, 17 November 1921, 9.

24 "Feminism on the Farm," 9. John Ewing Marshall also makes this point, conceding that farm women complained "with some justification." See *Half Century of Farming in Dufferin* (n.p., 1978), 16.

25 Feminism on the Farm," 9; and Ethel M. Chapman, "Machinery for Women – Why it Pays," *Farmer's Magazine*, 1 December 1918, 55; Jane B. Knowles, "'It's Our Turn Now': Rural American Women Speak Out, 1900–1920," in Wava G. Haney and Jane B. Knowles, eds., *Women and Farming; Changing Roles, Changing Structures* (Boulder, Colo.: Westview Press, 1988), 314; and "Feminism on the Farm," 9. With some contempt for his viewpoint, Ethel Chapman facetiously supposed that homemaking was to be "something that woman does unaided by the genius of her natural domestic instincts." See Chapman, "Machinery for Women," 24.

26 Chapman, "Machinery for Women," 55.

27 Bruere, "War on Drudgery," 550; Kenneth C. Cragg, *Father on the Farm* (Toronto: Longmans, Green and Co., 1947), 27; Bitz interview.

28 Carolyn Sachs, *The Invisible Farmers: Women in Agricultural Production* (Totawa, N.J.: Rowman and Allanheld, 1983), xii.

29 Mrs. T.H. Bass, "The Woman on the Farm," *O.A.C. Review* 24 (July 1912): 560–1; and "Farming for Women," *New York Times*, 13 April 1919, sec. 3, 3, in Monda M. Halpern, "'Our Mother Earth Has Called Us': A Study of the Woman's Land Army of America, World War I" (M.A. thesis, University of Western Ontario, 1988), 102. Also see Cragg, *Father on the Farm*, 10; Anne Higginson Spicer, "Training at Libertyville, Illinois," *Farmerette* 1 (January 1919): 2, National Agricultural Library, U.S. Department of Agriculture, in Halpern, "'Our Mother Earth has Called Us,'" 102; and Mrs W.M. Jull, "Ready Money Representing Real Profit Made by a Woman," *Farm and Dairy*, Third Annual Special Magazine Household Number, 5 October 1911, 3. Cragg recalled that his mother "claimed hens had to be fussed over." See Cragg, *Father on the Farm*, 46.

30 Kate Aitken, *Never a Day So Bright* (Toronto: Longmans, Green, 1956), 139; Dawson, "The Woman on the Farm," 405; and McDiarmid, "Should Farm Women go on Strike," 1136.

31 Dawson, "The Woman on the Farm," 405.

32 Terry Crowley, *Agnes Macphail and the Politics of Equality* (Toronto: James Lorimer, 1990), 7.

33 Dawson, "The Woman on the Farm," 405.

34 Uncle Peter, "Partners in the Business," *Farm and Dairy*, Third Annual Special Magazine Household Number, 5 October 1911, 21.

35 "Feminism on the Farm," 9.

36 Among white North American farm families of western European origin, tradition dedicated that the care of large animals and labour in the fields were men's work, while tending garden, small animals, the household, and children was women's unpaid work. Only during times of financial hardship or labour crisis, such as during the First World War, did women consistently, albeit temporarily, assume "men's work." See Joan M. Jensen, *With These Hands: Women Working on the Land* (Old Westbury, N.Y.: Feminist Press, 1981), 32; and Sachs, *The Invisible Farmers*, 3, 19.

37 "What is a Woman's Work on the Farm? A Discussion of this Oft Times Burning Question by Members of *Farm and Dairy*'s Home Club," *Farm and Dairy*, 8 October 1914, 7.

38 See, for example, Miss Yates, "Agriculture for Women," *O.A.C. Review* 21 (December 1908): 183; Sister Evelyn, "No Sympathy for Men," *Weekly Sun* 26 (May 29 1918): 6; Elizabeth Davis, in Allan Anderson, *Remembering the Farm: Memories of Farming, Ranching and Rural Life in Canada, Past and Present* (Toronto: Macmillan, 1977), 252.

39 Yates, "Agriculture for Women," 183; and Elizabeth Davis, in Anderson, *Remembering the Farm*, 252.

40 Bass, "The Woman on the Farm," 560. For a similar viewpoint, see Dream, "The True Homemaker Defined," *Farm and Dairy*, 8 October 1914, 7, 10.

41 Yates, "Agriculture for Women," 183.

42 A Worshipper, "The Farmer's Wife," *Farmer's Advocate* 44 (17 June 1909): 1000.

43 See, for example, ibid. Women's objections to outdoor

work were also premised on the belief that wives were already overworked and physically taxed. Men's objections were generally rooted in the concern that overwork would threaten women's reproductive health and thus the strength and fitness of future generations. See, for example, Mrs Breese, "The Woman upon the Farm," *O.A.C. Review* 24 (June 1912): 495; and Dot, "Let Us Give and Take, but –," *Farm and Dairy*, 8 October 1914, 7; Householder, "Farm Women and Outdoor Work," *Farmer's Advocate*, 7 March 1918, 370.

44 Mary Meek Atkeson, "Women in Farm Life and Rural Economy," in *The Annals of the American Academy of Political and Social Science* 143 (May 1929): 188. Atkeson insightfully pointed out that although the farm woman "was not allowed to ride the disc-harrow, or the reaper in the fields, no one objected to her working long hours over a steaming washtub, or cleaning the chicken house, or handling the deadly heavy cans of milk in the dairy, although this was a part of the heaviest work done on the farm."

45 "Cooperation in the Home," *Farm and Dairy*, Third Annual Special Magazine Household Number, 5 October 1911, 15. Because men's labour was not organized according to a weekly routine, a husband could often not distinguish the daily differences in a woman's work week. The diaries of men acknowledge women's work only "when it affected their own." See Neth, *Preserving the Family Farm*, 27.

46 "A Woman's Duty," *Farm and Dairy*, 8 October 1914, 10.

47 Ethel Hillier (MacDonald) Diaries, 1904–27, Collection of Elaine Bitz, London, Ontario [hereafter Hillier Diaries], 26 March 1923. Ethel Hillier, 1891–1984,makes no mention in her diary of which side won.

48 Cragg, *Father on the Farm*, 45, 167.

49 Densmore, *Seasons of Change*, 133.

50 "Should My Daughter Marry a Farmer?" was the question to be addressed by farm women in a 1922 essay competition sponsored by Manitoba's agricultural journal *Grain Growers Guide*. See Mary Kinnear, "'Do You Want Your Daughter to Marry a Farmer?' Women's Work on the Farm, 1922," in Donald H. Akenson, ed., *Canadian Papers in Rural History*, vol. 6, (Gananoque, Ont.: Langdale Press, 1988), 141.

51 Roxie Hostetler (b. 1889), interviewed by Ryan Taylor, 27 July 1982, tape 2, Oral History Tapes (OHT), OHT 132.

52 Hillier Diaries. See, for example, 10 August 1921, 20 June 1923, and 5 October 1923. Appreciation for the farm daughter's workload should have inhibited one man's advice that "girls should learn to do housework instead of sitting on rocking chairs and reading trashy novels from morning to night." See Edward Amey, *Farm Life As It Should Be and Farm Labourers' and Servant Girls' Grievances* (Toronto: Ellis and Moore, 1885), 13.

53 Bitz interview. In 1928, at the age of thirty-seven, Ethel gave birth to her only child, Elaine (Bitz).

54 Nephew Frank, "Would You Marry a Farmer?" *Farm and Dairy*, 8 October 1914, 7. Ethel Hillier married Thomas MacDonald in July of 1926. They moved to a farm six miles from her parents' home in Plympton Township. Bitz interview.

55 Alice A. Ferguson, "Should Daughters Be Compensated for Their Labor?" *Farm and Dairy*, 8 October 1914, 6.

56 Jennie A. Pringle, "What Girls Need Most in a Rural Community," *Canadian Countryman*, 15 (15 May 1926): 14, UGL, box 3309. This article was a winning letter in a contest to address this question. Pringle was born on a farm "in a long-settled district of Ontario" and as a young adult lived in Selby, Ontario.

57 Elizabeth McCutcheon, "The Single Woman in the Country[:] Can the Spinster Remain on the Farm and be Independent?" *Farm and Dairy*, 8 October 1914, 5.

58 Pringle, "What Girls Need Most," 14.

59 Edna I. Brown, "What Girls Need Most in a Rural Community," *Canadian Countryman*, 15 (15 May 1926): 14, UGL, box 3309. This article was a winning letter in a contest to address this question. The insistence by adult farm sons and daughters that they should be paid for their work on the family farm was a new development in early twenti-

eth-century Ontario. Before this time, they understood their labour as a debt owed to their parents for shelter, food, and clothing. See Joy Parr, "Hired Men: Ontario Agricultural Wage Labour in Historical Perspective," *Labour/Le Travail* 15 (Spring 1985): 97.

60 "Floy," "The Stay-at-Home Daughter," *Farmer's Advocate*, 65 (25 December 1930): 1883.

61 McCutcheon, "The Single Woman in the Country," 5.

62 Farm inheritance was based on the "patrilinear tradition," which dictated that fathers regularly pass their lands down to sons, all but excluding wives and daughters from ever owning property. See Michelle Boivin, "Farm Women: Obtaining Legal and Economic Recognition of Their Work," in *Growing Strong: Women in Agriculture* (Ottawa: Canadian Advisory Council on the Status of Women, 1987), 67; and E.A. (Nora) Cebotarev, "From Domesticity to the Public Sphere: Farm Women, 1945–86," in Joy Parr, ed., *A Diversity of Women: Ontario, 1945–1980* (Toronto: University of Toronto Press, 1995), 209.

63 "A Farmer's Daughter," "Independence for the Daughters," *Farmer's Advocate* 43 (23 January 1908): 129.

64 Ibid.

65 Ibid.

NUMBER 28

1 U.S. forces in Newfoundland peaked in 1943 at 10,882. Canadian forces also peaked in 1943, at 5,700. David Mackenzie, *Inside the Atlantic Triangle: Canada and the Entrance of Newfoundland into Confederation 1939–1949* (Toronto: University of Toronto Press, 1986), 79–80.

2 The wartime U.S. consul in Newfoundland estimated that between January 1942 and April 1944 there were 350 to 400 marriages between American men and Newfoundland women. Peter Neary, *Newfoundland in the North Atlantic World, 1929–1949* (Montreal & Kingston: McGill-Queen's University Press, 1988), 212.

3 Single mothers include all women with an illegitimate child, whether unmarried, widowed, separated, or living with a man without marriage. Statistics on illigitimate births are drawn from the *Annual Reports* of the St John's Child Welfare Association (hereafter CWA), 1942–45.

4 Cecelia Benoit, "Urbanizing Women Military Fashion: The Case of the Stephenville Women," in Carmelita McGrath et al., eds. *Their Lives and Times: Women in Newfoundland and Labrador, A Collage* (St John's: Killick Press, 1995), 118–19, 120.

5 Paternity suits were originally called bastardy cases, but after the 1931 Health and Welfare Act they were renamed affiliation cases. Since 1834, women could sue for child support, and the 1931 act gave the director of child welfare the authority to enforce child support. Linda Cullum and Maeve Baird, "A Woman's Lot: Women and Law in Newfoundland from Early Settlement to the Twentieth Century," in Linda Kealey, ed., *Pursuing Equality: Historical Perspectives on Women in Newfoundland and Labrador* (St John's: Institute of Social and Economic Research, 1993), 108. For the financial settlements of 1940s affiliation cases, see Provincial Archives of Newfoundland and Labrador (hereafter PANL), GN5/3/A/17, boxes 24–5.

6 PANL, GN38 s6/4/1 files 3–5.

7 The Mount Cashel Orphanage housed two hundred boys only; the smaller Methodist orphanage was only for girls. Stuart R. Godfrey, *Human Rights and Social Policy in Newfoundland 1832–1982: Search for a Just Society* (St John's: Harry Cuff Publications, 1985), 147–8.

8 PANL, GN38 s6/4/1, files 3–5.

9 Nancy Forestell and Jessie Chisholm, "Working-Class Women as Wage Earners in St. John's, Newfoundland, 1890–1921," in Peta Tancred-Sheriff, ed., *Feminist Research: Prospect and Retrospect* (Montreal & Kingston: McGill-Queen's University Press, 1988), 143, 152.

10 The single mothers who began affiliation cases from 1942 to 1947 ranged in age from 14 to 36, the average age being 21.7. PANL, GN5/3/A/5, box 8, and GN5/3/A/17, boxes 22–7.

11 PANL, GN13/2/A, box 404.

12 PANL GN5/3/A/17, boxes 24–5.

13 George D. Hopper, United States Consul General at St John's, to Secretary of State, Wahington, D.C., (SSW), 21 April 1944, Neary, Newfoundland, 211–12. Hopper's own research, using 1942–44 applications for children's visas, revealed that two-thirds of the children born to U.S. servicemen and Newfoundland women arrived within seven and one-half months of their parents' marriage.

14 Cullum and Baird, "Women and Law," 108.

15 PANL, GN38 S6/4/1 file 5.

16 Neary, *Newfoundland*, 210–13.

17 In the early 1930s St John's averaged fifty illegitimate births a year, compared to over two hundred a year from 1943 to 1945. CWA, *Annual Reports*, 1938–1946.

18 Birth control: Cullum and Baird, "A Woman's Lot," 129–30; condoms: Benoit, "Urbanizing Women Military Fashion," 120.

19 PANL, GN13/1/B #13, "instructions to censors."

20 Ellipses are from the original letter, which cites section 83 of chapter 35 of the Consolidated Statutes of Newfoundland, and section 9, schedule E of the 1938 Revenue Act. PANL, GN13/1/B, box 114 #95 "Indecent Literature."

21 A number of the oral accounts in a documentary film that claim the U.S. military deliberately shipped out soldiers when their girlfriends were expecting a child. *Seven Brides for Uncle Sam*, produced by Kent Martin and directed by Anita McGee, National Film Board of Canada, 1997.

22 PANL, GN38 S6/4/1, file 5; except chaplain: PANL, GN5/3/A/17, box 23.

23 By 1945 child-care facilities in Ontario served twenty-five hundred children. Ruth R. Pierson "Women's Emancipation and the Recruitment of Women into the Labour Force in World War II," in Susan Mann Trofimenkoff and Alison Prentice eds., in *The Neglected Majority: Essays in Canadian Women's History* (Toronto: McClelland and Stewart, 1977), 138.

24 PANL, GN38 S6/4/1, file 3b.

25 Newfoundland's first representative government was formed in 1832. One year later Newfoundland passed its first Support of Bastard Children Act. Godfrey, *Human Rights* 145–6.

26 Health and Public Welfare Act, 1931, chapter 12, section 636.

27 PANL, GN38 S6/4/1, files 3–5.

28 Dollar amounts from the summaries of the probation officers' reports: PANL GN38 S6/4/1.

29 The U.S. Army made affiliation account payments from a central office in New Jersey, but payments ended when the soldier left the service. PANL, GN38/S6/1/7, file 10.

30 Benoit, "Urbanizing Women," 121.

31 Section 145 of the Army Act, according to "Memorandum on Canadian Army Position and Practice with Regard to the Maintenance by Soldiers of Illegitimate Children" PANL, GN13/1/B, 43–6.

32 Letter from Major Gerald L.F. Page, Commander of the Combined Canadian and Newfoundland Forces in Newfoundland, 29 August 1942, citing section 145 of the Army Act. PANL, GN13/1/B, 43–6.

33 Jane Lewis and Mark Shrimpton, "Policymaking in Newfoundland During the 1940's: The Case of the St. John's Housing Corporation," *Canadian Historical Review*, 65, no. 2 (1984): 235.

34 Compensation for birth expenses ranged from zero to one hundred dollars. PANL, GN5/3/A, box 8.

35 PANL, GN5/3/A, box 8.

36 In 1892 the Anchorage opened as a "Rescue Home for Wayward Girls." Godfrey, *Human Rights* 148.

37 PANL, GN5/3/A, box 8.

38 *Evening Telegram* (St John's) 5 December 1944, 3.

39 Four types of homes for unwed mothers are examined in Marion J. Morton, *And Sin No More: Social Policy and Unwed Mothers in Cleveland, 1855–1990* (Columbus: Ohio State University Press, 1993).

40 PANL, GN38 S6/4/1.

41 Further legislative changes meant that after 1944 no child could be adopted without approval of the director of child welfare. Godfrey, *Human Rights* 161.

42 PANL, GN38 s6/4/1, file 3b.

43 *Evening Telegram* (St John's), 9 December 1944, 3.

44 PANL, GN38 s6/4/1, file 4.

45 In 1944 the average number of children per foster home was 6.7, but by using publicity and volunteer groups to attract foster families, the Division of Child Welfare was able to reduce the number to 2.6 in 1946. Godfrey, *Human Rights*, 162.

46 J.R. Smallwood, ed., *The Book of Newfoundland*, vol. 2, 299.

47 In 1944, owing to increased responsiblitities, this section was enlarged to become the Division of Child Welfare. The Child Welfare Act of 1944 gave the division the authority to remove children from their parental home if it was in their "best interest." Godfrey, *Human Rights* 160.

48 PANL, GN38/s6/4/1, files 3–5.

49 Helen and Margaret appear in the court records (PANL, GN5/3/A/5, box 5), as they both sued servicemen for support. Their addresses and daughters' names, as well as Josephine T.'s family situation, appear in the Census of Newfoundland and Labrador, 1945 (Nominal), vol. 44.

NUMBER 29

1 Janet Braide, *Prudence Heward (1896–1947): An Introduction to Her Life and Work* (Montreal: Walter Klinkhoff Gallery, September 1980), 23, lists Prudence as "Invited Contributor" in the Group of Seven exhibitions of 1928, 1930, 1931, and 1932.

2 Heward was a founding member of the Canadian Group of Painters and exhibited with the group in the 1930s and 1940s, until her death. She was also a founding member of John Lyman's Contemporary Arts Society in 1939.

3 Natalie Luckyj, *Visions and Victories: 10 Canadian Women Artists 1914–1945* (London, Ont.: London Regional Art Gallery, 1983), 34, lists the following exhibitions: *Exposition d'art canadien*, Jeu de Paume (1927); *Exposition UNESCO*, Musée d'art moderne (1946), Paris; *British Empire Exhibition*, Wembley (1925); *Exhibition of Paintings, Drawings and Sculpture by Artists of the British Empire Overseas*, Royal Institute Galleries (1937); *A Century of Canadian Art*, Tate Gallery (1938), London; *Exhibition of Contemporary Canadian Artists*, Roerich Museum (1932); and *Canadian Women's Exhibition Sponsored by the National Council of Women of the United States* (1947), New York.

4 Natalie Luckyj, *Expressions of Will: The Art of Prudence Heward* (Kingston: Agnes Etherington Art Centre, Queen's University, 1986), 121, lists *Exhibition of Canadian Art at the British Empire Trade Exhibition*, Buenos Aires, 1931.

5 Interview with Ann Johansson by the author on 14 October 1993 for the film *By Woman's Hand*.

6 Ibid.

7 "Group Exhibition," *Montreal Star*, 21 January 1921.

8 Kenneth Wells, "What You Don't See Looking at Modern Art," *Evening Telegram*, 25 November, 1933.

9 Letter from Prudence Heward to Isabel McLaughlin, 29 December 1943.

10 Letter from A.Y. Jackson to Prudence Heward, 11 April 1944.

11 The author wishes to acknowledge various members of the Heward family, Isabel McLaughlin, and Dr Naomi Jackson Groves for their valuable contribution to the compilation of information on Prudence Heward's life and work.

NUMBER 30

1 For a full discussion of the advice given by the quintuplet experts, see my article "Raising the Dionne Quintuplets: Lessons for Modern Mothers," *Journal of Canadian Studies* 29, no. 1 (Winter 1994–95), 65–85.

2 The highly publicized claim for damages brought against the Ontario government by the three surviving quintuplets in 1995 keeps their story alive for another generation of Canadians. The case was resolved in 1998, but was recently the subject of a judicial review, headed by Madam Justice Epstein.

3 Pierre Berton, in the 1978 National Film Board film, "The Dionne Quintuplets."

4 Pierre Berton, *The Dionne Years: A Thirties Melodrama* (Toronto: McClelland and Stewart, 1977), 13.

5 The column first appeared in 1938 and continued until 1941.

6 The Dafoe papers are available on microfilm at Archives of Ontario: Dr Allan Roy Dafoe Papers, 1934–1968, MS 598.

7 Dafoe Papers, B-1, vol. 1, letter from David C. Crouch, Harrisville, Ohio, 31 May 1934.

8 Ibid., B-2, vol. 9, letter from Ruby M. Dunham, Vancouver B.C., 2 February 1937.

9 Ibid., B-2, vol. 9, letter from Mrs Lee Wadleigh, Evanston, Illinois, no date.

10 Ibid., letter from Mrs A.H. Etehells (signature difficult to read), 29 January 1937.

11 Ibid., letter from Mrs Blanche Richter, Greenburg, Indiana, 2 February 1937.

12 Ibid., letter from Mrs Floyd Yates, Breckenridge, Texas, 29 January 1937.

13 Ibid., letter from Mrs B.R. Carin, Salem, Mass., 29 January 1937.

14 Ibid., "An Anxious Mother," 25 January 1937.

15 Ibid., letter from Mrs Marie Herbeck, St Paul, Minnesota, 28 January 1937.

16 Ibid., letter from Mrs Robt. Averbeck, 19 January 1937.

17 Ibid.

18 Ironically, the voice of the quintuplets' own mother, Elzire Dionne, is largely absent from the documentary record and hence from this article. For a fuller discussion of the role of Elzire Dionne, see my "Raising the Dionne Quintuplets."

19 Berton, *The Dionne Years*, 68.

20 Dafoe Papers, F 1, vol. 2, Dr Dafoe's column, King Features Syndicate, "The First Days of the Quints," 21 January 1939, 2.

21 Mrs Mary A. Austin, Toronto, letter to the author, 2 February 1992.

22 Thelma Bone, letter to the author, 3 February 1992.

23 Thelma Bone, letter to the author, 12 February 1992. I am grateful to all the people who responded to my inquiry, which appeared in the *Toronto Star*, 2 February 1992.

NUMBER 31

1 Recent examples of the historiography on maternalism include the pathbreaking work by T. Skocpol, *Protecting Soldiers and Mothers: The Political Origins of Social Policy in the United States* (Cambridge, Mass.: Belknap Press, 1992); G. Bock and P. Thane, eds., *Maternity and Gender Policies: Women and the Rise of European Welfare States* (London: Routledge, 1991); S. Koven and M. Michel, eds. *Mothers of the New World: Maternalist Politics and the Origins of Welfare States* (New York: Routledge, 1993); H. Marsland, L. Marks, and V. Fildes, eds., *Women and Children First: Maternal and Infant Welfare in International Perspective* (London: Routledge, 1992); S. Pedersen, *Family, Dependency, and the Origins of the Welfare State* (Cambridge: Cambridge University Press, 1993); M. Ladd Taylor, *Mother-Work: Women, Child Welfare and the State* (Indiana: University of Indiana Press, 1993). For Canada, see C.R. Comacchio, *"Nations Are Built of Babies": Saving Ontario's Mothers and Children* (Montreal and Kingston: McGill-Queen's University Press, 1993); K. Arnup, *Education for Motherhood: Advice for Mothers in 20th Century Canada* (Toronto: University of Toronto, 1994); and the essays in Arnup, A. Lévesque, and R.R. Pierson, *Delivering Motherhood: Maternal Ideologies and Practices in the 19th and 20th Centuries* (New York: Routledge, 1990). For Quebec, see D. Baillargeon, "Frequenter les Gouttes de lait: L'expérience des mères Montréalaises, 1910–65," *Revue d'histoire de l'Amerique francaise*, 50 (été 1996); A. Levesque (trans. Y.M. Klein), *Making and Breaking the Rules: Women in Quebec, 1919–39* (Toronto: McClelland and Stewart, 1994), esp. chap. 1. On Helen MacMurchy, see D. Dodd, "Advice to Parents: The Blue Books, Helen Mac-Murchy, M.D., and the Federal Department of Health," *Canadian Bulletin of Medical History* 8 (1991).

2 Dr J.H. Mason Knox, "Infant Care," CMAJ (*Canadian Medical Association Journal*) 29, no. 8 (1933): 151.

3 Charges of maternal ignorance and negligence run rampant through the medical and social service journals of

the early twentieth century. Some examples include Editorial, "Save the Children," *Canada Lancet* 40, (1907): 934; Editorial,"The Health of the Child," CMAJ 2 (1912): 704; Dr B.F. Royer, "Child Welfare," *Canadian Public Health Journal* 12 (1921): 293; and Dr H. MacMurchy, "A Safety League for Mothers," *Social Welfare* 13, (1931): 184. These themes are further developed in Comacchio, *"Nations Are Built of Babies."* See also Baillargeon, "Frequenter les Gouttes de lait."

4 Dr H. MacMurchy, *Infant Mortality: First Special Report* (Toronto: King's Printer, 1910); *Second Special Report* (1911); *Third Special Report* (1912).

5 On the role of doctors in social-moral reform campaigns, see A. McLaren, *Our Own Master Race: Eugenics in Canada* (Toronto: McClelland and Stewart, 1990), 8, 28–9; and M. Valverde, *The Age of Light, Soap and Water: Moral Reform in English Canada* (Toronto: McClelland and Stewart, 1991), 47.

6 On Quebec, see Baillargeon, "Frequenter les Gouttes de lait."

7 See, for example, Dr A. Brown and Dr G. Campbell, "Infant Mortality," CMAJ 4, no. 8 (1914): 693. Brown received his postgraduate training in paediatrics under the renowned American paediatrician Dr L. Emmett Holt, at the Babies' Hospital of New York; he was consultant to the Toronto Board of Health and the federal and provincial divisions of Maternal and Child Hygiene of the respective health departments; and he was physician in chief at Toronto's Hospital for Sick Children, 1920–50, chair of the Department of Paediatrics, School of Medicine, University of Toronto, and one of the founders of the Canadian Society for the Study of Diseases of Children (1920), later the Canadian Paediatric Society. Campbell did his postgraduate training at the Hospital for Sick Children and was the first director of the Division of Child Hygiene, Toronto Board of Health (1913–14).

8 National Archives of Canada, Records of the Department of Health, RG 29, vol. 991, file 499- 3-2, pt 2, Canadian Welfare Council, letter addressed to "Minister of Health," Mrs L.R., Wabewawa, Ontario. See Comacchio, *"Nations"*, chap. 7.

9 For one example of such arguments, see S.N. Pines, RN, "We Want Perfect Parents," *Chatelaine*, September 1928.

10 On the social influence of doctors in Canadian history, see W. Mitchinson, *The Nature of Their Bodies: Women and Their Doctors in Victorian Canada* (Toronto: University of Toronto, 1991); McLaren, *Our Own Master Race* 9, 28–9; M. Valverde, *The Age of Light, Soap and Water*, 47; Lévesque, *Making and Breaking the Rules*, 14. For the impact of medical regulation on the family, see C. Lasch, *Haven in a Heartless World* (New York: 1979); and J. Donzelot, *The Policing of Families* (New York: 1979).

11 Lasch, *Haven in a Heartless World*, and Donzelot *The Policing of Families*. For Canada, see the seminal work of N. Sutherland, *Children in English Canadian Society 1880–1920: Framing the Twentieth Century Consensus* (Toronto: University of Toronto Press, 1976: reissued by Wilfrid Laurier University Press, 2000). V. Strong Boag describes the tutoring in medicine to allay maternal "amateurism" in *The New Day Recalled*, 149. On infant and maternal mortality, see S. Buckley, "Efforts to Reduce Infant and Maternal Mortality Between the Wars," *Atlantis* 4 (1979); idem, "Ladies or Midwives?," in L. Kealey, ed., *A Not Unreasonable Claim: Women and Reform in English Canada* (Toronto: Women's Press, 1979); idem, "The Search for the Decline of Maternal Mortality," in W. Mitchinson and J.D. McGinnis, eds., *Essays in the History of Canadian Medicine* (Toronto, 1988); N. Lewis, "Creating the Little Machine," *B.C. Studies* 56 (1982–3); idem, "Reducing Maternal Mortality in British Columbia," in B.K. Latham and R.J. Pazdro, eds., *Not Just Pin Money: Selected Essyas on Women and Their Work in British Columbia* (Victoria: Camosun College, 1984).

12 The following are just a few examples of the advice literature: the federal government's Division of Child and Maternal Welfare produced *The Canadian Mother and*

Child; the Ontario government produced *The Baby*; the Canadian Welfare Council published a series of newsletters for mothers entitled *Prenatal Letters, Postnatal Letters,* and *Preschool Letters.* These circulated, with various updates, throughout the 1920s and 1930s; and *The Canadian Mother and Child* remains in print today. Advice manuals included Dr Alan Brown, *The Normal Child, Its Care and Feeding* (Toronto: Macmillan, 1923); and Dr F.F. Tisdall, *The Home Care of the Infant and Child* (New York, 1931). Brown and Tisdall, Canada's foremost paediatricians during this period, worked out of Toronto's Hospital for Sick Children; with Dr T.H. Drake, they were the creators of Pablum. See also J. Mechling, "Advice to Historians on Advice to Mothers," *Journal of Social History* 9 (1973): 65; V. Strong-Boag, "Intruders in the Nursery," in J. Parr, ed., *Childhood and Family in Canadian History* (Toronto: McClelland and Stewart, 1982), 169–73.

13 For examples, see the letters from dissatisfied mothers to the federal government's Division of Child and Maternal Welfare and the Canadian Welfare Council, expressing both their gratitude for information and for public health nurse visits and their belief in the need for real medical care, cited in Comacchio, *"Nations Are Built of Babies,"* 209–11. Similar letters from American mothers can be found in M. Ladd-Taylor, ed., *Raising a Baby the Government Way* (New Brunswick, N.J.: Rutgers University, 1993).

14 On the postwar generation, see D. Owram, *Born at the Right Time: A History of the Baby Boom Generation* (Toronto: University of Toronto Press, 1996).

15 See M. Ladd-Taylor, *Mother-Work*, 6, 189, for American developments paralleling these.

NUMBER 32

1 Alison Prentice, "The Feminization of Teaching in British North America and Canada, 1845–1975," *Histoire sociale/Social History* 8 (May 1975): 5–20, reprinted in S. Mann Trofimenkoff and A. Prentice, eds., *The Neglected Majority: Essays in Canadian Women's History* (Toronto:

McClelland and Stewart, 1977); Marta Danylewycz, "Sexes et classes sociales dans l'enseignement: Le cas de Montréal à la fin du 19e siècle," in N. Fahmy-Eid and M. Dumont, eds., *Maitresses de maison, maitresses d'école: Femmes, famille et éducation dans l'histoire du Québec* (Montreal: Boréal, 1983); Marta Danylewycz and Alison Prentice, "Teachers, Gender and Bureaucratizing School Systems in Nineteenth-Century Montreal and Toronto," *History of Education Quarterly*, Spring 1984, 75-100; Marta Danylewycz and Alison Prentice, "Teachers' Work: Changing Patterns and Perceptions in the Emerging School Systems of the 19th and 20th Century Central Canada," *Labour/Le Travail* Spring 1986), 59-80; and Alison Prentice and M. Theobald, eds., *Women Who Taught: Perspectives on the History of Women and Teaching* (Toronto: University of Toronto Press, 1991).

2 Alison Prentice, "Mapping Canadian Women's Teaching Work: Challenging the Stereotypes," in Alison Mackinnon, Inga Elgquist-Satteman, and Alison Prentice, eds., *Education into the 21st Century: Dangerous Terrain for Women?* (London: Falmer Press, 1998), 33. See Marta Danylewycz, Beth Light, and Alison Prentice, "The Evolution of the Sexual Division of Labour in Teaching: A Nineteenth-Century Ontario and Quebec Case Study," *Histoire sociale/Social History* 16 (1983).

3 See Susan Gelman, "The 'Feminization' of the High Schools? Women Secondary School Teachers in Toronto, 1871–1930," *Historical Studies in Education/Revue d'histoire de l'éducation* 2: 119–148, reprinted in Ruby Heap and Alison Prentice, eds., *Gender and Education in Ontario* (Toronto: Canadian Scholars Press, 1991)

4 See essay #36, Susan Gelman, "Educators Confront the 'Feminization of High Schools: The Problem of Women Secondary School Teachers in Ontario."

5 Ibid.

6 See Marta Danylewycz, *Taking the Veil: An Alternative to Marriage, Motherhood and Spinsterhood in Quebec, 1840–1920* (Toronto: McClelland and Stewart, 1987).

7 Michele Jean, "L'Enseignement supérieur des filles et son ambiguité: le College Marie-Anne, 1932–1958," in Dumont and Fahmy-Eid, *Maitresses de maison, maitresses d'école*, 143–70; Judith Fingard, "College, Career and Community: Dalhousie Coeds, 1881–1921," in Paul Axelrod and John G. Reid, eds., *Youth, University and Canadian Society: Essays in the Social History of Higher Learning* (Montreal & Kingston: McGill-Queen's University Press, 1989), 26–50; Jo Lapierre, "The Academic Life of Canadian Coeds, 1880–1920," *Historical Studies in Education/Revue d'histoire de l'éducation* 2 (Fall 1990): 225–46; Lee Jean Stewart, *'It's Up to You': Women at UBC in the Early Years* (Vancouver, 1990); and Guylaine Girouard, *L'admission des femmes à l'Université Laval, 1901-1945: Un compromis entre les objectifs féministes et les objections cléricales* (Quebec: Université Laval, 1993).

8 Enid Johnson Macleod, *Petticoat Doctors: The First Forty Years of Women in Medicine at Dalhousie University* (Laurencetown, N.S.: Pottersfield Press, 1990); and Mary Kinnear, "How Difference Made a Difference: Women Medical Students at the University of Manitoba in the 1940s," *Manitoba Medicine* 63 (1993): 135–6.

9 Judith Fingard, "Gender and Inequality at Dalhousie University: Faculty Women before 1950," *Dalhousie Review* 64 (Winter 1984–85): 687–703; Johanne Collin, "La dynamique des rapports de sexes à l'université, 1940–1980: une étude de cas," *Histoire sociale/Social History* 19 (November 1986): 365–85; Nicole Neatby, "Preparing for the Working World: Women at Queen's during the 1920s," *Historical Studies in Education/Revue d'histoire de l'éducation* 1 (Spring 1989): 53-72; Rebecca Priegert Coulter and Ivor F. Goodson, eds., *Rethinking Vocationalism: Whose Work/Life Is It?* (Toronto: Our Schools/Our Selves, 1993); Ruby Heap, "Training Women for a New Women's Profession: Physiotherapy Education at the University of Toronto, 1917–1940," *History of Education Quarterly* 35 (Summer 1995): 135–58; and Mary Kinnear, *In Subordination: Professional Women, 1870–1970* (Montreal and Kingston: McGill-

10 See also Diana Pedersen, "' The Call to Service': The YWCA and the Canadian College Woman," in Axelrod and Reid, *Youth, University and Canadian Society*, 187–215; Alyson King, "The Experience of Students in the 'New Era': Discourse and Gender in *The Varsity*, 1919–1929," *Ontario Journal of Higher Education*, 1994, 39–56; and Mona Gleason, "A Separate and 'Different' Education: Women and Coeducation at the University of Windsor's Asssumption College, 1950–1957," *Ontario History* 84 (June 1992): 119–32.

11 Margaret Prang, "'The Girl God Would Have Me Be': The Canadian Girls in Training, 1915–1939," *Canadian Historical Review* 66 (June 1985): 154–84; Elisabeth Smyth, "'A Noble Proof of Excellence': The Culture and Curriculum of a Nineteenth-Century Ontario Convent Academy," in Alison Prentice and Ruby Heap, eds., *Gender and Education* (Toronto: Canadian Scholar's Press, 1991), 269–90; Lucille Marr, "Sunday School Teaching: A Women's Enterprise. A Case Study from the Canadian Methodist, Presbyterian and United Church Tradition, 1919–1939," *Histoire sociale/Social History* 26 (November 1993): 329–44; Varpolati Aniko, "'Women Only and Proud of It!' The Politicization of the Girl Guides of Canada," *Resource for Feminist Research* 23 (Spring-Summer 1994): 14–23; Katherine Arnup, *Education for Motherhood: Advice for Mothers in 20th Century Canada* (Toronto: University of Toronto Press, 1994); Sharon Anne Cook, *'Through Sunshine and Shadow': The Woman's Christian Temperance Union, Evangelicalism and Reform in Ontario, 1874–1930* (Montreal & Kingston: McGill-Queen's University Press, 1995); Johanna M. Selles, *Methodists and Women's Education in Ontario, 1836–1925* (Montreal & Kingston: McGill-Queen's University Press, 1996); and Ruth Compton-Brouwer, *New Women for God: Canadian Presbyterian Women and India Missions, 1876–1914* (Toronto: University of Toronto Press, 1990).

12 See, among others, Jean Barman, "Schooled for Inequality: The Education of British Columbia Aboriginal Children," in Jean Barman, Neil Sutherland, and J. Donald Wilson,

eds., *Children, Teachers and Schools in the History of British Columbia* (Calgary, 1995), 57–80.

13 For other studies on minority groups, see Anne Gagnon, "'Our Parents Did Not Raise Us to Be Independant': The Work and Schooling of Young Franco-Albertan Women, 1890–1940," *Prairie Forum* 19 (Fall 1994): 169–88; and Lynn Marks, "Kaye Meydelach or Shulamith Girls: Cultural Change and Continuity among Jewish Parents and Daughters: A Case Study of Toronto's Harbord Collegiate Institute in the 1920s," in Prentice and Heap, *Gender and Education in Ontario*, 291-302.

14 Paul Axelrod, "Historical Writing and Canadian Education from the 1970s to the 1990s," *History of Education Quarterly* 36 (Spring 1996): 30, 36.

15 See, for example, Cecilia Reynolds, "Hegemony and Hierarchy: Becoming a Teacher in Toronto, 1930–1980," *Historical Studies in Education/Revue d'histoire de l'éducation* 2 (Spring 1990): 85–109; Alison Prentice, "Blue Stocking, Feminists or Women Workers? A Preliminary Look at Women's Early Employment at the University of Toronto," *Journal of the Canadian Historical Association*, 1991, 231–62; Margaret Gillet and Ann Beer, eds., *Our Own Agendas: Autobiographical Essays by Women Associated with McGill University* (Montreal and Kingston: McGill–Queen's University Press, 1995); Alison Prentice, "The Early History of Women in Physics: A Toronto Case Study," *Physics in Canada* 52 (1996): 94–100; Alison Prentice, "Elizabeth Allin: Physicist," in E. Cameron and J. Dickin, eds., *Great Dames* (Toronto: University of Toronto Press, 1997); and Isabelle Bourgeois's article in this section.

NUMBER 33

1 See, for example, *The Y.W.C.A. of Canada*, March 1912.

2 National Archives of Canada (NAC), YWCA Records, MG 28 I 198, vol. 10, Minutes of the National Executive, 5 December 1913.

3 Ibid, vol. 40, Report, September 1918–September 1919, Girls' Work Department. Ten of the fifteen Girls' Work

secretaries employed at different organizational levels of the YWCA by the end of the First World War were college graduates. For elaboration on the origins and early history of CGIT see Diana Pedersen, "'On the Trail of the Great Quest': the YWCA and the Launching of Canadian Girls in Training, 1909–1921," paper read to the Canadian Historical Association, Ottawa, 1982, and Margaret Prang, "'The Girl God Would Have Me Be': The Canadian Girls in Training, 1915–1939," *Canadian Historical Review* 66 (June 1985): 154–84.

4 See, for example, Gabrielle Blais, "'The Complete Personality': Female Adolescence in the Canadian Girls in Training CGIT, 1915–1955," M.A. thesis, University of Ottawa, 1986; Lucille Marr, "Church Teen Clubs, Feminized Organizations? Tuxis Boys, Trail Rangers, and Canadian Girls in Training, 1919–1939," *Historical Studies in Education/Revue d'histoire de l'éducation* 3 (Fall 1991): 249–314; and Prang, "'The Girl God Would Have Me Be,'" 154–84.

NUMBER 34

1 See Paula J.S. LaPierre, "The First Generation: The Experience of Women University Students in Central Canada" PhD thesis, University of Toronto, 1993); and AB. McKillop, *Matters of Mind: The University in Ontario 1791–1951* (Toronto: University of Toronto Press, 1994), 124–46.

2 For example, Sara Z. Burke, "New Women and Old Romans: Co-education at the University of Toronto, 1884–1895" (unpublished paper presented at the Annual Meeting of the Canadian Historical Association, St John's, Newfoundland, June 1997); Carol Dyhouse, *No Distinction of Sex? Women in British Universities* (London: UCL Press, 1995); Lynn D. Gordon, *Gender and Higher Education in the Progressive Era* (New Haven and London: Yale University Press, 1990); Helen Lefkowitz Horowitz, *Campus Life: Undergraduate Cultures from the End of the Eighteenth Century to the Present* (New York: Alfred A. Knopf, 1987); LaPierre, "The First Generation"; Johanna M. Selles,

Methodists and Women's Education in Ontario, 1836–1925 (Montreal & Kingston: McGill- Queen's University Press, 1996); and Lee Stewart, *"It's Up to You": Women at UBC in the Early Years* (Vancouver: University of British Columbia Press, 1990).

3 Compiled from various sources: University of Toronto *President's Reports*; University of Western Ontario "Registrar's Reports"; *Baptist Yearbooks; Canada Yearbooks*; and A.B. McKillop, *Matters of Mind*, 141, 234, 303, 433.

4 *Historical Statistics of Canada*, 2nd ed.

5 J.J. Talman Regional Collection (hereafter RCO), University of Western Ontario (hereafter UWO), CA9ONFOX114 10M36, box 14, Minutes of the Meeting of the Faculty of University College of Arts, 30 May 1929.

6 In *Cap and Gown*, November 1904 and November 1905.

7 *Western University Gazette*, February 1916, 19–22.

8 UWO, *The Year Book*, 1924, 42.

9 LaPierre, "The First Generation," 123.

10 Alison Prentice, "The Early History of Women in University Physics: A Toronto Case Study," *Physics in Canada/La Physique au Canada* 52 (March/April 1996).

11 Burke, "New Women," 10.

12 Hilda Neatby, *Queen's University, vol. I: 1884–1917* (Montreal & Kingston: McGill-Queen's University Press, 1978): 209.

13 Karen J. Blair, *The Clubwoman as Feminist: True Womanhood Redefined, 1868–1914* (New York: Holmes and Meier Publishers, 1980); Anne Firor Scott, *Natural Allies: Women's Associations in American History* (Urbana: University of Illinois Press, 1991); and Gillian Weiss, "The Brightest Women of Our Land: Vancouver Clubwomen, 1910–1928," in Barbara K. Latham and Roberta J. Pazdro, eds., *Not Just Pin Money* (Victoria: Camosun College, 1984).

14 *McMaster University Monthly* (hereafter MM), January 1892, 187.

15 MM, May 1893, 392; and Baptist Archives (hereafter BA), McMaster University, 5 and 7 October 1895, Minute Book, 1894–1915.

16 BA, 10 and 15 January 1896; and Literary and Scientific Society, Minute Book, 1894–1915.

17 BA, 27 March and 3 April 1914; and Literary and Scientific Society, Minute Book 1894–1915.

18 *In Cap and Gown*, November 1907.

19 Neatby, *Queen's*, 301–303; and *Torontonensis* 51 (1949): 224, and 43 (1941): 256–7.

20 Information from the early years is very sketchy. I have compiled the numbers from various sources: the Western University *Announcements* for the Arts Department, 1900–08; the Western University (later the University of Western Ontario) *Calendars*, 1909–30; Registrar's Reports, 1920–1930 (Registrar's Office, UWO, and Fox Papers, various boxes, RCO, UWO); *President's Reports*, 1928–1930.

21 UWO, RCO, Jessie Rowat Papers, CA9ONROW214 Y0S16, box 2. Notebook containing the constitution and minutes, from 8 October 1903 to 8 February 1905, of the Modern Language Club.

22 Legendre, "Baptist Contribution," 176; Elizabeth L. Profit, "Education for Women in the Baptist Tradition: An Examination of the Work of the Canadian Literary Institute, Moulton Ladies' College and McMaster University" (PhD thesis, McMaster Divinity College, 1987), 1–2.

23 *Baptist Year Book*, 1892, 106–22.

24 Estelle Freedman, "Separatism as Strategy: Female Institution Building and American Feminism, 1870–1930," *Feminist Studies*, Fall 1979, 514.

25 MM, November 1891, 89; and BA, Ladies Literary League (hereafter LLL) Minute Book, 1899–1911, 10 February 1899.

26 BA, LLL Minute Book, 1899–1911, 29 October 1907.

27 *Acta Victoriana*, October 1908, 21–22; see also *Queen's Journal*, 26 October 1900, 16.

28 BA, Student Body, Constitutions, Minutes, Treasurer, 16 March 1910.

29 Selles, *Methodists*, 34; G.A. Rawlyk, "A.L. McCrimmon, H.P. Whidden, T.T. Shields, Christian Higher Education, and McMaster University," in G.A. Rawlyk, ed., *Canadian Baptists and Christian Higher Education* (Montreal &

Kingston: McGill-Queen's University Press, 1988), 35.

30 BA, Literary and Scientific Society, Minute Book, 1894–1915, 20 December 1900.

31 BA, Chancellor's Reports, 1910–24, Report by William Findlay, 22 April 1922.

32 BA, Chancellor's Reports, 1910–24, Report of the Women Students, 1921–22.

33 BA, Chancellor's Reports, 1910–24, Chancellor's Report for 1917–18.

34 UWO, RCO, Fox Papers, Box 14

NUMBER 35

1 Anecdote courtesy of Judith Skelton Grant. Reports, letters, and papers of Margaret Addison are found in the Victoria University Archives (VUA), Toronto.

2 The only women teachers in the 1903–4 calendar are Clara Benson (assistant in the chemical laboratory) and Miss M. Downing (laboratory assistant in psychology). In 1903 Trinity College federated with the University of Toronto, and Mabel Cartwight was appointed lady principal of St Hilda's residence for women, but Trinity remained off-campus on Queen Street.

3 Report of 9 November 1922, VUA, fonds 2069, 90.064v, box 3, file 5.

4 Report of 4 June 1931, ibid., file 12.

5 Addison generally pointed out that ASGA had been modelled to some extent on the student government of Wellesley College.

6 Albert Carman, letter of 13 March 1912, VUA, Senate fonds, 87.221v.

7 Gertrude Rutherford, "Dr. M.E.T. Addison," *United Church Observer*, 15 January 1941, 29.

NUMBER 36

1 Alison Prentice, "The Feminization of Teaching," in Susan Mann Trofimenkoff and Alison Prentice, eds., *The Neglected Majority: Essays in Canadian Women's History* (Toronto: McClelland and Stewart, 1977), 48–63.

2 Susan E. Houston and Alison Prentice, *Schooling and Scholars in Nineteenth-Century Ontario* (Toronto: University of Toronto Press, 1988), 11, 347 n. 5.

3 R.D. Gidney and W.P.J. Millar, *Inventing Secondary Education: The Rise of the High School in Nineteenth Century Ontario* (Montreal & Kingston: McGill-Queen's University Press, 1990), 119.

4 A similar point was made with respect to elementary school teaching in Prentice, "The Feminization of Teaching," 50.

5 J.G. Hodgins, *Documentary History of Education in Upper Canada*, vol. 24 (Toronto, 1872), 180–6.

6 *Annual Report of the Minister of Education of Ontario*, 1873, 9–10.

7 Ibid., 1880–81, Tables A and B, 100, 101.

8 Ibid., 1889, 198–9.

9 Ibid., 1906, 615.

10 *Annual Report*, 1904, xxxiv, xxxvii–xxxviii.

11 Ibid., 1904, xxxvii.

12 S.W. Dyde, "Should There Be a Faculty of Education in the University?" *Queen's Quarterly* 21 (October 1904): 164–77.

13 *Report of the Royal Commission on the University of Toronto* (1906), 141–2, 184–6.

14 W.S. Ellis, Kingston, future dean of the Faculty of Education at Queen's University, 1907 to 1913, in *Report of the Royal Commission*, 184–6.

15 University of Toronto Archives, Education, Office of the President, Falconer, A67- 0007/62," Memo Re: A Faculty of Education in the University of Toronto for the Committee of the University Governor," 1906.

16 For a history of this, see Susan Gelman, "Women Secondary School Teachers: Ontario, 1871–1930" (PhD thesis, University of Toronto, 1994).

17 J.F. Macdonald, "Salaries in Ontario High Schools," *Queen's Quarterly* 17 (October, November, December 1909): 132–9.

18 *President's Report*, Dr W. Pakenham, 30 June 1918, 24.

19 University of Toronto Archives, Ontario College of Educa-

tion, A74-0011/005, October 1919.

20 *Annual Report* (1921), Inspector G.K. Mills, "Supply of Teachers," 29.

21 *Annual Report* (1922), R.H. Grant, minister of education, xi, xii.

22 Alison Prentice et al., *Canadian Women: A History* (Toronto: Harcourt Brace Jovanovich, 1988), 427.

23 Professor J.F. Macdonald, "Can First Class Honour Graduates Be Induced to Take Up Secondary School Teaching as a Life Work?" *University of Toronto Monthly* 31 (October 1930): 28–36.

NUMBER 37

1 See Bonnie G. Smith, *The Gender of History: Men, Women, and Historical Practice* (Cambridge, Mass.: Harvard University Press, 1998); and Joan W. Scott, *Gender and the Politics of History* (New York: Columbia University Press, 1988).

2 Isabel Skelton to Andrew Haydon, n.d. [1935], box 1, Isabel Skelton Papers, Queen's University Archives, Kingston.

3 Isabel Skelton, *The Backwoodswoman* (Toronto: Ryerson Press, 1924), preface.

4 Isabel Skelton to Oscar Skelton, 11 December 1924, box 1, Skelton Papers.

5 Isabel Skelton diary, 17 January 1924, in the possession of Dr Kenneth Menzies, Guelph, Ontario.

6 Isabel Skelton, *Thomas D'Arcy McGee, Issac Jogues, Jean de Brébeuf* (Toronto: Ryerson Press, 1928, 1930); and "Frederick Philip Grove," Dalhousie Review 19 (1939): and 147–63. See also Isabel Skelton, *Thomas D'Arcy McGee* (Ste Anne de Bellevue: Garden City Press, 1925); and Charles Murphy, ed., *1825 – Thomas D'Arcy McGee – 1925: A Collection of Speeches and Addresses* (Toronto: Macmillan, 1937). Isabel saw the latter book to publication after Charles Murphy died.

7 Isabel Skelton to F.P. Grove, 15 August 1939, ibid.

8 J.J. Talman to Isabel Skelton, 21 May 1948, box 1, Skelton Papers.

9 See Terry Crowley, "Isabel Skelton: Precursor to Canadian Cultural History," in Alison Prentice and Beverley Boutilier, eds., *Creating Historical Memory: Canadian Women and the Work of History* (Vancouver: University of British Columbia Press, 1996).

NUMBER 38

1 I would like to express my thanks to Rita Carrière and Lise Bourgeois for their contributions to this study. I would also like to thank Dr Sharon Cook for her encouragement and her comments on earlier drafts of this paper. All quotes were translated from French by the author.

2 The year 1948 marks the implementation of "special French" courses to French-speaking students registered in English-language public secondary schools.

3 A. Plante, *Les écoles séparées d'Ontario* (Montreal: Collection 'Relations,' 1952).

4 A. Godbout, *Nos écoles Franco-Ontariennes: Histoire des écoles de langue française dans l'Ontario* (Ottawa: Éditions de l'Université d'Ottawa, 1980).

5 For additional sources and support for some of the broader generalizations in this essay, see the following: L.G. Bordeleau, R. Lallier, and A. Lalonde, *Les écoles secondaires de langue française en Ontario: Dix ans après* (Ottawa: Éditions de l'Université d'Ottawa, 1980); S. Churchill, N. Frenette, and S. Quazi, *Éducation et besoins des Franco-Ontariens: Le diagnostic d'un système d'éducation* (Toronto: Le Conseil de l'éducation franco-ontarienne,1985); J. Costisella, *Le scandale des écoles séparées d'Ontario* (Montreal: Les Éditions de l'Homme, 1962); C. Deblois and A. Prujiner, *Les écoles françaises hors Québec: Rétrospective et prospective* (Quebec: Université Laval, 1991); M. Dumont, *Girls' Schooling in Quebec, 1639–1960*, Canadian Historical Association, Historical Booklet No. 49 (Ottawa: Canadian Historical Association, 1990); A. Godbout, *Origine des écoles françaises dans l'Ontario* (Ottawa: Les Éditions de l'Université d'Ottawa, 1972); Soeur Louise-Marguerite, s.c.o., ed. *Un Héritage: Réminiscences du Couvent de la rue*

Rideau et du Collège Bruyère – A Light Rekindled: Reminiscences of Rideau Street Convent and Bruyère College (Ottawa: Soeurs de la Charité d'Ottawa, 1988); and Soeur Paul-Émile, s.g.c., *Les Soeurs Grises de la Croix d'Ottawa* (Ottawa: Maison mère des Soeurs Grises de la Croix, 1967).

NUMBER 39

1 Dianne Hallman, "A Thing of the Past: Teaching in One-Room Schools in Nova Scotia, 1936–1941," *Historical Studies in Education/Revue d'histoire de l'éducation* 4 (Spring 1992): 115.

2 Donald J. Wilson, "'I am ready to be of assistance where I can': Lottie Bowron and Rural Women Teachers in British Columbia," in Alison Prentice and Marjorie Theobald, eds., *Women Who Taught: Perspectives on the History of Women and Teaching* (Toronto: University of Toronto Press, 1991), 112.

3 This private girls' boarding college was operated by a Roman Catholic religious order, the Sisters of Mercy. It was founded as a boarding school for young ladies in 1884 and elevated to the status of college in 1917.

4 A hectograph was a device, consisting of a gelatinous pad in a shallow pan, that duplicated printed matter. When paper printed with a special ink was placed face down on the pad, the gelatinous mixture absorbed the imprint. Numerous duplications were possible by placing fresh sheets of paper on the pad and rubbing gently, a process which absorbed the impression from the pad.

5 See F.W. Rowe, *The Development of Education in Newfoundland* (Toronto, 1952), 103.

6 Harry F. Wolcott, "The Teacher as an Enemy," in George Spindler, ed., *Education and Cultural Process: Anthropological Approaches* (Prospect Heights, Ill.: Waveland Press, 1977), 80.

7 My sincere thanks to all those who kindly assisted me with this paper through their remembrances.

NUMBER 41

1 "Early Education and the Margaret Eaton School: 1907," University of Toronto, Rare Book Collection (UT-RBC), Dora Mavor Moore Papers-207, box 29.

2 Alison Prentice and Marjorie R. Theobald, in their study of female academies in Canada and Australia during the nineteenth century, argue that these women's academies, seminaries and colleges played an important role in the history of education for women – a role that was neither trivial nor impractical. See Alison Prentice and Marjorie R. Theobald, *Women Who Taught: Perspectives on the History of Women and Teaching* (Toronto: University of Toronto Press, 1991). Contrary to traditional educational theorists, these scholars contend that female academies not only "finished" young women, but also provided serious foundational study in languages, the arts, and music, and enabled many of them to enter the teaching field as schoolmistresses and to open their own academies (247–68).

3 James Mavor was a British political economist who came to Canada in 1892 and accepted a position as a professor of political economy at the University of Toronto. He was interested in social reform and economic research, and critiqued the class-based aspect of the settlement movement. See Sara Z. Burke, *Seeking the Highest Good: Social Service and Gender at the University of Toronto, 1888–1937* (Toronto: University of Toronto Press, 1996).

4 *Globe*, "The School of Expression," 8 August 1903, 10.

5 *The Margaret Eaton School of Literature and Expression Calendar*, 1908–9, 10.

6 Emma Scott Raff, "Canadian Women in the Public Eye," *Saturday Night*, 11 September 1920, 26.

7 Paula Sperdakos, "Dora Mavor Moore: Her Career in the Canadian Theatre" (PhD thesis, University of Toronto, 1990).

8 Emma Scott Raff to Mr Eaton, 22 November 1915, Archives of Ontario, Eaton Collection, Series 22, box 6.

9 *The Margaret Eaton School Calendar*, 1923–4, 11.

10 Ibid., 1926–27, 5.

11 Mary G. Hamilton, *Call of the Algonquin: A Biography of a Summer Camp* (Toronto: Ryerson Press), 174.

12 Ibid., 72.

13 Ibid., 174.

14 *Calendar*, 1932–3, 5.

15 Ibid., 11.

16 Elizabeth Pitt Barron, interview by author, 28 May 1997.

17 Pitt Barron interview, 22 April 1994.

18 Pitt Barron, "A Strange Chronicle: The Power and Influence of Dr. R. Tait McKenzie" unpublished manuscript, Pitt Barron personal papers, held by author, 11.

19 Helen Plaunt, "The Awful Truth," *M.E.S. Amies*, 1937–38, 40.

20 Mariana Valverde, *The Age of Light, Soap and Water: Moral Reform in English Canada, 1885–1925* (Toronto: McClelland and Stewart, 1991).

21 Burke, *Seeking the Highest Good*, 53.

22 George S. Nasmith, "Commencement Exercise Address, 1918," in Dorothy Jackson, *A Brief History of the Three Schools* (Toronto: T. Eaton Company, 1953), 13.

23 Pitt Barron interview, 28 May 1997.

24 Ibid.

NUMBER 42

1 Deborah Gorham, "Flora MacDonald Denison, Canadian Feminist," in Linda Kealey, ed., *A Not Unreasonable Claim: Women and Reform in Canada* (Toronto, 1979). See also Carol Bacchi, *Liberation Deferred? The Ideas of the English-Canadian Suffragists, 1877–1918* (Toronto, 1983); C. Cleverdon, *The Women's Suffrage Movement in Canada* (Toronto, 1950); and Veronica Strong-Boag, "Ever a Crusader: Nellie McClung, First-Wave Feminist," in V. Strong-Boag and A. Clair Fellman, eds., *Rethinking Canada: The Promise of Women's History* (Toronto, 1997).

2 Linda Kealey, *Enlisting Women for the Cause: Women, Labour and the Left in Canada, 1890–1920* (Toronto, 1998).

3 This was not changed until 1946. Beth Light and Ruth Roach Pierson, eds., *No Easy Road: Women in Canada, 1920s to 1960s* (Toronto, 1990), 344.

4 Clio Collective, *Quebec Women, A History* (Toronto, 1987); Thérèse Casgrain, *A Woman in a Man's World* (Toronto, 1972); Marie Lavigne, Yolande Pinard, and Jennifer Stoddart, "The Fédération nationale Saint-Jean-Baptiste and the Women's Movement in Quebec," in Kealey, *A Not Unreasonable Claim*; and Susan Mann Trofimenkoff, *The Dream of Nation: A Social and Intellectual History of Quebec* (Toronto, 1982).

5 Joan Sangster, "The Communist Party and the Woman Question, 1922–29," *Labour/Le Travail* 15 (Spring 1985).

6 See Joan Sangster, *Dreams of Equality: Women on the Canadian Left, 1920–60* (Toronto, 1989); Susan Walsh, "The Peacock and the Guinea Hen: Political Profiles of Dorothy Gretchen Steeves and Grace MacInnis," in Alison Prentice and Susan Trofimenkoff, eds., *The Neglected Majority*, vol. 11 (Toronto, 1985); and Linda Kealey and Joan Sangster, eds., *Beyond the Vote: Women and Canadian Politics, 1920* (Toronto, 1989). On United Farm Women and Social Credit women in Alberta, see Alvin Finkel, "Populism and Gender: The UFA and Social Credit Experiences," *Journal of Canadian Studies* 27 no. 4 (Winter 1992–93).

7 Kealey, *Enlisting Women for the Cause*.

8 Ibid. On Jewish women workers, see Ruth Frager, *Sweatshop Strife: Ethnicity and Gender in the Jewish Labour Movement of Toronto, 1900–39* (Toronto, 1992); on Finnish women, see Varpu Lindstrom-Best, *Defiant Sisters: A Social History of Finnish Immigrant Women in Canada* (Toronto, 1988).

9 Patricia Myers, "A Noble Effort: The National Federation of Liberal Women of Canada, 1928–73," in Kealey and Sangster, *Beyond the Vote*; Veronica Strong-Boag, "Canadian Feminism in the 1920s: The Case of Nellie L. McClung," *Journal of Canadian Studies* 12 (1977); and Franca Iacovetta, "The Political Career of Senator Cairine Wilson, 1921–62," in Kealey and Sangster, *Beyond the Vote*.

10 Sangster, *Dreams of Equality*, 234. See also Georgina Taylor, "Gladys Strum: Farm Woman, Teacher, Politician,"

Canadian Women's Studies 7 (Winter 1986).

11 Light and Pierson, *No Easy Road*.

12 Julie Guard, "Women Worth Watching," 2000.

13 Ruth Frager, "Politicized Housewives in the Jewish Communist Movement in Toronto," in Kealey and Sangster, eds., *Beyond the Vote*; and Frances Syripa, *Wedded to the Cause: Ukrainian Canadian Women and Ethnic Identity, 1891–1991* (Toronto, 1992).

14 Constance Backhouse, *Dalhousie Law Journal* 17, no. 2 (Fall 1994): 299–362.

15 Dionne Brand, *No Burden to Carry: Narratives of Black Working Women in Ontario, 1920s to 1960s* (Toronto, 1991).

16 Nancy Adamson, Linda Briskin, and Margaret McPhail, *Feminists Organizing for Change: The Contemporary Women's Movement in Canada* (Toronto, 1988).

NUMBER 43

1 Canada, House of Commons, *Debates*, 29 March 1922, quoted in *Farmers' Sun*, 20 January 1927.

2 For further reading, see Terry Crowley, *Agnes Macphail and the Politics of Equality* (Toronto: Lorimer, 1990); and Joan Sangster, *Dreams of Equality: Women on the Canadian Left, 1920–1950* (Toronto: McClelland and Stewart, 1989).

NUMBER 44

1 Mrs E.B. Price, Calgary, Alberta, to Charles J. Doherty, K.C., Ottawa, Ontario, 15 June 1921, National Archives of Canada (NA), Department of Justice Records, RG 13, vol. 2425.

2 Private secretary for the prime minister, Ottawa, Ont. to Mrs Leila Geggie, Quebec, Que., 15th January 1923, Doherty papers, NA, RG 13, vol. 2425.

3 NA, Records of the Supreme Court of Canada, RG 125, vol. 563, file 5426, also featured in its "Treasured Memories Exhibition."

4 Ibid., 10.

5 Ibid., 14.

NUMBER 45

1 City of Toronto Archives (CTA), Central Neighbourhood House fonds, SC5 D, box 1, file 4, "The House by the Side of the Road" (pamphlet), June 1913.

2 Philip Abrams, "Notes on the Difficulty of Studying the State," *Journal of Historical Sociology* 1 (1988): 69, 76.

3 There are many excellent studies of the settlement movement, particularly as it manifested itself in Britain and the United States. See, for example, Standish Meacham, *Toynbee Hall and Social Reform 1880–1914: The Search for Community* (New Haven and London: Yale and London University Press, 1987); Allen F. Davis, *Spearheads for Reform: The Social Settlements and the Progressive Movement, 1885–1930* (New York: Oxford University Press, 1967); Mina Julia Carson, *Settlement Folk: Social Thought and the American Settlement Movement, 1885–1937* (Toronto: University of Toronto Press, 1990); and Cathy L. James, "Gender, Class and Ethnicity in the Organization of Neighbourhood and Nation: The Role of Toronto's Settlement Houses in the Formation of the Canadian State, 1902 to 1914" (PhD thesis, University of Toronto, 1997).

4 Robert A. Woods and Albert J. Kennedy, eds., *Handbook of Settlements* (Philadelphia: Wm F. Fell Co., 1911; reprint, New York: Arno Press, 1970), vi; Davis, *Spearheads*, 8; and James, "Neighbourhood and Nation," 6.

5 Ethel Dodds Parker, "The Origins and Early History of the Presbyterian Settlement Houses," in Richard Allen, ed., *The Social Gospel in Canada: Papers of the Interdisciplinary Conference on the Social Gospel in Canada, March 21–24, 1973, at the University of Regina* (Ottawa: National Museums of Canada, 1975), 86–121; Helen L. Hart, "Evangelical Social Settlement Work," *The Presbyterian Record*, June 1915, 255–6; and Elizabeth Neufeld, "The Training of an Immigrant for Canadian Citizenship," *Canadian Conference of Charities and Correction Proceedings* (Toronto: 1913), 23–7.

6 James, "Neighbourhood and Nation," chap. 7.

7 See Lorna Hurl, "Building a Profession: The Origin and

Development of the Department of Social Service in the University of Toronto, 1914–1928," *Working Papers on Social Welfare in Canada*, vol. 11 (Toronto: Faculty of Social Work, University of Toronto, 1983).

8 See James, "Neighbourhood and Nation," chap. 7.

9 Neufeld, "Training"; Hart, "Evangelical"; Edith Elwood, "The Social Settlement," in Twelfth Canadian Conference of Charities and Correction, *Proceedings* (Toronto: William Briggs, 1911), 31–2; and Arthur H. Burnett, "The Conservation of Citizenship: A Critique on Settlement Service," *Acta Victoriana* 35 (November 1911): 59–62.

10 A[lberta[S. Bastedo, "Fortnight at Evangelina [*sic*] House," *Varsity* 26 (11 October 1906): 21.

11 A.S. Bastedo, "A Visit to Evangelia House," *Varsity* 25 (19 October 1905): 43; CTA, SC5 D, box 1, file 2, Central Neighborhood [*sic*] House Year Book, 1912; Ethel Dodds Parker, "St. Christopher House: Stories of My Time," typed manuscript, 1962, United Church Archives library.

12 See James, "Neighbourhood and Nation," chaps. 5 and 6.

13 For one example of this approach to using the settlements, see Enrico Cumbo, "'Blazing the Trail and Setting the Pace': Central Neighbourhood House and Its Outreach to Italian Immigrants in Toronto, 1911–1929," *Italian Canadiana* 12 (1996): 68–93.

14 Philip Corrigan, Harvie Ramsey, and Derek Sayer, "The State as a Relation of Production," in Philip Corrigan, ed., *Capitalism, State Formation, and Marxist Theory* (London: Quartet Books, 1980), 10.

15 Bruce Curtis, "Policing Pedagogical Space: 'Voluntary' School Reform and Moral Regulation," *Canadian Journal of Sociology* 13 (Summer 1988): 298–9.

16 The research upon which this paper is based was supported, in part, by a doctoral fellowship from the Social Services and Humanities Research Council of Canada. I would like to thank William Westfall for his helpful comments on an earlier draft.

NUMBER 46

1 Judy Bedford, "Prostitution in Calgary, 1905–1914," *Alberta History* 29, no. 2 (Spring 1981): 1–11; Andrée Lévesque, "Le bordel: Milieu de travail contrôlé," *Labour/Le Travail* 20 (Fall 1987), and "Eteindre le Red Light: Le réformateurs et la prostitution à Montréal entre 1865–1925," *Urban History Review* 17, no. 3 (February 1989): 191–201; John McLaren, "The Canadian Magistracy and Anti-White Slavery Campaign, 1900–1920," in W. Wesley Pue and Barry Wright, eds., *Canadian Perspectives on Law and Society: Issues in Legal History* (Ottawa: Carleton University Press, 1988), 329; and Lori Rotenberg, "The Wayward Worker: Toronto's Prostitute at the Turn of the Century," in Janice Acton et al., eds., *Women at Work: Ontario, 1850–1930* (Toronto: Canadian Women's Educational Press, 1974), 33–69.

2 Christine Stansell, *City of Women* (Chicago: University of Illinois Press, 1987); Joanne Meyerowitz, *Women Adrift: Independent Wage Earners in Chicago, 1880–1930* (Chicago: Unviersity of Chicago Press, 1988); and Kathy Peiss, *Cheap Amusements: Working Women and Leisure in Turn-of-the-Century New York* (Philadelphia: Temple University Press, 1985).

3 Carolyn Strange, *Toronto's Girl Problem: The Perils and Pleasures of the City, 1880–1930* (Toronto: University of Toronto Press, 1995); and Mary E. Odem, *Delinquent Daughters: Protecting and Policing Adolescent Female Sexuality in the United States, 1885–1920* (Chapel Hill: University of North Carolina Press, 1995).

4 For example, see Judith R.Walkowitz, *City of Dreadful Delight: Narratives of Sexual Danger in Late-Victorian London* (Chicago: University of Chicago Press, 1992); and Phil Hubbard, "Red-Light Districts and Toleration Zones: geographies of female street prostitution in England and Wales," *Area* 29, no. 2 (1997): 129–40.

5 Andrée Lévesque, "Eteindre le Red Light: Les Réformateurs et la prostitution à Montréal entre 1865 et 1925," *Urban History Review* 17, no. 3 (February 1989): 191–201.

6 Ruth Rosen, *The Lost Sisterhood: Prostitution in America,*

1900–1918 (Baltimore: Johns Hopkins Press, 1982), 120.

7 Montreal Recorder's Court, *Annual Report 1923*, 12.

8 *Montreal by Gaslight* (pamphlet published in Montreal, 1889), 154.

9 Montreal Recorder's Court, *Annual Report 1898*, 14.

10 Committee of Sixteen, *Preliminary Report*, 1918.

11 Chief of Police Campeau agreed to swear in a Travellers' Aid worker temporarily if the WCTU were willing to pay her salary. Letter acknowledging receipt of the application, National Archives, Montreal Local Council of Women, Women's Patrols File, O. Campeau to E. Kohl, 20 February 1914.

12 NA, MLCW, vol. 7, Women's Patrols File, K. Chipman, "Report: Patrol Work for Three Months, Summer 1918."

13 *La Bonne Parole*, juin 1918, 14, and juin 1919, 2.

14 MJDC, 8 February 1924, #93

15 MJDC 13 January 1928, #1508; and 11 January 1930, #12.

16 MJDC, 3 April 1924, #284.

17 MJDC, 3 April 1924, #284; and April 1924, #235.

NUMBER 47

Author's Note: The author owes a debt of gratitude to Professors Rooke and Schnell, whose fine study of Charlotte Whitton's political thought, *No Bleeding Heart: Charlotte Whitton, A Feminist on the Right*, furnished many details on her career that are acknowledged throughout the text. The rest of the information on Whitton is drawn from the author's own research for her thesis on unemployment and relief in Ottawa, from her work as an archivist on the Whitton Papers, and finally from her own memories of growing up in Ottawa when "Charlotte" was always part of the political scene. Specific references are in the notes below.

1 P.T. Rooke and R.L. Schnell, *No Bleeding Heart: Charlotte Whitton, a Feminist on the Right* (Vancouver: University of British Columbia Press, 1987), 26–8. This study concentrates on the feminist aspect and political thought of Charlotte Whitton.

2 Ibid., 29, 43–6, 48.

3 Ibid., 68–9.

4 For a study of the larger context, see Joy Parr, *Labouring Children: British Immigrant Apprentices to Canada, 1869–1924* (Montreal & Kingston: McGill-Queen's University Press, 1980).

5 For a contemporary account illustrating the racial biases of the time, see J.T.M. Anderson, *The Education of the New-Canadian: A Treatise on Canada's Greatest Educational Problem* (Toronto: J.M. Dent, 1918). For historical perspective on prejudices against people of Jewish and Asian backgrounds, see Irving Abella and Harold Troper, *None Is Too Many: Canada and the Jews of Europe, 1933–1948*, 3rd ed. (Toronto: Lester Publishing, 1991); and Patricia Roy, *A White Man's Province: British Columbia Politicians and Chinese and Japanese Immigrants, 1858–1914* (Vancouver: University of British Columbia Press, 1989).

6 Katharine Arnup, *Education for Motherhood: Advice for Mothers in Twentieth Century Canada* (Toronto: University of Toronto Press, 1994), 71, 119. This book provides an in-depth analysis of the "advice to prospective and new mothers" books and pamphlets published by governments and private agencies.

7 Helen K. Exner, "Return to the Family in Community-Oriented Social Work," in William G. Dixon, ed., *Social Welfare and the Preservation of Human Values* (Vancouver: J.M. Dent and Sons, Canada, 1957), 164–5.

8 National Archives of Canada (NA), MG 28 I 10, *Records of the Canadian Council on Social Development*, vol. 43, file 213 – Ottawa – Federation Report 1931, as cited in Judith Roberts-Moore, "Maximum Relief for Minimum Cost? Coping with Unemployment and Relief in Ottawa during the Depression, 1929 to 1939" (M.A. thesis, University of Ottawa, 1980).

9 Rooke and Schnell, *No Bleeding Heart*, 87–88.

10 Ibid., 91.

11 Roberts-Moore, "Coping with Unemployment and Relief," 75–8, 83.

12 CCSD Records, vol. 122, file 1923: Work Schemes 1935, 1938–46, as cited in Roberts-Moore, "Coping with Unemployment and Relief," 83, 85.

13 Rooke and Schnell, *No Bleeding Heart*, 96.

14 Ibid., 93–7.

15 Ibid., 100.

16 Ibid.

17 The opening of the last volume of the Whitton Papers was reported on the front page of the *Ottawa Citizen*. See Dave Mullington, "Charlotte Whitton's Secret Letters," *Ottawa Citizen*, A1-A2, D1-D2.

NUMBER 48

1 Margaret Benston, "The Political Economy of Women's Liberation," *Monthly Review*, September 1969.

2 Betty Friedan, *The Feminine Mystique* (New York, 1963). On the domestic labour debates, see Bonnie Fox, ed., *Hidden in the Household: Women's Domestic Labour under Capitalism* (Toronto, 1980).

3 On the suffragists, see Carol Bacchi, *Liberation Deferred? The Ideas of the English Canadian Suffragists, 1877–1918* (Toronto, 1983). For an excellent American study that examines consumer protests and the labour movement, see Dana Frank, *Purchasing Power: Consumer Organizing, Gender and the Seattle Labor Movement* (Cambridge, 1994).

4 See Margaret Hobbs and Joan Sangster, eds., *The Woman Worker* (Canadian Committee on Labour History, 1999).

5 "Housing Conditions in Cape Breton," *Woman Worker*, July 1926.

6 "Mistress Housewife, What Does Your Husband Give You to Keep House?" *Woman Worker*, December 1926.

7 *The Worker*, 9 August 1924 and 15 January 1923.

8 Ibid., 30 January 1926.

9 Margaret Little, *No Car, No Radio, No Liquor Permit: The Moral Regulation of Single Mothers in Ontario, 1920–97* (Toronto, 1998); and James Struthers, *The Limits of Affluence: Welfare in Ontario, 1920–70* (Toronto, 1994). The

allowances were kept low to encourage women to take on other part-time work, return to wage work as soon as possible, or, the "best" possible solution, to remarry.

10 University of Toronto, Thomas Fisher Rare Books Room, Kenny Collection (hereafter U of T, TFRB, Kenny), box 13, 1938 Ontario Convention Report.

11 Communist Party of Canada, Eighth Dominion Convention, photocopy in author's possession.

12 Earlier housewives groups had existed, sometimes with a distinct ethnic membership. On a meat boycott organized by Jewish housewives in the early 1930s, see Ruth Frager, "Politicized Housewives in the Jewish Communist Movement of Toronto, 1923–33," in Linda Kealey and Joan Sangster, eds., *Beyond the Vote: Canadian Women and Politics* (Toronto, 1989).

13 *Daily Clarion*, 18 March 1938.

14 Ibid., 28 February 1938.

15 *The Worker*, 7 September 1935; *Daily Clarion*, 7 November 1936.

16 *Daily Clarion*, 29 August 1936.

17 *Daily Tribune*, 18 September 1943.

18 *Canadian Tribune*, 18 April 1942.

19 *Daily Tribune*, 14 November 1942.

20 Ibid., 18 September 1943.

21 *Daily Clarion*, 14 November 1942.

22 U of T, TFRB, Kenny, box 9, National Women's Commission, "Notes for International Women's Day," by Dorise Nielsen, 28 February 1948. Dorise Nielsen, an "independent" member of Parliament from Saskatchewan from 1940 to 1945, later joined the (Communist) Labour Progressive Party.

23 Ibid., box 57, Becky Buhay, "Women in the Fight for Peace and Socialism," 11.

24 *Canadian Tribune*, 10 June 1947.

25 Mona Morgan, quoted in Joan Sangster, *Dreams of Equality: Women on the Canadian Left, 1920–60* (Toronto, 1989), 188.

26 Julie Guard, "Women Worth Watching: Radical House-

wives in Cold War Canada," in D. Buse, G. Kinsman, and
M. Steedman, eds., *Rethinking National Security* (Toronto,
1999).

27 *The New Era*, 28 January 1938.

28 U of T, TFRB, Woodsworth Memorial Collection, Women's
Joint Committee Minutes, 12 May 1936.

29 On the WJC, see John Manley, "Women and the Left in the
1930s: The Case of the Toronto Women's Joint Committee," *Atlantis* 5 (1980).

30 National Archives of Canada (NA), Marjorie Mann fonds,
CCF Women's Conference Document, May 1947.

31 On the Provincial Women's Committee, see Sangster,
Dreams of Equality, chap. 7; Dean Beeby, "Women in the
Ontario CCF, 1940–50," *Ontario History* 74 (December
1982); and Dan Azoulay, "Winning Women to Socialism:
The Ontario CCF and Women, 1947–61," *Labour/Le Travail*,
36 (Fall 1995). Azoulay challenges feminist interpretations
of the PWC by Beeby and myself, arguing that there was
"no discrimination" against, or ghettoization of, women in
the party in the 1950s. Although his article unfortunately
tends to oversimplify and thus misrepresent the full argument of previous historians, his different emphasis on
women's integration into party building should be read
along with the earlier analyses.

32 *Ontario CCF News*, 25 March 1948.

33 NA, Co-operative Commonwealth Federation fonds,
Ontario Women's Conference, 1948.

34 Beeby, "Women in the Ontario CCF, 1940–50," 275.

35 One exception was a theoretical exposition on domestic
labour by an American communist, Mary Inman. Titled
Woman Power, these articles (later a book) were criticized
by the Communist Party at the time. Sangster, *Dreams of
Equality*, 183.

36 Feminist groups also appeared to be less sympathetic to
homemakers because of their opposition to fiscal and tax
policies that differentially favoured more affluent families
with women in the home. On second-wave feminists' policies vis-à-vis the family, see Margaret Eichler, *The Pro-
Family Movement: Are They For or Against Families?*
(Ottawa, 1985).

NUMBER 49

1 I would like to thank Susan Mann and Terry Cook for
helpful comments on earlier versions of this paper. Much
of the research was originally done for my memoir on
"Women Organized for Peace: Voice of Women, 1960-
1963" (University of Ottawa, 1985).

2 Gerda Lerner, *The Creation of Feminist Consciousness*
(New York: Oxford University Press, 1993), especially 47,
272, and 283. See also Carroll Smith-Rosenberg, *Disorderly
Conduct: Visions of Gender in Victorian America* (New
York: A.A. Knopf, 1985); and Candace Loewen, "'Liberat-
ing the Canadian Clio': Some Recent Archival Resources
on Women," *Resources for Feminist Research/Nouvelles
recherches feministes* 23 (Spring/Summer 1994): 31-4.

3 National Archives of Canada (hereafter NA), Lester B.
Pearson Papers, MG 26, n 2, vol. 91, part 1, draft of original
"Brief Concerning Motivation, Purpose, Methods of
Implement and Organization …," n.d.

4 Quote from VOW newsletter, as found in Kay Macpherson
and Meg Sears, "The Voice of Women: A History," in
Gwen Matheson, ed., *Women in the Canadian Mosaic*
(Toronto: Peter Martin Associates, 1976), 72.

5 NA, VOW Records, MG 28, I 218, vol. 1, file 2, from Mary
Thomas, 6 June 1960. See also letters from Margo Gamsby
and Betty May in the same file. VOW Records, vol. 1, files 1,
2, and 3 contain the letters the organization received from
May 1960 to October 1960.

6 Ibid., vol. 1, file 2, from Ursula McLennon, n.d.

7 Ibid., vol. 1, file 3, from Mrs Rene St Jacques, 16 October
1960. Edna D. Chamberlain wrote along the same lines,
saying, "For women to feel helpless is not really fulfilling
our true role in the world." Ibid., vol. 1, file 2, 24 July 1960.

8 Ibid., vol. 1, file 2, from Betty May, 24 June 1960.

9 Ibid., vol. 1, file 2, from Merle Keys, 6 July 1960.

10 Ibid., vol. 1, file 2, from Eleanor Thomson, 24 June 1960.

11 Ibid., vol. 1, file 2, from Merle Keys, 6 July 1960.

12 Ibid., vol. 1, file 17.

13 Ibid., vol. 1, file 2, Edith Steele to Josephine Davis, 26 June 1960.

14 Ibid., vol. 2, file 9, report prepared by the Hamilton branch, October 1962.

15 Ibid., vol. 2, file 14.

16 Catherine Sinclair's column in *Chatelaine* applauded the baby-tooth survey for radiation research. Teeth "no longer go to the good fairy," she wrote. *Chatelaine* 34 (October 1961): 4.

17 Barbara Frum, "You're Worried about Fallout? Air Pollution Will Probably Get You First," *Canadian Magazine*, 13 August 1966, 18, as found in VOW Records. Dr Franklin admitted failure in the VOW's efforts to persuade the government to decontaminate milk: "We failed, probably, because implicit in granting our request would have been an admission that fallout levels were indeed dangerous" (Frum, 18).

18 VOW Records, vol. 1, file 18.

19 Ibid., vol. 4, file 18, Ursula Franklin, "The Sad Subject of Peace Research," 28 November 1965.

20 Macpherson and Sears, "The Voice of Women," 76.

21 VOW Records, vol. 4, file 18, Ursula Franklin, "The Sad Subject of Peace Research," 28 November 1965. Some thought that government support would be beneficial for CPRI and others did not. Charlotte McEwen, VOW member in the early years, told the author, "They [CPRI] weren't giving us the hard data [and] research we wanted. We worked very hard on that, very hard ... Some people were afraid that CPRI would get government recognition." Charlotte McEwen, interview, 29 June 1984.

22 Thérèse Casgrain, one-time president of VOW, has written that "[d]emonstrating was one of our methods long before such actions became popular." Thérèse Casgrain, *A Woman in a Man's World*, trans. Joyce Marshall (Toronto: McClelland and Stewart, 1972), 164. See also Candace Loewen, "Thérèse Casgrain et la Voix des femmes," in *Thérèse Casgrain: Une femme tenace et engagée* (Montreal: Presses de l'Université du Québec, 1993).

23 Prior to November 1962, the VOW had suffered from bad press reports, especially in Quebec. Casgrain has written, "I was in the thick of the fray and target for attacks from the reactionaries of our province, especially the *Action catholique*, which in their paper on the fifth of April, 1962, described the Voice of Women as 'falsely humanitarian and misguided in their political aims.'" Ibid., 160.

24 VOW Records, vol. 1, file 8.

25 *Canadian Annual Review: 1962* (Toronto: University of Toronto Press, 1963), 143. See also VOW Records, vol. 1, file 18.

26 "La Voix des femmes revient à 'l'attaque' pour la paix," *Le Droit*, 2 November 1962; and "300 Irate VOW Delegates Demand Canada Voice Stand on Arms," *Globe and Mail*, 2 November 1962.

27 "La Voix des femmes est mécontente des réponses reçues du gouvernement," *Le Devoir*, 2 November 1962.

28 "300 Irate VOW Delegates Demand Canada Voice Stand on Arms," *Globe and Mail*, 2 November 1962.

29 VOW Records, vol. 1, file 8, Marjorie Bell to Josephine Davis, 28 November 1962.

30 Carol Chapman, "How Effective Is the Voice of Women?" *Chatelaine* 34 (June 1961): 116.

31 VOW Records, vol. 1, file 2, from Wilma M. McDonald, 25 June 1960.

32 Ibid., Josephine Davis to Pearson, 11 February 1963.

33 See note 11.

34 Of course, concerns other than worry for the world's future were behind VOW members' words and actions – political allegiances, religious impulses, ideological positions, and status considerations. For a fuller study of the VOW, its ideas, crises, and personalities, see Candace Loewen, "Mike Hears Voices: Voice of Women and Lester B. Pearson, 1960–1963," *Atlantis* 12 (Spring 1987): 24–30. A shorter popular version of the early VOW story is Candace Loewen, "Women for Peace: Voice of Women, the 1960s," *Horizon Canada* 7 (October 1986).

NUMBER 50

1 The concept of citizenship has not been fairly distributed to women throughout Canadian history. Indeed, Janine Brodie argues that "citizenship is an historically evolving concept that over time has carried different technologies of gender, meanings, contents and webs of inclusion and exclusion." Janine Brodie, "Meso-Discourses, State Forms and the Gendering of Liberal-Democratic Citizenship," *Citizenship Studies* 1 (1997), 239.

2 Alison Prentice et al., *Canadian Women: A History* (Toronto: Harcourt Brace Jovanovich, 1988), 109.

3 Nancy Adamson et al., *Feminists Organizing for Change* (Toronto: Oxford University Press, 1988), 10.

4 David Botchier, *The Feminist Challenge* (London: Macmillan Press, 1983), 66.

5 Sophie Watson, "The State of Play: An Introduction," in Sophie Watson, ed., *Playing the State: Australian Feminist Interventions* (London: Verso Books, 1990), 6–7. See also Carole Pateman, *The Disorder of Women: Democracy, Feminism, and Political Theory* (Stanford, Calif.: Stanford University Press, 1989), 128–30.

6 For further critiques of liberalism and liberal feminism, see Zillah Eisenstein, *Feminism and Sex Equality* (New York: Monthly Review, 1984); and Ian Forbes, "Equal Opportunity: Radical, Liberal and Conservative Critiques," in Elizabeth Meehan and Selma Sevenhuijsen, eds., *Equality, Politics and Gender* (Newbury Park, Calif.: Sage Publications, 1991).

7 Sue Findlay, "Feminist Struggles with the Canadian State: 1966–1988," *Resources in Feminist Research* 17 (3 September 1988): 6.

8 Florence Bird, as cited in Naomi Griffiths, *Penelope's Web* (Toronto: Oxford University Press, 1976), 209.

9 Canada, *Report of the Royal Commission on the Status of Women* (Ottawa: Queen's Printer, 1970), 3.

10 Equality of opportunity asserts that each person should have equal rights and opportunities to develop his or her own talents and virtues and that there should be equal rewards for those who deserve them. To allow this to happen, legal restrictions on the ability of individuals to compete with one another on the basis of equal opportunity should be removed.

11 Adamson, 191.

12 *Report of the Royal Commission*, 3.

13 Ibid.

14 Ibid., 161.

15 Ibid., 404.

16 Ibid., 228.

17 Ibid., 410–12.

18 Canada, Department of Labour, *Status of Women in Canada* (Ottawa: Queen's Printer, 1972), 2.

19 Carol Pateman, "Feminist Critiques of the Public/Private Dichotomy," in Anne Phillips, ed., *Feminism and Equality* (Oxford: Basil Blackwell, 1987), 103–4.

20 *Report of the Royal Commission,* 392–3.

21 See Caroline Andrew and Sandra Rodgers, *Women and the State – Les Femmes et l'État Canadien* (Montreal & Kingston: McGill-Queen's University Press, 1997); and Naomi Black, "The Canadian Women's Movement: The Second Wave," in Sandra Burt et al., eds., *Changing Patterns: Women in Canada* (Toronto: McClelland and Stewart, 1993).

22 Florence Bird, "The Royal Commission on the Status of Women: 20th Anniversary Edition: Introduction," *Ottawa Law Review* 22 (1991): 554.

NUMBER 51

1 Elsie Gregory MacGill fonds, National Archives of Canada (NA), MG 31 K 7, vol. 5, file: Biographical.

2 It is sad that Florence Bird died less than two weeks before the announcement of the federal pay equity decision of the Canadian Human Rights Commission, on 29 July 1998. She would have been pleased.

3 Telephone interview with Florence Bird by Judi Cumming, 3 April 1985.

NUMBER 52

1 Shirley Farlinger, "Rosalie Bertell: Political Activist and Grey Nun," *Status of Women News*, Winter 1984, 8–9.

2 Sam Totten and Martha Wescott Totten, *Facing the Danger: Interviews with 20 Anti-nuclear Activists* (Trumansburg, N.Y.: Crossing Press [1984]), chap. 2, 22.

3 Susan C. MacPhee, *Talking Peace: The Women's International Peace Conference* (Charlottetown: Ragweed Press, 1990), 16.

4 Ibid., 134.

5 Ibid., 132.

6 Rosalie Bertell fonds, NA, MG 31 K 39, vol. 4, "Women and the Environment," 4.

7 Ibid.

8 Ibid., 5.

9 Ibid.

10 Ibid., 7.

11 Ibid., 14.

12 Ibid.

13 Carol R. Berkin and Clara M. Lovett, eds., *Women, War and Revolution* (New York: Holmes & Meier, 1980), 260.

NUMBER 53

Author's Note: This paper is part of a major ten-year research program. I gratefully acknowledge research funding from the Social Sciences and Humanities Research Council of Canada and from a Saint Mary's University Senate research grant.

1 Source for all immigration flow data: Canada, Division of Immigration, *Immigration Statistics 1896 to 1961, Immigrants admitted to Canada by Ethnic Origin; Immigrants by Last Permanent Residence*, 1962–95; *Immigrants by Place of Birth*, 1980–98; *Annual Reports*, Sessional Paper. Fiscal years, 1904–5 to 1907–8; calender years, 1908 to 1991. Sex ratios were calculated from these data. For detailed tables, see Helen Ralston, *The Lived Experience of South Asian Immigrant Women in Atlantic Canada: The Interconnections of Race, Class and Gender*

(Lewiston/Queenston/Lampeter: Edwin Mellen Press, 1996), appendices.

2 Jogesh C. Misrow, *East Indian Immigration to the Pacific Coast* (Stanford, Calif., 1915), 1–2; and Norman Buchignani, D.M. Indra, with Ram Srivastava, *Continuous Journey: A Social History of South Asians in Canada* (Toronto: McClelland and Stewart, 1985), 5–6.

3 Robert A. Huttenback, *Racism and Empire: White Settlers and Colored Immigrants in the British Self-Governing Colonies 1830–1910* (Ithaca and London: Cornell University Press, 1976), 175.

4 PC 27 of 8 January 1908, National Archives of Canada (NA), RG 2, 1, Records of the Privy Council Office.

5 William Lyon Mackenzie King, *Report on His Mission to England to Confer with the British Authorities on the Subject of Immigration to Canada from the Orient, and Immigration from India in Particular*, 7–8 Edward VII., Sessional Paper No. 36a, 2 May 1908, 5, 7.

6 Statutes of Canada, Edward VII 1910, chap. 27, article 38 (a), (c).

7 Hugh Johnston, *The East Indians in Canada* (Ottawa: Canadian Historical Association, 1984), 10.

8 *Daily Province*, (Vancouver), editorial, 5 March 1912, 6.

9 *Vancouver Sun*, editorial, 17 June 1913, 6.

10 Buchignani et al., *Continuous Journey* 36–50; and Samuel Raj, "Some Aspects of East Indian Struggle in Canada, 1905–1947," in K. Victor Ujimoto and Gordon Hirabayashi, eds., *Visible Minorities and Multiculturalism: Asians in Canada* (Toronto: Butterworths, 1980), 70–2.

11 Emmaline E. Smillie, "An Historical Survey of Indian Migration within the Empire," *Canadian Historical Review* 4 (September 1923): 228; and Hugh J.M. Johnston, *The Voyage of the Komagata Maru: The Sikh Challenge to Canada's Colour Bar* (Delhi: Oxford University Press, 1979).

12 Source for South Asian Immigrants, by Last Permanent Residence, by Gender and Age Categories, 1962–1993: Canada, Division of Immigration, *Immigration Statistics*. Source for Census data, South Asians in Canada, by Sex,

1951–1991: Statistics Canada, *Census Canada*. For detailed tables, see Ralston, *The Lived Experience*, appendices.

13 Its terms were that, commencing 1951, there was to be an annual admission of 150 citizens of India; in addition, the wife, husband, or unmarried child under age twenty-one of a Canadian citizen of Indian origin was to be admitted. In 1957 the quota for Indian nationals was raised to 300 immigrants per year. The Department of Citizenship and Immigration came into force on 18 January 1950. "The regulation regarding Asian immigration was widened by Order-in-Council PC 6229 of 28 December 1950, which amended Order-in-Council PC 2115 of 16 September 1930, to provide for the admission of husbands of Asian racial origin in addition to the wives of Canadian citizens legally admitted and residents in Canada, and at the same time raised the age limit for unmarried children from 18 to 21 years of age" (*Annual Report* of Immigration Branch of Department of Citizenship and Immigration, 1951). The information about agreements with respect to admission of India, Pakistan, and Ceylon nationals is contained in this report and that of the following year, 1952. These agreements with the respective governments were incorporated in the immigration act that came into effect 1 June 1953. See also Alan G. Green, *Immigration and the Postwar Canadian Economy* (Toronto: Ryerson Press, 1955), xxi; and Freda Hawkins, *Canada and Immigration: Public Policy and Public Concern* (Montreal/London: McGill-Queen's University Press, 1972), 99.

14 Statutory Orders and Regulations/62–36, *Canada Gazette*, part 2, vol. 96, 14 February 1962, *Immigration Act* Immigration Regulations, Part 1, P.C. 1962–86, 126–39. See, especially, section 31.

15 Statutory Orders and Regulations/67–434, *Canada Gazette* part 2, vol. 101, 13 September 1967, *Immigration Act* Immigration Regulations, part 1, amended, P.C. 1967–1616, 1350–62. See, especially, Sections 31 and 32; schedules A and B.

16 Significantly, in January 1966 the Department of *Man*power and Immigration was created by bringing together the Immigration Branch of the former Department of Citizenship and Immigration and a number of components formerly with the Department of Labour.

17 Wenona Giles, "Language Rights Are Women's Rights: Discrimination against Immigrant Women in Canadian Language Training Policies," *Resources for Feminist Research* 17 (September 1988): 129.

18 Monica Boyd, *Migrant Women in Canada – Profiles and Policies*, Immigration Research Working Paper No. 2 (Canada: Employment and Immigration Canada, 1987), 19.

19 Ibid. My own research in Atlantic Canada and British Columbia has supported this immigrant entrance status of married women (See Ralston, *Lived Experience*, 55; and Helen Ralston, "Arranged, 'Semi-arranged' and 'Love' Marriages among South Asian Canadian Women: Intersections of Race, Class and Gender," unpublished paper presented at biennial conference of Canadian Ethnic Studies Association, Montreal, 20–23 November 1997.

20 Alma Estable, "Immigration policy and regulations," *Resources for Feminist Research* 16, no 1 (1987): 28; and Freda Hawkins, *Critical Years in Immigration* (Canada: McGill University, 1989), 69, 77.

21 I conducted interviews with 126 Atlantic Canada first-generation immigrant women aged fifteen years and over – one-tenth of the estimated total population of South Asian women of that age in the Atlantic region at the time. Interviews with 100 British Columbia women took place between November 1993 and December 1994. The samples were drawn in proportion to the census distribution of South Asians in the respective regions.

22 Anthony H. Richmond, *Immigration and Ethnic Conflict* (New York: St Martin's Press, 1988), 98–9.

23 See Buchignani et al., *Continuous Journey*, 72.

24 Citizenship and Immigration Canada, *Building on a Strong Foundation for the 21st Century: New Directions for Immigration and Refugee Policy and Legislation* (Canada: Minister of Public Works and Government Services Canada, 1998), Cat. No. Ci51-86/1998.

25 Ibid., 23.
26 Ibid., 30

NUMBER 54

1 Janice Hladki and Ann Holmes are members of the WCB Collective. They acknowledge that this essay is a partial narrative, and hope that it may stimulate the documentation of different versions/stories of WCB histories.
2 Women's Cultural Building Collection, Women's Art Resource Centre Archives (WARC), Toronto, document 2. Please note that "documents" references for this paper have been categorized numerically and are so labelled in the collection. WARC can be found at 401 Richmond Street West, Suite 122, Toronto, Ontario, M5V 3A8. Phone: (416) 977-0097; fax: (416) 977-7425; e-mail: matriart@warc.net; URL: www.warc.net.
3 Ibid.
4 WCB Collection, document 3.
5 Ellie Kirzner, "Feminist Arts Hit the Street," *NOW*, 3–9 March 1982, 7.
6 WCB Collection, document 3.
7 In Chicago's installation, a triangular table displayed thirty-nine place settings. Each celebrated a particular historic woman and featured an embroidered runner under a porcelain plate that was painted and sculpted in vagina designs. Many additional women's names were written on the tiles of the floor on which the table was installed.
8 Transcripts of these talks were published in *Parallélogramme* 8 (April/May 1983).
9 WCB Collection, "Some Notes towards a Festival," 25 January 1983, document 10.
10 WCB Collection, "Storefronting," document 11.
11 Randi Spires, "Feminism and Art in Toronto: A Five Year Overview," *Artviews* 13 (Spring 1987): 33.
12 Judith K. Brodsky, "Exhibitions, Galleries, and Alternative Spaces," Norma Broude and Mary D. Garrard, eds., *The Power of Feminist Art: Emergence, Impact and Triumph of the American Feminist Art Movement* (London: Thames and Hudson, 1994), 104.
13 WCB Collection, "Women's Cultural Building Presents a Festival of Women Building Culture," 1983, document 16.

NUMBER 55

1 Charlotte Canning, *Feminist Theatres in U.S.A.: Staging Women's Experience* (London and New York; Routledge, 1996), 13.
2 Gayle Austin, "Feminist Theories: Paying Attention to Women," *Feminist Theories for Dramatic Criticism* (Ann Arbor: University of Michigan Press, 1990), 1–2.
3 While what constitutes a feminist play, much less feminist theatre, is as varied as feminism itself, for the purposes of this analysis I will use Brown's definition, in which she suggests that the "feminist impulse" is expressed dramatically in women's struggle for autonomy against an oppressive, sexist society: "When woman's struggle for autonomy is a play's central rhetorical motive, that play can be considered feminist drama." See Janet Brown, *Feminist Drama: Definition & Critical Analysis* (London: Scarecrow Press, 1979), 1.
4 Amanda Hale, "A Dialectical Drama of Facts and Fiction on the Feminist Fringe," in Rhea Tregabov, ed., *Work in Progress: Building Feminist Culture*, (Toronto: Women's Press, 1987), 77.
5 For more on alternative theatres, see Robert Wallace, *Producing Marginality* (Saskatoon: Fifth House Publishers, 1990), 102.
6 Denis W. Johnston, *Up the Mainstream: The Rise of Toronto's Alternative Theatres* (Toronto: University of Toronto Press, 1991), 4.
7 Hale, "A Dialectical Drama," 81.
8 Ibid., 82.
9 Rina Fraticelli, *The Status of Women in the Canadian Theatre: A Report Prepared for Status of Women Canada* (Toronto: Status of Women Canada, 1982), 22–9.
10 Founded by Francine Volker, Diane Grant, and Marcella Lustig, Red Light was Toronto's first feminist theatre company.

11 Hale, "A Dialectical Drama," 84–5.

12 Cynthia Grant, interviewed by author, Toronto, 6 November 1993.

13 Ray Conlogue, "New Roles for Classic Heroines," *Globe and Mail*, 3 April 1988.

14 Nightwood Theatre press release, 24 October 1994.

15 Hale, "A Dialectical Drama," 87.

NUMBER 56

1 Wendy Mitchinson, *The Nature of Their Bodies: Women and Their Doctors in Victorian Canada* (Toronto: University of Toronto Press, 1991).

2 Gerda Lerner, *The Creation of Patriarchy* (New York: Oxford University Press, 1986).

3 Judith Leavitt, *Brought to Bed: Child-bearing in America, 1750–1950* (New York: Oxford University Press, 1986)

4 Beverly Boutilier, "Helpers or Heroines? The National Council of Women, Nursing, and 'Women's Work,'" in Dianne Dodd and Deborah Gorham, eds., *Caring and Curing: Historical Perspectives on Women and Healing in Canada* (Ottawa: University of Ottawa Press, 1994).

5 Kathryn McPherson, *Bedside Matters: The Transformation of Canadian Nursing, 1900–1990* (Toronto: University of Toronto Press, 1996).

NUMBER 57

1 Bloorview MacMillan Centre Archives, Toronto, Ladies Committee Meetings, 23 October 1899.

2 First Annual Report, November, 1900; Second Annual Report, 30 September 1901.

3 Ibid., 15 April 1901.

4 Ibid., 25 November 1901.

NUMBER 58

Author's Note: The article is based on material in the Margaret Scott Nursing Mission Collection, Provincial Archives of Manitoba, MG10 B9.

NUMBER 59

1 See Linda Quiney, "Assistant Angels: Canadian Voluntary aid Detachment Nurses in the Great War," *Canadian Bulletin of Medical History* 15, no. 1 (1998): 189–206. See also Linda Quiney "Canada's Voluntary Aid Detachment VAD Nurses of World War One," (Department of History, University of Ottawa, doctoral research).

2 See G.W.L. Nicholson, *Canada's Nursing Sisters* (Toronto: Samuel Stevens, Hakkart, 1975), for the most comprehensive history to date of Canada's nurses of the Great War.

3 Violet Wilson's narrative was recorded by Bill McNeil for his "Voice of the Pioneer" series, broadcast on CBC Radio from 1970 to 1984. All personal details regarding Violet Wilson's experiences in this account are taken from the interview. Deposited: National Archives of Canada (NA), R-09861, ACC 1981-0111, McNeil, Bill. Her service record in the U.K. and France is also recorded in the British Red Cross Society Archives and Library, *Personal Card Indexes*.

4 For an overview of women's activism and volunteerism in the late nineteenth century, see Alison Prentice et al., *Canadian Women: A History* (Toronto: Harcourt Brace, 1996), chap. 7. The enormous efforts of Canadian women during the First World War, both paid and voluntary, are too numerous to catalogue. See Ceta Ramkhalawansingh, "Women during the Great War," in Janice Action et al., eds., *Women at Work in Ontario, 1850–1930* (Toronto: Canadian Women's Educational Press, 1976), 261–307: and Prentice et al., *Canadian Women*, 230–4.

5 See note 1 above. These characteristics will be documented in a database being prepared as a basis for analysis of the VAD experience of the Great War.

6 See note 3 above. Violet recounts at length the deprivations and constraints she experienced during her boarding school years.

7 Government of Canada, Militia Council, *The Organisation of Voluntary Aid in Canada, 3 March 1914* (Ottawa: Government Printing Bureau, 1914).

8 Unlike the documented history of the Canadian experi-

ence, that of British VAD work in the Great War is extensive. Most notable is the experience of the British VAD, Vera Brittain. See Vera Brittain, *Testament of Youth: An Autobiographical Study of the Years 1900–1925* (London: Fontana, 1978 [c. 1933]). Dame Katherine Furse was instrumental in the organization and implementation of the British VAD scheme, which absorbed many Canadian applicants directly. See Katherine Furse, *Hearts & Pomegranates: The Story of Forty-Five Years, 1875 to 1920* (London: Peter Davis, 1940). See also Imperial War Museum, *Women at Work Collection* (British Red Cross Society, 1–25), "Furse Papers."

9 For the reasoning behind these policies, see NA, RG 9 III B 2, *CAMC Records*, vol. 3460; also MG 27 II D9, *Kemp Papers*, vol. 106, and MG 30 E 45, *Macdonald Papers*. There are no published studies concerning the military's aversion to the use of volunteers in its medical facilities abroad. However, Nancy Riegler's *Jean I. Gunn: Nursing Leader* (Toronto: Fitzhenry & Whiteside, 1997), chap. 5, outlines many of the concerns of trained nurses who feared a dilution of their professional status and standards if volunteer nurses were recruited for military work. The paper in note 1 above addresses this issue with regard to VADs specifically.

10 Records of Canadian VAD service are found in the British Red Cross Society Archives and Library, *Personnel Card Indexes*.

11 For an excellent discussion of the training and discipline required of graduate nurses, see Kathryn McPherson, *Bedside Matters: The Transformation of Canadian Nursing, 1900–1990* (Toronto: Oxford University Press, 1996).

12 The identification of "colonials" as troublemakers is also documented by Sandra Gwyn, *Tapestry of War: A Private View of Canadians in the Great War* (Toronto: HarperCollins, 1992), 452.

13 Canadian War Museum, *Grace MacPherson Diaries*, "26 April 1917." See also Gwyn, *Tapestry of War*, chap. 26.

14 See note 11 above. For a discussion of British hospital culture in the Great War era, see Stella Bingham, *Ministering*

Angels, (London: Osprey, 1979), chaps. 9–11.

15 The atmosphere in wartime hospitals, both in Britain and the war zones, is documented in the oral history in Lyn Macdonald, *The Roses of No Man's Land*, (London: Penguin, 1993).

16 See note 1 above.

17 Women who served abroad in a volunteer capacity for the British military were eligible for a variety of awards. Violet was accorded both the Victory and General Service Medals for service abroad in a theatre of war.

18 There were more than 1,789 Canadians and 51 Newfoundlanders (Newfoundland was then a colony of Britain) who served as VADs at home and abroad. St John Ambulance Brigade Overseas, *Report of the Chief Commissioner for Brigade Overseas, 1 October 1915 to 31 December 1917*, (London: Chancery of the Order, 1918), 35.

NUMBER 60

1 A good overview of the international literature can be found in Françoise Thébaud, "The Great War and the Triumph of Sexual Division," in Georges Duby and Michelle Perrot, eds., *A History of Women in the West*, vol. 5 of *Toward a Cultural Identity in the Twentieth Century* (Cambridge, Mass., London, England: Harvard University Press, 1994), 21–75.

2 See, for example, Margaret Higonnet, Jane Jenson, Sonya Michel, and Margaret Collins Weitz, eds., *Behind the Lines: Gender and the Two World Wars* (New Haven: Yale University Press, 1987); Susan Kent, *Making Peace: The Reconstruction of Gender in Interwar Britain* (Princeton: Princeton University Press, 1993); and Sharon Ouditt, *Fighting Forces, Writing Women: Identity and Ideology in the First World War* (New York: Routledge, 1994).

3 See for example, Ceta Rawkhalawansingh, "Women during the Great War," in Janice Acton, ed., *Women at Work: Ontario, 1850–1930* (Toronto, 1974), 261–307; Barbara M. Wilson, *Ontario and the First World War* (Toronto, 1977); Gloria Geller, "The Wartimes Elections Act of 1917 and the

Canadian Women's Movement," *Atlantis* 2 (Autumn 1976): 88–106; Kathryn Hearny, "Canadian Women and the First World War," *Les Cahiers de la femme/Canadian Women Studies* 13 (1981): 95–7; Barbara Ann Roberts, "Do women do anything to end the war? Canadian feminist pacifists and the Great War" (Ottawa: Canadian Research Institute for the Advancement of Women, 1987); Deborah Gorham, "Vera Brittain, Flora MacDonald Denison and the Great War: The Failure of Non-Violence," in Ruth Roach Pierson, ed., *Women and Peace: Theoretical, Historical and Practical Perspectives* (London, 1987); Diana Pederson, "'The Call to Service': The YWCA and the Canadian College Woman," in Paul Axelrod and John G. Reid, eds., *Youth, University and Canadian Society: Essays in the Social History of Higher Education* (Kingston, Montreal, and London: McGill-Queen's University Press, 1989).

4 On the historiography of Canadian nursing, see Ruby Heap and Meryn Stuart, "Nurses and Physiotherapists: Issues in the Professionalization of Health Care Occupations during and after World War I," *Health and Canadian Society/Santé et société canadienne*, 1995, 179–93. Kathryn Mcpherson has published since then the first monograph devoted to the evolution of the nursing profession in Canada. See her *Bedside Matters: The Transformation of Canadian Nursing, 1900–1990* (Toronto: Oxford University Press, 1996). Meryn Stuart is preparing with the author of this article a manuscript on the experiences of wartime nurses and physiotherapists. Linda Quiney, a contributor to the present volume, is completing a doctoral thesis on Canadian VADS.

5 The needs of war also spurred the growth of dietetics, another female-dominated profession, which was in its infancy at the time. A comprehensive study on the evolution of physiotherapy and dietetics in Quebec and Ontario, of which the author of this article is a co-author, has recently been published. See Nadia Fahmy-Eid et al., *Femmes, santé et profession: Histoire des diététistes et des physiothérapeutes au Québec et en Ontario, 1930–1980*

(Montreal: Fides, 1997). For a shorter discussion on the emergence of physiotherapy in Canada, see Ruby Heap, "Training Women for a New `Women's Profession': Physiotherapy Education at the University of Toronto," *History of Education Quarterly* 35 (Summer 1995): 135–58. There is presently no scholarly work devoted to the history of occupational therapy in Canada.

6 This study is part of a completed project on the history of nursing and physiotherapy during the Great War, conducted by the author and Meryn Stuart, with the financial support of the Hannah Institute on the History of Medicine and of the University of Ottawa. The results of this project will appear in a monograph presently in preparation.

7 After we began our project, the Canadian Physiotherapy Association (CPA) published its official history, which contains some information on the beginnings of the profession during the Great War. See Joan Cleather, *Head, Heart and Hands. The Story of Physiotherapy in Canada* (Toronto: CPA, 1995).

8 Desmond Morton and Glen Wright, *Winning the Second Battle: Canadian Veterans and the Return to Civilian Life, 1915–1930* (Toronto: University of Toronto Press, 1987).

9 Veronica Strong-Boag and Anita Clair Fellman, "Introduction," in their *Rethinking Canada: The Promise of Women's History*, 2nd ed. (Toronto, 1991), 7.

10 Thébaud, "The Great War," 24.

NUMBER 61

Author's Note: This article is drawn from my master's thesis, *Nursing for the Grenfell Mission: Maternalism and Moral Reform in Northern Newfoundland and Labrador, 1894–1938* (St John's: Memorial University of Newfoundland, 1997), supervised by Dr Linda Kealey. Financial support was provided by the School of Graduate Studies and the Department of History at Memorial University, the Hannah Institute for the History of Medicine, and the Smallwood Centre for Newfoundland Studies at Memorial University.

1 See S.J.R. Noel, *Politics in Newfoundland* (Toronto: University of Toronto Press, 1971), 21.

2 For examples of heroic biographies of Grenfell, see J. Lennox Kerr, *Wilfred Grenfell: His Life and Work* (New York: Dodd, Mead, and Co., 1959); and Basil Miller, *Wilfred Grenfell: Labrador's Dogsled Doctor* (Grand Rapids: Zondervan, 1965). Scholarly treatments of the Grenfell Mission include Ronald Rompkey, *Grenfell of Labrador: A Biography* (Toronto: University of Toronto Press, 1992); Ronald Rompkey, ed., *Labrador Odyssey* (Montreal & Kingston: McGill-Queens University Press, 1996); John C. Kennedy, "The Impact of the Grenfell Mission on Southwestern Labrador Communities," *Polar Record* 24, no.150 (1988): 199–206; and Patricia O'Brien, ed., *The Grenfell Obsession: An Anthology* (St John's: Creative Publishers, 1992).

3 Percentages were calculated through analysis of the "Reports of the Staff Selection Committee," which appear in the July issues of *Among the Deep Sea Fishers*, 1914–38. Comprehensive staff lists are unavailable for the years prior to 1914.

4 Provincial Archives of Newfoundland and Labrador, MG 63, part 2, Personnel Files, "Ethel Currant," Shnyder to Spalding, 23 September 1935. Please note that all subsequent references, unless otherwise indicated, are drawn from this file.

5 Currant to Spalding, 11 May 1936.

6 Currant to Spalding, 21 May 1939.

7 Currant to Spalding, 14 July 1939.

8 Currant to Spalding, 13 February 1937.

9 Currant to Spalding, 13 May 1938, and Currant to Spalding, 11 May 1936.

10 Although mission workers occasionally came into contact with Native groups, the resident livyers and fishers were their top priority.

11 Currant to Spalding, 11 May 1936.

12 Currant to Spalding, 24 May 1941.

13 Mariana Valverde, "'When the Mother of the Race Is Free': Race, Reproduction, and Sexuality in First-Wave Feminism," in Franca Iacovetta and Mariana Valverde, eds., *Gender Conflicts: New Essays in Women's History* (Toronto: University of Toronto Press, 1992), 4.

14 See Nancy Wolock, *Women and the American Experience* (New York: Alfred A. Knopf, 1984), 296–300.

15 Currant to Spalding, 15 January 1939.

16 Ibid.

17 Ibid.

18 When moving to new facilities at Englee in 1937, Currant was ashamed to have to cart a "terrible looking object" (of furniture) that a local man had made for the mission. See Currant to Spalding, 31 October 1937. Recounting a recent conversation with a local woman, Currant remarked that "in more intelligent company, the remark might have passed for sarcasm." In the same letter, she lamented her inability to sleep while staying overnight on a house call: "[I]t was not long before those abominable creatures started calling on me." See Currant to Spalding, 24 April 1939.

19 Seabrook to Currant (Bridge), 18 June 1970, and Bridge to Seabrook, 21 July 1970.

NUMBER 62

1 Edward Shorter, *A Century of Radiology in Toronto* (Toronto: Wall and Emerson, 1995), 50.

2 Ibid., 55.

3 P.J. Fitzpatrick, "Obituaries," *Clinical Oncology* 6 (1994): 66.

4 Untitled five-page draft document regarding Vera Peters, in Toronto Hospital Archives Edward Shorter fonds, file 2.2.5.

5 "Pioneering Hodgkin's disease," M.V. Peters in *Cancer in Ontario* (1982), 17, in Toronto Hospital Archives, Edward Shorter fonds, file 2.2.5.

6 Wilma Blokhuis, "Medical Pioneer Changed Treatment of Two Diseases," loose clipping in Toronto Hospital Archives, Edward Shorter fonds, file 2.2.5.

7 Joan Hollobon, "Radiologist Dr. Vera Peters Warns Doc-

tors: 'Discard this Robe of Ridiculous Mystery,'" *Globe and Mail*, 6 May 1976.

8 "Obituary: Vera Peters Changes Cancer Therapy," *Toronto Star*, 3 October 1993, A12.

NUMBER 63

1 Norah Toole's correspondence is in the Archives and Special Collections, Harriet Irving Library, University of New Brunswick. I thank the Social Science and Humanities Research Council of Canada for a Women and Work Strategic Grant, 1989–92, which made this research possible, and Barry Toole, Brigid Toole Grant, Janet Toole, Mary MacBeath, Mary Flagg, Doreen Estey, and David Ainley for their assistance.

NUMBER 64

1 Alice Payne, interview with author, Calgary, 1998.

2 Alice Payne, *CBC News Magazine*, 18 March 1998. See also Marianne Ainley, "Last in the Field? Canadian Women Natural Scientists, 1815–1975" in Marianne Ainley, *Despite the Odds: Essays on Canadian Women and Science* (Montreal: Vehicle Press, 1990), 25–62.

3 Marianne Ainley, "Women's Work in Geology: A Historical Perspective on Gender Division in Canadian Science," *Geoscience Canada* 21 (1995): 140–2.

4 R. Santi, *Women in Mining: The Progress and the Problems* (Ottawa: Department of Energy, Mines and Resources, MR 152 Mineral Policy Series, 1976).

5 E. Tina Crossfield, *Pride and Vision: The History of the Canadian Institute of Mining, Metallurgy and Petroleum, 1898–1998* (Montreal: CIM, 1998), 123–6; and "Women's Multiple Connections to the Canadian Minerals Industry: A Pilot Study," CRIAW report, November 1998, 26.

6 Payne interview

7 Ainley, *Despite the Odds.*

8 "The Playmakers: Alberta's 50 Most Influential People," *Alberta Venture*, July/August 1998, A14.

NUMBER 65

1 The John B. Ridley Research Library is located 160 kilometres west of Thunder Bay on Highway 11. For more information, contact the John B. Ridley Research Library, Quetico Park (QP), Atikokan, ON, POT 1CO.

2 Interview of Dinnah Madsen by Shirley Peruniak, 16 July 1982, QP 82–15.

3 Interviews of Tempest Powell Benson by Shirley Peruniak, September 1980–81, QP 81-24.

NUMBER 66

Author's Note: An earlier version of this paper was prepared for the Historic Sites and Monuments Board of Canada meetings in June 1998. I wish to thank Marilyn Barber, Jean Barman, Gail Cuthbert Brandt for providing advice on certain issues in the history of women and work at that time. Margaret Conrad, Dianne Dodd, Marsha Hay Snyder, Luce Vermette provided helpful comments on the original paper and an anonymous reviewer has assisted in the writing of this version.

1 *The Pocket Oxford Dictionary of Current English*, 5th ed., 1969.

2 The 1891 Census listed six "Non-productive" occupations: Indian chiefs, members of religious orders, paupers and inmates of asylums, pensioners, retired people, and students. *Census of Canada*, 1891, vol. 2, Table 12.

3 Dominion Bureau of Statistics, Canada (hereafter DBS), *Canada Census, 1891, Instructions to Officers*, 13, 15.

4 Elizabeth Fox-Genovese, "Placing Women's History in History," *New Left Review* 133 (May-June 1982), 26.

5 F.H. Leacy, M.C. Urquhart, and K.A.H. Buckley, eds., *Historical Statistics of Canada*, 2nd ed. ([Ottawa]: Statistics Canada in joint sponsorship with the Social Science Federation of Canada, *c.* 1983), series D107–D122; Statistics Canada Website, Labour force and participation rates, 1998.

6 Leacy, Urquhart, and Buckley, *Historical Statistics of Canada*, 2nd ed., series A10–124.

7 Statistics Canada, *Women in Canada: A Statistical Report*,

Catalogue #89-503E (Ottawa: Minister of Supply and Services Canada, 1985), Table 18. At this time over 60 per cent of divorced and separated women were in the labour force.

8 DBS, *Ninth Census of Canada, 1951*, vol. 1, Table 13.

9 Veronica Strong-Boag, "Discovering the Home: The Last 150 Years of Domestic Work in Canada," in Paula Bourne, ed., *Women's Paid and Unpaid Work: Historical and Contemporary Perspectives* (Toronto: New Hogtown Press, 1985), 55; Meg Luxton, *More Than a Labour of Love: Three Generations of Women's Work in the Home* (Toronto: Women's Educational Press, 1980), 18–23.

10 Marilyn Barber, "Immigrant Domestic Servants in Canada," *Canada's Ethnic Groups*, no. 16, (n.p.: Canadian Historical Association, 1991).

11 Marjorie Griffin Cohen, *Women's Work, Markets, and Economic Development in Nineteenth-Century Ontario* (Toronto: University of Toronto Press, 1988), 132–4; and John Bullen, "Hidden Workers: Child Labour and the Family Economy in Late Nineteenth-Century Urban Ontario," in L.S. MacDowell and I. Radforth, eds., *Canadian Working Class History: Selected Readings* (Toronto: Canadian Scholars Press, 1992), 273.

12 Cohen, *Women's Work*, 8–10.

13 Gail Cuthbert Brandt, "'Weaving It together': Life Cycle and the Industrial Experience of Female Cotton Workers in Quebec, 1910-1950, " in Alison Prentice and Susan Mann Trofimenkoff, eds., *The Neglected Majority: Essays in Canadian Women's History*, vol. 2 (Toronto: McClelland and Stewart, 1985), 160–73 and Tables 1 and 2.

14 Graham S. Lowe, "Women, Work, and the Office: The Feminization of Clerical Occupations in Canada, 1901–1931,' in Veronica Strong-Boag and Anita Clair Fellman, eds., *Rethinking Canada: the Promise of Women's History*, 2nd ed.(Toronto: Copp Clark Pitman, 1991), 272; and Graham S. Lowe, "Mechanization, Feminization and Managerial Control in the Early Twentieth-Century Canadian Office," in Craig Heron and Robert Storey, eds., *On the Job: Confronting Labour Processes in Canada* (Montreal & Kingston: McGill-Queen's University Press, 1986), 197, Table 1.

15 Lowe, "Women, Work, and the Office," 275; and Jane Nokes and Lisa Singer, "*Women in Banking: A Case Study of the Scotiabank,*" chap. 79 in this volume.

16 Lowe, "Women, Work, and the Office," 277–8.

17 Moira Armour with Pat Staton, *Canadian Women in History: A Chronology*, 2nd ed. (Toronto: Green Dragon Press, 1990), 83.

18 Ruth Roach Pierson, "Canadian Women and the Second World War," *The Canadian Historical Association, Historical Booklet* No. 37 (Ottawa: 1983), 14.

19 Ruth Schwarz Cowan, *More Work for Mother: The Ironies of Household Technology from Open Hearth to Microwave* (n.p: HarperCollins, 1983), 63–9.

20 Joanne Vanek, "Time Spent in Housework," *Scientific American*, no. 231 (November 1974): 116-20 .

21 Statistics Canada, 1996 Census *Nation* tables. Website.

22 Alison Prentice et al., *Canadian Women: A History*, 2nd ed. (Toronto: Harcourt Brace & Co., 1996), 144–6.

23 Pierson, "Canadian Women and the Second World," 8–14, 18.

24 Pierson, "Canadian Women and the Second World War," 19–27.

25 Prentice et al, *Canadian Women*, 258–60; and Margaret E. McCallum, "Keeping Women in Their Place: The Minimum Wage in Canada, 1910–1925," in Laurel Sefton MacDowell and Ian Radforth, *Canadian Working Class History: Selected Readings* (Toronto: Canadian Scholars Press, 1992), 433–58.

26 Gail Cuthbert Brandt, "The Transformation of Women's Work in the Quebec Cotton Industry, 1920–1950," in Bryan D. Palmer, ed., The Character of Class Struggle (Toronto: McClelland and Stewart, 1986), p.127.

27 Canada, Minister of Industry, Statistics Canada, *Canada Year Book, 1997* (Ottawa: Statistics Canada, 1997), 207.

28 Prentice et al, *Canadian Women*, 354–6.

NUMBER 67

1 Mrs Patricia Salciccioli, family history papers, 1998.

2 Marjorie Kohli, "Young Immigrants to Canada," Web page (Waterloo, 1995): http//www.dcs.uwaterloo.ca/~marj/genealogy/homeadd.html.

3 Joy Parr, *Labouring Children: British Immigrant Apprentices to Canada, 1869–1924*, 2nd ed. (Toronto: University of Toronto Press, 1994, 27, 34.

4 Claudette Lacelle, *Urban Domestic servants in 19th Century Canada* (Ottawa: Minister of the Environment, 1987), 71–7.

5 Ibid., 131.

6 Ibid., 98–100.

7 Mrs Beeton, *Mrs. Beeton's Every Day Cookery and Housekeeping Book*, 1865 facsimile by Gallery Books, 1984, imprint of W.H. Smith Publishers Inc. New York.

8 Lacelle, *Urban Domestic servants*, 133.

NUMBER 68

1 Marilyn Barber, "Sunny Ontario for British Girls, 1900-30," in Jean Burnet, ed., *Looking into My Sister's Eyes: An Exploration in Women's History* (Toronto: Multicultural Historical Society of Ontario, 1986), 56.

2 In 1902, for instance, the federal government spent $205,000 on advertising in Britain, $161,000 in the United States, and $60,000 in the rest of Europe. Howard Palmer, *The Settlement of the West* (Calgary: Alberta University Press, 1977), 71.

3 Marilyn Barber emphasizes the exhausting nature of the work and lack of social contact for domestic workers. Magda Farni, in turn, indicates that in addition to the hard work and stigma attached to domestic work, servants were often vulnerable to sexual harassment and assault by employers and family members. See Barber, *Immigrant Domestic Servants in Canada*, Canada's Ethnic Group Booklet series no. 16 (Ottawa: Canadian Historical Association, 1991), 18, 26; and Farni, "'Ruffled' Mistresses and 'Discontented' Maids: Respectability and the Case of Domestic Service, 1880-1914," *Labour/Le Travail* no. 39 (Spring 1997): 85.

4 Barber, *Immigrant Domestic Servants*, 9.

5 Mariana Valverde examines the influence of the social purity movement on the federal government's immigration policy. She notes its perception that Anglo-Saxons were superior in moral character to other races. This pervasive view at the time had a direct influence on the type of domestics admitted to Canada during the early twentieth century. See Valverde, *The Age of Light, Soap, and Water* (Toronto: McClelland and Stewart, 1991), 104–7.

6 Barber, *Immigrant Domestic Servants*, 2.

7 H. Gordon Skilling, *Canadian Representation Abroad: From Agency to Embassy* (Toronto: Ryerson Press, 1945), 16.

8 Harold Troper, *Only Farmers Need Apply* (Toronto: Griffin House, 1972), 7.

9 Jean Bruce, *The Last Best West* (Toronto: Fitzhenry and Whiteside, 1976), 5.

10 Canada, Department of the Interior, *Annual Report* (1910), 60.

11 Ibid., (1915), 78; and Canada, Department of Immigration and Colonization, *Annual Report* (1925), 37.

12 Department of the Interior, "Canada: The Opportunities Offered in the Dominion for Domestic Servants" (Ottawa, 1910), 3.

13 Department of the Interior, "Housework in Canada: Duties, Wages, Conditions and Opportunities for Household Workers in the Dominion" (Ottawa, 1926), 5.

14 Ibid., 9.

15 Patrick Dunae, "Promoting the Dominion: Records and the Canadian Immigration Campaign, 1872–1915," *Archivaria* 9 (Winter 1984–85), 81.

16 Department of the Interior, *Annual Report* (Ottawa, 1921), 35–6; and 1922, 46.

17 National Archives of Canada, RG 76, Records of the Immigration Branch, vol. 643, file 990380, pt 1.

18 Ibid., volume 38, file 839, pt 2.

NUMBER 69

Author's Note: I wish to acknowledge the financial assistance of the Institute of Social and Economic Research, Memorial University of Newfoundland.

1 The census category "Fish Canners, Curers and Packers" was standardized in 1971 with the *Occupational Classification Manual: Census of Canada 1971* (Ottawa: Ministry of Industry and Trade and Commerce, 1971), and was updated in 1980 with *Standard Occupational Classification 1980* (Ottawa: Statistics Canada, Standards Division, 1980). The 1991 Census figures are based on the 1980 classifications. This category includes occupations directly involved in the processing of fish, but excludes supervisors and graders.

NUMBER 71

1 On garment manufacturing, see, for example, Jean du Berger and Jacques Mathieu, eds., *Les ouvrières de Dominion Corset à Québec, 1886–1988* (Sainte-Foy: Presses de l'université Laval, 1993); Robert McIntosh, "Sweated Labour: Female Needleworkers in Industrializing Canada," *Labour/Le travail* 24 (Fall 1993): 105–38; James D. Mochoruk and Donna Webber, "Women in the Winnipeg Garment Trade, 1929–45," in Mary Kinnear, ed., *First Day, Fighting Days: Women in Manitoba History* (Regina: Canadian Plains Research Center, University of Regina, 1987); and Mercedes Steedman, *Angels of the Workplace: Women and the Construction of Gender Relations in the Canadian Clothing Industry, 1890–1940* (Toronto: Oxford University Press, 1997).

There are no comprehensive studies of the dressmaking and millinery trades for the Canadian experience to compare with Wendy Gamber's book on the eastern United States: *The Female Economy: the Millinery and Dressmaking Trades, 1860–1930* (Urbana and Chicago: University of Illinois Press, 1997). However, a few works touch on the topic: Christina Bates, "Wearing Two Hats: An Interdisciplinary Approach to the Millinery Trade in Ontario, 1850–1950," *Material History Review* 51 (Spring 2000);

Jacqueline Giroux, *Yvette Brillon, femme de coeur et femme de têtes* (Longueuil: La société historique de Marigot de Longueuil, 1989); Christine Godin, "Les femmes au chapeau," and "Créer des chapeaux" *Cap-aux-diamants* 4 (Summer 1988): 25–8, 51–4; Joleen Gordon, *Handwoven Hats: A History of Straw, Wood and Rush Hats in Nova Scotia* (Halifax: The Nova Scotia Museum, 1981); Musée du Château Ramezy, *Les chapeaux feminins d'heir et d'aujourd'hui/Women's Hats Yesterday and Today* (Montreal: La société d'archeologie et de numismatique de Montréal, 1989); Mary Anne Poutanen, "For the Benefit of the Master: The Montreal Needle Trades during the Transition, 1820–42" (MA thesis, McGill University, 1985); and Dianne R. Smith, "Dressmaking Occupations in Edmonton, 1900–1930" (MSC thesis, University of Alberta, 1987).

2 A selected list of manuals includes Anna Ben-Ysuf, *Edwardian Hats: The Art of Millinery* (1909; reprint, Mendocino, Calif.: R.L. Shep, 1982); Julia Bottomley, *Practical Millinery Lessons* (New York: Illustrated Millinery Co., 1914); Violet Brand and Beatrice Mussared, *Millinery* (London: Sir Isaac Pitman and Sons, 1935); Edna Bryner, *Dressmaking and Millinery* (Cleveland, Ohio: Survey Committee of the Cleveland Foundation, 1916); Agnes Campbell, *Lessons in Millinery* (Winnipeg: Manitoba Farmers' Library, 1920); Isabella Innes, *Scientific Dressmaking and Millinery* (Toronto: I. Innes, 1913); and Women's Institute of Domestic Sciences Instruction Papers, *Millinery for Mature Women* (1923), *The Millinery Shop* (1923); *Millinery for Misses and Children* (1924), (Scranton, Pa.: "Women's Institute of Domestic Arts and Sciences).

3 Sources other than those used in this essay could include oral histories, mail-order catalogues, newspapers, fashion journals, and written personal accounts.

4 Marjorie Griffin Cohen, *Women's Work, Markets and Economic Developments in Nineteenth-Century Ontario* (Toronto: University of Toronto Press, 1988), 142–6; Gerald Tulchinsky, "Hidden among the Smokestacks: Toronto's Clothing Industry, 1871–1901," in David Keane and Colin

Read, eds., *Old Ontario: Essyas in Honour of J.M.S. Careless* (Toronto: Dundurn Press, 1990), 257–84. A classic study of the trend towards mass production of clothing is Claudia Kidwell and Margaret Christman, *Suiting Everyone: The Democratization of Clothing in America* (Washington D.C.: Smithsonian Press, 1974).

5 On changing millinery fashions, see Éliane Bolomier, *Cent ans de chapeau: 1870–1970* (Chazelle-sur-Lyon: Musée du chapeau de Chazelles-sur-Lyon, 1993); Dilys E. Blum, *Ahead of Fashion: Hats of the Twentieth Century* (Philadelphia: Philadelphia Museum of Art, 1993); Fiona Clark, *Hats* (London: Anchor Press, 1982); Madeleine Ginsburg, *The Hat: Trends and Traditions* (New York: Barron's Educational Series, 1990); Mildred Doris Lintner, "The Height of Fashion: The Construction of Ladies Fashion Headwear, 1830–1914" (PhD thesis, University of Michigan, 1979); and Florence Muller and Lydia Kamitsis, *Les chapeaux: Une histoire de tête* (Paris: Syros Alternatives, 1993).

6 E.M. Knox, *The Girl of the New Day* (Toronto: McClelland and Stewart, 1919). On the realities of the girl of the new day, see Veronica Strong-Boag, "The Girl of the New Day: Canadian Working Women in the 1920s," *Labour/Le travail* 4 (1979): 131–64.

7 *Vocational Opportunities in the Industries of Ontario: A Survey*, Bulletin 3: *Dressmaking and Millinery* (Toronto: printed by the Ryerson Press for the Ontario Department of Labour, 1920); Women's Institute, *Millinery Shop*; and Lorinda Perry, *Millinery as a Trade for Women* (New York: Longmans, Green and Co., 1916), 27–43.

8 Bureau of Statistics, *Fifth Census of Canada*, 1911, vol. 6, 166–7, 264–464; *Business and Professional Directory of all Cities in Ontario* (Ingersoll, Ont.: Union Publishing Co., 1902–3); Ontario Gazeteer and Directory (Ingersoll, Ont.: Union Publishing Co., 1905–6).

9 *Dry Goods Review*, 19 March 1914, 20.

10 Marjorie MacMurchy, *The Canadian Girl at Work: A Book of Vocational Guidance* (Toronto: A.T. Wilgress, 1919), 50.

11 "Royal Commission on Industrial Training and Technical Education," vol. 4, *Sessional Papers* (1913), 1974–5, 2015–159, 2347.

12 *Vocational Opportunities*, 14.

13 MacMurchy, *Canadian Girl*, 50–1.

14 *Dry Goods Review*, September 1924, 77.

15 "Royal Commission on Industrial Training," 1978; *Vocational Opportunities*, 14–15; *Wages and Hours of Labour in Canada*, 1920–1928, Department of Labour, Report 12 (Ottawa: F.A. Acland, 1929), 100–1; Knox, *Girl of the New Day*, 240; MacMurchy, *Canadian Girl*, 51–2; National Council of Women of Canada, *Women of Canada: Their Life and Work* (1901), 100–1; and Kathryn McPherson, *Bedside Matters: The Transformation of Canadian Nursing, 1900–1990* (Toronto: Oxford University Press, 1996), 136.

16 MacMurchy, *Canadian Girl*, 109; *Vocational Opportunities*, 16; and Strong-Boag, "Girl of New Day," 146–7.

17 Cohen, *Women's Work*, 119.

18 *Vocational Opportunities*, 15; and Strong-Boag, "Girl of New Day," 137.

19 *1911 Census*, 166–7; Bureau of Statistics, *Sixth Census of Canada, 1921*, 640–1; and Tulchinsky, "Hidden among the Smokestacks," 261, 279.

20 *Vocational Opportunities*, 15; and McPherson, *Bedside Matters*, 136.

21 *Dry Goods Review*, March 1923, 67.

22 *1911 Census*, 166–7, 264.

23 The *Dry Goods Review* and the *Canadian Milliner* reported frequently on the wholesale millinery business, see also *Vocational Opportunities*, 11.

24 *Dry Goods Review*, 1 January 1912, 152–4.

25 There are few references in secondary sources to this major change in women's hat materials and construction in the early twentieth century. A discussion of the problems with the low prices of cloches by a wholesale milliner appeared in the *Dry Goods Review*, December 1932.

26 Correspondence with Lyn and Dave Dennis, Petrolia (on file, Canadian Museum of Civilization); *Advertiser-Topic* (Petrolia), 2 December 1946 and 30 May 1968; *Sarnia*

Observer, 14 March 1919; Edward Phelps, *Petrolia 1874–1974* (Petrolia, Ont.: Petrolia Print and Litho Co., 1974), 10, 25, 95; and Lambton County Archives and Library (Wyoming, Ont.), Newton Hat Shop File, 6DF (letters), 9ED-JDF (account book).

27 *Dry Goods Review*, April 1933, 22. Unlike many of her sister milliners, Gertrude Mantell had a long millinery career. She closed her shop in 1958 after over forty years in the millinery business.

28 Ibid.

29 *1921 Census*, vol. 4, xli; and Bureau of Statistics, *Seventh Census of Canada, 1931*, vol. 7, 496; vol. 10, 505, 513.

NUMBER 72

Author's Note: The author would like to thank co-curators Naomi Sawada, Minnie Hattori, and Suzi Nitta Petersen; Dr Midge Ayukawa and Dr. Michael Wilson for their excellent advice and editing assistance; the staff and volunteers at the Japanese-Canadian National Museum and Archives Society; and the individuals who shared their stories and assisted us with this project: Ruth Hamaguchi, Sayoko Hattori, Bev Inouye, Tokuko Inouye, Yosh Kariatsumari, Ayako Kohara, Kimiko Matsunaga, Chizu Nakamura, Yayoi Negishi, Mary Ohara, Kimiyo Oshikawa, Mary Otto, Chie Oya, Ritsuko Saimoto, Marie Saito, Mary Seki, Joe Tatebe, and Kay Tatebe. Dedicated to preserving and presenting the history and experience of the Japanese-Canadian community, the Japanese-Canadian National Museum and Archives is located in Vancouver, B.C., and is awaiting construction of its new home in the National Nikkei Heritage Centre in Burnaby, B.C., in 2000.

1 The term Nikkei refers to any persons who are of Japanese origin; I use the terms Nikkei and Japanese-Canadian interchangeably throughout this paper.

2 Telephone interview with Kay Tatebe, June 1996.

3 Dr Michiko (Midge) Ayukawa, "Yōsai: Western Sewing," *Nikkei Images* (newsletter of the Japanese-Canadian National Museum and Archives) 1 (July 1996): 3–4.

4 "Report of the Survey of Second-Generation Japanese in British Columbia," published by the Committee for the Second-Generation Japanese in British Columbia, the Canadian Japanese Association; Japanese-Canadian National Museum and Archives Collection, Campbell, Brazier, Fisher and McMaster Barristers and Solicitors, 97/086.

5 Interview with Tokuko Inouye, June 1997.

6 *The New Canadian*, 22 August 1941, 3

7 Mary Otto, personal correspondence, June 1996.

8 Interview with Sayoko Hattori, June, 1996.

9 Interview with Ayako Kohara, June, 1996.

10 Charles H. Young and Helen R. Reid, *The Japanese Canadians*, (Toronto: University of Toronto Press, 1938), 74.

11 Mary Otto, personal correspondence, June 1996.

12 Marie Saito, personal correspondence, June 1996.

NUMBER 73

Author's Note: I would like to thank the following individuals for their assistance: Mr Réne Phillipe Hecht for donating Federica's scrapbook to the Royal Ontario Museum (ROM); Angelina Fabbro for her time and archives now at the ROM; and Mrs Leo Harrison for permission to use the photograph taken by the late Leo Harrison.

1 Luigi Settembrini, "From Haute Couture to Pret-à-Porter," in *The Italian Metamorphosis, 1943–1968*, organized by Germano Celant (New York: Guggenheim Museum, 1994), 485–7.

2 Bettina Ballard, *In My Fashion* (New York: David McKay, 1960), 250.

3 Settembrini, "From Haute Couture," 488.

4 Ornella Morelli, "The International Success and Domestic Debut of Postwar Italian Fashion," in *Italian Fashion*, vol. 1 *The Origins of High Fashion and Knitwear*, ed. Gloria Bianchino, (Milano: Electra, New York: Rizzoli International Publications, 1987), 62.

5 Settembrini, "From Haute Couture," 486.

6 Susan Porter Benson, *Counter Cultures: Saleswomen, Man-*

agers, and Customers in American Department Stores 1890–1940 (Urbana and Chicago: University of Illinois Press, 1986), 105.

7 Interviews with Angelina Fabbro, 13 October 1988 and 19 May 1999.

8 This information was gathered from Federica. However, Angelina informed me that her job was actually more like that of the head saleswomen and did not involve designing.

9 Interview with Angelina Fabbro.

10 Interview with Federica Hecht, 13 June 1992.

11 Interview with Angelina Fabbro. Her cousin was Teresa Massarelli. Her clients purchased their own fabric in Bari, at a store called Minuzzi. The textiles were Italian, from Como. Angelina attended a cutting school run by Professere Panaro, in Bari.

12 Interview with Mrs E.G. Burton, 22 August 1990.

13 The Association of Canadian Couturiers (ACC) was a national organization that was founded in Montreal in 1954, with the aim of promoting Canadian textiles through fashions designed by Canadian couturiers. Angelina became a member. See Alexandra Palmer, "The Myth and Reality of Haute Couture: Consumption, Social Function and Taste in Toronto, 1945–1963" (PhD thesis, University of Brighton, 1995), chaps. 6 and 7.

14 Interviews with Federica Hecht and Angelina Fabbro.

15 Interview with Jeanie Hersenhoren, 4 March 1991.

16 Ibid.

17 Interview with Angelina Fabbro.

18 Interview with John Artibello, 15 February 1993.

19 Angelina Scrapbook, Olive Dickason, "Recipe for High Fashion," *The Globe Magazine*, 27 May 1961, 20. These papers are currently with Angelina Fabbro, but the ROM is in negotiation to acquire them.

20 Interview with Angelina Fabbro.

21 Interviews with Federica Hecht, and John Artibello.

22 Interview with Angelina Fabbro.

23 Interviews with Cornelia Berceller, 14 March 1991, Federica Hecht and John Artibello.

24 Interview with Federica Hecht.

25 Interview with John Artibello.

26 Angelina Scrapbook, "The Difficult Road to $10,000 a Year," *Globe and Mail*, 4 July 1963.

27 Angelina Scrapbook, "Canadian Women to Show New Chic in Dressing for Latest Visit of Royalty," *Globe and Mail*, 13 June 1959.

28 Angelina Scrapbook, Lillian Foster, "She'll Be Seen with the Queen," *Telegram*, 23 June 1959.

29 Interview with Federica Hecht.

30 Interview with Jeanie Hersenhoren.

31 Federica Scrapbook, newspaper clippings, unidentified photo.

32 Angelina Scrapbook, newspaper clipping.

33 Interview with Federica Hecht. Mrs George Marshall began "Marina Creations," named after the Duchess of Kent, in 1955. It encouraged a group of approximately sixty skilled female workers to use hand labour on goods that were pre-designed by local artists. See Florence Schill, "New Industry to Help Homebound," *Globe and Mail*, 17 September 1955, 14; and "Marina Creations," *Globe and Mail*, 24 November 1960, 17.

34 Angelina Scrapbook. Newspaper clipping, "Model Program Girls."

35 Examples include 1952 Cornelia fashion show for the Ladies Auxiliary of Toronto Hotel Proprietors, on the Roof Garden of the Royal York Hotel, with Rosemary Boxer commentating, *Globe and Mail*, 16 January 1952, 10; Rodolphe's 5 February 1958 fashion show at the Royal York Hotel, sponsored by the Young Women's Canadian Club, *Globe and Mail*, 7 February 1958, 8 (photo); Federica's second solo fashion presentation in October at the Crystal Ballroom Royal York Hotel in aid of charity, Federica Scrapbook.

36 Federica Scrapbook, undated article by Olive Dickason.

37 Federica Scrapbook, "Designers First Sportswear Shown in Summer Collection," undated clipping. Prices: shorts

$ 3.95; shirt, $6.95; pedal-pushers, $7.95; slim jims, $10.95; car coat, $17.95.

38 Federica Scrapbook, Olive Dickason, "Figures Play a Prominent Role in Custom Knits," *The Globe Magazine*, 24 December 1960,

39 Interview with Angelina Fabbro. See her Scrapbook: Heather Rodger, "Shifts, Crinolines Little Girl 'Looks.'" *Toronto Daily Star*, 8 May 1962; and article Helen Palmer, "Now Pre-Teens Have Fashion "Collection," *Toronto Star*.

40 Angelina Scrapbook, unidentified clipping. She designed a dress and Cornelia a suit.

NUMBER 75

1 Michele Martin, "Capitalizing on the 'Feminine Voice,'" *Canadian Journal of Communication* 14:42–62.

NUMBER 76

1 This quotation and much of the biographical information used in this essay came from a personal communication with author, 12 May 1999.

2 See, for example, Dorothy Harley Eber with Pitseolak Ashoona, *Pitseolak: Pictures Out of My Life* (Montreal: Design Collaborative Books, in association with Oxford University Press, Toronto, 1971); and Peter Pitseolak and Dorothy Harley Eber, *People from Our Side*, 2nd ed. (Montreal & Kingston: McGill-Queen's University Press, 1993).

3 For work by Ann Meekitjuk Hanson, see "Your Inuit Hosts," in *The Baffin Handbook: Travelling in Canada's Eastern Arctic* (Iqaluit: Nortext Publishing Corporation, 1993); "Good Memories," in *Inuit Women Artists, Voices from Cape Dorset* (Hull: Canadian Museum of Civilization, 1994); and various articles on Inuit culture, music, and language in *The Nunavut Handbook: Travelling in Canada's Arctic* (Iqaluit: Nortext Multimedia, 1998).

NUMBER 77

1 Although various sources give different dates of birth for Macbeth, ranging from 1878 to 1883, the official register of births in the Philadelphia Municipal Archives reveals that she was born on 6 November 1878.

2 The "New Woman" was a nineteenth-century term coined to refer to the undomesticated career woman who worked outside the home, travelled without a male companion, and was sexually liberated. The figure of the New Woman threatened those in patriarchal societies who feared the changing role of women. See Carol Gerson, *A Purer Taste: The Writing and Reading of Fiction in English in Nineteenth-Century Canada* (Toronto: University of Toronto Press, 1989), 148–9; and Misao Dean, *Practising Feminity: Domestic Realism and the Performance of Gender in Early Canadian Fiction* (Toronto: University of Toronto Press, 1998), 57–76. For Macbeth's desire to be a New Woman, see her *Boulevard Career* (Toronto: Kingswood House, 1957), especially 32 and 69.

3 Madge Macbeth fonds, National Archives of Canada (NA), MG30 D52, vol. 2, Correspondence-1924. See also Constance Skinner's review, "Wanted – A Literature," in *The Literary Review*, a supplement of the *New York Evening Post*, 5 January 1924, 419.

4 Some Canadian writers who lived and worked elsewhere are Arthur Heming, Constance Lindsay Skinner, Sara Jeannette Duncan, Charles G.D. and Theodore G. Roberts, Frank Packard, Robert Service, Basil King, Arthur Stringer, Bliss Carman, A.J.M. Smith, and Leon Edel. The expatriation of Canadian literary talent continues today. See Graham Carr, "'All We North Americans': Literary Culture and the Continentalist Ideal, 1919–1939," *American Review of Canadian Studies* 17 (1987): 145–57, especially 151.

5 For more on the history of literary copyright in Canada, see Lyn Harrington, *Syllables of Recorded Time: The Story of the Canadian Authors Association 1921–1981* (Toronto: Simon and Pierre, 1981); and George L. Parker *The Beginnings of the Book Trade in Canada* (Toronto: University of Toronto Press, 1985).

6 Madge Macbeth, "A New Psychological Approach to Home-Keeping is Needed," *Saturday Night*, 15 April 1944,

38; and "Raise Her Status and the Worker May Return to the House," ibid., 22 April 1944, 32. For an example of an early Canadian writer employing the metaphor of nation as family, see Agnes Machar [Fidelis], "Patriotism Versus Cosmopolitanism," *The Week*, 7 October 1886, 716.

7 See Macbeth, *Boulevard Career*, 30–1, 16–17. See also a short autobiographical piece written by Macbeth for the *Ottawa Journal*, 13 July 1950, titled "Ottawa Woman's Serial Story Begins in *The Journal* Saturday," available in the Madge Macbeth fonds, vol. 15, Scrapbook 1941–1950.

8 For Anglo-American definitions of feminisms, see Maggie Humm, *The Dictionary of Feminist Theory*, (Columbus: Ohio State University Press, 1990).

9 Madge Macbeth, "'Until Love Dies' or the Courts Us Do Part," *Chatelaine* 1 (November 1928): 4.

10 For a complete list of Macbeth's books, see Carole Gerson's entry on Macbeth in W.H. New, ed., *Dictionary of Literary Biography*, vol. 92: *Canadian Writers, 1890–1920* (1990). Macbeth also wrote and published a great number of short stories, serialized novels, and articles, as well as a few poems. She kept a ledger of her submissions to periodicals between 1907 and 1918; see her papers at the City of Ottawa Archives, Collection MG 59, vol. 5, file 10. See also the *Canadian Periodical Index* for her works from 1920 to 1964.

NUMBER 78

1 Jill Downie, *A Passionate Pen: The Life and Times of Faith Fenton* (Toronto: HarperCollins, 1996); Barbara M. Freeman, *Kit's Kingdom: The Journalism of Kathleen Blake Coleman* (Ottawa: Carleton University Press 1989); Freeman, "Framing Feminine/Feminist: English-Language Press Coverage of the Hearings of the Royal Commission on the Status of Women in Canada, 1968," *International Journal of Canadian Studies* 11 (Spring 1995): 11–31; and Nancy Adamson, Linda Briskin, and Margaret McPhail, *Feminist Organizing for Change: The Contemporary Women's Movement in Canada* (Toronto: University of

Toronto Press 1988), chapter 2.

2 Freeman, *Kit's Kingdom*, chaps. 2, 3, and 5; Coleman quotation on 144–5.

3 Fenton quotation in *Empire* (20 May 1893), 7. Coleman quotation in *Mail*, 18 August 1893, 5; Freeman, *Kit's Kingdom*, 144–8; Downie, *A Passionate Pen*, 180, 209.

4 Paul Rutherford, *A Victorian Authority: The Daily Press in Late Nineteenth Century Canada* (Toronto: University of Toronto Press, 1982), 81; Minko Sotiron, *From Politics to Profit: The Commercialization of Canadian Daily Newspapers, 1890–1920* (Montreal & Kingston: McGill-Queen's University Press, 1997), chap. 8; and Daniel Schiller, *Objectivity and the News* (Philadelphia: University of Pennsylvania Press, 1981).

5 On practice, see Curtis D. MacDougall, *Newsroom Problems and Policies* (New York: Dover Publications, 1963), chaps. 1, 2, and 6. For analysis, see Teun A. Van Dijk, *News as Discourse* (Hillsdale, N.J.: Lawrence Erlbaum Associates, 1988).

6 Freeman, "Framing Feminine/Feminist," 15.

7 Barbara M. Freeman interview with Yvonne Crittenden, Toronto, 25 September 1995. On the *Telegram*'s politics, see Ron Poulton, *The Paper Tyrant: John Ross Robertson of the Toronto Telegram* (Toronto: Clarke, Irwin, 1971), 70–147; and Maggie Siggins, *Bassett* (Toronto: James Lorimer, 1979), chap. 6.

8 Siggins, "Man the enemy is downtown," *Telegram*, 1 May 1970; and Barbara M. Freeman interview with Maggie Siggins, Montreal, 25 August 1995.

9 Freeman interview with Crittenden; and Crittenden, "One report Ottawa can't ignore," *Telegram*, 1 October 1968.

10 Maggie Siggins, "Gents open doors for feminist philosophy," *Telegram*, 28 April 1970; and Freeman interview with Siggins.

NUMBER 79

1 J. Douglas Gibson and Joseph Schull, *The Scotiabank Story: A History of The Bank of Nova Scotia, 1832–1982*

(Toronto: Macmillan, 1982).

2 The Bank of Nova Scotia Archives, Circular and Manual
Control – Manuals, series 1, files 1–17.

3 "Next – The Lady Bank Manager?," *Scotiabanker*, Spring-
Summer, 1953, 1–3.

4 Ibid.

5 "Marcellus and Giles: A Banking Tradition Shattered,"
Scotiabanker, September-October 1961, 38–9.

6 Ibid.

7 "Task Force Studies Advancement of Women at Scotiabank," *Scotiabanker*, October 1993, 8.

8 Ibid.

NUMBER 81

1 D. Fraser, "Elsie Gregory MacGill: Aeronautical Engineer,"
Archivist 14 (January–February 1987): 8–9.

2 Ibid.

3 Elsie MacGill, copies of letters to the family, 7 and 27 May
1938, National Archives of Canada (NA), MG 31 K 7, Elsie
Gregory MacGill Papers.

4 "Girl Designs New Trainer," *New York Times*, 13 October
1940.

5 G. Burkowski, *Can-Car: A History 1912–1992* (Thunder
Bay: Bombardier, 1995).

6 Elsie MacGill, draft of speech to West Algoma Local
Council of Women, NA, MG 31 K 7, vol. 15, file 11. See also
"Plane 'Plant Rumors False and Unjust' Says Miss
MacGill," *Port Arthur-News Chronicle*, 28 March 1942.

7 Ibid.

8 Fraser, "Elsie MacGill," 9.

9 See, for example, "Girl Engineer to Speak Here," *Globe and
Mail*, 1 February 1940; "Aircraft Boss," *The Standard Pho-
toNews*, 27 July 1940; and "Canadian Woman is Aeronautical Engineer," *The Evening Telegraph*, 20 November 1942.

10 For a discussion of representations of women working in
war industries at Canadian Car, see essay #84 in this volume.

11 "She Debates Plane Design Just Like Recipe for Pie," *Star*,
8 February 1940, 4.

12 Ibid.

13 James Montagnes, "Girl Designs New Trainer," *New York
Times*, 13 October 1940.

14 "Queen of the Hurricanes. Elsie MacGill," no author cited,
NA, MG 31 K 7, vol. 16, file 7, 17–21.

15 Ibid., 21.

16 Ibid. It is interesting to note from our oral history
research (see #84) that none of the Canadian Car workers
remembers such an event taking place. It was more likely
the figment of the cartoonist's imagination employed to
feminize the image of MacGill.

17 John J. Green, "Obituary-Elizabeth (Elsie) Gregory
MacGill, FC AS1, 1905–1980." unpublished text from
Memorial Service held in Knox College Chapel, University
of Toronto, Wednesday, 26 November 1980, University of
Toronto Archives.

18 See correspondence between Elsie MacGill and L.D. Gard-
ner, secretary of the Institute of Aeronautical Sciences,
May–June 1936, NA, MG 31, K 7, vol. 15, file 10.

19 See, for example, Elizabeth M. MacGill "Position of
Women in Canada in the Engineering Profession," *Saturday Night*, 19 October 1946; and newspaper reports on her
address to Regina B and P Club, "Women 'Natural' Engineers," University of Toronto Archives, Department of
Graduate Records, Elsie Gregory MacGill.

20 Elsie Gregory MacGill, "A Blueprint for Madame Prime
Minister," address to the 14th Biennial Convention of the
Federation of Business and Professional Women's Clubs,
Toronto, Ontario, 27 July 1954.

21 Ibid., 4.

22 Alison Prentice et al., *Canadian Women: A History* (Toronto: Harcourt Brace, 1996), 416– 19.

23 Government of Canada, *Report of the Royal Commission
on the Status of Women in Canada* (Ottawa: Information
Canada, 1970), 281, 287, 303–5, 413, 429.

24 Ibid., 429.

25 Green, "Obituary," 4.

26 Ibid., 1.

27 Elsie G.M. MacGill, *My Mother the Judge* (Toronto: Ryerson Press, 1953).

28 "In Memoriam. Elsie Gregory MacGill, 1905–1980," no author cited, Memorial Service Program, University of Toronto, 26 November 1980, 4.

NUMBER 82

1 Interview with Jenny (Whitehead) Pike and Dorothy Robertson conducted by Donna Porter, 19 September 1998.

2 Edward R. Paquette, and Charles G. Bainbridge, *Honours and Awards: Canadian Naval Forces, World War II* (Vancouver: Project Gallantry, 1986), 356.

3 Ibid.

4 National Archives of Canada, MG 30 E 391, Adelaide Sinclair Papers, newsclippings, 1942–43, Report re the Women's Royal Canadian Naval Service Organizations and Problems, c. December 1945.

NUMBER 83

1 For more on this topic, see Terresa McIntosh, "Other Images of War: Canadian Women War Artists of the First and Second World Wars" (MA thesis, Carleton University, 1990).

NUMBER 84

1 G. Burkowski, *Can-Car: A History 1912–1992* (Thunder Bay: Bombardier, 1995), 85.

2 Sherna Berger Gluck, *Rosie the Riveter Revisited: Women, the War, and Social Change* (New York: Penguin, 1988), xv.

3 K. Anderson and D.C. Jack, "Learning to Listen: Interview Techniques and Analyses," in S. Gluck and D. Patai, eds., *Women's Words: The Feminist Practice of Oral History* (New York: Routledge, 1991), 11.

4 Ibid., 24.

5 See T. Tronrud and A.E. Epp, eds., *Thunder Bay from Rivalry to Unity* (Thunder Bay: Thunder Bay Historical Museum Society, 1995).

6 T. Tronrud, "Building the Industrial City," in ibid., 113.

7 Burkowski, *Can-Car*, 6, 23.

8 Ibid., 28.

9 Ibid., 49, 53, 74.

10 For a discussion of the national trend, see Ruth Pierson, *"They're Still Women After All": The Second World War and Canadian Womanhood* (Toronto: McClelland and Stewart, 1986).

11 Evidence from the oral histories indicates that awareness of this hiring policy led at least some women to not disclose that they were married or had children when applying for jobs at CanCar, to improve their chances of being hired.

12 Burkowski, *Can-Car*, 85.

13 Ibid., 85.

14 CanCar Interview #12, 27 January 1997.

15 Burkowski, *Can-Car*, 85.

16 CanCar Interview #4, 13 November 1996.

17 Burkowski, *Can-Car*, 96.

18 E. MacGill, draft of speech to West Algoma Local Council of Women, 27 March 1938, National Archives of Canada (NA), MG 31 K 7, Elsie Gregory MacGill Papers.

19 Howard Reid,"People," *Chronicle-Journal*, 27 September 1996, A2. Our thanks to Mr Reid for his interest in, and support of, the project.

20 Many of the women interviewed have expressed gratitude for the interest and attention being given to their war work and life stories through the project. As most have noted, family, friends, and professional researchers have rarely asked them about their wartime contributions and reflections.

21 Project files include copies of Staff House Rules and Regulations, as well as minutes of various Wartime Housing Incorporated meetings related to the establishment and management of wartime housing for women workers. See NA, Defence Construction Limited Records, RG 83, vol. 70, Wartime Housing Ltd., parts 1 and 2; NA, Defence Construction Limited Records, RG 83, vol. 71, Wartime Housing Limited Manual Rules and Procedure, "Staff House

Rules and Regulations," 1–19 to 1–22.

22 Burkowski, *Can-Car*, 88.

23 In response to queries about her pay rates while at the plant, one respondent briefly excused herself, climbed up on a stool, and proceeded to rummage about on the top of a tall kitchen cupboard. With an exclamation of "Ah, there it is!" she picked up and dusted off a small green bundle wrapped in a faded orange elastic band. Much to our delight, the "bundle" contained the complete set of her CanCar pay stubs, from the first day and shift worked to her last day on the job. The pay stubs contain a variety of useful information, from pay rates and their increase through time, to hours and shifts worked, the departments worked in, pay deductions for Victory Bonds, and so on.

24 For a more detailed discussion of the *Aircrafter*, see H. Smith and P. Wakewich, "Representations of Women and Wartime Work in the Canadian Car and Foundry Company Newspaper, *The Aircrafter*," *Papers & Records* 25 (1997): 64-77; and "'Beauty and the Helldivers': Representing Women's Work and Identities in a Warplant Newspaper," *Labour/Le travail*, Fall 1999, 71–107.

25 See G. Evans, *John Grierson and the National Film Board: The Politics of Wartime Propaganda, 1939–1945* (Toronto: University of Toronto Press, 1984).

26 See Smith and Wakewich, "Representations of Women and Wartime Work."

27 See, for example Pierson, *"They're Still Women After All"*; J. Sangster, *Earning Respect: The Lives of Working Women in Small Town Ontario, 1920–1960* (Toronto: University of Toronto Press, 1995); M. Susan Bland, "Henrietta the Homemaker, and 'Rosie the Riveter': Images of Women in Advertising in Maclean's Magazine, 1939–50," *Atlantis* 8

(Spring 1983): 8; Y. Mathews-Klein, "How They Saw Us: Images of Women in National Film Board Films of the 1940s and 1950s," *Atlantis* 4 (Spring 1979): 18–33; and S J. Wilson, "The Changing Image of Women in Canadian Mass Circulating Magazines, 1930–70," *Atlantis* 2 (Spring 1977): 34–44.

28 D. Montgomerie, "Reassessing Rosie: World War II, New Zealand Women and the Iconography of Femininity," *Gender and History* 8 (April 1996): 108. See also Smith and Wakewich, "'Beauty and the Helldivers.'"

29 We would like to thank Tory Tronrud of the Thunder Bay Historical Museum and Gordon Burkowski of Bombardier Inc. (formerly CanCar) for their assistance in locating archival material for the project, and retired newspaper columnist Howard Reid, whose newspaper article on the project generated numerous contacts for the oral history interviews. We would also like to acknowledge the work of research assistants Tina Davidson and Mary Maurice, who aided with library research and cataloguing of materials. Our biggest debt of gratitude is, of course, to the women workers themselves, who have been generous with their time, their memories, and their memorabilia, and who have provided ongoing support and encouragement for the project.

NUMBER 85

1 Clyde Sanger, *Lotta and the Unitarian Service Committee Story* (Toronto: Stoddard, 1986).

2 National Archives of Canada, Records of the Unitarian Service Committee of Canada, MG 28, I 322, vol. 244, file "Speeches–1973."

Selected Readings

LIVING WOMEN'S LIVES

Baillargeon, Denyse. *Making Do*: *Women, Family and Home in Montreal during the Great Depression*. Trans. Yvonne Klein. Waterloo: Wilfrid University Press, 1999.

Boutilier, Beverly, and Alison Prentice. *Creating Historical Memory: English-Canadian Women and the Work of History*. Vancouver: University of British Columbia Press, 1997.

Cook, Sharon Anne. *"Through Sunshine and Shadow": The Woman's Christian Temperance Union, Evangelicalism and Reform in Ontario 1874–1930*. Montreal & Kingston: McGill-Queen's University Press, 1995.

Danylewycz, Marta. *Taking the Veil: An Alternative to Marriage, Motherhood and Spinsterhood in Quebec, 1840–1920*. Toronto: McClelland and Stewart, 1987.

Dumont, Micheline, and Nadia Fahmy-Eid, eds. *Les Couventines: L'educationdes filles au Québec dans les con-grégations religieuses enseignantes, 1840–1960*. Montreal: Boreal Express, 1986.

Heap, Ruby, and Alison Prentice, eds. *Gender and Education in Ontario: An Historical Reader*. Toronto: Canadian Scholars Press, 1991.

Kinnear, Mary. *In Subordination: Professional Women Women 1870–1970*. Montreal & Kingston,: McGill-Queen's University Press, 1995.

Lang, Marjory. *Women Who Made the News: Female Journalists in Canada, 1880–1945*. Montreal & Kingston, McGill-Queen's University Press, 1999.

Lévesque, Andrée. *Making and Breaking the Rules: Women in Quebec, 1919–39*. Trans. Y. Klein. Toronto: McClelland and Stewart, 1994.

– *La norme et les deviantes: Les femmes du Québec pendant l'entre-deux guerres*. Montreal: Les éditions du Remue-Ménage, 1989.

MacMillan, Carrie, Lorraine McMullen, and Elizabeth Waterson. *Silenced Sextet: Six Nineteenth-Century Canadian Women Novelists*. Montreal & Kingston, McGill-Queen's university Press, 1993.

Murray, Hilda. *More than Fifty Percent: Women's Life in a Newfoundland Outport, 1900–1950*. St John's: Breakwater Books, 1979.

Sangster, Joan. *Earning Respect: The Lives of Working Women in Small-Town Ontario, 1920–1960*. Toronto: University of Toronto Press, 1995.

Smart, Patricia. *Writing in the Father's House: The Emergence of the Feminine in the Quebec Literary Tradition*. Toronto: University of Toronto Press, 1990.

Strong-Boag, Veronica, and Carole Gerson. *Paddling Her Own Canoe: The Times and Texts of E. Pauline Johnson, Tekahionwake*. Toronto: University of Toronto Press, 2000.

Tippett, Maria. *By a Lady: Celebrating Three Centuries of Art by Canadian Women*. Toronto: Penguin Books Canada, 1992.

FAMILY AND THE HOME

Arnup, K. *Education for Motherhood: Advice for Mothers in 20th Century Canada*. Toronto: University of Toronto Press, 1994.

Arnup, K., R. Pierson, and A. Lévesque, eds. *Delivering Motherhood: Maternal Ideologies and Practices in the 19th and 20th Centuries.* London: Routledge, 1990.

Baillargeon, D. *Ménageres au temps de la Crise.* Montreal: Les Editions du Rémue-Ménage, 1991. Translated by Y. Klein under the title *Making Do: Women, Family and Home in Montreal during the Great Depression.* Waterloo: Wilfrid Laurier University Press, 1999.

Comacchio, C.R. *Nations Are Built of Babies: Saving Ontario's Mothers and Children, 1900–40.* Montreal & Kingston: McGill-Queen's University Press, 1993.

– *The Infinite Bonds of Family: Domesticity in Canada, 1850–1940.* Toronto: University of Toronto Press, 1999. Kealey, L., ed. *A Not Unreasonable Claim: Women and Reform in Canada, 1880s–1920s.* Toronto: Canadian Women's Educational Press, 1979.

Lemieux, D., and L. Mercier. *Les femmes au tournant du siecle: 1880–1940: Ages de la vie, maternité, et quotidien.* Quebec: Institut québécois de recherche sur la culture, 1989.

Lévesque, A. *Le Norme et les déviantes: Des femmes au Québéc pendant l'entre-deux guerres.* Montreal: Les Editions du Rémue-Ménage, 1989. Translated by Y. Klein, under the title *Making and Breaking the Rules: Women in Quebec, 1919–1939.* Toronto: McClelland and Stewart, 1994.

Owram, D. *Born at the Right Time: A History of the Baby Boom Generation.* Toronto: University of Toronto Press, 1996.

Richardson, T.R. *The Century of the Child: The Mental Hygiene Movement and Social Policy in The United States and Canada.* Albany, N.Y.: State University of New York Press, 1989.

Strong Boag, V. *The New Day Recalled: Lives of Girls and Women in English Canada, 1919–1939.* Markham, Ont.: Penguin, 1988.

Sutherland, N. *Children in English Canadian Society, 1880–1920: Framing the Twentieth Century Consensus.* Toronto: University of Toronto Press, 1976; reissued by Wilfrid Laurier University Press, 2000.

– *Growing Up: Childhood in English Canada from the Great War to the Age of Television.* Toronto: University of Toronto, 1997.

TEACHING AND LEARNING

Arnup, Katherine. *Education for Motherhood: Advice for Mothers in 20th Century Canada.* Toronto: University of Toronto Press, 1994.

Axelrod, Paul, and John G. Reid, eds., *Youth, University and Canadian Society: Essays in the Social History of Higher Education.* Montreal & Kingston: McGill-Queen's University Press, 1989.

Barman, Jean, Neil Sutherland and J. Donald Wilson, eds. *Children, Teachers and Schools in the History of British Columbia.* Calgary, 1995.

Compton, Brouwer. Ruth, *New Women for God: Canadian Presbyterian Women and India Missions, 1876–1914.* Toronto: University of Toronto Press, 1990.

Cook, A. Sharon. *Through Sunshine and Shadow: The Women Christian Temperance Union, Evangelicalism and Reform in Ontario, 1874–1930.* Montreal & Kingston: McGill-Queen's University Press, 1995.

Danylewycz, Marta. *Taking the Veil: An Alternative to Marriage, Motherhood and Spinsterhood in Quebec, 1840–1920.* Toronto: University of Toronto Press, 1987.

Dumont, Micheline, Nadia, Fahmy-Eid with Johanne Daigle. *Les Couventines: l'éducation des filles au Québec dans les congrégations religieuses enseignantes, 1940–1960.* Montreal: Boréal, 1986.

Fahmy-Eid, Nadia, and Micheline Dumont, eds. *Maîtresses de maison, maîtresses d'école: femmes, famille et éducation dans l'histoire du Québec.* Montreal: Boréal, 1983.

Heap, Ruby, and Alison Prentice, eds. *Gender and Education in Ontario.* Toronto: Canadian Scholar's Press, 1991.

Kinnear, Mary. *In Subordination: Professional Women, 1870–1970.* Montreal & Kingston: McGill-Queen's University Press, 1995.

Prentice, Alison, and Marjorie Theobald, eds. *Women Who

Taught: Perspectives on the History of Women and Teaching. Toronto: University of Toronto Press, 1991.

Selles, M. Johanne. *Methodists and Women s Education in Ontario, 1836–1925.* Montreal & Kingston: McGill-Queen's University Press, 1996.

WOMEN'S ACTIVISM AND THE STATE

Bacchi, Carol. *Liberation Deferred: The Ideas of the English Canadian Suffragists, 1877–1918.* Toronto: University of Toronto Press, 1982.

Bashevkin, Sylvia. *Toeing the Lines: Women and Party Politics in English Canada.* Toronto: Oxford University Press, 1993.

Burt, Sandra. "ReThinking Canadian Politics: The Impact of Gender." In Michael Whittingham and Glen Williams, eds., *Canadian Politics in the 1990s.* Scarborough: Nelson, 1990.

De Seve, Micheline. "The Perspectives of Quebec Feminists." In Constance Backhouse and David Flaherty, eds., *Challenging Times: the Women's Movement in Canada and the United States.* Montreal & Kingston: McGill-Queen's University Press, 1992.

Dumont, Micheline. "The Origins of the Women's Movement in Quebec." In Backhouse and Flaherty, *Challenging Times.*

Fiske, JoAnne, "Carrier Women and the Politics of Mothering." In Gillian Creese and Veronica Strong-Boag, eds., *B.C. Reconsidered: Essays on Women.* Vancouver: Press Gang, 1992.

Fournier, Françine. "Les femmes et la vie politique au Québec." In Marie Lavigne and Yolande Pinard, eds., *Travailleuses et feministes: Les femmes dans la société québécoise.* Montreal: Boreal Express, 1983.

Kealey, Linda, and Joan Sangster, eds., *Beyond the Vote: Canadian Women and Politics.* Toronto: University of Toronto Press, 1989.

Native Women's Association of Canada. *Native Women and Self-Governance: A Discussion Paper.* Ottawa: Native Women's Association of Canada, 1992.

Sangster, Joan. *Dreams of Equality: Women on the Canadian Left, 1920–60.* Toronto: Oxford University Press, 1989.

HEALTH CARE AND SCIENCE

Ainley, Marianne Gosztonyi, ed. *Despite the Odds: Essays on Canadian Women and Science.* Montreal: Vehicule Press, 1990.

Arnup, Katherine, Andrée Lévesque, and Ruth Roach Pierson, eds. *Delivering Motherhood: Maternal Ideologies and Practices in the 19th and 20th Centuries.* London and New York: Routledge, 1990.

Comacchio, Cynthia R. *"Nations are Built of Babies": Saving Ontario's Mothers and Children 1900–1940.* Montreal & Kingston: McGill-Queen's University Press, 1993.

Dodd, Dianne, and Deborah Gorham, eds. *Caring and Curing: Historical Perspectives on Women and Healing in Canada.* Ottawa: University of Ottawa Press, 1994.

Hacker, Carlotta. *The Indomitable Lady Doctors* (Toronto and Vancouver: Clark Irwin, 1974.

Innis, Mary Quayle, ed. *The Clear Spirit: Twenty Canadian Women and Their Times.* (Toronto: University of Toronto Press, 1966.

McPherson, Kathryn. *Bedside Matters: The Transformation of Canadian Nursing, 1900–1990.* Toronto: Oxford University Press, 1996.

Mitchinson, Wendy. *The Nature of Their Bodies: Women and Their Doctors in Victorian Canada.* Toronto: University of Toronto Press, 1991.

Strong-Boag, Veronica. "Canada's Women Doctors: Feminism Constrained." In Linda Kealey, ed. *A Not Unreasonable Claim: Women and Reform in Canada, 1880s–1920s,* 109–29. Toronto: Women's Press, 1979.

EARNING THEIR BREAD

Acton, Janice, et al. *Women at Work: Ontario, 1850–1930.* Toronto: Canadian Women's Educational Press, 1974.

Bourne, Paula, ed., *Women's Paid and Unpaid Work: Historical and Contemporary Perspectives.* Toronto: New Hogtown Press, 1985.

Bradbury, Bettina. *Working Families: Age, Gender, and Daily Survival in Industrializing Montreal.* Toronto: McClelland

and Stewart, 1993.

Cohen, Marjorie Griffin. *Women's Work, Markets, and Economic Development in Nineteenth-Century Ontario.* Toronto: University of Toronto Press, 1988.

Errington, Elizabeth Jane. *Wives and Mothers, School Mistresses and Scullery Maids: Working Women in Upper Canada, 1790–1840.* Montreal & Kingston: McGill-Queen's University Press, 1995.

Kinnear, Mary. *In Subordination: Professional Women, 1870–1970.* Montreal & Kingston: McGill-Queen's University Press, 1995.

Lacelle, Claudette. *Urban Domestic Servants in 19th Century Canada.* Ottawa: Environment Canada, 1987.

Latham, Barbara K., and Roberta J. Pazdro. *Not Just Pin Money: Selected Essays on the History of Women's Work in British Columbia.* Victoria: Camosun College, 1985.

Luxton, Meg. *More Than a Labour of Love: Three Generations of Women's Work in the Home.* Toronto: Women's Educational Press, 1980.

Nadel-Klein, Jane, and Dona Lee Davis, eds. *To Work and to Weep: Women in Fishing Economics.* St John's: Institute of Social and Economic, 1995.

Parr, Joy. *The Gender of Breadwinners: Women, Men and Change in Two Industrial Towns, 1880–1950.* Toronto: University of Toronto Press, 1990.

Pierson, Ruth Roach. *"They're Still Women After All": The Second World War and Canadian Womanhood.* Toronto: McClelland and Stewart, 1986.

Van Kirk, Sylvia. *"Many Tender Ties": Women in Fur Trade Society, 1670–1870.* Winnipeg: Watson & Dwyer, 1980.

Contributors

EDITORS

Sharon Anne Cook is a professor and director of teacher education in the Faculty of Education, University of Ottawa. She taught for sixteen years in the secondary school system, completing a PhD in history in 1990. Her publications include articles in teacher education, the history of education and women and religious movements. Her most recent academic book with McGill-Queen's University Press is entitled *'Through Sunshine and Shadow': The Woman's Christian Temperance Union, Evangelicalism and Reform in Ontario, 1874–1930.* 1990

Lorna McLean is an assistant professor in the Faculty of Education, University of Ottawa. She holds an Ontario Teaching Certificate and after many years of teaching entered graduate school and completed her PhD in history. She has authored and co-authored articles on women's history and archival sources, and co-edited the book, *Historical Perspectives on Law and Society in Canada.*

Kate O'Rourke has been working in archives since 1988. She began at the National Archives of Canada as a student. She worked in the Documentary Art and Photography Division as an art archivist from 1992–1996. In 1996 she moved to the Archives of Ontario, where she currently works as an archivist in the Agriculture, Transportation and Photographic Records portfolio,

specializing in documentary art. She has a master's degree in Canadian Art History from Concordia University.

CONTRIBUTORS

Marianne Gosztonyi Ainley is a professor of women's studies/gender studies, University of Northern British Columbia. Her interests include a feminist biography, the history of Canadian women and science, First Nations women and environmental knowledge, and the history of natural history and ornithology.

Katherine Arnup is an associate professor at the school of Canadian Studies, Carleton University. She studies the history of motherhood and child rearing in twentieth-century Canada; the history of child custody and divorce in Canada; and lesbian mothers, both contemporary and in the 1950s and 1960s.

Jody Baltessen is the head of Textual Records and Public Service, Private Records Section, Provincial Archives of Manitoba. She is interested in women writers, in particular, lesser-known or locally known writers, focusing on autobiography, life-writing, and biography.

Christina Bates is an Ontario historian at the Canadian Museum of Civilization. She studies Ontario history, women's history, and the value of artifacts, especially clothing, to explore these themes.

Pierrette Boily is the curator of the Musée de Saint-Boniface, Winnipeg, where she assisted in the production of the exhibit "By Their Deeds … : Women of French Manitoba."

Isabelle Bourgeois is a graduate student in educational sciences at the University of Ottawa. She is interested in educational measurement and evaluation.

Lise Brémault is the curator of the exhibit "By Their Deeds … : Women of French Manitoba" and is currently employed as assistant curator and collections manager at the Musée de Saint-Boniface, Winnipeg.

Lara Campbell is a doctoral student at Queen's University. She is completing her dissertation on the Great Depression in Ontario, its impact on gender and the family, and the relationship between the family and the emerging welfare state.

Jim Catton has a master's degree in English from Carleton University and is a research assistant assigned to the Oncology Education Department of the Princess Margaret Hospital in Toronto. He studies the medical founders of the Oncology Program of the Princess Margaret Hospital.

Pamela Catton is a radiation oncologist and director of oncology education at the Princess Margaret Hospital. As coordinator of the Heritage Visiting Professor Program, Dr Catton administers the biennial Vera Peters Professorship, under which distinguished physicians are invited to visit the Princess Margaret Hospital to lecture, teach, and meet with staff.

Kathryn Lorraine Church is an independent researcher and community-based scholar. She works for groups and organizations comprised primarily of people who experience long-term poverty and are involved in the psychiatric survivor movement.

Cynthia R. Comacchio is an associate professor of history at Wilfrid Laurier University. She studies childhood and family, adolescence, health care and social policy as pertaining to women and children.

E. Tina Crossfield is an independent scholar of Canadian science and technology, history, biography, and women's studies.

Terry Crowley is a professor of history at the University of Guelph. He studies the history of women and of rural society.

Judi Cumming is a senior project officer of the Economic and Public Archives Section, Manuscript Division, National Archives of Canada. Her interests include women's history in Canada, with an emphasis on environmental activism; and women's rights in the nineteenth century.

Helen M. Diemert is professor emeritas in the Faculty of Fine Arts, University of Calgary, Calgary. She studies theory in art as an academic discipline.

Patricia G. Dirks is an associate professor in the Department of History at Brock University. She studies religious/citizenship training programs for children and adolescents in early twentieth-century Canada.

Dianne Dodd is a historian at Parks Canada Agency. She studies women and technology, women and medicine, and public history.

Kirstin Evenden is an art curator at Glenbow Museum in Calgary. She has a particular interest in feminist art history and curated several exhibitions in this area, including Mary Is Here: Alrene Stamp (2000) and Women's Work: Art by Women from Glenbow's Collections (1996).

Pepita Ferrari is an independent film director, writer, and researcher. She studies women in history, such as Victorian women travelers in Canada. She is currently writing a script on Sarah Emma Edmunds, Canada's civil war heroine.

Barbara M. Freeman is an associate professor, School of Journalism and Communication, Carleton University. Her research includes media history, gender, and the news media.

Susan Gelman holds a PhD in the history of education from the Ontario Institute for Studies in Education. She is currently teaching, operating her own tutoring agency, and working as an independent scholar. Her interests lie in the history of women teachers and teacher education in Ontario.

Monda Halpern is an assistant professor of history at the University of Western Ontario. She is studying Canadian and American women's history, and has a special interest in rural women.

Sonia Halpern is an instructor in art history at the University of Western Ontario. Her interests lie in feminist art history.

Ruth Haywood is currently completing her master's thesis at Memorial University. Her study examines moral regulation and venereal disease control in St John's during the Second World War.

Ruby Heap is associate professor of history and the director of the Institute of Women's Studies at the University of Ottawa. She studies women and education, and women and the professions.

Janice Hladki is an assistant professor in the Women's Studies Program, McMaster University. An artist, activist, researcher, and educator, she has collaborated on numerous feminist projects and is interested in the tensions arising from social differences in practices of collaboration and collectivity.

Ann Holmes, a former art educator, has worked at the Ontario Women's Directorate since 1984 making space for girls in math, science, and technology. With Janice Hladki and six other women, she co-curated the Women's Cultural Building Archives show at the Women's Art Resource Centre in February 2000.

Brenda Hornby is a writer and teacher. Her contribution to this book came from a six-month assignment she had with the Nelson Museum and Historical Society to archive the stories of women of Nelson's past (1880-1950).

Grace Maurice Hyam is an archivist in the manuscript Division at the National Archives of Canada.

Cathy Leigh James works at the National Academy of Education, where she is a Spencer Post Doctoral Fellow. She is also a visiting scholar in the Department of Theory and Policy Studies, Ontario Institute for Studies in Education, at the University of Toronto. She studies the history of higher education and the history of women and social reform, 1880–1940.

Jo Fraser Jones is a retired French immersion teacher and librarian. She currently volunteers as a writer and researcher at the Vernon Museum and Archives in Vernon, B.C. She studies local and women's history in the Okanagan Valley.

Margaret Christina Kechnie is an associate professor of women's studies at Thorneloe College, Laurentian University and is coordinator of the Women's Studies Program. She studies women's history, history of farm and rural women, and the history of women in ministry in the Pentecostal Assemblies of Canada.

Peggy Kelly is a doctoral candidate at the Department of English, University of Alberta. She studies Canadian literature, cultural studies,and feminist theory.

Alyson E. King holds a PhD and works as an independent researcher and historian. She examines the history of women and higher education and the use of the Internet for research, teaching, and learning.

Christine Lalonde worked at the National Gallery of Canada as acting assistant curator of Inuit art from 1966 to 1999. She writes on topics dealing with the exhibition of Inuit art and the ways in which it is understood by scholars and public alike.

Anna Hildegarde Lathrop is an associate professor, Department of Physical Education, Brock University, St Catharines, Ontario. She studies the history of physical education and sport, the history of women in higher education, and women and sport.

Majorie Edna Cunningham Levan received her BA in history from McMaster University and a master of education degree from Queen's University. Her research interests focus on the experience of her family as missionaries in China.

Candace Loewen is senior project officer, Government Archives and Records Disposition Division, National Archives of Canada, and general editor of *Archivaria*. Her research interests include women and the peace movement, women and the environment, and archival theory on electronic records.

Jeanette Lynes is an associate professor of English at St Francis Xavier University. Her books include the edited collection, *Words Out There: Women Poets in Atlantic Canada*, and a collection of poetry, *A Woman Alone on the Atikokan Highway*. She has published numerous articles on contemporary Canadian literature.

Wilma Jean MacDonald is an archivist at the National Archives of Canada. She studies oral histories and oral tradition, and the history of women, families, and aboriginal people.

Marie Suzanne Brigitte Caroline Martel is an MA student in media studies at Concordia University, where she is studying to be a documentary filmmaker. Her interests focus on telephone operators in Quebec.

Alan Bruce McCullough is a contract researcher. He studies western Canada, industrial history, and women and work.

Ellen Easton McLeod is an independent scholar and the author of *In Good Hands: The Women of the Canadian Handicrafts Guild*. She is interested in art history, women's history, and craft and decorative arts.

Tamara Miller is a doctoral candidate at the University of Manitoba, specifically looking at childbirth in the Canadian health-care system.

Wendy Mitchinson is a professor of history at the University of Waterloo. Her research interests are the medical treatment of women in Canada, in particular the history of childbirth.

Tamara Myers is a doctoral candidate at the University of Winnipeg and a member of the Montreal History Group. She studies juvenile justice and the history of modern Quebec.

Nicole Neatby is an associate professor at the University of Prince Edward Island. Her research interests include the study of female university students at Queen's University during the 1920s and university students in Montreal during the 1950s.

Anne Newlands is an art educator at the National Gallery of Canada. She has published several introductory texts on Canadian art with an interest in making it more accessible to the general public.

Dawn Nickel is a PHD student, Department of History, University of Alberta. Her interests include the following: women's history (western and prairie history), the social history of medicine, and the history of death and dying.

Jane Nokes is the corporate archivist for the Scotiabank Group. She also coordinates the Group Fine Art Collection, is the director of Dance Collection Danse, and chairs the Silverthorn C.I. School Advisory Council and the Etobicoke Public Art Advisory Committee.

Jean O'Grady is an associate editor of the Collected Works of Northrop Frye at Victoria University, where she studies Margaret Addison, the history of Victoria University, Northrop Frye, R.E. Knowles, John Stuart Mill, and nineteenth-century England.

Ellen O'Reilly is an assistant professor at St Francis Xavier University. Her research interests include conceptions of gender and sexuality, moral and ethical practice, and the historical roots of female physical activity.

Alexandra Palmer works as the Nora E. Vaughan Fashion Costume Curator in the Textiles and Costume Section at the Royal Ontario Museum. Her current research is on twentieth-century couture consumption and trade in Toronto, and the influence of American and European styles and tastes on Canadians.

Jill Perry is a student in the Faculty of Law at the University of Victoria. Her research interests are women's issues and criminal law.

Charlene Porsild teaches in the Department of History at the University of Nebraska. Her recent book, *Gamblers and Dreamers: Women, Men, and Community in the Klondike*, won the Western History Association's W. Turrentine Jackson Award and the Canadian Historical Association's Clio Prize.

Donna Porter holds a BA from Mount Allison University and an MLS from Dalhousie University. She was employed by the Directorate of History and Heritage, Department of National Defence, as a naval archivist and now works at the National Archives of Canada as a standards officer.

Alison Prentice is professor emerita at the Ontario Institute for Studies in Education, University of Toronto, and is adjunct professor at the University of Victoria.

Linda Joan Quiney is a PHD candidate at the Department of History, University of Ottawa. She studies women and the First World War, and nursing and women's social service in pre–Second World War Canadian society.

Helen Ralston is professor emerita of sociology, Saint Mary's University. Her books and articles focus on women in India and South Asian immigrant women and their daughters in Canada, Australia, and New Zealand.

Judith Roberts-Moore is a senior project officer, Appraisal and Special Projects Section, Government Archives and Records Disposition Division, National Archives of Canada. She studies issues related to archives and archival records and Canadian history, especially social and political history as well as the history of Ottawa.

Corinne Rusch-Drutz is a PhD candidate in the Graduate Centre for Study of Drama, University of Toronto. She studies feminist theatre and dramatic theory, Canadian theatre, female spirituality, and Jewish feminism and spirituality.

Joan Sangster is a professor of history and women's studies at Trent University. She has published articles and books on working-class and women's history, including *Dreams of Equality: Women on the Canadian Left*, and *Earning Respect: The Lives of Women in Small-Town Ontario*. Her current research is on women and girls in conflict with the law.

Mairuth Sarsfield continues to work on writing and editing. Her recent activities have included readings and workshops on literacy with young people in prison.

Ellen Scheinberg received her BA and MA from Queen's University. She is currently undertaking a PhD in history at the University of Ottawa. She has worked as an archivist at the National Archives of Canada and is currently working at the University of Toronto Archives.

Lisa Singer is an archivist in the Special Collections Unit of the Archives of Ontario, Agriculture, Transportation and Photographic Records Portfolio. She has a master's degree in Archival Studies from the University of Manitoba.

Susan Michi Sirovyak is a collections coordinator at the Japanese Canadian National Museum and Archives. Her research interests include Japanese Canadian studies.

Helen Smith is an assistant professor at the Department of History and Women's Studies, Lakehead University. She does historical surveys of intellectual ideas surrounding menstruation and studies representations and lived experiences of women's wartime work and identities.

Elizabeth Marian Smyth is an associate chair, Department of Curriculum, Teaching and Learning at the Ontario Institute for Studies in Education, University of Toronto. She studies gender and education, history of education in Canada, women religious, and teaching.

Kimberly Speers is a PhD candidate at the University of Alberta. She studies women and politics, and public and financial management and administration.

Shelagh J. Squire is an associate professor, Department of Geography and Environmental Studies, Carleton University. Her research interests include tourism and gender, western Canadian women's history, and cultural and interdisciplinary studies.

Veronica Strong-Boag is a professor of women's studies and educational studies at the University of British Columbia. She studies Canadian women and children in the nineteenth and twentieth centuries.

Jessica Tomic-Bagshaw is a fourth-year art history student at Carleton University. Previously she graduated from a cultural industries training program held at the Inuit Art Foundation. She works at the Inuit Art Foundation.

Patricia M. Trites is the project coordinator at the Canadian Public Health Association, where she does health-related research.

Catherine Vye is an archivist at the National Archives of Canada. She studies the history of commercialism and the visual depiction of gender, popular culture, architectural history, the decorative arts, and Victorian funerary artifacts.

Pamela Wakewich is an assistant professor of sociology and Women's Studies at Lakehead University. She studies oral history and narrative analysis, women and work during the Second World War, and changing perceptions of health and embodiment.

Edith Wheeler was born in England but in 1906 moved with her family to Winnipeg, where she received her education. In 1929 she and her husband made their journey west. Edith now lives in a retirement residence in Toronto.

Anne White is a PHD candidate at the University of Calgary. She is a sessional instructor in the Department of Religious Studies. She studies women in religion with an emphasis on Christianity.

Marilyn Färdig Whiteley is an independent scholar. She studies the history of women in Canadian Protestantism and edits the papers of Annie Leake Tuttle.

Kathleen Wilker is from Scarborough. Her poems celebrate life in the suburbs as well as female creativity and community. She teaches literature at the Universidad de Sonora in Hermosillo, Mexico.

Andrea M. Winlo has a master's drgree in history from Concordia University. Her research interests are in sport and women's history, particularly skiing.

Miriam Wright is an SSHRC post-doctoral fellow with the Department of History, University of British Columbia. Her research interests include Atlantic and Pacific coast fisheries and twentieth-century Canadian history.

Madga Zakanyi currently holds the position of archives coordinator at the Bloorview MacMillan Centre (rehabilitation and chronic-care facility for children). Her research interests focus on disabled children and their families at the turn of the century.

Christine Elizabeth Zaporzan is a former education and marketing coordinator for Glanmore National Historic Site. She works as a marketing assistant at Hastings and Prince Edward District School Board.